The Atlantic and Its Enemies

NORMAN STONE

The Atlantic and Its Enemies

A Personal History of the Cold War

A MEMBER OF THE PERSEUS BOOKS GROUP

NEW YORK

For Ömer Koç

Books published by Basic Books are available at special
discounts for bulk purchases in the United States by corporations,
institutions, and other organizations. For more information, please contact
the Special Markets Department at the Perseus Books Group, 2300 Chestnut
Street, Suite 200, Philadelphia, PA 19103, or call (800) 810-4145,
ext. 5000, or e-mail special.markets@perseusbooks.com.

A CIP catalog record for this book is available from the Library of Congress.
LCCN: 2009944216
ISBN: 978-0-465-02043-0

10 9 8 7 6 5 4 3 2 1

Contents

List of Illustrations

Introduction

Books on the twentieth century tend to be either encyclopedias or tracts. I have a certain weakness for the tract approach: it makes for readability, because, as Pirandello said, facts are like sacks, which do not hold up unless you put something into them. If asked to recommend a book on this subject, I always suggest Paul Johnson's *Modern Times*, written from – on the whole – the Right, or Eric Hobsbawm's *Age of Extremes*, written from a head-shaking Left. Each is very good on the vices of the other.

I am not a tractarian. This book began life as a history of the entire twentieth century, but I soon realized that the task was too great, not least because the two halves of the century were so different. Churchill and Hitler were old-fashioned figures, looking back to the nineteenth century, but 1945 was, as the Germans called it, *Stunde Null*, when things started anew. There had been a three-cornered international battle, between Fascism, Communism and what, for want of a more accurate word, we have to call liberalism, i.e. the free-market-democracy world of which the USA became the pre-eminent representative. Fascism lost, and quite soon the other two were fighting the Cold War, which ended fifty years later. 'Capitalism' was not in splendid shape, and it lost various tricks in the fifties. Of course, in 1989, it won, and even triumphed: as a Soviet marshal said, the Soviet Union had lost the third world war without firing a shot. However, the triumphalism of 1989 did not really last for very long, and, with financial and other troubles, the world was back, in a sense, to the doubts and compromises that had marked the 1970s. Back then, it was the Left that, on the whole, might appear triumphalist, and it is as well to be reminded of the swings and roundabouts in these matters.

In the fifties, a great many people assumed that the Soviet system was superior. Perhaps the greatest symbol of this was *Sputnik* in 1957, the first man-made satellite in space. It came from a country which, back in 1914, had been by European standards well behind – two thirds of the railwaymen illiterate, for instance. But the concentration on education in Soviet Russia was extraordinary, even reaching far into backward Central Asia. One of my earliest semi-adult memories is a visit to the Brussels Exhibition of 1958, taken there by a splendid French family with whom, for a month at a time over four years, I did an exchange. They, the Simottels of Brest, were well-off, and we, my mother school-teaching in Glasgow, an RAF war widow, were not: Madame Simottel understood, and was superb (and even sent me to a Franco-German establishment in Lindau, on Lake Constance, where I learned to massacre German in the French manner). The bus from Brest to Brussels stopped off in Amiens, and we went to the cathedral, which, since I knew that Amiens had been the main town for the British army in the First World War, moved me greatly. In Brussels, where the exhibition was marked by an 'Atomium' – there was a European Atomic Community, though it never took off – the various states showed off, and the Soviet one was best.

The British Pavilion was not bad, not bad at all, but it was very old-fashioned (not a bad thing – subsequent efforts, as with the Dome, verged on the farcical, and the British should just stick to old formulas: it was stained-glass windows, Benjamin Britten, and a general air of reverential hush; it got the third prize). The French one dwelled on the wonderful things that France was doing in Algeria (they were *all* going to leave, in four years, and at fifteen I had made myself unloved in Brest by predicting this). The American one was boring; kitchen equipment or something. The Soviet one had *Sputnik*, I suppose, but I remember a room with recordings of Oistrakh doing the Tchaikovsky violin concerto, and, at seventeen, you are forgiven for succumbing. Nowadays, I have what must be a complete collection of everything that Svyatoslav Richter ever played, though nothing could ever replace those live performances, and I have never forgotten the *Hammerklavier* that he performed at King's College, Cambridge, in 1975 or 1976, peace to his rather tortured soul. As things have turned out, it was the Michael Jacksons (his rather mercenary obsequies proceeding as I write, in late July 2009) who won. Why, is a good question, to which I wish I had a dogmatic answer. A Russian in New York asked, in bewilderment, why *is* it that, with a system of education five times better, we have an economy five times worse? In this book, I have tried to answer such questions. The Atlantic world won, warts and all.

In this book, Communism is central, but so is the other great theme, the extraordinary vigour of the 'capitalist' (Hayek tried to find another word, and failed) world. It has helped that I have been here before. In some ways, this book is a continuation of an earlier one, *Europe Transformed 1878–1919*. In that period, free-market democracy, or whichever word you want to use, spread, and the British were at the centre of the world system. Even then, something of an Atlantic system was building up, the British by far the largest investors in the United States, although, as the great economic crash of the early 1930s was to show, the Americans were not yet up to the world-wide responsibilities that their economic weight entailed. It was particularly absurd to slap a tariff against the exports of countries that owed money to the USA and could not pay, except if they exported, but other things went wrong as well, including the collapse of thousands of banks. It was only in the later thirties, and especially during the Second World War, that these matters were responsibly managed, and after 1947 (when my book really starts) there was an extraordinary boom in the West, the Atlantic world of my title. Its symbol has been the extraordinary growth of English, the language, as a French ambassador sagely remarked, that is easiest to speak badly. Nowadays, when I have to introduce this subject to Turkish students, I ask them to bear in mind that they use the language, wear the clothes, and – sadly – listen to the music or eat the fast food (in a superior version) of the Atlantic.

The post-1947 era has had a great many resemblances, of a great-grandfatherly kind, to the present. Marvellous inventions, ultimately the computer and the internet, are part of the story. However, before we succumb in admiring speechlessness, it is worth remembering that the later nineteenth century was there before us, so much so that

I refuse to regard 'globalization', an ugly word in any event, as
something new. By 1890, there had been wonderful inventions: horses
and carts to aircraft in a generation. One of my earliest memories is of
being taken by my mother to see a friend of hers, whose grandmother,
aged about a hundred, was bed-ridden but otherwise in good order.
She told me what it had been like to have a dental operation, in rural
Scotland, in what must have been about 1848. The story went: barn-
yard table, two large glasses of whisky, string round tooth, other end
attached to door of barn, slammed shut; half tooth off; more whisky,
then stable chisel used to extract rest of tooth (little girl then lives for
ever). By 1900, there would have been ether to knock her out. By
1948, when my own dental visits started, a drill worked by the dentist's foot, and I still dread a visit to the dentist, but my splendid Turkish dentist now understands why I need a jab even for tooth-cleaning.
Andrew Wilson, in his *Victorians*, rightly remarks that these improvements in dentistry are one of the few elements of progress that can be
welcomed without reservation: with others, there have been great
drawbacks. At any rate, the years 1878–1914 saw an enormous jump
in progress, as measured by the positivist standards of the era. This left
writers, often, strangely gloomy, and Orwell teased them: quoting, say,
Ernest Dowson's 'I have been faithful to thee, Cynara', he remarks,
'hard cheese, old chap'. But the Dowsons were right. That world of
progress came to an end in 1914, with the First World War, and the
following generation saw the great disasters. The thirties were indeed,
as an old student of mine, Richard Overy, calls them, 'morbid'. It is
salutary to remember that the 'research' of Dr Mengele at Auschwitz
– he ended up, tail-waggingly, carting a box of eyeballs to his professor
at Frankfurt through the mess of 1945 Germany and was very hurt
when his university deprived him of his doctorate – was paid for by the
Rockefeller Foundation (though the story is more complicated).

At any rate, the West, in 1947, resumed the progress that had happened before 1914. I write, 'progress', but there is much over which
heads can be shaken. It has gone together with a vulgarization and a
coarsening of things, although before 1914 reactionaries had also
complained of this. The decisive year seems to have been 1968, when
there were babyish revolts, terrifying enough to bureaucracies for

them just to capitulate: the universities of Europe, to which the world had beaten its path in 1914, collapsed into near irrelevance. I had direct experience of what happened to the great university of Louvain in Belgium in that, thirty-five years ago, I was asked to translate an admirable official history, for presentation of honorary doctorates to the usual suspects (Isaiah Berlin, Raymond Aron) by an institution that had become Flemish. It was an exceedingly interesting task, but also depressing: in Louvain, if in some public office, even a telephone box, you were required to speak Flemish, even if you explained that you were foreign. Being from Glasgow, and speaking decent German, I could more or less make it up, and the resulting hilarity ensured that my messages got through, but the growth of provincial nationalism is an absurd phenomenon, and in this book I make my protest by using 'England', often enough, to cover a country generally known, in passport-ese, as 'UK'. We say 'Holland' to cover Zeeland, without resorting to 'The Netherlands', which is anyway inaccurate. *Pace* Glasgow, England saved us from civil war, and I owe her a considerable debt.

If there is a single country of which admirable things can be said in the era after 1947, it would of course be Germany. Success is boring, and Germans shake their heads, but their recovery has been remarkable. The world of late nineteenth-century progress came to an end when Germany kicked over the board, and went to war in 1914. It was an exercise in intelligent craziness that ended with Hitler's Bunker in 1945; *Downfall (Der Untergang)* is, after *The Third Man*, Graham Greene's Vienna of 1947, one of the grand films (and quite accurate, as I know from having seen the interrogations, in Moscow, of the Bunker witnesses). It is extraordinarily interesting to watch the counterpoint, over the centuries, of Germany and England. I would even claim that the best historians of Germany are English, and I seem to have taught German to them, from Richard Overy and David Blackbourn to Harold James and Niall Ferguson. I cut my own teeth as historian by looking at Austria-Hungary, and if I rationalize about that, now, I can see that I was really looking at two important questions, which, in the early 1960s, I was hardly able to appreciate. You are looking, in the first instance, at the question of nationalism: why, as a Yugoslav remarks, do the peasants grow up and hate their nearest neighbour, and what can be done about it? The other question is more difficult: given that Prussia ended in disaster, why was the Catholic, Austrian, alternative not more successful? In the end this is an old nineteenth-century question, boiling down to the relationship of Catholicism and Liberalism – not a happy story. An old Cambridge colleague, Tim Blanning, in his *The Pursuit of Glory*, produces some answers. It is about the third Germany, great-great-grandfather of the *Bundesrepublik*, those prince-bishoprics that were very worthy and thought that the Thirty Years War had been a mistake. The prince-bishoprics – harmless souls – took over in 1949, and have done incredibly well. 1989, the fall of the Wall, was a deserved tribute, though the Lutheran Church rather characteristically forbade the tolling of bells in celebration. Margaret Thatcher – one of the none-too-many heroic figures in this book: my others would be Charles de Gaulle and Helmut Schmidt – worried that some sort of Fourth Reich was emerging, and invited me to Chequers, along with other historians, to lecture her on the subject. I was able to reassure her that, in taking over East Germany, the West Germans were just getting six Liverpools. We shall see what they make of it. Yes, the European Union is German-dominated, but this is not necessarily a bad thing.

However, the creativity has been Atlantic, not European, and that involves messiness. This was most obviously on display in England. It had been rather spoiled, post-war, and for a very long time, well into the eighties, a tiresome self-satisfaction reigned. At Oxford, I used to dread having to mark the examination scripts covering the ultra-modern period of British history, because they all beta-plusly said the same things about the 1945 Labour government (of which I had, of all oddities, been an agitprop exhibit, photographed winsomely clutching a bunny and a blanket in advertisement of crèches to help the working mother). Very, very few undergraduates managed to write originally about that period, the best of them an Italian, of Communist background, and the real reason was that none of them knew how much better matters had been organized on the Continent. That England came to grief in the seventies, when, of all oddities, the very heartland of Atlantic capitalism had to go cap in hand to the International Monetary Fund. Helmut Schmidt shook his head, and Germans in Scotland could not believe the level of poverty. And then came the remarkable turnaround. England is a place gifted with tissue regeneration. In 1979 Margaret Thatcher became Prime Minister, and there was a very bumpy period as she turned things round, in the teeth of endless criticism, often contemptuous, from the powers that had been. I myself drew some flak for writing in the press, fairly frequently, in support of her. So be it: I was right. Nowadays there are 400 German students at Oxford, the largest foreign contingent, and they are not there because the truth is in the middle.

Of course, the United States, in it all, was the great creative force. All along, you need to read American books (while I am on the subject, here is a curious fact: in the Cambridge University library, where, unlike the Bodleian at Oxford, you can go round the stacks, the books on 'Reaganomics' are almost never taken out). For some reason, they are much more interesting on defeat – Vietnam – than on victory, and the enormous biographies of presidents are a considerable though necessary bore. I have had to read enormous amounts of dross, have made a vow never ever again to read a book by a man with a beard, and sometimes think that America abolished feudalism only through making serfs think they were free. Still, it has huge bursts of creativity, and serious thoughts about the modern world come from there: there is a strange fact that the stars whom I have taught, with Harold James or Niall Ferguson or David Blackbourn, ended up there. America follows from *Europe Transformed*, and Niall Ferguson was quite right to explore the British parallels.

As is inevitable with a book of this sort, it brings back my yesterdays. Much of what I say about England has had to be wrenched out. It was a very good place in the fifties and I can remember what it was like, going to the old Cambridge schol. exam, through the last great fog, by a steam train from Glasgow Central Station. The Head Porter at Caius, in a top hat, an ex-sergeant major frequently mistaken for the Master, received you, and then, at 9 a.m. in the Old Schools in Benet Street, you were confronted with an examination, beautifully printed, which read, 'For translation into French'. The passage would read: 'choppingly, the blades flashing in the wan sunlight, the queen's skiff moved through a brisk north-easterly towards the port of Leith

(A. Fraser)'. In those days there was an interesting battle between the examiners and the schoolmasters, and I had an enormous advantage, in that I had been taught by the siege-master extraordinary, Christopher Varley, at Glasgow Academy, who had no thoughts at all – he read Balzac for the vocabulary, a siege-engine of some power, which enabled you to turn the tables on the interviewers, who would be lost as you trotted out words such as *balivot*, or is it *baliveau*, meaning a tree marked one year to be cut down the next, in English, 'staddle'. The examiners were wiped out, but, once at Caius, I realized I could not handle literary criticism (admittedly there was some excuse: they expected me to read Gide, to whom 'hard cheese, old chap' was indeed the only possible response). I switched to history, and was again very lucky, in that I fell under the control of Neil McKendrick, a teacher of genius. He taught me a version of history which was an updated version of the Whig Interpretation, and I have been struggling ever since to get away from it. I remember my first supervision. I had written some drivel about the Dutch Revolt, as to how the breasts of free men could not be whatever-it-was against Inquisitions and what-not. He said, do not forget that torture can be quite efficient. I am still not sure about the Whig Interpretation of English history. The experience of the 1980s showed that there was a huge amount to be said for the Whig Atlantic, warts and all. The warts are horrible – Michael Jackson and the rest – but the Atlantic won, and is now spreading to, of all places, China. Chinese students are now all over Oxford, learning English. The resurrection of that extraordinary civilization must count as the best thing in the modern world.

There has been another resurrection: Turkey. I have been teaching there for some fifteen years, and very happily so: my university, Bilkent, a private one, was established a quarter-century ago in the teeth of considerable resistance. Its founder, İhsan Doğramacı, had a very good idea as to what was going wrong with universities in the 1970s. Inflation had been a disaster, and Turkey was one of the centres of the troubles of the 1970s. However, she too is a country with tissue regeneration, and though I was much criticized by left-wing friends for being a sort of monkey in a fez jumping up and down on the Bilkent barrel organ, they now admit that I was right. In the latter part of this book, concerning the 1980s, I have written a good bit about Turkey, because there is much interest in a process that has turned the country into a considerable economic power, with a resonance throughout Eurasia. When the country started off, in 1923, you could not even have a table made, unless by an Armenian carpenter, because the legs wobbled, the Turks not knowing how to warp wood. Now, they make F16s. Today, aged not far from seventy, I still look forward to marching into a class of Turks, the best being excellent, and the others decorative and polite. As ever, I owe much to my Rector, Professor Ali Doğramacı.

I have a great many other debts of gratitude, a book of this scope needing a great deal of outside support. The London Library is a wonderful institution, and my assistants, Onur Onol and Yasin Yavuz, have been helpful way beyond the line of duty. My agent, Caroline Michel, has been magnificently encouraging, as have Simon Winder at Penguin and Lara Heimert at Basic Books. Rupert Stone, as ever my target reader, made encouraging comments, and Christine Stone has splendidly put up with the bad patches that come up when sails flap listlessly in windlessness. Over the years I have of course learned a great deal from friends in various countries, and I can here only acknowledge a few. Manfred Bruncken, of the Hanns-Martin-Schleyer Foundation in Cologne, Francine-Dominique Lichtenhan in Paris, Sergey Mironenko in Moscow, Rusty Greenland in Texas and, on matters to do with business in England, Robert Goddard have all been especially informative and helpful. In Turkey I have as ever relied especially upon David Barchard, Andrew Mango, Sean McMeekin, Hasan Ali Karasar, Evgenia and Hasan Unal and Sergey Podbolotov. As regards the significance of the 1980s, I have been fortunate to be able to discuss them at length, and at all levels, with Niall Ferguson, Nick Stone and Robert Skidelsky. There is one final debt. Towards the end of her time in office, Margaret Thatcher took me on as speechwriter, and these were rather dramatic occasions. She did not exactly throw things, but she made her point, and you did not spend five minutes in her company without having a memory to chalk up. She represented a force of tissue-regeneration that, in the 1970s, I had not expected.

I

The War of the British Succession

The winter of 1946–7 sank into the memory of anyone who lived through it. A contemporary, the historian Correlli Barnett, writes that it was 'a catastrophe of ice and snow'. It started early, and on 20 January produced a:

> savage east wind that cut through every cranny in British houses and froze all within [and] the blizzards began to sweep in across the country again and again through the rest of January and on through the coldest February for three hundred years. In the hills nearly a third of the sheep perished. In East Anglia the snowdrifts piled to a height of fourteen feet. Off the Norfolk coast ice-floes eerily converted the North Sea into a semblance of the Arctic.

In London the temperature fell to sixteen below, and the railways were paralysed; coal could not be moved from the pitheads, and the power stations' stocks collapsed. By February 2,500,000 people were idle because of power cuts. This lasted until the end of March (and was followed by a drought). Yet the British climate was generally quite mild, and matters were made worse because of the strange way in which the British preferred inefficient coal fires ('cosy') to central heating, and put up, every winter, with the phenomenon of burst pipes. Later on, George Orwell, though not complaining at the time, blamed that winter in London for the appalling condition of his lungs, which later killed him.

On the European continent that winter was still worse the further east you went. In Germany the frozen waterways and paralysed (or shattered) railways could not move stocks at all. The bombing damage had not been made good and people lived in cairns of rubble, freezing and starving; they did business by barter or in crumpled *Reichsmark* notes, marked with endless noughts. Such were the scenes that the American Secretary of State, George C. Marshall, saw from his train window as he went to a conference of foreign ministers at Moscow in the middle of that winter. In England, there had been bread rationing since the previous summer (500 grams per week for working men, half that for most others) and rations were low otherwise – 50 grams of tea and bacon, the same for mousetrap cheese, with about 250 grams for fat and sugar. Dried egg was an item of that period, eked out with water into an at least edible paste. The British were even then much better off than the French, whose official rations were considerably less. In Germany there was outright starvation, and an unknown number of people just died – maybe 9 million, in addition to the 6 million men who had gone in the war. In 1946, 6 million of them had been expelled, carrying a suitcase each, from Czechoslovakia and Poland, and they had been dumped in makeshift camps over the new German border.

Most of continental Europe was in dreadful shape. France had been fought over, and more comprehensively than in the First World War, which had affected only thirteen of the north-eastern and northern departments, whereas the Second affected seventy-four. She had also had a robber baron Nazi occupation for four years, and the outcome was terrible – with almost 10 per cent infant mortality at Tourcoing, for instance, and a whole range of growth troubles associated with vitamin deficiency, such as rickets. The railway system was so badly run down that you needed fifteen hours to go from Paris to Strasbourg and there was constant inflation, as paper money chased an industrial output less than one third of that of 1929. In Paris rations amounted to 1,500 calories per day in May 1945, as against an otherwise minimum 2,000, and the daily bread ration in the Marshall winter was at 250 grams and even at times 200. In 1946 France had to get half of her coal from the USA, not the Ruhr, and there were terrible shortages of fuel. There were shortages of grain because cattle, not people, were fed on it: the peasants would not sell grain for the paper money. In Italy, though she was spared the worst of the weather, matters were even worse. Much of the south was starving; the peninsula had been fought over; there had been a civil war in the north; there were millions of refugees; and in 1947 1.6 million were out of work. Those in work had seen their wages cut in half by inflation and survived often enough only through a subsidized canteen, eating meat only once a week. Italy was backward by other European standards, and there were millions of peasants; malaria was still a problem; and relations between the great landowners and their peasants in the south were sometimes tense, to the point of violent occupations of land, and counter-killings by the armed police.

Politics in both countries were at boiling point, and a Communist Party became the largest one, taking a third of the vote, and running the trade unions. In early March 1947, as General Marshall journeyed to Moscow through this devastated scene, he was well aware that Communist coups could be launched, to take over western Europe. Already, that had happened to the east, where only Czechoslovakia stood out as a parliamentary and democratically run country, but even there the Communists had taken two fifths of the vote. The Moscow conference that he attended – one of several, of foreign ministers, devoted to the subject of central Europe and especially Germany – dragged on for weeks and went nowhere. And now there was a very obvious problem, that the USSR would use the emergency to encourage the spread of Communism. Over Germany, the Soviet idea, said Ernest Bevin, was to 'loot Germany at our expense'. The Russians wanted huge reparations for the damage caused to them in the war, and they also meant to keep Germany permanently down. Maybe, even, the Germans would vote Communist so as to save themselves from this miserable fate. There was no peace treaty as yet, but at the turn of 1946–7 such treaties with other countries had been settled, and Communists had won support in, say, Romania or Poland when they promised land at the expense of Hungary or Germany.

The Second World War had been, in western Europe, a civil war as well, and Communists were very strong in the resistance movements. When Marshall returned from Moscow, he could see that France and Italy were in no condition to withstand the effects of the winter of 1946–7. In fact Stalin had even been preening himself at the Americans' discomfiture. Controlling as he did the Communist parties, he knew well enough that western Europe might be lost for the Americans altogether. The Americans might be the strongest military power, but they would be powerless if western Europe fell naturally into Communist hands, and in any case there would be an economic crisis in America once the demobilized soldiers tried to find jobs in an economy that could not export, given the collapse in Europe. He was of course informed of what was happening by spies in high positions – Donald Maclean, second man at the British embassy in Washington; Kim Philby, one of the chiefs of British Intelligence; Henri d'Astier de la Vigerie, in the immediate entourage of General de Gaulle, who in 1945 headed the French government; Anthony Blunt, also excellently informed as to British Intelligence; John Cairncross, chief civil servant in the London Cabinet defence committee, who revealed the secrets of the atomic bomb; Alger Hiss and Harry Dexter White in the US machine: so many, in fact, that Stalin gave up reading what they wrote, because he could not believe that such men were real spies. When Maclean defected, he was simply sent to teach English in a remote Siberian place, and was drinking himself to death until a bright young foreign ministry man, Alexandr Lebedev, rescued him. Expecting Communism to triumph, Stalin and Vyacheslav Molotov, his foreign minister, refused to try to make that Moscow conference work. They dragged it out, haggling over details, and the Americans were struck by the confidence of Stalin's tone. But this time the Americans were going to take up the challenge.

They did so much more robustly than before because of a further crisis. When the Second World War ended, there was no idea of their staying for long, and millions of soldiers went home. There was an American occupation zone in Germany and Austria, but it was not the chief zone (the British took over the industrial areas of the northwest) and it was supposed to be run under the general auspices of an Allied Control Council, at which the Russians were strongly represented. At Yalta, early in February 1945, there was a famous meeting of men who were known in the news as the 'Big Three'. Franklin Delano Roosevelt and Joseph Stalin undoubtedly deserved the title. The American war economy had been extraordinarily productive, with one mass production miracle after another – especially the 'Liberty ships' turned out in six weeks, partly prefabricated. The USA fought wars in two hemispheres but even managed to improve the home population's standard of living as well. Stalin for his part controlled a huge war machine which had recovered from disastrous defeats, and, from the summer of 1943 onwards, had rolled into central Europe and the Balkans, flattening all before it. The third of the 'Big Three' was Winston Churchill, who had defied Hitler from the start, and who now counted as the great hero of the Second World War. But Great Britain had suffered, and was really kept going by American troops and money. Churchill did not have the strength to resist Stalin, and the Americans did not have the will. The old man had been forced to fly, very uncomfortably, in stages over Malta and Cairo to the Crimea, and even then, on arrival, had an eight-hour journey by road, through high hilly country, to a residence some way away from the main palace, where the other two were installed. He had put a good face on things, waving his trademark cigar, but the real business was done despite his wishes. The Americans – Marshall was there, as Chief of Staff of the Army – wanted Soviet help to finish the war with Japan. As things turned out, they did not need it. On 6 and 9 August they dropped two atomic bombs, on Hiroshima and Nagasaki, and that brought a Japanese surrender, but until then everyone had expected the Japanese to fight on and on, fanatically and suicidally, as they had done for the past three years in a chain of Pacific islands (some individuals had still not surrendered, decades later, and had gently to be persuaded that the war had been lost). But in February 1945 no-one foresaw this: the atomic bomb was not successfully tested until July. The American–Soviet deal had already been in the air at an earlier conference, held at Teheran in November 1943. Now it was confirmed. Stalin could control much of central Europe and the Balkans. There were other concessions. The United Nations was set up, with a five-country Security Council, in which each member had a power of veto. There were suggestions of the Soviet Union's joining in the new world financial arrangements, with a large American loan; for a time, consideration was even given to a sharing of the secrets of the atomic bomb. Great Britain did not rate such treatment. The Americans of course supported her, but they did not mean to help the British maintain their empire. At the time, that accounted for a quarter of the world's land surface, and most Americans did not like it.

To start with, in 1945 the USA assumed that Great Britain would take the main responsibility for Europe, and American troops left, in droves. She also halted the economic help, 'Lend-Lease', that she had been giving, and ships were even turned back in mid-Atlantic. But the winter of 1947 saw crisis in Britain as well. There had been five and a half years of fighting, and the start, in 1940, had been Great Britain's finest hour, when she did indeed stop Nazi Germany from taking over Europe, and probably Russia as well. As the war went on, the American share in it became more and more important, and there was a decisive moment late in 1944, when American troops outnumbered British ones on the battlefield in France. The Americans also had the money, because the US economy had prospered greatly with production for war, and in 1945 it accounted for fully half of the entire world's manufactures. But, still, the British thought that they would be an equal partner, together with America and Russia, in making the post-war world. Even very sober, disillusioned commentators thought so. George Orwell, who had reported the troubles of London, the dreadful food, the unpredictable bombs, to the American *Partisan Review*, assumed that his country would still have a decisive voice in the settlement of the world after the war. So did a very clever European expert, Hugh Seton Watson, whose father, after the First World War, had had some influence over that peace treaty. They very soon realized the limits of British power. The fact was that the country was bankrupt, and the war had left it with enormous responsibilities and not nearly enough strength to take them on. The physical destruction had not been nearly as great as on the Continent and the British standard of living was much higher than there: overall health had even improved during the war, and British industry accounted for roughly half the output of western Europe for the next three or four years. But, otherwise, the problems abounded.

Twelve million tons of shipping had been sunk. Imports stood at six times the figure for exports, and, with such demand, American prices rose by 47 per cent in 1946. There was a large debt. The country's overseas assets, most of its foreign investment, had been sold off for the war effort. The worldwide prestige of the wartime leader, Winston Churchill, was vast, and he was treated with respect and affection almost everywhere, but he was a very old-fashioned figure – an aristocrat brought up in the imperial Victorian certainties, and now presiding over a country that had greatly changed. Wartime arrangements were carried on for years to come. For example, you registered with a grocer and handed over stamps which entitled you to a loaf every three days. There was a South African fish called snoek, which could be bought without dollars: its taste was revolting but there was not much alternative at the time. This world, of permits and privation, went on for several years after the war had ended (until 1954), and one could hardly recognize the country. The novelist Evelyn Waugh – his trilogy about wartime England, *Sword of Honour*, is the best book on the subject – felt that the country was under a sort of foreign occupation. Many bright sparks simply emigrated. Denis Hills was an Englishman of a peculiar but typical sort. After a standard middle-class education (in Birmingham) he went, in the thirties, to Poland and during the war worked with the Poles. In Italy at the end, the Poles having been heavily involved in the reconquest of that country, he was helpful to various unfortunate Soviet citizens who had ended up fighting on the German side: he got them away from Soviet captivity, and death. He fell foul of the military authorities, getting tipsy in front of the military governor's palace in Trieste, and left the army. Then it was home, to an impoverished England where nothing worked and the climate added to the gloom. An advertisement caught his eye, for a post as teacher in Ankara College, an establishment in Turkey where the teaching was carried on in English.

As with Denis Hills, bright British emigrated, but the reason was not just the privation. In 1945 a Labour government had been elected with a landslide, and it proceeded with social revolution. 'We are the masters now' was the claim (characteristically it was said, and is generally slightly misquoted, by an upper-middle-class lawyer, Hartley Shawcross, who subsequently moved to the Right). The world gasped that the great Churchill had been overthrown, but events were moving in the direction of Labour. The Conservatives were associated with the 1930s, with mass unemployment and also with the attempts to buy off Hitler, 'appeasement' as it was called. Most people were persuaded that if the Western Powers had stood up to Hitler in 1938, he could have been stopped, and the most powerful writers argued in this sense. Then there was the English class system, an outcome of England's peculiar history. There were 'two nations' which dressed, spoke, ate and were educated differently. Orwell told his American readership that Lord Halifax, British ambassador to the USA early in the war, was as representative of his country as a Red Indian chieftain would be of the United States. In 1945 class resentment was strong, at least in the big cities, and it affected even many solidly middle-class figures themselves. Labour drew its strength from the trade unions, but there was an important element made up from men who had a background in grand schools or at Oxford (or, more rarely, Cambridge, which was less politically minded). They resented the sheer inefficiencies that the class problem entailed. Woodrow Wyatt, with an Oxford background and a good war behind him, was typical of such men, largely because he believed that fairness and efficiency could be combined.

In the election of 1945 Labour swept in and it had a radical programme. It nationalized the heavy industries, coal, the docks, the railways: what were called 'the commanding heights' of the British economy. Education had already been made costless, even for parents who could afford some fees. Health was to become so, under a National Health Service (inaugurated on 5 July 1948, but debated since 1946). It replaced earlier charitable or for-profit arrangements, and also the extensive private insurance schemes which had grown up since the nineteenth century (under the 'Friendly Societies' which sprang straight from the respectable working class and much of the lower-middle class). Curiously it did not abolish private (or 'public' as they were bizarrely called) schools, which were a key element in the class structure. If the State supplied a decent and costless education, then why bother to abolish them? In any case Labour believed in equality, and the tax arrangements were such that equality was largely attained. Paying school fees became a problem for families that traditionally could afford them.

There was an argument behind all of this – that the State would do better than private arrangements ever could. The basis for this lay in the thirties, when private enterprise had indeed been associated with mass unemployment. But there was also the example of the war itself, and, there, the British were pleased with themselves, supposing also that their example was one to be widely followed as some sort of 'third way' between American capitalism and Soviet Communism. Early in 1945 Michael Foot, later to lead the Labour Party, told Parliament that the country was at the summit of its power – with 'something unique to offer', combining the 'economic democracy' of Communism and the 'political democracy' of the West: socialism without labour camps. Rationing had worked quite well, and health improved vastly during the war because working-class children were given rations of vitamin-rich food – orange juice, for instance – and had to do without sweets. Many children attended day nurseries because their mothers were working; the diets of these nurseries were supervised by doctors who had a power that they had not previously experienced, and the health of that generation was far better than that of its predecessors. Women had been brought into wartime employment, often classed as 'national service', and most remembered these years as a good time. There was an almost universal belief that the war economy had been very successful, despite German bombing and submarine attacks on shipping. One third of it had been devoted to the great Bomber Offensive, and Germany's smashed cities were a testimony to its success. For the State to take over, to plan, and to develop a Welfare State therefore seemed sensible.

People who argued to the contrary were in a small minority – derided by the historian A. J. P. Taylor as similar to 'Jacobites at the court of Louis XIV', men who had lost any connection with the reality back home as they tried to support the lost cause of the Stuart dynasty – but even in the later 1940s these supposedly half-demented figures were starting to have reality on their side. It struck with a ferocious blow, in the second post-war winter. The money began to run out, and the government became quite badly divided as to priorities. A saying at the time was that 'France is getting order through chaos; England chaos through order', and, even now, a classic post-war problem with trade unions emerged.

The nightmare winter of 1946–7 went on well into April; brief thaws only added to the problem in that they created small ice-rinks. In all of this, the miners went on strike, and their output generally, let alone individually, was considerably below what it had been before the war. Then the dockers went on strike as well, such that exports were badly affected: without these there would be none of the vital imports (though it was maybe characteristic of the era that more dollars were spent on tobacco than on machinery: cigarettes were regarded as a vital import, as almost everyone smoked and there would probably have been a general strike if tobacco had given out). London, still with huge areas of bombed-out buildings, was a very depressed and depressing place as that winter went ahead. Rations now meant that you could get a pair of socks every four weeks. There had already been, in 1946, an American loan of $3.75bn. That had in effect allowed dollars to be spent – even on the import of timber for 'social' ('Council') housing – but it had come with the condition that the pound could be changed into dollars, free of wartime restrictions. The historian Kenneth Morgan even claims that it made the Labour programme possible. There was an implication, too, that the Americans would be able to trade freely with the British Empire, which, in places, had vital raw materials still priced in pounds.

In 1947 convertibility was introduced, and foreigners, in droves, changed their pounds into dollars. Almost £200m was being lost every week. The Labour government was in effect broken by this: there was never the same drive in it again; its huge majority collapsed at the next election, in 1950, and in 1951 it lost. The money ran out, but it had already been so programmed domestically that there was no room for going back: the various reforms that constituted the 'Welfare State' were mainly in place. It is notable that no other country copied the British formula in these matters, or at any rate not without substantial emendation of it. The Germans in a way were fortunate, in that they experienced that winter before any post-war social reforms had taken place: their state was constructed without the illusions of 1945.

However, the worst position for a Cabinet minister to be in was probably the Foreign Office. The country may have been badly weakened internally but there was no end to its responsibilities, and these were turning very sour. The problems went back to the first post-war period, in 1919, when men had joyously assumed that Empire made them rich, and the British Empire, already enormous, received a considerable extension in the Middle East. In 1929, the world slump in the end particularly affected agricultural prices, such that lambs were simply slaughtered rather than eaten, because the profit margins were lost in transport costs. India, 'the jewel in the Crown', became instead a liability and the nationalist leader there, Gandhi, rightly said that the Empire consisted of millions of acres of bankrupt real estate. But the British were nevertheless responsible for these problems. Of course, they tried hard to keep order, and they often inspired considerable loyalty, being uncorrupt, and holding the balance among various peoples. The Governor of Uganda was a much loved figure who got about on a bicycle. But the bottom had dropped out of the Empire, and a war for succession was under way – in India, between the Moslems who eventually set up Pakistan ('land of the pure') and the others, including Moslems living in southern India. In Palestine, there was a three-cornered war between the British, Arabs and Jews. Then there were the problems of Europe, and the drain of hard currency into Germany – £80mn in 1945–6 alone. Even in 1945 there had been some desire for a joint Anglo-American zone in Germany, but the USA was not minded, then, to do much more than leave Europe to sort itself out, maybe with the aid of the new IMF and World Bank. True, early in 1946 George Kennan, who was a very influential diplomat in Moscow, famously warned as to Soviet policy (Stalin had made a threatening speech in February), but even when Churchill talked of the 'Iron Curtain', Truman was careful not to associate himself with the idea. Crisis was needed, if the Americans were to intervene. The British had tried to attract support by showing themselves worthy of it. Now they used a different tactic. They would just collapse.

The Foreign Secretary, Ernest Bevin, was an old trade unionist, whose ways ran very counter to those of the old imperial Foreign Office, but he inspired much loyalty and admiration. Though born illegitimate, and lacking schooling, he was literate (using phrases such as 'with alacrity') because, like so many of his class at the time, he could and would make use of the after-hours workers' education libraries and self-help mechanisms without embarrassment. He was an astute trade union leader, and that gave him some insight into the ways of Communists, who would exploit an industrial crisis for their own political ends rather than for the workers' own good. Bevin ran his machine well at the Foreign Office, and he needed to, because his in-tray was a very gloomy one. Was Great Britain bulldog or bullfrog, ran one question.

After 1945 the Western empires fell apart. The Japanese had already broken their prestige, the 'charisma' that had kept, say, British India going. There, apart from the army, there had been only 60,000 British in a subcontinent of 400 million, and a unique combination of circumstances kept them in control for an extraordinary length of time. A good part of the story had to do with divisions within India (Churchill said that it was 'no more a nation than the Equator'), but there was also the army, which worked remarkably well almost to the end, and the British themselves respected the rule of law (with one or two notorious lapses). In 1904 a Viceroy, Lord Curzon, who was not at all a stupid man, remarked that the British should stay in India 'as if . . . for ever'. But by the 1930s the formula was coming apart. A nationalist intelligentsia emerged, men such as Nirad Chaudhuri, a Bengali whose English and whose knowledge of literature were better than most Englishmen's, and whose life story, *The Autobiography of an Unknown Indian* (1951), is one of the classics of the era. Chaudhuri started off as a nationalist – precisely the sort of Brown Briton who, if Indian independence had developed as, say, Canada's had done, would have been a paladin of Commonwealth and Empire. Instead, he became rapidly disillusioned when his cause had won. His admiration for England was immense, but men of his stamp sometimes had to put up with absurd humiliations: a Cambridge-educated Burmese rugger player told he could not use the common bath with the British players; a Chinese millionaire in Singapore being invited by the Governor-General to dine at the chief club, and the Governor-General receiving a letter of protest from the committee the following day; George Orwell crossing the road in Rangoon if he heard Scottish voices, so far did they bear overtones of crudity. The heart of Indian nationalism had been in Bengal, itself a special area (and the oldest part of the British *raj*). But when the British went down, so, too, did Bengal: a festering mass of hatreds was soon revealed, and they were to wreck Indian independence. Chaudhuri emigrated to an England which he also found culturally impoverished by the loss of Empire.

In the later 1930s it was clear enough that the British would not be staying. The great difficulty was to find a successor element on which to rely, and, here, the war made problems much worse. The Japanese invaded Burma, causing hundreds of thousands of refugees to flee to the already overcrowded north-east. Boats were wrecked, so as to deter further Japanese invasion over the sea. In 1942 the main Indian nationalist movement demanded immediate independence and refused to have any truck even with sympathetic British politicians who asked them to wait until the end of the war. A movement of civil disobedience was put down with some harshness in the same year, and was broken in effect only when a great famine broke out – partly a consequence of the Burmese disaster, partly because of a terrible cyclone that wrecked the rice crop, partly for lack of transport, and partly because the British gave priority to war transports rather than to civilian needs. The (Indian) government of Bengal itself proved none too efficient, and 3 million people starved to death. India had been radicalized, the prestige of the *raj* broken; in 1946 government buildings were routinely being destroyed, and there were even alarms for the loyalty of the army. In the event, the great tragedy of modern India soon emerged. Getting the Hindu-dominated Congress to agree with the Moslem League proved to be impossible, and a partition was hurriedly agreed. It was, in the words of the very sober Christopher Bayly, 'a crazy geographer's nightmare'. Bengal, 25 million Hindus to 35 million Moslems, was almost impossible to partition, and 8 million people moved. However, 'East Pakistan' without Calcutta was 'an economic disaster area', with the jute production separated from the mills, and it was itself separated from the rest of Pakistan by a thousand miles. The division of the Punjab in spring and summer 1947 turned out to be savage, whole train-loads arriving with corpses that were burned or disembowelled, as the Punjab was mixed, with a large Sikh population that was to be split between India and Pakistan. By the summer of 1947 the British had neither the money nor the will for a fight, and the army did not carry out proper policing; besides, the timetable was absurdly short, and maddened people grabbed what they could when they could. On independence, in mid-August, New Delhi itself was seething, while in Calcutta 7,000 tons of rubbish built up, even at the gates of the stock exchange, the leading financial institution in Asia. It was a dismal end to the British *raj* and even then showed something of what was soon to happen in England herself. The last Viceroy, Lord Mountbatten, was indeed the gold filling in a rotten mouth – a jibe later on made about the role of the monarchy itself. Not a British life was lost in the departure, but quite soon India and Pakistan were at war over a vast disputed area, Kashmir.

Of all oddities, the British had been at work in 1945 even trying to extend their empire. British troops were present in Vietnam and Indonesia, where they were dragged into support for the existing French and Dutch rulers. In order to do so (and in Burma as well) they were driven to use the hundreds of thousands of Japanese prisoners of war to put down risings by the local nationalists. The French and the Dutch somehow understood even less than did the British that the European position was hopelessly lost: the Foreign Office adviser on Mountbatten's staff told him that the Dutch were 'mentally sick' and 'not in a fit state to resume control in this vast area'; it was not until 1948 that the Dutch abandoned Indonesia. But the British were also fantasizing, though less bizarrely. In the second half of the 1940s they were trying to create a new form of empire, in this case one based on Malaya. Here, they had a certain amount of justification, in that Malayan rubber earned a surplus of £170m for the sterling area – more than a third of its income (the Gold Coast supplied another quarter). Malaya was put together in a novel way, together with Singapore, but this did not solve the three-cornered problem of Indian, Chinese and Malay cohabitation. A civil war soon developed, with a Communist insurgency that was largely Chinese, and Malaya was not stabilized until 1960. The Americans faced problems of the same sort in the Philippines, to which they gave an independence with certain limits.

The nightmare of nightmares was Palestine. Whatever the British did would be wrong. As with India, it is obvious that a few more years of Empire would have been desirable for an orderly transfer of power to occur. But to whom? Here again, as with other parts of the British Empire, there was much strength in the argument that the Empire kept order, tried to assure legal rights, and sent out honest people. But there was an original sin at the centre of the Palestinian question, and it lay in the context of the Balfour Declaration of 1917, which had offered the Jews a national home in what was then Arab (or Ottoman) territory: the aim being essentially to keep the French away from the Suez Canal. The British then found themselves responsible for keeping order in a small area claimed by both sides, and there was a further problem, in so far as the native Palestinians were themselves very divided. Partition was an obvious solution, and even then the transfer of Palestine to Jordan would have made sense, but there were vast problems as regards Jerusalem. The British muddled, swung to one side and the other with pressures of terrorism, and thus encouraged the terrorists to do their worst. There were some particularly horrible episodes, such as the blowing up, in an operation of sinister brilliance, of the King David Hotel, British headquarters in Jerusalem (March 1946), or the hanging of two sergeants, whose bodies were then booby-trapped, and the British were much criticized for stopping the emigration of Jews from the concentration camps to Palestine. The Americans were loud in their criticism, and in February 1947 the British threw the affair at them and the United Nations. The Mandate was abandoned; an unworkable plan for partition came up; ethnic cleansing occurred, and 700,000 Palestinians fled from their homes. On 14 May 1948 Israel was proclaimed as a state, and a war then followed, until 1949, when an unsatisfactory boundary was set up through an armistice. This period is full of questions: was there ever any possibility that proper partition, or even a single-state solution, might have been established? At any rate, here was another problem, involving Moslems, that the British simply could not manage. They 'scuttled', as in India or Greece.

Those dreadful winter months of 1947 were decisive and the issue which caused the decision was the least of the problems: Greece. She had a very important place in British imperial strategy. Control of the eastern Mediterranean was essential for any power concerned with the Suez Canal and the shortest routes to Asia, and there had long been a British interest in the whole area – it had led to the Crimean War, and in 1878 to the taking over of Cyprus. The British were preponderant in Athens and in 1944 Churchill had struck a bargain with Stalin to keep it that way. The Red Army was conquering eastern and much of central Europe, and the resistance movements were heavily influenced by Communism – in Yugoslavia especially, but also in Greece.

Greece was indeed almost a textbook case of the sort of country most open to Communist takeover. She was backward and largely agrarian; the Orthodox Church, unlike the Catholic Church, was not solid as regards resistance to Communism (it had not been much of a focus of reaction against the Bolsheviks in the Civil War); the non-Communists were badly divided between monarchists and republicans, and, besides, they were dominant in different parts of the country. There were also minorities, whether Albanian, Bulgarian (or Macedonian) or Vlach (or Romanian), and, decisively, a quarter of the entire population consisted of refugees – people, destitute, who had fled from the collapse of the Greek invasion of western Turkey after 1922. Salonica and its hinterland had been populated by them, as the local Moslems also emigrated to Turkey and that city, very heavily Jewish, was the capital of Greek Communism. Its leader, Nikos Zachariadis, had even once been a dock-worker at Galata, the port of Istanbul. The Communists had been a political presence in the 1930s and kept an organization even under the military dictatorship that ruled Greece. When the German army invaded in 1941 and occupied the country, Greek Communists eventually became foremost in the resistance movement and when the Germans withdrew, late in 1944, they nearly took over Athens. British troops prevented this, but there was a more important factor: Stalin instructed the Greek Communists not to take power but to make an agreement with the British and with the monarchists whom they supported. This was Stalin's part of a bargain that otherwise provided for the British not to resist Communist takeovers elsewhere (Romania and Bulgaria, expressly, though the implications as regards the other parts of Soviet-dominated eastern Europe were menacing enough). In 1946 the Greek Civil War flared up again, and this time the Communists had help from Yugoslavia (there was a substantial Macedonian Slav minority in northern Greece) and bases in Albania.

Here was the first of a set of Cold War crises in which the Great Powers fought each other by proxy in some place, extremely complicated on the ground, with a colonial past, a divided native middle class, no tradition of stable government, a strong Communist Party and a foreign intervention that had happened more by incident than design. There was a very ugly encounter (each side hijacked the other's children with a view to re-education). The British were divided as to what they should do. One thing was plain: they could not afford another imperial war, and they shrank from the unpopularity that was accruing. The Chancellor, Hugh Dalton, disliked the Greek policy and warned that there was in any event no money for it: 'we are . . . drifting . . . towards the rapids'. On 21 February 1947, in the middle of that terrible winter, the British ambassador in Washington announced to President Harry S. Truman that the British would terminate their involvement in the Greek Civil War. The United States would have to sort things out. It was at this point that the War of the British Succession broke out, with Americans and Soviets the chief contenders for the succession.

2

Cold War

The British collapse in that terrible winter of 1946–7 coincided with a worsening of the domestic problems of western Europe, but it also coincided with the start of the Cold War, an expression that now entered the world's vocabulary. The tensions grew in central Europe, and especially Germany. Here was the greatest economic power in Europe, but in 1945 Germany was prostrate. The smashing of Germany's cities was a very cruel business, and was carried on almost to the very end of the war, quite without necessity. In July 1944 the British and Americans fielded their maximum bomber strength – 5,250 – with a capacity to drop 20,000 tons of bombs over any target in a day, and overall, from D-Day to the end of the war, a million tons were dropped on German cities and towns, even smaller ones. The last RAF raid took place, appropriately enough, on Potsdam, the heart of 'German militarism', where 500 aircraft went in on 14–15 April and killed 3,500 people. Even places far from the front line, which were also famous centres of German civilization, were attacked. They included the Wagner headquarters of Bayreuth, which had once been a scene of nationalist pageantry. The Festspielhaus was missed but the place was looted by American soldiers shortly afterwards, and Wagner's house, the Villa Wahnfried, has (or had), among its exhibits (its point unclear – or perhaps too clear), a photograph of a black American soldier playing the great man's piano.

In April 1945 the Russians were already besieging Berlin, and a terrible vengeance descended on Germany. She lost 1.8 million soldiers, dead, in the defeats of 1944, and that did not include civilians. The fighting in 1945 cost another 1.4 million dead, again not including civilians. Even before the final capitulation on 8 May 1945, the dis-integration that marked the post-war years had set in – valueless paper money, churned out by an official printing press that could only be backed by the execution squads or the concentration camps; a paraly-sis of transport, people huddled in the rubble. Cigarettes replaced money as the store of value, and the working classes increasingly rejected money wages for them. Hitler, a fanatical anti-smoker, banned them. Oddly enough, that was how the public came to learn that Adolf Hitler had died. He had immured himself in his great bunker, far underground in the gardens of the Reich Chancellery that had been built for him in his days of greatness, and, there, the machinery of government ran to the end – heels clicked, trays presented by white gloves, titles adhered to. The Soviets were only a few hundred yards away when Hitler at last committed suicide. His private pilot, crossing the garden above, became aware of cigarette smoke coming through the ventilator shafts, and he realized that Hitler must have died. Once he had died, the various adjutants and secretaries put on dance music, attacked the wine cellars, and lit cigarettes. The whole episode has been brilliantly captured in *Downfall*.

At the film's end there is a scene of genius. One of the young women from the Bunker, desperate to escape without being raped, comman-deers a lost boy, and marches boldly through the Soviet ranks with him. She gets away, and under a bridge the boy discovers an aban-doned bicycle. She peddles off, with the boy on the handlebars, you assume to safety, to a new life, and overall recovery from the catas-trophe that the film has shown. It is a well-chosen, symbolic end, because the recovery of Germany was one of the great themes of the half-century that followed. At the time, not many people foresaw this (one of the few was Dr Hjalmar Schacht, held as a prisoner for the war crimes trials to come, at Nuremberg: he told his interrogators that Germany would of course rise again).

That mistake was forgivable. Germany had had the fate of Genesis' Sodom and Gomorrah, brimstone and fire, and on the Dutch border there were signs reading, in English: 'Here ends the civilized world'. Two out of five boys born between 1915 and 1925 were dead or missing. The 10 million surviving Wehrmacht men were herded into makeshift camps behind barbed wire, and another 10 million non-Germans, released from the camps or from forced labour, were wandering around at will. Another 10 million evacuee Germans went back from the countryside to the stricken towns and cities. On top of all this, in the summer of 1945, Germans from the east had to be settled. Some had taken part in the 'trek' out of areas that were about to be taken by the Soviets but others, in the summer and winter of 1945, had been expelled from their homes in Poland or Czechoslovakia. Coal production had collapsed, and what little was produced could not be moved. Food supplies fell to the point of near starvation. The problem was made all the worse because the Allies did not know, at first, what to do. There was even a decree ('JCS 1067') to the effect that there must be no fraternization with this savage people. However, that broke down very quickly, and in any case an element of the biblical Sodom came up: there *were* 'righteous men'. From internal or external exile, and even in some cases from the camps, men appeared, willing to help in the creation of a decent Germany – on the whole, Catholics and Social Democrats, both of whom had faced persecution under the Nazis. Some sort of administration might be set up, locally. The symbolic woman-boy-and-bicycle in *Downfall* made, here, their first and halting moves forward. But the end of the Third Reich was followed by two years' penury, and the winter of early 1947 worsened it. The British had been responsible for the industrial north-west, and had been parting with food to keep it going at a time when their own rations were poorer than during the war itself, when the Americans had helped out. On 1 January 1947 they agreed to put their own zone together with the American one, based on Frankfurt: the result, most of what was to be West Germany, was called 'Bizonia', but that too did not work any too well.

The German problem went together with others, worldwide. Japan, her capital almost flattened, and two principal cities nuclear ruins, was prostrate; European colonies in south-eastern Asia were hardly governable. Especially, a vast civil war was brewing in China. The Chinese Communists had acquired a solid base, with Soviet help and with captured Japanese weaponry, in Manchuria, and it was traditionally from there that China was conquered. But Stalin was probing in other areas as well. Himself from the Caucasus, he wanted to reassert Russia's old dominance in the northern Middle East, a dominance that had been lost after the First World War, and he prided himself on restoring the Tsarist empire. It had collapsed, ran the thinking, from backwardness and exploitation by foreigners, with native collaborators. Communism had re-established the empire, and now he aimed at the Istanbul Straits, the most important waterway in the world, Europe's way to Asia. During the war there had been a British and Russian occupation of Iran, and Soviet troops stayed there. The north of the country was largely Azeri and Kurdish, and Stalin encouraged both elements: Soviet Azerbaidjan, centred on the oil of Baku, was in theory an independent place, but the real Azerbaidjan was mainly in old Persia, and Stalin urged on Azeri nationalism. He did the same with the Kurds of northern Iran, some of whose tribesmen briefly declared a republic. This might have been the nucleus of a Kurdistan that would have taken Turkish territory; and Stalin anyway threatened Turkey, which had entered the war only at the last moment, with an insultingly worded demand for bases, along with a further demand, that the Turks should give back three provinces in the northeast that had once belonged to Tsarist Russia. For the West this was a step too far, the eastern Mediterranean being a very sensitive spot, and it was over Turkey that the first Cold War crisis came up. In spring 1946 the Americans sent warships to the Straits, and Stalin, his hands already full with Germany, backed off.

The Communist takeover of what came to be known as 'eastern Europe' was becoming a fact, and the process was very ugly indeed: a blanket tyranny was falling on countries that had already been semiwrecked by the war. In the Soviet zone, there had been an orgy of killing and rape; the concentration camps themselves were still open, sometimes for Germans quite innocent of involvement with Nazism; and in some countries liberated by the Red Army, there were outright massacres. Later on, 'Yalta' became a code-word for the willingness of the Western Allies to consign half of Europe to Stalin.

Churchill had agreed in 1944 that the British would take scant interest in the fate of Romania or Bulgaria, but he wanted security in the eastern Mediterranean above all, and that meant Greece, or, to some extent, Yugoslavia. The latter occupied a strategic position on the Adriatic, and in the war the British had been the essential element in supplying arms to the Communist partisans who, in 1945, took over. Their leader, Marshal Josip Broz Tito, was a man of infinite guile, whose chief ambition in 1945 was to take over the great port of Trieste from Italy; and that mattered to the British, the more so as an Italy deprived of Trieste might easily be tipped over into Communism. It is tempting to think, though the evidence is conjectural, that relations between the British and Tito carried on surreptitiously, through such men as Sir Fitzroy Maclean. He had been dropped into Yugoslavia to make contact with the partisans and he knew them as brothers – or comrades: some were women – in arms. He had also been foremost in getting weapons for them from British rather than Communist sources, and, like so many others, he believed that Yugoslavia was the only possible answer to the problems of nationality in the western Balkans. Here were half a dozen quite different but often intermingled peoples, and the alternative to coexistence was endless mutually hostile tinpot nationalistic states. A great many people on the ground agreed (a prominent Croat writer, contemplating folklore dances and fancy invented words, said, 'God save us from Serbian bombs and Croat culture'). In 1945, as the partisans tried to take over Trieste and parts of south-eastern Austria, there were clashes with British troops, but personal contacts remained and in 1948 came to life again (Maclean was given a house on the island of Korčula in the Adriatic and wrote one of the war's classics). Tito himself was quite capable of singing in different keys. He had been in Moscow, and had worked as an agent for the NKVD, or People's Commissariat for Internal Affairs. He knew his Stalin: suspicious and murderous. Churchill had got Stalin to approve a fifty-fifty deal over Yugoslavia, and in due course – in 1948 – that became reality.

Elsewhere, in 1945 and 1946, the Communists took over. The techniques of takeover amounted to a choreography which they had learned mainly in the Spanish Civil War: indeed, some of the people they used had had experience in Spain. There, the Communists had had to play a complicated game – how to infiltrate trade unions, to destroy anarchists, to exploit minority nationalism, to keep poor peasants and middle-class progressives in step, to gull the foreign press, to recruit concealed agents (one of them, the Spanish foreign minister himself). Controlling the media was important, and there were specialists in this: before the war Willi Münzenberg had built an empire on Moscow money and, carefully keeping a neutral face, lined up the grand intelligentsia of Europe and America at prominent platforms on the Left. Tito himself had been involved in this, and so, in Hungary, was Ernő Gerő; Georgy Dimitrov, who took over Bulgaria, had been secretary of the Comintern, managing much of the game from Moscow. Grim bare-floorboard Party schools taught Marxist political science, and it was often enough quite accurate. It was also ruthless against the rest of the Left. Anarchists, moderate socialists, trade unionists only wanting better wages and lower hours: all might be enemies. In Spain, to the disgust of George Orwell, the Communists in Barcelona had killed or imprisoned members of the POUM, an independent Communist organization that wanted revolution there and then, which did not fit with Soviet Communist purposes. In Spain, Stalin's real aim was not victory, but a continuation of the civil war. It divided Italy and Germany from Britain and France. He sent weaponry to the Republicans when they seemed likely to collapse, and stopped deliveries when they were winning. He also used Catalan nationalism, which the POUM opposed. It was a cunningly played game, and had lessons for the men and women who emerged from the Party schools to take over central Europe.

That sophistication was not needed in the Balkans, where there was not much between lord and peasant. There, the choreography was simple, brutal, and short: terrorize any opposition, offer land reform and grant property to new Party members. They were easy enough to recruit: disgruntled peasants (the village bad-hats) and the local minorities, including gypsies. In Romania some of the Hungarian minority were mobilized, and there were always Jews, though not of course the religious Jews, who suffered as much persecution as did other religious. However, even with religion, there were hatreds that could be exploited. Most Orthodox followed their own Patriarch, but there were other Orthodox – the Uniates, especially strong in Romania and the western Ukraine – who followed the Pope. The Communists might gain Orthodox support by campaigning against Uniates, and they did so. Elections in such circumstances were a sinister pantomime. The presence of Western representatives did mean, in Bulgaria and Romania, that some token elements from the old order were permitted to stay on. Some might be straightforward opportunists, such as the one-time Romanian foreign minister Gheorghe Tătărescu, who, with thirties manners, perfect French, and a habit of adultery, could be indulged or blackmailed into acting as a non-Communist front man. Even the young king of Romania was kept going until early in 1948, when he was bullied into abdicating and sent (not penniless: four automobiles of his collection, and some jewels, accompanied him) abroad. But these figureheads were powerless and were soon eliminated. Stalin got the Balkans, and a tyranny emerged: deportations in the hundreds of thousands, public executions, concentration camps, rigged elections and purge trials. Albania and Yugoslavia did not even need the Moscow bargain: they had strong Communist movements which took power as soon as the Germans had retreated, and they disposed early enough of the non-Communist furniture. The Western Allies were not consulted (in Bulgaria, Marshal Fyodor Tolbukhin, chairman of the supposed Allied Control Council, attended only once and otherwise did as he pleased) and there was some shabby behaviour, as when the British revealed to Moscow what their agents had been told by non-Communist Romanians, or threw a would-be Bulgarian refugee out of their embassy at 2.30 a.m. People's Republics soon emerged. But a Communist takeover elsewhere was more difficult, requiring a more complicated choreography. The media had to be controlled, and you had to win elections that might be supervised by foreign observers. There were middle-class sympathizers to be brought along, and you had to make some appeal to peasant farmers who were not obvious Communist supporters. The trade unions mattered, especially, because they could mobilize hundreds of thousands of demonstrators or strikers, and if, say, you wanted to shut down an opposition newspaper you could do it either by rationing its paper quota or by getting the printers to strike against 'anti-democratic' writings. A secret police, keeping a close eye on it all, therefore became very important and even central. These things happened, with variations, in Poland and Hungary. Czechoslovakia came later, early in 1948.

The British had gone to war in alliance with Poland, and had even guaranteed her territory. However, Stalin wanted to annex a good part of the Polish east – lands that were mainly Ukrainian or Byelorussian, which he could attach to the Soviet republics of those names, for the sake of what he himself called a Bolshevik version of Pan-Slavism. Since the Red Army occupied the area in 1944, and went on to occupy the entire country in 1945, there was not much that the British could achieve on the ground. Churchill tried. The deal which the British had in mind was a sacrifice of the eastern lands in exchange for western lands taken from Germany, and that deal was implicitly agreed at the Teheran conference late in 1943. The British wanted the Polish government in London exile to accept this, with a further guarantee that the country, no doubt neutral, would have its independence respected by Stalin. But there was too much bad blood. Stalin, occupying the Soviet part of the country in the early part of the war, had behaved atrociously, murdering 15,000 Polish officers at Katyń and elsewhere, and deporting hundreds of thousands of people. Almost no Pole was prepared to cede the historic cities of the east, and even when Churchill was in Moscow in October 1944 to negotiate over the issue, one of the Polish delegates, a professor, chose to lecture him for a long time on the historic rights of Poland in that region. It is just thinkable that, in exchange for an agreed cession of the eastern territories, Poland might indeed have been neutral and independent.

An equivalent such deal was successfully done over Finland. The Russians had attacked her in the winter of 1939–40, with a view to seizing lands north of Leningrad; after several months, in which blundering Soviet soldiers were outmanoeuvred by white-clad Finnish soldiers sliding on skis from ambushes, the Finns had had to surrender; they lost the lands, but, when Hitler attacked the USSR, joined up with him to take them back. If they had then cut the supply line to Leningrad, that city would have collapsed, and would have faced the utter extinction that Hitler had promised it. However, the Finns' leader, Marshal Carl Gustaf Emil Mannerheim, knew his Russia – he had been a cavalry general under the Tsar – and told his intimates that if the Finns acted 'they will never forgive us'. The Finns stopped, dragged their feet, maintained a link to Moscow through Stockholm, got out of the war in September 1944, and fought the Germans in their far north. In the resulting peace, Finland lost land, had to pay reparations (mainly in timber), conceded a Russian base and proclaimed neutrality. But there was no Soviet occupation, and parliamentary democracy was maintained at the cost, now and again, of grubby concessions (would-be Soviet defectors were, for instance, handed back).

The London Poles did not give way and it may not anyway have made a difference. Poland was much larger than Finland, in a much more strategic position – on the way to Germany – and in any case strongly anti-Soviet or even just anti-Russian (at Potsdam, Stalin openly said that a free election would mean an anti-Soviet government). Sad battles went on in the eastern territories as the Red Army settled in, and local Lithuanians or Ukrainians tried to establish themselves in the historic Polish cities: very young Polish hotheads were killed in defence of Vilna, for instance, and are remembered with cheap iron crosses in the old cemetery; and there was a battle in Balzac's old haunt, Wierzchównia, in which the entire village was wiped out by Ukrainian partisans. Five million Poles were expelled from these regions as the Red Army cleared them out. They were settled in turn mainly in the formerly German lands that had been assigned to Poland as compensation, from which 3 million Germans had themselves been expelled. Shattered Warsaw was reoccupied by 1.5 million people. Inflation was rife, and in 1945 and 1946 the average monthly wage in Poland bought ten pounds of meat or sugar; bottles were currency; there were epidemics of venereal disease. Late in 1945 an amnesty brought 30,000 demoralized men from hiding. The non-Communists were in no position to resist with any force. On the other hand, Poland had 'a mass of manoeuvre' in the sense that the population was greater and the territory quite large; besides, the Western embassies had treaty rights, and the Communists had public opinion in the USA to consider. Also, there was Catholicism, and that required some management. Still, at Yalta the Western powers had given way, in exchange for a guarantee that the Soviet Union would

help against Japan. There were supposed to be free elections but everyone knew what these would entail. When Roosevelt told Stalin that
the American Lithuanians might object if their country were taken
into the USSR, Stalin said, 'You want a referendum? It can be
arranged.' With a near 100 per cent 'yes' vote, this duly happened.
The British and the Americans (though not the Vatican or the Irish)
recognized the Communist-based Polish government, provided that
some (unimportant) ministries went to non-Communists. It was now
up to Stalin's Polish collaborators to manage the takeover.

The people who did the stage-managing were acute and energetic
enough, and Marxism was a useful training. They were widely hated,
and eventually lost, but many lived on to a great age, and an enterprising journalist got them, in retirement, in small, overheated, book-
lined flats, to talk. The head of the Secret Service, responsible for
espionage and lengthy prison sentences, was Jakub Berman – forty-
four in 1945, son of a Warsaw commercial traveller with five children,
and he went on to higher education. Most of the family were wiped
out by the Nazis at Treblinka, though one brother managed, as secretary of the Jewish resistance organization, to escape, eventually to
Israel. Berman himself had the advantage of talking Russian, because
he had attended the main Warsaw Russian school, and he reached the
Soviet zone early on. Then he went through the grim and dedicated
political school, and attracted the attention of a Comintern chief,
Dmitry Manuilsky, and lived in a chauffeur's room on the fifth floor
of the Hotel Lux (there was a telephone in the corridor, which no-one,
for fear that it might be the NKVD police, dared to answer; it was
part of the sinister surrealism of the place that when he did eventually
answer an insistent ringing, someone asked him about a Polish Communist writing on Africa). Berman then cultivated the obviously up-
and-coming Soviet officials Nikita Khrushchev, in the western Ukraine,
and Boris Ponomarev, in Byelorussia, who was to be head of the International Department of the Central Committee, the successor to the
Comintern. As the Red Army moved forward, Berman was one of
the very few Poles whom Stalin trusted, and in Warsaw he took over
the Security Service, the UB, with its networks everywhere, and he
was a main architect of the new regime, arranging for the persecution

and silencing of opponents. In case such men might let him down, Stalin would be a constant presence, even telephoning at midnight to catch them off their guard. But there were figures ostensibly less sinister than Berman. The press chief, Stefan Staszewski, had had a terrible history. Born in 1906, son of a Jewish small tradesman, he became a law student, joined the Communist Party, went to the Comintern school in Moscow for three years, and then served as youth secretary in south-east Poland, where the Party tried for an alliance with Ukrainian nationalists. He was arrested, fled to the USSR in 1934, and was sentenced there to eight years in a camp, in the terrible frozen Kolyma. A brother was murdered in the USSR; his mother was murdered at Treblinka. A man such as Staszewski only really had the Party as a mental and emotional focus, and in 1948 he was its press chief. Or there was Roman Werfel, socially above Staszewski, in that his father was a prosperous lawyer in the chief city of the south-east, Lwów, when it was one of the great places of the Austrian empire. There was a portrait of the Emperor on the wall and the family spoke German at home. Roman – like so many other boys of this class – despised religion, ate ham sandwiches at school, and was beaten up by other Jewish pupils. Then it was Vienna and Communism, followed by Berlin and a return to Poland, where he organized strikes on the noble Sapieha family estate at Rawa Ruska, where the peasants were generally Ukrainian. In 1939 he escaped to the Soviet zone, and joined up with the Moscow Communists as head of the ideological section. As such, he came to run much of the educational and cultural side of Polish Communism, but he was very erudite, and he did use his influence to help people who, in, say, Prague, would have been cleaning boilers. There were others who followed the Stalinist line and who were as much its captives as its advocates, and their loss of office later on probably came as a relief. Of the people the journalist spoke to, the only unrepentant figure was Julia Minc, widow of the one-time economic chief. Her past was part prison (for membership of Communist Youth, in 1922), part France, part Samarkand, where her husband, during the war, taught economics. Her interview with the journalist was pure agitprop, delivered with contempt, and when the journalist demurred, she told the dog to bite her.

In 1945 and 1946 the Communists entrenched themselves, working out how to take power. In the summer of 1946 the matter became urgent. The failure of the Council of Foreign Ministers to agree as to Germany's future was followed, that September, by the speech of James F. Byrnes in Stuttgart, to the effect that a German state in the west was under examination; Bizonia had already been announced, and its economic council was to be the nucleus of a West German government. Poland, in her strategic position, was then taken over by Stalin. It was important to discredit the non-Communists in Western eyes, and of course old Poland could be caricatured as a place of great estates and downtrodden peasants. There was some truth in this, but not much: the country had made considerable but unsung progress between the wars. Anti-semitism could also be used to discredit the anti-Communists, and there were indeed murderous clashes as Jews returned, trying to recover their property. The Cardinal Prince Sapieha himself was tactless, saying after an incident in the summer of 1946 that there were too many Jews in a government 'the nation does not wish'. In saying this he was only echoing a widespread peasant opinion that *rząd jest zażydzony* – 'the government is judaized' – and at a time when almost all of Western opinion sympathized with the Jews, such lines were not helpful.

The Communists mobilized their supporters, awarding them lands and houses evacuated by the three million Germans in 1945–6, whether in Silesia, Pomerania or southern East Prussia, and by April 1946 were being pressed by the Western ambassadors for proper elections. These could be postponed for a time, with reference to the endless movement of people, but not for ever; they needed preparation. In June there was a dress rehearsal – a referendum, containing three questions inviting the answer 'yes' (e.g. whether to approve of the new western borders). That allowed a drawing up of electoral lists, and a noting down of who was who. The next stage was to gain the alliance of left-wing elements outside the Party, much as the Bolsheviks had done in 1917, with the Left of the Socialist Revolutionaries. The Communists took over the trade unions, with endless detailed manoeuvering in committees where the agenda was 'fixed' by a Communist nominee. That way, 'the organized discontent of the masses' could be deployed against any independent voice. Besides, the Communists allocated land and housing, and could therefore arrange for whole blocks and factories to vote in unison. 'Anti-Fascism' was a weapon to use against opposition, and a dissident party was simply outlawed; with some left-wing socialist help a new electoral law was passed in September. Another scheme was to establish dummy parties, pretending to be properly Catholic or Liberal or Peasant; the real ones could then, again, be outlawed; and opposition media could be silenced. There were even some supposedly realistic Catholics, such as the journalist Stefan Kisielewski, who called for a Catholic bloc acceptable to both sides. When the election occurred, 'List Three', 'the Democratic bloc', won 80 per cent of the vote with 90 per cent participation, whole factories and housing blocks voting together: there had been 15,000 arrests and 10 per cent of the opposition (PSL) offices were simply closed. The non-Communist ministers, still theoretically in charge of their second- and third-rank ministries, found their telephones disconnected and their secretaries sabotaging correspondence. The Western embassies collected tales of all this and protested, but the Communists could weasel out. When the parliament met, in January 1947, with its handful of real opposition deputies, these behaved bravely, but, fearing for their lives, fled abroad.

In Germany, Soviet policy somewhat varied. On the one side were demands for reparations, and much of industry in the Soviet zone was dismantled. But on the other, the zone was supposed to be an advertisement for socialism, or, at the very least, to show that a neutral, unified Germany would have nothing to fear from Moscow, somewhat in the manner of Finland. In 1945 revenge was the dominant note. All along there had been friction in the German capital. Almost as soon as they occupied the city, the Russians had flown in old German Communists from Moscow, with an idea of controlling their zone through apparently democratic methods. To start with, the Communists announced that they would co-operate with other anti-Fascist parties and not insist on a full-scale Communist programme. They would, for instance, have a land reform, but one designed to break up the estates of the 'reactionaries' and grant land to small farmers (who were expected, as in Poland or the Czech lands, then to support the Communists). But elections did not go their way – hardly surprisingly, since at the time the Red Army had acquired a terrible reputation for looting and raping, and a quarter of the industrial installations of the zone were being dismantled. When free elections were held in Austria and Hungary (November 1945) the Communists did badly, and in Hungary had to be given an artificially powerful place in the government (controlling the police). One solution would be to force the Social Democratic Party (SDP) (and the trade unions) into a Communist framework – a united workers' party – and to muzzle any other parties. That last was easy enough, and the leaders (of the Christian Democrats and the Liberal Democrats) were just expelled, while dummies took their places. No more opposition from that quarter. The Social Democrats, collecting roughly two thirds of the vote, were more difficult, and the picture was complicated. Most Social Democrats were not unsympathetic at least to co-operation with the Communists. They regarded the recent German past with horror, some had spent time in concentration camps, and almost all felt that the failure of the two working-class parties to collaborate against Hitler had been a main cause of the Nazi catastrophe. In some cases, there was an idea that the Soviet Union alone offered a real chance that Germany could be a united, democratic and neutral country, like an enormous version of Finland, and maybe there would be concessions as to the border with Poland. Gustav Dahrendorf, who had been a member of the Reichstag before Hitler came to power, dallied with such ideas in 1945 and early in 1946. But the Communists behaved in a devious and bullying way, repellent to democrats, and they also resorted to force, kidnapping opposition figures. Meanwhile, they activated a form of the Nazi system of local control. Under the Nazis, each block of flats had its political supervisor, who snooped and bullied. The Communists reintroduced the system. When it came to political or trade union meetings, they were also skilled at the tactics employed by revolutionary minorities throughout history: 'packing' key committees with their own placemen, putting essential details into the small print, preventing opponents from attending meetings, deploying boring and lengthy speeches as a way of emptying a hall of moderate opponents and then taking a snap vote, provided they had the chairman in their pocket. In that way the trade union elections in Berlin produced a Communist majority (just as had happened in Russia, with the Soviets, in the later months of 1917). In any case, there was the Soviet military presence, as a great threat: the Social Democrats were forced to hold all meetings jointly with the Communists, Russian officers in plain clothes, with stenographers, in attendance. The Russians forced out opposition SPD figures, replacing them with men who supported fusion. Late in 1945 the SPD passed a firm resolution that there would have to be a fusion of the parties at national, not zonal, level, though they refused to present a joint list of candidates at the next elections. In this way, the Social Democratic Party of the eastern zone was fused with the Communist one in April 1946.

Hungary went the same way, in September 1947, with a unified Workers' Party in 1948. Hungary in 1945 had reached the end of the line. Budapest had had its moment of glory, around 1900, and, with Glasgow and Sydney, was among the greatest of the Victorian cities. But Hungary had consistently chosen the wrong side, had lost territory all around, and had fought the war to the bitter end: the siege in February smashed the great bridges between Buda and Pest, the Royal Castle on the Buda side was a ruin, and from the top floor of one of the grandest mansion flat buildings in Pest there stuck the fuselage of a bomber. Crammed into the ghetto area, there survived still about 250,000 Jews, whose lives had been spared because there were considerable limits to the anti-semitism of Hungary; but there was bitterness and privation all around. The Soviet authorities had promoted a sort of last-moment National Front and anti-Nazi coalition, and then set about recruiting Communists in a country that did not, by nature, produce very many. However, land reform was a serious cause in a country still dominated by great (and quite efficient) estates; there was at least a peasant radical movement, and, given the large and sometimes foreign-owned factories in Pest, there was at least the beginning of a labour movement.

To begin with, Stalin had not quite known how to handle Hungary, and allowed a free election in November 1945 – calculating no doubt at first, as with East Germany, that the triumph of the Red Army would cause Communism to become popular. But there was an overwhelming vote for the Peasant Party. It formed a government, but the Soviet occupiers gave control of the police and the Security Service (AVO) to Communists. Most of these were Jewish, their leader, Mátyás Rákosi, soured and made crafty by long experience of pre-war prison. Others had survived in Moscow (where Stalin had had several of their associates murdered) by treachery and guile.

Two young men in the new apparatus, Vladimir Farkas and Tibor Szamuely, had had characteristic Hungarian lives. As a young adept in AVO, Vladimir Farkas, born in 1925 in that selfsame region of what had been north-eastern Hungary that produced Robert Maxwell, distinguished himself as a zealot: the headquarters, on one of the main boulevards of Pest, had its complement of torture instruments, and there was a whole office to listen in on telephone conversations or to open letters. When he was born, his father, a Communist (and later on head of AVO), was in prison, and when he came out the family disintegrated. Father left for Moscow and worked for the Comintern, remarrying with a German woman and living in the celebrated Hotel Lux with the other Comintern families. Mother did not get on with grandmother, tried to kill herself by jumping into the river Hernad with her child, and then left for France, where eventually she joined the Communist resistance. She and Vladimir briefly met again only in 1945. He grew up in a sometimes flooded cellar with his grandmother, who took in washing; as a child he took meals to German Communists in the prison. The old woman, hitherto Orthodox Jewish, decided that there was no God after all, and when the Hungarians reoccupied the place sent the boy off to join his father in Moscow, having baked a favourite cake called *Linzer Karikak* which had raspberry jam inside and nuts outside. She was to die in 1945 and was buried in the Jewish cemetery, but her son, by this time head of the Hungarian Communist security system, would not have a proper tombstone put up. The boy, now fourteen, went on a Hungarian Jewish network to Prague, Warsaw and Moscow in 1939. His first (and characteristic) experience of the USSR occurred when the customs officials split open his apple to find out if anything had been concealed in it. Then he stayed, ignored, with his father and stepmother in the sinister Lux. In October 1941 the Germans arrived outside Moscow, and the Comintern people were evacuated to Samara, then called Kuybyshev. The lift wheezed up and down from the fifth floor, where the Farkas family lived in a set next to the Gottwalds from Czechoslovakia. Father and stepmother piled in with suitcases, leaving no place for the boy, and father pressed the button. Boy ran down the stairs and arrived at the lobby just as father's bus pulled out. He did get himself to the train after an odyssey through trudging refugees, and travelled for a week, fed from sardine tins by a Hungarian Communist woman, Erzsébet Andics, who, looking like Madeleine Albright, urged her charms on all and sundry. Then that Comintern political school, all pseudonyms, water, relentless Marx and no sex. Vladimir went to Hungary late in 1944 with a view to organizing the Communist takeover. With him went another Moscow product, Tibor Szamuely. Szamuely was the nephew of the man who had set up the Hungarian equivalent of the Cheka, the secret police of revolutionary Russia. They were called the 'Lenin Boys'. They had fled in 1919, and ended up via Vienna in Moscow. Young Tibor was sent to Bertrand Russell's progressive school, and was therefore bilingual in English (of which he was a superb writer). Back in the USSR, such people went to camps, and he did as well, but war liberated him and he too arrived in Budapest with instructions concerning the takeover. Both men ended up on the other side. Tibor Szamuely kept his cards hidden and arranged an appointment in the end as ambassador to Ghana (of which he remarked that the anthem should be 'aux arbres citoyens') and defected to London with all of his belongings. Vladimir Farkas was imprisoned in 1953 for his misdeeds and was let out in 1961, returning to his grand apartment on the Orsó utca in Buda to see his little daughter and his wife, who slammed the door in his face.

As Farkas says, 'the parliamentary democratic order was condemned to collapse on the day the November election results were published.' For a time, the Hungarians were told that they might have favourable peace terms in return for good behaviour: the eventual peace treaty, at the turn of 1946–7, went against them, as all of the lands awarded to Hungary by Hitler were returned to her neighbours. Then there was an inflation – the worst ever experienced in a European country, including Weimar Germany. By July 1946 there were 50 million million million *pengő* in circulation, and you survived by doing deals with the Communists, who controlled things. Dealing illegally in dollars was also possible, but it gave the Communists an apparently legitimate way to try to sentence anyone who was involved, including, as things turned out, the Cardinal himself, József Mind-szenty. But Hungary was not Poland. The Church did have its support-ers, but there was a large Protestant element, itself divided between Lutherans, Calvinists and Unitarians; there was no basis here for the passive resistance that Poles could put up, or for the Christian Democ-racy that emerged in Italy to defeat the Communists. Indeed, strict Calvinists, hating the Catholics, supplied useful men for the Commun-ists, including a pastor, Zoltán Tildy, who even became president for a few years. Meanwhile, the Communists infiltrated the trade unions, where there was supposed to be parity with the Social Democrats, and the trick was, as in Czechoslovakia, to identify a left-wing element. This was not altogether difficult. In the first place, there generally was, among the non-Communist left-wing elements, one that would always argue for appeasement: the Communists would behave better if col-laborated with. But there was terror, and there was bribery, and there was cynicism; and in the hopeless condition of Hungary in 1945, many people (including among the intelligentsia) saw Communism as the way forward. There were vast demonstrations of 'the organized discontent of the masses' in Budapest, and in 1946 'conspiracies' were unearthed, by which the non-Communists could be discredited (there is a heroically mistimed – 1986 – Communist book on this period, by Jakab and Balogh, which announces grandly that 'the competent authorities of the Ministry of Home Affairs' 'discovered the existence of an anti-republican illegal organization'). In Hungary, there was a further factor. In 1920 she had lost many of her old and historic lands, Transylvania especially. With Hitler, some of Transylvania had been recovered; and there was a hope that, with collaboration, something could be saved from the wreckage. Not until early in 1947 were the 1920 borders reconfirmed, Romania taking back Transylvania, and Czechoslovakia or the USSR an equivalent region in the north-east.

In 1946 the non-Communist government had very limited power, given that the Communists held the Ministry of the Interior, i.e. the police, and the security services. Besides, the Red Army was in occupation, and it simply carried people off for forced labour in the USSR; meanwhile, the economy, such as it was, was now dominated by Soviet cartels, and the foreign factory owners were powerless. The government was in any case easy to divide, because some of its following remained doggedly faithful to free markets, whereas others were sympathetic to the Left; and the religious division was still so strong that, in 1947, there were vicious fights over the presence of religion in schools. With their stories of 'conspiracy', the Communists could arrest, torture and deport even quite prominent Peasant Party politicians, and then extract confessions from them which would incriminate the prime minister himself. The government was only really able to let people escape to the West, including, in spring 1947, the prime minister, whose little son (now a New York banker) was held hostage. At the same time, with mass demonstrations in public, and secret police threats in private, sections of the governing party could be isolated and banned ('salami tactics', as they were called). The Allied Control Commission, dependent upon its Soviet chairman, was powerless. In 1947 a left-wing stalwart of the Peasant Party, István Dobi, took over, a man so demoralized and given to drink that, when he headed a delegation to Moscow, Molotov simply slid the bottle contemptuously down in his direction. There was then a coup against the Social Democrat and trade union 'Right'. An apparatus of dummy parties emerged, and in the elections of September ten parties fought, seven of them splinters, one of them so absurd as to be allowed to function openly: the 'Christian Women's Camp'. A Communist-dominated coalition with Social Democrats and Peasant Radicals easily won, and by March 1948 the Social Democrats had been forced into fusion with the Communists, as the 'United Workers' Party'. In 1949 this won '95.68 per cent' of the vote, and Stalinism descended.

Its local face was that of Mátyás Rákosi, born as József Rosenfeld in Bácska, to a family of twelve children from a small trader. He had won scholarships to Hamburg and London, had been a prisoner of war in Russia (at Chita, where a Countess Kinsky had helped) and had then experienced, on and off, but more on than off, prison. He knew how to act. He had a superb voice and had charm of a sort; he was also very vain, and at his sixtieth-birthday celebrations had special shoes constructed so that he could appear taller than Anastas Mikoyan, the Party vice-chairman, who bore birthday greetings from Stalin. Thirty-three prominent writers managed to write assorted items in praise of him, at a celebration in the Opera. Rákosi was hideous, the very exemplar of the French line that at forty you are responsible for your face. For the next five years, until the death of Stalin, Rákosi ran Hungary.

As Churchill said, an 'Iron Curtain' had indeed descended, and though there were still Soviet sympathizers, they lost the battle for public opinion as the facts seeped through the Curtain. Greece at least had been saved from the Communist takeover because of Churchill's bargain with Stalin in 1944. But, as ever, Churchill's side needed American backing.

3

Marshall

When the British announced on 21 February 1947 that they could not go on in Greece, the American reaction went far further than they had expected – 'quick and volcanic' was the expression used. In 1945 the Americans had hardly expected to be much involved in the eastern Mediterranean, though they had oil interests in Saudi Arabia. They had not meant to be heavily involved in Europe, even. But now, in February 1947, Greece caused a sea-change. The new Secretary of State, George C. Marshall, spoke – even then, to complaints at his moderation – for the entire Truman administration when on 27 February he said, 'It is not alarmist to say that we are faced with the first crisis of a series which might extend Soviet domination to Europe, the Middle East and Asia.' He had spent the previous year in China, where there was a civil war in progress, and had been fooled by the Communist leader, Mao Tse-tung. The behaviour of Stalin was still more provocative. Everyone knew that the Soviet Union needed peace in order to recover from the devastation of the war, and American help was on offer. Instead, after a brief interlude tyranny had been reimposed, with starvation and in places cannibalism, while millions of people were worked to death in the camps, and Stalin had told Marshall to his face that Communism in Europe would win. But by March 1947 the Americans had had enough.

Marshall himself was an old military man, straight, austere, not given to panic, but also unwilling to tolerate untruths. Now he spoke for almost the entire American establishment. Dean Acheson, also a man of much integrity, told the Congress leaders that a Soviet penetration of the Near East 'might open three continents to Soviet penetration'. The need now was to convince a largely apathetic public of the danger, and on 12 March, at a joint session of Congress, Truman made what was referred to as the 'All-Out speech': 'It must be the policy of the United States to support free peoples who are resisting attempted subjugation by armed minorities or by outside pressure.' Large majorities gave Truman what he wanted: $300m for Greece, $100m for Turkey. There followed a deliberate American strategy to contain Communism by using the economic weapon.

As Marshall returned from the exhausting and fruitless Moscow conference, without even an Austrian, let alone a German, deal, he could see that the Greek problem was just a small version of a much larger one. Western Europe desperately needed help, and the British themselves were unable to go on shouldering the burden as before. The three western zones in Germany were producing hardly one third of their pre-war level and yet they had been the source of one fifth of Europe's entire industrial output, including the heavy machinery for which Germany had been so famous. On the official market an egg in Hamburg cost a day's wage. The former President Hoover had been sent in 1946 to study the food question, on which, with Belgium in the First World War and Russia after it, he was a considerable expert. Early in 1947 he reported that the whole problem was insoluble unless Germany were once more part of a wider European economy.

When Marshall returned he had a flurry of memoranda on the European crises and various officials had been sounding the alarm for some time. The fact was that the Europeans were importing far beyond their capacity to pay, and a businessman, William L. Clayton, who had become assistant for economic affairs in the Secretaryship of State, had written that 'Europe is steadily deteriorating. The political position reflects the economic. One political crisis after another merely denotes the existence of grave economic distress. Millions of people in the cities are slowly starving ... The modern system of division of labour has almost broken down in Europe.' The American trade surplus by March 1947 ran at over $12m, and American prices themselves rose by 40 per cent in 1946–7, such that imports from Europe themselves declined and made her overall balance of trade even worse. The US wartime deficit ended in 1947, with a budget surplus of $4bn.

Had this been peacetime, no doubt banks could have been mustered for relief, or the European currencies could have been devalued, to make imports in the USA cheaper – a device eventually used in 1949. But in the immediate post-war era, and especially with the terrible winter of 1947, these escape hatches were blocked, and besides, the fledgling World Bank and International Monetary Fund, set up in 1944 for such emergencies, were too small to be effective (the IMF made a small loan to Denmark and was otherwise not heard from). Everything depended upon the Americans' attitude, and in spring 1947 the British Chancellor complained, '[they] have half the total income in the world, but won't either spend it on buying other people's goods or lending it or giving it away on a sufficient scale'. Here he was quite right, and they even still maintained high tariffs, pricing out such European goods as could be sold. Getting round Congress over such matters was not easy, even if the administration itself clearly saw what needed to be done. Stalin greatly helped: the USA would have to act or Europe might fall to Communism. Marshall understood, and as Daniel Yergin says, 'the anticommunist consensus was [now] so wide that there was little resistance or debate about fundamental assumptions'. Private businessmen would have to be deterred from pulling out of Europe altogether, as was happening.

In June 1947 Marshall spoke at Harvard and launched into a speech that entered history as one of America's most positive contributions ever. Veteran diplomats who knew Russia drafted it (Kennan and Bohlen) and their words were carefully chosen – for instance, there was no overt anti-Communism and the Russians were invited to the initial conference (in Paris) to discuss things. The Marshall Plan was ingenious. It was presented as a design to put Europe back on its feet, thousands of millions of dollars being on offer, generally as a gift. That in itself offered hope in the bread queues, and the USA at the time counted as a land of milk and honey, a place of wizardry in typewriters and refrigerators. That in itself would counter any appeal that Communism might have. But the Plan also squared another difficult circle. Western Europeans blamed their own lack of recovery on the failure of the Americans to deliver reparations from Germany, and the Americans had let this happen (in May 1946) because they would have had to pay still more for a stricken Germany. But if Germany were allowed to recover, there were many, many Europeans who would fear the worst, given the German past. But without German recovery, as Hoover had stressed, there would be no overall European recovery given that, for instance, half of Holland's exports generally went there.

Marshall presented German recovery in the context of overall European recovery, and in the summer of 1947 the Americans informally discussed the political unification of 'Bizonia' with the British. This was the restart of Germany: in April, at Frankfurt, an 'Economic Council' of fifty-two delegates chosen by the *Länder* parties had met. 'Reparations' were scaled down to permit the Germans to produce 10.7 million tons of steel. 'Bizonia' was formally included in the European Recovery Program, as the Marshall Plan was formally called, and after a conference of sixteen European nations in July, including Turkey, a project was submitted in September for increased output and exports, for financial stability and cross-border co-operation. The cost was put at $20bn. The winter had vastly weakened ideas of 'socialism', and liberalism, as the Europeans understood it, was coming back again. Marshall obviously meant capitalism, New Deal style, and it floated in on the tide of $40bn that the Americans disbursed in the second half of the forties. This was needed the more because the summer turned out in its way to mark more disaster: there was a drought, and the French had the smallest wheat crop for 132 years; extra rations had to be given to the Ruhr miners in a desperate effort to increase coal production. Importing food, France and Italy found their dollar reserves melting, and such private capital as was free to do so shifted to the USA. There was a run on the pound sterling, and as Truman wrote, 'the British have turned out to be our problem children now. They've decided to go bankrupt and if they do that it will end our prosperity and probably all the world's too.' Late in September he told congressmen and said that some interim help (before the Plan started) was essential, 'or ... for all practical purposes Europe will be Communist'. A new international Communist organization had been set up, Cominform, and the French and Italian parties had been instructed to start disruption through strikes and industrial trouble: in fact, news that 'in France the subway and bus strike is spreading' caused congressmen to accept Truman's proposal for a special session, at which the American people could be persuaded to endorse the Marshall Plan. A special session did then authorize a further $600 million as interim aid to Austria, France and Italy.

There was a final postscript when the next Council of Foreign Ministers assembled in November in London. By then, Marshall had no expectation of Russia: she would try to 'get us out of western Germany under arrangements which would leave that country defenceless against communist penetration'. One such 'ruse' would obviously be to accuse the Western powers of dividing Germany, with the establishment of a separate state there (and some Germans did argue that siding with Russia would mean a united and neutral Germany). In due course Molotov was utterly intransigent, and, now, the French came round to the American side, at last willing to accept the principle of a sovereign Germany. Such plans included a currency reform, which would obviously mark off the western zones from the east, which would retain the old, managed, currency. At American initiative, the Council was broken off on 15 December. European reconstruction, under the Marshall Plan, now went ahead.

Over a five-year period, $13bn was given to European countries, including Turkey, and that amounted to 2.5 per cent of the entire American economy. In the first year – 1948–9 – over $5bn went, in accordance with the recommendation of a committee set up under Averell Harriman. For a government to collect sums of that sort was remarkable enough but so too was the degree of international co-operation involved. The European Recovery Program (ERP) financed about one third of all exports, and a central office in Paris, the Committee for European Economic Co-operation, collected the statistics of what was needed, and allocated the dollars to pay for them (in April 1948 it became 'Organization' and subsequently became the Organization for Economic Co-operation and Development, today's OECD). That took time, and a large staff, some of them working in the various countries to check on the statistics and the needs. The Plan operated properly only in 1948–9, when it made a significant contribution to the overall GNP of between 5 and 10 per cent. An

Economic Co-operation Administration (ECA) was opened in Washington to supervise the statistics-collecting and co-ordinate it with American spending. There were some grumblers on the Right who did not like this government largesse. Certainly, it amounted to a subsidy for American producers, and the lobbyists got to work – half of the ERP shipments to go in American bottoms, and a quarter of the flour to be sent ready-milled.

German industry was essential, and the Economic Council in Frankfurt became a proto-government, with six 'directors' as technical ministers. By February 1948, when the European Recovery Program got under way, there were 104 deputies and by June 1948 there was a prototypical central bank, with the unwieldy name 'Bank of German Lands', the 'the' omitted because the 'lands' did not include the eastern-zone ones. In May 1947 the Christian Democratic Union emerged as a *Bürgerblock* dominated by Konrad Adenauer. Quite soon, in July 1948, the ministers-president of the *Länder* were authorized to set up a constitutional convention, and 'Bizonia' had its own people in the Marshall offices in Paris. There were still wrangles with the French, who wanted the Saarland's coal, and there were still debates about 'reparations' in 1949, but these were echoes of old shouting, and in summer 1948 the French Zone was to be added to the other Western ones, as a 'Trizonia'. An agreement at Washington in April 1949 agreed the bases for a new Germany.

The Marshall Plan counted as enormously successful. There were some imponderables. For Americans at that time, Europe was a place of endless interest. As a young CIA man of the time, Michael Ledeen, said, its films, wines and women were endlessly fascinating and stood at great contrast to the tea and cookies on offer at home. It was a sort of emancipation. Nan Kempner, wife of a banker stationed in London, was full of admiration for the stoicism of her British friends, giving dinner parties in the midst of severe rationing; she said she found a way of leaving money on the mantelpiece discreetly; Zara Steiner, then studying at Oxford, also found the place exotic, as champagne fountains flowed for summer balls in bread-rationed and then drought-ridden 1947. Fifty thousand people applied for ECA jobs, of which there were 3,701, 2,612 abroad. There was a further imponderable.

The myth of Roosevelt grew as time went by. In his lifetime, he had had enemies. But in the later 1940s and 1950s he came to be seen in a golden glow. The New Deal had made for superb propaganda, as public money was poured, with conviction, into the sort of giant engineering projects that distinguished America – especially the Tennessee Valley Authority, designed to irrigate a huge area with dams or river diversion (the original plan was, as it happens, Hoover's, and has subsequently been much criticized for its effects on the ecology). The New Deal of the 1930s may not have immediately solved America's problem with unemployment, but the Second World War certainly had, and the American war economy had been one of the world's wonders. This war economy, thought the people who managed it, just showed what could be done if the government and business co-operated, with government applying controls (as over petrol rationing) when this had to be. A young economist, John Kenneth Galbraith, rose to positions of power and influence. He had trained at Cambridge with J. M. Keynes and had been beguiled by the ease with which Keynes, himself apparently a grandee, took on the grandees of the 'orthodox', stuffy financial world, associated with the old and staid virtues. Galbraith, who went on to write very good books and convincing articles about the modern economy, had controlled some prices during the war. He was, instinctively, a believer in the power of government to liberate people from the bad barons or wicked capitalists or stupid bankers who might attempt to rule their lives. Roosevelt had died in April 1945, just before the end of the war in Europe. But his soul went marching on. The Americans who came to Europe in the Marshall Plan period had a wonderful time. Their attitude ('can do') came straight from the New Deal and the war. Now it was on display in Europe. Especially in Germany, it went down very well indeed. The Marshall Plan was the application of New Dealing to Europe. The thirties had been a bleak decade for foreign trade, with quotas, exchange controls and highly complex trade agreements between one country and another, striving for balance, and consuming vast amounts of paper in the effort to work out how many exported turnips translated into an imported locomotive. Exports in 1946 stood at only 60 per cent of the figure for 1938 – itself a poor year, given rearmament and the near withdrawal of Germany from the international arena. That was set to change.

To make the Plan popular, the ECA had a public advisory board on which sat trade unions, Rockefellers, General Motors, the New York 'Fed'. There were also American businessmen of the classically successful type. Joseph Dodge was a banker, later credited with the restoration of Japan. Paul Hoffman, the administrator of the ECA, was originally a car salesman, had made a million dollars by the time he was thirty-five, and rescued Studebaker. Lucius Clay, Eisenhower's deputy and then military governor, was an engineer by training and had worked on the Red River Dam and on airfields; at sixty-five, in 1962, he was to become a merchant banker. Averell Harriman, in charge of a committee to popularize the Plan, was a banker, with abrasive manners that irritated the British, who kept trying to prevent him from dominating Paris sessions. His associate David Bruce similarly had a background among what critics called 'Wall Street wolves'. William Clayton was a Texan oil man, looking everywhere, intelligently, for practical solutions and no-nonsense ways. The operation of the Marshall Plan did involve a great deal of paperwork, with typewriters and carbon copies, as the various government agencies set priorities – food imports, machinery or, more simply, dollars to fend off a crisis with foreign reserves, as was, by and large, the British concern. Foreign trade was generally run by governments, and there was strict exchange control. Cutting through that bureaucracy took energy, and the Americans had it. Already by 1949 a European recovery was going ahead, and the fifties saw a vast rise in prosperity.

But the Marshall Plan was to work as intended only for two years – 1948–9 and 1949–50, when the bulk of the $13.5bn was spent. The $10bn had more or less sufficed to deal with the European deficit and quite soon the Europeans were exporting again. The further $4bn that had been intended was diverted because the Plan, if not derailed, was greatly changed in emphasis, partly because of its own logic, and partly because of international crises. By the end of 1947, the USSR had turned its satellites into fully Communist countries, without any but a formal vestige of opposition.

There was a final decisive moment in February 1948, when Czechoslovakia fell under total Communist control, the 'Czech coup', as it was known. This was not at all easy, because the vital ingredients were missing: there was no Red Army occupation, and there was a functioning democratic state – and not only that, but one unlike the others in the Soviet bloc. The Czechs had serious heavy industry, and there were world-class firms such as Bat'a for shoes and Škoda for machinery; there was a substantial middle class, and, uniquely in the bloc, a large and organized working class. Czechoslovakia before the war had been roughly on the same level as Belgium, and even the capitals' architecture had points in common, especially the ingenious twenties additions. In ordinary circumstances, the trade unions and the Social Democrats would no doubt have co-operated with some farmers' party, whatever its name, to profit from the Marshall Plan and leave Czechoslovakia associated with the West – a sort of Austria or Finland. Such a solution to the Soviet problem was clearly in the mind of the Czech leader in exile, Edvard Beneš. He did not go down the Polish path, to challenge Moscow; instead, he went out of his way to reassure Stalin, and made no trouble when, at the end of the war, the Soviet Union annexed a strip of land on the Carpathians that had a Ukrainian population. He maintained good relations with the Czech Communists who had chosen exile in Moscow, and his ambassador there even turned out to be a Communist agent. A Czech force, again commanded by a man who turned out to be an agent, operated on the Eastern Front – all of this in absolute contrast to the behaviour of the Poles. The counterpoint was of course that the Red Army would not occupy Czechoslovakia, and in due course it did indeed depart. In May 1945 a five-party coalition took over the government, and a year later there was a free election. Prague, undamaged by war, struck a Polish journalist, Stefan Kisielewski, as a miracle: quite unlike grim Warsaw, its shops were full, the lights were working, the hotels were functioning, and even the old aristocracy could be seen making their way through the cobbled medieval streets in black tie, to this or that dinner party in some Schönborn or Lobkowitz Palace. 'Our Communists are not like the others' was a line that foreign diplomats or journalists often heard, and some of them were quite impressed by the fluent and knowledgeable minister of culture, Václav Kopecký, who could talk about film and much else. When the British historian A. J. P. Taylor visited Prague, his old London acquaintance, Beneš, showed him the undamaged Prague skyline with pride: 'all my doing'. He had even sent a 'plane-load of senior non-Communists to Moscow to negotiate terms with the Communists there, and Stalin, at a farewell banquet, had assured them, "We will never interfere in the internal affairs of our allies." '

But circumstances would prevent Czechoslovakia's becoming Austria or Finland, let alone Belgium. In 1945 there was indeed a sort of Popular Front regime, as the Communists understood it – an alliance with the Social Democrats and with the 'progressive' elements of the middle class (for historical reasons, one element was called 'National Socialist', essentially anti-clerical and anti-German). But the two chief political parties had been knocked out because of their behaviour during the war. Hitler had taken over the rump of the Czech lands, as a 'Protectorate', and there had been a collaborationist government run by the old Agrarian Party, the chief Czech party before the war. Collaboration had gone so far that the Czech lands, along with Belgium, were the only parts of Nazi-occupied Europe in which industrial production had gone up, not down. Its chiefs were put on trial and the party was banned. Slovakia had been even more heavily involved in collaboration. She had been given independence, and a nationalist or even Fascist regime had followed in 1939, under a priest, Mgr Jozef Tiso. With the blessing of the Yalta conferees, only 'anti-Fascist' parties were now allowed into parliaments, such that the two largest elements in Czech and Slovak politics were banned. Slovakia might, as today, otherwise have remained independent, and it was really only Soviet support for the integrity of Czechoslovakia that kept the country together.

On the face of things, restored Czechoslovakia was a functioning democracy, complete with cabinet and parliament and debates. However, the real centre of power lay in the 'National Front', a body on which were represented, by appointment, the five permitted political parties, and the administration consisted of 'national committees', again not elected. Not only this: the party members in the supposed parliament were under orders to vote as they were told by the National Front. In its regional and local committees, there was not much opposition to the Communists and they had a vast prize to offer. With Stalin's support, the 3 million German inhabitants of the country were expelled in 1945–6, with a suitcase each. In German-inhabited towns (in Slovakia, to a limited extent, the same happened with Hungarians), placards went up, couched in the same insulting language that had been used by the Nazis as regards the Jews: 'All Germans, regardless of age or sex', were to collect in the town square and be marched off or in some cases moved by train, and dumped in shattered Germany. Unknown numbers died, and their property was free for the taking. However, since the Communists controlled the relevant administration, anyone aspiring to take over these lands and houses, including many gypsies, would have to register with the Communist Party (as happened in Poland). The non-Communist elements in the National Front did not object to this – quite the contrary, they were even more vociferous about the process than the Communists themselves, and one of the chief 'National Socialists' (or 'Radicals', a more suitable translation), Peter Zenkl, argued for the abolition of 'capitalism', by which he meant foreign-owned plants and farms. A land reform took over 5m hectares, one fifth of them forest, and three fifths of industrial output was taken over by the State, again with the blessing of the non-Communists. Even the Communists argued for a slower speed of change and put themselves forward as protectors of 'the small man'. Meanwhile, on any national issue, including irritating little territorial claims against Poland, the five parties were glued together. This mattered very greatly in anything to do with Slovakia. Where the Czech lands were prosperous and modern, Slovakia was in many ways backward: still heavily peasant and Catholic, the educated element often Hungarian and Jewish or, where Slovak, part of the small Lutheran minority. When Slovakia had declared independence in March 1939, it had been a vast blow to the Czechs, hitherto the dominant people, and there was still much resentment at the Slovaks' behaviour during the war, when they had been pampered favourites of the Third Reich. Since it was Stalin and the Communists who in effect kept the country together, they received Czech support.

This made for the other unique (or, given Chile much later on, almost unique) feature in the case of Czechoslovakia: the Communists were by a long head the strongest party. As part of his deal with Stalin, Beneš had already allowed them a great deal of weight in the National Front, where they took a leading role in Security, the Interior, and (though their man was theoretically non-Party) Defence. They used their weight quite cleverly to make sure of the police and the security services, the StB; they wormed their way into the trade unions; they set up 'organizations' for resistance fighters and the like which (as in France) they could parade as democratic and anti-Fascist bodies. In particular, they set up militias based on factories which, if there ever were a clash, could easily dominate the streets, given that neither police nor army would intervene. A free election in May 1946 revealed their strength. In the Czech lands they took 40.17 per cent of the votes, three other Czech parties taking 15–24 per cent each; of these, the Social Democrats contained an element that could easily take the Communists' part and therefore even give them a slight Czech majority. In Slovakia the proportions were very different. There, a Slovak Democratic Party gained three fifths of the vote, the Communists under a third, which gave them, all in all, 38 per cent of the seats – still the largest party by far, but potentially a minority just the same.

In 1946, as tensions rose in Germany, Czechoslovakia still appeared to be an island of peace and even prosperity. Exports went ahead; Western visitors came and went; Czechs put themselves in the world's newspapers with this or that far-flung expedition. There were political wrangles as the parties fought over one proposal or another, and the non-Communists managed to win one such, a proposal for a wealth tax that would have damaged small enterprise. But Czechoslovakia, her borders reaching far into the bloc, and even, for a few miles, contiguous with the Soviet Union's, was no Finland, and there came a moment of truth in the early summer of 1947. George C. Marshall proposed his Plan, and the British joined him in inviting all European governments to attend a conference at Paris. The invitations went to the Soviet bloc, and the Russians did indeed appear in great numbers. The Czechs, and even the chief Polish economist, were anxious to go along with Marshall. But Stalin denounced the Plan, as a plot by which imperialists could take over weak economies such as those of central Europe and the Balkans; the bloc states, including Finland, refused to accept Marshall's terms, and a Czechoslovak delegation in Moscow was also instructed along these lines. Czechoslovakia therefore missed out on the developments that were to turn neighbouring West Germany, in a short space of time, back into a great trading industrial power.

As that development went ahead, Stalin could see that a rearmed West Germany, part of an imperialist bloc, would be on his doorstep, and an order went out for the Communist parties everywhere to respond. In August, at Szklarska Poręba in Silesia, a one-time German spa called Schreiberhau, in a manor house that had been turned into a secret-police sanatorium, a meeting of the main Communist parties was held, and was harangued by Andrey Zhdanov, the cultural commissar. There would be an end to 'Popular Front' tactics, i.e. alliances with treacherous middle-class or peasant politicians; trouble should be made, through strikes or whatever in western Europe, especially France and Italy; a union should be forced through of Social Democrats and Communists, and a one-party regime imposed, with all the paraphernalia of relentless propaganda and faked elections. This programme had already gone through in the Balkans and East Germany; Poland was nearly there; Hungary was about to undergo it, with the September elections. Czechoslovakia stood out but the secretary-general of the Czech Communist Party, Rudolf Slansky, soon had a plan ready. There were two possible routes to takeover. Power might simply, Bolshevik-fashion, be seized. But that would be too obvious, and would shock western European opinion. Better 'Trojan Horse' tactics, infiltrating the enemy parties. That programme now went ahead.

It was helped by circumstances – the harsh winter, followed by a severe drought, made for discontent, and there was a fall in exports (even food was imported from the Soviet Union). There was also much grumbling among the intelligentsia, whose wages had fallen quite drastically whereas elsewhere, as the economy recovered, there were patches of prosperity. The Communists blamed the machinations of 'capitalism' and the effects of the Marshall meeting; they proposed to head these off with a tax on 'millionaires' but suffered an early and misleading defeat. The other parties, recognizing it to be futile, blocked it, and the block succeeded because the Communists had not yet established their own manipulable element among the Social Democrats. On 10 September came a mysterious development: the despatch of parcel bombs to three prominent non-Communist ministers, including the one responsible for Justice, Dr Prokop Drtina. But the essential manoeuvre came over Slovakia. There, the Communist-controlled Secret Service discovered an alleged conspiracy, of exiled 'Fascists' colluding with Democrats. There followed 450 arrests, and the trade unions went into action to demand a suppression of the Slovak governors. They were replaced by a commission, in which the 'organizations' were represented; and though there was of course opposition in Slovakia, it was in some degree divided by religion (Catholic and Lutheran) and in any case could not challenge the police and the trade unions, who muzzled the media. Later on, the archives of all of this became open, and were written up in somewhat surreal circumstances by Karel Kaplan, who revealed that there had been spies, known in code (agent V101 etc.), in the Catholic ranks. Slovakia had been corralled by November, and there was a great block of opinion in the Czech lands that now saw the Communists as guarantors of the unity of the country against the treacherous Slovaks. Especially, a decisive element among the Social Democrats drifted towards the Communist side, and was led by one of the wartime chieftains, Zdeněk Fierlinger, who had probably been a Communist agent all along. Meanwhile, in Prague, there were barrages of Communist propaganda, and displays of 'the organized discontent of the masses', and these hundreds of thousands of people, complete with threatening banderoles, were imposing enough. How were the non-Communists to respond?

In January 1948 a provocation was carefully set up. The parcel bomb incident was investigated by the police, at the behest of the Minister of Justice, Dr Drtina (in his memories, he is, Austrian-fashion, punctilious about recording the title 'Dr', even when applied to executed war criminals or Communist agents). They dragged their feet, and did so insultingly, as Czech officials knew very well how to do; the incident was used too as an excuse to plant 'bodyguards' on the non-Communist ministers, and the state security service by now contained men who had been given a Soviet training. Drtina's investigation led towards two police officials, whose arrest by the Minister of the Interior (and police) he now demanded. The affair reached the cabinet, and its chairman, Klement Gottwald, refused to act. We know the sequel from both sides – memoirs on the one, secret archives on the other. Stalin advised confrontation, once he was assured by Gottwald that the Red Army would not have to intervene, and he flew into Prague his long-term Czech expert, the former ambassador Valerian Zorin. On their side, the non-Communist ministers talked to the American and British ambassadors, and conferred among themselves or with President Beneš. Beneš told them not to risk a battle, but they themselves wanted one, in the expectation that early elections would be called, which, given the Marshall Plan as support, they would win. In fact elections were due that May, but Drtina and his friends feared that the Communists, being in charge of the arrangements, would bring off the sort of coup that had worked in Poland, with the fraudulent referendum. So they forced a crisis, and resigned. If a majority of the ministers had resigned from the government and from the National Front especially, there would indeed, formally, have been a government crisis, compelling Beneš to act. On 18 February they threatened to resign, and on 20 February twelve of the twenty-six ministers did indeed do so.

This was not a majority. The Social Democrat Fierlinger stayed on, and so, fatally, did the foreign minister, Jan Masaryk. In his way, he represented the tragedy of the Czechs: vastly talented, an excellent linguist, a good pianist, a bibulous charmer with a long string of affairs and funny stories, and contacts all over the world; but in the end a weak and selfish man, the shadow of his far tougher father, the founder of the republic. Beneš was very ill, not likely to live much longer; the last thing that he now wanted was any kind of crisis. He would bow to force, whether that now shown by the Communists with their militias in the street, or by the Red Army; he dressed this up with reference to the West, which he alleged was forcing him to choose between Germany, which he hated, and Russia. Jan Masaryk thought that he would be Beneš's successor, and stayed on. Gottwald could hardly believe his luck and said, 'At first I couldn't believe it would be so easy. But it turned out that they had resigned. I prayed that this stupidity would go on and that they wouldn't change their minds.' They did not. Gottwald now had an opening, to nominate men to the National Front who would replace the resigning ministers, and were ostensibly from the same parties. Thus the Catholic (People's) Party leader, an aged priest, Dr Jan Šrámek, was replaced by a colleague, Mgr Josef Plojhar, who had been in Mauthausen and no doubt learned, there, to co-operate with Communists; and there were stooge Radicals or Social Democrats as well. The way was clear for Gottwald to proclaim the Communist takeover, which he did, overlooking the statue of Jan Huss from the balcony of the Kinsky Palace on Old Town Square, on 25 February.

Poor Drtina had tried to make amends, saying the day before that 'the most important guarantee of security rests in close collaboration with the USSR'. But it was too late, and two days later he tried to commit suicide, in a manner befitting the native tradition, by jumping out of the window. Badly broken, he was kept in hospital for a while and then imprisoned, spending long years in this or that castle dungeon, often together with German war criminals or Slovak Fascists whom he himself, in his great days as minister for 'retribution', had sentenced. In 1960 there was at last an amnesty and he was released, staying on in Prague until his death, aged eighty, in 1980. The new Communist regime showed its character in other cases. The aged Šrámek, a tough old peasant-priest who had spent the war years as part of the exile government in London, tried to escape on a French aircraft and was held at the airport. He too faced years of dungeon and prison, dying, aged eighty-four, in 1956. Jan Masaryk had a fate all his own. He stayed on as foreign minister, living alone in the official flat at the top of the Czernin Palace, the foreign ministry building (which had also housed the Nazi Protectorate staff). On 12 March he was found splayed on the road, below the bathroom window of that flat. Suicide? Murder? No-one knew, and neither the investigation of the time, nor a subsequent investigation by an American journalist twenty years later, when witnesses were still alive and evidence still warm, cleared up the matter. There were signs of a struggle in the bedroom, and there was blood all over the bathroom, which had only a small window, through which it would have been very difficult to manoeuvre Masaryk, a big man. Perhaps the affair can be explained by drugs. LSD, which had been discovered in Switzerland at the end of the 1930s, can cause a sort of birth trauma: a foetus, struggling inside the womb, then making, head-first, for a small opening through which it has to fight its way. Jan Masaryk, a fashionable thirties figure, probably used the then fashionable drugs of high society in the West, and, no doubt demoralized by what he had done and what had happened to his friends and colleagues, this time overdid the dose. He could have saved his country if he had been less vain. As things were, he deserved the epithet uttered by a celebrated British journalist, Malcolm Muggeridge, who had known him in London, and who knew (from a year in Moscow) his Communists: the window dressing fell out of the window. Beneš himself lingered on for a month or two at his country retreat, then died. In Czechoslovakia, the barbed wire went up along the frontiers, complete with barking dogs, watchtowers, minefields and searchlights – 'the Iron Curtain' that Churchill had spoken of. A peculiarly harsh and durable version of Communism descended and Prague acquired an enormous statue of Stalin, on a bluff above the river. It was the start of a military confrontation of East and West.

The Czech coup went together with a further Stalinization of the Soviet bloc. In Hungary, the preceding September, there had been a sort of parade ground version of a fraudulent election, complete with dummy parties, useful idiots and double voting; the unlovely Rákosi had taken over, and the Socialists were forced into union with the Communists. This, and the Berlin blockade, caused blood at last to flow through the bureaucratic arteries of western Europe, and ideas of unity began to take shape.

The British had even supported a Western Union, complete with a Council of Europe and a Court of Human Rights at Strasbourg. The motive was essentially anti-Communist, to lay down guidelines that would prevent governments from putting citizens into camps. There was a grand meeting of a 'Congress of Europe' in May 1948, with over 700 delegates from thirteen countries, graced with the presence of anti-Fascist warhorses and of course the lionized Churchill. Parliaments sent delegates to the Council of Europe which then emerged. However, there was no economic content to this. At the time, the British were trying to revitalize their empire, and concentrated above all on dollar-earning exports; the French had their Plan, of which fuel was a vital component – whether through exploitation of the German Saarland or development of nuclear energy. Currencies were subject to exchange control, and all but a tiny fraction of trade was carried out by barter, with mountains of paper in ministries. For this Europe to develop an economic character, French fears over Germany would have to be overcome, and this took time: for the moment, the French aimed mainly to take the coal of the Saarland for themselves, and, if possible, to loot the Ruhr. It was the great heavy-industrial powerhouse, and for the moment it was still operating far below par, partly because of trade controls, partly because the French feared German resurgence, and partly because of British maladministration – the Germans said that it caused greater damage than the bombing had done. But its relative inactivity was harming everybody else. Next-door Holland, half of the economy of which depended upon Germany, was still in poor shape. Two things were needed. Germany would have to be reintegrated into the European economy, and the various countries would have to trade with each other. This needed practical steps, far beyond a Western Union.

It was here above all that the Marshall Plan mattered. In the first two years, with roughly $5bn each for essential goods, and food in particular, it had amounted to a vast charitable enterprise, built upon the already considerable American transfers of the immediate post-war period, when UN Relief and Rehabilitation Administration (UNRRA) and Cooperative for American Remittances to Europe (CARE) parcels had kept body and soul together. That had been vitally necessary, because of the terrible winter of 1947 and the dollar shortages and the inflation which, in most countries, but especially in Germany, had wrenched trade into the black markets and below the counter. But for various reasons the Plan changed character after the first two years. To begin with, each country had taken its handout and kept the money in the bank. But trade was the real engine of growth, the dollars being used as a basis for that, not with the USA but over European borders. That meant the Rhine; the immediate point was German integration, through an increase in European trade. As the international crisis developed, there was a further element of great importance: American defence expenditure shot up, from the $13.5bn of 1949 to the $50bn of 1950, and a good part of this went to Germany, where forty American divisions were now stationed, and which produced the essential steel. The Ruhr wheels turned, slowly, again, and the great smokestacks emitted. Marshall money also saved the French Plan, which, again, required German coal and steel. The British, still attempting to refloat their empire as a bloc, were much less intimately involved. They used the dollars just to pay off debts.

It was on continental western Europe that the Marshall Planners concentrated, and its unity, in that sense, came in the (considerable) logistics trains of the American army. The essential was trade liberalization, and that could not be managed unless there were some means of payment, i.e. recognition of the various paper currencies. The old Bank for International Settlements at Basle in Switzerland – originally set up to handle the Reparations payments of the First World War – was revitalized, with a European Payments Union (in 1950). This again followed an Atlantic example. In 1944, at Bretton Woods in New Hampshire, the Americans and British had developed institutions that were meant to stop the collapse of world trade that had occurred in the Great Slump of the 1930s. The collapse – two thirds – had been a disaster, causing unemployment in millions and millions, and bringing dictatorships in dozens, the worst of them Hitler's. A chief reason for the disaster had been monetary – the loss of a common standard of exchange, in this case gold, when the British ran out of reserves and neither the Americans nor the French, who had gold, would move in to support the system. In 1944, the Americans recognized that they would have to use their economic weight sensibly, and an International Monetary Fund (IMF) was established (with a World Bank) so that countries importing more than they exported could be tided over with foreign reserves until they could bring their payments back into balance. This was a good idea, but in the first post-war years, as western Europe went through near calamity, the IMF did not have much of a role, and could not, until the various trading currencies had established themselves. With the European Payments Union, there came a limited version. It did not, at the time, seem to be at all simple. Most countries lacked earnings in dollars, the real currency. The Belgians, still controlling the mineral resources of the Congo, did have a dollar surplus, and had to be persuaded to use it for the common good; the British, who needed their European surplus to pay dollar debts, were in a still greater odd-man-out position, and made difficulties.

The Americans lost patience with it all, and preached the virtues of their own big and unified market. Marshall's successor as Secretary of State, John Foster Dulles, knew his Europe from the old days, when he had been an international banker, and said that unification was 'an absolute necessity'. More, the Americans lost patience with national currencies and said there should be a common one. This was formally suggested by the deputy director-general of the ECA, William Foster, in June 1950: call it the 'Europa', he said, or perhaps the 'Euro'. The Marshall people saw each country's storing its Marshall dollars in some bank or other, not using them to trade with, across the various borders. In response, there were indeed ideas of trade areas within Europe, but there were still fears as regards Germany. In part these were French, but the real difficulties were made by the British, fearing German competition. Various phantom schemes came up, to combine Britain, France, Scandinavia, Italy and the Benelux countries as a free-trade area: 'Fritalux', 'Finebel', 'Uniscan', none of which were worth much without the Ruhr. But in October 1949 the Federal Republic of Germany emerged, and the French had to rethink.

There now came an interesting affair, indicating the shape of things to come. The western Europeans received a further fillip, and one that, at least formally, did more for economic recovery than anything else: they devalued. The pound especially had been overvalued, partly to enable the British to pay off dollar debts, and partly to let them reconstitute their pre-war investments (which, strangely enough, by 1950 amounted to more than in 1939). Since trade was strictly controlled, the artificially high exchange rate was not menaced by any great imbalance of exports and imports. However, with the Marshall Plan, trade went ahead, and there was considerable difficulty in controlling it, because an exporter and an importer could connive to make 'false invoices', the money held in surreptitious foreign accounts. But the pound was a soft currency, given the size of British wartime debts, and foreigners sold it when they could – at that time, even more dollars were going back to the United States than were coming into Europe through the Marshall Plan. In the summer of 1949, there was a run on the pound. The Labour government that had swept into power in 1945 had become tired and divided: New Jerusalem had not happened, and the severely rationed British were now living at a lower standard than most liberalized Germans. If they were to rejoin the international trading network, to export, then the pound would have to be devalued; if the pound were again to become an international trading currency, alongside the dollar, then Atlantic co-operation would be needed. After discussion with the Americans, the pound was devalued by a good 30 per cent (to $2.80) on 18 September. The International Monetary Fund was not involved in this, and the German Mark was also devalued, but only by 20 per cent – the hardest sign so far of a rift between the Common Market to come and the British.

British exports did in fact do quite well, in part because other countries were still restocking with machinery, and a modest boom was under way by 1950, but the real boom started in continental Europe. The Germans did indeed restock, and for a time had a drastic problem as regards the balance of imports and exports: they had some difficulty in meeting their obligations under the Payments Union, and there was some question, for a time, of their dropping out. But the managers of the German economy held out, and the Americans as ever gave support. For a few months, the other Europeans accepted German IOUs. And then the German economy, on the basis of exports, boomed, and boomed. Then it boomed again, in 1955 overtaking British figures. In fact even by 1951 the export surplus amounted to more than the entire Marshall Plan had done. Now, surplus Germans could carry indebted Italians, whose economic recovery also got under way. There is an interesting question in this period, as to how far the Marshall Plan really produced the European recovery. The 'dollar gap' was greater in 1950 than it had been back in 1947, but no-one bothered; the sums spent under Marshall were quite trivial, in comparison with the proceeds; there are German experts who consider that the economy was recovering quite well, under the regulated and semi-socialized regime of 1946, and that it was the terrible winter of 1947 that caused the problem. Later on, international aid programmes, set up on Marshall lines, had very questionable results. Perhaps the answer lies straightforwardly in the presence of those forty US divisions: behind that shield, western Europe recovered.

By 1950 the Europeans had indeed understood that intra-European trade would have to be promoted. A key, here, lay in Paris. Late in 1948 an international authority had been set up for the Ruhr, an attempt to square the various circles – coal, coke, steel being allocated between exports (partly to France) and the Germans' own needs. But its budget was limited – under $300 million. The French were not going to be able to control German raw materials in that way, and they would have to alter their strategy. In 1949 the American desire to relaunch Germany was clear enough, and the main point of the French Plan was therefore hopeless. The fact was that Marshall and other money alone let the French import the machinery with which their own Plan could work, and the French needed direct access to the raw materials in Germany (or Belgium).

In 1949 there was rethinking, not least in the head of Jean Monnet, architect of the Plan, and a considerable opportunist. He, like so many of the initial Europeans, was an interesting and even a rather fascinating man. He had not bothered to finish school, made money by selling brandy to Eskimos, got a Soviet divorce, and admired American business (he spent both world wars in the USA, acting for the British or French governments). He would as easily have been director of a French five-year plan as founding father of a sort of New Deal Europe, and his influence was formidable. There were by now many Frenchmen arguing that some closer association with booming Germany was essential. The foreign minister, Robert Schuman, was one (he came from Lorraine and had even served in the German army in the First World War) and he talked comfortably not just to Adenauer but to the Italian, Alcide De Gasperi, who had been a deputy in the Austrian parliament before 1914, when Trieste had been an Austrian port.

In 1949 Monnet and Schuman sensed that France must change course, and make an effort to capture the new Germany before she went off in a completely Atlantic direction. Monnet was already irritated at the French metallurgical industries' inability or unwillingness to compete. Trade with Germany would put an end to that, and Franco-German reconciliation became the order of the day. Even in the twenties, there had been efforts at co-operation, for French steel, and during the war intelligent technocratic heads – Albert Speer, as German munitions minister, and tubby little Jean Bichelonne, head of industrial production for the Vichy French – had talked 'Europe', though the sheer clumsiness of the Nazis had caused French workers to run away and hide. Now there were better-organized Germans, and the Ruhr was working again. Collaboration could go ahead without the old collaborators – in fact, on the French side, the Free French had just stepped into their shoes. The French proposed a European Coal and Steel Community, in May 1950, and told the British only at the last minute, just as the British had informed them of the devaluation of 1949 at the last minute. The Germans had agreed in advance. True, their industrialists did not necessarily want to have their hands tied, but a political argument was all-important: 'Europe' would be Germany's way of becoming respectable again. Konrad Adenauer, anyway a product of the western-leaning and mainly Catholic Rhineland, therefore overrode objections.

The heavy industry of western Europe was to be run through some multinational body. It would take charge of coal and steel, set prices, govern cartels, allocate production quotas and generally preside over trade, which would of course be free of tariffs. At this time, Belgium and Luxemburg were major producers of coal and steel, and their adhesion was important; at the same time Italy, re-emerging, and surprisingly strongly so, as an economic power, also needed access to coal and iron, of which she had little. As with all such international arrangements, the details were difficult and complicated, because in each country there were lobbies and interest groups wanting special treatment. The French metallurgical industrialists had long been used to protection; the Belgians subsidized wages in the older, and sometimes nearly obsolete, mines of the French-speaking Borinage country, around Mons and Namur, so that the miners there could match those of the Kempen district, where the mines were very new, productive and in Flemish-speaking country. Such subsidies could not be squared with the rules of competition of an international community, supposed to create 'a level playing field'. An equalization fund would have to be set up, so that in effect the Germans compensated the Borinage miners whose coal sold at a loss. Even Luxemburg made for difficulties, as its iron and steel needed protection from the Ruhr. In 1951, after difficult negotiations on such points, a treaty established the European Coal and Steel Community. There was a High Authority, sitting in Luxemburg, in some pomp and grandeur, interpreters chattering away. There was a court of arbitration. There was a ministerial council, taken from member country governments, and an assembly of deputies. There were provisions for the Authority to store, say, scrap metal in case prices fell below a certain level. The organization even had a flag – blue for steel, black for coal, six yellow stars representing the member countries (Italy had joined). With adaptations – the black was dropped, as it stood for political Catholicism – this became the flag of the future Europe.

4

The NATO System

'The Czech coup' brought an immediate hardening of Western attitudes, and the ratchet effect of the Cold War moved on: in three years,
it led to a full-scale war, though not the one that had been expected. In
1947 there had already been a military side to this. In March of that
year, the British and French concluded an alliance, the Treaty of Dunkirk. It was supposedly designed against Germany, but its real point
was of course defence against the Soviet Union, and there was a further concealed point of importance: no-one entirely trusted the Americans, who were extracting hard bargains for any economic help that
they gave, and who were even, still, imposing 50 per cent tariffs on
European imports. The British and French responded with efforts to
refloat their overseas empires, and again feared, quite rightly, that the
Americans were not in sympathy. Again, there was the nuclear element.
The British had taken the decisive steps in the making of the atomic
bomb, and had presented the secret to the Americans, a good year
before they had come into the war, but they had then cut out the
British, who proceeded with a bomb of their own. France, lacking coal,
was also extremely interested in nuclear energy (and proceeded very
successfully with it). Dunkirk therefore had an anti-American aspect.

More generally, ideas of European unity were in the air: Churchill
had made a well-publicized speech at Zurich in September 1946 calling
for it and in January 1948 the Foreign Secretary, Ernest Bevin, echoed
him, after the London conference on Germany had failed. This time
round, given Soviet intransigence, the Americans sympathized. In
December 1947 the three Western foreign ministers reviewed the whole
situation and agreed as to the problems – Greece under great pressure,

Germany still in collapse, the Italian Communist Party perhaps on the verge of taking power at the next (April) election. In effect Bevin was proposing an American military alliance, and had secretly made this proposal late in January. The Americans had told him that they would do nothing unless the Europeans themselves united, and it was in that sense that Bevin spoke. He was adamant as to the nature of the Soviet threat, of police state totalitarianism, and proposed a rather vague 'Western European Union' which did indeed develop in 1948–9 (and became less vague six years later, when Italy and Germany were included). Now, in March 1948, a Brussels Pact brought in the Low Countries, 'Benelux', with a permanent committee of defence ministers, and in September a staff was set up, at Brussels, under Field Marshal Bernard Montgomery. In April there was already an Anglo-Canadian draft plan for extension of the Pact to the USA, though the American role was mainly financial, to help rearmament, and without provision for an American command, let alone bases on European soil. But a US military mission was present and in July it took part in deliberations. There was a formal problem, that the USA could not make peacetime alliances, but that was got round by the 'Vandenberg Resolution' (June), which – with some sleight of hand as to the wording – allowed the USA to make them after all, provided they were undertaken in connection with the United Nations.

In that context, the Americans publicly announced that they would co-operate in the Brussels Pact. The American guarantee was an essential ingredient for the French as well – they would accept the German state, creation of which had been formally resolved upon at London, on 4 June – provided that there were an American presence to prevent the Germans from growing too independent. Now, the old Second World War associations came alive again: Eisenhower, Montgomery, the French all knew each other well, and they co-operated again. Here was the start of NATO, and of much else, as Atlantic ties multiplied and thickened. Trade unions co-operated in a free association. The American trade unions (the AFL, or American Federation of Labor, had merged in 1946 with the CIO, or Congress of Industrial Organizations) were now strongly anti-Communist (their leader, Walter Reuther, having worked for two years at a Ford plant in Nizhny

Novgorod, and thus knowing his Soviet circumstances) and the Western trade unions set up an organization of their own, challenging the older international one, which the Communists had taken over. There were generous provisions for cross-Atlantic student exchanges and scholarships, particularly with Britain, so that the elites could get to know each other, or even that foreign students in the United States would go back to their own countries and teach the natives how to do things. To win over the intelligentsia, American subsidies went to *Preuves* in France and *Encounter* in England (via Melvin Lasky, who had a German wife). These magazines were very good indeed, and writers appeared in them for prestige, not for the fees. On another level, *Reader's Digest* promoted simple-minded American patriotism and anti-Communism, and was translated into many languages. It paid well, and was widely read. After the fall of Communism, a famous American commentator, at the time something of a fellow-traveller, remarked that *Reader's Digest* had been a better guide to what was going on than anything else. The CIA, set up on a British model, also came into its own around this time.

One vital part of the new order was a restored Germany. The London conferences in February–March and April–June had recommended this on 4 June. One great difficulty was with France: would her parliament accept this restitution of the hereditary enemy? The American Senate's adoption of the Vandenberg Resolution on 11 June was reassuring: there would be an American presence in Europe to contain Germany, and the London recommendations went through Paris, though by only eight votes – one of the deciding moments of French history, in that the main danger was now recognized as Soviet, and the way forward, the elaboration of a pan-European system which the French would have a lead in managing. In July the German federal states were authorized to set up a 'parliamentary council' which would write a constitution. In this period the Allies received another great fillip. The Italian elections of mid-April 1948 were decisive, and the Communists lost. There were (and are) cries of 'foul', because of covert activity by CIA men such as Michael Ledeen or Edward Luttwak, who knew the country well. But there had already been the considerable counter-example of the Czech coup to deter anyone on the moderate

Left from voting for the Communists, Marshall aid was at stake, and, besides, the Americans were in a position to save the Italian minority of Trieste from absorption in Yugoslavia. The Christian Democrats, under the European-minded De Gasperi, swept the board.

The Cold War took a further ratchet in Germany, and a configuration was then set, for the next two generations. 'Trizonia', now that the French (formally in April 1949) had included their zone in 'Bizonia', was being turned into a state, but this could not be done with the old Reich currency, which had become dramatically valueless. The whole economy was distorted, as banks could not operate with it, and a vast proportion of exchanges took place in the black market, with which by now all Germans were familiar. Controls existed on food prices but the result was that food vanished from the shops: sellers could not afford to sell at these giveaway prices, and the same was true for most other goods. As ever with inflations, cheats and parasites were rewarded; far from there being a social revolution in Germany, people with property were rewarded for just sitting on it, as it went up in value. But there would be no economic recovery – outside the black market – until the currency was reformed; at a British suggestion, this was undertaken, and in great secrecy new banknotes were printed for the *Deutsche Mark*. This turned out to be an enormous success, because shop windows all of a sudden were filled, at last, with goods.

Would it be extended to the western sectors of Berlin? All along there had been friction in the German capital, as the Russians attempted to force Social Democrats and Communists into a single party, which they could control. In the western parts of the city, a referendum at the end of March 1946 rejected it by an enormous majority. Early in 1946 there were still many people in the British administration who reckoned that they should just cut their losses and concede Berlin to the Russians, while building up their own zone, and even the American commander, Clay, who became a subsequent West German hero, was not sure. Late in 1946 there returned (from exile in Ankara) a remarkable soon-to-be Lord Mayor, Ernst Reuter. He and his rival Willy Brandt were strongly anti-Communist, having (like Bevin) had ugly experiences of their tactics, and even the Popular Front nostalgics in the SPD were silenced as the Soviet oppression and kidnappings went ahead. Besides, the British were having to pay £80 million per annum for their own occupation zone, and Soviet reparations demands seemed designed to wreck the economy, or even to make the British pay more. The Western Allies could not give up Berlin if they wanted to remake a Germany of their own, and a British adviser, Alec Cairncross, was responsible for the new currency. On 20 June 1948, a Sunday, the new *Deutsche Mark* came in, the old *Reichsmark* was scrapped. Money savings were almost wiped out but each German got forty of the new Marks.

It was the signal for collision. By now western Berlin was seen by the Western powers as part of their own territory, and the currency was to be introduced there as well. The Soviet zone operated along entirely different principles, and there prices did not play the same part: such goods as were available were paid for in the old paper in any event, and prices were fixed by decree or Plan. The Russians protested against the process, and on 30 March began to make difficulties for Allied vehicles going to and from West Berlin. On 16 June they walked out of the *Kommandatura*, the joint body managing affairs for Germany, cut the railways on 23 June, and on 10 July closed the canals. Here, there was a difficult point, because there were no treaty arrangements as regards Western access by land to Berlin. There was, however, legally a right to passage by air, and there followed a remarkable episode. By air, with aircraft landing, skimming the rooftops, every few minutes, two and a half million people were fed and even heated by coal over eleven months by an Anglo-American effort. American warplanes, capable of delivering nuclear bombs, now reoccupied the wartime airfields in eastern England, and there were rumours of war. From full-scale war, Stalin shrank, and he never turned off Berlin's water supply, which would indeed have caused the place to surrender. But he had done enough to make the Americans formally support the new military structure being set up at Brussels, and in the following year it was turned into NATO, the North Atlantic Treaty Organization, with an American commander. There was almost no opposition to the demands for rearmament that were now heard in the United States. The 'National Security State' emerged, in later years much bemoaned, but at the time an apparently obvious outcome of the Soviet challenge.

In May 1949 the affair was uneasily settled. Stalin now half froze West Berlin. There were strict controls as to Allies' access but traffic went ahead, and the half-city survived as an island. The West built it up, and turned it into an advertisement: it was artificial and heavily subsidized, but, because of its peculiar status, Germans wanting to escape to the West could easily just pass through Berlin, and millions did. In the end it became a slow-acting embolism in the entire arterial system of European Communism. In that sense the West had won.

Now there were better-organized Germans, and the Ruhr was working again. The European Coal and Steel Community became a much more practical step towards European unity than anything proposed by the British. They themselves, invited to join, refused. At the time, British miners' wages were much higher, and the British were looking at different markets. They feared competition from lower-cost Continental coal (in practice, American coal was cheaper) and Bevin, when consulted, just said that the Durham miners would not stand for this. Later on, the British attitude to this emerging Europe seemed purblind, foolhardy. But Britain, with still strong imperial or ex-imperial connections, with exports booming, with an important position in Atlantic affairs and a sizeable force fighting in Korea, had solid interests elsewhere, and in 1951 very few people took developments in Europe with the seriousness that they, in hindsight, merited. No-one in 1950 foresaw the rapidity with which England would decline.

In practice the ECSC was not particularly successful. In a world of trade liberalization, it was at the mercy of imports, and, of all paradoxes, American coal imports were needed in Germany because the speed of her recovery meant that she needed all of her own coal. Much the same happened with metal: there was a 'scrap mountain' because it could not be sold at the cheap rates on offer elsewhere. The Korean War brought a boom for steel: 50 per cent of Belgian output was exported and, as the historian Alan Milward says, the ECSC 'virtually collapsed'; without the formal creation of a European Economic Community later on, it 'would probably have been unable to find a common course of action'. Another British commentator, John Gillingham, is even more dismissive. So was Jean Monnet himself. He recognized that the organization was not going anywhere, went to Luxemburg less and less, and faced attempts even to push him out. He did in fact resign in 1955.

There was another blind alley. What was to be done with Germany on the international level? France was divided; both Right and Left opposed any forward move. Nevertheless, a centrist government, at American prompting, went ahead. Monnet's deputy, René Pleven, by now prime minister (though not for long) proposed another supra-national arrangement, a European Defence Force (it went back to 1950, and Monnet urged this in part because he wanted another iron in the fire during the lengthy and arduous negotiations over the ECSC). At first the idea was to delay German rearmament, but then came another ambition, to put German troops under French officers in a European Defence Community (EDC), in its way not dissimilar to the ECSC. On its own the EDC arrangement was hardly necessary. It was to be small, and would not operate independently of NATO; in any case in 1953, even before the treaty was to be ratified, the Americans had adopted a new strategic doctrine, that of enormous nuclear response to a Soviet attack, such that any European Defence Force (EDF) would only be of trivial importance. On the other hand, the EDF would be supported by a proto-government with four ministries and a great deal of money to spend on armaments – a European 'military-industrial complex' as President Eisenhower later called the American version. The foreign ministers of the six ECSC nations initialled this treaty in May 1952. The French socialists insisted on the EDC's having a political supervisory body, and negotiations started for a European Political Community out of that, with the same paraphernalia as the ECSC. Defence budgets doubled in the first year of the Korean War (to $9bn) and in a 'Mutual Security Program' the US supplied defence aid as well, in fact not much less than the Marshall Plan itself. It was really the Americans who pushed for the EDC, and no-one was enthusiastic. In July 1954, after two years' acrimonious exchanges, and two months after France's catastrophic defeat at Dien Bien Phu in Vietnam, the French parliament failed to ratify it. 'Europe' had been foiled again, it seemed, but in fact the EDC was superfluous. German rearmament went ahead anyway, Germany joining NATO in

1955, and NATO itself did what the EDC had been supposed to do. On Christmas Eve in 1954 the French assembly rejected German membership of NATO but then, on 30 December, bizarrely allowed Germany into what was now to be called the 'Western European Union' under the Brussels Pact. A threat that there would be a separate treaty with Germany then allowed her into NATO as well. There had been a crisis in the alliance, but not one, in the end, of any significance. Dulles greatly exaggerated when he remarked that a 'disaster' had been avoided, of an 'isolated' France and a 'neutralized' Germany, Europe dominated by the Russians. The crisis such as it was was easily enough settled. But again Monnet and his friends had been disappointed, and they needed something else.

There was another strand to 'Europe', and it also closely involved France. Monnet could see that nuclear energy was becoming important, and France, lacking coal, had been forward with it. Now he proposed a European Atomic Community, 'Euratom' (the Brussels Exhibition in 1958 with the huge 'Atomium' as its centrepiece). This was a step too far. The American atomic agency preferred to deal separately with the European countries and they anyway lacked the uranium and the specialized knowledge, which the Americans, outside diplomatic circles, were not inclined to share. Euratom never achieved anything. But the idea of a customs union now came up again – yet another idea that was originally American and even went back to 1947. The Benelux countries were at the mercy of their larger neighbours, Germany especially. They were enthusiastic about anything that made for a supra-national authority that would bind France and especially Germany, and they were also anxious that the British should be involved as a counterweight. Now, the Dutch foreign minister proposed a customs union.

The suggestion was taken up by an Italian foreign minister with a desire to lay down supra-national rules that would prevent Italian politicians from indulging in sharp practices. With a constituency in Sicily to impress, he invited major representatives to discuss the Dutch idea. They met in an old Dominican monastery near Messina, at Taormina, in May 1955. The French wanted German machinery; the Germans wanted respectability; and Euratom was at least worth discussing. As ever, the British hung back. They sent an intelligent, well-informed and linguistically talented official, Russell Bretherton, who sucked an avuncular pipe in some scepticism as the others talked in their high-flown way; then he wished them well and took his leave. Later on, there was much criticism at this missed opportunity. Of the failure to link up with the ECSC, Alan Milward remarks that the then Labour government was 'too complacent and too much a product of British history to understand what was happening in France'; besides it suspected 'neo-liberalism', i.e. Erhardian anti-socialism, in the various 'European' ideas. As to Bretherton's departure from Messina, other commentators also shake their heads, and suggest that Great Britain missed a chance to create a 'Europe' that would have suited its purposes better than the Europe that did emerge. There is truth in these criticisms, but in the end they are anachronistic. In the mid-fifties the British were doing quite well, were even selling fashionable motor cars, were reconstituting their foreign investments, even beyond the pre-war level. The trading agreements with the Commonwealth worked quite well, and food was quite cheap, while markets were available for exports.

At any rate the other Europeans came quite quickly to an agreement, and set up a conference at Venice for the following May and June to work out details. Experts settled these and on 25 March 1957 the Treaty of Rome (strictly speaking, 'treaties') established the European Economic Community, or EEC (and the ineffectual Euratom). It entered into force on 1 January 1958. The preamble, a sort of Catholic aftershave, stated grandly that the aim was integration and even unification within a set period. Institutions were taken from the ECSC – a council of ministers, an arbitration court and a High Authority, though it was called a 'Commission' because by now most people had had enough of Monnet's ambitiousness. The first president – such was his title – was German. Adenauer would have preferred Wilhelm Röpke, a good liberal who had had much to do with the remaking of Germany but instead had to make do with Walter Hallstein, who taught commercial law. He was a chilly figure who, asked what he should be called, said he would prefer it if he were called 'Professor'.

He was too frosty to deal with the French combination of acuteness and arrogance that he now encountered. The new Community, as with its predecessor, followed French lines. The Germans were simply anxious to be accepted. Provided that the customs area, free trade and competition meant what they said, they would accept French proposals as regards institutions. These reflected French ways, which meant 'top-down' behaviour, complete with 'directives' that were composed by functionaries on high and then communicated for obedience by the member states' governments. French civil servants referred to the people as *les administrés* and in French circumstances, given the periodic ungovernability of the country, this was not inappropriate. But these institutions were conceded because the other member states recognized that France faced particular difficulties with a customs union. She still had a large African empire, and had made some effort to integrate it with the French metropolis. Much of her agriculture was very poor and backward, and would not face competition. Some of her industry – Lorraine steel, for instance – had flourished but there were still large parts of it that would collapse if exposed to German and even Italian trade on level terms. There was a further French fear that, given the capital mobility that a customs union must mean, there would be yet another 'flight from the franc'. At varying intervals, the bourgeoisie famously put its money into suitcases and headed for the Swiss border: this had happened when a left-liberal and anti-clerical government (led by Émile Combes) took over in 1905, and had been repeated with the Popular Front government of 1936. With the troubles of 1947, it had happened again, and French governments knew very well that their best-laid plans could go awry because the money fled. This was one reason for their readiness to devalue, a course of action that at least made the suitcases (some of them no doubt filled with black-market profits from the war) lighter. One way and the other, the French were not wholehearted about the Community, and they had to be placated. There were also fears for the 'social benefits' which had been awarded to French workers after the war. These were expensive for the *patrons* and they thought that cheaper-wage countries would have an unfair advantage. The 'benefits', such as wage equality of the sexes, would have to be 'harmonized'. Few people in France were therefore particularly enthusiastic about a customs union, and on the whole the idea went ahead mainly because, otherwise, it was clear enough that France was going nowhere; it was Germany that led the pack. In 1954 France had been humiliated in Vietnam, and now she was being further strained as a vicious terrorist war went on in Algeria. France needed friends. It helped that in 1955 a lively anti-European figure, Pierre Mendès France, lost office at this time, punished for being right. It also helped that the head of the French delegation, Robert Marjolin, was a remarkable man with long experience as head of the Organization for European Economic Co-operation (OEEC), and he managed the negotiations very well – tacitly telling the other Europeans what they should say, so that he could manage the French behind him.

He extracted the concessions, and the French interest ensured that the Community would not just spend its money in Brussels, its supposed capital, but in Strasbourg and, for some matters, Luxemburg as well, which, in time, meant absurd amounts of time wasted on travel. At a dramatic turn in the negotiations, Adenauer went to Paris in secret, agreed that the French empire could be associated, and that Germany would contribute to a development fund for it; he then in public overrode the German delegation and told it to make progress on 'harmonization', i.e. say 'yes'. There were further plans for the EEC tariffs to be reduced, and for a common external tariff to be imposed even against other Europeans' goods within four years. The French peasant was to be looked after by a common policy, i.e. artificially high prices for food, and a Common Agricultural Policy did indeed emerge in 1962. It made food prices inside the EEC greater than outside by half again, and is still with us, making a cow or even a tree more expensive than a student.

When the British representative at Messina had left the discussions early, it was because he could see no future for them as far as his own country was concerned. In the first place the British imperial or ex-imperial territories still looked promising, and they had preferences as regards tariffs. Apart from anything else, this meant that food in England was cheaper than elsewhere, because New Zealand and Australia had low-cost farming. But in any case it was a peculiarity of

British history that the rural or village population was vastly smaller than that of any other European country – in 1900 only 8 per cent, whereas in France the figure stood closer to 50 per cent and even in industrialized Germany 40 per cent. It was a decisive difference, explaining everything else, from the weakness of the native culinary tradition to the Industrial Revolution. The English, though not the Scots, had never had formally to abolish serfdom, because it just went, and the last vestige of it, an archaic exchange of labour rent called copyhold, went in 1925 (whereas slavery, in the sense of owning a slave on English soil, had been declared illegal in 1772). In other countries the call for protection of the farmer was loud and clear, and supported by millions of votes. In Great Britain, not. Cheap food came partly from the Commonwealth countries or the Argentine, but British agriculture was more efficient, because it was relatively mechanized, whereas elsewhere the peasant farm prevailed. However, now, in 1956, it was becoming clear to the British that a customs area was emerging in Europe, from which they were to be excluded: exporters would have to pay tariffs and face other obstacles to trade which could be just as effective in pricing them out. They responded, without any sense of urgency, with a counter-proposal: a free-trade area to include all of Europe, including such countries as Denmark and Austria which needed an outlet for cheaply produced agricultural exports, or which, as small and specialized economies, did not want to be cut off from world markets. Britain, and six such countries, now set up the European Free Trade Association, a version of 'Uniscan', which was run in a way quite unlike the EEC, without much regulation and with only seventy officials. Left to themselves, Germany and Benelux would probably have been happy enough with such an arrangement. However, the peculiarities of the Franco-German relationship meant that the six EEC countries took a different road. As matters turned out, it was a road to a prosperity that made Britain, a decade later, seem backward. But, in 1955, no-one in high places foresaw this.

5

Communism in China

Stalin may have backed down in West Berlin but in the short term he had achieved what suited him: the attention of the Americans had been hugely diverted from developments in Asia that were of far vaster significance for the future. The other great European crisis also showed its effects. Greece was proving to be what Lawrence had said of Balzac, a sort of 'gigantic dwarf'. The British had given up on the extraordinarily complicated but in the end quite simple little country, in February 1947, and Truman had picked up the pieces with his 'doctrine' (like most such, civilian or military, in effect a one-liner) a month later. The Americans shouldered up non-Communist Greece. But at exactly the same moments, the British were throwing in their hand over Palestine, over India, even over Indonesia and Vietnam. There was now a general crisis in that huge area of the world that had been dominated, until very recently, by British and Japanese imperial power, and the largest of the problems occurred over China. In the late winter and early spring of 1947, there were terrible headlines, one after another, throughout this region of British implosion, and the Cold War encountered what was to prove the greatest of its dimensions. The British decision of February 1947 over Greece was the pebble announcing the avalanche.

Greece now became symbolic on a worldwide scale once more – a symbol of developments over the next two generations. Empires were to be replaced by nation states, the world over, and an immense problem came with the modernization of the backward places that escaped from empire. Nineteenth-century Europe had introduced as a universal principle the nation state, and Greece had been launched, freed from the Turkish empire, early on, though only as a small kingdom, based on the Morea (a name meaning 'mulberry'). She was modernized as such things were then understood: a constitution, a Bavarian megalomaniac as king, professors enthusiastically making up words for the new national language, one far beyond anything that the peasants could understand ('laundry' was *katharsis* and 'foreign travel' *metafora esoterika*). She had, even then, a further pioneering role: she attracted footloose, romantic intelligentsia, obsessed with foreign liberations that they perhaps did not understand any too well. The English (or Scottish) poet Lord Byron, his finances not in good shape, his talents ebbing away, the latest mistress sent back to her elderly husband, betook himself there, was widely stolen from, and was be-scened by a page boy, one Loukas, who extracted from him a coat of gold cloth which he wore when astride the donkey with which he followed Byron around. In 1824 Byron turned his face to the wall and died. The subsequent history of Greece was not very happy, and in 1945, though she had the appurtenances of a nation state, she was in many ways closer to what was soon to be called the 'Third World'. In that respect, she was, on microscopic scale, a model, and, there, as on the far greater scale beyond Europe, British imperialism came to grief.

'Third World' – at one time covering countries as different as Haiti and South Korea (of which, in 1960, the only export consisted of wigs) – was itself an expression that became worse than useless, but after the Second World War large areas of the world were indeed backward and poor, with millions of illiterate and superstitious peasants scratching the soil and making immense families. Running democracy in such countries was a precarious business, and in politics they wobbled between military coups and would-be revolution. Between the wars, Greece had been on the edge of anarchy. A quarter of the population consisted of minorities, themselves very varied, and another quarter had arrived twenty years before as penniless refugees from Turkey. Often enough, they were exploited, not so much by great landowners as by village headmen and especially by middlemen on a small scale who bought and sold for them. The State was a major employer, and clans fought over the resulting jobs, or the meagre fruits from corruption that came with them. There was indeed some industry, mainly to do with ships and tobacco-processing, but not much.

But Greece developed a Europeanized educated class, with English and especially French schools; there was also a large diaspora in the eastern Mediterranean, Alexandria especially, which produced more in the way of European civilization than did Athens herself. Communism developed, particularly in Salonica, where dockers, minorities and refugees congregated – a miniature Shanghai. Here was imperialism (British) in alliance with a grasping native bourgeoisie (Aristotle Onassis, Taki Theodoracopulos) and an exploited peasantry; here as well was an army with a political role; and here too was an intelligentsia which could lead that mass of dock workers and porters and servants-of-servants and bargees who were too poor, disorganized and mistrustful to produce a trade union movement of their own. Here, the Party would come into its own. It would be the 'vanguard'. Of course there was absurd oversimplification in seeing all such countries as the same. Later on, development economists fell for similar oversimplifications. But the fact is that there was often much of substance to what the Marxists said, and their diagnoses were often not wrong at all. The prescriptions turned out to be another matter. They created more havoc and mayhem than anything the banana republic alternatives would have done.

The failures of the Communists were some way in the future, and meanwhile in 1946, in that huge swathe of the world that was coming free of European empires, there was near chaos. The war had caused even more death and destruction in Asia than in Europe, the great symbol being the dropping of the atomic bomb on Hiroshima, on 6 August 1945. The Japanese had taken a lead in showing that the Western powers could be defeated by their own technology. A Japanese fleet had annihilated a Russian one in 1905; Japanese commerce had taken over Western markets; then at the turn of 1941–2 superior Japanese air power had produced catastrophe for the British at Singapore and the Americans at the naval base of Pearl Harbor. Japanese occupation of an enormous area of eastern and south-eastern Asia had followed. The peoples involved – Vietnamese, Burmese, Malayan, Indonesian – produced independence movements that the Japanese (clumsily) encouraged, and when the war came to an end, these national movements had a force that could not, as events soon showed, be stopped. True, the Americans' atomic bomb did indeed demonstrate that Western inventiveness was still ahead, or even far ahead. The casualties from that single bomb, about ten feet long and just over two feet in diameter, ran to 140,000 (direct and, through radiation, indirect); even the birds in mid-air were burned, and two thirds of the city's buildings were destroyed. The West was still hugely superior in the most advanced forms of engineering (or 'technology' as it became known), but there were by now great limits to the effectiveness of this. Asia was at least learning 'intermediate technology', and though the West might win great land wars, winning small and scattered ones was another matter. Empire was over, though it fought a rearguard action that now seems very weird.

Such was the condition of the Far East as the Cold War got under way in 1947. So far, the Far East had already influenced events in Europe: at Yalta, the Americans had been willing to concede a great deal in eastern and central Europe in order to get Soviet help against Japan. But that meant a full-scale Soviet invasion. It struck a China already in endless convulsion. During the war, thanks to the American alliance, China had been very unsteadily returned to independence, had even been granted nominal Great Power status, with membership of the Security Council of the new United Nations. But she was in the grip of civil war, and Stalin patronized (or bullied) the local Communists, under Mao Tse-tung. The Berlin blockade was a very good device for diverting the attentions of the Americans away from China; they were surprisingly weak on the ground in the Far East, and were altogether unsure as to how to proceed. When the civil war began in China, American support for the non-Communists was limited and sometimes reluctant, and by 1949, when the Berlin blockade was ended, the Communists were well on their way to victory. This was a greater disaster than even the Second World War, but it began with good intentions and with Western sympathizers who, for all their extraordinary knowledge and sympathy, now look foolish.

Chinese Communism had started off as a reflection of Russian Bolshevism, and there were Chinese intellectuals – including the young Mao Tse-tung, then a librarian – who had looked at socialist or at least progressive literature. They seethed with resentment, or even hatred, at what had happened to old China: important seaports just seized by this or that foreign power, the Japanese in bullying mode, finances in a mess, native collaborators coining it in. In 1912 the old empire had been abolished, but no solid state had then followed: on the contrary, local warlords divided the country up. There were also some 6,000 Protestant missionaries, setting up hospitals and even universities some way into central China: Yale developed a connection. But this activity just called attention to Chinese backwardness: the awful poverty of the peasants, the degradation of women (in China little girls had their feet crushed so that, in later life, they would walk daintily), the illiteracy that was bound to follow from a script in which each word had its own character, sometimes of forty different brush strokes. Even the Americans' record was not spotless: they imposed such restrictions against Chinese immigration that a team of Chinese representatives trying to set up their pavilion for an international exhibition at St Louis were roughed up as they came through. Shanghai was an international city, with tens of thousands of foreigners in their own settlements, from which Chinese were kept out; and when there were riots in the twenties, foreign policemen fired into the crowds. Russia had also been dominated by more advanced countries; Lenin had just refused to pay the debts, and in 1919 was defeating the foreign invaders trying to collect them and to return Russia to her previous status. In Peking, Chinese took an interest, and a Communist Party soon followed.

Of course, this was in some degree fanciful. Old Marx did not really have very much to say about such countries, regarding their economic and social arrangements as fossils. There was not much of an industrial working class in China, either. However, Lenin had made his revolution in a Russia that also had only a limited number of industrial workers: the 'people' were Volga boatmen, dockers, hawkers, servants-of-servants and especially peasants, and especially again peasants who had been pushed into military uniform in pursuit of a very badly managed war with Germany. There were at least the beginnings of that pattern in China, and some of the intelligentsia understood as much. The cause was even inspiring, and Chinese students, getting married in France, solemnly had photographs taken to record them in their wedding finery, jointly holding up a copy of *Das Kapital*. France, appositely enough, was the principal source for the spread of Marxist ideas: in the First World War, to create some gratitude on the part of the imperialists, the Chinese government had sent 100,000 labourers, each with a welded dog-tag, to the Western Front: this was known to the British as the 'sausage machine'. Students, who also undertook to work part-time, also went to France, where, unsurprisingly, they picked up revolutionary ideas. Some of Mao Tse-tung's most prominent colleagues were among these students: Chou En-lai and Deng Xiaoping, for instance. Later on, as French academe moved Left, the Sorbonne attracted many more such, from all countries.

On the worldwide scale, there was of course a potential Bolshevik alliance with victims of imperialism, and, quite soon after the Revolution, representatives of these, from India or China, began to appear in Moscow. The Communist International – Comintern – set up a school for them, and sent its own people to offer sage advice. Mao Tse-tung (the name means 'shined-on east') did not go to that school, and did not in fact go to Moscow at all until after his own victory, much later. But his cause was revolutionary, and he belonged to a type that, worldwide, produced revolutionaries: for he was a student teacher from a peasant background less dismal than others, and had ambitions to count as a scholar, which had been frustrated by an irascible, bullying father who made him work in the fields. The province in which he was born (in 1893), Hunan, was on a military road, and it was relatively open to foreign influences: in 1903 it had the first girls' school in China and its capital was also chosen by Yale University as the place for an educational programme, on which American missionaries were very keen. In fact Mao was first noticed by an American, the president of Yale-in-China, as an agitator in 1924. It was easy enough for the young Mao to regard China with contempt. Why had such a civilization, the most ancient of all, come under Western domination? Mao cut off his pigtail, broke with his domineering father, and took up links with Peking intelligentsia who became interested in the Russian Revolution.

It was not just Communists who wanted to get rid of these things. There was a progressive-nationalist movement, the Kuomintang, initially dominated by Chinese Christians, with support from the merchants and students. They, too, were prepared to collaborate in the anti-imperialist cause with the Bolsheviks, and developed close relations with a Moscow which, to start off with, regarded the Kuomintang as the desirable ally. The overall notion was that China was too backward and rural to produce a proper Communist movement, and that the likely revolution would be anti-Western but also fuelled by peasants wanting their own land and merchants wanting to corner trade: these would be useful to Moscow, though they might also, on the ground, be hostile towards Communists. The Russians sent advisers and even set up the Whampoa Military Academy, near Canton. Its graduates, led by Chiang Kai-shek, set about unifying the country, which had fallen under various warlords, each with his protection racket (often involving opium, of which there was an epidemic). Moscow instructed the Chinese Communists to co-operate with Chiang, and the labour unions in Shanghai did so. He, however, had other ideas, and mercilessly butchered them, sometimes, to save ammunition, just binding them in batches of ten, taking them out to sea, and throwing them overboard. The origins of the Sino-Soviet split, a vastly important element in the end of the Cold War much later on, go back to this period. The Communists were decapitated, and Mao kept much of the nucleus together in remote, difficult, mountainous country; he did get help from Moscow, but not very much – in effect only enough to keep him going (in one decisive battle, his troops could fire their machine-guns only for ten minutes). Meanwhile, Moscow co-operated with Chiang Kai-shek, since the Kuomintang had taken over most of the country and especially the cities. Even when the Kuomintang eventually lost the civil war, in 1949, and evacuated Shanghai in conditions of much disarray, the Soviet ambassador accompanied it to the very last stage of exile.

Mao Tse-tung turned out to be a guerrilla leader of genius, and kept his forces together for years of harsh living and very hard fighting against an enemy far stronger. As Leszek Kołakowski says, he 'was one of the greatest . . . manipulator[s] of large masses of human beings in the twentieth century'. The ideology was 'a naïve repetition of a few commonplaces of Leninist-Stalinist Marxism' and in places hardly said more than 'what goes up must come down'. But it did lay stress on the peasant side, and it possessed the necessary degree of hating-ness, as required by Lenin. In later life, he became grotesquely vain and self-indulgent, producing a 'Little Red Book' that the masses were supposed to chant ('The world is progressing, the future is bright and no-one can change this general trend of history' and the like) and he was always neurotic (suffering from chronic constipation). But he had a Stalinist mixture of guile and ruthlessness, and even when he was travelling through remote territory, carried on a bamboo litter with two senior colleagues and followed by a bedraggled horde carting weaponry along muddy tracks, he had an idea as to which of the two colleagues needed to be knifed by some show trial held in some hut of wicker, roofed and walled with yak dung. He also seems to have had the measure of the Soviets, knowing how to extract help from them and what to expect. It was at a Party meeting at which Stalin's hench-man Lominadze presided that Mao made his most famous remark, that 'power comes from the barrel of a gun'.

In China, the generation that surfaced with Mao Tse-tung around 1920 took up the revolt of the peasants, the downtrodden rural masses, oppressed by landlords and by village usurers. When these matters were properly examined, the downtreading was limited, or, rather, was a matter of overall poverty. There were no doubt usurers who made money out of the poor, but the landlords themselves were badly off, in most cases not far above the rest of the peasantry: in fact, when Mao set about land distribution, expropriating the land-lords, each peasant came away with one sixth of an acre, or hardly more than a suburban garden. True, there were absentee landlords in the towns, and their rent collectors were hated, especially when they arrived at a bad time, but in every village there were problems between peasants or other inhabitants, and it was here that Mao excelled. Col-lecting army mutineers, village bad-hats, bandits and dirt-poor peas-ants in an isolated mountain area in Hunan, he applied himself to studying what a peasant revolution would really be about: prices, profits, networks, diets, the incomes of watch repairers, the num-bers of prostitutes (thirty in a population of 2,684 in one locality). 'On hearing that a borrower has sold a son, lenders will hurry to the borrower's house and force the borrower to repay his loan... "You have sold your son. Why don't you repay me?"' Mao thus represented the Party with at least some cohesion and force, whereas the Shanghai and southern components had been hopelessly weakened; later, he escaped to an even more remote area, where he set up the 'Jiangxi soviet', one of those Communist islands that appeared with all wartime resistance movements, complete with its own secret police, its own re-education arrangements and its own machinery for exploiting gullible foreigners. In any village there would be a confiscation committee, a recruitment committee, a 'red curfew committee' etc., and even a children's corps. An economy developed, too. Curiously enough the area was a big source of tungsten, and exported it through a state bank run by Mao's brother to Canton; peasant women were made to cut their hair short such that their hair-pins – their savings – could be taken in for war finance. There was, however, primary school education for the first time, and Mao gained a favourable press, with romantic American journalists such as Edgar Snow to be flattered or lied to (when the Sino-Soviet split occurred, he was refused a visa to Moscow). There were other little Red bases, such as Hailufeng on the south coast, that counted as a 'Little Moscow' with its own Red Square and a gateway copied from the Kremlin, the leader of which, Peng Pai, had 10,000 people killed, burning down 'reactionary villages'. He was then chased away, and when the remnants of such defeated forces reached Mao he took them over and expanded his own force: he could now defy the Shanghai leadership (which wanted to dismiss him) and impress Moscow. It needed him: relations between the USSR and Kuomintang China were not straightforward. The Kuomintang were nationalistic, not inclined to give way over foreign concessions, and in 1929 there was a Soviet–Chinese crisis when the Nationalists tried to take back the vast railway concession in Manchuria, including Harbin (this was the largest of the foreign concessions, at 400 square miles). The Soviets set up a Far Eastern army under Vasily Blyukher, who had been adviser to Chiang Kai-shek, and Mao was encouraged to divert the Nationalists by campaigns 1,250 miles to the south. His real strength lay in his having the largest Red Army outside the USSR. Stalin's tactic was to keep the Communists in play, but never strong enough to win (the same tactic applied over the Spanish Civil War). Mao was helped in this because he was soon joined by Chou En-lai, who knew a great deal about foreign circumstances (he had studied in Japan and in 1921 had been in France). In Shanghai he had been associated with the Comintern representative, Gerhart Eisler, and he had even been at the Whampoa Military Academy, as director of the Political Department when the Soviet Blyukher directed the officer cadets. He turned out to have a genius for operating in clandestine conditions and in Shanghai he had set up the Chinese equivalent of the Cheka (the later KGB). A man of icy and elegant presence, he became an essential prop for the brutal Mao, and was especially important because he knew well enough what could be expected from the USSR.

No doubt if matters had been normal, the Communists would have been defeated; Chiang Kai-shek had vast superiority, and controlled the cities; and Kuomintang China, despite the troubles, was making remarkable progress with railways, banks, education, industry and even health. But matters went far beyond control in the early 1930s. The world economic depression caused great turmoil, bankrupting producers of raw materials, and drying up foreign investment; and in 1931 cataclysm occurred, with an attack by Japan. She – or rather, her military – were now determined on empire, and took advantage of China's confusions to take over Manchuria, industrially the richest part of the entire country, with raw materials such as coal that Japan did not possess. With truces now and then, the Japanese fanned out over the next few years, occupying eventually a third of China and usually defeating the disorganized Chinese, who in any case, with the Communist presence, had a civil war on their hands. Even without the Japanese, Chiang Kai-shek had local challengers, would-be warlords to put down, and Mao was able to use them, on occasion, as allies. He himself claimed to fight the Japanese in the name of national unity but in practice did so fairly seldom, and sometimes even made secret arrangements with them.

It was in that context that Mao constructed the founding legend of the Party: the 'Long March'. In September 1933 Chiang Kai-shek mustered half a million men for the fifth 'annihilation' expedition against

Mao's Ruijin state base. In May he had agreed a truce with the Japanese to do this and he surrounded the area with an ever-tightening net of blockhouses – 'drying the pond and then getting the fish'. Each side had its Germans: on Chiang's were two very prominent generals of the First World War, Hans von Seeckt and Karl Litzmann, and on Mao's, Otto Braun (who had to be assigned a 'wife') and Manfred Stern, who emerged later on in the Spanish Civil War as 'Kleber', one of the main agents of the undercover Communist takeover. Mao was driven to break out, and he showed himself a leader of genius, even using the 28,000 wounded and sick as a rearguard, and dumping the wives and children as well (he was himself a neglectful and even cruel father). Mao managed to keep his force of 90,000 men together, at least in part because he kept the treasure, hidden in a cave, and thereby defeated possible rivals. The whole episode required ruthlessness and cunning. One of the Nationalist chieftains was bought off with a deal involving the local tungsten, unreliable men and women were hacked to death and pushed into pits before any move was made, and there was a pretence that action was going to be taken against the Japanese. Instead, in October 1934, Mao's whole force, laden with weapons and machinery, undertook a vast and circuitous move towards the north-west. Chiang himself was something of an accomplice, in that he wanted the Communists out of the way, so that he could control the south-west, including Sichuan and Yunan (where, in the event, during the Second World War, he established a Kuomintang government) and it suited him for the Communists just to make off, on a 6,000-mile trail that depleted them, to the far north-west, in barren Shanxi, where there already was a Red 'pocket' of some million souls. The area was quite widely Moslem, and Turkic, and Communists had already shown how they could use such minorities. In this case, Mao's men even forswore pork. Otto Braun said with wonder that 'the hospitality astonished me greatly'. Nationalist planes attacked and there were marches of 25–30 miles per day but Mao was able to trudge back and forth, and even to force his way across an old bridge leading into Tibet: an episode that was crowned by legend, as even the veteran American journalist Harrison Salisbury wrote it up (in 1985) as heroic: the bridge was alleged to have been burning. Later biographers regard this as 'complete invention'. By October 1935 the Red armies at last consolidated,

Mao's in a dysentery- and louse-ridden state, but there were supplies, and the new base was not far from Soviet territory. Foreigners such as Edgar Snow were there to conduct public relations with the West, especially the United States, and they were remarkably successful in presenting the Communists as progressives in the American sense: land reformers, emancipators of women, etc. One such was Anna Louise Strong, in Malcolm Muggeridge's words 'an enormous woman with a very red face, a lot of white hair and an expression of stupidity so over-whelming that it amounted to a kind of strange beauty'. Such people, marching across the Sinkiang swamps, had a wonderful time playing outlaw with foreign passports to save them, and in the case of Miss Strong the Maoist convictions were strong enough to land her in a Soviet prison, as a spy (Muggeridge adds that 'her incarceration proved to be brief – I imagine that even in the Lubyanka her presence was burden-some'). At any rate, Mao had excellent relations with Moscow and with the USA, whereas Chiang Kai-shek, facing Japanese invasion and the need to respect Western pieties, had other concerns. By October 1935 Mao was in safety, recognized as leader by *Pravda*, and able to profit from Chiang Kai-shek's mistakes and misfortunes.

The Japanese did much of Mao's work for him. They smashed a good part of the Chinese army and air force, and Chiang Kai-shek tended to keep his best troops in relative safety, in the south-west (thus alienating Churchill, who thought that he was not seriously fighting the war at all). Japanese depredations (which had included the killing of hundreds of thousands in the Nationalist capital, Nanking) caused chaos, and the war ended only with the Soviet invasion of August 1945; it had taken 20 million lives and caused 100 million refugees to flee. When the Japanese advanced on Chiang's headquarters at Chungkin they even dropped fully one third the tonnage of bombs on it that the Americans used on Japan.

Chiang Kai-shek was under strong pressure from the Russians as regards arms deliveries and had more or less to do as he was told, but he was also pressed by the Americans, who looked at him patroniz-ingly. Roosevelt had a network of informers who included Edgar Snow, while the British ambassador, Clark Kerr, said that Chou En-lai was worth all the Nationalists rolled into one. Chiang Kai-shek's regime could be portrayed in much the same way as, say, the exiled Polish government in London, representative of 'reaction', capital, landlords, etc., and when Ernest Hemingway submitted a report comparing the Communists' tactics with those he had observed in Spain, it was sidelined by a White House economic adviser, Lauchlin Currie, who said that the Chinese Communists were just 'socialists', and that the White House approved of 'their attitude towards the peasants, towards women and towards Japan'. It was also Currie who chose as American representative Owen Lattimore, a considerable expert (he even spoke Mongolian) but also forthrightly sympathetic to the Chinese Communists (as was another considerable expert, the Englishman Joseph Needham: both men looked somewhat foolish when the truth emerged). Chou En-lai now devoted his energies to the Western powers, persuading Mao that they could be far more useful than Mao had realized. Meanwhile, the Communist base was strengthened financially through sales of opium, grown on 30,000 acres in Yenan and marketed in part through a Nationalist general to the north. This at least allowed Mao to ease up on the exploitation of the peasants. Later on, another considerable expert, Gunnar Myrdal, was to observe a village in that area, and to offer wide-eyed praise at the 'traditions' being observed. Mao had the grace to burst out laughing.

He meanwhile built up his party (it now had over 700,000 members) and many were well-educated volunteers from the Nationalist areas as they arrived (40,000 of them) in Yenan. In 1945 an effort was made to bridge the gap towards well-intentioned neutrals, schoolteachers for instance, because Mao would need 'cadres' to run things. He himself was by now wholly in charge, chairman of the top bodies of the Party – Central Committee, Secretariat and Politburo, having, Stalin-fashion, eliminated all of his rivals and several others for good measure; all opposition had been swept aside, and when in April 1945 the seventh Party congress was held, of the 500 previous delegates half had dropped out, whether by suicide or nervous collapse or arrest. But still, in this period Mao could present himself as *the* genuine reformer, and was accepted as such by many foreigners; he went out of his way to emphasize that he would not discriminate too far and his lieutenant, the then young Deng Xiaoping, announced that 'our policy towards the rich peasants is to encourage their capitalistic side, though not the feudal one' ('rich', 'capitalist' and 'feudal' being entirely relative terms). The Kuomintang, by contrast, counted as corrupt and tyrannical; the wayward and vainglorious Chiang Kai-shek – his mausoleum in Taiwan must count as the greatest ever monument to failure – did not impress. Besides, the Chinese Communists were given a great shot in the arm when the Soviet Union intervened in the Far Eastern war.

At Yalta Stalin had been given the Far Eastern railway and two major ports in Manchuria (presented as reparations from Japan) in return for the promise to intervene. When the atomic bombs were dropped, the invasion occurred, and Soviet troops moved into the north-east; they swept all before them. Stalin as ever played both sides. He recognized, and had an alliance with, the Kuomintang government because it had in effect ceded Outer Mongolia to him and because he thought he could manage it. But he also helped Mao. The Communists took areas only a hundred miles north-west and north-east of Peking, secured the northern half of Korea, and took over Manchuria, which had coal, iron and gold, with giant forests and over two thirds of China's heavy industry; it also had a border with Siberia that was well over a thousand miles in length. The Russians at once gave Japanese weapons stocks to the Red Chinese, who also conscripted troops from the puppet Japanese government in 'Manchukuo' (along with the titular emperor, who ended up as a gardener in the palace of his ancestors).

The sequel showed how well Chou En-lai had understood the weakness of the West. Chiang's best troops were in Burma and southern China and he could get them north only in American ships – and the Americans insisted on negotiations with Mao. In late August Mao did go to Chungkin (he insisted on the American ambassador's accompanying him, as an insurance against an air accident) for six weeks followed by a treaty that the foreign embassies wanted. Chiang and Mao even met over a breakfast. But as soon as Mao was back in Yenan in October 1945 he started operations in Manchuria. At the turn of 1945–6 matters did not go well for the Communists – Chiang Kai-shek's troops had had experience of fighting the Japanese and once they came north gave a good account of themselves, thousands of Communist troops deserting. The Soviets left Manchuria in early May 1946, and Mao made an initial error of trying to hold the cities, whereas his real strength lay with the peasants. The Nationalists did well, chasing the Communists to the north; at one stage Mao even planned to give up Harbin and retreat into Siberia. But in Jonathan Spence's account the rush into Manchuria was a mistake: Chiang should have concentrated on building up China south of the Great Wall, not on a complicated adventure into territory where the Communists had ready Soviet support. However, Chiang was desperately anxious for victory, and at the same time unwilling to use his tanks and heavy weaponry; he neglected the countryside and mismanaged Manchuria when he ran it in 1946–7. Kuomintang finances went into an inflationary spiral, and even the Shanghai business people were alienated, while troops deserted for want of proper pay.

The Communists were in effect also saved by the Americans. President Truman did not want a fight over China, would grant dollars, would help with shipping, but believed he could insist on the Chinese co-operating. He sent George C. Marshall in December 1945 – a hugely respected man, who had some knowledge of the country from service there in the twenties. He took against Chiang Kai-shek because of his relatives' corruption and his own dissolute doings (although Chiang had become a Methodist and a reformed character), and a subsequent American envoy, though more sympathetic, was a buffoon. To the American professionals, Mao and Chou had little difficulty in portraying themselves as efficient popular-front democrats, and Marshall himself was impressed when he saw them at work in Yenan, in March 1946. In any case, at this moment the Americans had enough on their plate. Europe was by far the greatest problem, but in Asia they faced one conundrum after another: what *were* they to do with Japan; the Philippines had to be sorted out; Korea was a muddle; the British, still influential, feared what a Nationalist government might do in Hong Kong. The last thing that the Americans wanted to see was a Chinese civil war, and for a time Marshall accepted what Mao told him. He stopped the Nationalists at a decisive moment. Chiang might have destroyed the Communists in Manchuria but on 31 May

Marshall told him not to go on: Chiang Kai-shek was getting American aid – $3bn in all – and he was in no position to defy Marshall. Truman wrote to Chiang, admonishingly, and under American pressure the Nationalists set up an assembly that wasted time and attracted endless criticism for sharp practice: the Americans making exactly the same mistake as they were to make in Vietnam twenty years later, of assuming that democracy Western-style needed to be introduced at once. A truce was proclaimed, just as Mao prepared to abandon Harbin and the railway link to Siberia.

The upshot was that the Communists were left in control of Manchuria, an area twice the size of Germany, and they used these four months to consolidate their hold over it, using Japanese weaponry supplied by the Russians (as well as Japanese prisoners of war who even served as flight instructors). They took over 900 aircraft, 700 tanks, 3,700 guns and much else, together with 200,000 regular soldiers, and North Korea, which the Russians had occupied, was also a useful asset for Mao. In June 1946, when matters were going badly, he was able to send his wounded and his reserve materiel there, and when the Nationalists split Manchuria in two, North Korea was the link between the Communists in the north and the south, who would otherwise have been divided. The other decisive Soviet contribution was the remaking of the railway, which was linked up with Russia again in spring 1947. In June 1948 when Mao was preparing for his final push into all of Manchuria a Russian railway expert, Ivan Kovalev, supervised the work – over 6,000 miles of track and 120 large bridges. This was all done in very great secrecy and not even acknowledged in Party documents, where the general line was that the Communists romantically had only 'millet plus rifles'. Soviet help was decisive, though it came at a grotesque price: the export of food from a starving country.

When Marshall imposed his ceasefire in June 1946 the Nationalists were greatly superior, with over 4 million troops to Mao's 1.25 million; and they expelled the Communists from most of their strongholds in China proper, with Nanking again the capital. In October 1946 Chiang Kai-shek did attack Manchuria but by then the Red bases had become too strong and Mao's chief general, Lin Biao, proved to have much military talent (it was also the hardest winter in living memory, and his troops were made to carry out ambushes in fearful cold, at −40 degrees: they lost 100,000 men from frostbite). In January 1947 Marshall left China and it was the end of American efforts at mediation.

The collapse in China was astonishingly rapid, given the size of the country. The Kuomintang had become demoralized; some even of the senior commanders were secretly working for the Communists (using contacts from Whampoa, dating back to its Soviet period, when Chou En-lai had been head of its political department). In April 1947 Mao did win two surprising victories near Yenan as the Nationalist commander sent his troops in the wrong direction, or lost them to intensive shelling in a narrow valley; he even lost his base with all reserve supplies. A first-class artillery park fell to the Communists (now 'People's Liberation Army') and Yenan was mainly retaken by them. East-central China was thus lost by spring 1948. There was another strange choice as commander for Manchuria, a man whom the Americans had supported as a liberal (he seems to have fought well in Burma) but, when appointed, he let Mao know, via Paris, and then failed to secure his line of retreat. Only 20,000 of half a million Kuomintang troops managed to escape from Manchuria, and that man lived on untouched in Mainland China until his death in 1960. Lin Biao was now free to move south for the Peking–Tianjin campaign, reckoned to be the second decisive one of the Civil War – again encountering a general who seems to have been surrounded by agents, perhaps including his daughter. This general had lost faith and in any case did not want to see Peking destroyed; he was on the edge of a breakdown, slapping his own face. But he kept his command, even though his forces were outnumbered two to one by Lin Biao's 1.3 million men. Tientsin fell in January 1949 – the third-largest city in China. This general too went on to collaborate with Mao until his death in 1974.

At the same moment there was a great fight going on, this time for the heartland of China north of Nanking, the Nationalist capital. By mid-January 1949 Mao had taken the whole country north of the Yangtze, where four fifths of the Nationalist troops had concentrated: the way was open to Nanking and Shanghai and the Nationalists were in utter collapse. Here, a pattern built up that had been seen ever since the Russian Whites had imploded in 1919; the pattern was detectable again in Vietnam and even, in 1978, in Iran. There was vast corruption, food-hoarding, mismanagement of the currency (in this case an absurd exchange rate for the Japanese puppet government's currency and a ridiculously variable rate for the dollar, which allowed speculators to make small fortunes just by moving from town to town). Enormous American imports were profitably sold off, as in Vietnam later on, and an investigation into Chiang Kai-shek's in-laws reckoned that $380m had been illegally converted. On top of everything else there was American criticism of inadequate democracy, whereas the central point about Mao was a pitilessness that the Nationalists could not emulate, as when he starved out a Manchurian city in summer 1948, for five months, involving half a million civilians who were desperate to escape. More people were killed in this way than by the Japanese at Nanking in 1937. As the Reds moved in they would stage rallies for what they called land reform, which in reality affected quite small people, who were subjected to tortures. The terror expert was Kang Sheng: 'educate the peasants . . . to have no mercy . . . There will be deaths', and children were encouraged to join in against 'little landlords', – all of it deliberate terror that was a copy of the Cheka's in 1919. An essential point was that the Party people themselves would be implicated in the terror and Mao's own son was sent around with Kang, though in his diary he protested at what he saw. The Nationalists were unsubtle in response – they arrested and tortured students and intellectuals.

On 20 April 1949 1.2 million men started to pour across the Yangtze and Nanking fell three days later. The Soviets helped, by mowing down a Moslem cavalry army from the air near the Gobi Desert. Chiang Kai-shek and what was left of his army made for the port of Canton, taking away the great treasures now preserved in the Taiwan museum; a medley of Confucian scholars, grasping generals, old-fashioned lecturing liberals, Canton and Shanghai bankers and merchants fled, just as their Russian counterparts had done at the port of Novorossiysk back in March 1920, towards safety. In this case, there was an invulnerable fall-back position on the island of Taiwan, which was relatively unscathed from the wars; Chiang's men had made certain of the island, severely controlling the native population, and there they established themselves, eventually with American naval protection. Taiwan, as the state was called, became in its way the alternative China. Despite isolation and, to begin with, severe poverty, it was to become the fourteenth greatest trading nation in the world – a sign of what might have happened in Kuomintang China if events had turned out differently. But for the moment, the hour was Mao Tse-tung's. On 1 October he stood on top of Tiananmen Gate and inaugurated the People's Republic of China (PRC), as ruler of 550 million people. An appalling destructive energy reigned, though it was directed with a great deal of cunning.

China under the Communists was to go through another terrible generation, but she started out with a good deal of international sympathy. The Kuomintang had few admirers, and any observer of the terrible sufferings of the Chinese people at Japanese hands was prepared to give the Communists the benefit of the doubt. British recognition was almost immediate; and a man such as Joseph Needham, devout Anglican, distinguished Cambridge biochemist, and then the great historian of Chinese science, spent years in China at the worst time and was devoted to her; there were children of missionaries such as the American writer Pearl S. Buck, who won a Nobel Prize for her thirties novel about the life of the Chinese peasant (a New York wit wrote, not inaccurately, that of the seven American Nobel laureates for literature, five had been alcoholics, the sixth a drunk, and the seventh Pearl S. Buck). Many men in the American State Department had assured their superiors that Mao Tse-tung was just a well-meaning socialist. Besides, to begin with, Mao and his team were relatively moderate. All of this was of course to descend into frenzied nightmare, and the first stage came with China's involvement in an absurd, bloody and long-lasting affair, the Korean War. When it ended in 1953, with a loss of 750,000 Chinese lives, it concluded almost thirty years of internecine and international war, further interspersed with famines and epidemics (brought about, in one instance, by the release of plague-bearing rats which the Japanese had raised in a biological warfare establishment in Manchuria, and then, upon surrender, released). It was small wonder that Mao and a very large part of the population did not respond altogether rationally to international events.

There was another factor: relations with the USSR. China was of course dependent upon foreign aid, and her Communists' admiration for the Russian Revolution went back to the very beginning. True, Stalin had played a game between Mao and Chiang, but he counted as all-powerful and there were Soviet agents even in Mao's closest entourage – his doctor, for instance. Stalin had wanted Mao to remain north of the Yangtze so as not to provoke the Americans. Disapprovingly, he delayed for weeks on end as to inviting Mao to Moscow, treating him as once the Khan of the Golden Horde had treated obscure, grubbing princes of Muscovy when they were supposed to turn up with their tribute to his vast tent-palace on the Volga. Stalin fobbed off Mao with the preposterous excuse that the grain harvest had to be brought in before a proper meeting could occur (summer 1948), and there was a minor row before Chiang Kai-shek fled to Taiwan, because his successors asked for peace, which Stalin said should be explored by the Chinese Party whereas Mao stood up for himself. The Russians still benefited from the 'unequal treaty' that gave them a sovereign role on Chinese territories in the north-east, linking Moscow with eastern Siberia, and they wanted controlling rights in Outer Mongolia as well, a very sensitive area that abutted on a Chinese Moslem region that was not necessarily loyal to Peking. Stalin fired some warning shots – arresting poor old Anna Louise Strong, who was stranded in Moscow; and, when Mao claimed some sort of ideological headship over questions of imperialism, Andrey Orlov, Mao's doctor from the Main Intelligence Directorate, was arrested and tortured by the Ministry of State Security's grand inquisitor, Viktor Abakumov (and several other contact men died strangely: even Mikhail Borodin, who had managed Comintern affairs in Shanghai, was picked up). Stalin sensed a rival, and when finally Mao did go to Moscow (by train) in December 1949 he was only one of several leaders greeting Stalin on his seventieth birthday (and for weeks he was belittled by his treatment – he even had to write a crawling letter to ask what was happening).

At length Stalin agreed to make a new treaty with China; Chou En-lai arrived – by train rather than plane for fear of 'accidents' – together with various experts who would work with the Russians to make China a major military power. A treaty did come about in February 1950 with a loan (much of which was subtracted in assorted ways). There were to be fifty major industrial projects and 'the bases for strategic co-operation'; in exchange the USSR in effect took Outer Mongolia, or, as the Chinese saw it, half of Sinkiang and Manchuria, and through 'joint ventures' it had very favourable terms for tungsten and other materials important for armament. The Chinese had to pay large salaries for the technicians, who were exempted from Chinese jurisdiction. Both Stalin and Mao had come an enormously long way from their remote and bullied infancies. They had waded through tidal waves of blood, and, though neither was an ideologist of any seriousness, they did know that Communism was a formula for victory on an unimaginable scale. Under it, Russia had developed an empire far more powerful than that of the Tsars; and Mao had accomplished a feat still greater, to restore the power of the ancient Chinese empire. There was of course already an implicit rivalry, given that Tsarist Russia had been foremost among the European powers in stealing this or that march on China, ever since 1689, when Jesuits on both sides had negotiated the Treaty of Nerchinsk, laying down a common border. That rivalry broke out into the public gaze in 1960, but in 1950 it was still confined, given Mao's dependence on Moscow, and given also his satrap-like admiration for the achievements of the Kremlin.

But Mao could at least test the old imperial waters. He could, for instance, consider Vietnam, where was now a common border. There, a battle had developed between the French empire, obstinately holding on, and the Communist resistance to it, under Ho Chi Minh. Stalin had shown little interest in this (he did not answer Ho Chi Minh's telegrams in 1945) but matters changed once Communist Chinese troops were on the border late in 1949. Ho had fluent Chinese (having lived in China for ten years) and he made a dramatic entrance at the final dinner for Mao in Moscow in mid-February 1950. The two men went back by train (sandwiched between dismantled MiG-15 fighters and military technicians who were to advise as to the aerial defence of coastal cities). The first agreed step was for Mao to build up the link to Vietnam. New roads were created such that by August 1950 the French lost control of the border region to the better-armed Vietnamese Communists; and Chinese help meant that Ho Chi Minh could establish the same sort of 'little-soviet' base as Mao himself had had after the Long March. But there was another and more important part of the old Chinese imperial inheritance to consider: Korea.

Korea had a strategic position, as a south-eastern peninsula of Manchuria, pointing towards Japan. She also had a torn history at Japanese hands. However, she was a poor country, and in 1945 her fate was fairly casually decided: Soviet troops, invading from the north, would stop in the middle, at the 38th Parallel, and Americans would be established to the south. Rival regimes then emerged. A leathery Methodist, Syngman Rhee, was promoted in the South, while Communist North Korea formally became independent in 1948 under Kim Il Sung, a figure (also with a Protestant background) who emerged from Chinese shadows and had trained for a time at Khabarovsk in Siberia. Kim had megalomaniac qualities (he eventually proclaimed himself 'President for Eternity') and went to Moscow in March 1949, as Mao was winning in China. He wanted help to seize the South, where consolidation, with a small American presence, was ramshackle (as happened in Japan, there was a considerable enough Communist element there). That was refused: Stalin's hands were full with the Berlin blockade. However, Mao was less discouraging, though he wanted action only 'in the first half of 1950', by which time he would control all of China. He even said that Chinese soldiers might be sent in, because the Americans would not be able to tell them apart.

In January 1950 Stalin did tell him that he was 'prepared to help him' but also said to rely on Mao. War in Korea would offer some advantages to the Soviets. They could test their own new technology as against that of the USA; Stalin told Mao in October 1950 that there was a brief opportunity to fight a big war as Germany and Japan were out of action and 'if a war is inevitable then let it be waged now and not in a few years' time'. There was another motive, to do with Japan. The USSR (and in the main the British) had been roughly shouldered aside by the American military when Japan was occupied. For a time, MacArthur ran Japanese affairs very high-handedly, comparing himself favourably with Julius Caesar, whereas Moscow felt that Japan was close enough to the Soviet eastern lands for Soviet interests to be taken into account.

Initially American policy in Japan was muddled and naively punitive; Japan sank into a morass of epidemic, starvation, black marketeering and crime that was worse than Germany's: inflation reached 700 per cent in so far as there were goods with prices to be inflated. Then, in 1948, the American learning curve made its usual advance: Japan would have to be run not according to American New Deal principles, but according to her own patterns. Besides, there was a serious enough Communist presence in Japan, and by 1948 there was an even more serious Communist presence just over the water, in China. An equivalent of Konrad Adenauer, Yoshida Shigeru, emerged in politics, with a clean record, and the Americans co-operated. In December 1948 Dean Acheson, Marshall's successor, saw that Japan would have to be the American industrial 'powerhouse', now that China was falling to the Communists, and he sent a banker, Joseph Dodge, to produce a (rough) equivalent of Ludwig Erhard's plans for West Germany: currency stabilization, resistance to union wage demands, trade credits and a very low exchange rate for the yen against the dollar. The Korean War, breaking out a few months later, created a demand for Japanese goods and services, and injected $5,500 million into the economy. As with Germany, the new programme went together with relaxation of war criminals' imprisonment; some were quietly rehabilitated and restored to the bureaucracy, and one (Shigemitsu Mamoru) even became foreign minister. All of this needed a regularization of Japan's international position, i.e. a peace treaty, and discussion of this was in the air in 1950 (although formal negotiation only started in 1951, ending that same year with a San Francisco Treaty that not only gave the Americans several bases, but also foreshadowed Japanese rearmament). A rearmed Japan was an obvious threat to both Mao and Stalin; on the other hand, in mid-January Acheson had said in public that the outer line for the USA would not involve the Far Eastern mainland. Taking advantage of this, in April 1950 Stalin encouraged Kim. He would not help directly; Mao would have to do it. On 15 May Mao agreed to help if the Americans came in.

In the meantime, an election had been proclaimed in South Korea, in a context of upheaval; and there already had been bloody fighting on this or that occasion across the 38th Parallel, as the North Koreans tried to deter or terrorize non-Communists in the South. On 25 June, presenting these battles (which had already caused 100,000 casualties) as provocations, the North Koreans invaded. They had 400,000 men, 150 Soviet tanks, 40 modern fighters and 70 bombers, whereas the South Koreans had 150,000 soldiers, with 40 tanks and 14 planes. There were few American troops, and the immediate results were disastrous – Seoul, the Southern capital, captured on 28 June, and the Southern army disintegrating. However, Syngman Rhee did not surrender, and the Americans reacted very quickly. They were given a present: at the United Nations, the Soviet representative had been boycotting meetings of the Security Council, to protest at the exclusion of Communist China. He was therefore not present when Truman asked the UN to resist the aggression; accordingly, the Korean War was not just an American one, but formally concerned the United Nations; in effect, it became a NATO affair, with even a Turkish contingent.

However, the North Koreans' advantage lasted for some time. By early August they had taken 90 per cent of the South, and there was a desperate fight for the area around Pusan; an American force was overwhelmed and its general captured. But the American shuttle from Japan started to operate, and strategic B29 bombers shattered the North's communications and supply dumps. General Douglas MacArthur then launched a very bold amphibious operation at Inchon, on Korea's western coast, near Seoul. Against difficult weather, over a sea of mud, and with tides that required very precise timing, it succeeded; only a few thousand of the North Koreans escaped entrapment, and in October 1950 the Americans invaded North Korea. MacArthur's weakness was vainglory, and he advanced, without considering the risks, to the Yalu river and the Chinese border, no doubt dreaming that he could reverse the verdict of the Chinese civil war (American warships were also now protecting Taiwan).

On 29 September Kim asked Stalin for 'volunteers' from China, and Mao ordered his forces to be ready, even calling his Politburo for a discussion (though he later said that the decision to intervene was taken by 'one and a half men', the latter being Chou En-lai. They gambled, as it turned out, rightly, that the Americans would not use the bomb, that Chinese superiority in sheer manpower would prevent defeat (and many of the hundreds of thousands to be sacrificed were anyway former Nationalist soldiers). Chou and Lin Biao went to see Stalin on the Black Sea on 10 October, talked through the night and obtained a guarantee of equipment though not of direct air support. On 19 October Chinese intervention did occur, as Mao mobilized his millions, moved them by stealth, in fact enlisted some Soviet fighter support (which proved to be very effective) and confronted American troops on 1 November. Now came the great surprise: these Chinese troops, lightly equipped and able to move fast, defeated the Americans. One division marched at night over mountain roads and managed eighteen miles per day for nearly three weeks on end, and with such feats the Chinese brought about the longest retreat ever undertaken by an American army; a vast evacuation had to be carried out at the end of 1950. The line stabilized, roughly along the 38th Parallel where it had started out, and Seoul was retaken, in utter ruins, in March 1951. In some desperation, MacArthur publicly suggested an aerial attack on China, with hints that the atomic bomb might be used as well. Was Korea worth a nuclear war? Truman's allies were appalled, and that gave him an excuse to remove MacArthur from command. His more prudent successor elected to stay on the 38th Parallel.

Under the nuclear umbrella, wars of this sort developed the surreal quality that George Orwell had foreseen in *Nineteen Eighty-Four*. A stalemate, in horrible terrain and terrible weather, went on and on, punctuated by offensives that got nowhere and were probably not really meant to get anywhere. Meanwhile, American air power was used, and wrecked much of North Korea, though of course without affecting the Chinese bases. Stalin could sit back and rub his hands with glee at the discomfiture of America, and Mao could rejoice in the return of China as a military power: a very far cry from the days of yore, when the junks of the imperial navy had been smashed to matchsticks and the ports of the Mandate of Heaven had been grabbed by foreigners selling opium.

An effort, also surreal, was made at peace. At Panmunjom, between the front lines, teams of negotiators haggled for two years, while the war went on outside the barbed wire and the huts. Thousands of the Chinese and North Korean prisoners did not want to be repatriated at all, but the Communist side insisted, expecting that American public opinion (which had turned against the war) would eventually rebel. Delaying tactics were used: there were a few deluded souls in Chinese prisons who volunteered to stay there (they trickled back, crestfallen, decades later) and various well-meaning Western scientists, including Joseph Needham, were deployed to accuse the Americans (wrongly) of biological warfare.

This slow-moving but murderous farce went on until the Americans started to use nuclear language. Ostentatious test flights went ahead; the new President, Dwight D. Eisenhower, visited Korea late in 1952, and used harsh language. The threat of the bomb was real enough, but the key moment came in March, when Stalin died. His successors had had enough of direct confrontation, and sent peaceable messages to the West. In Korea, finally, on 27 July 1953, on an Indian proposal, a ceasefire was proclaimed at Panmunjom. 'Only the provisional is lasting,' says the French proverb, and so it proved, again in surreal circumstances, the armistice negotiation teams remaining in their huts, decades in, decades out, thereafter, while North Korea became the weirdest country on the globe, and South Korea became an extraordinary first-world success story. The Korean War ended, where it had begun, on the 38th Parallel, with hundreds of thousands of dead on the side of the South and the Americans, and millions on the side of the North and the Chinese. But it had a side-effect, not foreseen by Stalin. The Korean War created Europe.

6

The World at the Death of Stalin

When the dictator's death was announced, his subjects reacted first as if stunned, and then with mass hysteria. A great silence is reported to have fallen almost everywhere in the huge empire that he had dominated, from Rostock on the Baltic to Vladivostok, ten time zones away. Stalin had been in the tradition of despots who had ruled Eurasia, the most recent of whom had been Genghiz Khan and Tamerlane, threatening the Balkans, Persia, China, one sign of their capital a pyramid of skulls. Stalin had their type of absolute power since 1929, but with modern methods of communication, and the USSR had been convulsed. The old peasantry had been destroyed, 40 million of them crammed into towns and cities in a few years, many other millions starved to death or deported, and the rest living a scratch existence. A vast industrial machinery had been set in place, then there had been more millions of deaths in the course of political troubles, the 'Purges'. Then had come the Second World War, another near 9 million deaths in the armed forces alone, and no-one knows how many further civilian millions. In 1945 had come the great victory over Nazi Germany, with Soviet troops conquering Berlin. Russians, for generations looked down on by Germans as backward and lazy, now saw tens of thousands of these same Germans marching through the streets of Moscow as prisoners, some of them losing control of their bowels in fear. Later on, seven elaborate skyscrapers went up in the capital, built by the captive German labourers, who were regarded as better bricklayers than ever the Russian natives would be. (In 1953, 3 million of these prisoners of war were still working, as forced labour; of the 90,000 men who had surrendered at Stalingrad, only 9,000 ever managed to return.)

Then, in 1949, Communism made another enormous demonstration of its strength. The Soviet Union exploded its first bomb. In China, after a long civil war, Mao Tse-tung defeated the anti-Communist Nationalists, and came to Moscow to celebrate, to get his orders. So too at intervals did some Mátyás Rákosi or Klement Gottwald from Budapest or Prague, fresh from some intra-Party knifing, their capitals grimly Stalinized. In the whole empire, factory chimneys fumed, proclaiming forced industrialization; in southern Russia there had been cannibalism; in places there were still shadowy guerrilla wars. But Stalin had not just survived Hitler; he had turned Russia into a superpower, her capital the centre of a hemispheric empire.

It was Stalin's seventieth birthday, 21 December. In the preceding months, there had been endless tributes in the newspapers. Stalin was certainly a well-read man, but he claimed to dominate whole ranges of scholarship – even, at the time of the battle of Stalingrad, contributing an article to a zoological journal about a particular rock-fish that his rival, Trotsky, had apparently discovered (in Turkish exile). Now, scholars, artists, intellectuals, writers praised and imitated him: you had to open any article, more or less regardless of subject, with quotations from Stalin and Lenin. On 21 December Stalin's face was shown on an enormous balloon above the Kremlin, and there were parades throughout the country, with floats to glorify 'the greatest genius of all times and nations'. That evening, in the Bolshoy Theatre, there was a grand gala. On stage was a huge portrait of Stalin, and in front sat the leaders of Communism: Mao Tse-tung, fresh from his triumph; leaders of the various countries that the USSR had taken in 1944–5 in central Europe, including a bearded and weaselly little German, Walter Ulbricht; a veteran of the Spanish Civil War, 'passionate' Dolores Ibárruri, who had been the chief mouthpiece of the defeated left-wing side (her granddaughter in time became Russian interpreter for the king of Spain); and a small troop of hard faces from western Europe. The British, with a tiny Communist Party, were hardly represented (though, in 1953, for the funeral, a rich Communist-sympathizing London barrister, John Platts-Mills, did manage to attend, in his private aircraft), but the French were slavish and the Italians flattered. In the auditorium sat thousands of delegates, carefully ranked, with the senior families in the front rows, and, as first to enter, the family of Lavrenti Beria, who ran the security empire, with the millions of slaving prisoners. It was he who had stamped the Soviet atom bomb out of the ground, partly with internment camps, *sharashki*, where nuclear physicists worked as convicts. Speeches were then made, for hours on end, and a rising star was Nikita Khrushchev, whom Stalin had promoted (he was seated on the left, Mao Tse-tung on the right). Khrushchev's speech ended with: 'Glory to our dear father, our wise teacher, to the brilliant leader of the Party of the Soviet people and of the workers of the entire world, Comrade Stalin!'

Stalin had sunk monstrously into the consciousness and subconsciousness of the world, or at any rate the part of the world that he dominated. For eight years, since the end of the Second World War, his picture had been everywhere, huge statues had gone up to him, and secret-police chiefs all through the empire were kept vigilant at the idea that he might make a telephone call to them in the middle of the night – for his own working hours were strange. In the end, they killed him.

In 1953 Stalin was seventy-three and age was showing. The suspiciousness grew, and when his physical health seemed to be weakening, suspicion caused him to have his own doctors arrested, imprisoned, tortured to make them confess that there was a medical plot afoot. Then came signs that he was planning another culling of chief subordinates – Beria especially. In the 1930s, he had killed off three quarters of the Central Committee, along with much of the senior military establishment and then, for good measure, the chief of security who had organized it all. Now, the senior men could read the telltale signs that the old man was meditating another great purge. On the face of things, he could still be affable and welcoming, and on the night of 28 February/1 March he did stage one of his dinner parties, at which he liked people to get drunk (on one occasion a British ambassador had to be carried out). He told the servants not to wake him: he was usually around by midday in any event. But on 1 March, no. The bewildered staff did not know what to do, and, again because of the suspiciousness, there was no chief domestic secretary to take any responsibility; he had been carted off months before. The servants, with the 1,500 security guards posted all around, waited. A light finally did go on, at about six o'clock, in the quarters he had chosen for the night (out of suspicion, he changed his bedroom regularly, to foil would-be assassins). Then nothing more. Finally, since a document had arrived for him to read, a maid was sent into Stalin's room. She found him on the floor, obviously victim of a stroke. He could hardly move or speak: only the terrible, malignant eyes had life in them.

Still no-one was prepared to take responsibility: the servants, the ministers they telephoned; only Beria could react. He told them to remain silent about the stroke, and arrived that night. The system being so strange, Stalin had remained for ten hours or so without medical attention, and now they had to go and ask his chief doctor in the special prison what he would advise. Beria himself at first told the guards to go, that Stalin was 'sleeping', and by the time doctors arrived, Stalin had been unattended for twelve hours. Did Beria do this deliberately? Stalin's drunken son burst in, on 3 March, shrieked that they had killed him, and according to Molotov, Beria said as much: 'I did away with him, I saved you all.' As the old man slid into and out of coma, Beria did not bother to hide his hatred; by 3 March the doctors pronounced that there was no hope, and death came two days later, with a final scene that his daughter remembered:

> He literally choked to death as we watched. At what seemed like the very last moment he suddenly opened his eyes and cast a glance over everyone in the room. It was a terrible glance, insane or perhaps angry and full of the fear of death . . . He suddenly lifted his hand as though he were point-ing to something above and bringing down a curse on us all

– the old housekeeper in hysterics, on her knees the while, as members of the Party executive came and went, and Beria, at the end, hardly able to control his glee.

Between themselves, before Stalin died, they managed to cobble together an agreement to take over the government, without any immediate fuss, and Beria emerged as the main man, with the Minis-try of the Interior, to which would be attached the Ministry of State Security. Division of these two had been one of the signs that Stalin intended to strip Beria of his full powers, whittle him down and then eliminate him. In the same way, the new men reversed an arrangement that Stalin had made, to expand the size of the Party's leading body, the 'Praesidium' (the old Politburo), to twenty-five as against an original ten. The ten older members would have been swamped by the new ones – an obvious way in which the old man could prepare to get rid of them. With at least some agreement, the new leaders were prepared to let the people know, at last, of Stalin's death. The body was embalmed and laid out, and crowds upon crowds came to see it. Pandemonium followed, and hundreds of people were crushed to death in the middle of Moscow.

What were the new leaders to do? They were themselves Stalinists, involved in all of his doings, with hardly a scruple to be detected. The one with the worst record was obviously enough Beria, and the others had every reason to fear the power that he could use against them: one of the first things that he had done, when Stalin began to die, was to go and remove top-secret documents from the dictator's desk. What did they contain? Already, said Khrushchev in his memoirs, his colleagues were wary, with little signs to each other of apprehension as to what Beria might do. They apportioned the various offices among themselves, and Khrushchev got what seemed to be the least of them – he was one among eight other secretaries of the Central Committee – while Georgy Malenkov took Stalin's seat as head of the Council of Ministers. In the system, and the problem grew more complicated without a dictator, offices sometimes lacked the power that their names should have meant. Did the Party govern, and what was the role of the State in that event? And which part of the Party really had the power – the police or security element, later known as the KGB? These questions came up as soon as Stalin had died, and a struggle for power duly commenced.

However, to start with, there was a somewhat strange business. The Stalin tyranny began to be whittled down, and elements of liberalization came in. People started to come back from the huge prison camp network. Some, when arrested, had had the kind of acute intelligence that Communism fostered – a matter of survival, to guess what to do – and had confessed to crimes that were manifestly ridiculous. Thus, the director of the Leningrad Zoo had confessed that he had staged ballet rehearsals outside the cages so as to drive the monkeys mad. Any commission looking into 'crimes' would of course at once spot a preposterous one, and release the man. But there were other pieces of relaxation that touched on the two central themes of Soviet history from then onwards. These had to do with the non-Russian peoples on the one side, and relations with Germany on the other. Both themes now came up, and it was a measure of the strangeness of the system that the liberalizer, in both, was Beria, the man of Terror whom his colleages feared. However, given that this was a system in which information was very carefully doled out or distorted, the secret police were the agency best able to know what was going on, through a huge network of spies, and experts on various foreign countries. Beria knew well enough that the country was poor, sometimes famished, living in often disgusting conditions. Oppression at home and abroad cost an enormous amount, distorting production. Liberalization would solve some of this. Half of the USSR's population consisted of non-Russians, and these had generally been run, tyrannically, through Russian Communists. In the Ukraine, where there had still been nationalist partisans fighting in the forests until very recently, Russians, not Ukrainians, had been trusted and in the Caucasus, the Baltic, Central Asia, it had been much the same. Whole peoples had been transported, in any event – the Chechens, for instance, to far-off Kazakhstan, along with the Tatars of the Crimea, who lost half of their population in the process (the Chechens, once they arrived, decided to reintroduce polygamy, so that their population could be restored). Now, Beria allowed some non-Russian Communists to take over, locally. Even in 1953 it caused head-shaking in Moscow. Stalin had survived Hitler's attack largely because he put himself at the head of a Russian national movement, as distinct from a Communist one. What would happen if loyal Russians were now displaced by slippery Georgians and, worse still, Central Asians, who would use their power to instal their brothers and their cousins and their uncles through some hidden tribal or even sectarian network? Playing off the nationalities against Moscow was dangerous; in the end it brought down the USSR. There were pre-echoes of that in Beria's post-Stalin months.

But he also had a sense of strategy in foreign affairs. Stalin may have been absolute master at home, but he had the modern countries all against him, and a war was going on, pointlessly, in the middle of Korea. In 1945, when Hitler's Germany had been smashed, the USSR had been in alliance with the West, and various arrangements for the post-war period had been drawn up. From Beria's viewpoint, these had gone very badly wrong: the West had been misplayed. NATO now existed and it united western Europe, despite the existence in France and Italy of strong Communist parties; West Berlin was a leech attached to a main artery of the Soviet system; West German industry was recovering fast and would clearly be used for the rearmament of the country. The same was coming to pass in Japan. What had the USSR got in return for this? Peasant countries on her borders, each quite complicated. It had also gained East Germany, now dressed up as the 'German Democratic Republic', but everyone knew that it was a fake state. The chief element was that American troops were stationed in western Europe, that nuclear weaponry was in the air, that western Europe was overcoming the post-war crises, and American officials were all around, to encourage freer trade, both within Europe and with the USA. From Moscow's viewpoint this was all very alarming, maybe presaging a general attack, and in his last years Stalin himself expected a war. Beria knew different: no-one knowing, through the extraordinarily highly placed Soviet spies, what was really being calculated in the West could have any serious idea that it would go to war. If NATO existed, if the Americans maintained a military presence in Europe, this was purely in response to Soviet provocations – a long list of cruelty and unnecessary aggression, including even the continued use of old Nazi concentration camps. There were still some idealists who chose to go and live in the 'German Democratic Republic', or 'the other Germany' – Bertolt Brecht the main one, though there were other men and women who had detested California. Disillusionment followed.

At this stage, German reunification was still a matter for diplomatic competition. The West argued for free elections, and meanwhile got the United Nations, which the West at the time controlled, to set up a commission to study the subject (it was refused entry to East

Germany). At the time, there was also question of a German contribution to defence – the European Defence Community being the chief
vehicle for this, and part of the post-Marshall arrangements that were
the basis of the later European unification. This of course worried
Moscow – she had always feared an alliance against her of the entire
West, Germany included. Now, some of those same German generals
who had reached Leningrad, Moscow, the lower Volga and the Caucasus were apparently being groomed again for an attack. Stalin himself had responded with a note, of 10 March 1952, which became
famous, and over the interpretation of which some foolish historical
statements have been made. He proposed the formation of a German
government, to include the East; it would be recognized for the purposes of a peace treaty; Germany would be neutral, i.e. would not join
any Western organization at all, including the economic ones; and
might have her own army; and would be able to return civil and political rights. East German Communists proudly assured the Left-leaning
Italian socialist Pietro Nenni that they would soon be in much the
same position as the Italian Communist Party, i.e. waiting in the wings
for power. Stalin also still had millions of prisoners in his thrall, whose
return would be a considerable gift. The aim, overall, was at German
national sentiment – there was even mention of giving political rights
back to SS men – at the very moment when treaties signed in Bonn
and Paris for a European army were supposed to be ratified, and the
timing was not coincidental. The three Western powers consulted, and
they then put the question as to free elections; they also said that a
future German government should be free to choose alliances. The
exchanges went on until September, always failing on these two points,
since the USSR would never accept a united Germany, allied with the
West, and despite some effort with the small print, never accepted that
the elections would be really free. Anti-Cold War historians held the
Stalin note up as evidence that the man was sincere about German
neutrality and unification, 'Finlandization' as it came to be called, but
subsequent evidence shows that he gave the matter much thought –
the note went through fourteen versions, three of them annotated by
him – and seems to have been possessed by the notion that he could
deliver a Communist Germany, just as Czechoslovakia had produced

a strong Party. The Party of Socialist Unity (Sozialistische Einheits-partei Deutschland, or SED) in East Germany was groomed for con-trol of the entire country, and was told to accelerate 'the construction of socialism' in April 1950. The next Party congress, in July, went ahead with collectivization of agriculture, heavy-industrial plans and the extinction of small-scale trade and workshops. If Stalin did not get the Germany he wanted, he would in other words at least get his bit of Germany to fall into line.

In any event, the West Germans quite clearly preferred their free-dom to their national unification. Adenauer, the Christian Democratic leader, was certain that there could be no honest arrangement with the USSR and was determined to go ahead with the Western programme, even if that meant accepting a divided Germany. He worried that the West might let him down, with some Allied conference that would leave Germany at Moscow's mercy – some European security arrange-ment of the sort had even been suggested by an American Secretary of State (James F. Byrnes) in 1946. He also had an argument, that a pros-perous and democratic West Germany would in the end act as a mag-net for the East as a whole: and so indeed it did, though Adenauer (and the Frenchman, Schuman) were reckoning on up to ten years, and not nearly forty. The West Germans went ahead with rearmament plans and even conscription, although many of the Social Democrats detested the idea, as for that matter did some of the Christian Democrats. The French, too, had swallowed their doubts, despite threats of 'Guns for Huns'. The Soviet side had offered (and Molotov stressed the offer again in 1954) some European security system that would include the USSR but exclude the USA and of course NATO Germany. This idea, to be launched with the sort of large international conference that the USSR could quite easily manipulate (the other countries being divided among themselves, with a number of small ones to cause trouble), was now in the air. It was 'Europe for the Europeans', and it later grew nuclear-free extrapolations; in time it became 'our common European home' – a famous enough expression, later on, under Gorbachev, but promoted before him by much harder men. The idea was not unpopu-lar in some circles in Germany and elsewhere, and even had attractions on the Right. But there was one unshakably strong argument against it: Stalin and all his works, particularly the repulsive little state in East Germany. Its capital, East Berlin, had been rebuilt in homage to Moscow. The centre, the Alexander-Platz, was a gigantic field of concrete, and off it marched the Stalin-Allee, another hideous boulevard of concrete, with a peculiar smell, partly made-up of local low-quality coal and partly of the Soviet method of oil refinery. Along it went lorries, packed with rubble, and occasional large, curtained, black cars, carrying the unlovely Communist bosses. There was another peculiarity to East Berlin. Bomb damage did not mean that old buildings were torn down, as in the West. Instead, they were patched together, at least in areas such as the Schönhauser Allee or the Vineta-strasse, outside of the international gaze, ripe for 'gentrification' two generations down the line, but at the time almost uninhabitable. No German in his senses would want to live there.

The tensions of 1952 were such that Stalin was obviously thinking of a war, and he told Mao to prepare for one. Then came, perhaps in preparation for it, a new 'purge', both at home and in the satellite states, to dispose of potential traitors before they had time to act. He did not trust Jews at all, and they were, in the main, eliminated from leading positions in the satellite states, and from influential ones in Moscow, though the Budapest ones had an adhesive quality, and he sacrificed some gentiles instead. Paranoia of an extreme kind reigned, but Stalin was untouchable, had knees knocking, and his nominees, while secretly hating the system, could only wait for his death.

Such was the position on 5 March 1953. Beria, with understanding from Georgy Malenkov, now moved into the vacuum, took charge of things, and had a strategy of his own. In the first place, Stalin's crude challenges to the West had left no room for the divisions within it. We now know, for instance, that the Americans were not really using West Germany as a tool against the USSR: up to 1950, they regarded Bonn as a provisional solution, and one that had been forced upon them; they still used the machinery set up at Potsdam. But then had come the Korean War, and in 1952 Eisenhower was elected President on a strongly anti-Soviet platform: he seemed even to be saying that the USA should make use of its then enormous superiority in nuclear weapons. The Germans themselves were divided, and the one argument that

Adenauer could always use was that East Germany was a tyrannically run place – no advertisement for life under 'socialism'. The new leaders were clearly anxious to soften the line, and various things followed from this – on 27 March a limited amnesty (10,000 people, including Molotov's Jewish wife); on 4 April, release of the imprisoned doctors of the 'plot'; on 10 June, dropping of Soviet claims against Turkey; in June, resumption of relations with Yugoslavia and even Israel; in the same period, the Chinese at last made the vital concession in Korea, with an armistice declared in July. In fact, on 19 March the new leaders, including the true Stalinist Molotov, agreed that the Korean War must be stopped, and the Chinese foreign minister, Chou En-lai, got his orders to that effect on 21 March, in Moscow.

To all of this there was a nuclear background: the USSR was weak in that respect, and needed respite from Stalin's warring, his turning every neighbour into an enemy. The essential question remained Germany, and here there were divisions, with Molotov following the Party line, to the effect that a Communist East Germany was a necessity. Beria had other ideas, and probably regarded the Party with contempt. Why not try a new tactic altogether: prepare to get rid of East Germany, Walter Ulbricht and all, in exchange for a Germany that would collaborate economically and politically? Such was the model of Rapallo, the Italian town where, in 1922, the USSR and Republican Germany, bizarrely represented by elderly homosexuals in pyjamas, had entered upon semi-alliance. Then, the two countries, isolated, made an agreement that even included considerable German help for Soviet industry and for that matter Soviet help for the German military. A normal and parliamentary Germany, detached from the West? A sort of Finland? And if it meant getting rid of little Ulbricht, why not?

Of course, in the then Soviet system, such things were not written down, and when eventually 'revelations' from the archives emerged, they did not really reveal anything more than would have been known to readers of the *Reader's Digest* at its purest. Even Walter Pieck, a lieutenant of Ulbricht's, kept a diary in a code of a code of a summary. Stray lines in memoirs alone ensured that something of the truth emerged. Once Beria started to suggest sacrificing East Germany for a new Rapallo, a strange episode followed. East Germany had been whipped into following the Soviet course, and half a million of her people left, through Berlin. Walter Ulbricht was asking for Soviet economic assistance and was told to move more slowly with 'the construction of socialism'. The Praesidium discussed this on 27 May and sent a Note to the East Germans. Such documents had a character all their own. There would be a thick framework of 'wooden language', unreadable if you were not initiated. Men who sat through six-hour speeches of industrial statistics at enormous Party gatherings, applauding at the right moments, with stewards lining the wall, holding stopwatches, and indicating 'stop' when the designated speaker's designated applause had been completed, were indeed initiated. If they just listened, they would find that at some point there would be a passage meaning something. This was a way of demonstrating the leaders' power (similarly, if one of them gave an interview, the technique was to answer a question at enormous length, boring the interviewer into the ground).

On 2 June the Soviet Note said the East German leadership should, 'to make the present political situation more healthy and to consolidate our position in Germany and the international arena, act over the German question such as to create a united, democratic, peaceful and independent Germany'. This was referred to as a 'new course' and there was to be some liberalization in East Germany; some of the 'construction of socialism' measures were to be cancelled, and the Soviet Control Commission would be replaced by a civilian, Vladimir Semyonov, political adviser to the Control Commission, a member of the NKVD and close to Beria. He was to replace Ulbricht with more pliable figures – Rudolf Herrnstadt, editor of the Party newspaper, and Wilhelm Zaisser, head of East German security, also close to Beria. After all, even East German Communists were sometimes uncomfortable with being hated and lied to. At the same time reparations were ended, and the Soviet firms set up to exploit East Germany were disbanded. Beria was in effect giving some sense to the Stalin Note of March 1952 – not intending full-scale Communization of Germany but, instead, looking for co-operation or 'Finlandization'. From 2 to 4 June there was a conference at Berlin, 'the new course' being explained to Ulbricht. He went ahead with some concessions as far as small trade and farmers were concerned, and he released a few hundred political prisoners, but he did nothing to lessen the load on the industrial workers. His goal was a Communist Germany. That had been the whole purpose of his life, and he probably had some sort of encouragement from within Moscow. Ulbricht knew how the system worked. He resisted the pressure, and instead launched a 'provocation' (meaning, in Continental and Communist parlance, an action designed to produce its opposite). He decreed at once, in mid-May, that each worker must produce 10 per cent more, while rations went down – equivalent to a drop in wages and an increase in hours worked. The provocation duly provoked trouble. On 16 June there were demonstrations in the very centre of 'the construction of socialism', by builders working on the grotesque Stalin-Allee. Did Beria's enemies stage a provocation, to discredit 'the new course' and Beria, in collusion with Ulbricht and Pieck, who had been trotting in and out of Soviet offices? Or were the demonstrations just what they purported to be, a rising against exploitation? On 17 June the unrest spread, with workers in the big factories in other centres of industry joining in. That day, the Soviet authorities declared martial law and sent in tanks; some 200 people were killed. The whole episode gave the West, and West Germany in particular, excellent propaganda.

It also discredited Beria. A conspiracy now grew against him, and it was inspired by Nikita Khrushchev. He had the very useful talent, in that system, of threatening no-one. He had risen through the Party, some of the time as manager of Moscow (where he tore down many old buildings). He was fat and piggy-eyedly jovial, and had a rustic air: his colleagues wrote him off as second-rate. When they agreed on the post-Stalin arrangements, their idea was to return to the days when the secretary of the Central Committee was just a technician, drowning in files. But Stalin himself had used that administrative post to great effect, because the other men in the Politburo ignored him while they fought among themselves; he controlled appointments to this or that Party function, and knew who was who. Khrushchev also knew how to do this, promoting men who would later be very useful allies. Meanwhile, given the fear of Beria that existed among the others, there was some response to Khrushchev's prompting when he told them that

Beria must be overthrown. The Berlin affair gave him a very good excuse. He had another useful ally. The war hero Marshall Georgy Zhukov had been sidelined by Stalin, and the successors brought him back as deputy defence minister: that meant troops on their side. The plotters were careful never to talk openly, there being informants or 'bugs' all around; they behaved towards Beria as if all were normal, even chaffing him about his spies, and in Khrushchev's case accepting lifts in his car.

On 26 June a meeting of the Praesidium of the Council of Ministers had been called by Malenkov, who had been left in the chair. He was programmed to say at some stage that Party matters should be discussed, and that Beria's office needed to be rationalized. Beria's men were sitting outside the room as usual, and they had to be neutralized: that was done by Zhukov's men, who had had weapons smuggled in. Beria arrived (as usual) self-important and late, with a briefcase. Malenkov opened up, questioning Beria's role, and when Beria opened the briefcase, intending to take out papers, the conspirators feared that he would produce a gun and called in Zhukov's men. They arrested him and, when dusk fell, smuggled him out of the Kremlin, wrapped in a carpet. He went off to a military prison, where he was soon joined by his closest collaborators, the torturer Viktor Abakumov especially. Written pleas, hysterical in tone, went out from the cells to Malenkov, but after a secret trial Beria was executed the following December. His crimes were publicly denounced by his ex-colleagues. Indirectly, he was taking the blame for what Stalin had done, and they were distancing themselves as best they could from the tyrant: Communism was to have a human face.

Khrushchev, the least regarded of these colleagues, did indeed have a human face, though pachydermic, and he was now asserting himself. In appearance, Malenkov had the chief role, but he had been Beria's associate, and the next stage was for him to be eliminated. Yet again, Khrushchev was underestimated: he now became, in September, first secretary of the Central Committee, and thereby controlled agendas and appointments, and so low did the others rate him that his nomination came only after several other apparently more pressing items on the Central Committee's list of topics for the day. Meanwhile,

Malenkov had his own ideas as to liberalization. Prices were cut, and peasant taxes also; he even proposed allowing peasants to have small plots of their own, whereas in Stalin's time all of the land was supposedly collective in case peasants were tempted to work privately, for themselves. Other ideas came up. For instance, there had long been a tension between Party and State, in the sense that the machinery of the State did not have any independence, operating as the Party wanted, and through Party nominees (the *nomenklatura* of people 'cleared' by the Party). This had economic consequences, in that industry might be shaped by some powerful boss, to build up his own empire, regardless of economic sense, and there was similar trouble with appointments, as square pegs were put into round holes. Late in 1953 Malenkov told the Party that some government agencies must be removed from its control, and made himself very unpopular. Besides, Khrushchev set himself up as the agricultural specialist, and made little effort to conceal the truth – that Russians were eating less well than they had done before the Revolution itself. In 1954 Malenkov was gradually effaced, Party defeating government; early in 1955 he was formally demoted by the others. Khrushchev had won.

Nikita Khrushchev was of just the generation to think that Communism would triumph, worldwide. He was born of peasant stock in a small town of the Ukraine, Yuzovka (now Donetsk), his family straight from the land, mostly illiterate. Yuzovka took its very name from foreign capital, in that the man who developed its mines was a Welshman called Hughes, and the young Khrushchev went down the mines. But the family did not drink, his parents pushed him, he acquired an education because his mother enlisted the help of a priest (Khrushchev, like so many Bolsheviks, was a good mathematician), and when the Revolution came, he joined in and worked his way up. This was all quite standard for the USSR in the twenties and thirties: the peasant Khrushchevs displaced the Jewish intellectual Trotskys who had originally led the Revolution (a quarter of Party deaths in the early twenties were suicides). Stalin controlled whole waves of men like Khrushchev, and was very cunning in setting them against each other. He also made sure that they had to take their share of responsibility in his rule of murder and mass imprisonment, and

Khrushchev's own career shows that he joined in without demur. But he was himself quite cunning, and learned that, if you wanted to advance in Soviet politics, you needed not to be a threat to anyone, even not to be taken seriously at all. His role at the top level was to play the buffoon who nevertheless somehow got things done. In manner, Khrushchev was that Russian figure, the clown, but, as Arthur Koestler said, a clown can look very sinister, seen close to.

Khrushchev was not the type of man to have doubts about the eventual victory of Communism. It had catapulted him from Yuzovka to the Kremlin, of course, but it had also catapulted Russia. In the days of Yuzovka, she had counted as backward, filled with illiterate peasants, and she had lost a war against Germany. After the Revolution, she had become a great industrial country and defeated Germany. There was much wrong with this very simple picture, but that would not have crossed Khrushchev's mind: Communism had started off with a meeting, of about forty people, in 1903, and now look where it was – dominating more of the world than the British Empire had done. Khrushchev himself, the former peasant and apprentice miner, now had an educated family, with a grand apartment overlooking the Moskva river, and grand offices in the Kremlin. He could snap his fingers, and the President of the USA would jump. Not bad for a boy from Yuzovka: the Revolution would win.

7

Khrushchev

In the middle fifties, when the American historian Richard Pipes was in Leningrad, and travelled by crowded tram through the rubbish-strewn and crumbling imperial quarter of the old Tsarist capital, a woman muttered to him, 'We live like dogs, don't we?' They did. There were queues, filthy and overcrowded living quarters, a fatty diet, and beyond the palaces, St Isaac's Cathedral, the Admiralty spire, there was foul smoke from the huge factories which disfigured the suburbs over the Neva. There was a plan even just to knock down the old city, to erase its memory. Meanwhile came propaganda from the regime to the effect that the Soviet Union was a model for the universe, and the city bosses rode along the boulevards in curtained black cars, at high speed, insured against the resentments of their subjects, though not against the envy and intrigues of their colleagues. With Nikita Khrushchev, this began to change. Russia entered upon what the St Petersburg poetess Anna Akhmatova called 'one of our vegetarian periods'.

She herself had undergone the carnivorous ones, living in the urine-stinking corner of what had once been a grand mansion block, losing two husbands, murdered by the system, and having her son imprisoned by it for years. In 1914, when there had been life and hope in St Petersburg, she had been the subject of a superb portrait, by Nathan Altman, and there had been others, in the early twenties, in the period when the Revolution still allowed an innovative cultural life. These paintings, like so many others of that period, had been shoved into basements of the Russian Museum, stored by heroic men and women who knew the secret, and they reappeared only two generations later. Anna Akhmatova's own poems only officially came back to life in

1987, though they were of course well-known by word of mouth before then. Around the time of Pipes's visit, not long after Stalin's death, victims of the system had begun to reappear: products of the camps that were dotted around the north and east of this enormous country, their faces gaunt and toothless, expressing ruined lives. There were tens and then hundreds of thousands of them, and everyone knew what had happened to them. Khrushchev was associated with their release, and in later years he took great pride in it, even regarding this as the main achievement of his life. That was right.

On 25 February 1956, at the 20th Party Congress, he gave one of the most famous speeches ever made. In it – it was put together at the last minute, was being scribbled even after the congress had started – he denounced the 'cult of personality'. This was code for the monstrous crimes that Stalin had committed against the Party (the even more monstrous ones against society as a whole were ignored). He repeated this five years later, and this time together with the removal of Stalin's corpse from the Kremlin Mausoleum. Lenin was to reign alone in it, though most of the corpse was made of wax, the original having been attacked by a fungus when it was wrapped in the flag of the Paris Commune, presented by the French government. Khrushchev wanted to get back to Lenin, and especially to the Lenin of 1921, who had carried through economic reform and a flexible response towards the West.

He himself hardly looked like one of Anna Akhmatova's 'vegetarians': on the contrary, a coarse little man, bullying in style, embarrassingly ignorant of Russian culture. As Party boss in Moscow, he tore down old buildings with a vengeance, and when he ran Kiev or Lvov in the Ukraine, he behaved brutally and sometimes, as he himself admitted, murderously. He had survived in Stalin's closest circle because he could act the peasant clown, and because he could handle the drink that Stalin poured into men, in the expectation that at some point their eyes would flash the truth, as to what they had in mind. His name was not on the mental list drawn up by Stalin for the last great purge, and he played his game carefully, not asserting himself too much and too early. He ostentatiously talked about reform in agriculture and in the Party, to which he wanted the secret police to be subordinated; and he showed willingness to talk to the West, with disarmament in the air. Then Khrushchev kept the powerful interests in check, because he maintained, as apparent equal as head of state in 1955, the blockheaded Nikolay Bulganin, in the name of conservatism and even friendship with China. It was not really until 1957, when he crushed a last-minute rebellion by the old guard, that Khrushchev had power enough to run the Party and the State, in the style of Stalin. But at least he was determined that the Soviet peoples should not have to go on living like dogs. He could show that Stalin had been grossly mistaken, that Communism could both go on developing its power and would also improve the Russians' miserable standard of living. Why did they live like dogs, whereas their system could put a living dog into orbit round the Earth?

A Khrushchev would have things to think about. Aside from the grand apartment overlooking the Moskva river and offices in the Tsars' Kremlin, he had elaborate semi-palaces to which he could retire, whether in the Moscow suburbs or at Pitsunda, on the Black Sea. The Pitsunda place had a huge swimming pool with a view out over the sea, and its glass front could be opened and shut at the touch of a button. Communism had proved itself: it had turned Russia into a superpower, able to defeat Germany at last. Again and again he would go back to this theme, and lectured the Americans that, when they had seized Alaska, they could only do so because the Russian army was feeble, its soldiers flapping in baste shoes. The whole Stalin epic had changed that, though he thought the cost was unnecessarily, cruelly high. Khrushchev therefore had some cards to play and he could look the American President in the eye. In October 1957, timed for the fortieth anniversary of the Revolution, there was a symbol: *Sputnik*, the first man-made satellite, fired into orbit round the Earth. That little spot of light, moving visibly at night at some speed in the sky, was the calling card of Communism and of Russia's emergence at last. The Americans had tried to compete, but had failed, farcically, to put even a football-sized one into space: their rocket had risen for a few yards and then settled back on its socket. In other matters, again, the USSR impressed. The violinist David Oistrakh and the pianist Svyatoslav Richter were household names in western Europe and at the Brussels Exhibition of 1958 the Soviet pavilion, with its recordings, caused spines to tingle, whereas the American one just showed off creature-comforts. Khrushchev beamed, and a 21st Party Congress solemnly announced in January 1959 that the USSR would 'catch up' by 1970. In October 1961 that turned into '1966'; by 1980 there was supposed to be 'super-abundance', a claim answered by an historical laugh when the time came. But there were many people in the West who agreed, including the British Prime Minister, Harold Macmillan (in his diary).

In fact most of it came from the pre-revolutionary world. There was a superb mathematical and musical tradition in old Russia, and *Sputnik* owed most to equations produced by a Tatar-Polish theoretical physicist called Konstantin Cholkovsky in 1903: even in his native Kaluga at that time, electro-magnetism and the name of James Clerk Maxwell were known. The Bolsheviks had some understanding of what was going on, and did not, initially, make problems for men such as Cholkovsky (who died in 1935 at a great age). Another learned man of the old order, Vladimir Vernadsky (born in 1863: his brother, a notable historian of Russia's Tatar aspect, emigrated) stayed on, and in 1922 guessed that there was 'a great revolution' coming, 'a source of power' that would have something to do with radium, on which he became an expert. Scientific institutes were important to the Bolsheviks, and the 17th Party Congress in 1934 announced that the Soviet Union was to be 'the most technologically advanced state in Europe'. There was some international collaboration (most notably with Piotr Kapitsa, born in 1894, who spent twelve years at the Cavendish Laboratory in Cambridge, in the era of Rutherford and the splitting of the atom; but of course there was a strong German link as well). The scientific intelligentsia of that era were extraordinarily well-rounded men and women, good on their music and literature (one of the outstanding Soviet nuclear physicists was Yuli Khariton, born in 1904, who had studied at Cambridge, like Kapitsa, and, back home, had to do with the founding of the Writers' House). Of course they took their role very seriously indeed, Kapitsa writing to Stalin to say that scientists were the new patriarchs – patriarchs having become quite obsolete.

Vladimir Vernadsky seems to have been the model for Professor Preobrazhensky in Mikhail Bulgakov's *Heart of a Dog*, a splendid satire on the Dictatorship of the Proletariat. In it, a gynaecologist of the old school and a man of broad culture (including the proper qualities of vodka and the *zakuski*, or caviar, to go with it) keeps a large and well-appointed flat in Moscow because he can rejuvenate sexual organs and powerful Party people use his services. He implants the testicles and other glands of a drunken thug into a lovable dog, creating a monstrous dog-man who fits in with the local Communist cell. The book was read out to a chosen audience that contained an informer, who in outrage recorded that the Vernadsky–Preobrazhensky figure complains that Communism had meant the theft of galoshes from the communal hallway, and that this had caused 'deafening laughter'. The book then vanished, known only to a few people. In Khrushchev's time, characteristically, the circle in the know grew wider, but the book was not properly published until 1987. A regime capable of such absurdities of censorship would not in ordinary circumstances have been able to produce anything of much sophistication, let alone a pioneering bomb and missile programme. In fact engineers were initially put in charge, and they were so sceptical that they regarded uranium just as a rock, and irradiated themselves. Without the men and women of the late-Tsarist educational system, science and for that matter cultural life of any but the most primitive sort would not have survived. Matters even then became very difficult for many of them, the writers especially, and it was the war that saved them; even the aeronautics expert Sergey Korolev was sent to Kolyma camp, and both A. N. Tupolev and the designer of the *katyusha* missile system, V. N. Galkovskiy, were imprisoned in a specialist camp, a *sharashka*. But the scientists were badly needed, and they were given organization (and motivation) that they might otherwise have lost. It is also true that the first Soviet bomb owed something to Western examples, known through espionage, a glory of the regime. Some of the nuclear physicists were anxious for the West to give the secret to the USSR, which they much admired (for some reason, natural scientists lost their minds when it came to the Soviet Union: Sir Julian Huxley had written a particularly silly book about Soviet science, comparing it very favourably with British, just as the British produced penicillin, radar, the cathode-ray tube and the atomic bomb). But the essentials were Russian.

The USSR set up a bomb remarkably quickly. The Americans always had superiority of numbers – nine in 1946, thirteen in 1947, fifty-six in 1949, 1,161 in 1953 – but it had meant an enormous expense (during the war, \$2bn, though much of this was on buildings). The Soviet system, with far fewer resources, responded rapidly and the first uranium plant was ready by the end of 1945, with a design similar to that of Enrico Fermi's atomic pile at Chicago. Uranium (of which the Western powers had cornered 97 per cent in the Belgian Congo and elsewhere) was available at the Jachymov mines in Bohemia (strangely enough its German name, Joachimsthal, lent itself to a silver coin, the *Thaler*, i.e. 'dollar') and convicts were set to work in them. The research was carried out in an old monastery, 250 miles east of Moscow, and the monks' cells became the laboratories; columns of convicts trudged through it all, and the guards were primitives who thought that plutonium was just old iron. It was there that Y. B. Zeldovitch, an inspired and versatile mathematician, worked out the depth and range of the explosive power, in microseconds; and within three years, in August 1949, the first bomb was successfully tested at Semipalatinsk. Next came the thermonuclear or hydrogen bomb which the Hungaro-American expert Edward Teller likened to the Sun itself, an atomic device being used to trigger a vast explosion. In this, the Russians (in 1952, with the first test) proved to be ahead of the Americans, although they exploded an even more powerful, and immediately usable, one in 1953 (and a later test killed several Japanese fishermen eighty miles away). Soviet tests were also murderous, though this was concealed at the time; they caused the most prominent physicist, Andrey Sakharov, to have his first doubts as to the whole thing; and Igor Kurchatov himself, the director of the Soviet atomic-weapons programme, wrote to Molotov in 1954 to say that war would mean the end of the world. Molotov did not punish him, or publicize the letter, one of Khrushchev's reasons for subsequently getting rid of him. More generally, a doctrine came up of the 'nuclear deterrent', which would make war unthinkable. One of the chief Soviet physicists, Lev Landau, also had doubts as to the morality of the whole enterprise, and he was eavesdropped on in his house by the KGB. He was heard to remark that the first lives to be saved by the nuclear deterrent had been those of the Soviet scientists.

At any rate, *Sputnik*, launched on 4 October 1957, was followed in November by a dog, and then in 1961 by the first man in space, Yuri Gagarin. *Lunik* landed a red pennant on the Moon, and was first to photograph its hidden side. Still, whatever these triumphs, there was always Anna Akhmatova's slum of a city. Food and housing were dismal and the USSR's transport system was primitive – fewer railways than India. Communism was hated in much of central and eastern Europe; it was maintained only by a Moscow tyranny, and the local powers depended on the Soviet embassies. At home, there were millions of slave labourers (Khrushchev reckoned ten), and once Stalin died there were great revolts among them, as the famous places – Vorkuta, Karaganda, Norilsk – went on strike, organized by Chechens, Ukrainians and Balts. What was Khrushchev to do about it all? Change in the Soviet Union was exceedingly difficult, especially given the presence, in the Politburo and elsewhere, of the old Stalin guard. He did indeed set about reforms, and these were to become compulsive and very deeply unsettling, but in the first instance there was one thing Khrushchev could do, more or less in agreement with the Politburo, and that was to improve relations with the West. It was to be called the 'first détente', a word meaning 'relaxation of tension', though it also happened to mean 'trigger'. Experience was to show that the first meaning led straight to the second.

As Khrushchev contemplated the West, what did he see? He hardly knew it at all (unlike Stalin, who in his revolutionary youth had briefly been in London) but there were certain main lines in his understanding of it, and his younger advisers were clever. Stalin had managed to unite it, with NATO and the pacts that linked almost all of the Soviet Union's neighbours, however disparate. In 1955, at a meeting of the Politburo, Khrushchev made some sarcastic remarks at the expense of Molotov, whose 'no' in international gatherings had become famously obstructive. The USSR under Stalin, he said, had managed to make enemies of *everybody* – even countries such as Iran and Turkey, which had been friendly since the Revolution and were now allied with the West. Yugoslavia, too, a faithful Communist ally, had been alienated – quite absurd because the place had a strategic position and it could also have been a sort of showcase. Yugoslavia contained seven different and sometimes very different peoples, and had inherited a good bit of poisoned history. Lenin had decreed how such problems should be dealt with: get rid of capitalism, and the brotherhood of peoples would prevail. In Yugoslavia a serious effort was made. Tito, a Croat, had led the resistance, and his partisans, drawn from all the peoples of Yugoslavia, had liberated much of the country even before the Red Army arrived. Tito then 'built socialism' in the Moscow-approved manner. However, there were signs of independence that Stalin did not like, and suspicion reigned: a quarrel became open in summer 1948, and the Yugoslav Party was expelled from Cominform. However, this did not break Tito at all. Instead, he gained strong domestic support, approached old allies in Great Britain, received financial and other help from the West, crushed his Stalinist opponents, and proclaimed neutrality. For a very long time to come, Yugoslavia received adulation in the West: all of it, said an apologetic Khrushchev, the fault of Stalin and Molotov.

And now there was also a Germany, again needlessly alienated, firmly anchored in the West, and being rearmed. Moscow might justly take pride in its leaders' understanding of the dynamics of power politics, and Lenin had known which buttons to press. When in 1919 the international revolution failed to happen, he had made up to the Germans, and played off the Western powers against each other. German officers had trained secretly on Russian soil: German bosses had built up Russian industry during the first Five Year Plan. Why not dangle the carrot of unification before the Germans, in return for economic co-operation and neutrality? For Khrushchev, the time had come for a relaxation of the tensions that had so unnecessarily been built up. It was called 'peaceful co-existence', and coincidentally helped him to get rid of Molotov, packed off to run a power plant far away.

The United States had also been misplayed. Left to itself, America would have got on with business, but Stalin had done his work, and the Americans had built up a formidable war machine that had become an important and even indispensable part of American business life. Weapons research and production made California rich and kept universities going; exports of weaponry or aircraft became important for the balance of payments, and a whole political and media machine developed to foster these. Various pacts, underwritten by the American taxpayer, now linked nearly all of the Soviet Union's neighbours against Moscow. Without Stalin's ominous threats, that taxpayer (paying a marginal rate of 94 per cent) might have rebelled against this system, but as things were, even Eisenhower growled nuclearly over Korea. In January 1954 Dulles laid out a new 'doctrine': the USA would use its enormous nuclear superiority if the Russians attacked in Europe, ran the threat, subsequently modified.

Then there were the British and French. The British had had to go it alone as regards nuclear weaponry, although they could hardly afford it. They had exploded their own first bomb in October 1952 and were obviously looking for some independent role. In the first place, Churchill himself hoped to have a last grand international moment, reconciling the USSR and the rest, and in the early fifties, before German competition properly started, British exports boomed, and there was some life in the British Commonwealth. A third of the world's trade was conducted in pounds, and money therefore came back to the City of London: Churchill could imagine that he had an independent role. With the French, matters were simpler. There was a large Communist Party; there was a great deal of resentment against Germany; there was cultural resentment of American domination; and there was a colonial war going on, in Vietnam, where Soviet help might be helpful. To have pushed all of them together, in NATO, had been extraordinarily clumsy. Once the Soviets decided to be more cunning the Korean War was wound up within weeks, and a year later, at Geneva, the parallel war in Vietnam was stopped, again with a division in the middle. What of central Europe?

In the air there was the question of disarmament. War might lead to the victory of the proletariat, but it could wipe out the planet as well. Malenkov had said as much, but was driven out by Khrushchev for saying it. Now, accompanied by an old-order totem, Bulganin, Khrushchev started to do his world rounds, visiting the United Nations, England, the USA and elsewhere, and saying much the same things as Malenkov had been overthrown for saying. He had a sort of rough charm, and was at any rate memorable, dropping peasant wisdoms like a caricature Russian: socialism was to have a human face again, and Stalin's mistakes had to be made good. The moment was quite propitious. A business-minded Right, now mainly dominant in the West, had various uses for the USSR. It could for a start neutralize the public opinion that backed it. When Eisenhower won the election of 1952, he did so on a strongly anti-Communist platform, and his Vice-President, Richard Nixon, had made a name for himself as persecutor of Communists in general. The period of Joseph McCarthy was not long over, and public opinion in some places was strongly in favour of the use of American power: General MacArthur himself had argued for a nuclear strike against the Chinese ports, though Truman had sidelined him over this. In practice, the death of Stalin came as a huge present to Eisenhower, and let him off the Korean hook. He really wanted to go down in history as the man who had stopped a nuclear war. Business should be done.

How should the USSR respond? It mattered that Khrushchev himself had great faith in Communism, and was confident of the future, but for the moment he needed calm. After all, the USSR had made enemies of all of her neighbours except China, and China was a potential rival: Mao wanted the bomb. This time, in the context of possible German reunification, a new idea emerged in Moscow: a 'security plan' that involved 'security guarantees in Europe' and 'a project for a treaty of collective security in Europe'. It was meant to establish permanent pan-European institutions, and not to include the Americans or NATO; foreign forces were to be withdrawn. The proposals were intelligent enough, and the immediate aim was clearly to prevent any European Defence Community. Appeal needed to be made to German pacifism – to rope the Germans into some overall European 'structure', which would be neutral. Beyond that lay the hope of detaching Europe from the USA. The Russians were generally agile when it came to managing these large-scale multinational bodies, their own foreign affairs being on the whole less messily conceived and executed than other countries'. Eventually, Molotov's plan, put forward again and again, was realized with the Helsinki Conference of 1975, and it had some temptations in a Europe that might otherwise be the scene of nuclear war and was anyway on occasion resentful of the Americans. In 1954, in the very short run, the Molotov suggestion was successful enough in France, when the Paris parliament failed to ratify the EDC on 30 August. But that failure was not very significant: German rearmament was anyway going ahead.

Khrushchev needed to show that Communism did not need to mean labour camps. His Stalin speech was symbolic: rules would prevail henceforth. The Party, which was the essential institution, would be restored, whereas Stalin had considered just abolishing it and Beria had meant to turn it into a sort of baroque Scout and Girl Guide organization. The Central Committee, expanded by one third to 340 souls, met more often (six times in 1958) and congresses were held every four years, although the speeches, vetted beforehand, were ritualistic and, to an outsider, an ordeal: as John Keep says, 'only by close examination could one detect here and there a slight emphasis that reflected some local or occupational interest'. Even the word *glasnost* was used, when its proceedings were published, but its real nerve was a secretariat, employing thousands, that operated in extreme secrecy. There was a Department of Agitation and Propaganda which covered the media and cultural life generally, and the number of people involved rose from 6 million in 1957 to 36 million in 1964. Party members doubled, to 12 million. The proportion of 'specialists' – engineers, for instance – went up, and there was more room for men in their thirties. At the 20th Congress, that of the Stalin speech, more than half of the eighty-four national or regional secretaries were replaced, and Khrushchev finally defeated the old guard in 1957 because over half of the Central Committee members were new appointments. In 1960–61 he repeated the anti-Stalin drive, and replaced fifty-five of the (now) 114 national and regional secretaries. At any rate, the personnel, if not the structure, was de-Stalinized, and there were no more mass killings. When Khrushchev was finally overthrown in 1964, he took pride in the fact that he had not been killed. That went together with a certain cultural liberalization, in that books open about some of the horrors of Stalin's time were published, though there were limits. Still, whatever these limits, observers in the West could safely conclude that things were getting better, that business could be done. By 1955, when Khrushchev had established his authority, a half-thaw occurred in the Cold War.

The first sign of movement in Moscow came when on 8 February 1955 Molotov at last said that there might be a *Staatsvertrag* ('state treaty') over the restoration of Austria – no need to wait for a German treaty, he said. Earlier, the USSR had refused any Austrian arrangement: the country was on the Czechoslovak and Hungarian borders, and might make these countries unstable. But Austrian independence was a useful carrot to have on offer. Now, fearing that the western zones of Austria might be incorporated in the new western Germany, and wanting to show the Germans what might be achieved, the Russians recognized and evacuated Austria. A *Staatsvertrag* was signed in the Belvedere Palace on 15 May, and the Red Army moved out quite quickly. The Austrian chancellor, Julius Raab, spent three days in Moscow discussing these arrangements, and Austrian neutrality was solemnly declared by the parliament in October. In this case, the neutrality meant certain rewards – for instance, the placing of international bodies (including the new Atomic Energy Commission) in Vienna – but it also had its questionable side, in that Vienna became something of an espionage capital, and, like Finland, a place where Moscow might maintain agents of influence. The most obvious of these was one Kurt Waldheim, who slipped and slithered his way from the staff of an Army Group in the Balkans to the Austrian foreign ministry, where he connived in the Soviet invasion of Czechoslovakia and was rewarded to become secretary-general of the United Nations. In this same period, the Soviet bases in Finland were also given up, partly on the grounds that they made the Swedes nervous, and caused them secretly to co-operate with the West. This again, as with Austria's Waldheim, was to prove its uses with Sweden's Olof Palme. In May 1955 Khrushchev visited Tito, in an attempt to make up, but there, one Communist seeing through another, he had a guarded welcome, and Tito was enjoying his role as arbiter between East and West; Yugoslavia also became an important pioneer of the 'Third World', made money out of Arab shipping, oil and construction, and was cheerfully represented as every country's favourite neutral. West Germany was once more well and truly on the map, and in 1955 Adenauer was invited to Moscow for resumption of diplomatic relations – one present being the return to Germany of the prisoners of war who had been cruelly kept back, including the few thousand survivors of Stalingrad and the men who had been in Hitler's Bunker to the very end.

At any rate, here was a grinning Khrushchev going round the West, even being received with rapture by ambitious hostesses in California and talking agriculture with prominent American farmers. A machinery for East–West relations was coming into existence. At the United Nations and in foreign ministries, a bureaucracy was to emerge, with an interest in common matters, such as disarmament talks or 'summits', which were supposed, generally quite wrongly, to make for personal friendships that would solve the various international problems. Quite soon, American farmers were saving the Soviet population from the consequences of Moscow's misdeeds over agriculture (in 1914 Russia had been the greatest grain exporter in the world). Grain exports started in 1955, and were generally paid for, through a credit system, by the American taxpayer. However, there was an obvious problem, in that the People's Democracies that Stalin had set up were considerable counter-propaganda. The contrast between Austria and Hungary was illustrative. Vienna was remaking itself as an historic city. Budapest, its twin, was still pockmarked by bullet holes, the splendid boulevards of nineteenth-century Pest dimly lit, empty, and marked only by occasional dingy shops. Any appeal to the West would mean getting rid of the little Stalinists who ran these places, each with its own miniature Iron Curtain, complete with savage Alsatians (a stuffed one, in heroic biting mode, was on display in the Prague museum of the security police, which occupied part of the old German university).

Getting rid of these little Stalinists was not easy. Czechoslovakia had her own native Communist movement of some strength, but in Poland and Hungary Communism was the imposition of a small minority. The local Communists kept power by Stalinist methods – in Hungary a labour camp at Récsk, in Romania a much larger one in the foetid Danube Delta – and crammed peasants into collective farms or towns and cities, which were swamped. Cracow, an historic baroque town in southern Poland, Catholic and middle-class in character, acquired a huge steelworks, Nowa Huta, to introduce a proletarian element. To combat religion, sport was used: Katowice had a huge smog-bound stadium in its centre. Churches, independent organizations of all sorts, contacts with foreigners or emigrants all came under severe censure, and a secret police, the UB, had its spies everywhere. In East Germany the situation was still harsher. Meanwhile, a good proportion of anything that these countries produced went to the USSR. The cities were dominated by lorries carting building rubble around, spewing out Soviet-refined oil, which had its own unmistakable smell. In Stalin's last years, there had been grotesque political trials, in which senior Communist stalwarts, generally Jewish, were tortured into confessions as to British espionage and the like. The problem here was the example of Tito, whose enmity Stalin himself had created, but whose example, as an independent national-minded Communist, might prove tempting to other of the satellite country leaderships.

Now, as part of a strategy to make the USSR less repellent in Western and especially German eyes, Khrushchev attempted to make conditions in the People's Democracies less oppressive. He would try to find popular and national Communist leaders to replace the various Stalinist oppressors. Even in 1953 there were modest changes: George Soros visited Budapest, for instance. The chief idea (Molotov did not like it) was to make Communism less unpopular, by associating it with nationalism (and Khrushchev went to Warsaw and Prague in 1954, also with a view to minor relaxations). The local Stalin-appointed leaderships got in the way; the furniture would have to be changed. This was not easy. The satellite leaders each had his own network and support system, and in Czechoslovakia, which was still quite an advanced country, with a genuine proletariat, Klement Gottwald and his successor, Antonín Novotný, were not at all easy to shake. Even, they could claim to have taken over the country because of electoral popularity rather than through the Red Army. The country was anyway made up of two nations, Czech and Slovak, and in so far as there were 'national' Communists, they were likely to be Slovak, men such as Gustáv Husák and Alexandr Dubček. Poland was the greatest headache – the largest of these countries, and, as everyone knew, likely to be strongly anti-Soviet if freed from Moscow's control. Hungary, though much smaller, was similar. As with Poland, she was tightly controlled by a small knot of mainly Jewish Communists – Mátyás Rákosi, a veteran of pre-war prison; Ernő Gerő, a veteran of the Spanish Civil War and much else in particular; others, including a female or two. These people were an embarrassment and the Hungarians' security police, the AVO, were famously horrible. On the other hand, once they were removed, who else? Khrushchev interfered, but not with much forcefulness. One of the worst AVO men, Vladimir Farkas, was removed. More, a man with long associations in Moscow was moved back into a position of power. Imre Nagy was not Jewish. He was of a poor and provincial Protestant background, and in Hungary the Protestant minorities in the past had been substantial, creative, the backbone of the national cause and, before 1867, sometimes persecuted by the Catholic establishment of the Austrian empire. Nagy as a young soldier had been made prisoner by the Russians in the First World War and, like many such, including figures as diverse as Tito in Yugoslavia and Ernst Reuter, mayor of Berlin at the time of the blockade, had become a Communist. In the 1930s he had lived in Moscow, and had survived the killings that Stalin launched against foreign Communists not protected by their own embassy. Nagy was widely assumed to have been an informer – perhaps trying to get rid of rivals within the Party, such as its leader, Béla Kun. He came back to Budapest in 1945, and was minister of agriculture. As such, he protested against the grotesque misuse that was made of farmers, and was sidelined; under pressure from the USSR, he was reinstated, as prime minister, in 1953, but he did not replace Rákosi as Party secretary, and, since in that system the Party constituted the real power, he was rapidly pushed aside through committee manoeuvring by the Rákosi–Gerő team. In the same way, on a much grander scale in Moscow, Malenkov, head of the government, was outmanoeuvred by Khrushchev, who ran the Party. But now, Khrushchev wanted to be rid of Rákosi.

The long-accepted account of the Hungarian national uprising that followed ran along heroic lines. In 1848 there had been a great revolt against the Austrian empire, and it had had an operatic quality – barricades, student demonstrations, public rhetoric, epic poems by writers and, behind the scenes, calculations by clever aristocrats. Updated, this meant the masses, bare hands against tanks. This was legend: manipulative noblemen had been at work. The same, in much different form, happened again: 1956 was a stage revolution that got out of hand. The Stalin speech in February 1956 was supposed to have been secret, but Khrushchev did not mean or expect this to remain the case, and the rumours of it spread. Upsetting Rákosi meant organizing some well-placed demonstration against him, and a useful forum was the Writers' Union. Under Communism, writers were a privileged breed, with special restaurants and guaranteed royalties, and their union was a natural home for writers who knew that they were not in the first class. It was also heavily bureaucratized by the Party. On the anniversary of the start of the 1848 uprising, a national day, some students – their union, too, heavily bureaucratized – laid a national flag at the statue of the great poet of 1848, Sándor Petőfi. The writers followed, with a carefully worded resolution as to the need for this or that alteration of the Party's ways. Rákosi, dented, carried on, but the new developments were obvious enough. Then came news of events in Poland, which stimulated the opposition to continue.

The Stalin report had given the visiting Polish leader, Bolesław Bierut, a heart attack; of which he died. Khrushchev went to the funeral, and stayed for the election of Bierut's successor. He tried both to excuse his own Stalinist past, and to explain how the monster had ruled; when someone anonymous broke out with a 'no', Khrushchev retorted, quite accurately, that that kind of objection, to a Soviet leader, would have been unthinkable before his, Khrushchev's, report, and, 'as the saying goes, the fool becomes smart afterwards'. Khrushchev then vastly alarmed his Polish audience when he praised Stalin's imposition of a quota – 2 per cent – for Jews in important places, including the universities. What, in a very muddled and offensive way, he was doing was to make his audience elect as leader a 'national' and non-Jewish figure. They did not know what to do; the interim successor figures toyed with change, and events then brought on a crisis. Tito had arrived in Moscow early in June and at the end of the month, at Poznan, working-class restiveness resulted in a huge anti-Soviet demonstration and a strike that was only crushed by tanks and security troops in thousands; over seventy people were killed, and hundreds wounded. It mattered that, in Poland, there was a very widely popular Church which had a long tradition of working-class Catholicism. The priests were politically, by implication, far more powerful in Poland than elsewhere in the bloc and they became important in the sequel. The Communists themselves did not even, for years, imprison the Cardinal, as had happened in Hungary, and only latterly kept him under house arrest in the southern mountains.

When the Poles met to elect a new Politburo on 19 October, they elected Władysław Gomułka. He, back in 1948, had had some popularity (he was not a Jew, though his wife was), had been expelled from the Party for the usual heresies, and in 1951 was arrested (though, again, interned rather than purge-tried). Now he was brought back, to enormous waves of public enthusiasm, and when Khrushchev wanted an invitation to Warsaw it was refused. He came, uninvited, with a retinue of senior Soviet politicians and generals, in full-dress uniform; he threatened to order the troops into Warsaw. There was a high scene at the airport, but Gomułka won Khrushchev round: there would be yet another enormous Polish rising unless the Polish Communists were allowed to order things their own way. Khrushchev flew back to Moscow, still in two minds but in the end resigned. There was to be a Polish 'national Communism', with Gomułka in charge (and the Cardinal always there to advise prudence). There were tempestuous scenes in Poland, and they were transmitted to Hungary. On 23 October Budapest exploded as well, this time organized by the students. Thousands strong, they moved towards the parliament, and towards the radio station, where they wanted to be on air; they tore down the huge Stalin statue in the Városliget. There was firing by the AVO that evening, but the police were overwhelmed and fled. The fact was that there was no Church to calm tempers; nor was there a Gomułka. The Hungarian Stalinists were hated, and Hungary as a country had faced vast humiliation, whereas, though Poland had been ruined, she had at least counted among the victors, and the Communists, though detested, had had their human face. Khrushchev detected that the Hungarian situation would be much more explosive and, though he did encounter criticism, moved in troops on 24 October. But they met resistance from Molotov cocktails and the like, and the Hungarian army went over to the rebellion. Gerő speedily went, replaced by János Kádár, who, like Gomułka, had been a victim of the

Stalinists, but the fighting went on, with hundreds of dead Hungarians and Soviet soldiers. Even Marshall Zhukov now thought that the troops should be withdrawn, and others in the Politburo agreed. On 30 October Khrushchev was ready to withdraw from Hungary altogether and issued a placating statement. But by then events in Budapest were out of control and a mob sacked the Party headquarters; the AVO men were identified by their light-coloured shoes, and lynched (hanged from the trees). Hungarian tanks defected and Nagy now said he would leave the Soviet alliance, the Warsaw Pact. Mikoyan and Mikhail Suslov, the head of ideology, were in Budapest, and Nagy also talked to them about a Soviet withdrawal from Hungary. Khrushchev had been very much in doubt up to that point, and now he began to see the dangers in further concession – as he said to Tito, it would mean 'capitalists' on the Soviet border. To begin with, the Chinese had been all for a Polish solution but Mao Tse-tung, too, urged force on the evening of 30 October, when he learned of the lynchings and on the 31st Khrushchev told the Praesidium that the USSR must restore order. Several days before, Khrushchev had noted that the British and French were embroiled in Suez and had said the USSR should not be similarly embroiled. But he went ahead. Mikoyan protested. Khrushchev just said that 'bloodshed' then would spare much worse bloodshed later on.

Then he went off to talk to the Poles (at Brest-Litovsk) and to Hungary's neighbours. They were worried that a non-Communist Hungary would make trouble over the borders with the Hungarian minorities. In the 1920s and 1930s, there had been an alliance of Czechoslovakia, Romania and Yugoslavia against Hungary, known as the 'Little Entente', and it now made a shadowy reappearance. Khrushchev made an especial appeal to Tito, who made him fly to his country retreat on the island of Brioni, one of the Quarnero group at the head of the Adriatic, where storms frequently blew. He flew into a terrible one over the mountains, and then had to cross a wild sea: Malenkov was very ill. Tito – himself recently revealed to have been, like Nagy, a one-time agent of the NKVD – gave the Russians his support, and their troops would move in on Budapest again. It took several days of fighting for Budapest to be brought back under control, under a new government, Kádár's, which started off with severe repression, while 200,000 people fled the country. Nagy was shabbily tricked into the Yugoslav embassy, with other leading figures, was promised asylum, and was kidnapped to Romania, where he was kept for two years in seclusion. Then, bizarrely, he was tried and executed – his remains thrown into an unmarked prison grave. He said, before his death, that history would rehabilitate him; the only thing he feared, he added, was that it would be his executioners who did the rehabilitating, and there he was completely right. His eventual rehabilitation, in 1989, was part of the Communists' struggle to survive. But 1956 had another curious effect, that Moscow would from now on handle the Hungarians with a certain amount of care.

8

Europe and the Wider World

Hungarians in the West demonstrated outside Soviet embassies in protest at the crushing of Budapest; there was an exodus from Western Communist parties. However, there was never any question of Western intervention in the affair; on the contrary, it confirmed the existing borders. Besides, the rising in itself caused the Soviet hand to be less heavy. Khrushchev hoped that a more national character in the People's Democracies would make them less unpopular, and for a time that did indeed succeed – even, eventually, in Hungary, the leader of which might well echo an old line of central European politics, that 'I have no ambition in politics beyond the attainment on all sides of a supportable level of dissatisfaction.' Khrushchev, for his part, was still full of himself. True, western Europe had not fallen – quite the contrary. But there was the rest of the world, and Moscow was now discovering it.

The justification for Stalin had been that semi-colonial backward peasant countries could remake themselves in a generation, through industry, and defeat the Western imperialists. Mao Tse-tung was applying what he took to be Soviet lessons, and in 1955 Khrushchev had been quite generous as regards help, though he stopped short at nuclear secrets. Progressive intelligentsia the world over took the Soviet example seriously, and studies of the whole subject in the West were dominated by E. H. Carr's multivolume history of the Revolution. Carr, who had earlier written a book arguing that, since Hitler had power, Britain should side with him, now noted that Stalin had power, and that Britain should accommodate him. His account of the Revolution showed how that power had been obtained, and it took the whole experience of Five Year Plans and the collectivization of agriculture very seriously. He waved aside with contempt any suggestion that Russia in 1914 had not really been so backward after all; his history of the Revolution hardly bothers with the subject, and begins rather bewilderingly and at length with arguments between a few dozen socialists in exile. The Soviet example had acquired world-wide resonance; now Latin America was in the offing, and so also was the Middle East. Khrushchev went onto the world stage.

The Middle East, with oil, had an importance for the world that went far beyond its stage in development; and this was all the more so as the Suez Canal was still, in the 1950s, the essential artery for Western trade. British interests reigned over the oil, which was then very cheap (at around $1 to the barrel, there being seven barrels to the ton) and that made for prosperity in the industrial countries, where the motor car was both a cause and a symbol. The once great Ottoman Empire had collapsed in the First World War, replaced by supposedly national states. The only successful one turned out to be Turkey, based on the Ottoman heartland in Anatolia; the others were semi-colonies. In 1948 another nation state emerged, Israel, which had been carved out of Ottoman Palestine as a Jewish national home; it fought a war against Arab armies, and the native Arab or Palestinian population mainly fled. The implantation of Israel, as a Western outcrop, stood almost as a symbol of Arab weakness, but that was also shown in the French occupation of North Africa or the British semi-occupation of Egypt. The Europeans often took pride in what these occupations achieved, but they tended to co-operate either with a Westernized upper class or with minorities of various sorts, of which the Middle East contained a great many: Christian Copts in Egypt, Assyrian or Chaldean Christians in Iraq, Beduin in Transjordan, diaspora Greeks or Armenians throughout. They also introduced the deadly principle of nationalism and by 1950 that was gaining much ground. In the early 1950s the British and French were losing. In June 1956 the British withdrew the garrison from Suez.

The beneficiary was an Egyptian army officer, Gamel Abdal Nasser, whose ambition it was to put Egypt at the head of an Arab nationalist movement. He had emerged in 1952, when the monarchy was overthrown; at the same time the Iranian Mohammad Mossadegh seized

British oil installations (he was, with CIA intervention, overthrown). Nasser now made trouble throughout the Middle East, and especially for the French in Algeria. In 1954 Algeria had erupted, and by 1956 there was a savage war there; he also interfered in Iraq, and its prime minister – very soon to be brutally murdered – told the British that they must get rid of Nasser or he would finish them: 'It was life and death for the West as well as for Nasser.' Intelligence did indeed reveal that Nasser had such a plan, and it would of course mean the elimination of Israel as well; he also had his eyes on the revenues of the Suez Canal, through which 80 per cent of western Europe's oil had to flow. That would mean an Egyptian hand on the windpipe. The British tried to tame him. An anti-Soviet Baghdad Pact existed, linking a 'northern tier' of Middle Eastern countries; he was invited to join it. But he was well alive to the new possibilities that the Cold War had presented to countries such as his own. There was now a league of 'non-aligned' states, states that had in most cases been recently decolonized, and in 1955 their leaders held a conference at Bandung in Indonesia; preachy Indians loomed large, and so did Yugoslavia. These states now had votes at the United Nations, a body taken seriously, and could play on the guilt that many people in the rich West felt about their imperialist past. At this time, and partly because of the huge success of the Marshall Plan, the idea of government-to-government aid was dominant, and the Bandung countries looked for this. In Nasser's case, the aim was for technology and specialists to construct an enormous dam on the upper Nile, at Aswan. It would control the waters, prevent devastating floods, allow irrigation of a much larger area on either side of the lower river, and so promote agriculture and especially cotton, which was a principal Egyptian export. Later on, the whole notion of government-to-government aid came into question, and so also did the notion of gigantic dams, but in 1956 both counted as 'Progress', and the British had themselves built the first Nile dam, in 1902. Nasser asked them and the Americans for finance, but in 1955 he also took weaponry from the Soviet Union (via Czechoslovakia – 200 planes, including MiG-15s and Il-28 bombers). The target was of course Israel, and Nasser meant to head a sort of counter-crusade, which would also have the effect of eliminating rivals such as King Abdullah in Jordan, who co-operated with the Israelis in the hope of reaching a sensible solution. He was indeed murdered.

Building a dam was very expensive indeed, and if the money came from outside, Nasser could use his own for armaments. In 1955 he had been busy enough. The very future of Israel was under question, as the Egyptians closed the Gulf of Aqaba and the Suez Canal to Israeli shipping, and there were constant border raids – the killing of fifty here, fifty there, with reprisals and counter-reprisals. Jordan, controlling Jerusalem, was also becoming unstable, as Palestinians took refuge there and made life difficult for the new, very young, British-educated king, Hussein. Nasser's agents now entered the picture, offering a pan-Arab and supposedly socialist nationalism that would sweep away client monarchies such as Hussein's, and the king had a very hard balancing act to perform. One piece of it was to make a show of independence from the British, and dismiss the legendary Glubb Pasha, who commanded the also legendary Arab Legion, in March 1956. How were the British to handle all of this? Their own self-confidence had considerably recovered in the middle of that decade, as exports were (misleadingly) booming and the domestic economy recovered at last from the post-war emergencies. NATO gave them apparently solid American backing: they had their own nuclear bomb. Why give in to blackmail from a jumped-up Arab nobody? Churchill's successor, Anthony Eden, was anxious to show his worth, and the Suez challenge put him into an almost hysterical condition. A visit to Cairo in 1955 had not been a success, Clarissa Eden regarding Nasser as a seedy waiter. Nasser had kept his Soviet options open, refused to join the Baghdad Pact, and obviously meant to overthrow Arab kings. He threatened to nationalize the Suez Canal and take the dues that came in from the world's trade, but he also prompted the Americans to give him the money for the Aswan Dam.

There was indeed an air of surrealism in what followed. Eden was ill, and bile entered his system; the pain could only be controlled by drugs that slowed him down, and these could only be countered by doses of Benzedrine, not a happy combination. Besides, Eden had always laboured under the mighty shadow of Churchill, who was still a physical presence, always communicating doubt as to whether

'Anthony' could really do the job. The influential press tended now to dismiss Eden as a weakling, and his relations with senior Cabinet men were difficult. Now, from Nasser, came an insulting rebuff to a country that still claimed status as a Great Power. Eden would act. It was a sad end to what had been a very honourable career. Eden had been a brilliant Oriental linguist at Oxford, had had a very good First World War and, being utterly uncorrupt, had money worries for much of the time. He had also been morally on the right side in the 1930s, when he wanted to stop Hitler and Mussolini before they truly got under way. But now his judgement went, and a strange petulance governed affairs. Nasser was, he said, another Mussolini. The leading journalist of the period, Malcolm Muggeridge, had it right when he sneered that in any manual for Men of Destiny, invading Egypt was Exercise One, as Eden shrieked into telephones that he wanted Nasser destroyed. There was no thought for the consequences – who would follow Nasser. Eden said he did not care. He and many others seemed to think it would be easy to dispose of the jumped-up Nasser and expressions of such over-confidence are legion. Public opinion was strongly in favour of some action: it did not mind being challenged by Russians, but drew the line at Egyptian Arabs. The problem, familiar to Marxists, was that the Americans were against it.

The final provocation to Nasser came in July when Dulles indicated in an insulting way that money for the Aswan Dam would not be forthcoming. The Americans too were hostile to Nasser, but they were also not anxious to support British imperialism in the area, and CIA men were even encouraging Nasser, to their own ambassador's dismay (Eisenhower later said that what happened at Suez was his greatest regret). On 26 July Nasser suddenly announced that he would nationalize the Suez Canal, and his men took over the offices of the international (and mainly Anglo-French) company that ran it. This was in breach of an old convention, but these old conventions had been agreed back in the days when such countries were helpless before British strength, and the Egyptian public was delirious.

What followed was a disaster, in all respects including the fact that the disaster was limited. The French went on to a disaster, to do with North Africa, but it delivered such a shock to their system that they abandoned it, and experienced an economic miracle to rival Germany's. Suez did not have such an effect in England, and marks the start of a national decline that continued for the next generation. Whitehall still thought imperially: an often quoted comment, and not from Eden alone, was that England could not possibly go the way of Holland. As things turned out, she should have been so lucky: Holland indeed lost an empire, but hers had been a low-wage and heavily agricultural economy, and after the loss of Indonesia she became rich, a major exporter and a well-managed place.

Reservists were mobilized (the Queen signed the document, squaring it on a horse's rump at Goodwood). Then – in such situations, a very bad move – they were kept waiting around, away from employment and family. Delays mounted. The Americans were consulted, and wartime solidarity was invoked between an Eisenhower and an Eden who had known each other in the old days of glory. Dulles sometimes encouraged, but more often the American line was that force should not be used – instead, a process of negotiation should start, and subversive methods tried. Eden said that Nasser's hands were on the West's windpipe and he seems to have thought that if he presented the Americans with a *fait accompli*, they would have to support him, and he went ahead with military plans. The French, enraged at Nasser's appeal to Arab nationalism in Algeria, joined in. As negotiations dragged on the two governments reckoned that they needed a pretext for intervention, and a ghost in the machine came to their rescue. There were constant tensions and skirmishes on the Egyptian–Israeli border, as on the Jordanian–Israeli one. The Israelis had a plan to strike, and had bought up-to-date French fighter aircraft with a view to this. They and the French got together: Israel would attack, and claim she was merely anticipating an Egyptian attack; a French admiral came to London looking to give 'those damned Arabs the lesson they long needed', and on 19 September, just as Dulles's backing appeared to weaken, the French and Israelis appeared ready to go ahead on their own. Eden jumped in, and an absurd plot took shape, the British Foreign Secretary wearing a false moustache and a French general suggesting that the Israelis should bomb one of their own cities to give a pretext for Anglo-French intervention. In the event, a secret 'Sèvres Protocol' established an agreement: the Israelis would attack on 29 October and the British and French would pretend to intervene to keep the peace and guarantee the Canal's workings.

The Israelis staged a very clever operation, carried out with panache. Four Mustangs, flying only twelve feet from the ground, cut Egyptian telephone connections, and a few hundred paratroops secured the essential desert pass. By 5 November the Israelis were on the Canal, occupying, also, the entrance to the Gulf of Aqaba from which their shipping had been banned. It no doubt helped that, on 31 October, the British bombed Egyptian air bases. The day before, Eden had told the House of Commons that the Israelis and Egyptians would be told to stop while an Anglo-French force occupied the Canal Zone. He even tried to claim that this was not 'war', but 'armed conflict', and of all absurdities suspended deliveries of arms to Tel Aviv. Almost at once, problems emerged. The dollar reserves were declining, and in any case mobilization was a very slow business: the British had put resources into nuclear weaponry, and had run down the effectiveness both of their army and of their navy. They could not get troops to the Suez area inside a month, and though they did have troops at a base in Libya, they shrank from using these, for fear of offending wider opinion. In fact the Chiefs of Staff objected to an immediate action, threatening resignation: they were just not ready. A British force did eventually leave from Malta and Cyprus – bases both too far distant, given that speed was so essential: the world, confronted by the fact on the ground of an immediate occupation, might have accepted it (as Dulles later said, 'Had they done it quickly, we'd have accepted it' and Eisenhower shook his head: 'I've just never seen Great Powers make such a complete mess'). Four days' delay occurred, while British and American diplomats had a public wrangle. The First Lord of the Admiralty, Lord Mountbatten, showed his usual instinct for the possible, and was only narrowly stopped from resigning as he sensed the unfolding fiasco. The Americans became incensed at being told such obvious lies by men whom they imagined they could absolutely trust, and as the Anglo-French force steamed forth, the American fleet in the area disrupted its radio communications and used submarines to shadow it. Then disaster went ahead. The Canal was blocked by the

Egyptians, and oil imports dwindled, prices rising. Junior Foreign Office people threatened mass resignation. The Americans at the United Nations denounced the expedition, and that body produced a resolution in which all countries but a faithful few condemned the British and French: Eden even received a letter from Moscow on 5 November, vaguely threatening retaliation, just as the paratroops at last landed. That was bluster, but a further move was not bluster. The pound sterling was an artificially strong currency, and now the Americans refused to support the pound. It fell – reserves dropping by $50m in the first two days of November, and by 5 per cent of the total in the first week. At that rate, there would be none left by the early weeks of 1957. The end was humiliating, as the American Secretary of State told the United Nations that he could not support his allies. Just as he said so, the landings at Port Said finally occurred on 5 November, but by then it was far too late, and a ceasefire had to follow by the evening of the next day. The broken Eden retired ill to the house on Jamaica where Ian Fleming wrote his James Bond books – one imperial fantasy meeting another. The conclusion at once drawn in London was that never again would the Atlantic link be risked.

The conclusions drawn in France were rather different. She had entered upon Suez because she blamed Nasser for problems in North Africa: he supported, and inspired, an Arab nationalism there, and especially in Algeria. French governments after the war faced colonial troubles. Burke had remarked that political life was a partnership of the dead, the living and the yet unborn, but in France the dead predominated. The theory – very theoretical – behind French republicanism had been that, regardless of origin, all citizens of the republic were French. This was very far from being senseless, and even went back to the Revolution itself, when Robespierre had declared that the colonies might perish, provided that justice survived. The rising socialist François Mitterrand himself talked of a France 'from Flanders to the Congo', and representatives of the overseas departments or colonies sat as of right in the chamber, sometimes attaining cabinet rank. Determined, after the terrible experience of German occupation and liberation by the Americans and the British, to reassert France's status in the world, post-war governments let themselves be dragged into a hopeless struggle to retain Vietnam. That ended with the defeat of Dien Bien Phu in May 1954, after which a (brief) sensibly run government, under the Radical Pierre Mendès France, gave up. But far worse was to come in Algeria. North Africa had been taken over by the French at various stages. Tunisia and Morocco were taken over in 1881 and 1912 as protectorates, their native rulers kept intact, though controlled by the French. They were not colonies in the strict sense, nor were there many French colonists. For France to give independence in return for useful economic and cultural links was therefore not very difficult, and in 1956 this duly happened. Algeria was different. French rule went back to 1830, and the country at that time had been both vast and empty. It was also quite varied in composition, and the French could divide and rule easily enough. They developed the country, and by 1950 there were a million colonists, known as *pieds noirs*, apparently because their feet, after trampling the grapes for the wine harvest, turned black. Many of these *pieds noirs* were not French at all but came from all over the Mediterranean coasts and islands. There was much Arab immigration as well, and as medical improvements got under way, that part of the population greatly expanded (as it has continued to do). In republican ideology, Algerians were French citizens, but on the ground matters were very different: the natives – by origin in many cases no more native than the *pieds noirs* – had far less political weight, and in the 1930s French governments were dilatory about reform. In effect they were captured by the *pieds noirs*, and very few of these were prepared to concede anything to the Algerians. As often happens in such situations, from the United States through Ottoman Greece and British India, the opponents of change did have some right on their side: once the empire went, the way would be open to slavery, or ethnic cleansing, or absurd religious divisions. In any case, almost all Frenchmen were convinced that they were carrying out a civilizing mission in Algeria, and even the Communists supported *Algérie française*, though of course expecting that differences between Moslems and others would be vastly reduced in scale once the revolution applied, as in the Soviet Union, its solutions to the national question. Governments in Paris were overthrown just for suggesting reform, which came tardily. Riots and repression followed and educated Algerians, rebuffed, looked to Arab nationalism, to the example of Egypt, where Nasser had established himself at Anglo-French expense in 1952.

In any case, the collapse of the French position in Indo-China showed what might happen: Dien Bien Phu was rapidly followed by a revolt in Algeria, which started with a characteristic atrocity on All Saints' Day. On 1 November, La Voix des Arabes from Cairo announced, 'Today, on the fifth day of the month of Rabii of the year 1374 ... at one o'clock in the morning, Algeria has begun to live an honourable life ... A powerful group of free children of Algeria has started the insurrection of freedom against the tyrannical French imperialism in North Africa.' What had happened was that, in a remote part of the country, a bus had been ambushed, a protesting village headman machine-gunned, a French schoolteacher shot dead and his wife badly wounded. The ambushers waited around for a while, in order to shoot any rescuers who arrived, but since none did, they left. The French followed this with severe repression, harassed relatively moderate Algerians, dropped bombs, and sent in troops who were only too anxious to avenge the defeat in Vietnam (where the French lost some 90,000 men). Mendès France had been sensible over Vietnam but even he reacted, in the first instance, with an 'Ici c'est la France.' But it was not so simple. Now, the 'National Liberation Front' was in a much stronger position than had been Algerian rebels in the old days, when Foreign Legionaries could romantically hold desert forts against camel-riding raiders. Several of the rebels had fought in the French army; arms could be supplied across the Tunisian border, or even as it turned out from Yugoslavia, where Tito was in full leader-of-unaligned mode; Nasser was bidding for leadership of the Arab world; and the Americans especially were not in sympathy with French colonization (on a later occasion, the American cultural centre in Algiers was burned down by enraged *pieds noirs*). Algiers itself was the scene of a foul battle in 1957, when random terrorists provoked retribution, and the French parachutists, under an implacable general, Jacques Émile Massu, restored order. One method was torture. By 1958 the army had in its way won, but the cost was enormous – in fact, a degree of hatred between the two sides (and among the Algerians themselves) that made a solution impossible. The *pieds noirs* were possessed of a collective rage, and so was much of the army. Meanwhile in Paris the politicians, facing condemnation even from allies, were facing the headache of paying for the unending war, and some of them knew that in an era of decolonization there were other ways of saving France's position in Algeria. Oil had been discovered in the Sahara and that could be obtained easily enough through collaboration with an independent Algeria. In mid-April one government fell and a moderate, Pierre Pflimlin, took the succession. At the very hint of compromise, Algiers exploded. On 13 May the *pieds noirs*, who all along felt that metropolitan governments were not nearly harsh enough against the rebels, struck; the governor-general's palace was stormed and sacked; parts of the army clearly sympathized; even, Massu was asked to set up a 'Committee of Public Safety', an emergency institution that went back to the days of the great Revolution when France had been invaded. A few days later, a parachute unit from Algeria seized the island of Corsica. There was strong pressure in Paris for a return of de Gaulle, the supreme national figure, and the Algerian French supposed that he would impose an *Algérie française*. There were enormous demonstrations in Algiers (in which a great number of Moslems joined: as ever, in such situations, the Algerian revolt was itself a civil war, and even more Moslems were killed by Moslems than by the French, whose own losses – 30,000 – were surprisingly limited for an eight-year war of this savagery).

The crisis in Algeria and the threat of an army putsch against the government itself at least put an end to the preposterous government crisis. De Gaulle had been thinking. The almost universal belief was that the colonial crises were causing the paralysis of the State. De Gaulle came to the belief that this order should be reversed – that the institutions had to be radically changed for some sensible solution to these interminable conflicts to be found, as after all the British had, more or less, managed. Vietnam stood in very stark contrast to Malaya, where the British had had to fight a long and difficult war but had been very careful to cultivate local allies who were essential to the winning of it. The fact was that a great many of the politicians more or less agreed that the institutions were absurd, and asked only to be put out of their misery in a dignified way. There was some screeching alarmism. The president of the Council of Europe, a standard-issue Belgian socialist, set the tone for many such pronouncements in the future and announced that 'I am struck by the analogy between the Algiers insurrection and the beginnings of Franco in Spain.' Some French opponents, and the official Communist Party, spread alarms as to a new version of the Second Empire or even of Vichy France. To that, de Gaulle had an easy answer: he was sixty-seven, not an age at which a man aspires to be dictator. In fact he was soon joined by great numbers of politicians from several parties. He agreed, for form's sake, to address the existing assembly, did so briefly and to the point: there was crisis in everything. A new constitution was needed, with a strong executive. He was given full powers. A referendum in September endorsed what he did, and the 'yes' vote included about one third of the Communists' usual number.

Changing constitutions – as French experience showed – is not always worth the effort. As Benjamin Constant, one of the many wise defeated liberals whom France produced, remarked, 'on change de situation mais on transporte dans chacune les tourments dont on espérait se délivrer'. But in this case the constitution also represented a France that was becoming very different indeed from the France of the nineteenth century and of the interwar period. There were children; the rural masses were being broken up; industry could develop even with German competition and there were new sources of energy to supplement France's none-too-many and none-too-rich coal mines. The historic problem, that the Right was divided, was being overcome. With de Gaulle, a conservative element became united enough at last to form a stable government (though the name of the party changed, over and over again, from UNR (Union pour la Nouvelle République) to RPR (Jacques Chirac's Rassemblement pour la République) and whatever). It had its dissidents, but the power of the presidency was such that the spoils of office which had made governments so unstable before were now transferred in effect to the Élysée Palace and a coterie round presidents. Spoils of office remained, but at least there was governmental continuity.

Given as much, the Algerian problem was solved in so far as its abolition can be described as a solution: the *pieds noirs*, almost all of them, left in 1962. When he went to Algeria, de Gaulle had given a strong impression that he would fight for *Algérie française*, and he proclaimed economic measures that would contain some of the disastrous unemployment that came partly from the sheer terror of the war, and partly from the demographic explosion on the Moslem side. But after a year he was outlining a new policy: Algeria for the Algerians. At that, the army started to rebel again and de Gaulle produced another of his masterpieces: a television address – he practised his quite extraordinary style with much care, to be fondly remembered ever after by caricaturists – in which he began, 'Eh bien, mon cher et vieux pays', appealing for popular support. The army leaders were isolated in Algiers, much of the army dissociating itself, and they backed down. In control, de Gaulle could now move towards a settlement with the Algerian rebels, with whom there had been secret negotiations in Switzerland. He could always threaten that, if they went too far, the country could be partitioned, the French retaining a coastal strip. In the event, in July 1962, France recognized Algeria, retaining some rights over the Sahara oil. There had been a final outburst from the unrelenting elements in the army, four senior figures carrying out a putsch in 1961 and then going underground, striking out brutally and almost at random. But they had no future: nor perhaps did they want or expect one. In the summer of 1962, under a broiling sun, a million French settlers now left, leaving Algeria to an unhappy future.

9

Europe 1958

General de Gaulle is supposed to have said, when Algeria left, that the moment had come for 'Europe'. There, France would be remade. It mattered that French self-confidence had taken a battering in the middle of the 1950s. French post-war aims, of taking over German resources, had been frustrated, and the Monnet Plan had not worked, at least not in the intended sense. There was a constant shortage of dollars for imports, and the franc was devalued again and again. This all became much worse because of the political system. It reflected the concerns of the old France, and the politicians of 1945 were scared enough by the authoritarian ways of the Vichy regime – and the potential authoritarianism of de Gaulle – not to want a strong executive. The parliamentarians kept decisive powers in their own hands, and arranged for a powerless presidency. This was made worse because the party that held the balance of power – the Radicals – had not been solid. Even their constitution said that they were in effect allowed to split, and they reflected local realities that often had little to do with national matters. Snap votes could destroy a government's majority, if a prime minister were inept, and a government crisis would duly follow. Then the politicians failed to agree, and governments kept changing in a way that might have been harmless if times were easy, but now appeared ridiculous. There was one government after another – when the final crisis of the Fourth Republic began on 15 April 1958 it was the seventeenth or the twenty-second, depending upon how you define 'crisis'. Five weeks went by before a Félix Gaillard assembled a thin majority to replace a Maurice Bourgès-Maunoury on 5 November 1957, and the crisis that began with Gaillard's over-

throw on 15 April 1958 had still not been resolved when the final act of
the Fourth Republic began on 13 May. As the historian René Rémond
comments, there was a sort of liturgy involved as each of the participants
– president, party leaders, etc. – knew how the ceremonial went, and
it developed its own vocabulary: lifting the mortgage, wiping the slate,
testing the slopes, sending back the lift, etc. Karl Marx, asked why it
was that the non-socialists produced so many divisions, answered,
thunderously, 'It is in the nature of the petty bourgeoisie to be subject-
ive.' The Algerian affair brought about change, at last (as, curiously
enough, the beginnings of French rule there, in 1830, had coincided
with a domestic half-revolution).

The chief beneficiary of Gaullism was generally the bourgeoisie.
This expression covered much more than its nearest equivalent, 'middle class', could possibly do in English. It had been the dominant class
of the earlier Third Republic, had supplanted the aristocracy, and had
been more different from it than had the English middle classes. Alain
Besançon's *Une génération* manages to paint that world in brief
sketches: there is a great deal of property, with a very large private
house in Paris, grandmothers in grand flats, on the rue du Faubourg-
Saint-Honoré and the boulevard de La-Tour-Maubourg, driven in a
Hispano-Suiza; and there are two country properties, one with
hundreds of acres of grounds, well laid out by devoted gardeners.
There is a whole *familia* of servants; and young Besançon gets to
know the endless varieties of pears (Williams, *beurres Hardy*, *beurres
Lebrun*, the *doyennes du Comice*, etc.). As he says, though he is not
quite clear what 'bourgeoisie' means, it is simply not present in any
literature other than French. He describes it as a matter of language
and dress; it was a matter of family, too, the aristocracy being much
more distant with each other. It was also a happy business, with much
to do. Richard Cobb remembers the same phenomenon though he
encountered it in a different form. He was sent at fifteen in the mid-
thirties to a family that looked after him devotedly, and fell in love
with France; then, after the war, he fell in with two eccentric brothers
bizarrely occupying a house near the Lycée Saint-Louis ('grimmest of
Paris schools'). Bourgeois France went through a bad time: the killing
fields of 1914, the interwar Depression (which gave France negative

growth rates longer than in any other major country), and then the years of Occupation and Vichy, which led almost to its collapse. Besançon remembered the period of the fifties as 'sale et pauvre'; the house yards uneven, plaster falling off, the porters' kitchen foul-smelling, of cabbage and urine; 40-watt bulbs were used in the cafés, hanging from a wire, and their lavatories were of the Turkish type, with thick newspaper on a string; even the coffee was muddy and the wine was vinegary. It had been the end of a period of disaster when the bourgeois certainties had gone by the board. But with de Gaulle these returned in a peculiar way: there was a distinct bourgeois revival, partly based on glossy state institutions, and partly on the newly successful world-class economic activities. The new Citroën DS, majestically inflating as it was started up, was as much a symbol of sixties Paris as had been the canvas-and-tin *deux chevaux* of the fifties.

Now that de Gaulle had united the historically divided Right enough to establish a durable government, quite soon France was going to overtake England, for the first time since the French Revolution itself. Charles de Gaulle was truly the man of the decade. As he said in his memoirs, in one of the great first lines of literature, all his life he had had a certain idea of France, and now, in his late sixties, he would restore her greatness. He had gone through the First World War, had been wounded and taken prisoner, had lived through the humiliations of the thirties, when Paris became, in George Orwell's words, half brothel, half museum. Then had come defeat in 1940, and the German occupation. De Gaulle, going to London with a few companions, had kept the idea of France going, and had become in 1944 the man of the hour. He had repeated the feat in 1958, and, by 1962, a great man known around the globe, he would give France the self-confidence and influence which in his opinion his country deserved. This was very far from being fanciful. France was one of very few European countries from which people did not emigrate: quite the contrary, many foreigners wanted to move there, whether Italians and Spaniards in search of employment, or Englishmen anxious to escape from the taxes and the weather and the babyish restrictions back home. Literature, film, wine, history – everything spoke for France.

There had been one long-term problem, again a uniquely French experience, in that her people since the great Revolution had made fewer and fewer babies. In the seventeenth century there had been more Frenchmen than Russians, but by 1914 there were almost five times as many Russians (or subjects of the Tsar). Why, is a good question: the answer is probably to be found in the French Revolution, which gave land to the peasant, and the *Code Napoléon* which forcibly divided inheritances among children. There was enough to keep one child, and the size of the farm meant that only one extra pair of hands was needed, while only one extra mouth could be fed. In the slump of the thirties, as everywhere else, parents stopped producing babies, and the French population hardly went up, except through immigration, after 1870. The war, and the Occupation, changed this, for mysterious reasons: in 1949 there were almost a million births, one third more than in 1939, which was itself one of the better years for births, and by 1960 the young in France once more outnumbered the old. Families now produced three children, not one. De Gaulle, though himself elderly, spoke for a new generation, and French self-confidence began to recover.

De Gaulle's prestige ran very high because, since 1958, France had flourished, and this was shown in the very considerable power of his new presidential office. In the summer, there had been consultation over a new constitution, which was supposed to do away with the political swings-and-roundabouts of the Third and Fourth Republics. Then, because the politicians did not want an authoritarian figure as head of state, the presidency was a mainly ceremonial office. Now, the president had much greater power (the historian Jean Lacouture remarked that the executive had such power that 'this republic' tends to be 'on the frontiers of the democratic world'). The prime minister in the Matignon Palace also had power, though less of it, and there was a potential for conflict, but in 1958 this did not matter. De Gaulle had the constitution approved by an enormous majority with a referendum. On 21 December 1958 he got nearly 80 per cent of the vote, as president. On the whole he chose resistance men for his team, and Georges Pompidou, though now at the Rothschild Bank, was marked with great favour as he did as he was told.

Once in office, de Gaulle ran affairs in grand style (he once terminated an interview when the woman journalist crossed her legs), though often with a human touch, like a good commander-in-chief keeping up with his men. He also disciplined his time: curiously enough he used to read *Le Monde* cover to cover, though he did not regard it as 'national' and generally disliked the press. He loved the James Bond films and television in the evening but also kept up with his reading, always punctiliously thanking in his own hand authors who sent their books. Someone said of him that in moments of idleness he was like a Henry Moore statue. Twice a year was the press conference, when de Gaulle would speak for up to one and a half hours, very well-rehearsed beforehand, and exhausting, like a theatrical performance or, as his press secretary said, like a woman giving birth. On television he had 'the eyes of an elephant' and a face like Rodin's Balzac. His courage was not in dispute, and at Kennedy's funeral he behaved characteristically – waving aside the insistent offer of an armour-plated limousine so that he could walk at the side of Kennedy's widow and son, when other statesmen behaved with self-preserving prudence. At any rate, an indisputable charisma.

He himself was such a figure as to conceal the possible problems – that power would be transferred from a fractious and difficult assembly to a presidential court, far less visible from the outside, and therefore likely to be very corrupt; and there was a further problem that, without formal opposition, informal opposition in the streets would grow – as was to happen, within a few years. But de Gaulle himself was utterly incorruptible (in the fifties his wife had discreetly made ends meet by selling heirloom silver as she otherwise had to make do on a colonel's pension). A. J. P. Taylor rightly noted that only one man in French politics had emerged from office significantly poorer, de Gaulle, and one man in English politics significantly richer, Lloyd George (since then, Blair has joined the little list). Even then there were complaints that the State dominated the media, especially television, and at one ceremony foreign journalists – hated figures, given the Algerian problem – were kicked and manhandled. In the event, even Communists voted 'yes': the total 'no' vote being a million short of their own 5,500,000 in the elections. There followed the lengthy effort at peace in Algeria together with self-assertion in matters European, and this marked the whole presidency.

The November elections of 1958 proceeded in a two-stage form that greatly damaged the Left – though even now a problem emerged, that there were two conservative or right-of-centre parties, de Gaulle's UNR with almost 200 seats, and a second group with 132. They had won under two fifths of the vote, but had two thirds of the new assembly, and were therefore not forced into unity of action. In time, this was to become a problem. The French Right was given to splitting, as some would-be stalwart, feeling slighted, would round up the out-ins against the loyalists, and even launch a new party which, by making a nuisance of itself, could menace the government's existence. Such was the basis of the career of Valéry Giscard d'Estaing and of several others since. However, de Gaulle commanded by his presence, and there was also a distinct strategy: in effect, the old *résistants* stepped into the shoes of the unlovely Vichy technocrats. The first prime minister, Michel Debré, was an old *résistant* who in the end could not follow de Gaulle's policy in Algeria, but who loyally carried through the first measures. It had been obvious since 1945 that inflation and protectionism went together with institutional trade union power, itself heavily under Communist influence, and the new government, installed in the summer of 1958, had a priority to change matters radically. Georges Pompidou, who had started life as a French teacher, had moved into banking and was now Debré's chief of staff, had as much in mind, and the new finance minister was the rigid Antoine Pinay (de Gaulle did not much care for him but he did have the confidence of the financial world). His chief idea was to make the franc stable, and to dismantle the protectionism that allowed such inefficiency in French industry.

De Gaulle had little time for economics, and saw it in terms of national confidence. Pinay was dry and prudent (he even objected to the plan being launched in his name, but was overruled by the General); the real architect of the reform was the perennially right-but-repulsive Jacques Rueff, and his priority was to stop inflation. An immediate loan was launched, successfully, and a team of experts set about the problem of the franc, recognizing that no country with self-respect could tolerate more than two zeroes on the notes. But that meant far deeper changes: the Bank of France (and the nationalized banks in general) must not go on giving preferential medium-term credit at low interest rates for industry and housing; the Treasury should just take money from the market, now that one existed. The Rueff reform took a line in financial stabilization that has been familiar since 1923, when Dr Hjalmar Schacht took it in Germany; budget decreases, tax increases, a liberalization of foreign trade and a devaluation of 15.45 per cent. It is political arithmetic, dressed up, and is currently called the 'Washington consensus'. But the whole was accompanied by a measure that caught the world's attention – introduction of the 'heavy franc', at 100 to one. Now, with a money that could be converted at will, producers were to be stimulated by competition, and this indeed was to happen: France created some world-class industrial concerns in a short time. The five socialists wanted to resign, but de Gaulle browbeat Guy Mollet into staying on patriotic grounds. The General was by now a master of television performance: he understood that ham acting was his stock-in-trade but he 'sold' the plans: without them, he said, 'we would remain a backward country, perpetually between crisis and second-rateness'.

In a descant on similar German debates as to Marshall and Erhard, the economic recovery of France divides opinion. Was it caused by the Monnet Plan, and the devastating omniscience of the great and good? Certainly, there were institutions to give a strategy to the new self-confidence. In 1962 the reputation of the Plan stood high. Intelligent technocrats had, it appeared, waved a wand, and French backwardness was no more; nuclear energy heated and lit, where coal had once been too poor in quantity and quality to do anything of the kind; there was a French bomb as well. The specialist 'great schools' took the best and the brightest, and trained them for the job of managing the State – the Polytechnic, a military institution, to produce engineers; the National School of Administration to produce civil servants who understood town planning or transport or energy, whereas in England their equivalents behaved with terrible obtuseness. The standards of education were still extremely high, and French technocrats of that generation were clever, sure of themselves and their mission. In 1960 they got rid of many of the clogging obstacles that dated back to the post-war experiments in socialism: France was set for a boom, for the creation of modern industries in automobiles or chemicals or food-processing. Anti-Americans might scoff at the space programme and claim that it only resulted in an unforeseen spin-off in the shape of 'Teflon', a new plastic used to make frying-pans 'non-stick'. This had in fact been invented by DuPont in 1938 but was picked up by a French company, Tefal ('aluminium') in 1956; by 1961 that company was selling a million frying pans per month in the USA alone. There were many other such French successes: motor cars, aircraft, nuclear energy and even, at last, steel. There is an imponderable in such things: how far did the sheer matter of national morale play its part in the business recovery? To be French in de Gaulle's early years was no longer to be part of a picturesquely backward country, and French businessmen could travel the world with a certain pride. Even the French peasants ceased to be the figures of grim fun, 'Robespierre with twenty million heads', as Balzac had said, a remark echoed in their own ways by Zola and Flaubert (whose parody of a minister of agriculture's speech at a rural fete in *Madame Bovary* is timelessly exact).

'Europe' helped, was even ruthlessly exploited in the interests of French agriculture. The spirit of the Treaty of Rome was one thing; but from lofty considerations to economic arrangements meant months and months of detailed haggling over tariff rates on various goods. The presiding spirit was not that of Napoleon or Bismarck, who, anyway, when asked as to Europe's identity, just said, 'Many great nations.' Rather, it was that of a Baron von Itzenplitz who, in the 1830s and 1840s, had led the customs union in Germany, the *Zollverein*, which had allowed the industry of the northern and northwestern, Prussian, parts of the country to dominate the rest. Especially, agriculture was very difficult to handle. Some regions were go-ahead and mechanized, not needing anything more than a sensibly run bank with credit to offer. Others were very backward, their inhabitants only needing to go away. A policy was not agreed until 1962. A Dutchman led negotiations that produced the principles, and two further years were needed to work out the details for 'commodity regimes' governing grain, cattle, milk and the rest. For over three weeks at the very end, there was 'non-stop haggling', with two heart attacks and one nervous breakdown, until finally a crenellated machinery whirred and flailed its way off the ground, in 1962. It was called the Common Agricultural Policy (CAP), and was designed to meet the problems of the 1930s, preventing food prices from collapsing: the CAP, with most of the European Economic Community's budget, would buy up 'surplus' stocks at an agreed price above the world level, and store them somewhere. There were complicated arrangements to subsidize exports and to hinder imports of cheaper food and wine.

Critics pointed out that this would impoverish would-be sellers in poor countries with nothing else to offer. They were answered by the Lomé Convention of 1963, which offered the governments of these poor countries – essentially the old French empire – development aid. These arrangements turned out fairly badly, the development money being mainly wasted or stolen (or, on a later occasion, presented to a successor of de Gaulle's, Giscard d'Estaing, in the form of diamonds, by a beneficiary of the Lomé loot named Jean-Bédel Bokassa, by now emperor of Central Africa). Still, the Common Agricultural Policy became one of the wheels and levers by which France, in weight second class, became a great power again. Europe was pouring money into French agriculture, and if there were protests, de Gaulle just had his people boycott European Economic Community affairs until (by the 'Luxemburg Compromise' of 1966) a national veto as to important matters was built into Community dealings, in place of the compromises that had been the rule up to that point. For many years, little progress was made towards unity, ever closer and closer, as the makers of the Treaty of Rome had intended, and even the attempt to put the Economic Community together with the two obsolete other communities, defence and nuclear, took years of negotiation (until 1967, when the EEC became the EC).

De Gaulle had not originally been at all enthusiastic about the Common Market, and preferred a 'Europe of the states'. In his time the 'construction of Europe' was a painfully slow business, which took the absurd form of setting standards for each and every product marketed across borders (cucumbers, for instance, had to be straight

so that you could fit an identical number of them into identical packages, and such matters were solemnly passed from in-tray to out-tray
in Brussels). But France could not go alone. If she had seriously to
offer a way forward between the world powers, she had to have allies,
and Germany was the obvious candidate. This was not just a matter
of political strategy. Over the Common Agricultural Policy de Gaulle
had Chancellor Adenauer's support. The German peasant also grasped.
He had been an even more baneful figure in the country's modern history: he had even torpedoed democracy. To buy his support, politicians of the Centre and Right had agreed upon tariffs that would keep
out cheap foreign food, and agreed such devices as making whale-oil
margarine so repulsive in colour – that of the Reichstag skirting board
– that it would deter buyers and cause them to choose dearer peasant-
made butter instead.

Gaullist France profited hugely from the new partnership with West
Germany. The outstanding feature of post-war Europe was of course
the 'German economic miracle': the moonscape of 1945 had been
utterly transformed. As the Treaty of Rome took effect on 1 January
1958, the various restrictions on money exchange were dismantled,
and the dollar could invade any market that its owners chose. Now,
the institutions that had been thought up towards the end of the war
came into their own: 'Bretton Woods' to run world trade and foreign
exchange, through the World Bank, the International Monetary Fund
and the General Agreement on Tariffs and Trade (GATT), which regularly assembled to discuss the liberation of commercial exchange. The
European Payments Union lost its function, though the Bank for
International Settlements at Basle in Switzerland carried on as a sort
of catch-all institution.

Here was an enormous and essential difference with the post-war
of 1919. Then, the American banking system was simply not up to a
world role. But all other advanced countries had been wrecked by the
Great War, and the British – with huge debts – were in no position to
finance world trade as they had done in the previous century. The
United States' banking system did not even include a central bank
with much power: the 'Fed' – or 'Federal Reserve System' – had been
set up only in 1913, did not spread to more than a dozen of the states,

and was not by any means under government control. American lending was essential but irresponsible – huge outflows one year, huge inflows another – and foreign countries had no way of responding short of putting up the barriers, as happened in the early 1930s, when world trade shrank by two thirds and strict exchange controls were brought in. But that same waywardness in the American system had also provoked a great slump in the United States, where thousands of banks went bankrupt (the trigger for the entire Depression had come when marshland in Florida, with alligators, had collapsed in price). A further pernicious element had been the exposure of Congress to lobbies, often corrupt. In 1930 these had insisted on a new tariff to make it difficult for foreign goods to enter the American market and thus be used to pay off debts. All of the then noteworthy economists had protested. They were waved aside by the Congress majority. That majority, what with the ensuing Slump and the disasters of 1945, had learned: as the Turkish proverb has it, 'One disaster is better than a thousand pieces of advice.' In the later 1940s, US intervention was very positive and largely logical. The golden fifties resulted.

In 1958 the ending of exchange controls went with an extraordinary European boom; for this, the Americans could take credit. West Germany was in the lead. At the time, it was called the 'German economic miracle', and that was how it struck contemporaries, although the expression itself went back to a Swedish book published in 1936 about the success of Hitler's reduction of mass unemployment in Germany. Then, too, the success was symbolized by motorways and motor cars. The 'people's car', *Volkswagen*, had been designed then by Dr Ferdinand Porsche, who had made his reputation with a four-wheel drive that had carried artillery across mountain passes, in snow, on the Italian front. It was a small and serviceable family car, which Germans would have bought on credit if the war had not broken out. Porsche's factories were still in existence in 1945, though the buildings had been damaged. Quite soon, they were put into service again, with the help of a British officer who expected them to turn out cars for British use. Instead, two thirds of the personnel were lengthily de-Nazified, and, when British automobile firms were asked whether they could use the design, they replied that no-one with any dignity would be seen dead in a car that looked like a large bug on wheels (an early model had been captured intact in North Africa and sent back home for comment). The British equivalent, the Morris Minor, attempted the sort of truncated grandness that characterized much of British doing in that era and cost twice as much; when they realized their mistake, in the 1960s, the designers attempted to be cute instead and were none too brilliant at that, either. They could not compete with the VW. Already in 1956 the Germans were making more cars than the British, and exporting more. The VW symbolized Germany's recovery, with growth rates of 8 per cent and sometimes twice that figure, right into the 1960s. The Marshall Plan was widely given the credit, and certainly the atmosphere it generated – the United States to the rescue – was important in giving the Germans hope for the future (though the contribution now seems quite small: Germany had less than France or Britain, and the amount received was less than had flowed in in the early 1920s, when American bankers speculated in the then wildly inflationary Mark). The presence of energetic American businessmen backed by generals who understood something of engineering was no doubt also important, but the essential was their insistence upon intra-European trade. Already in 1952 the great German firms were back on the European scene – Mannesmann, Krupp, BASF, Hoechst, BMW, Siemens-Schuckert, their chemicals and engineered goods popular worldwide. The German recovery then rolled on, with hardly a break, for the next quarter-century, but it was only the most striking example of an overall phenomenon in Europe. France, then Italy, experienced similar 'miracles'. With the USA and Japan, western European countries became the richest on the globe.

The growth in foreign trade – at 6 per cent after 1948 – went faster than that of the GDP. Later on, foreign direct investment and capital mobility also rose faster. In Germany, for instance, the economy grew by two thirds between 1950 and 1958, but foreign trade nearly tripled, and exports rose from a quarter to two fifths of total output. What caused this boom in trade? Financial security mattered, of course, because the pound and the dollar had fixed parities. So did technology – much cheaper and more efficient (and uglier) ships. A sales team could travel by aircraft, and petrol was very cheap, at not even one dollar per barrel. But an important factor was the willingness to trade, to get rid of the tariffs that got in the way. The GATT was another of the post-war institutions, and in 1947 its first and most important meeting was held at Geneva. In the context of the Marshall Plan the Americans recognized that they must not stop Europe from selling in their market, and reduced their own tariffs by 35 per cent, though the previous heights had been absurd and the tariffs still remained strangely high by other standards. Overall, there were 123 agreements between trading countries, covering 45,000 different items, which corresponded to about half of world trade. There were two further GATT 'rounds' up to 1951, but they were less important, and mainly just confirmed what had been done. The central institution of the Marshall Plan, the OEEC, was now adapted to follow this, and changed its name to the Organization for Economic Co-operation and Development (OECD, with us still). When the European Payments Union (EPU) started, it too was an engine for liberalization. At the time, currencies were quite strictly controlled – the British could take only £25 if they went abroad, the sum being marked in their passports – and the EPU existed to convert the one into the other in a closed system. The Marshall Plan provided a loan of $350m for the basic capital, and otherwise member countries contributed according to their resources and requirements. In the fifties it was a more than qualified success and the Code of Liberalization (for trade and investment) was the enduring monument to the Marshall Plan. It was proclaimed in September 1949, after the devaluations had set up manageable exchange rates. Overall OEEC countries' exports increased by 1.7 times between 1948 and 1955, and trade within the OEEC bloc by 2.3 times. Countries were now competing, instead of sheltering themselves from more efficient producers, and the result was, apart from other benefits, low inflation.

West Germany was the locomotive. She became the largest market for the exports of all her western neighbours, and Italy. An export surplus might have led to inflation, as the profits returned to a domestic market, and the answer to that was to import so that domestic producers trying to increase their prices would face competition from abroad. Under Ludwig Erhard, Germany had a director pledged to liberalization there as well, even if in the short term it might harm some local producers. Erhard, like other prominent economists of that period, had learned from the Nazi era, when protection had been the rule, and Joseph Schumpeter (a brilliant economist who had once been Austrian finance minister before proceeding to a Chair at Harvard) even said that Germany in 1931 had ceased to be a capitalist country because so much was regulated by the State. An ex-NCO, thumbing through your underwear on a border, in search of paper money, said it all.

But, beyond that, there was a whole school of German historians and commentators who appreciated that what had gone wrong had something to do with the monopoly-capitalistic and protectionist ways of the last generation before the First World War. It had been called 'The alliance of Iron and Rye'. Behind protectionist tariffs the great heavy-industrial works on the one side, and estate-agriculture on the other, had had a charmed life; finance capital, since the banks were part of the charmed circle, had joined in. Some crumbs from this table had been thrown to millions of peasants. Accordingly, there was a majority bloc in the Reichstag in favour of protection, and Germany had not been part of the world's trading order on the same terms as, say, Britain or Belgium. Germany might have developed as a normal Western country, a sort of huge Netherlands, but instead, in politics, liberals and social democrats were in a large but hopeless minority; and some outstanding interpretative works on German history have been written in exposition of this (Lujo Brentano, Ralf Dahrendorf, Alexander Gerschenkron and, today, David Blackbourn). Now, with 'Iron' under a Ruhr Authority or an ECSC, and 'Rye' occupied by the Russians, there was a chance for a normal Germany, and Erhard well understood what he was doing. He had a strategy. Like so many other good financial managers, he was not a good politician, was happiest with businessmen, themselves generally none too good with politics, and was impatient with men less intelligent than himself. He needed Konrad Adenauer, who had the right and complementary gifts.

It was a measure of the change in Germany that Ludwig Erhard, a Bavarian Protestant, and Adenauer, a Rhineland Catholic, worked together, because the religious divide had been vastly important and even, in its way, a reason for the Nazis' rise (the third of Bavaria that was Protestant had voted quite heavily Nazi, the Catholics, hardly at all). Erhard at least had a clean record, and had acted as an obscure adviser to some retailers. He emerged as executive director of the Economic Council for Bizonia, which the Allies set up in summer 1948 as a prototype for a West German government. His appointment was a fluke – one man's resignation had been forced, and the politicians could not agree on anyone else. The fluke meant that Germans, at last, had a lucky break. All the other candidates were thinking only of more efficient rationing and some reduction of the tidal wave of paper money; then they would go over to a planned economy, such as the French and British were supposed to be doing. Erhard said no. He would 'jump into the cold water' of the market, would deregulate, would scrap much of the rationing, and would introduce a new currency altogether. The old one, with its endless noughts, would be abolished, and holders of these notes would get only limited compensation. That way, the entire wartime and pre-war debt would be wiped out; the tidal wave of paper money would become an orderly stream, and people who set prices would be free to do so without government dictation. After an uncomfortable moment or two, West Germany prospered, but there was another vital difference from the past. Erhard did not try to beggar his neighbours if they fell into deficit trouble because German competition undercut their goods and weakened their currency. By 1955 the EPU had become a machine for taking German money to pay for the trade deficits of other Western countries, and especially France. This was the financial base for the various meetings that led up to the Treaty of Rome. Erhard could have exchanged his winnings for dollars, and for a build-up of reserves. But Germany was now European – the solution that so many intelligent central Europeans had foreseen.

If a country were to be judged by its institutions, Germany was a nearly perfect place. The makers of the constitution were wise men of the Philadelphia class (some of whom had in any case been German). They had a truly dreadful precedent from which to learn. The republican constitution set up in 1919 at the historically enlightened town of Weimar had been designed to show the Americans how very democratic Germany had become. This was an effort at gaining American sympathy in Germany's hour of defeat, and the men of Weimar proceeded with a literal-minded clumsiness that had a majority of Germans voting either for the Nazis or for the Communists within a dozen years of relentless elections, proportional representation, referenda, constitutional-court cases and the paraphernalia of self-destructive democracy. The method of decentralization had given the country seventeen different governmental spending and borrowing points, and finance soon became a headache: a hugely destructive inflation early on, an even more destructive deflation ten years later. Now, the wise men in Bonn composed a very sensible and even a model document. It was quite short, as these things go. There was decentralization of a sensible kind. States – eleven *Länder*, Bavaria the largest – were set up, and they competed in a healthy way over cultural matters and, as things turned out, decisively for the better over education. Bavaria and Baden remained conservative as regards this, and defied American attempts to set up comprehensive schools that would somehow be more democratic than the existing selective ones. In time, the south German *Länder* were thus to reverse the historic pattern, and become considerably better off than the northern ones.

The rules for politics were also sensible – a system of proportional representation, but not one that allowed tiny local parties to enter parliament. Rights of a basic kind were spelled out, and these included those of small children to be brought up by their mothers: tax was not to fall so heavily on the father that the mother would have to go out to work. Then again, Germany had the great benefit of not having a single capital, sucking in all of the wealth and talent of a country, as were London and Paris. Hamburg, Cologne, Munich were the chief cities, and Berlin was kept going, but the government was confined to little Rhineland Bonn: the assembly originally met, and it was a sign both of the weaknesses and of the strengths of the new Germany, in a schoolroom undamaged in the latter stages of the war. Giving government a city of its own is generally a good idea: it allows other cities to be more interesting. But the common sense attached to the German Basic Law – it was not called a 'constitution', because its makers were acting on behalf of all Germany, not just the Federal Republic – spread elsewhere. Knowing what had done so much damage in the days of Weimar, the trade unions accepted sensible reforms: there were only twelve unions, they had considerable privileges as regards management, and they built up a considerable interest of their own in the fortunes of 'capitalism'. They therefore had every interest in making sure that the system worked, such that they would be flexible as regards the introduction of new machinery, even if it meant a loss of old-fashioned or obsolete jobs. True, the position of the trade unions was in a sense quite weak in the early years because of the huge numbers of hungry immigrants. Twelve million of them poured in from the east, latterly from the Communist-run Soviet zone (3.2 million of them, four fifths of them aged between eighteen and twenty-five, 20,000 of them engineers and 4,500 doctors). Finally there was the Federal Bank as it was soon called. It was independent, or at any rate as independent as human wisdom could make it in the circumstances. Its brief was to avoid the inflation that had twice shattered the country's finances. It managed to do so quite successfully. One result was that the Germans saved: they saved and saved, at twice the British rate. There was therefore money for investment, and German business duly invested, taking a long-term view, which the lack of inflation again made possible. German business, much of it medium-sized and family-run, flourished, and, when it had to deal with exports, would behave quite sensibly, in establishing a chamber of commerce that knew the market. Germans of course had been determined never to repeat their past mistakes, and they were sometimes very literal-minded in applying the lessons. Nevertheless, a remarkable country emerged from the years of the Marshall Plan.

Broadly speaking, the country was twice as rich as in 1950, itself a year much better than its predecessors. By 1959 Germany was producing half of Europe's steel (30.6 million tons) and 50 per cent more than Britain; it was then the vital element in a manufacturing economy. By 1957 Germany had become the chief producer of automobiles in Europe, with 1.5 million to Britain's 1.4 million and France's 1.1 million. The Volkswagen was economic in fuel, not expensive, had an air-cooled engine and could be parked in a small place: it was popular worldwide. The fifties saw a world in which stable families took a joy in the wave of consumer gadgets that were coming on the market, at more and more affordable prices, such that refrigerators or washing machines or telephones or typewriters or new electric coffee-machines marked the decade. By 1959 German exports overtook British.

10

The Sixties

In the outcome of the great dramas of 1956, the Americans could be quite content. The European empires were finished; the West had been refashioned in America's interest, or at any rate in the interest of most Americans. NATO took firm shape, as the Communist threat in western Europe receded; the fifties were a time of American trium-phalism, and the immensely popular new President, General Eisen-hower, was an apt and genial symbol. Eisenhower could as easily have been elected as a Democrat if he had chosen, but the Republicans, whose chief platform was tax-cutting, got in first. America had become very prosperous; her trade and investments boomed. By 1965 the USA produced 119 million tons of steel, almost as much as France, Germany (37 million, as against the maximum 10 million generously allowed in 1948), Great Britain and Japan put together, and it easily led in the consumer goods that marked the age – nearly 8 million television sets to very few German, for instance. The Europeans were catching up, but even in 1969 American workers earned over twice as much as German workers ($460 per month as against $209, and $199 in the British case). Three million Europeans emigrated to the USA in the fifties. However, Europe was becoming more united, and the impetus was really American: the European Economic Community contained the arm spiritual of NATO. Besides, for all of the talk of a European bloc, it was open to cheap and very rewarding investment.

The USA did very well out of this. The conglomerates such as IBM spread abroad. Investment ran at $2bn per annum in these years, and in 1956 American private investment abroad exceeded public spend-ing there for the first time since the twenties. From 1946 to 1950 US foreign investment rose from over $7bn to nearly $12bn and by 1958 $25bn, and spread from mining and trade into more sophisticated fields such as petroleum-linked industries and manufacturing. The investment was dominated by the 'multinationals', firms which set up in western Europe to take advantage of lower costs or a growing market, or to escape from the tariffs that would otherwise have hit them, and some of the great American companies became worldwide names, the products ranging from soap to oil tankers. They were regarded as models of efficiency, with headquarters of plate glass and concrete, abstract sculptures and fountains well to the fore, and they developed a large research-and-development infrastructure. Their managers were also, often enough, teachers: IBM became something of a model, even, in the 1960s, for Romanians whose Communist government was then trying to become less dependent on the USSR. There was much alarm at the time about the allegedly predatory nature of this, but in 1950 there were higher western European investments in the USA than vice versa and in the later 1950s the USA had a positive balance of payments, despite the NATO spending. In the fifties and sixties – at any rate their first half – American business had a formidable reputation: it could do what Europeans could not imagine themselves doing, because the quality of management was so high. Some explanation is needed. In the twenties, when the phenomenon had first struck Europeans, it had seemed inhuman – workers like cogs in a machine, much exploited and put upon, turning out the same bit of a machine or an automobile on an assembly line, and not able to take any pride in the craftsmanship of a completed product. Fritz Lang, in the Weimar cinema, or Charlie Chaplin, captured this hostility, though it had roots in the England of Blake ('dark satanic mills'). But it resulted in a huge flow of goods, and in high wages; during the war it had produced the extraordinary American production miracles, whereas for much of the time German workers, putting together a first-class piece of aeronautical engineering in craft groups, might take pride in the product but did not make nearly enough of it. In Europe in 1948 there was not a single continuous strip steel mill, because small firms and cartels resisted it, such that the cheap steel needed for refrigerators or automobiles was much more expensive than in the USA. A washing machine cost eight man-hours in New York, and 500 in Paris. But it was American management that shone.

It had quite long origins: even in the 1830s, Stendhal, for instance, has throw-away and dismissive lines about American business and dollar worship, and the Teamsters, a famous union mainly on the docks, took their name from the mule-drivers of yore. In the 1850s Sam Colt was able to assemble a first-class gun in thousands, because he made each part the same, to within a thirty-second of an inch to start with, and then a five-hundredth, so that they were interchangeable, and Linus Yale, of locks fame, goes back to that period. Machines were soon made with interchangeable parts, and the tools that produced these became an American specialty, keeping British war industries going in both of the world wars. Henry Ford famously transferred this to motor cars that were therefore cheap. Various explanations have been offered: unskilled immigrant labour, needing to be given simple and repetitive tasks within their capacity; expensive labour, putting pressure on firms to diminish their costs by use of machinery; practical education, such as was plentifully on offer; the peculiarly classless atmosphere in the USA, where ordinary workmen would co-operate on friendly terms with an owner when it came to reporting faults and taking an interest in machines, whereas elsewhere workmen regarded them as an enemy and in Britain were notoriously reluctant to accept them, because they would be tended by fewer workmen and might depress wage rates. In the Marshall years British trade unionists went to the USA to learn about productivity and the results were generally depressing. But the essential seems to have been the quality of management.

In Europe at large this was misunderstood, because of business schools; and it was a curious fact that they did more damage than good. Any true businessman regarded them as pernicious or at least useless: Sir James Goldsmith remarked, for instance, that he would never hire anyone for senior management who had failed to leave school at sixteen. One trouble was that those who could not manage, taught, and sometimes preached. Real managers have better things to do, and asking them about theories of management is equivalent to asking a first-class golfer to lecture on ballistics. There was even around

1900 a group of men who wanted to make business academically respectable and Harvard acquired a business school that its founders expected to rival the law school. Frederick Winslow Taylor (1856–1915) invented the time-and-motion study, in which white-coated experts studied the performance of the workforce, and, with slide-rules, criticized. Early on, the application of these methods caused demoralization and in the Ford plant at Dearborn turnover of the workforce stood at 900 per cent a year. Taylor's claim was to 'mathematize' everything, and though himself a failure as a manager of men, he was the ancestor of the management consultant, and even the originator of a notion that management could be learned from books as distinct from experience. He and later followers referred to their creed as 'Scientific Management', and this suited some modern production methods, by 'flow', i.e. of workers each, on a slowly moving belt, assembling one part and moving it on to another worker who would add something to it. To manage men doing this mechanical stuff was not at all easy: in fact Taylor himself once remarked that he preferred a 'little Dutchman' for a pig-iron job because what it needed was 'the mental make-up' of an 'ox'. In the USSR later on, 'Taylorism' was thought to be a good doctrine to follow. As things turned out, it was not, because it was so machine-like and inhuman. One reason for the failure of the USSR in the end was that it copied what it thought to be the most successful, because nastiest, method of managing labour. It merely demoralized, and created drunks.

America's businessmen managed in fact in different ways and in the fifties they were very successful. One striking aspect was the in-house research laboratory. The Dupont Company, the first of America's great ones, already employed a hundred technicians in gleaming new buildings, and the example was followed by General Electric, where a mathematical genius tinkered away at Schenectady in New York State, and helped produce the cathode tube and the high-frequency alternator which made commercial broadcasting possible. General Electric then set up the National Broadcasting Corporation. Bell Laboratories was the research side of AT&T and it produced sixteen Nobel Prizes over the half-century: even the theory of information technology came from there, with a paper in 1948 called 'A Mathematical Theory of Communications', by

Claude Elwood Shannon (like other mathematicians a considerable eccentric, who rode along the corridors on a specially made bicycle which enabled him along the way to juggle balls). As Kenneth and William Hopper say, these vastly successful companies 'achieved a delicate ... balance between ... share-holders, employees, managers, suppliers, customers – and researchers'. They also attracted young scientists, who somehow gave of their best, because they were well-led, by men with knowledge and enthusiasm. Productivity growth per man-hour was 3 per cent per annum in the fifties and sixties, an extraordinary and unmatched figure.

Alfred Chandler analysed the success story – two men at the top, one a chairman, complementing each other; both, products of the business itself, and sometimes with a very lowly start in it; a readiness for long-term thinking rather than short-term profits. A rule was 'one man, one boss'; employees would be given as good a guarantee as possible of long-term work: the middle manager was seen as the 'key-stone of the managerial arch' because, through him, information could be collected and passed up. The great companies survived the 1930s because they had carefully avoided debt; they were able to shift resources towards the new products that distinguished that decade, despite the general blackness: radio, telephones, commercial aircraft, electrical goods. The Slump stimulated them as slumps are meant to do – 'the only cause of prosperity is depression,' said the economist Clement Juglar, a student of the business cycle. They cut costs and made intelligent adaptations towards new goods. IBM did not borrow on any scale until the 1970s, and Gillette had an office in an old factory with bare brick walls. When it came to war, there was further extraordinary adaptability – a peacetime economy created aircraft-carrier-borne fighters that outdid the Japanese Zero by 1943, and the nature of the Pacific war changed overnight. The Mustang, which transformed the bomber campaign in Germany through precision attacks, unperturbed by German fighters, had its prototype within six months of the designing, and had few troubles in testing. This economic machine, so successful at home, now turned abroad. Ford, IBM, General Motors, Chrysler, General Electric, Xerox became household words the world over.

When did 'the sixties' begin? The obvious moment to choose would be January 1961, when John F. Kennedy, aged forty-four, became President of the United States. But definitions of decades can only be ragged, and in a sense the sixties began in 1956. That year launched Elvis Presley; the London theatre was assailed by 'angry young men', especially John Osborne; Hollywood was stunned by James Dean, the 'rebel without a cause' who starred for sullen teenagers, was rated sixth most sexually attractive film star ever, but had died in a car crash the year before, aged twenty-four. On an altogether different plane, 1955 had been the last year in which world prices fell generally, as, from time to time, classical economics expected to happen: thereafter, prices just went up, overall. There was a mysterious sea-change, in other words, away from the old world. In the short run, it had obviously enough to do with the prosperity that was spreading so extraordinarily fast, as domestic tools made life much easier, food and energy became cheaper, television spread and spread. In another perspective, the sea-change had to do with a 'youth culture' which reflected the rise in population in the Anglo-Saxon West, where, in place of the sometimes negative growth rates of the troubled interwar years, it became normal again for families to produce three or four children. They were growing up and, because the necessities of life were costing less, they had money to spend. Youth, at least in the media world, had its decade in the sixties. Student revolts occupied the headlines; student thoughts were taken seriously; the vote was given to people aged eighteen, though in many places they were forbidden to buy alcohol until they reached the age of twenty-one. All of this was emerging in Eisenhower's second period, and the elderly golfing President, with his occasional troubles with long words, was not the man of the hour. Deeply honourable, in defence of the dollar, Eisenhower accepted three recessions, one of which in effect cost Nixon his succession. John F. Kennedy succeeded him in January 1961, and seemed indeed to be the man of the hour. He too had to defend the dollar, but it was characteristic of him and indeed the sixties as a whole that he imagined it could be done without pain.

Chateaubriand had remarked of Talleyrand that he was 'a nineteenth-century parvenu's idea of an eighteenth-century great nobleman'. In the same way, Kennedy, with his fairy-tale looks, money and wife, was a hairdresser's Harvard man. He was easily adaptable to a television age that older men had found uncomfortable. Next to the glowering, charmless, permanently unshaven-looking Richard Nixon, his election opponent, he shone, and especially entranced the intelligentsia of the East Coast. They, culturally still overshadowed by Europe, were often embarrassed by their own country, in some ways still very naive and simple. A visiting English grandee, Harold Nicolson, had gone on a coast-to-coast lecture tour in the USA to rescue his finances, had addressed Midwest ladies in cherried hats as to how the two democracies stood shoulder to shoulder facing the foe to the east, had taken yet another train to yet more ladies offering tea and cookies, and had gone back to London and told his friends that it had been 'like a month at a servants' ball'. The New York intelligentsia in their way agreed. They had not much cared for Eisenhower, who played the golfing Republican buffoon; and Norman Mailer set the tone for many writers to come when he dismissed the fifties as 'the worst decade in the history of mankind'. Most writers really respond to conditions a generation before, did not feel at home in mass prosperity, and made fools of themselves when they pronounced on politics. But pronounce they did, and the sniggering or resentment of the intelligentsia had effect. Kennedy appeared. He was less well-read and was certainly less musical than Truman (who was a good pianist) or even Eisenhower, but the image was far better: he could pretend, and perhaps even believe in the pretence. Kennedy, a Catholic, and sprig of a corrupt Boston-Irish dynasty, was not by nature a convinced friend of the left-wing intelligentsia, and he had even, for a time, gone along with Joe McCarthy's persecution of the crypto-Communists among them. That had helped Kennedy's father, notoriously crooked, in effect to buy a Massachusetts Senate seat, which was retained by the longest-surviving Kennedy brother, Edward, for decades, despite a reputation that included manslaughter. Kennedy's own electoral victory came only with a tiny margin, which he owed to the slippery practices of the man whom he chose as Vice-President, Lyndon B. Johnson, who had managed Congress for Roosevelt and understood how Texas worked. Almost everything to do with Kennedy was, in other words, false. In practice, as Johnson said, he 'never did a thing ... It was the goddamnedest thing ... his growing hold on the American people was a mystery to me.' However, he was the man for the decade to come.

Kennedy proclaimed a 'New Frontier'. The reference to Roosevelt's New Deal was obvious, and Kennedy took office with a promise of new energy. Fashion clothes and concert pianists appeared in the White House, and clever academics made up a good part of the new presidential team. Was there any substance? 'New' is not generally a word to use in politics. It is exhausted before it even begins: it generally means that the user of it has no ideas of any depth, and runs out of steam early on. However, when he began, Kennedy symbolized quite well what were to be the great makers of the decades to come. Apart from anything else, he was the first, and very, televisual politician. That instrument was to give politics an altogether new shape, or, rather, it vastly spread what had already been a vice of the cinema, to oversimplify to the point of caricature. William Blake had prophesied this a century and more before, and in their way the medieval iconoclasts had done so, as well. 'They ever will believe a lie who see not with but through the eye', said Blake, and St Bonaventura had announced that 'the ears communicate faith and the eyes, fervour'. But there were other inventions that shaped the sixties and beyond.

The 1960s were indeed a new age. In 1958 the world economy was revolutionized, because the main currencies became convertible one into another: that created a true world economy, almost independent of national governments or at any rate putting a great strain upon them, because money would just move out if they defied its rules. But other things of revolutionary importance were coming about. Most ages are marked by some invention or other: as Orwell wrote in a ten-second summary of world history, the castle defeated the knight, gunpowder defeated the castle, and the chequebook defeated gunpowder (he went on that the machine-gun defeated the chequebook). In 1960 such inventions came onto the mass market – the fax machine and the contraceptive pill. The first sent money round the world far faster than ever before. It had long and disputed origins, but came into its own because the Japanese could use it. Their language was almost impossible to type, for there were a great many characters, each needing a different combination of many pen strokes.

These could now be quickly scribbled by felt pen, and sent by fax, not typewriter, and as Japan started on her long economic boom, towards the middle of the 1950s, faxes to banks and importers made it possible. She developed into a world economic power, second or third in weight. That example was followed, later on, by Taiwan, a desperately poor country that became fourteenth trading nation in two decades, and by South Korea, devastated by the war. Now, the money exchanges became very busy, no longer dependent on mail, and the amounts of money that went round the world made trade itself of less and less apparent weight. The later effects of the computer have been just a continuation of that process, though on a much greater scale.

The Pill's effect on the relations of the sexes was, said Conrad Russell, like that of the nuclear bomb on international relations. On 1 June 1961 it came on the market in Germany (through Schering AG). It had origins going back to the early twenties, a time when 'race improvement' (eugenics) was fashionable, and the poor or stupid were supposed to be discouraged from procreating (in Sweden, up to the 1970s, Lapps were being sterilized on the grounds that they drank too much and were not very bright). German scientists received grants from American foundations for such research (the money was frozen in Germany under Hitler, and was used to pay for the experiments of Josef Mengele, at Auschwitz). Preventing ovulation had been done by natural methods in the past – in Mexico, for instance, women knew the qualities of wild yam in this respect; the ancient, Hippocrates, had recommended a wild carrot known as Queen Anne's Lace. In 1951 Carl Djerassi, of Bulgarian-Jewish and Viennese origin, working in Mexico and connected with the Swiss chemical firm Ciba, took out a patent, and experimented with the first synthetic compound in 1956 in Haiti. Germans marketed the Pill first, but it spread very rapidly. Freeing women from unwanted childbirth was equivalent to a new dimension in world history. Before 1914, in England, women doctors had not been allowed to contribute to medical journals because this was thought to be immodest, indicating an interest in the body that was improper. Fifty years later, women were establishing themselves in a man's world – probably the single greatest change, among the very many that set in after the Second World War. In the next generation, even mothers of small children were going out to work, some of them very successful, and many others left with no choice but drudgery. Feminism became a fashionable cause.

In some ways, what followed was a natural enough outcome of the sheer silliness with which conservatives defended their not indefensible world. They had been, in a way, spoiled by their own success against Communism. There was of course a conservatism that the following decade sneered at – churches got a billion dollars for building, twice what public hospitals got. The fifties ended with optimism and in retrospect seem to have been the last gasp of the old world. Families stayed together, women in the home or aiming to be, and the laws governing divorce or contraception were sometimes ridiculously difficult. A Catholic hierarch in Paris remarked that it was all very well to say that an extra child might break the family's budget and starve; it would die surrounded by love. This business of course provoked unthought-out reactions. Republican women in Connecticut had to fight a (Catholic-inspired) law against birth control all the way to the Supreme Court and that resulted in the easy-abortion arrangements of *Roe* v. *Wade* in 1973. Homosexuals in England faced worse persecution than in the days of Oscar Wilde, as the police could gain promotion points if they provoked an approach in a public place, and got more convictions from magistrates' courts than they had in the 1930s. There was still censorship, at a comic level, as when a lawyer, prosecuting Penguin for publishing D. H. Lawrence's (unreadable) *Lady Chatterley's Lover*, enquired in what he thought was a devastating way as to whether such a book could be read by the servants. Education was also rigidly unchanging, and everywhere operated unpredictably and unfairly, with, in most universities, a hierarchical professoriate that was all-powerful and old-fashioned. Sexual differences were enforced with ridiculous pinpricks. As late as 1968, at Trinity College, Cambridge, a 28-year-old graduate student was expelled when he was found by the porters 'with a woman in his room', and even in the 1970s, at Corpus Christi College, the Master's wife was refused a key. When a distinguished French historian, Marc Ferro, wanted to bring his wife to stay at Jesus College, Cambridge, two seniors found an argument to stop them from using the main (and splendid) guestroom. The room was used for Boat Club breakfasts. Breakfasts meant toastcrumbs, difficult to vacuum-clean away. Men getting out of bed with bare feet might be expected to put up with the discomfort; women, not. Therefore no Madame Ferro. In the United States, such conservatism, picturesquely tiresome elsewhere, was deadly, because it worsened what was already the worst blot on the country, its treatment of Negroes, as they were then generally called. In New York, if you took a Negro friend to dinner in a restaurant, you telephoned the management beforehand. Even when Kennedy's Vice-President went round Texas with his cook in a motor car, she could not use the roadside lavatories, and had to squat at the side of the road. Such things bred rebellion on the one side, contempt on the other, and guilty consciences in the middle.

Towards the end of the decade there was an international exhibition in Moscow, and the Americans showed off their kitchens. Vice-President Richard Nixon appeared, and there was a famous row between him and the Soviet leader, Nikita Khrushchev, who said that such things had nothing to do with justice or culture. Though he was not himself an expert in either field, a good part of the intelligentsia might have agreed with him. There was no question about it: Soviet high culture was far richer than American. There was now a Soviet challenge, in that the Soviet space effort appeared to be more successful than the USA's where science, applied to space and weaponry, was concerned. *Sputnik* caused national alarm, and a new national effort by America (in Great Britain the alarm was similar if less effectual) was apparently needed. This coincided with a two-year slowdown in the economy, when it grew by 2 per cent and unemployment came close to 6 per cent, then thought excessive. These questions gave Kennedy his narrow margin at the end of 1960, and when he took over, early in 1961, ambitious academics advised as to how the challenge was to be met. There were some famous and influential books, and conservatism had a bad time. These new writers analysed problems, and often suggested easy-sounding solutions, one mark of the sixties. John Kenneth Galbraith's *Affluent Society* (1957) noted that private people had money and governments none the less produced squalor: New York gorged with money, yet the roads were potholed and a good part of the population lived in poor conditions. Two decades later governments had a great deal more money and were still producing squalor: what conclusion was to be drawn, that governments should have even more, or that they just could not help producing squalor? Vance Packard's *Status Seekers* (1960) described the American business rat race. Jane Jacobs, looking at the wreckage caused by the San Francisco freeway system, wrote *The Death and Life of Great American Cities* (1961) and she foresaw that housing estates for the poor would turn into sinks of hopelessness worse than the slums that they were to replace; she also foresaw that city centres would become empty, inhabited only by tramps. Betty Friedan's *The Feminine Mystique* (1963) spoke for the bored housewife. Michael Harrington discovered that there were many poor Americans: *The Other America* (1962). David Riesman looked at the American rat race in *The Lonely Crowd* (1961) and shook his head at the two-dimensional misery of it all. René Dumont considered international aid, and thought that there should be much more of it; Gunnar Myrdal saw American race relations in the same light. Germaine Greer wrote *The Female Eunuch* (1970) saying that for women life was a bitter picture from the cradle to the tomb.

The answer was: spend money. Here, the presiding genius was Maynard Keynes. He had been contemptuous of the orthodox balance-the-budget financiers who had run things in the 1930s (and who were still running them in the 1950s): they reduced the National Debt and tried to run a budget surplus. An enlightened State, borrowing and spending, could easily be beneficial, especially if it helped poor people at the expense of the better-off. 'Demand' – the ability to buy – would stimulate supply, the provision of goods. It was just selfishness on the part of the rich that got in the way, and a measure of sheer stupidity. The great Slump of 1929 had discredited capitalism and especially bankers in many intelligent eyes, and Keynes had made easy conquests of intelligent young men and women, who would probably have agreed with the grandfather of a well-known Italian journalist, Indro Montanelli, in the sentiment that 'it is possible for an honest man to have dealings with whores, but with bankers, never'. If making life better for people beyond the prosperous circles of the fifties meant spending money, then that was a worthy cause. Galbraith had been involved in price control during the Second World War and never did understand why his critics regarded the State as wasteful, corrupt and inefficient. The war economy had been extraordinarily successful, thought he and his like: even petrol rationing, which made life very difficult in the more isolated places, had been very widely accepted. Why bother with out-of-date economic rules?

Economists of the younger generation were convinced that they were the legislators for mankind, and even that they had abolished all problems. Keynes himself would never have agreed with this, but his younger disciples, among them splendid writers such as Galbraith, did not have doubts. Economists were the Druids of the age, and the message that, overall, they gave was very comforting: if governments spent money, problems would be solved and the good life (whatever that meant) would duly happen. As a profession, economists had been rather caught out in the interwar Slump, because they had preached austerity and virtue – saving, cuts in welfare spending. That had not cured the Slump – far from it, at least in the popular mind. On the contrary, it had worsened matters, to the point where, in Germany, Hitler came to power. Galbraith wrote a book on the Slump that blamed bankers, and it was a bestseller. Now, economists were associated, on the whole, with easy answers. How widespread their effect was can be seen from an aside by the English historian A. J. P. Taylor, in his book about the origins of the Second World War. Hitler's economy had produced mild inflation, he said, and had thereby produced full employment in a country that, in 1933, had had 8 million men out of work; Taylor added that everyone now knew that mild inflation was a cause for prosperity. A dozen years after writing this, when, nearing old age, he saw his savings consumed by inflation, and the streets outside scattered with litter, he told a different story. But the essence of the sixties was a belief that there were easy answers, so long as grumbling old men got out of the way. Kennedy was inspired by Roosevelt, but the ghost of Keynes stalked his corridors (although when Keynes met Roosevelt in the 1930s, and tried to discuss his theory, the meeting was not a success). It is strange, looking back, how easy the solutions appeared to be. Cambridge, where

Keynes had reigned, was still the leading centre in the world for economics, and one of the few dissidents with a sense of publicity, the young Milton Friedman, from Chicago, went there for a spell. He was a good mathematician, and his work might have proved useful to the economists there. Instead, he was in effect frozen out by a grand old dame of Cambridge economics, Joan Robinson (who padded around King's College in a bizarre Chinese peasant costume: but she was the daughter of a reactionary general who had fallen foul of Lloyd George in 1918, and the granddaughter of a considerable Victorian poet). There were of course dissident voices, but they were few, and they were unfashionable. Milton Friedman published a key article, 'The Quantity Theory of Money', which warned that there was a danger of inflation with the then current practices. He was waved aside, and when in the early 1960s Alan Walters – much later on, a recognized authority on both sides of the Atlantic – applied for a grant to develop statistics as to how much money was being created in England, he was turned down. At the time, economists were fighting their last war, in this case against unemployment, and an engineer-turned-economist, Alban Phillips, who had worked on a long run of data, produced one of the great symbols of the decade, the Phillips Curve. Wage rises and unemployment were related, with only one variable, import costs (as in the Korean War). In England, welfare benefits stopped wages from falling too low, and so demand for goods was kept up; government must surely maintain that demand to the point at which unemployment would never rise above 2.5 per cent. That way, there would be price stability, and men such as Alan Walters, wanting to make complicated calculations as to how much credit there was in the system were simply wasting time. The Phillips Curve dominated academic economics (or 'discourse'). If anything went wrong, ran a further assumption, then price controls could be used – after all, they had been so used during the war, and operated, even by J. K. Galbraith. In ultra-prosperous Sweden, prices and wages were controlled by law. Why not elsewhere? So the economists, on the whole, assumed that they either had the answers or would have them.

There would in ordinary circumstances have been something of a problem with foreign exchange. If governments produced paper money in excess of other governments' production of it, then the rate of exchange between the virtuous currency and the vicious one would clearly be affected. Why should Germans, their money prudently run by the Bundesbank, have to exchange their solid Mark at twelve to the dollar? The answer lay in the post-war system loosely (and not altogether accurately) known as Bretton Woods. The dollar was the anchor currency, taking most of the role of the British pound in its imperial days, and it had a fixed value in terms of gold: if foreigners wanted to exchange their dollars for gold, they were (in theory) free to do so, and the Americans, at Fort Knox, had laid up an enormous treasure of it. The fixed dollar had been associated not just with the fifties trade boom, but with the recovery of western Europe; the system therefore seemed sacrosanct, the more so as the American military undertook the burden of defence in western Europe.

With Kennedy, there was the first small step towards the weakening of this structure. He began the debauching of the dollar – what would have been called coin-clipping in earlier times, as rulers surreptitiously reduced the amount of silver in their coins (the milled edge around some modern ones is a survival from that era, showing that the coins had not been clipped). Quite outside the economists' advice, there was temptation towards this course, because the dollar was in such a strong position that the USA could in effect just pay its foreign bills by printing pieces of paper. There was a minor recession in 1958–9 and the government's finances were dented. A deficit appeared. Kennedy did not reduce spending, and reduced taxes that were still remarkably high, because of post-war responsibilities and the level of arms-spending. The pound sterling was by now being moved closely in concert with the dollar. They were the world's trading currencies, and in the past the pound had been a true anchor. It could be exchanged, on demand, for gold, and the world's prices had on the whole been stable while the gold standard was in force. Now, the pound followed the dollar, and in 1958 the Macmillan government also took an unorthodox financial course, of spending when there was no money to back it. Three Treasury ministers resigned in protest, and this was dismissed by Macmillan as 'a little local difficulty'. It was, but it was a sign of great crises to come. By 1971 the post-war economic order, the very underpinning of fifties prosperity, was in disarray.

Even in 1960 the dollar was the victim of its own success. The real problem was to get the Americans to let the dollar be used as the world's currency. That meant the printing of dollars for world (especially European) purposes. If any country bought more abroad – mainly of course in the USA – than it sold, its currency might become weak, and an International Monetary Fund came into existence, mainly with American contributions, to lend that country money to tide it over while it managed its affairs better, and sold more. The classic case of that was Germany, though the money came not from the International Monetary Fund but from other sources such as the Marshall Plan or the European Payments Union. There was also, from Bretton Woods, a World Bank ('International Bank for Reconstruction and Development') with, at the time, very limited resources. These institutions were meant to encourage world trade, made a brave start, encountered the Cold War and the troubles of western Europe, and stalled. Under the European Payments Union, a more limited system did emerge, and trade between the recovering (or booming) European countries was greatly promoted by it. If any country was in deficit on trade, its currency was supported by the country with the surplus. That way, the weaker country could go on buying. That system worked in the 1950s only in Europe. At the time, European currencies were still weak, and there was very limited credit; neither Frankfurt, the German financial capital, nor Paris had well-developed financial institutions such as a stock exchange, and in Germany most firms notoriously raised their own money from a bank or even from family savings. The system was closed to the dollar, as the European currencies could not be converted into dollars without enormous bureaucratic involvement. However, as trade grew, and as European prosperity rose, these restrictions came under pressure. In the first place, the Americans, using paper dollars, invested in Europe – in 1956 private dollars more than government ones. Conversion was therefore much easier for Europeans, especially Germans. But there were also easy ways round the restrictions: false invoicing, for instance, by which buyers and sellers agreed as to the recording of a figure for a purchase that was not true, the hidden balance then transferred, in dollars or Swiss francs, to some bank outside the system, in Switzerland for preference, though Luxemburg also made itself useful.

The Germans had been exporting successfully to the USA – their surplus on trade in 1958 amounted to $6bn – and had collected dollars. But dollars also went from the USA to Germany (and other European countries) because of the profits that investors could make there – greater than in the USA. There was a further problem. Some very large American firms established themselves overseas, partly to take advantage of cheaper labour costs, and partly to get over protectionist barriers. In France, especially, a desire to build up native industries meant that foreign goods were kept out. It was obvious, in that case, for the first of the great American electronic-computer firms, IBM or Xerox, to set up factories in France and elsewhere. These firms also represented a dollar outflow to Europe. The result was that in Europe there were large sums of money in dollars, the 'eurodollar'.

In theory these dollars could be exchanged for gold, at $32 per ounce, and efforts were made to control the gold market somehow. If these dollars were at any stage sent back to the USA, with a demand for them to be exchanged into gold at the fixed rate, it might go beyond what the USA could stand. This eventually happened in summer 1971, and it was the end of the extraordinary quarter-century of prosperity that had followed the Marshall Plan of 1947. To stop this meant the Americans' keeping their own government spending in reasonable bounds, and it also meant international co-operation: the European banks would have to buy up the spare dollars. A Belgian economist, Robert Triffin, who had migrated to Yale, had foreseen this problem – the Americans, required to send dollars abroad, would lose control of their own currency, and it could then slide in value. By 1960 eurodollars were already greater in value than the gold held in reserve at Fort Knox. With the British pound, which still accounted for half of the world's trade, the problem was much greater, given the weakness of the British economy and the extent of British overseas commitments, with garrisons 'east of Suez' to keep some kind of control over the petrol reserves, or, for instance, to deter the Indonesians from invading Malaysian territory. As Europe recovered in the 1950s, these problems were under control, but by 1958 there was a deficit in the American balance of payments – $5bn – and $2bn went abroad in foreign investment.

American business was still enormously successful and the great firms – Ford, which was all over the place, but many others – were all doing well, setting up overseas. The eurodollar problem was still easily under control, and the problem would have gone away altogether if a dollar devaluation had been allowed, or some revaluation of the Mark, which was anyway very low. The German exporters themselves did not want such a revaluation, because they thought that, if their prices rose, they would lose customers; and in any case holders of eurodollars did not want their value to be reduced. Instead of a serious readjustment, various hand-to-mouth expedients were used. The International Monetary Fund's resources were too low to be very useful – they were still, in 1958, at the same level as ten years before, despite the huge increase in trade. Instead, a group of trading industrial countries was set up, the G10, in 1960. This happened just when, for the first time, people sold their dollars for German Marks. Gold on the free market also rose above $32 per ounce. This did not worry Kennedy. In his first year, a decision was taken to increase spending, and to take on a deficit. It was the first point at which post-war financial management broke with old prudent ways. Not many people objected, at the time. As a leading expert, Barry Eichengreen, comments, it was all rather clumsily done, yesterday's problems being solved by the creation of tomorrow's. He adds, 'the array of devices to which the Kennedy and Johnson administrations resorted became positively embarrassing. They acknowledged the severity of the dollar problem while displaying a willingness to address only the symptoms.' Americans were not allowed to own gold coins; visas became easier to encourage tourism, the virtues of Disneyland advertised. Besides, the low official price of gold, and the difficulties set up about using it, discouraged output and so made the potential problem worse. In the USA inflation in the sixties ran to 30 per cent, the very problem that Keynes's critics had identified.

What was at stake, in these very technical transactions, was the base of the enormous prosperity that the fifties had seen. Oil cost $1 per barrel – almost absurdly cheap, and fuelling a great automobile boom in the West, especially Germany and the USA (where cars became boat-like). Other raw materials were also very very cheap, partly because the market had been glutted, partly because, during the war, men had understood how to make more of them go round. Once the dollar fell in value, those raw materials would rise in price. Wise old heads did shake, but this was not a period when wise old heads counted for much. Keynes had sneered at them as the 'orthodoxy'. In the 1960s the world financial system, which in a sense he had inspired, did work. The central bankers regularly met, at the Bank for International Settlements in Basle, and they knew the rules. The dollar and pound were the essential trading currencies for the world, and if their value became unclear, trade might suffer. Therefore, the central bank of a country with a strong currency, the Mark being the obvious one, would not sell a currency that others ('speculators') might already be selling: instead, the central banks would buy it and so keep up its value. They did not exchange dollars for gold, and in 1961 there were 'swap arrangements' for immediate support of the pound ($1bn, with another $3bn in 1964). The Germans refused to revalue the Mark, thinking that their trade might suffer, but they did forbid the payment of interest on foreign accounts and they (like the Swiss) co-operated to keep the dollar price of gold at or near the low official rate (the 'Gold Pool'). Of course, the basis of it all was that the Americans were chief defenders of the West in NATO with the British as loyal seconds, and when the whole system became weak later on a German chancellor even spelled it out – in supporting the dollar the Germans were defending themselves. NATO developed its own military-financial complex, and the central banks were part of it. The 'American Peace' ruled and the world gave Kennedy a good welcome. The 'New Frontier' books became bestsellers, endlessly discussed, and the *New York Review of Books* made the timing. But do these books now survive, except as remembered titles?

There was trouble ahead. The new team in Washington was self-consciously Rooseveltian, as they understood it, and that meant action against poverty at home, and an assertion of American power abroad. Curing poverty and removing the dreadful blot on the USA that the Black problem amounted to caused much enthusiasm, and at home there was an impetus for change. Spending on education rose, partly to counter the supposed advantage that the Soviet Union had acquired in natural science, as displayed with *Sputnik*. Kennedy preached 5 per cent growth in 1960: it was the federal government's responsibility to abolish poverty, and Kennedy duly put up government spending, though not by very much. Less noticed at the time, he also lowered taxes, which had been at very high, wartime levels, and something of a boom followed. However, the New Frontier ran into difficult country. Kennedy also had to deal with foreign problems and one of these now developed. It was in fact a combination of problems – the whole nuclear structure on the one side, and the question of the West's relations with what was turning into something of a nightmare, the 'Third World'. Kennedy's team were impressed by the sheer success of the Marshall Plan, as they understood it, and a Marshall Plan, applied worldwide, could, in their view, sort out the whole problem of underdevelopment (as it was then known).

11

Berlin–Cuba–Vietnam

The fifties ended with two symbolic places: Berlin and Cuba. Over these, West and East duly collided. As Khrushchev looked at the world in 1957 – the fortieth anniversary of the Revolution – he could be quite optimistic. True, the Soviet people lived much less well than the Americans, and West Berlin was a permanent demonstration of this, but as Khrushchev angrily explained to the visiting American Vice-President, Nixon, man did not live by up-to-date kitchen equipment alone. The anniversary of the Revolution was triumphalist, with huge thermonuclear tests in the offing, and Khrushchev beamed: 'It is the United States which is now intent on catching up.' A 21st Congress in January 1959 announced that the USSR itself would 'catch up' by 1970. On the other side, Cuba was in its way a showcase of things that went wrong in the American hemisphere, and to this day the hero of Latin American revolution, Che Guevara, agonizes over T-shirts. In the view of Khrushchev, and not his alone, Russian Communism was the right formula to turn Cubas into modern places, without the unemployment and racism that came with capitalism. At the turn of the fifties and sixties, Cuba and Berlin meshed to cause crisis.

Khrushchev now lived in a very dangerous mixture of inferiority complex and megalomania, and that was only confirmed by events at home. He had taken time to secure his power and had needed the alliance of men of the old order, including Marshal Kliment Voroshilov and Molotov. But they and other seniors were alarmed at Khrushchev's extraordinarily impulsive ways and they had never been happy with the denunciation of Stalin: whatever next? Wild reform schemes came up early in 1957, because, like Stalin before him, Khrushchev resented having to deal with the Party, and, like Malenkov and many others, would have liked to build up a state machinery with its own rules, as in normal countries. However, that would have meant (and, in the event, did mean) substituting a fabulously multiplied bureaucracy. He put up tower blocks in the cities, doubled Party membership to 12 million, shut an eye to rural migration, and thus created his own clientele. As matters turned out, he fashioned a huge and self-replicating bureaucracy, the leaders of which had their own clientele in the various national republics. In 1958 he was quite popular, and though the intelligentsia regarded him as a clown, he knew well enough how to square them: release of a critical novel, toleration of a critical poet, visas abroad, would get them going. Meanwhile, the Moscow ruler received visits that Moscow rulers had had in the past – envoys from China, from India, from Iran, from the West, all wondering what they might do to please.

He had boasted somewhat earlier of intercontinental ballistic missiles (ICBMs), though in that – rather fatefully – there was less substance to the boast (only in the 1960s were they operational and even then there were only four of them). Khrushchev, who had sneered back at critics that he had no education beyond some lessons that the local priest had given in return for a present of a sack of potatoes, had done far better than any of them. Foreigners might look down their noses at his armpit scratching and his gobbling, spluttering table manners, but he was the leader of what would soon be the most powerful country on earth. At any rate, Khrushchev's ascendancy was now beyond challenge, and he looked to foreign affairs. Here was pabulum for megalomania, as the world trumpeted the 'Soviet achievement' and wondered how to emulate it. Had the time come to get the perennial German problem out of the way? Stalin had tried force. Khrushchev applied the Leninist tactic, first used in 1922, of pretending to be just another ruler of just another state. 'Dictatorship of the proletariat' could be passed off as just a piece of picturesque titling, on the lines of 'King of Kings'.

Late in 1957 the Americans had placed limited-range nuclear weapons in Europe but there were evident disagreements in the West. True, it had a Cold War to fight, but each country fought its own version.

The British were by now rapidly losing the substance of their power and could be expected to play up the shadow of it at international gatherings: classically ripe for flattery, and in any case not really willing to fight for, of all things, West Berlin. The Germans might be isolated, and might even come to terms, which, for Moscow, was the great prize. Adenauer had been shaken by the Americans' abandonment of their allies over Suez, and there were fears in Germany that the Americans would not even reply with a nuclear strike to a land invasion of Central Europe: why should they risk an attack on their own cities? Adenauer approached Moscow with a vague suggestion that there might conceivably be an Austrian solution for East Germany. Khrushchev aired the possibility of a nuclear-free Europe and there was a Geneva conference as to the ending of nuclear tests, in October 1958. Meanwhile other tensions developed. The Middle East had been boiling since Suez, and Nasser was showing off. He proposed an Egyptian–Syrian union, then inspired a coup in the Lebanon, and then another, particularly gruesome, one in Baghdad. Finally there was another and rather strange trouble, the emergence of a sinisterly independent-minded Red China.

Khrushchev was not the only Communist leader to be showing off: Mao Tse-tung had his own remarks to pass. This time round, he had encouraged the intellectuals to criticize and promised to tolerate this (an episode known as 'a hundred flowers bloom'). Nationalism was thus encouraged and the Chinese attacked India, a friendly country, over a trivial frontier dispute in the high mountains. Khrushchev had not supported this. Late in August 1958 there was a further crisis in the Far East, when Red Chinese artillery pounded the islands of Quemoy and Matsu – quite insignificant in themselves, but close to the Chinese shore and still occupied by the Kuomintang forces of Chiang Kai-shek in Taiwan. Eisenhower responded, had his navy escort supply ships and even threatened to use nuclear arms (though he also made Chiang Kai-shek promise not to attack Red China). The crisis then ebbed away. However, this crisis created much more trouble than it appeared to. There were under-the-surface disagreements between Khrushchev and the Chinese because he told them not to invade Taiwan: there were to be no more Koreas. In 1959 he refused them a prototype bomb. Thereupon the Chinese started denouncing what they called 'revisionism'. They were angry at the vilification of Stalin, whose statue still stood in the middle of Peking, and they especially resented, or claimed to resent, Khrushchev's doctrine that nuclear war would be too destructive to be contemplated ('peaceful coexistence'). Mao remarked that if 500 million or so people in the Communist bloc would be wiped out, the price might be worth paying for the utter end of capitalism and imperialism. The arguments between the two sides, couched in the usual wooden language, became public, as each side tried to convince other Communist parties of the correctness of its view. The depth of the disagreements became clear abroad only in 1963, and even then they were sometimes dismissed as part of some game to fool the West, 'disinformation', but they were real enough, and even caused one of the Soviet-dominated parties to defect, that of little Albania, fizzing with resentment at the preferential treatment accorded by one and all to Tito in Yugoslavia, which contained its own Albanians. Khrushchev now tried to stop China's development, and in July 1960 withdrew his specialists. He had been clumsy – giving the Chinese too much in 1955 and then taking too much back five years later. The quarrel was to do with the role of war and revolution in an ideological world filled with such hatreds. At any rate, here was competition for Moscow, and Khrushchev responded adventurously. Off he charged, over Berlin.

Something needed to be done. The Western zones had become an open sore. The problem could be solved if a great wall were put up around West Berlin, thus preventing escapes into it. But it might also be solved if there were a deal with Germany; it might even be solved through a grand deal with the Americans, who (with the British and French) might be prepared just to abandon the place in return for some bargain over arms limitations or whatever. The East German leader, Walter Ulbricht, was cunning and repellent, a product of Comintern weasellings in thirties Moscow, and he understood that Khrushchev would dump him and his state if that were the price of a neutral Germany, detached from NATO, and 'Finlandized' on an enormous scale. Khrushchev himself well knew that walling in West Berlin would be wonderful propaganda for his enemies, in fact the crowning piece in the showcase that the West had built up. He strictly told Ulbricht not to take that step, but at the end of 1958 he threatened to sign a separate peace treaty with East Germany, and offered to let Berlin be a Free City inside it. But he wanted a Western military evacuation; and the West would have to recognize East Germany if it wanted to continue dealings with West Berlin. In January 1959 a draft peace treaty for two disarmed and neutral German states was sent off, and an emissary in Washington suggested that negotiations might go over Adenauer's head.

All of this had military overtones, to do with German rearmament, and Eisenhower himself had had considerable, often very unpleasant, experience of what that might mean. In fact the old general was now quite seriously minded to enter history as the man who had done most to stop nuclear destruction. True, Eisenhower played the golfing old buffer, and his wife was plain cooking. But he saw well enough what was going on, and produced a line, 'the military-industrial complex', that summed up the realities of warfare and militarized economics better than ever Norman Mailer did. Might he not decide that Berlin was not worth a fight? Oddly enough, it was the French who were most firmly in favour of defending Germany, their new associate in Europe. To exploit the differences, in May 1959 Khrushchev agreed to drop his ultimatum in return for a general conference at Geneva, scene of the earlier and quite satisfactory conference that had settled the French war in Indo-China. The new conference might lead to realization of Molotov's old scheme, a conference on European security, from which the Americans could be excluded by definition, and which the USSR would then dominate (the phrase 'our common European home' comes from this period, and not the 1980s).

In September 1959 Khrushchev went to the USA and talked with Eisenhower, drawing the conclusion that here was weakness to be exploited; the two agreed on a 'summit', as these gatherings were irritatingly called, for May 1960, in Paris. The clowning but at least not block-like Khrushchev even had a certain success as regards public relations, holding his own quite well in a roomful of Rockefellers and Harrimans. A string of Western concessions followed – East German control was accepted over the access routes, rather than Soviet; even a promise not to spy. Khrushchev waved these things aside, for they only convinced him that with another show of Soviet power the Western powers would fall apart in disarray. He always was brutal in his ways – on one occasion, at the United Nations, taking off his shoe and banging it on the table in rage – and now he was accidentally presented with an excuse for more temper. The Americans used special planes, the U2s, to spy on the Soviet Union, and one of these was shot down. The pilot survived and talked. Eisenhower at first clumsily denied that U2s were flown, because he had expected the pilot to swallow the poison pill supplied to him. This denial caused a gleeful Khrushchev to present his evidence; Eisenhower was duly humiliated; the Paris conference was cancelled. Eisenhower missed his chance to be the man who had saved the world.

He was succeeded by an altogether different figure, Kennedy, a considerably younger man who took time to find his feet. They were found for him. The US budget for ICBMs and Polaris went up to almost $10bn, and such missiles, hidden in submarines, enabled a crippling 'first strike' to be made. In other words, provided that there were no warning at all, the Soviet capacity to strike back significantly would be destroyed, and the USSR would be helpless. At the same time the military advisers (Maxwell Taylor in particular, but also two up-and-coming academics, Henry Kissinger and Albert Wohlstetter) were adamant that there should be a powerful non-nuclear force as well, i.e. a strong army in western Europe. It was therefore in a very tense atmosphere that the Berlin crisis went ahead. Kennedy and his advisers would probably have settled for some agreement with Moscow over their allies' heads, and Walt Rostow, one of Kennedy's academics, went to Moscow and explained Kennedy's interest in disarmament. This was not the best background for negotiation over Berlin – it was in fact a considerable mistake, given Khrushchev's peasant megalomania. In June 1961 Kennedy and Khrushchev met in Vienna, and Khrushchev posed as the wiser, older man – he despised Kennedy's youthfulness, enhanced all the more because the new President did not even look his age. Besides, just then, Kennedy had been involved in an absurd humiliation. In Cuba, which was in effect an American colony, there had been a revolution bringing a native radical, Fidel Castro, to power at the turn of 1958–9. He had attacked American interests and the Americans had mounted a coup against him, by exiles based in Central America. The coup fell to pieces at the Bay of Pigs, in April 1961, and Khrushchev, conqueror of Hungary, could shake his head patronizingly, and instruct Kennedy as to how the USSR was far better for the 'Third World' than was American capitalism. The Vienna meeting therefore turned out badly.

There was now no apparent solution to the Berlin problem, and Ulbricht had been pressing: if the flight of people, especially the skilled people, went on, then East Germany would implode (in which senti-ments he was a generation later to be triumphantly confirmed right). For a time, Khrushchev demurred, hoping for some outright division among the Western powers; had he played the game more subtly, that might even have occurred. He told Ulbricht to wait, not to take any such step as building a wall. Ulbricht then announced publicly that he would not take it, and his subjects, used to such things, left in greater numbers than before – 2,000 every day in the spring of 1961, adding to the 3 million who had already gone. Khrushchev now gave way, thinking that, at the very least, there would be no opposition if a wall went up, and on 13 August 1961 it did go up. Barbed-wire entangle-ments appeared, and behind them came a whole defensive system complete with searchlights, swept fire-zones, Alsatians and minefields. In the shortest of short terms, Khrushchev was proved right, in that the West confined itself to verbal protests, and the Americans, later, in March 1962, even sent proposals that amounted to a Soviet–American condominium in Europe. But Khrushchev was after bigger game. He exploded a monstrous 50-megaton bomb on 30 October, expecting to browbeat West Germany into neutrality, and at the same time show the adolescent Kennedy who was the master. He would place missiles on Cuba, a few dozen miles from Florida.

'Third World' was a concept that made sense in the sixties, when there were economies of various sorts that appeared to need mod-ernization. Even then, it only had meaning for the United Nations or the World Bank. Japan had already shown the emptiness of the idea, in that as early as 1905 she had Westernized far enough to defeat the Russians and take over a good part of the east-Asian trade.

Now, countries as disparate as Korea and Haiti were included. Latin America was in an odd position. In places, the 'First World' was present, for in Mexico City or Buenos Aires you could think that you were in Europe, but if you travelled four stops down the tramway you were in a different world altogether, where ex-peasants huddled in boxes, and the obvious problem was that the progress of medicine meant that they could produce children who survived. In the suburbs of any city, the poor pullulated, as in a Dickens slum. Some fought their way out, but others gave up, went on making children for want of any alternative. The Soviet Union offered a path to modernity that had been quite successfully applied, and a good part of the intelligentsia of Latin America was sympathetic.

What, after all, could be done with a country like Haiti? To Europeans of the Left in the nineteenth century, Haiti was what Cuba was to become in the middle of the twentieth. She had become independent in 1804 as the outcome of a vast slave revolt against the French. After several years of murderous struggle, the former slaves had managed to set up their own state. It was called 'Haiti' after the old Carib name, and the chief figure in its making was Toussaint L'Ouverture, the black leader. It was one the many Haitian tragedies that he was not present when the country began: the French had hoodwinked him and imprisoned him in the frozen Jura, where he soon died. Toussaint had been a good man, and it was to him that Wordsworth addressed his lines on 'man's unconquerable mind'.

Eventually, Haiti was taken over by the Americans, for twenty years. They did not make very good imperialists, unlike the British, who were more used to taking over other people's countries. Their chief, Admiral William B. Caperton, was a wooden and leathery Virginian, who could see no virtues in the place and who, when besought to co-operate with the Haitian elite, asked whether these were the ones who wore shoes. Still, there was justice, and some roads and schools went up; a black lower-middle class did emerge. Then when the bottom dropped out of tropical agriculture in the Slump, the Americans withdrew (in 1934) leaving a thin crust of collaborationist mulattos in charge, in the wedding-cake presidential palace. In 1946 they were challenged by a black who talked leftist language, whereupon the mulatto elite found their own black army officer to manipulate, one Paul Magloire, who was overthrown by a junta in 1956. At this point, the Americans insisted on an election. By now, the results of their earlier occupation were coming through: roads, and even a form of national transport, multicoloured vans called *tap-taps*, connected town and country more than before; and there was also a tremendous demographic explosion which began to fill Port-au-Prince, as was to happen with so many other cities in both hemispheres. A left-wing candidate, Daniel Fignolé, endeavoured to speak for them. A Belgian-educated mulatto, Louis Dejoie, spoke for the old French-oriented Haiti. The Americans found a convenient third force, as they thought: a little black doctor, François Duvalier, a product of the provincial lower-middle class (his father was alleged to be a schoolteacher from Martinique) whom the Americans had brought into existence. He knew the villages, where he was known as 'Papa Doc', and had spent a year at Michigan; he seemed quiet and manageable, and received support from the Syrian business element that had been cold-shouldered by the mulatto establishment. His private secretary, and link with the Americans, was a Therese Jones, daughter of a Welsh missionary (she had spent a year getting chilblains at an ecclesiastical establishment in forties London), and an American Anglican bishop also gave Duvalier his blessing: 'Papa Doc' would be pro-American but vaguely progressive and would not be a tool of the French (who still exercised influence). Duvalier was triumphantly elected in 1957.

Duvalier's regime then turned out to be a legendary worst in the history of Central America. In fourteen years, he wrecked the country. Waves of ignorant blacks, with a thin layer of mulatto collaborators, swept into power, and stole. Roads turned into potholed tracks, impassable when it rained. The *tap-taps* took seven hours to travel the thirty or so miles from Port-au-Prince to Saint-Marc, and Jacmel in the south was cut off except by sea. The telephones mainly stopped because the copper wire was stolen, and rats gnawed at the rest (as happened with the national archives). The educated classes fled abroad or made their peace by bribery or gaining the ear of Therese Jones (whose husband, Franck Thébaud, ran the customs as the only honest man in the regime; his brother Fritz was finance minister, built a hotel, failed to bribe in the right quarters and found himself in the terrible prison of Fort-Dimanche periodically, later to resurface as development minister). Duvalier and his men in the provinces used voodoo for legitimacy; and from time to time there would be a burst of social energy – the Simone O. Duvalier Hospital and the like; there was even a miniature Brasilia, a huddle of concrete in the (originally Polish) village of Cabaret which was mainly given over to cockfighting. Haiti was in its way a gigantic dwarf, and it attracted the attention of Graham Greene. One of the characters in his *The Comedians*, set in Haiti, remarks that the government has claimed that illiteracy has declined in the north; he concludes that there must have been a hurricane. The country was run by a paramilitary outfit known to the peasants as *Tontons Macoutes*, 'bagmen' from the villages or the urban rabble, who dressed in blue denim (homage to Franco's fake-proletarian *Falange*, though blue was also a good-luck colour in voodoo) and, sign of sinister sophistication, dark glasses. Fort-Dimanche and the other prisons filled up with their victims; in 1963, when the Americans attempted to get rid of their creation, a man was shot in a chair outside the airport, and was left there to greet arriving tourists.

Duvalier was aware of his growing unpopularity, and turned for inspiration to any or every dictatorship, however horrible. There was Mao ('mon petit livre vert'); there was Hitler ('un chef, un peuple, un pays'); there was Mussolini ('le chef a toujours raison'). Slogans such as the emperor Dessalines's 'Je suis le drapeau haïtien' would be put up in neon on the port-side, some of the sections then failing to light up, thus leaving some bits of incomprehensible tubing flickering dimly when the electricity was working. All of this was orchestrated by a strange figure named Gérard de Catalogne, a Guadeloupian *quarteron* who had picked up his knowledge of Fascism at first-hand, since he had served in the secretariat-general of the youth movement of Vichy France. A sense of survival had caused him to find an appointment in Tahiti. There he met a lady, the daughter of the Norwegian consul in St Petersburg and his Russian wife (who had gone into a camp). She was interpreting for General MacArthur. The two married, looking for a sympathetic refuge. Santo Domingo turned out to be overcrowded; across the border in Haiti, Duvalier offered a more promising outlet.

They founded a newspaper, *Le Nouvelliste*, and advised Duvalier as to ideology. Curiously enough, the official name of the *Tontons*, 'Volontaires de la Sécurité Nationale', came from Mussolini's 'Volontari per la Sicurezza Nazionale', who had also confused national security with the operation of protection rackets on small grocers.

It is impossible to get rid of such dictators if they are ruthless enough, and so it was with Duvalier. He forestalled palace coups by exiling his son-in-law as ambassador to Paris and, over the radio, organizing the execution of his best friends. He himself died in his bed, after a long and painful illness, on 22 April 1971. His illness was a secret, though everyone knew; on the morning of the death, there was a strange calm in the town, as even the dogs somehow did not bark, or the cocks crow, as they generally and cacophonously did. It was a palpable *grande peur*, as in the start of any revolution. It was clear that the old brute had finally died when, on the radio, they played their classical record, of all oddities the K464 Mozart string quartet which had been Beethoven's favourite. This only happened at times of national emergency, such as a hurricane or an invasion scare. The record had a crack in it, so that the same phrase was repeated again and again, though no-one noticed. Then, hour after hour, those Duvalier speeches were replayed, meandering through all the platitudes of twentieth-century megalomania: 'je, je, je, moi, moi, moi', 'des anarchisses', 'le pèple', 'la politik que préconize mon gouvernèmon', 'contre les mersses demokratik' etc. The Americans and the usual smooth mulatto middlemen managed, to everyone's surprise, to organize a transition of power to Duvalier's teenage son, Jean-Claude.

Duvalier's funeral had a mass turnout. He lay in state in the presidential palace for rather too long, given the heat and the power cuts, and was then escorted to a vast mausoleum. There were some alarms in the crowd as it shuffled through the dust and the ruts. An aircraft hopping between Nassau and Kingston was thought to be bringing vengeful exiles; the wooden balconies, overloaded with spectators, sometimes let out pistol-like cracks; and a little gust of wind, a miniature tornado, suddenly swept the street rubbish into a column. In voodoo superstition, this means that a soul is entering hell, and it momentarily disconcerted the shuffling, blue-denimed or evening-coated procession. Life then got back to genial normality for a while. 'Baby Doc' liked parties with his young mulatto friends. He was first run by his mother, known as 'La Cornélie du siècle' from her overweight Gracchus, and then by his wife, who took her friends on shopping expeditions to Paris by private plane while the going was good. Hope there was, that light industry – sewing baseballs – and the use of Creole for elementary instruction by missionaries would help the country to progress. Instead, the rule was *ampil pitit*: a plague of children, swamping the outskirts of Port-au-Prince. These were the dragons' teeth of *la partie française de l'île de Saint-Domingue*, and many sensible people might well look across from Môle Saint-Nicolas in the north-west, from where, at night, you could dimly make out the flickering lights of Cuba, across the narrow gulf.

There had been another revolution on Cuba, and it was set to have a vast effect on Latin and Central America because it stood for liberation from the American imperialism shown in those lights. The island had been taken from its Spanish masters by the Americans in 1898 and though it was independent that independence was limited, in that there was a permanent American base at Guantanamo, and the economy was more or less captured by the USA. It did make much progress: Cuba was the most developed of countries south of the USA in terms of literacy, medicine, etc. But there was something of a revolutionary tradition and for a good reason, much of the island having nothing else to think about. It was in one sense condemned to a semi-colonial status because of its chief and even only crop, sugar. Cuba was the largest producer in the hemisphere, and it was the Americans who bought it up, by a fixed arrangement which helped when world prices were low and and not when they were high. Sugar occupied half a million acres, and there were huge factories for grinding; transport took much labour. The revolts of the past had been for rent reductions, and there had also been revolts against the cattle-breeders or tobacco-growers: the landowners generally feared another Saint-Domingue, but anti-imperialism was a powerful enough cause, and had produced its local hero, José Marti, who had denounced the Americans. Their initial occupation had been contemptuous.

The GDP per capita figure was not too bad, but there was an enormous income gap. Sugar had the disadvantage that the cultivation and harvesting of it took six or seven months, and sometimes just four, after which the workers had nothing to do, especially given the heat of the climate, and if they did not develop a habit of saving, then they would be in debt for much of the year and would have trouble repaying out of the next year's proceeds: a classic debt-spiral known throughout the peasant world (the real meaning of the word *kulak* is not 'rich farmer' but 'usurer'). This was complicated again by the existence of a black minority, descended from the slaves that Spain had kept going even after the French had freed them (in 1848). The sugar-owners lived well, and Havana was a famous capital, with noble Spanish colonial architecture. It attracted literate Americans. But it also attracted gangsters, who took over the gambling and the prostitution: Havana became a place where the repressed Americans of that era could escape from the world of the Eisenhowers. Cuban politics was dominated by these interests, and there was much nation-alist resentment of this. In 1933, an army sergeant of mixed blood, Fulgencio Batista, with Communist associates, led off with a cam-paign against the rich, then retired in 1944, but returned after a coup in 1952, this time just greedy; gambling franchises were given out freely, and required contributions towards Batista's own funds; he became very rich. Meyer and Jack Lansky, as Mafia capos, became notorious. On the other side peasants in shanty towns might be evicted for small debts owed to grocers. Meanwhile a university did go up, and middle-class children often became disaffected in it, as they watched Havana obey the Americans. There was a strong enough cur-rent of discontent in Havana, much of it among students.

One such was Fidel Castro, illegitimate son (by his father's cook) of a prosperous (and grasping) farmer who had emigrated from Galicia, the Scotland of Spain. He went to a religious school and like other revolutionaries of the Latin world – including France – seems to have taken an anti-clerical line early on because he was badly treated (in his case by Jesuits). His fellow students (in the law faculty) looked down on him because he was a flashy upstart. At this stage he was not a Com-munist and even had Mussolini's *Works* in a dozen volumes on his bookshelves (for a time Mussolini himself had counted as a left-wing figure and had had good relations with the USSR), but in any case the

Communist Party itself said that Batista should be supported. In 1953 (26 July) Castro and a few companions tried to seize the Moncada army barracks in Santiago, the rival city of Havana, the atmosphere of which Castro did not like. As with other such pre-revolutionary gambits – Hitler's *Putsch* in the Munich beer-hall, or Louis Napoleon's landing at Boulogne in 1840, when, unable to find an eagle as a symbol, his little group, before being rounded up by the police, made do with a parrot bought at a chandler's in Southampton – Castro's affair was near farce, but it gave him another essential revolutionary credential, prison (1953–5). That might have been the end of that, but Batista's ways were such that opposition built up, from army officers, students, trade unions and even the Church in Santiago; the Americans themselves were uncomfortable, and pushed for improvements. Castro was released under an amnesty; a banker gave him support, and so did an exiled politician. He then escaped to Mexico and Guatemala, where the Americans had overthrown a left-wing movement (led by Colonel Jacobo Arbenz) in 1954 ('a Soviet beachhead in our hemisphere', Eisenhower had said, though rumour had it that keeping the low wages paid to the local Indian banana-cutters also counted for something). There, by chance, he met a young Argentinian rebel medical student, Ernesto 'Che' Guevara – a one-time sickly youth with a very pious mother who gobbled up stacks of literature. He was trying to make a living as an itinerant photographer. Anti-Americanism and then Marxist ideas were their medium, and the two young men went on to Mexico, where there was a real Left; Castro talked, and talked; he came to dominate a small group of Cubans.

The two gathered some eighty associates, planned a revolution and with $20,000 set off for Cuba in the *Granma*, a vessel meant for twelve. It landed in December 1956, got some immediate help from a cattle thief and set up in the Sierra Madre, on the south-eastern coast. The invasion began badly. The pilot had fallen into the sea, and most of the men were rounded up; the peasant rising did not occur, and on the contrary the locals were hostile. Castro moved on to a poor region, Oriente province, the poorest in Cuba (with a black population: the black Juan Almeida became a token figure later on) and attacked this or that demoralized, badly paid government post – not a threat taken very seriously to begin with but requiring in the end some response. Batista was clumsy. He had the police beat up people who sang the national anthem after Mass, and the like. It was again part of a pattern that the old order – if that is the right name for Batista's regime – would make stupid mistakes of this sort, and present the revolutionaries with gifts. Castro was a good enough student of such things, and knew how a guerrilla movement could insert itself into local peasant affairs (as Mao had done) whereas Batista's men were generally ineptly led conscripts.

When finally Batista's men did make an effort, they moved up a river valley without securing the ridges on either side and were surrounded, Castro taking much weaponry from them but also releasing the 263 prisoners as a goodwill gesture. In the meantime he had attracted American attention, in June 1958 taking hostage some twenty-four sailors on leave from Guantanamo. He held on to them to deter Batista from using American rocketry. The trick worked: Batista grounded his air force. But there was another important element. Many Americans had a guilty conscience, and a sympathetic journalist, Herbert Matthews, had arrived early in 1957 to live with this new charismatic rebel: he put Castro on the map, himself striking poses of a kind used by Hollywood later on to portray the journalist-as-hero. Senator Mansfield, a warhorse in the making, spoke for an arms embargo against Batista, and, as had happened with the Kuomintang, there was now pressure for human rights, which made for trouble in Havana in 1957. Here, Castro was cunning. He did not want successful rivals, and therefore withheld help from the anti-Batista strikers and the Havana underground; it was not he but the Americans who, on 10 December 1958, told Batista that he should go. There was a final New Year party, and Batista used it as a blind: he got away (to Santo Domingo) beforehand, and early that morning, the Batista women in their finery had to escape by plane to Miami. The chief judge of the Supreme Court, Manuel Urrutia, agreed to take over as temporary president and a general strike in Havana ensured Castro's arrival in the city. It was a *joyeuse entrée* of a new ruler, and he began quite well: there was not even much out-of-hand killing of the Batista men.

But this moment did not last for long. Very early in 1959, Castro at once took over from the Havana people, and Urrutia escaped, disguised as a milkman. Castro was not just aiming to succeed Batista and proclaim yet another exercise in radicalism. There was to be a social and by implication an anti-American revolution. The first steps involved rent reductions, wage increases and on 1 May 1959 the establishment of a militia. American property was taken over, and there were fights with Esso and Shell. But Castro was popular enough on the Left, and that included much of the American Left, which saw in him only a sort of Jacksonian democrat. Beards ruled (as they had done ever since the 1830s, as a badge of the Left: thus Marx). Writers and artists popular-fronted themselves in the thirties Comintern manner: Juan Goytisolo appeared; Picasso applauded; Le Corbusier offered to design a proper prison provided Picasso's murals were not used; a well-known French agronomist, René Dumont, offered his services but was expelled for criticizing Castro's plans for huge collectives to grow pineapples that could not compete with those of Abidjan. Pablo Neruda appeared but, out of jealousy, the local poet, Nicolás Guillén, tried to sabotage the visit. Castro had read some books, and he did impress men such as Graham Greene, who had lived for a time in Haiti and recognized the problems involved in the Caribbean. At this stage Communists were only tangentially involved: only one, Carlos Rodríguez, had joined Castro, at the last minute, in the Sierra, and even he had been a Batista minister. However, Castro made international waves as the fight against American interests grew, and in February 1960 Mikoyan appeared. He warned against precipitate action, but got the measure of Castro's vanity: he 'can't stand not being front-page news'.

Radicalism proceeded apace. The trade unions were taken over, and a land reform was proclaimed (maximum holding: 67 acres). Castro refused to hold elections, and his brother Raúl appeared as a Saint-Just figure, shrilly and self-righteously denouncing opposition: it grew, even among the peasants, but was divided and in any case there was an expectation that the Americans would come to the rescue. They were certainly provoked, as their business interests were taken over, and as Castro refused, for weeks, even to see the ambassador (he himself ran affairs chaotically, from a hotel floor, and addressed million-strong crowds with hours-long speeches). Eisenhower was bewildered: he meant well enough and so did Christian Herter, the new head of the State Department, but early in 1960, with cattle ranches being invaded, there were television rantings by Castro as to the expropriation of property: American companies, including General Electric and Remington Rand, had $200m at stake in October 1960. Trials in public started, in the sports centre, with public executions, and Castro vastly resented the criticism. By May 1960 there were huge anti-American rallies, but there was also a small flood of refugees, at 2,000 per day on occasion. The free press was now closed down, the printers refusing to print it ('anti-democratic') and in July the US Congress voted to let the President reduce Castro's sugar quota. Castro responded by expropriating all foreign property, and there were demonstrative foreign displays, as in the Organization of American States and in New York, when Castro visited the United Nations, stayed in a Harlem hotel, and met Khrushchev.

Either Castro gave way, or he went on. He went on. A single Marxist-Leninist Party was set up, in 1961, with the usual paraphernalia, including revolutionary fancy dress and a theoretical journal, *Cuba Socialista*, edited by an old Comintern hand. Castro made a show of associating himself with the 'non-aligned' leaders, including the Algerian Ahmed Ben Bella (who came on a visit in September 1962), Kwame Nkrumah of Ghana, Sukarno of Indonesia and the inevitable Tito. The USSR took a serious hand, and agreed to buy (at half the price) the sugar that the Americans were not taking, lent $900m (by 1964) and educated 4,000 Cubans. It was now that Castro, abroad, generally appeared in his guerrilla rig-out, no doubt an example for Yasser Arafat of the Palestine Liberation Organization later on, and that the CIA, with Richard Bissell and under Allen Dulles, began to plot Castro's overthrow.

Relations were broken off, and a plot to use Cuban counter-revolutionaries went ahead. By now there was a new President, John F. Kennedy, and he allowed the plan to proceed. Preparations went ahead for a landing at the Bay of Pigs; but in Guatemala, where a hundred different Cuban exile groups were represented, there was an atmosphere of black farce: a brothel was built for them, while the American trainers, arrogant and speaking no Spanish, lived apart and better, and their commander, a colonel, simply said, 'I just don't trust any goddam Cuban.' The counter-revolution turned into a huge version of the U2 fiasco. Of course, it needed some preparation from the air, but that was kept very limited, as Kennedy did not want to expose his involvement too far and anyway feared criticism from Castro's friends in New York. Two planes attacked each of the airfields – warning of something coming, but not enough to affect the issue and, despite precautions of a clumsy sort, very obviously not the work of exiled Cubans. The landing at the Bay of Pigs in mid-April was music hall floundering. It occurred on a reef coast, which damaged the ships, and the deep water swamped the invaders' mobile radios ('walkie-talkies'). The coast was not, as expected, deserted: on the contrary there were charcoal burners at work, and they spread news of the landings. Almost at once the exile force – 1,500 men – was pinned own. Kennedy would not use air power to help; 1,200 men were taken prisoner (they were bought out, late in 1962). Here was another opening for Khrushchev: he would now pose as the protector of the People's Cuba.

Cuba made for legend: Che Guevara agonizing on student T-shirts and posters the Western world over. But those T-shirts could as well have had a thermonuclear cloud instead, because the collision of the USA and the USSR over this and other 'Third World' matters did for a time threaten the ultimate disaster. Cuba now provoked this. Castro was full of himself, and so was Khrushchev: they had stood up to the Americans and their proxies, and in the United States Castro had many sympathizers who even blamed America for his turn to Communism: he had been, they said, just a sort of Jacksonian democrat, and it was only the vicious and interest-bound hatred in Washington that threw him into alliance with the Soviet Union. The truth was of course more complicated. The Soviet machine was used to dealing with such matters as national liberation fronts, had managed their precursors in the Spanish Civil War of 1936–9, and had handled European resistance movements. Raúl Castro and Guevara himself had been members of the Party and in April 1959, weeks after the capture of Havana, they sought Soviet military help: it came, through Czechoslovakian weaponry, and with mediation by the KGB, the resident of which in Havana subsequently became Soviet ambassador (in general, the affair was handled not by the Soviet foreign ministry but by the KGB and the Central Committee's International Department). By March 1960 Castro himself was approaching Moscow, suspecting that the Americans would intervene. Khrushchev spoke out against American intervention early in July, described the Cuban revolution as 'national-democratic' (i.e. a step towards socialism, according to his own understanding of Lenin) and in January 1961 made a famous speech in which he offered Soviet protection for movements of national liberation, such as Castro's. The speech came before Kennedy's own Inaugural, which offered help to any nation saving itself from Communist takeover (an echo of the 'Truman Doctrine' of 1947). Then came the Bay of Pigs, in April 1961, which threw Cuba and the USSR together, and Castro, with KGB help, ruthlessly suppressed opposition.

Khrushchev was in forward mode: he had just exploded an ICBM, but needed to make up, he thought, for the Americans' superiority there (and the moratorium on tests, of 1958, had been broken, first by himself, then by the Americans). Placing intermediate rocketry on Cuba would allow him to reach two thirds of American territory directly. In any case, the rockets were something of a counterpart to the American Jupiter missiles that had just been placed in Turkey. Khrushchev used this as an argument with the Politburo in May 1962 for the placement of Soviet missiles on Cuba (which the experienced and cautious Mikoyan thought risky). In July Raúl Castro came to Moscow and the despatch was agreed – Khrushchev insisting on secrecy, which meant disguising ships and sailors; not a realistic notion, given the U2 flights, which recorded everything serious. The Soviet Union sent far more than was until recently thought – 50,000 men and eighty-five ships, not 10,000 – and there were eighty nuclear weapons of differing range. In other words the operation went far beyond a simple defence of Cuba.

On 14 October an American spy plane did record the missile bases that were being constructed. Khrushchev wanted the secret kept so that Kennedy would not be forced into a public confrontation – the Soviet missiles could in private just be passed off as equivalent to the

Turkish ones – and he intended, when he went to the UN in New York in November, to make a grand public announcement. This was completely to misunderstand Kennedy. There was an election in the offing, and the Republicans made a great fuss about the arrival of Soviet troops – at which Khrushchev ordered more missiles, including tactical ones, to be sent to Cuba (7 September). The Americans called up 150,000 troops, in part for Berlin purposes, and prepared for an invasion of the island. Kennedy told the visiting Algerian president, Ben Bella, that he could accept a Caribbean Yugoslavia, but not more, and stepped up his response, setting up a group named 'Excom' under his main lieutenants, including General Maxwell Taylor. There were ideas of simple invasion, to dispose of Castro, but the technicians warned that not all missiles would be wiped out by an initial strike and on 18 October it became clear that the position was worse than had been suspected – even the American ICBM sites were under threat. That evening Gromyko called; and he greatly angered the Americans by lying outright that there were no offensive weapons on Cuba. They did not say anything, and he sent a reassuring telegram back, such that Khrushchev did not take fright, as he might have done.

October the 20th was the decisive day, when Excom agreed that there should be a blockade around Cuba to prevent Soviet ships from delivering any more missiles, and on 21 October Kennedy saw the British ambassador and revealed his thinking – air strikes would have alarmed the allies; a blockade, technically called 'quarantine' because the legality of a blockade was dubious, was to be imposed. Next day Kennedy revealed to the public, on television, that missiles were on Cuba and announced his response: 'quarantine'. His behaviour, now, was sound enough because the difficulties were formidable, given that substantial parts of Western opinion were against him: what was so wrong about Cuba, given Turkey, and why risk all-out war over this? The Politburo was at first relieved on the 23rd that there would at least be no invasion of the island, and agreed to stop some of the ships; but a few others, to complete the missile preparations, would proceed on course. That day, Soviet forces were put on alert. Khrushchev sent a message that he would not respect the blockade. At the same time, American forces were also put on alert (24 October) with many nuclear-armed bombers permanently in the air. Would the USSR try to force the blockade? October the 25th and 26th marked the height of the crisis. Khrushchev realized that Kennedy was entirely serious, that he would invade Cuba, and was not bluffing. A letter was then composed – the Soviet missiles would be withdrawn, in return for an American pledge not to invade. A further letter was sent on the 27th, and seemed in part to revoke the concessions, this time read out over the radio – a condition was added, that American missiles should be withdrawn from Turkey. Khrushchev had claimed that if these missiles were indeed withdrawn, then it would be a Soviet victory. That evening, Robert Kennedy indicated that they might indeed be withdrawn, but not at once and not in public, since other allies might feel let down. On the 28th, a deal was done and revealed at 9 a.m. on the radio – no American invasion, and withdrawal in due course of Jupiters from Turkey; Soviet withdrawal of missiles from Cuba. The United Nations would inspect. Castro himself was enraged (he broke a mirror), especially at the last proposal, and refused; the American commitment was therefore never made formal, but at least a new code of conduct grew up around these potentially disastrous confron- tations. Mikoyan was sent to calm down Castro and discussions as to nuclear disarmament – or control – went ahead. But the episode had vastly alarmed Khrushchev's associates: so much for his 'peaceful coexistence'. Plotting began, to be rid of him. In 1964 he was duly overthrown. He was replaced by safe pairs of hands: no more adven- tures. Kennedy, by contrast, was assassinated on 22 November 1963, the end of the post-war period, but the start of a very troubled period in the history of the United States.

12

America in Vietnam

In strange symmetry with his enemy Che Guevara, John F. Kennedy became an icon, film attached. He had been – at least given the infuriating late-fifties cult of Youth – the best-looking President ever, and, like Che, he had had a tragic, mysterious fate. When he was assassinated in 1963, the date – 22 November – became one of the very few that have sunk into the mass memory. The funeral was a very solemn and tragic affair, as the widow, herself a strikingly good-looking woman, veiled in black, held her three-year-old boy's hand, as with his slightly older sister she walked towards the funeral service in the cathedral. The little boy touched the world as he saluted his father's coffin. It is, again, an image that has never quite left the world's retina.

It was a most extraordinary murder, in its way a descant upon the American dream, in the sense that a 'loner', Lee Harvey Oswald, product of a (very) broken home, failed volunteer for the military and the CIA and the KGB, acquired a gun, thanks to America's lawlessness in that regard (he got it by mail order), and, his brain full of confusion, thought of murder. Kennedy rode in an open car through Dallas, Texas. Oswald fired, and killed. He was then himself caught, and was shot by a man with Mafia connections who himself was dying of cancer. There was easily stuff here for an Oliver Stone film, and for contorted conspiracy theories: even the considerable British historian Hugh Trevor Roper set himself up as an expert in ballistics to endorse one of these, as, towards the end of his life, he endorsed a preposterous forgery, 'The Hitler Diaries' (he had an addiction to betting on horses, generally unsuccessfully, perpetually needed money, and, in an otherwise distinguished career, made absurd blunders). Few people in the commentating classes could see, as did I. F. Stone, that Kennedy had been 'an optical illusion', and the outpouring of histrionic grief that followed upon his death was not equalled until the death of Princess Diana, grasping and manipulative, a third of a century later. But the neon enlightenment cast shadows. The strangest concerned his own family. The corrupt old father, Joseph, had a stroke in 1961 which confined him, fully conscious, to a wheelchair, and he lived for another twenty years. One daughter with depression had a lobotomy that went wrong and made her a vegetable (she too lived on and on). His oldest son had been killed in the war, two others were murdered, and another daughter, Marchioness of Hartington, was killed in a plane crash with her lover, Earl Fitzwilliam. The last son, Edward Kennedy, was lucky to avoid a charge of manslaughter; and the generation further on has also suffered. John F. Kennedy's own son, the poor little boy of 1963, was killed while semi-trainedly flying an aircraft, carrying his wife (whose family then sued the Kennedys). It was the British writer Malcolm Muggeridge who as ever spoke for common sense with an inspired essay in the *New York Review of Books*, when he mocked the obituary literature as 'plaster pyramids' and showed Kennedy to have been a creation of the new media. Later biographies – Victor Lasky, Nigel Hamilton – left nothing standing of the legend. Besides, Kennedy's legacy led to disaster.

Johnson was a politician from Texas who, like the fabled Mayor Richard J. Daley of Chicago, understood how to play Democratic Party games: between them, they had concocted Kennedy's sliver of a majority in 1960. But Johnson was Texas-machine, on a vast scale, and he had been Roosevelt's manager; he wanted to go into history as a new version of the great man. Kennedy had already referred to the 'New Frontier'. What this would mean in practice was a sixties version of the Roosevelt New Deal in the thirties. The federal government would override the separate states and use the Supreme Court to bypass Congress in pursuit of general emancipation; it would spend money, even if that meant bending the constitutional rules, as Roosevelt had done. As things turned out, the deficits that then came up put a huge strain on the world's financial system, which collapsed in

August 1971. This led first to a fourfold and then an eightfold rise in oil prices, with baleful consequences all round. Kennedy began this.

The background was a great shift in American politics. The parties began – in part – to reverse their natures without changing their names. The Republicans were generally speaking Protestant in origin, their leadership East Coast and well off; now, some Republican parts of America, the north-east and its counterparts – migrant territory, such as Illinois – in the Midwest were gradually turning Democrat. The Democratic Party, historically, was a very odd alliance of Northern Catholics and Southern Baptists, whose chief concern was the rights of their generally backward states. Now, the Democrats of the South tended, more and more, to ally with Republicans on many vital matters such as states' rights – meaning, in this case, racial segregation, and a general fear of the overriding power of the Supreme Court to change states' ways. The Democrats, though still formally holding southern fiefdoms for some time to come, thus tended towards left-liberalism, and they adopted the Kennedy image, whereas the Republicans, though also divided, acquired what would later be called a conservative wing. In 1964 its candidate was Barry Goldwater, a senator from Arizona, who was made to seem almost ridiculously right-wing though he was no stupid bigot, and was personally a kinder and more upright man than Johnson (in Phoenix, Arizona, he had been good at stamping out corruption and had had a brave career in the air force, over the Himalayas, for instance). Still, he had only managed to win the nomination because the other candidate, Nelson Rockefeller, scored black marks for divorcing his wife of thirty-one years, and Goldwater manoeuvred himself into what appeared to be grotesquely reactionary positions – the abolition of graduated income tax, the bombing of North Vietnam, a denunciation of Eisenhower's administration as a 'dime store New Deal'. His electoral ship sank with all hands, though Ronald Reagan found a lifebelt.

The mood was now for political change, though, looking back, it is difficult to see quite where the urgency for this lay. The racial problem in the USA was indeed a great blot, and had been seen as such even in the days when the Constitution proclaimed equality. But there was much to be said for taking things carefully, even just applying the existing laws that protected individuals in the Anglo-Saxon manner. Health care was another great problem, and everyone had a horror story, though again there were not really any instant solutions that did not produce further problems of their own. That was not, in the sixties, a fashionable approach. In the first place there was a very powerful emerging weapon, television, which simplified everything, and the 'conservatives' did not shine there. Besides, the modern economy, and the American way of easy divorce, had resulted in a growth of what were later to be derided as the 'soft professions'. The typewriter was already known as an instrument of female emancipation: secretarial jobs. The computer, though in its early adolescence, was even more to be such an instrument, and women were about to abandon the wife-and-mother role in millions. However the sea-change is to be explained, it happened, and Lyndon Johnson was very agile in riding it. He spent, and did so with the blessing of the fashionable economists. Politics was going to be polarized, in a battle between those who depended on public money, and those who paid it.

Johnson was a master at knowing when to cajole, when to bully, when to threaten. His energy was gigantic – working from 6.30 a.m. until 2 p.m. and again after 4 p.m. – and so was his Jupiterian temper. By Kennedy's standards he was an exceedingly crude man, given to receiving bureaucrats and politicians for interviews on the lavatory, and there were gruesome anecdotes about his behaviour – urinating on his own grave plot while drunk and the like. He announced in Michigan University that 'In your time we have the opportunity to move not only towards the rich society and the powerful society but upward to the Great Society.' This was a response to Khrushchev's ambitious claims, and it became the chief theme of his presidential campaign of 1964. Johnson pushed through a whole set of measures that remade the United States. To Congress in March 1964 he had said that 'for the first time in our history it is possible to conquer poverty', as his wife, Lady Bird, urged him to become a sort of Truman and Lincoln and Roosevelt rolled into one. Money was then used almost as a sort of internal Marshall Plan, with 2 per cent of the GDP to be spent, or $2bn per annum. The analogy was with the various New Deal agencies, and the men appointed were almost classic second-generation New Dealers – McGeorge Bundy (from an old Boston family), Robert McNamara from the Harvard Business School, and Walt Rostow from MIT: each one of them versatile and from the very top of academe. Harvard had an enlightened system, by which such brains were supposed (as, at the time, with Research Fellowships at Oxford and Cambridge) not to have to bother with the drudgery of a Ph.D. thesis, a chore for lesser talents ('Mr' was *the* honourable title) and Bundy was not only firmly 'Mr', but the youngest Harvard Dean in history. Rostow was an extremely interesting man who wrote a characteristic book of the age, now seeming rather naïve: *Stages of Economic Growth* (1960). It identified a moment of industrial take-off, when countries saved enough of their GDP to foster investment and thence an industrial revolution, and development economics went ahead, with an assumption that squeezing peasants would mean investment for big industry. This was a period when academics were supposed to have answers, and not just to be an interest group like others; university education was vastly promoted as an engine for progress. It was all rather good politics, in the sense that it made the Republicans appear to be in favour of poverty, which, said Johnson's rival, Hubert Humphrey, would, if allowed to go on, become hereditary. It turned out, despite his efforts, that that indeed happened, the inheritance being from the lone-maternal side: a later book, by Allen Matusow, had the title *How Not to Fight Poverty* (1985). As Ronald Reagan later put it, 'We declared war on poverty, and we lost.' But such discoveries were a good decade in the future.

Roosevelt had had much trouble with the Supreme Court in the later 1930s. Johnson found that he could get around this, because he had an astute legal ally, Abe Fortas, and he could in effect 'pack' the Court. States' rights were overborne, and so too, on occasion, were the provisions of Congress. But Medicare and Medicaid followed, paying for the elderly and the poor, both becoming much more expensive than any other system of health care, and yet also excluding many millions of people. A Mass Transit Act committed $375m of federal funds to subsidize public transport, particularly railways. A Higher Education Act gave funds for the education of the poor, in

1965, and in 1966 a Demonstration Cities Act gave funds for the abolition of ghettoes; a Housing and Urban Development Act followed, in 1968. Urban transport, landscaping, etc. were to be supported, at first in six cities, then in others. It all meant bureaucratic expansion, the more so when large areas were declared environmentally secured, and the arts ('National Endowment for the Humanities and the Arts') came up as well. Under Johnson, the educational spending rose from $2.3bn to $10.8bn and health spending from $4.2bn to $13.9bn. The costs of all this grew hugely, from $5.5bn in 1964–5 to $144bn by 1993. The 'disadvantaged' (as the poor, given the odd American addiction to euphemism, were now called) saw their share of overall spending rise from $12.5bn to $24.6bn in the sixties. But it all went together with spending on defence. That had risen tenfold since 1949, reaching $114.5bn by 1979 and running at about 4 or 5 per cent of GNP. America was heading for a great deficit problem, and in the sixties was already producing considerable inflation as the paper dollars were churned out. 'The Great Society' ran very sour, and for it all 'Vietnam' became the symbol. If it had not existed, it would have had to be invented. It too, despite the legend of JFK, had started with him.

The Vietnam problem had emerged in the first place from the collapse both of France and of Japan. There had been other, similar cases – similar, at least, in the sense that they all looked the same if you judged things with the wrong criteria, as, increasingly, number-obsessed American managers, with no particular knowledge, were inclined to do. The European empires in Asia had collapsed, but the American record in the area had not been bad – not at all: Japan, Taiwan and South Korea were starting to flourish, and, in the Philippines, American military intervention had quite successfully put down a Communist rebellion. The British had done the same in Malaya, had in fact had a legendary success in doing so. Why Vietnam was different is still an interesting question. For a start, it was not a unity, but until 1954 a French colony, acquired in the later nineteenth century, as a sort of failed stepping stone to China. The complications even began with the name. The French had called it Annam, a Chinese word meaning 'conquered place'; Cochinchine, as the south was known, came from a Portuguese word that was itself a misreading of the Chinese characters for 'Vietnam'. The French also used Tonkin for the northern part, and stressed the divisions, so as to rule more easily; and there were two associated countries, Laos and Cambodia, the whole being known as French Indo-China. Indian and Chinese influences had shaped the country, and Buddhism of various types reigned, but Catholicism had also been brought to bear. There was even a Moslem minority, the Chams, who spoke a language that was the link between the version of Thai spoken in southern China and Indonesian. There was rice, there was rubber, and the geography, from the great Mekong Delta in the south to the mist-swathed mountains of the centre, was very varied. Much of the trade was in the hands of the Chinese minority, who had a symbiotic relationship with river pirates who managed to develop a religious sect all their own. The French managed things easily enough in the days when they had the machine-guns and the Vietnamese did not. There was even an emperor, supplying picturesque legitimacy to the French presence. Then the Vietnamese acquired machine-guns.

They also acquired, and again courtesy of French lessons, a leader of genius who had much the same understanding as Mao had had, as to how technique from the West could be used to subvert the West. The Comintern had its adventurers, men and women who went from language to language and country to country stirring up trouble. Ho Chi Minh was the strangest. He started out with the usual twixt-and-between origins of so many Comintern stalwarts: his father, son of a concubine, nevertheless a mandarin; his schooling, from a French Foreign Legionary with a foul temper; an escape, as stoker, to France, where there was a spell of market-gardening, and then London, where he assisted the great Escoffier in making pastry for the Savoy. In the First World War the French shifted 100,000 Annamites to dig trenches, and Ho picked up Marxism from two Hungarian-Jewish brothers who ran a hostel. The French socialists split in 1920 as to whether they should link up with the victorious Communists in Russia. Ho attended the conference that decided in favour, and signed the document. Then it was the Oriental Workers University in Moscow, where the Comintern taught its people how to take over countries, what were the levers of real power. Ho then moved east – Bangkok as a Buddhist monk, Hong Kong as a cigarette-seller. There, the police picked him up, and he had to be released when appeal was made on his behalf by a prominent British left-wing figure, Sir Stafford Cripps. In 1941, when the Japanese invaded Vietnam, he walked back in. This extremely thin, ascetic, chain-smoking figure with his TB and malaria, his multiple pseudonyms (of which Ho Chi Minh was one, and meant 'bringer of light') soon met another clever product of French Marxism, Vo Nguyen Giap, who turned out to have a superb talent for underground warfare. In May 1941, in a small hut, with bamboo tables, they staged the 'eighth plenum' of the Vietnamese Communist Party. Ho, chairman, sat on a wooden box and drafted the introductory statements, which are not inflammatory reading. The new organization, essentially popular-front Communist, had the name *Viet Nam Doc Lap Dong Minh*, or Vietnamese Independence League. It was shortened to 'Vietminh' and was then known as 'Vietcong'.

In 1945, when the Japanese collapsed, Ho Chi Minh could claim quite simply to be the leader of a nationalist resistance. Giap had organized resistance cells among the peasantry, five to a cell, and, in accordance with the usual practice, did not reveal cells' existence to other cells. They just took their orders from an unknown source – that committee meeting in a bamboo hut. Having used non-Communists in the resistance, Ho and Giap set about eliminating them when the Japanese surrendered (including all Trotskyists, who had illusions that there might be a 'native' revolution independent of Moscow). Ho knew very well that help from Moscow would be decisive, but here, as a pawn in Moscow's game, he needed to be careful. After all, the French were far more important, as potential allies, than any Vietnamese Communists and until 1947, when the Communists were expelled from the Paris government, Ho was required to co-operate with the French. They were very clumsy, not appreciating that their end of empire was upon them, and Ho gained allies. In 1949 China became Communist, and help was forthcoming from that quarter. It gave the Vietminh a commanding lead. By 1952 the French were facing an extremely difficult war, with brittle allies and uncertain American support; in May 1954 they lost a final battle at Dien Bien

Phu, in the north. No doubt if Ho had been left to his own devices, he would have gone on to conquer the south. However, in 1954 the Soviets, anxious to spare France in case she signed up to the European Defence Union, pushed for negotiations at Geneva, and a South Vietnamese state came into existence. Ho's North Vietnam established itself in the usual way, with a million refugees, mainly Catholic, fleeing from collectivized agriculture and the one-party militarized state. There were 100,000 executions.

Saigon, the Southern capital, was then a backwater of French colonial architecture, with its Hôtel Caravelle on the rue Catinat, where Graham Greene talked Pascal to despairing French officers in the stink of rotting vegetation in the marsh heat. It was not at all well organized, and there were battles of some depth between Buddhists and Catholics, while protection rackets pretended to be religions, and the drugs trade flourished. The picture was further confused because there were still French influences, and the refugees from the North made everything difficult. Some wished to take land, and that opened up a dimension of the Vietnam imbroglio which made it, for some academics, romantic: like Cuba, Vietnam was supposed to be having a 'peasant war'. This was a situation well understood by Ho, perhaps via Mao, but certainly through his Comintern background. It was not so much a matter of class confict between poor peasant and rich peasant, but between poor peasants and their creditors; besides, within and between villages there were generally deeply felt and sometimes hereditary grievances that could be exploited by Communist guerrillas who knew the ground. By the later fifties, guerrillas from the North were infiltrating the South, carrying out attacks on landowners and government servants. As ever, the Communists presented at least an organization, whereas the Saigon regime, preoccupied with internal fighting, was helpless; it appealed to the Americans.

Kennedy's advisers, in 1960, were unanimously in favour of giving help and in 1961 7,000 Americans appeared, giving instruction in 'state-building', i.e. teaching the Vietnamese to be democratic in the American manner. Beefy, gold-braided Americans now had to deal with the South Vietnamese ruler, Ngo Dinh Diem, and found him very difficult: an austere, chaste figure, given to lecturing them about a fashionable

French Catholic substitute ideology, 'personalism'. He had taken over the insufferable loftiness of the French higher administrative style, and he had worked out that the way to avoid awkward questions was to talk and talk. He talked and talked, and the power at court was his sister-in-law, who banned divorce. Still, the Americans had had to deal with tiresome Asiatics in the past; these were not to get in the way. Strangely enough, it was only Johnson who had his doubts: 'I don't think it's worth fighting for and I don't think we can get out.' De Gaulle ('a rotten country') also advised him against going in, but the academic advisers were all adamant.

This had been successfully – very successfully – done elsewhere in Asia, most obviously in the case of a Japan that was now lifted off on an extraordinary trajectory that would make her a world economic power, but also with South Korea and Taiwan. Colonization was not part of the programme: on the contrary, the American ambassador was expected to be avuncular and helpful, not domineering, and as a sign of this the embassy itself was not much protected – easy access and no bombproof windows. 'Hearts and minds' programmes taught English and showed Hollywood movies; a famous photograph showed a very slender Vietnamese boy wielding a baseball bat almost his own size at the behest of a protein-stuffed and well-intentioned soldier. Dollars flowed into Vietnam; so did advisers with the latest wisdoms of political science (in 1966 they staged a constitutional convention, as the country fell to pieces around them: some of the people present had even designed three constitutions and Samuel Huntington immortally remarked upon the 'consensus-making bodies . . . viable institutions for power-sharing which would gradually lead to the legitimation of the entire governmental framework'). In all of this, security of body and soul naturally came first, and the Vietcong would have to be contained and defeated, the Americans helping where necessary. But some means to gain the peasants' loyalty was also of elementary importance.

At the time, influential writers were saying that the central problem of 'Third World' countries was the great imbalance in land ownership – huge estates, downtrodden peasants. The peasants, dirt-poor, could not buy anything, so native industry did not develop; the rich just imported goods via some comprador class. Such was Sicily in the nineteenth century, such was Latin America in the twentieth (Barrington Moore is an outstanding writer on these subjects). The answer was for governments to intervene and give land to the peasant. Japan and Taiwan had had land reforms, for political reasons, and these were thought to have been successful, in that societies with an element of equality had emerged. There was much more to this story than met the eye. The most successful agriculture was practised (outside the great empty plains of America) in England, which even in 1930 had more land under the cultivation of great estates than Tsarist Russia in 1916. But in the decolonizing era, landowners were an obvious target for expropriation, and the contented, picturesque peasant made for good propaganda. In South Vietnam the growers of rice for export had thrived in the French period, and they were influential in Saigon. That they were Catholics, and the peasants generally not, mattered; the prevalence of the Chinese minority in the whole trade also mattered; and sometimes there was not even a language in common between lord and peasant.

Diem knew the complications, but his Army of the Republic of Vietnam (ARVN) was ragtag and his writ hardly went beyond Saigon. Efforts at land reform went slowly and badly, and the Vietcong, launching guerrilla attacks, made matters far more difficult. Peasants were herded into *agrovilles* and had to walk for hours to reach their plots; there was much bribery in the sale of, for instance, rat poison, and it was sometimes difficult for peasants to stop squatters from occupying their land. Surrounded by barbed wire, but badly defended, the peasants became demoralized, and the Vietcong knew how to exploit the situation. One of their first acts was to murder people who had the peasants' confidence, such that, leaderless, they would be an open target. The reform programme, never enthusiastically pursued, was largely abandoned, and in Long An province only 1,000 tenants out of 35,000 received any land at all; many were expected to buy it whereas the Vietcong 'gave' it. Diem, surrounded by relatives – half of his cabinet – hardly knew what to do, beyond keeping the old system going, however bad, on the grounds that anything else would have been worse. The rural scene would no doubt have got better, as peasants moved to towns, reduced overpopulation and sent money home, as happened in happier climes. That was not to be. As the journalist Neil Sheehan says, 'the Americans . . . were not gaining the communities of controlled peasants they sought. They were instead fostering temporary encampments of peasants motivated as never before to support the Vietcong.'

How were Americans to deal with assassins, clutching an old rifle, waiting for hours in ambush, their feet rotting in the rice paddy slush? Guerrillas who moved with great cunning to terrorize peasants in their huts? There were very good American officers, and one such was Lieutenant-Colonel John Vann, who had made his mark in Korea, and went to Vietnam as adviser – a man of enormous energy, a good organizer and brave without being foolhardy. He knew only too well what was going wrong in Vietnam. He had to deal with a Colonel Huynh Van Cao in the Plain of Reeds, the north-western corner of the Mekong Delta. It was close to the Cambodian border, where the Vietcong had sanctuary, and was a vile place to fight – swamp, waist-high reeds, clumps of bush and woods, stretching over two provinces. There were concrete blockhouses at the bridges, with rusting barbed wire, among fields of sprouting sugarcane, with canals, ditches and, in the season, a steady downpour. It was easy enough for the Vietcong to hide, where necessary in the water, breathing through a hollow reed; and they could come and go, noiselessly, on flat-bottomed boats. They would wait patiently, suddenly emerging to fire. The Saigon government had in effect lost the southern delta, and the northern delta, with its 2 million people, supplied much of the country's food.

Colonel Cao had written a novel and talked windy French ideology; the French had not trained Vietnamese officers until late in the day and the soldiers, paid ten dollars per month in Saigon piastres, were not enthusiastic for the cause. On night patrol, for instance, they would cough, to warn Vietcong to keep away. If trouble came, American air power would be used, and the peasantry suffered from such indiscriminate firing. Vann became especially angry when a battle went hopelessly wrong at a village, Ap Bac, in the eastern part of the Plain of Reeds, early in 1963. The Vietcong had suffered from American helicopters in particular, but wished to show the peasantry that they had not been beaten. They had studied the situation, and worked out that, if they aimed in front of a passing helicopter, they would hit it; and they used captured American machine-guns. Now, holding a well-camouflaged zigzag line along irrigation ditches, which had small embankments and a dike on the outer edge, they threatened the South Vietnamese positions. On that side, what could go wrong, did – artillery firing inaccurately, American helicopter pilots resenting direction by South Vietnamese, landing in the wrong place, there to be shot to pieces; armoured vehicles pushed across impossible swamp; napalm dropped on peasant straw huts; Colonel Cao going into a huff and refusing to fight at all. A total of 350 Vietcong defeated four times their number, at that with fighter bombers, and five helicopters were lost. Reuters and Associated Press had been present to see the mess, and John Vann, in private, briefed them. He had been especially dismayed at the remoteness and serenity of the senior Americans – General Paul D. Harkins, swagger stick, gold braid, impeccable uniform, playing the part in a Hollywood movie about the Pacific war; the Secretary of Defense, Robert McNamara, extraordinary two-dimensional energy, suit, writing down every figure he could in a little notebook for transfer into some machine that would mathematize everything (and produce the inevitable conclusion that the United States would win).

By 1963 much of the countryside was ungovernable, unsafe to travel in, and the Americans' support encouraged the Catholics in charge of affairs to act high-handedly. In the summer, surrealism supervened. To the Catholics, the Buddhists were backward and absurd – a dozen and more squabbling sects, 750,000 monks who were, strictly speaking, parasitical. Their involvement in the sectarian protection rackets was dangerous, and they had links with the Vietcong. The Diem regime tried to control the Buddhists; a 73-year-old monk adopted the lotus position, arranged his saffron robes, covered himself in petrol, and struck a match. His example was followed, and Madame Ngo Dinh Nhu – wife of the president's brother and adviser – clapped her delicate little hands in glee at the 'barbecue'. Ugly episodes followed – the police manhandling protesting nuns, students, even young girls from school, some of them children of well-placed officials. That summer, there were further self-sacrifices by monks, and into this stepped forceful Americans, their patience barely under control. The ambassador, Henry Cabot Lodge, talked to the generals, and Diem was killed after a coup led by Duong Van Minh and despite an American safe-conduct. When, three weeks later, Kennedy was killed, his wife received a barbed letter of condolences from Madame Nhu.

The South Vietnamese now fell back, often enough, on passivity, expecting the Americans to do everything. One immediate conse-quence was an overloading of the American machinery: for instance, security had been left to the South Vietnamese, and a suicide car-bombing at the embassy in Saigon killed twenty and wounded 126, mostly Vietnamese, in summer 1965. Not even the glass had been reinforced, or covered with plastic. As Vietcong authority grew, so too did the number of Americans. By the spring of 1965 the South Viet-namese were taking $500m per annum, but this somehow did not give them a workable government. As William Bundy, a foreign affairs adviser, said, the government was 'the bottom of the barrel, absolutely the bottom of the barrel'. There was even briefly a nonagenarian in charge. The problem as regards Buddhists continued – they sacked the American library in the city of Hue, for instance. It was not until the summer of 1966 that the Buddhist movement was (bloodily) crushed, but in towns and cities such as Hue it was the Vietcong that profited from the resulting hatreds. Meanwhile, South Vietnam became mem-orably corrupt. Import licences for cement were such that the entire country could have been paved over; theft from the PX was gigantic, even involving a computer worth two million dollars. Inflation had wrecked government salaries, so that corruption became the only means of survival – a provincial chief, with a family, could not survive on $200 per month, and there were networks of black-marketeering, involving wives, often enough, such that the Vietcong could obtain anything they wanted. Some Americans understood the situation well – Vann's associate, Douglas Ramsay, who spoke the language, acquired the locals' confidence, became a target for the Vietcong, and survived seven hellish years in their prison cages. The *guerrilleros'* grip on the countryside was such that the roads to Saigon were mined, again and again, and Vann himself rode around in an unmarked pick-up, without ostensible defences.

The Saigon government considered just abandoning the five north-central provinces, more or less difficult to hold, given the enemy's safe supply road through Cambodia. In black pyjama-suits, the Vietcong could even infiltrate American airbases and use mortars against them, knocking out a dozen planes; at the end of 1964, undetected, they encircled Saigon and planted a bomb in an American hotel for officers on Christmas Eve. The bombers had perfect intelligence, had had South Vietnamese uniforms, had even studied how these soldiers smoked. A little later they brought off a similar coup against an airbase at Pleiku. Against such an enemy, the American tactics of bombing and aerial machine-gunning from gunships were ineffectual, or even made the problem worse, because peasants, their homes wrecked, would support the Vietcong.

Johnson could not quite understand the passions that went into the Vietnamese resistance: why could Ho Chi Minh not just be bought off, with some enormous project to develop the Mekong Valley (1965) in return for concessions to end the war? He would have, with great reluctance, to increase the American commitment. In August 1964 he profited from an incident of naval attack in the Gulf of Tonkin to take authority for the war – Congress gave it, with few serious dissidents – and was determined to Americanize the war altogether: 'power on the land, power in the air, power wherever'. On 8 March 1965 came a decisive moment. The Marines landed at Da Nang, on the central coast, and heavy bombing began against the Ho Chi Minh Trail, a network of tracks through the jungle. Overall, the plan was to bomb North Vietnam in such a way as to show Ho Chi Minh that he must give way, and three times the weight of bombs used in the Second World War was duly dropped – 6 million tons. On the other hand, Johnson was very anxious to spare civilians, and every Tuesday he held a lunch where he himself specified the targets and bomb weights. Quite often – sixteen times – he ordered pauses in the bombing, hoping that the North Vietnamese would come to terms as, in the end, the North Koreans had had to do. There were seventy-two 'peace initiatives'. None had any effect. The American ambassador in

Moscow at one stage sent a letter inviting negotiations, and it was returned unopened.

By the middle of 1965 there were 50,000 American troops on the ground, who had been well-trained for the wrong war, and the military authorities said they needed many more. By November 1965 there were 250,000. Soon there would be half a million. Their arrival transformed the country. A colossal effort was made, with extraordinary ingenuity in engineering, to build a base at Cam Ranh Bay, 200 miles from Saigon, with six panoramic jet bases, carefully protected from infiltration. The Mekong Delta was dredged, to create a 600-acre island used as a secure camp site; six deep-draft harbours were rapidly set up, the pieces, prefabricated, towed across the Pacific. The base had forty ice-cream plants, and enormous deep-freeze facilities, such that on alternate days the electricity in Saigon was shut off. All the Americans' food was flown in, and the enormous PX arrangements (at Cholon, on the scale of Bloomingdale's in New York) meant that there was an equally enormous black market in stolen American goods of all sorts. Saigon itself became disgusting – heaps of uncollected rubbish, dogs and cats rooting in them; rats and stray dogs everywhere; drug-dealers, whores, GI bars, refugees pouring in from the stricken countryside. By 1971 the Pentagon said one third of the men were on drugs.

At this stage, the Americans' tactics were simple enough. As Sheehan rightly said, men of limited capacity, who knew their limits, would just go on doing what they knew they were good at; anything different would bewilder them. General William Westmoreland was one such. He replayed the Korean War. 'Operation Rolling Thunder' went ahead, with huge quantities of explosives dropped on what were known as 'free zones'. Westmoreland gave press conferences at which he outlined the stages in which the war was supposed to come to an end – in this case, quite precisely, November 1968, while McNamara busied himself with his mathematics on the subject, and his deputy, Cyrus Vance, established an air-mobile cavalry division, with Huey gunships, firing rockets from side-pods. In November 1965 there were already battles of some scale with North Vietnamese regular soldiers who had come down the Ho Chi Minh Trail, and, given the patience and ingenuity with which these troops waited in ambush, with Soviet weaponry, the battles were testing for the Americans. Their firepower could reduce fishing villages to rubble but there was nothing they could do to prevent the Vietcong from reoccupying the rubble, and there were grotesque episodes in which tactics of attrition were used in rice paddies, complete with 'Zippo jobs' on thatched village huts that could be ignited with a flick of a cigarette lighter. There was not much, either, to be said for the use of herbicides ('Agent Orange') to destroy vegetation, and hence cover for the enemy. Immense areas of forest were destroyed every year – in the whole war, 12 million acres, together with 25 million of farmland. B52s, in waves of three apiece, would attack a 'box' of two miles' length and 1,100 yards' breadth, with huge bombs, dropped at will. The aircraft also never flew lower than 3,500 feet, and thus were unable to pinpoint their targets.

Even the army Chief of Staff complained how 'indiscriminate' had been 'our use of fire-power . . . I think we sort of devastated the countryside.' By 1966, there had been 2 million refugees and Saigon itself rose in population from 1 million to 3 million – rubbish cities, impossible to patrol or govern, except through mafias, of which the Vietcong were obviously one (Samuel Huntington remarked that 'in an absent-minded way the United States in Vietnam may well have stumbled upon the answer to wars of national liberation' – i.e. clear out the peasants who were then thought to be their principal support). All in all, up to 1974, there were 1.16 million civilian war casualties, at least half of them by US action from the air. By the time of the January 1973 ceasefire, an area the size of Texas had received three times the bomb tonnage dropped on Europe in the Second World War (though the air force complained that it had been forbidden to touch essential targets – Hanoi itself, or the port of Haiphong, or the Red River dykes, the collapse of which would have destroyed the country).

The North Vietnamese put up an extraordinary effort. They faced an exceedingly difficult situation, in that their Soviet and Chinese patrons were at odds – the 'Sino-Soviet split' which had the two sides bombarding each other with insulting messages and at one stage even produced combat over a disputed border. The Vietcong inclined towards the Chinese, and from them acquired, in 1962, 90,000 rifles and machine-guns. There was a prodigy of effort involved in the Ho Chi Minh Trail which brought weaponry to the *guerrilleros* in the South. At first the trail had been primitive, but in 1964 a railroad was constructed: in 1964 10,000 soldiers had gone south every month, but by 1967, 20,000. The Trail became a very elaborate network, with tunnels and several branches; it supported 170,000 North Vietnamese troops in the South. The heart of the military problem, for the Americans, was that they had to move out in small groups, probing for a much larger Vietcong force that would withhold fire – in May 1968, at Hue, even with 500 Americans set against 20,000 Vietcong in difficult country. Besides, the weakness of their allies meant that Americans had even to do small-scale patrol work. Now, they also had to undertake what resembled a frontal war, as the North Vietnamese came in via the tunnels or through Cambodia. There were set-piece battles in the absurdly named DMZ ('demilitarized zone').

Giant bombing raids were astonishingly ineffective, against North Vietnamese troops that could continue with slender resources – a mere fifteen tons every day – and the entire electricity supply of North Vietnam was only a fifth of that in Alexandria, Virginia. The dockers in the North learned how to cope with the threat of bombs, and imports from China more than doubled between 1965 and 1967 (to 1.4 million tons): barrels of oil went by barge along the canal network. The attrition campaign in effect damaged the Americans more, in that they lost 700 aircraft by the end of 1967. The Americans compounded their own problems by sending draftees home after a year, which meant a constant influx of inexperienced and, in the end, very reluctant young men, and it was remarkable enough that they did not run amuck, as such soldiery could easily have done. Of course, they resented the local people ('staring at us as if we were from Mars', said one) and there was a celebrated incident in March 1968 when at a village called My Lai peasants were killed by American soldiers, enraged at the endless obstinacy and guile of the enemy. McNamara had been obsessed with his 'bottom line', in this case dead enemy. The corpses were supposed to be counted, so ambitious soldiers gave

him them. There was even an absurd system for spotting concentrations of urine below in the jungle, and many peasants died therefrom.
One consequence was what gave Huntington his preposterous look-
ing-on-the-bright-side. There were 2 million refugees in the cities,
especially Saigon, by 1967. The Hao Hoa sect-gang did a deal with
the Vietcong in order to operate a black market in the products distributed under the aid programmes: tractors were simply bartered.
Meanwhile in Saigon Westmoreland presented multicoloured charts
for the press, some of which was beginning to adopt derision. He
defended the tactics with an all-American metaphor: that the alternative was like using a screwdriver to kill termites: if you overdid it you
brought the house down. It was all an invitation to revenge, even
suicidal revenge. The Americans had scotched their snake, not killed
it, and it bit back.

In the early hours of the morning of 31 January 1968 two ancient
vehicles drove up to the American embassy compound, and nineteen
men jumped out, to plant explosives in the wall. The guards shot back,
but one of the Vietcong managed to reach the embassy building itself,
and got in. The shooting went on all night, until, finally, one of the diplomats killed the infiltrator. The Vietcong had prepared very thoroughly
– smuggling the explosives in rice lorries, and using, as agent, a chauffeur who had worked for the Americans for years. Nor was this the
only attack: the radio station itself was seized by fourteen men who had
been training for three months, and there were lesser troubles all over
Saigon, the worst when the Vietcong broke into the house of the chief
of police, shot him, and slit the throats of his wife and six children.
Another police officer, who had been godfather to one of the children,
caught one of the men, held a gun to his temple, and fired. The young
man's face, freezing at the very moment of death, made one of the most
famous photographs of the war. The godfather's reputation never recovered from this characteristic photographic lie (the photographer later
'apologized'). These attacks and many more like them were called 'the
Tet offensive', and it counted as a humiliation for the Americans. By
then, opposition to the war had been building up inside the United
States. It was based largely on conscripts' unwillingness to go to a
Vietnam the scenes of which were nightly shown on television. 'Tet' was

the Vietnamese New Year, which began in February, and the American generals had previously been very optimistic: but for the Vietcong to be able to attack so widely, and to reach targets that were not only spectacular, but also happened to be within easy reach of television cameras, appeared to be a tremendous coup.

But the reality was different. In the first place, there was a classic piece of fraud. A truce had been arranged for the New Year, for the sake of the ordinary people, and it was broken; many Americans were celebrating, and firecrackers masked the sound of gunfire. Besides, the attacks, however spectacular, all failed, with heavy loss of life to the attackers, and there was no popular uprising. General Frederick C. Weyand, near Saigon, had expected the truce to be broken, had prepared for an attack, and fended it off easily. In the north, on the border, 6,000 Marines held a base at Khe Sanh for seventy-seven days of battle, and this was presented as another version of Dien Bien Phu, the great French defeat in 1954. But the truth was that the Marines, in holding the place, lost on average three killed and twelve wounded every day, whereas the Vietcong casualties were much heavier, and in any case the essential problem at Dien Bien Phu had been the failure of the French over supply, whereas at Khe Sanh the C123 transports had no such problem. The 'Iron Triangle' north of Saigon was notoriously difficult to defend because of the relative freedom of approach roads for an attack, and the Americans had done well in the circumstances. Qualified observers have since said that the Vietcong's southern element was dealt a tremendous blow by their losses, and that, thereafter, the North Vietnamese regular army predominated.

The curious aspect was that the American media presented Tet as a terrible failure. *Newsweek* talked of 'the agony of Khe Sanh' and Walter Cronkite on CBS referred to it as a 'microcosm' of the South Vietnam 'problem'. Later on, Vietnamese Communists themselves admitted that Tet had been a disaster – 60,000 killed, as against 10,000 Americans and South Vietnamese (though also 14,000 civilians). Two American writers, very hostile to American intervention, Don Oberdorfer and Frances Fitzgerald, note that Tet was a failure, though of course very spectacular. Why did it have such an effect on American educated opinion? It did, and the role of the media was analysed in extraordinary detail by Peter Braestrup. Part of the problem was purely technical, in that getting a 'story' out meant seventy-two hours over thousands of miles: satellite broadcasting was still in a very early stage. Accordingly, journalists in Saigon – 464 of them, tending to repeat each other – were best placed to send out film of the various troubles in the capital, and as one of Braestrup's informants said, 'the networks see no harm in running a stand-up piece ... by a guy who has just come in the country two days earlier'. The many positive aspects were ignored – the fact, for instance, that there had been no South Vietnamese defections. Was a central problem the fact that the American military did not know how to 'manage' the news? Westmoreland himself breathed confidence, and came across as a buffoon.

A war started between the media and the White House, and there were grand defections, including John Kenneth Galbraith, high priest of the Rooseveltian New Deal, and even Senator J. William Fulbright, who had done much for the spreading of democracy under an American aegis. The younger generation of the Johnson team broke off, and Johnson himself became demoralized, sometimes breaking down in tears. McNamara himself broke off, and went to head the World Bank, though his ministrations did not make a positive difference in all but two of the economies he treated. The fact was that Johnson's nerve had already been badly weakened by the failure of the 'Great Society'. He had been overawed by the grand Galbraiths and McNamaras; now they were making him take the blame.

The disaster was clear: America was losing, and doing so at much cost. There were to be nearly 50,000 battle deaths, over 150,000 cases of wounds severe enough for hospital, and over 2,000 missing. Two million Americans saw service in Vietnam but even then it was a selective business: conscription ('the draft') was theoretically universal, but in practice seldom hit young men who could ask for deferment on grounds of education, and education was a very broad church. The army took a dim view of homosexuals and exempted them: there were volunteers for that. Blacks and the working classes (and the inevitably enthusiastic Virginians) were disproportionately represented in the draft, which took 100,000 men for Vietnam in 1964 and 400,000 in

1966. There were protests across the land, and the universities, though not in truth much affected, were in ferment. Demonstrations and the media desertions caused collapse in Johnson, whose hopes for the reputation of his presidency were smashed. In March 1968 he made a dramatic announcement on television that he did not intend to run for President again.

13

Nixon in China

The withdrawal of Johnson introduced a period of surrealism in American affairs, a surrealism that became grotesque. A President, soon to be hounded from office for telling complicated lies about a matter of no importance, was seen on the Great Wall of China; he had come there as part of a fantasy game, had been received by a Chairman Mao who had ripped the hospital tubes out of his post-stroke body in order to exchange fifty minutes of exhausted and interpreted platitudes with his knees-pressed-together visitor. Mao was, said André Malraux, a colossus contemplating death. Of death, the colossus had seen much. His People's Republic had turned into a sort of huge, failed version of anything that the Bolsheviks had ever tried, beginning with War Communism in 1919. Thirty million people had starved to death in one of his campaigns, when, trying to stop birds from eating grain, he had ordered peasants to bang pots day and night to stop the birds from landing. They flew about, as planned, until they dropped. Insects were then deadlier to the grain than the birds had been, and Mao's peasants were eating bark.

In the same period, the dollar turned into paper, and the financial structure that had saved the West collapsed. There was a consequence: oil producers quadrupled their prices, and then octupled them, causing mayhem. Stock exchanges imploded and banks failed; Keynes's famous line, that modern ideas reflected defunct thinkers, boomeranged back at him. The period even managed to start off with a villa belonging to the modernist French painter Fernand Léger, who had bequeathed it to the French Communist Party, which then offered it as a place where peace negotiations could be concluded (a ceasefire over Vietnam was eventually signed there). These were another Panmunjom, endless haggling over tiny details while hundreds of thousands went on dying.

In November 1968 a presidential election, by a small majority, brought to office the Republican candidate, Richard Nixon, whose reputation was for fierce anti-Communism. He seemed to be entirely pledged to winning the war. Nixon's presidential career was bedevilled from the start by media hostility, which he was extraordinarily clumsy in handling – bullying one moment, cloyingly and with obvious insincerity making up at another, and then, when both tactics had failed, relapsing into paranoia. Nixon was no patrician from the East Coast – quite the contrary, he counted as a weaselly provincial reactionary, and his assistants were charmless effigies of the American virtues. Hanoi sensed blood. Not long after Johnson's announcement, what appeared to be negotiations on a ceasefire took place in Paris. Johnson had been desperately trying to arrange these, and offered to stop the bombing in return for North Vietnamese acceptance. It was given, as a propaganda gesture, but it was empty, and very irritating. There were indeed endless different 'peace initiatives', a 'charade' according to Gabriel Kolko: none had any effect. The North Vietnamese were adamant that the Americans should just pack up and go, and they ignored Johnson's offers. The fact was that they did hold some cards. The North Vietnamese army was battleworthy and ruthlessly led; unlike the South Vietnamese one, it did not have to rely on ethnic-minority conscripts; it had supplies from one or other of the Communist giants; it had safe areas in ostensibly neutral countries only a few miles from Saigon. Besides, the Americans' hands were firmly tied. They had too few troops for a very complicated political geography, those few often quite untrained, and therefore reliant on aerial bombardment.

But Johnson could not really bomb the essential targets, because he feared the resulting gruesome publicity, and because he did not want to provoke either Moscow or Peking. The fact was that the Americans were anxious not to push China too far: in 1964 she had exploded an atomic bomb, and in 1967 a hydrogen one (though at the time, in the middle of the 'cultural revolution', the country was widely in chaos).

There were also great difficulties as regards the United Nations, then taken seriously as a 'forum' for 'world opinion'. Even in 1975 only some two dozen of its 144 member states counted as democracies, and from 1945 to 1991 'Third World' states were run, for half of the time, by their armies. Nevertheless, the organization – at least, capable of 'peacekeeping' – had some uses and had to be respected. In any case the North Vietnamese could bite back. They had acquired powerful defences, with 250 interceptors and 8,000 anti-aircraft guns, and one American plane was downed for every twenty-five sorties (whereas, later on, in the Gulf War, the figure was one in 700). The US air force bombed forest, smashed villages, and just caused the locals to hate the Americans all the more (a hatred returned with considerable sincerity). But the North also had the vast advantage that there was a safe supply line, the Ho Chi Minh Trail, which went through an area of Cambodia that jutted out towards Saigon itself, the 'parrot's beak'. The Americans had too few men to cover these long borders, and in any case they were not the light infantry that might have been effective.

To start with, just the same, events appeared to go in Nixon's direction. In the first place there was the Americans' always considerable learning curve. After Tet there was a period when the war seemed to be moving the Americans' way, and a British expert (from his days in Malaya), Robert Thompson, gave sage advice: the war would have to be 'nativized' in the sense that the South Vietnamese should take over as far as possible; their army was given training of a sort. Whether this worked is still debated: there is evidence for and against, but the Northern Communists were certainly not popular, as the huge number of refugees always showed. There was also an American programme of 'counter-insurgency', 'pacification' – i.e. a carefully controlled reaction, involving the civilian population. Guerrillas or for that matter infiltrators could only really be countered if their areas of support were liquidated, whether by the physical movement of the potentially supportive population, or by that population's inclining towards the anti-guerrilla cause. The Americans studied these matters, and had an educated team. Robert W. Komer came in May 1967 to head the Civil Operations and Revolutionary Development Support office, or CORDS, run by men who subsequently made considerable careers in the 1980s and even beyond, when the Right were again in charge in sensitive areas (Komer himself becoming ambassador to Turkey). The programme was called by the CIA 'Phoenix', an evocation of a Vietnamese symbolic bird, the Phung Hoan (the equivalent of the Central American Quetzal). One of the great problems hitherto had been the endless targeting of competent South Vietnamese officials, of whom tens of thousands had been assassinated. There was to be a riposte – the careful targeting of North Vietnamese 'cadres'. In 1970–71, 10,444 of these were killed, generally in fire-fights.

Pacification would have meant an infantry war, and the generals did not want this. For a start, they had too few men to cover the long borders with Cambodia and Laos, and of their 540,000 men, only 200,000 were actually fighting. In fact the Marines did quite well with small patrols; and William Colby, Komer's successor (in 1968), claimed over 20,000 killed, 30,000 captured and 180,000 defections by 1971. Much of the country did become quiet again, and foreigners could travel by road from Saigon to the coast, where there was a protected holiday resort. The watchword was now 'Vietnamization' because the Americans were expecting to withdraw, and Westmoreland's successor, Creighton Adams, was under instructions to release troops as fast as he could. Vietnamization might have worked: however, one of the decisive elements in this pacification would have been mixed American–Vietnamese units, and Westmoreland was adamantly opposed to their existence: only a few thousand such mixed troops operated in the field. Relations were not good – resentment on the one side, contempt on the other, with linguistic barriers to complicate matters. At any rate, by spring 1970 there was a regular war and not a guerrilla one: the North Vietnamese were able to keep troops in great force in Cambodia and their army held what amounted to a regular front line through the mountainous and jungle territory on the official borderline. From there, they could strike at the old imperial capital (most of it was in reality nineteenth-century pastiche architecture), Hue. By stealth, Nixon – infuriated by the endless nonsense of the Paris talks – decided to strike there, together with the South Vietnamese army, which, Thompson said, was now capable of action. There was much military justification for this, given the North

Vietnamese army's closeness to Saigon, and that it was preparing an attack. The Americans' attack itself did not go badly – much equipment destroyed, food supplies captured, and US casualties falling from ninety to fifty per week – but there was an explosion of rage inside the USA.

This war had now, in a sense, to be won at home. American opinion was in places violently, hysterically, hostile: 1967 had seen 100,000 march on the Pentagon and there were arson attacks in several universities, including Stanford, where the Institute of Social Anthropology was burned down. The National Guard was called out, and over-responded, in panic: in May 1970 at Kent State University four protestors were shot, two of them girl students on their way to lectures. Four hundred and fifty colleges were closed down. Nixon responded violently to 'bums blowing up campuses' and famously got support from building workers at one demonstration in New York (he invited their leaders, ingratiatingly, to coffee at the White House; on another occasion he smarmed at student protestors whom he encountered by chance in the early hours on a visit to the Lincoln Memorial). By 1972 the administration was simply held in derision by almost anyone in the United States who could read and write. At the same time, Nixon alienated his own bedrock supporters.

The opposition to the Vietnam War does not, now, look very impressive. After they had won, in 1975, the Communists massacred a quarter of the population of Cambodia, and threw out the 'boat people' from Vietnam, hundreds of thousands of the population, forced onto refugee boats, many sunk or destroyed by Malay or Thai pirates before they reached long-term refugee camps in Hong Kong. At the time, the American opposition was saying that the North Vietnamese were just another version of Tito's Yugoslavians, potentially neutralist and in effect social reformers in the Henry George sense of one peasant, one plot. There are long lists, of the best writers and scholars in the country, who blundered – and who would, very soon, be disavowed by the very people they thought they were defending. John K. Fairbank of Harvard and *The Cambridge History of China* thought that Mao was 'one of the best things that has ever happened to China'. The doyen of Asian studies in the USA, Warren Cohen, agreed. His principal target was Dean Rusk, craggy provincial Protestant with a moral sense: who now looks right? Barbara Tuchman said that America was repeating the mistakes of the fourteenth century, when paranoia and the Black Death stalked the land; she wrote in *Foreign Affairs* that Chiang Kai-shek had been wicked, that in China famine had been 'eliminated'. Marilyn B. Young recycled Leninist propaganda (*The Vietnamese Wars 1945–1990* (1991)) to the effect that peasants with a back garden of rice-land were 'exploiters', and 'concerned Asian scholars' talked nonsense of the same sort. When the anti-Nixon people took over, their performance was lamentable. The fact was that a million people fled the North when independence came and a further million and a half when the Communists took over in the South. One of the Asian scholars was Chalmers Johnson of Berkeley, who complained of the student opposition that they never took his books out of the library. David Halberstam, who became the veteran journalist in the South, blamed the McCarthy persecution of the 'Asia hands' for the American inability to understand what was going on. Even a well-made film such as *The Killing Fields*, about the Cambodian horrors, somehow fails to mention Communism as the cause of them.

Nixon's response was to withdraw American troops, promising to 'Vietnamize' the war. This had mixed results. The Delta was made safe again, but there was now in 1970 a full-scale war going on along the borders, and the North Vietnamese were quite well equipped to fight it – T54 tanks, 130mm anti-aircraft artillery and 350,000 Chinese to back them up. Cambodia was almost safe reserve territory for them, because King Sihanouk, in 1964, believed that 'all of south-east Asia is destined to become Communist', and he allowed the Vietcong tacitly to use his port, Sihanoukville, where better-off Cambodians made money from smuggling to the Vietcong. In 1969 Nixon had stealthily bombed the Cambodian trails while the Vietcong trained Khmer Rouge (12,000) as *guerrilleros*, whereat mobs in Phnom Penh sacked the Vietnamese embassy and killed local resident Vietnamese. Sihanouk went to Moscow and Peking to have the Communists taken out of the country and was himself exiled – taking up an alliance with the Khmer Rouge even though they went on to kill some of his children. Nixon deviously supported the man who replaced him, a general by the name of Lon Nol (even the CIA heard about this only when Nixon announced it on TV). The bombing in 1970 shattered just huts, and Nixon had acquired another brittle and touchy ally (when Lon Nol was offered sanctuary in the embassy when it all collapsed he refused, blaming the Americans for scuttling from the scene); an attempt to use South Vietnamese troops broke down when they were ambushed. In February 1971 another effort was made, this time to cut the Ho Chi Minh Trail at Lam Son, and this was even worse. The Vietcong knew what was coming, and when the South Vietnamese had lost 3,000 men, President Nguyen Van Thieu ordered a retreat, but without telling the Americans. The retreat turned into a rout, fleeing soldiers clinging desperately to the skids of helicopters, and being torn to pieces by the treetops. There were even anti-American demonstrations in Saigon, and by now the Americans themselves were widely demoralized: to counter the use of heroin, urine tests had to be imposed on the army. In 1972 the North Vietnamese made a great effort to break the South. In March 40,000 men attacked over the 17th Parallel into the DMZ. In the first two weeks, there was a South Vietnamese collapse, made much worse because the roads were clogged by fleeing civilians and soldiers' families – in fact by now there were 5 million refugees in a population of 17 million. An important base, Quang Tri, fell, and only vast US bombing stabilized the front.

Maybe South Vietnam could have been saved, but by 1971 the chief foundation of the American hegemony was collapsing: in mid-August 1971 Nixon refused to honour the gold bills of the dollar. This opened the way to a general crisis of the West, and in that Vietnam hardly counted, except as a symbol. The man who understood this was Henry Kissinger, who, for want of local solutions, looked for transcendental ones. Since the North Vietnamese were impossible, another dimension would have to be opened up on the board, and, here, geopolitics had its part to play. Kissinger had written an admiring book about Prince Metternich, the chief statesman of the post-Napoleonic period in Europe, when there had been forty years of peace, despite the emergence of international problems that were later on to cause great wars. He came to the White House with a formidable academic reputation, and he had qualities that made him dominant there. He had, in the first place, that central European accent that held lecture audiences spellbound. Hannah Arendt, who lectured in the style of the Metro-Goldwyn-Mayer lion, had the same trick, in her case of building castles of long words with an air of having something of vast importance to convey, which none of the audience afterwards could remember. Kissinger by contrast had content. There were, in post-Napoleonic Europe, problems that simply could not be solved on the ground. Of these, later on, Yugoslavia became the classic example, because it just broke up into unworkable fragments but at the same time could not be held together. Metternich knew when to haggle, when to browbeat, when to bore stiff, and it was a success. Kissinger – who was, after all, a refugee from a central Europe that had indeed produced all of the horrors and more that Metternich had foreseen – greatly admired him: the answer to insoluble problems was to internationalize them. That was what, over Vietnam, Nixon and Kissinger now tried to do. It was a huge face-saving device: America would get out. She did, and the fall of Saigon at the end of April 1975 was one of the subconscience-entering scenes of the post-war world, perhaps its greatest.

The hope was in détente. Stalin had conceded Italy and Greece in return for this and that, at Teheran or Yalta. Could another such bargain be struck? But this time round there was China as well. There was increasing trouble between these two Communist giants; it could be exploited. In 1967 Kosygin had visited Johnson, who noticed the obsession with China, and even Nixon wrote an article hinting that US relations with China might be improved. In March 1969 Soviet and Chinese forces clashed on the river Ussuri, over a border question, and Moscow asked Nixon to condemn the Chinese nuclear tests; there were hints at a nuclear strike to destroy the Chinese 'facilities'; and the Chinese were refusing the Russians the right to fly supplies to Vietnam or to use their airfields. The Chinese needed America against Russia. There was room, here, for clever-cleverness, and in April 1971 the world was surprised when an American table tennis team went to Peking. It was even more taken aback a year later, when Nixon followed, on 21 February 1972. Through de Gaulle, Ceauşescu and others, approaches were made, along with indications that Taiwan would be formally derecognized. The Sino-Soviet split was real enough, and the Chinese (themselves barely recovering from economic and cultural convulsions) were anxious to fend off a Soviet attack. Moscow had made plain enough what it would do to Communists who took their own 'path to socialism', which Peking ineffably had done. Kissinger travelled incognito to Peking in July 1971, and in mid-July Nixon told television that he had accepted an invitation there. In February 1972 he went, and met a Mao who had insisted on leaving his hospital bed. There was a bargain: China would be protected from Russia; Taiwan would be left alone but downgraded; the Chinese would cease to support the North Vietnamese.

Then came Moscow's turn, and the offer – suitably preceded by a bill to set up an anti-ballistic missile system – was of negotiations over 'strategic-arms' limitation, again handled by Kissinger by stealth. After news of the planned visit to Mao, in July 1971, the Soviet ambassador asked for Nixon to visit Moscow first, but he went in fact later, in May 1972. In September 1971 there was even an agreement about access to Berlin. Despite the various crises of the sixties, there were always US–Soviet discussions as to nuclear weaponry – disarmament. Cuba had frightened both sides (and everyone else) and there was a possibility that war might break out by accident over this or that difficult-to-manage international quarrel. In the Middle East there was one such crisis, the Arab–Israeli war of June 1967, when the clients of both sides came to an armed clash and the Israelis won a smashing victory. After Johnson and Leonid Brezhnev met in June 1967, a 'non-proliferation treaty' was concluded (July 1968) and this was supposed to stop the chief signatories from passing on nuclear secrets to countries without the bomb, while these countries also agreed not to take them. The chief idea was of course to prevent Germany (or China) from acquiring them. At the same time, negotiations began on the limitation of numbers of strategic arms – SALT (Strategic Arms Limitation Talks) – and were permanent after 1969, even the chief matter of US–Soviet relations, though they were held up now and again by political crises. When Nixon and Brezhnev met in Moscow in May 1972, a vast conference on security and disarmament was indeed agreed, but contrary to earlier Soviet ideas it was also to include the North Americans. Preparatory negotiations started in 1973, and led to the Conference on Security and Co-operation in Europe (CSCE), which assembled in Helsinki in 1975.

These went in tandem with the SALT. The Americans had proposed these in 1964, but the USSR showed serious interest only after Nixon became President in 1969, obviously with a programme of anti-Communism; by now they were greatly worried about China, and in November 1969 the negotiations began for two agreements – an ABM treaty limiting anti-ballistic missiles and a SALT treaty limiting offensive nuclear weaponry. The Soviets were overtaking the Americans in offensive weapons and their interest lay in limiting the Americans' superior defensive capacity (ABMs), which reduced the effectiveness of their ICBMs. With the US, the interest was the converse, since by 1972 the USSR had over 1,500 missiles to the United States' 1,054, and, with a first strike, could incapacitate the silos and completely destroy any nuclear balance between the two sides. In May 1972, with Nixon's visit to Moscow, the ABM and SALT I treaties were signed. There were to be two ABM bases only, with 100 launchers each, one to defend the capital (the 'Galosh' system around Moscow, maybe maintained against China) and one to contain the ICBMs. In fact the ABMs of the era were not effective, because their first explosion would block the Americans' own radar, and the treaty further stipulated that defensive weapons in space, with the use of lasers (where the Americans had a great advantage), would be banned. This greatly assisted the Soviets, the more so as, not subject to democratic controls, they could proceed anyway with secret tests.

There was a further problem, more important later on, in that the disposal of weaponry might include stuff that was obsolete and was anyway due for the junkyard (a ruse used by the Americans when they solemnly withdrew Jupiter missiles from Turkey in the outcome of the Cuban crisis). Besides, what was to happen with inspection, to make sure that the agreements were being kept? This invited trouble, especially on the Soviet side, where there was a mania for secrecy that even divided the Soviet negotiating team: their military refused to divulge information to the civilians, and would only do so to the US military. They now refused any inspection rights, such that satellites would have to be used, and these could not spot concealed weapons on land. In Washington these treaties, whatever their defects, were desired because they led to 'stability', then a much prized commodity. The SALT I treaty was a provisional agreement for five years, to keep things at the then level, and affected intercontinental ballistic missiles with a range of over 5,500 kilometres and submarine-based missiles. Bombers, in which the Americans had a considerable advantage, were not affected. The treaty allowed the USSR 1,620 ICBMs and 950 submarine-launched ballistic missiles, and the USA 1,054 and 710 respectively. But it was quite limited – MIRVs (multiple independently targeted re-entry vehicles) were unmentioned, and so were Cruise missiles, which the Americans put into service the following year, weapons with a precision that altered nuclear warfare. The Soviets continued to have the more powerful warheads (one megaton or more, whereas the Americans had a few hundred kilotons) but there was a mathematical formula for the effect of an explosion, which varied according to the negative cube of distance but only according to the square of the power. Qualitative, not quantitative, matters then began to count.

But the value of the treaties was essentially political. It was translated into a high-sounding document about peaceful coexistence and mutual respect, which amounted to a declaration that the USA recognized the USSR as a legitimate and equal partner, and not as a bandit state. The same Moscow 'summit' not only agreed the establishment of the CSCE, but also a conference on MBFR (Mutual and Balanced Force Reductions on the conventional-weaponry side). There was even a commercial counterpart, a commission assembling for the first time in Moscow, with an agreement as to the sale of American grain, and in 1975, following an agreement on space, two manned spacecraft solemnly met up. The grain trade opened the way for bank credit and sales of factories or technology, and in the 1970s the Eastern bloc developed quite quickly because of Western credits (though, much to the fury of the Soviets, the USSR was denied most-favoured-nation status by the Jackson Amendment, which made this dependent upon free emigration of Jews: the effect was to multiply the administrative side, customs and insurance, of US–Soviet commercial exchanges).

The apogee of this period was reached with Brezhnev's journey to the USA, on 22 June 1973, when another high-sounding declaration was made, at Soviet insistence, that there would be co-operation to ensure that the two sides would collaborate if there were any danger of a nuclear war. Some Europeans saw this as a step towards US–Soviet condominium.

When Kissinger went to Moscow in September 1972 he laid out the programme – Helsinki on European security (i.e. borders, etc.) in November, Vienna on reciprocal conventional disarmament (MBFR) the following January. The Helsinki negotiations led to a conference of foreign ministers in July 1973, and to the CSCE in July 1975, also at Helsinki. There were of course various hidden concerns on both sides, and since Congress at the time was very close to desiring absolute withdrawal from Vietnam (Senator Mansfeld's amendment to that effect was rejected only by two votes in 1973), the Americans were operating under considerable pressure from public opinion – perhaps the worst side-effect of Vietnam being its effects on that. At any rate, the attempt to appeal to Moscow did lead to just the attempt at a huge conference that the Soviet side had been wanting since 1954. This also set up a machinery for détente, with bureaucracies on both sides that came, increasingly, to adopt a mutual understanding which meant, in 1990, that there was no real revolution against Communism: the intelligent Communists sacrificed the stupid ones, and remade their own careers very profitably, contacts intact.

The meeting of foreign ministers that initiated the CSCE in Europe assembled in Helsinki on 3 July 1973 (the experts met in Geneva). There were three great topics to be discussed – 'baskets', as they were called – the third being in effect human rights, i.e. free circulation of ideas and people, the other two concerning politics and economics. In April 1974 the West made an essential concession, official recognition of the borders of 1945, and the Americans were apparently happy enough to dispose of subjects that were uncomfortable for the Soviets, because they were proceeding with the beginnings of SALT II. The Europeans preferred to let the negotiations last, over the 'third basket' (at French insistence), and in any case the Americans had to bear in mind their own eastern European constituency, at times incandescent.

Nixon's successor, Gerald Ford, suddenly took up the 'third basket', no doubt as compensation for what had happened over the 'first', political one. In the event, differences between the USA, France and Germany, each of which had its own emphasis, were resolved, the French having pushed the 'third basket' because they wanted to give satellite governments a lever to prise open the 'Iron Curtain' as and when they wanted to, and the Germans, less concerned with this, concerned to avoid having borders defined as 'intangible' as distinct from 'inviolable'. At the turn of July/August 1975 thirty-three heads of state (Europeans, with the USA, Canada, the USSR) signed the 'Final Act' of the CSCE – recognition of borders, certain precautionary measures in military affairs, promotion of trade, free circulation of people and ideas. It was a considerable success for the USSR, which had wanted reognition of borders since Potsdam, and Brezhnev told the Politburo that it had needed 'thirty years of colossal efforts' to reach that point. Besides, there had been a Soviet condition as regards free circulation of people and ideas, that this would have to reflect 'national legislation'. The Soviets had wanted to establish a permanent 'organ' for the CSCE, which of course might have established them as part of a security structure, as distinct from NATO, but the West managed to substitute, simply, permanent arrangements for conferences (to which Brezhnev proposed, in 1977, various additions as regards ecology, energy, transport). The CSCE had been part of a strategy to draw western Europe towards Moscow.

Georges-Henri Soutou poses the question as to whether recognition of 'human rights' mattered more, in the longer term, than the recognition of borders, and of the legitimacy of Communist rule in eastern Europe. It is a good question. As regards 'human rights' – a clumsy Atlantic, bureaucratic rendering of the French 'Rights of Man' – the Soviets were indeed, for a time, embarrassed. But then they hit on a useful device: there were blemishes, and more than that, on the Western side. If the fate of a dissident Yuri Orlov or Leonid Plyushch were mentioned, the Soviet representatives could wax indignant as to the rights of women in Micronesia. How were such matters to be covered? What Vladimir Bukovsky calls *une bureaucratie droits-de-l'hommarde* grew up, and could easily be used against the interests of the West, or even to break up countries such as Turkey. And the KGB knew how to manage 'dissidence', to use it, even in the 'satellite countries'. One writer-martyr, Andrey Sinyavsky, turned out to be one of its agents.

This clever-clever management of world affairs because of the Vietnam problem was not rewarded with forbearance on the part of the North. Between Kissinger's journeys to Peking and Moscow, the North Vietnamese attacked (spring 1972). There were now very few American troops on the ground, and the South Vietnamese were exhibiting all the signs of rout. This began in March and went on until June with attacks from Laos and Cambodia as well as North Vietnam, and there was fierce fighting in the Mekong Delta. By now there were only 10,000 US combat troops present (400,000 had been taken out) and the ARVN had superior numbers, but the forces were mismanaged in defensive positions without reserves and refugees clogged the roads. Without the B52s there might have been collapse (Pleiku-Kontum). Nixon began to think only of great air strikes in the North at last and secretly approached Brezhnev, who wanted a 'summit' on arms control. Kissinger did not even tell the ambassador. Nixon was widely condemned, but Moscow went ahead with the Brezhnev meeting and Dmitri Simes, there on the Soviet side, said that Nixon handled the meeting perfectly, not 'moralizing' as Carter was later to do.

Bombing seemed to be the only way to save South Vietnam, and Nixon, in the face of much opposition within the Cabinet, went ahead to mine Haiphong and bomb the supply depots and railways. He was now rewarded for his efforts over Vietnam. Perhaps Chinese pressure meant that the North made a serious move for peace; in any event, Hue had not fallen and by mid-September 1972 Quang Tri had been retaken. A presidential election was due in the United States, and Nixon sent a message via Andrey Gromyko, the Soviet minister of foreign affairs, that after the election he would go much further in attacking the North. On 8 October Kissinger reported from Paris that there had been a great shift: the North were at last seriously talking peace. Nixon celebrated with Lafite-Rothschild but matters then dragged on because the proposal did not suit the South Vietnamese leader, Thieu, at all: he could see that if troops were left as they were on the ground (the proposal for ceasefire) then Saigon was under great pressure. In the event he had to be threatened by Nixon with complete abandonment before he gave way, and the North also prevaricated. Kissinger was infuriated and called its team 'tawdry, filthy shits'. Nixon then sent in waves of B52s against the Hanoi–Haiphong area from 18 to 30 December, dropped 40,000 tons of bombs, and received an appalling press, the ineffable little Kennedy saying it should 'outrage the conscience of all Americans'. Congress moved to cut off funds. In reality the bombing had not been marked by much 'collateral damage': the bombs were (as the Soviet experts noted) of a new and 'smart' kind and the military installations were indeed hit. This sufficed: on 9 January 1973 Le Duc Tho accepted the conditions proposed in November. Thieu himself was obstinate – the agreement was not at all favourable to him, as it left the North in a position to strike at will – but Nixon, both threatening the end of all aid, but also promising a bombing campaign if the North Vietnamese broke the truce, overruled him, with a deadline of 20 January 1973 (his own inauguration) for the ending of the war. This finally caused the North Vietnamese to appreciate that they would have to wait for final victory, and on 27 January 1973 the agreement was at last signed. It left a messy situation on the ground, half war, half peace, and Thieu used it to clear the Delta, while the Vietcong moved heavy weaponry through jungle roads and developed an ultra-modern radio network.

In these same weeks Nixon secured a landslide electoral victory, almost as great as Johnson's. He was handed it easily enough. This was partly because – an admiring biographer, Jonathan Aitken, does not quite see how devastating this was – he had procured short-term growth, prosperity and even tax cuts by coin-clipping the dollar itself. But in any event the Democrats, true to form for the Vietnam opposition, made fools of themselves, reconstructing their party statutes on lines that allowed any fringe grievance-struck group a say, conducting their affairs childishly in public, and finally putting forward the classic loser candidate. At the heart of matters was a vast change in American politics symbolized by the Southern Democrats and the switch of old Republicans in the north-east: there were new coalitions at work. Nixon's 'silent majority' speech of November 1969 had it right: there was indeed an almost unnoticed America that was very far from sharing the concerns that made the headlines, and they voted for Nixon.

However, this did not matter, as by now in Washington there was what, later, in England, was called 'a media feeding frenzy'. A sort of civil war developed in the USA, Nixon being in some quarters hated (with, even twenty years later, an Oliver Stone film to perpetuate the black legend). The administration's own men could not be trusted, and in June 1971 the *New York Times* had started to serialize the 'Pentagon Papers', a huge collection of government documents, studies commissioned by McNamara in 1967, and 'leaked' by a one-time McNamara recruit from Harvard (Daniel Ellsberg: he had been at King's, Cambridge, moved on to Harvard, and even served in Vietnam – precisely the McNamara sort until he had his moment of truth against the war). The studies were not binding, merely indicating how the administration thought, but the overall effect was to make Nixon conclude that 'the media' were against him and he was extraordinarily clumsy and brutal in his underhand dealings. Ben Bradlee of the *Washington Post* had been the object of gruesome flattery; now the Nixon machine went into clumsy reverse. He ordered wire-taps on thirteen telephones of his own officials. He did not trust his people, including Kissinger, and had every word recorded that was spoken in the White House. Kissinger was furious about the Ellsberg leak, and absurd prosecutions followed; newspapers were not just frontally attacked in this way, but were also surreptitiously harassed over television licence renewals and the like. Kissinger, similarly, devised foreign policy without letting the State Department know what he was doing, or even, as regards Moscow, telling the US ambassador.

For the re-election of 1972–3 Nixon's war chest was flowing over in contributions, hundreds of thousands of dollars in safes. These could be handed out in generous bundles, and in the middle of a triumphal campaign Nixon hardly noticed at all what his lowest subordinates were doing: in this case a break-in to the Democrat headquarters in the Watergate Building on 17 June 1972. Nixon had been extraordinarily vindictive about the anti-war liberals – 'We'll get them on the ground where we want them and we'll stick our heels in, step on them hard and twist' – and he tried very hard indeed to destroy Ellsberg: even a special small team called 'the plumbers' (one of the White House security officers had a mother who wrote to him proudly that his grandfather, a plumber, would have been so pleased at his rise) was set up to find out what could be discovered from his psychiatric records. A list of enemies was drawn up, including Gregory Peck and the president of Harvard, and the telephone recordings whirred away. In the event, Nixon tried to weasel out of his ultimate responsibility, was caught up in a network of blackmail and blustering, and was eventually impeached by a Congress that had always had a Democrat majority. Not long after the Vietnam peace, he too was out, succeeded by a nonentity, Gerald Ford, who had not even been Vice-President, but who had to step in because the Vice-President had been caught in assorted illegalities as well.

14

Unravelling

The course of the Vietnam War worried the Europeans: did it mean that the Americans had given them up? Germany was now a fat target, but lacking her own nuclear weapon, and the Berlin crisis in 1961 had shown that the Americans were not anxious to move, whatever Kennedy said. Why, anyway, should the USA risk the obliteration of Chicago for a West Berlin of which American bombers had already made a considerable mess? In any case, the USA very obviously did not mean to let West Germany have a finger on any nuclear trigger, and the arms control proposals put to Moscow in spring 1962 amounted in effect to joint American–Soviet control, with only face-saving clauses for the NATO allies. Was this a moment for united Europe to assert itself? It had recovered from the war, and the Common Market was proving to be a great success. The old European world, with great numbers of peasant farmers, was rapidly going, and the towns boomed through hard-working rural migrants – a sure-fire formula for success in all economies except the Communist ones. Prosperity of an American sort proliferated – more cars, domestic tools, holidays in the sun. But what did it all signify?

In the immediate post-war decades, civilization was still defined by Europe. British and French writers and restaurants, Italian filmmakers, the Vienna Staatsoper dominated the stage. The great universities of Europe were still vastly attractive to foreigners, who learned French or German as a matter of course; American graduate students came to Cambridge to take an undergraduate degree and American academics, visiting European institutions with their families, found that their children, at school, were a year or two behind. True, this cultural Europe did not extend into mass culture, which had been Americanized, and was to become ever more strongly so. As to this there was resentment. At this stage the Germans were in no mood to contest the American empire politically, but, especially in the Catholic south, they resisted the cultural side-effects and despite the best efforts of a would-be democratizing occupation education expert, one Zink, they had been able to retain the old divisions in education, as between academic and technical. If you opened a German newspaper, you were going to be instructed. The various German states competed with each other in cultural matters, and supported outstanding museums or opera houses; Wagner's Bayreuth returned to the world's stage, with command performances on traditional lines from Birgit Nielsen or Hans Hotter, and the Austrians, even more conservative, maintained the standards of the Vienna Opera or the Salzburg Festival, where Karl Böhm and Herbert von Karajan drew audiences from around the world; the Wiener Philharmoniker still excluded women. That world resisted Americanization, but Americanization was very difficult to resist.

It affected language. The bestselling weekly journal in Germany was *Der Spiegel*, which had been set up in British-occupied Hamburg after the war, with advice from the British (along with the left-liberal *Die Zeit*, modelled on the *Observer* in London, owned and run by David Astor). It did not express itself in the standard German literary style, lengthy verbs-at-the-end-sentences and all: it aimed for English brevity, and in time *Spiegeldeutsch* was such that the magazine could only be understood if you knew American English quite well. There was a bestselling book in France at this time, Étiemble's *Parlez-vous franglais?* It is a long book, giving many examples of the corruption of French, not just by Anglo-American words, but even by Anglo-American usages – for instance, the translation of the World Bank's formal title to include *développement*, whereas *mise en valeur* gives a better understanding of the English original. There was some justice in the French campaign. After all, up until very recent times French had indeed been a dominant language, and when de Gaulle appeared at a state visit in London in 1962, and was accompanied by the Comédie-Française and the great Racine actress and director

Marie Bell, the London theatre was enthusiastically full up for her productions of *Bérénice* and *Britannicus*, austere alexandrines in a language that, today, even most of the French would find testing. As it happened, Étiemble (who was of peasant origin) had spent seven years in Chicago and had hated much about it. A French West Indian academic colleague had come to see him at home, and the landlord had nearly thrown him out; he remarks, of 'the American way of not living', 'how can you not deplore the great sexual misery of a people with frigid, obsessive, puritanical and bossy women for whom the men stupifiedly kill themselves with work and alcohol?' and asks what might be done with 'the infantile cuisine to which the Yankees are reduced and which they take such joy in'. He adds that he would never be attracted by a woman wearing jeans. Étiemble (who lived to an immense age) had no illusions as to what might be done: he recognized that French writers were simply not as interesting as they had been even in the recent past, when French theatre had had worldwide resonance, and he would soon have had to admit as well that the great French cinema was producing mainly clichés. Such campaigns were all too easy to ridicule. At least Luther in the sixteenth century had been robust and not long-winded, but in the 1880s there had been an absurdly pompous effort to prevent words such as 'telephone' entering the German language directly: 'far-speaker' (*Fernsprecher*) was substituted, and 'round-spark' (*Rundfunk*) for 'radio' (an even more absurd Croat effort to avoid that word came up with *krugoval*, 'round-spark' in South Slavonic). This was a hopeless business, and Étiemble had the humiliation of seeing ambitious Frenchmen and Frenchwomen of a sort he detested make the standard trot to Harvard or Stanford business school, there to be deracinated into unmemorable miniature Jean Monnets.

There was another famous French book at this time, another of those silly-clever sixties bestsellers, Jean-Jacques Servan-Schreiber's *Le Défi américain*. He, in a later work, suffered from strange notions, that, to stop Indian textiles from competing with their own, the British in India had cut off the little fingers of Hindu girls' hands. However, the earlier title made at length the point that the Americans were buying up Europe: multinationals such as IBM were moving in; they were taking advantage of cheap labour, and yet by setting up in France they could duck under the French protectionist walls and thereby keep French industry from developing. However, they could do this because they could quite literally just print off dollars on paper which everyone else had to accept as if it were real gold. As had been feared from the start of the new system devised at Bretton Woods, in 1944, American paper money was international legal tender because two thirds of trade was conducted with the dollar (the pound sterling accounting for most of the remainder). In theory it could be converted into gold, at the famous formula of $35 per ounce, but even in 1960 the American gold reserve at Fort Knox was less in value than the number of dollars kept abroad and especially in Europe. What was to stop the Americans from just printing pieces of paper and buying up Europe? This was a fraudulent point, because the same system, triumphantly and perhaps perversely in the case of the British, enabled Europeans to invest in the USA. 'S-S', as he was called (he produced a would-be French version of *Time* magazine, became an internet-is-the-answer bore, and had his children brought up in Pittsburgh, generally at the business school), also failed to notice that French industry, far from languishing, was doing better than it had done since the 1890s, when the arrival of electrical energy had enabled it to bypass the coal in which France was poor. Quite soon France was going to overtake England, for the first time since the French Revolution itself.

All of this allowed de Gaulle to appear as a world statesman, to put France back on the map. Now, he, many Frenchmen and many Europeans in general resented the American domination. There was not just the unreliability, the way in which the USA, every four years, became paralysed by a prospective presidential election. France's defence was largely dependent upon the USA, and, here, there were fears in Paris and Bonn. They did not find Washington easy. The more the Americans became bogged down in Vietnam, the more there was head-shaking in Europe. They alone had the nuclear capacity to stop a Russian advance, but the Berlin crisis had already shown that the Americans' willingness to come to Germany's defence was quite limited, and they had not even stood up for their own treaty rights. Now, in 1964, they were involved in a guerrilla war in south-east Asia and were demonstrably making a mess of it: would Europe have any priority? Perhaps, if West Germany had been allowed to have nuclear weaponry, the Europeans could have built up a real deterrent of their own, but that was hardly in anyone's mind. The bomb was to be Anglo-American.

At the turn of 1962–3 the British Prime Minister, Harold Macmillan, had met Kennedy (at Nassau) and agreed to depend upon a little American technology on condition that the French got even less. There would be no Franco-British nuclear link and as far as de Gaulle was concerned, France would have to make her own way forward. He got his own back. The Americans were trying to manoeuvre Great Britain into the EEC, and, conscious now of their comparative decline, the British reluctantly agreed to be manoeuvred. At a press conference in January 1963, de Gaulle showed them the door. Europe was to be a Franco-German affair, and de Gaulle was its leader. France could not go alone. If she had seriously to offer a way forward between the world powers, she had to have allies, and Germany was the obvious candidate. Adenauer, too, needed the votes of what, in a more robust age, had been called 'the brutal rurals', and the Common Agricultural Policy bribed them. In return for protection and price support, they would vote for Adenauer, even if they only had some small plot that they worked at weekends.

France, with a seat on the Security Council and the capacity to make trouble for the USA with the dollar and much else, mattered; the Communists were a useful tool, and they were told not to destabilize de Gaulle. He was being helpful to Moscow. In the first instance, starting in 1964, the French had made problems as regards support for the dollar. They built up gold reserves, and then sold dollars for more gold, on the grounds that the dollar was just paper, and inflationary paper at that. There was of course more to it, in that there was no financial centre in France to rival that of London, and the French lost because they had to use London for financial transactions; by 1966 they were formally refusing to support the dollar any more, and this (an equivalent of French behaviour in the early stages of the great Slump of 1929–32) was a pillar knocked from under the entire Atlantic financial system.

De Gaulle had persuaded himself that the Sino-Soviet split would make the USSR more amenable, that it might even become once more France's ideal eastern partner. There were also signs, he could see, of a new independence in eastern Europe. The new Romanian leader, Ceaușescu, looked with envy on next-door Tito, cultivated and admired by everybody. Romania had been set up by France a century before, and French had been the second, or even, for the upper classes, the first language until recently. Now, de Gaulle took up links with her, and also revisited a Poland that he had not seen since 1920, as a young officer. In March 1966 he announced that France would leave the NATO joint command structure, and the body's headquarters were shifted to Brussels, among much irritation at French ingratitude. In June the General visited the USSR itself, and unfolded his schemes to Brezhnev: there should be a new European security system, a nuclear France and a nuclear USSR in partnership, the Americans removed, and a French-dominated Europe balancing between the two sides. He had already made sure of Europe's not having an American component, in that he had vetoed British membership of the Community. Now he would try to persuade Brezhnev that the time had come to get rid of East Germany, to loosen the iron bonds that kept the satellite countries tied to Moscow, and to prepare for serious change in the post-war arrangements. Brezhnev was not particularly interested, and certainly not in the disappearance of East Germany; in any case, although France was unquestionably of interest, it was West Germany that chiefly concerned Moscow, and there were constant problems over Berlin. De Gaulle was useful because, as Brezhnev said, 'thanks to him we have made a breach, without the slightest risk, in American capitalism. De Gaulle is of course an enemy, we know, and the French Party, narrow-minded and seeing only its own interests, has been trying to work us up against him. But look at what we have achieved: the American position in Europe has been weakened, and we have not finished yet.'

Europeans, and Germans especially, had built up a trade surplus, storing their dollars as reserves; they, this time mainly British, had also invested in the USA. What would happen if their holdings of dollars were so large that they outnumbered the Americans' own reserves?

And then they sold, as de Gaulle was to do? There was a free market in gold, partly in London, and the Swiss were also not bound by the rules. What would happen if dollars were sold for gold, at a price different from the official one? It would weaken the dollar, make it unstable, and less useful as the medium for world trade, upon which the prosperity of the Western world depended. And if the producers of oil especially, but also other essential raw materials, realized that their dollars were just paper, would they not react by raising their prices? In the sixties there were moments of trouble, as dollars built up in private hands, and the dollar's junior partner, the pound sterling, looked weaker and weaker as the British economy lagged behind the German and then the French.

However, there were still too many important interests involved in the existing system for it to be easily abandoned. In the very first place there was defence – largely American, but with a not insignificant British contribution, whether in central Europe or 'east of Suez', where a British presence guaranteed important areas in the Arabian penin-sula and South-East Asia. The drain of dollars and pounds was partly accounted for by the military spending that went on abroad, a prob-lem that the Germans themselves did not now have to face. One answer to the particular difficulties of the dollar might have been just to increase the value of the Mark, to take account of the Germans' export surplus. There was resistance in Germany, where the Bundes-bank and exporters feared what might happen if exports became more expensive, though with much heaving and puffing, small increases (revaluations) of the Mark were agreed in 1961 and at the end of the decade. Meanwhile, if speculators sold dollars, Germans bought them up at the fixed and increasingly artificial price. This did not address the fundamental problem, that more and more dollars were held outside the system, and the problem kept coming back. In the early 1970s, the dry and technical debates of ten, or even twenty-five, years before sud-denly took on a hectic life. There always was a central problem, that the dollar was in the end just paper, and would appear to be such if the Americans produced too much of it. That was what happened. Viet-nam had to be paid for, but so also did the expense of Johnson's vast public spending programme.

Nixon, though supported, electorally, by opponents or at least critics of Johnson's spending, carried on with and for that matter increased
it: when a new chairman of the Federal Reserve System was introduced in July 1970, Nixon said he wanted 'low interest rates and
more money ... I have very strong views and ... hope that he will
independently conclude that my views are the right ones.' Whether he
did or did not, he allowed Nixon to continue the Johnson programmes
and to expand them. The result was a rising budget deficit and a rising
national debt.

The national debt had reached $271bn in 1946. It fell in propor-
tion to the GNP until 1965 and then boomed. Under Johnson deficit
financing became the rule, and in 1968 his Treasury Secretary, Henry
Fowler, protested because of the strain for the dollar. A successor, John
Connally, dismissed arguments of this sort: the dollar is our currency
and it's their problem. The Great Society programmes were greedy,
and by 1975 federal spending had reached $332bn, the deficit being
$53.2bn. By then, federal spending had reached almost 25 per cent of
gross domestic product (in 1950, it had been 16 per cent). The dollar
had a tenfold inflation after 1956. At the time the sixties economists
were still confident enough of their ideas and in any case the Western
world's most prosperous elements almost had to support the dollar,
and so the deficits marched on and there were regular meetings of
international experts to supply funds with which to buy up the excess
dollars. Wise heads shook, though they shook in the wrong direction,
absurdly conjuring up a 'liquidity crisis', and deflation, in which they
were quite wrong, because the problem was that there was a glut of
money, and an inflation that rocked the entire system. At any rate,
tinkering happened. A G10 group of the industrial nations was formed
to defend the dollar (and a Basle one for the pound) and they could
lend to the IMF, which allowed special drawing rights of immediate
credit to defend a currency under threat. The IMF thereby, at last,
acquired a role. NATO members were encouraged to spend dollars in
the USA and to deposit cash there; American citizens were forbidden
to own gold coins (1965) and the GATT round of 1958–62 even
allowed countries with threatened currencies to impose an import
surcharge of 10 per cent (as happened with the British in 1961 and

1964). American visas were made easier, to encourage tourism in the USA; Germany and Switzerland refused to pay interest on foreign bank holdings (though that was very difficult to arrange and anyway only encouraged countries such as Luxemburg to take them instead). It was all small beer in comparison with the two great problems – the German surplus and US government spending, with a deficit in 1971 of $10bn.

The dollar itself was badly weakened by all of this, and after making constant noises, with suggestions that a form of the old gold standard might be reintroduced, in 1966 de Gaulle stated that the French bank would henceforth want gold instead. This was not just anti-Americanism. At the time, Paris did not much count as a financial centre, so this was easier for France to do than for, say, London, where credit functioned more efficiently (the French banks had been nationalized in 1945). But the pound itself came under constant pressure in the 1960s as speculators based in Switzerland appreciated that it was overvalued, while British spending overseas (partly for military purposes) put it under strain. In the autumn of 1967 there was a threat that the Suez Canal would be closed and therefore unusable for British oil imports. At the existing rate, the British could not exchange harder currencies without seeing their reserves wiped out and the pound was at last devalued, from $2.80 to $2.40. That shifted pressure onto the dollar, and the oil producers sat up.

The Germans also had their reasons for complaint. The Bundesbank had as a primary aim the control of inflation. One cause of that would be an inflow of dollars, swapped for Marks. The exporters liked their undervalued Mark; the savers, as represented by the Bundesbank, their stable currency. The temper of international meetings as to the future became acrimonious and everyone blamed everyone else – Americans, Germans for saving too much; Germans, British and Americans for not saving enough; Swiss, the others for having crooked tax systems; the others, the Swiss, for receiving stolen goods. Japan was now emerging as a large and fast-growing economy, and she like Germany saved: there was not, as in the Anglo-Saxon countries, the sort of consumer boom that sucked in imports. In 1970 there was a brief respite, as the British and Americans balanced their budgets, but the tidal-wave overhang of paper dollars was too great, and was being added to with every breath that Americans took.

Bad news from Vietnam no doubt did not help, but in 1971 a great inflow of dollars into Switzerland, Germany and Holland occurred. The German government decided it would have to float (followed by the Dutch) in order to make Marks more expensive for the speculators. There were rumours that other governments, including even the British, would buy gold at the now giveaway price of $35 per ounce. Fort Knox would be drained dry. What would Nixon do? He retired to Camp David with his advisers and announced, on 15 August 1971, at the end of the weekend, that the dollar's formal gold link was ended. He even imposed a 10 per cent import charge, and did not even tell the IMF what he was doing. Maybe he did not even know himself. But this was the end of the Bretton Woods system. It was also the end of much else.

One of the bases of Western prosperity after 1947 had been cheap oil. It cost a dollar a barrel in the early fifties and then crept up to two. Transport in the past had been one of the great obstacles to progress, since horses ate 26 pounds of grain every day, and were frequently sick as well as temperamental; wooden wheels needed constant maintenance (hence in all countries 'Wheeler', 'Raeder', 'Charron' is a common surname) and roads were maintained by convict gangs or serf (*corvée*) labour. The internal-combustion engine, using very cheap petrol, was revolutionary, and even before the First World War the cities of the West knew all too well the meaning of 'traffic jam'. In the 1950s the ownership of cars spread, and, with international competition, they became cheaper. The Volkswagen was the symbol of Germany's economic recovery, quite soon putting even the great British makers almost out of business. Cheap transport of course allowed manufacturers to drop their costs, at least relative to other goods, and at the same time allowed ordinary consumers to spend on something else the money that they saved on travel. Besides, an automobile industry was very productive of other jobs – maintenance, spare parts, garages, roadside restaurants and hairdressers, and on and on.

The Americans had a very strong hand as regards oil. In the first place, their own reserves were very large. If any effort had been made to put up the world price the Americans would just flood the markets and bring the price down. Then again, oil technology was expensive and very demanding; there was a large investment to be made, and there had to be excellent teamwork, with first-rate management, itself of course expensive, and the Anglo-Americans in that respect were irreplaceable. Just how vital such things were was shown in the 1930s. Mexico had oil; she acquired a revolutionary government that was hostile to the USA. It nationalized oil, offering insultingly low compensation to the American owners. Nationalized oil did not thrive. Men were appointed for political reasons, the state invested in misguided and sometimes corrupt ways, and the labour union was spoiled – too many employees, paid too much. The result was that Mexican oil could not easily compete on the world markets, and the employees (inflation having taken its cull of real value) ended up worse off than they had been before nationalization. The example taught Venezuela (for now), the other great Latin American producer, to behave more prudently: the State, there, took just a fifty-fifty share of the profits. In the Middle East, local rulers were persuaded without much difficulty that they should co-operate with British and American oil firms – in Iran, a nationalist who sought more, Mohammad Mossadegh, was expelled by a coup in which the Shah co-operated with the British and the CIA; Anglo-Iranian thereafter held 40 per cent of the oil, and in Saudi Arabia there were no problems at all, as oil installations spread over the desert, and local rulers who had started off with camels and tents suddenly found themselves rich.

In the later 1950s oil entered a new era. The supply grew from 8.7 million barrels per day in 1948 to 42 million in 1972. American output almost doubled (to 9.2 million barrels) but its share fell from two thirds to one fifth, whereas Middle East output rose from a million barrels to 20 million. Known oil reserves showed the same pattern – the American share falling from one third to 10 per cent (38 million barrels, to the Middle East's 367 million). The Shah became greedy, and wanted Iran to be a 'great power'. An ambitious Italian proved willing to take only 25 per cent of the profit, whereas the Anglo-American share had been 50 per cent (the 'seven sisters' were Exxon, Chevron, Mobil and Texaco, with the British Gulf, BP and Royal

Dutch-Shell). The Japanese also indicated to Saudi Arabia that they would take less than half (though defining 'profit' after various expenses was not easy). In 1958 Nasser at least in theory united Egypt and Syria, thus controlling the Suez and Mediterranean pipeline routes for oil; and that year there was a coup in Iraq, when the king was overthrown and his prime minister was lynched, his body hauled through the streets of Baghdad and flattened to a pulp as a car was driven back and forth over it. Arabs began now to talk about what they might do to expand their control, and use it against Israel. At that point, an angry Venezuelan took a hand. He had been embittered by American support for an army dictatorship, had spent years of impoverished exile, and had finally left the USA for Mexico because he did not want his children to be Americanized. In 1959, in charge of oil, he had asked the Americans for preferential treatment: Venezuelan oil cost much more to produce than Middle Eastern oil (80 cents per barrel to 25) but it had a strategic location. This time, the Americans refused – they were protecting their own, and anyway gave preferential treatment to Canada and Mexico. The Venezuelan then went to the Middle East and discovered that the Saudi expert had done his training in Texas, and had been taken for a Mexican and sometimes refused entrance to hotels. At the time, oil prices were naturally falling, as supply grew. The companies had been absorbing the trouble out of their own profits, and not passing any of the load back to the states, through lessened royalties. At this point the USSR entered the field, doubling oil production in the later fifties and displacing Venezuela as second-largest oil producer. Soviet oil was also cheap – at Odessa, one half the Middle Eastern price. The oil companies now said that the states should take some of the load, or allow cutbacks in volume. There was much rage: when Standard Oil high-handedly announced a price cut, Venezuela took up an alliance with the Saudis; the Shah sympathized; and the Iraqis, though they were rivals of Nasser's Egypt, also came in. In 1960 OPEC was set up, the 'Organization of Petroleum Exporting Countries'. The five founding members controlled 80 per cent of crude oil exports.

Sixties prosperity in the West nevertheless went ahead, and oil became cheaper and cheaper – by 36 cents per barrel. From 1960 to

1969 the price fell by one fifth, or, in value, two fifths, because of general inflation in the decade. This was because supply, and variety, greatly increased. There was now a large Algerian field, which the French, when recognizing that country's independence at Evian in 1962, cornered. Libya turned out to have reserves of high-quality oil that could easily be converted for aircraft and for low-sulphur-content crude oil which suited the now emerging 'green' concerns. Libya by 1965 had become the sixth-largest exporter, producing over 3 million barrels per day in 1970. Meanwhile, American policy was in disarray: the companies could probably not cut back production without infringing anti-trust laws, and the government behaved bewilderingly, preventing tankers from importing oil but allowing trucks to do so. The tankers therefore arrived and deposited the oil in trucks, which went over the border and then turned back again over it, to avoid tariffs. This decisively discouraged oil prospecting. The system of protection depended upon oil companies each adhering to a limited quota, as regulated by the government, and such quotas belonged only in a world of potential oil glut. That world had gone.

But the Western world, America in the lead, deserved such misman-agement, because it was becoming extraordinarily self-indulgent – in Shakespeare's words, like rats that ravin down their proper bane ('and so we drink, we die'). From 1948 to 1972 American consumption trebled, to 16.4 million barrels every day. In western Europe it went up fifteen times, to 14.1 million and in Japan to 4.4 million. Housing was put up with hardly a concern for fuel economy: centrally heated, air conditioned and above all dependent on motor cars – of which the USA was the prime example, the 45 million of 1949 becoming the 119 million of 1972. There was also a new petrochemicals industry, which produced plastics of ever greater sophistication (coal had been at the start of this: in the 1890s, a great Belgian industrialist, Ernest Solvay, had made his fortune by using by-products of coal to produce the first plastic, Bakelite, named after its Belgian-born inventor, Leo H. Baekeland). There was a proliferation of gigantic-scale technology, producing larger jet aircraft and ever larger tankers; petrol stations and motels multiplied, turning more and more of the Western world into a huge version of the 'ribbon development', the bland snaking of ugly roadsides, of which Orwell had complained in the later 1930s. In *Coming Up for Air* (1938) he had even foresaw the advertising techniques for junk food – in this case fish sausage, eaten by a smug Brylcreemed man on a large hoarding. The fish sausage more or less predicted McDonald's.

It had an indestructible relationship with motor cars; in 1948, in California, two brothers found that food could be produced by the same very simplified assembly line methods that had given the American war economy such triumphs, and after 1954 'fast food' took off. This had feedback effects on agriculture, as cows could now be bred that grew more meat more quickly per hoof – the tower block of beef. Puritans complained that Americans were becoming obese – sitting in motor cars, eating fatty fast food, and then sitting in front of televisions. The Eisenhower years saw a great burst of motorway construction, beginning with the Los Angeles Freeway in 1947; in 1956 came the funding for an interstate network, and the claim was made, with perverse pride, that the concrete involved would have produced eighty enormous dams.

There was a further problem for energy consumption, with the emergence of Japan as a great economy. By 1960, Japan – where firewood had been more important than oil – had become a major consumer; it went together with an extraordinary exporting drive, with the economy growing at over 10 per cent per annum. In 1955 the Japanese had made 70,000 cars, but in 1968 the figure was 4.1 million. Huge Japanese tankers, of 300,000 tons, were now being built. There was an alarm in 1967, at the time of the Six Day War between Israel and Egypt, but at the time the Arab countries were desperate for oil money and attempts at an oil embargo on the West failed; in any case, the Shah, now obsequiously courted by the Americans, would not join it, and rivalries between the various producer states meant that no serious co-operation was possible. Still, the hourglass was running out; and one sign that the West would be badly caught out occurred in 1971, when the British withdrew their forces from the Gulf. This saved a small sum – $20m – and opened up Kuwait, especially, to threats from neighbours. It was – with severe competition – the silliest decision made by a British government of that era.

Various other factors came into play. The first was the weirdness of American policy. Oil had been protected against cheap imports, because it was a strategic commodity, and under Harold Ickes there had been sensible regulation – reserves were created, from the surplus, and in the war crises of 1951, 1956 (Suez) and 1967 the reserves had been used, to offset interruptions in supply and keep prices down. From 1957 to 1963 the surplus had amounted to 4 million barrels per day. However, the artificially high price, through protective tariffs, of imported oil then made it profitable for reserves to be used, and these ran down, falling to one million barrels as against an output of over 11 million. If for whatever reason prices suddenly rose, then there would be no American reserve with which to flood the market and bring prices down again. In March 1971 the Texas authority for oil allowed full-capacity use for the first time. Imports followed. The world was in effect becoming dependent upon Middle Eastern oil – demand had risen to 21 million barrels per day, and the Middle East, producing 13 million barrels more, was therefore in the position of meeting two thirds of the rise in demand – despite the emergence of other fields, in Nigeria and Indonesia. Besides, alternative fuels were either undeveloped, or under attack.

Various ideas had already appeared for the use of wind or solar power: they involved much trial and error and great expense at a time when oil was cheap. The fact that there were oil reserves in Alaska was known, but by now the environmentalists were at work and the technology, given the geology and climate, was exceedingly difficult and expensive. In 1972 human genius went into a discovery that there were reserves under the oceans – the North Sea, for instance – but, again, there were environmental fears, as an oil slick destroyed thirty miles of Californian beach. In 1972 the Club of Rome – an informal but weighty international group, supposed wise men of the world – issued a warning called *The Predicament of Mankind*, which took the consumption figures for that year and reckoned that 'sometime within the next hundred years' energy and food would run out because the population was growing so fast and 'the limits to growth on this planet will be reached'. There were also alarms as to the effect of industrialization, in its modern form, on the climate, as carbon dioxide built up in the atmosphere. Nuclear power was in some quarters regarded as an answer – the Soviet Union and France went ahead – but elsewhere there were fears of accidents and in any case, in some countries – Great Britain especially – coal had an almighty presence. There, a mixture of bad conscience (the miners had been chief victims of the British Slump of the 1930s) and misbegotten policy ensured that coal would have a predominance that prevented the development of a nuclear policy such as the French (to Margaret Thatcher's subsequent admiration) had had. But coal itself was under some threat, because of environmental considerations. There had been a great 'smog' in London in the late autumn of 1958, the last of the Dickensian 'London partiklars', and a Clean Air Act had followed, inhibiting domestic use of coal. More oil, in other words. As things were, America, through the quota system, had made matters doubly bad. Oil was not produced, in order to keep prices artificially high. The major companies just agreed among themselves, and took the profits without much effort. On the other hand, world prices were low, and this discouraged exploration of, or at any rate investment in, new sources of oil. There already were alarms – power cuts in the harsh winter of 1969–70. By summer 1973 the USA imported 6 million barrels every day, as against 3 million three years before.

The final element in all of this was financial: the dollar. The Shah, for instance, had embarked upon a colossal attempt to modernize Iran and turn it into something commensurate with the Indo-European (as distinct from Arab or Turkic: 'Iran' instead of 'Persia' is itself something of an artifice, since it refers to 'Aryan', as in blue-eyed, blond, etc.) origins of the Persians, as he understood them. In 1971 he had even staged a great ceremony, inviting anyone interested, at the old capital of Persepolis, complete with Peacock Throne and elaborate use of tiles and gold. His view of the history of Persia was a hard-luck story: on the one side elaborate white clothing, dignified attitudes, elegant and moving poetry, imposing architecture, and on the other side (mainly) Turks, bringing to the work of destruction a glee that civilized Persians could not have been expected to resist, the more so as their potential allies had stabbed them in the back. That the modern-day Turks had made a considerable success of national independence and Westernization was another tiresome element: the Shah would show the Middle East how it could be done. Now, the dollars with which he had been doing his accounts were proving unsafe. Prices per barrel of oil were low enough, in any event – $2 – and inflation was already proceeding in the West at a noticeable pace. The Kuwaiti oil minister said, 'What is the point of producing more oil and selling it for an unguaranteed paper currency?' Indeed.

OPEC was by nature divided. But this time agreement was easy enough, and there was a ready excuse to hand. One thing worked on the surface in the Arab world, advancing the anti-Zionist argument. Israel: the great enemy of the Arabs; seemingly successful only because of American support; oil properly used would create such trouble in the West that it would just stand by and let Israel be crushed. So long as oil-producing Arab countries were ruled by pliant monarchies, such arguments remained largely hot air. However, in Libya there was a coup against one such monarch; an army officer, Muammar al-Gaddafi, came to power, in 1969, with the intention of extracting as much as he could from the oil companies who exploited Libya's high-quality oil. He could quite easily play one country off against others – particularly, his neighbour and former colonial master, Italy, could be used – and into the whole picture there now crept a malignant figure, Armand Hammer, whose appearance at anything generally meant trouble. He had made money out of revolutionary Russia, and profits from that let him buy up coal and oil in America, when prices were at their lowest in the Depression. His company, Occidental Petroleum, no doubt benefited from advance notice of Soviet sales, as these would affect prices on offer in particular markets; and Hammer in return offered services to the Communist Party. Later on, Robert Maxwell did much the same. Unlike Maxwell, Hammer was not found out: though in reality he, too, had built up a mountain of debt, which was concealed by apparent philanthropic activities (they did not extend to his sister-in-law, who had borrowed $15,000 from him; in his will he gave instructions that every cent was to be re-extracted). Hammer had already built up a Libyan connection, perhaps through his Soviet allies, and Gaddafi wanted to have a better deal. Libyan oil supplied a third of the European market, and Hammer allowed him 55 per cent of the profit – a decisive breach of the fifty-fifty principle that soon had Iranian and Venezuelan feet tapping (September 1970). As the dollar declined, there were further demands for price rises, and the position of OPEC became quite strong, since America was now a net importer, and by April 1973 the surplus capacity within the USA was down to a week's consumption.

At this point, the various oil countries began to threaten even a form of nationalization – 'participation', i.e. a share of the oil resources previously covered by concessions. The companies resisted but were not supported by their own governments – the time for gunboats, or even covert operations of the type that had overthrown Mossadegh, was past, and the Americans relied on the Shah. In fact Libya went ahead with nationalization: Hammer was thrown out. It was upon this tense scene that the Israeli–Arab war (Yom Kippur) of October 1973 broke out.

Nasser himself had died in 1970. His successor, Anwar Sadat, was deeply cunning (and during the Second World War had had a minor role as a German spy against the British). It was now obvious that the Middle Eastern oil producers had a very strong case for raising the oil price. In real money, as against paper dollars, they were getting much less than before, and world demand was pushing hard against capacity. Nasser himself had left Egypt in a calamitous condition. He had detached it from the Western world, led it into a disastrous war with Israel in 1967 (with lesser campaigning thereafter) and, with 'Arab socialism', driven out the creative minority of Greeks and many of the Coptic Christians who had allowed trade to flourish. He had also taken up a Soviet alliance, and there were 20,000 Soviet citizens, including advisers, in the country; these advisers were often very robust in saying what they thought of Egyptian ways. In July 1972 Sadat had them expelled, though he continued the close relationship with Moscow. But how could he escape from it? If the USA supported Israel, then, given public opinion in the Arab world (which appeared to believe that everything wrong was the Jews' fault), there was no chance. He must make the Americans force the Israelis to negotiate seriously as to a settlement of Arab–Israeli problems. How? The answer seemed to be, a war. Won, it would end the existence of Israel.

Not won, but sufficiently alarming, it would force some movement. Maybe, talking to Kissinger, he realized that he had an equally devious possible partner. The game was in effect to use Soviet help to make any further Soviet connection unnecessary, and solve the Palestinian problem that bedevilled Israel's relations with Egypt and so deprived Egypt of the link that she needed in order to become a rival to Iran. In the winter of 1972–3 Sadat came up with a scheme for a surprise attack on Israel, in concert with Syria, and told no-one except King Faisal in Saudi Arabia.

The Saudis had by now become the oil producer of reserve – that is, if they produced more of their potential, oil prices would fall, and if not, not. Earlier, that 'switch' position had been America's. Faisal also approved of Sadat, whereas Nasser had been a threat to the monarchies – not a man to support. Religion, the sacred position of Mecca, the ancient glories of the caliphate, in many quarters a vainglorious belief that Arab civilization, so long despised as useless, would triumphantly return, white horses included, to down the infidel and particularly the Jewish enemy (Mohammed's first target 1,400 years before, as it happened) – all of it really about those paper dollars. In mid-September 1973 OPEC met in Vienna and advanced a new deal with the oil companies, which were to lose their property substantially: an ultimatum followed. Then on 6 October the oil companies nervously offered a price rise of 15 per cent at Vienna; and OPEC demanded 100 per cent. That very day, Egyptian and Syrian troops had launched their surprise attack on the Israeli lines.

The Yom Kippur war had its origins in 1967, when Nasser had been humiliatingly defeated essentially in the first hours of that war. Before it Israel had seemed more or less indefensible, along the 1949 armistice line, but in 1967, with the West Bank and the Sinai, her territory had been rounded off and even Jerusalem was safe from Jordanian artillery. Meanwhile the Arabs had fought among themselves and King Hussein of Jordan only just survived attacks by the Syrians and Palestinians, who regarded him as a traitor: in 1967, thanks to having been let down by allies, he lost half his kingdom. But the 1967 war itself had twisted origins. There was, in the first place, Nasser's extraordinary vainglory. The Suez affair had counted as a tremendous victory, a defeat for the traditional imperialist powers, Great Britain and France. That had been followed by Algerian independence from France in 1962, another triumph that Nasser was supposed to have inspired.

In 1960 he set himself up as leader of all Arabs, disposing of rivals or Western associates, if need be by murder. In 1960, accepting Soviet help, he had gone over to 'socialism', complete with concentration camps and a Five Year Plan, and took over land and businesses: he tried to corral the *ulema*. What kept the regime together was external aggrandizement as Nasser tried to take over the Yemen; there was constant vainglorious anti-Israeli rhetoric. Soviet arms and money gave him the wherewithal: between 1954 and 1970 Egypt, Syria and Iraq received more than half of Soviet military assistance and Egypt alone got significant amounts of ground and air weapons. In 1967 he was caught on his own rhetoric: the Soviet Union provoked him into a war with Israel, suggesting that the Israelis were preparing an attack, and Nasser could hardly resist. A week before the war, at the end of May 1967, he trumpeted:

> We are confronting Israel and the West as well – the West which created Israel and which despised us Arabs . . . They had no regard whatsoever for our feelings, our hopes in life or our rights . . . We are now ready to confront Israel . . . If the Western powers . . . ridicule and despise us, we Arabs must teach them to respect us.

This blustering led to a fiasco, the Six Day War, which, on 5 June, the Israelis won in about three hours, destroying 309 of 340 serviceable combat aircraft, including all the long-range Tu-16 bombers, twenty-seven Il-28 medium-range ones, twenty-seven Su-7 fighter bombers and 135 MiG fighters. Nasser's successor, Sadat, had learned a lesson or two when, in October 1973, he launched the next round.

Here was to be another humiliation, or at least a serious reverse, for the Atlantic system. This time it was the Israelis' turn to be vainglorious. The Egyptians struck in the midst of Israeli triumphalism. There had been a grandiose parade to mark the country's twenty-fifth anniversary on 15 May 1973 and hardly anyone took the threats of the new Egyptian ruler, Sadat, seriously: the Suez Canal was guarded by prodigious fortifications. The Egyptian army now appointed educated men as officers, some of whom learned Hebrew; soon after the great defeat a Soviet delegation came to offer reconstruction, which took place in six months. Low-level warring went on, as did the usual failed peace processes; but Sadat now at least saw that he should take up links with the Americans, and in July 1972 asked the Soviet advisers to go. What Sadat really wanted was the involvement of the Americans, who could force Israel towards a deal. However, he needed some sort of victory in advance, and reckoned from the plain evidence in Vietnam that the USA would be pliable. Meanwhile, he could rely on some degree of Soviet support: the USSR was not going to let Egypt go. Port facilities would allow for transfer of resources from Russia, which sent the latest technology; and in any case the Russians were well into Syria, Egypt's ally. In March 1973 shipment of SCUD missiles (with a range of 180 miles) began. Sadat then conspired with Hafiz Assad in Syria, with whom he had nothing in common, and got finance from the Saudis; with the Soviet help, he did bring off the initial victory, and became the 'Hero of the Crossing'.

The attack came on 6 October, Yom Kippur, a religious festival when Israeli preparedness might be expected to be low (reservists were indeed absent); and the tides of the Suez Canal would also be right at that time. Syria and Egypt would attack together, at 2 p.m., when the sun was in the enemy's eyes. Yet the Suez defence zone was formidable enough and the Canal itself was about 200 yards wide and up to sixty feet in depth (it has since been deepened to accommodate tankers, by Israeli–Egyptian agreement). The tides vary vastly, changing the depths, and both sides had built ramparts – the Egyptian ones higher, such that they could spot more easily. There was an ingenious Israeli device for spraying the Canal with oil that could be ignited, but it did not work because the pipes had bent under the weight of earth, and though a new commander wanted to activate the system he was actually demonstrating how this should be done when the Egyptian shells fell. The Egyptians had learned from previous experience and had prepared a deception very well. In the first place they had again and again staged emergencies, the first such at the end of 1971, when there appeared to have been a plan for an air strike, and another major mobilization a year later involving paratroops. In spring 1973 there was another, so the further one of September/October was not rated highly by the Israelis. There were similar problems with Syria (thirteen of her aircraft had been shot down in what had seemed to be a fairly routine affair). Even the Israeli media were distracted because at the time there was a row involving Palestinians holding up a train carrying Jews to Vienna on the Austro-Czech border, whereat the Austrian chancellor, Bruno Kreisky, agreed to close the Jewish transit centre in exchange for release of hostages and gunmen alike. The Israeli prime minister, Golda Meir, had been so preoccupied by this that she went to Strasbourg to address the Council of Europe.

Now, the Egyptian army (800,000 men with 2,200 tanks and 550 first-line aircraft) went into action. One key was that the Israeli air force would not be permitted to establish itself: in February 1972 the Egyptians were told in Moscow that they could have Soviet surface-to-air missiles – SAMs – that would constitute a 'wall' as well as the SCUD missiles that could land far in Israeli territory, to deter the Israelis from deep raids into Egypt. They arrived in May and Sadat started planning for war in January 1973. The Russians delivered fifty SAM batteries to Syria as well. Rumours were put about as to the Egyptians' poor preparedness, and the mobilization just looked like another manoeuvre. There were arrangements in place for Soviet back-up, and in the meantime Sadat had co-ordinated with King Faisal that war and the oil weapon could go together. Secrecy was such that 95 per cent of the officers taken prisoner by the Israelis said that they only knew this would be a real attack on the morning of 6 October. Surprise was complete: 240 aircraft crossed the Canal to attack airfields, 2,000 guns opened up and fired 10,500 shells in the first minute. Tanks moved up the ramps and fired point-blank at the fortifications and then the first wave of infantrymen crossed at areas not covered by the Israeli strong-points: they had practised the manoeuvre dozens or even hundreds of times, sometimes by numbers. Such infantry could not be expected to act or learn otherwise. Ten bridges were to be thrown across the Canal. The Egyptians had expected up to 30,000 casualties on the crossing but these were extraordinarily light – 208 – and the bridges were ingeniously constructed so that a damaged section could easily be replaced. By midday on 7 October an Egyptian division was across and it prepared for counter-attack. But 'the Israeli armour mounted what looked like old-fashioned cavalry charges' which 'made no sense whatsoever in the face of the masses of anti-tank weapons that the Egyptians had concentrated on the battlefield'. General Moshe Dayan himself gave a pessimistic briefing to the editors of the Israeli press and hinted that he might have to withdraw out of the Sinai altogether. However, the Egyptian follow-up was poor, and further attacks failed: the way was open to an Israeli counter-attack that reached even west of the Canal. But these three days had marked an Egyptian victory, for the first time ever, and that was Sadat's essential point. A real victory would be the prelude to some settlement.

However, by 12 October the Israelis were receiving an American airlift to make up for the unforeseen losses and use of ammunition and aircraft. On 8 and 9 October Brezhnev appealed to other Arab states to join in and on the 10th set up an air bridge to Syria (Tito gave permission, saying it was for Sadat not Brezhnev that he agreed). On the 9th the Americans agreed to supply the Israelis, especially with electronic materiel that allowed Israeli planes to escape missiles, and to begin with the Israelis did the transporting, but the US air force did it from the 12th, as Israeli aircraft were not enough for these supplies. The decisive moment occurred on 14 October. There were 1,000 Egyptian tanks on the east bank, and they launched one of the largest tank battles in history: the missiles were out of range and so the Israeli air force could act decisively. The Egyptians lost 264 tanks, the Israelis ten. The SS11 anti-tank guided missiles had been important and the Israelis' tanks were also well prepared – in fact the Egyptians had attacked only in response to appeals from Syria, where the fighting was not going well: on the Golan Heights there was a desperate battle but 867 Syrian tanks were left there. Now the Israelis could plan their own crossing of the Canal, succeeding on the 16th, and the Egyptians began to collapse. Within two days an Egyptian army was under threat of being cut off and the USSR proposed a ceasefire, the proposal being agreed between Brezhnev and Kissinger and presented through the United Nations. On the 24th a second UN resolution was put through because the Russians could foresee the collapse of their allies, and under American pressure the Israelis accepted it, their forces now even threatening Cairo. The Russians had mobilized airborne divisions for a move to the Middle East when the ceasefire came, but Sadat himself was not enthusiastic. Of course, it was yet another Arab defeat, in the end, but there was something to show for it. The upshot of the Yom Kippur war was not clear-cut. The French and the Germans made difficulties for Israel; Bonn refused the Americans an air bridge over Germany. At the end of the year all sides did meet for the first time and in mid-January 1974 there was a new arrangement – a neutral zone on the east bank. Egypt restored diplomatic relations with the USA in 1974 and broke with the USSR in 1976; two years later, on American territory (Camp David, the President's official retreat), there was an Egyptian–Israeli peace. Israel evacuated Sinai.

It was now Arabs who used the oil weapon. On 16 October 1973 they put up prices by 70 per cent and on the 17th OPEC announced a reduction of output by 25 per cent and an embargo on the USA and Holland. On 23 December there was a doubling of Persian Gulf prices. OPEC announced that the price would rise to $5.11, and there was a further threat, that production would be cut by 5 per cent every month – the claim being that this was necessary for the Americans to force Israel into serious negotiations. Kissinger, in his aircraft, even learned that the Saudis would join the embargo on oil sales to America and her allies because of President Nixon's public offer of $2bn in aid for Israel. On 21 October the Arabs stated that they would nationalize the oil companies if they failed to join the embargo against the USA, the whole affair occurring in the context of the Watergate revelations, and Nixon had just lost his corrupt Vice-President, Spiro Agnew, over tax fraud. The oil embargo went ahead, against Holland (which had stood up for Israel's cause) and the USA, and even against the American ships supposedly protecting the Saudis. The price climbed and production fell back – from over 20 million barrels early in October to 15 million; and although Iran stepped up production somewhat (600,000) overall supply by December had fallen by 4 million barrels per day. This was about a tenth of consumption, but since consumption had been rising at 7.5 per cent per annum, the dent was more severe, and in any case panic caused damage, as the companies realized what was happening. They bid for any oil on the market, anywhere – in Nigeria, in November, $16 and then $22.60; in Iran, $17. The official price went up, from $1.80 in 1970 to $2.18 in 1971, $2.90 in summer 1973, $5.12 in October and $11.65 in December. By 23 December the Gulf States had doubled the price, and of course the rise in oil and natural gas prices much profited the Soviet Union. Boris Ponomarev, of the International Department, thought the crisis of capitalism was at hand. The centre was not holding.

15

1968: A Generation

This disintegration of the Marshall–NATO world had a cultural aspect. The biggest sign of this by far was in France, and perhaps not by chance. De Gaulle had greatly angered the Americans, with his withdrawal from NATO and his torpedoing of the dollar. France, in 1968, appeared to be extraordinarily successful, but de Gaulle received, out of the blue, a vast humiliation. In a moment that summed up the sixties, the students of Paris rebelled against him, and would have brought him down if the Communist Party had not, for Moscow's sake, saved him. The episode in itself was farcical, but it was farce with a sinister side, edging into terrorism; it also did great damage to education in general, and particularly to European universities, which since then have declined. In 1914, as a foreigner, you beat your path to Paris or Berlin if you wanted to study anything of seriousness. By 1980 American universities were all the rage, and foreigners made for the universities of France or Germany only if they had no American (or at least British) alternative.

As so often, it was in Italy that the European starting gun was fired. She, much poorer than France, had nevertheless been another European miracle in the sense that her exports boomed. The Italian State was another matter. Parents cared about schools, which were very good, as was the press, but universities were of much less interest, and here Italy, living in the tailwind of a demographic storm, faced a crisis. Student numbers had doubled, from 1959 to 1969, to nearly half a million, while the curriculum remained the same, and there were no textbooks or classrooms. The extension of the school-leaving age to fourteen had gone together (in 1965) with abolition of university entrance examinations.

Governments as ever found it easy to economize on education, because at least in the short term it could not mobilize discontent, and headlines as to educational improvements made for good politics. The university system, according to Paul Ginsborg, was therefore in 'an advanced state of malfunction': Rome had 60,000 students, Naples 50,000, Bari 30,000 – each institution designed for 5,000. There were too few lecturers, and they also gave few lectures – one per week; and examinations were oral, no poorly paid lecturer wanting to spend time on thousands of scripts. It was true that there was much failure, but a merciful providence decreed that the failures could go on repeating years, perhaps with some part-time job to keep them going. Even middle-class students in the then fashionable subjects of sociology or psychology would easily find that they had no job at the end of it all. Therefore the universities simmered. An absurd cult of 'Che' developed from 1967, when the university of Trento was occupied; then came troubles at the Catholic University in Milan and then again at Turin, in opposition to entirely sensible reform. All of this came with the usual paraphernalia of lumpish clothes and ready-made 'anti' talk: thus R. D. Laing's remarks, critical of the family, in *Sanity, Madness and the Family* (1964), had much resonance in family-bound Italy where one graffito read, 'I want to be an orphan'. Such students could at least claim partnership with 'the workers' – a matter generally fanciful elsewhere. One and a half million metalworkers struck; they wanted a forty-hour week and equal wages. Other workers, including state and local government ones, followed, sometimes with a view to keeping their relatively higher wage levels.

France was next. One of the wisdoms of the age was that education produced prosperity. The logic was simple enough: university = knowledge = technology = prosperity. *Sputnik* was in the end a deadly weapon, because it destroyed the Western university. Bureaucrats could brandish statistics of expanding education at each other, quite independently of the deeper factors involved, which were not subject to measurement. All advanced countries therefore saw a vast increase in the number of students, a raising of the school-leaving age, and a proliferation of institutions of higher learning. The number of teachers also increased, though not as fast, and the overall budget rose less fast again. French higher education had been both very exacting and unfair: there had not even been a retiring age for professors until the 1930s and aged, comic figures occupied posts at which the aspiring young resentfully gazed. They, meanwhile, would have to undergo examinations that were not just extremely demanding, but were even competitive, meaning that, to pass, you had to be classed in the top twenty or whichever number the organizers reckoned was needed. It was called *agrégation*, and qualified you to go on with research. Even then, if a place did not fall open, you would have to go and teach in a school. This was not in itself a bad thing, because the highest forms of a French school were themselves, in terms of what was expected, a sort of junior university, and discipline in the class was kept by a special supervisor while the teacher concentrated upon the lessons. There were other routes to success, particularly through the selective 'Grand Schools' which were designed to produce an elite – engineers in the Polytechnic, administrators in the École Nationale d'Administration (ENA) (others, some fifty, great and small, covered transport, bridges, archives, etc. and business schools followed). ENA had been supposed to be classless but in practice, with, somewhat later, business schools, became a near preserve of the bourgeoisie. Young would-be academics worked in the highest two years of a secondary school towards the École Normale Supérieure, which produced school-teachers. It was a hard life, made tolerable by a sense of mission, and that sense was overtaken by ENA's. Not surprisingly, the schoolteachers were on the Left. University teachers had similarly undergone an ordeal. There was a diploma that took ten years, and you could be under some old tyrant; if you were lucky, it might be Professor Labrousse, who saw his students on a Sunday morning or a Saturday afternoon. If you were senior you got the less uncomfortable chair, otherwise you were *posé du bout des fesses* far from the professorial desk and hoped for patronage in a system that was generally far from transparent in its workings. Again following a Soviet model, research was partly detached from the university system, with a Centre National de la Recherche Scientifique (CNRS) to sort it out, and of course that body was prey to politics. Communists were particularly good at the game, and in time the great historian Fernand Braudel (who had taught once upon a time in a school in Algeria) ran his section of the CNRS like a Valois court, all over you one minute, the trapdoor the next.

Out of the blue in 1968 came troubles that caught world headlines: there was a mass revolt in universities, Paris easily in the lead. The immediate cause was the mishandling of educational expansion. France in 1958 had had a quarter of a million students and ten years later 630,000. Student–staff ratios stood at 15:1 in Germany in the Humanities, but 27.5:1 in Law, whereas in France the figures were close to 60:1. Then again, academic staff was expanded but quality declined: in France there had been 5,600 teachers in 1956 but there were 22,500 in 1967, and their salaries had not kept pace with the times. Nor had buildings. The temper of the times was made concrete in the new university of Nanterre, miles away from the centre of Paris, in an area of migrant shanty dwellings beset by mud and wire. It was hated, as Annie Kriegel remembers:

> un horrible cul-de-basse-fosse où grouillaient, aveugles et sourds aux bruits du dehors, des humains anonymes qui se ressemblaient tous par l'accoutrement, la tenue avachie, une langue de bois formée d'onomatopées, de sigles et d'injures ordurières, et des discours insensés.

In all countries, new universities (and hospitals) became bywords for expensive ugliness: they were crammed with students; taught by men and women appointed all of a sudden in great numbers, without regard for quality. The humanities came off least well, and yet the expansion with relatively new subjects, such as economics, sociology and psychology, meant that there were young men and women a-plenty who imagined that they had the answer to everything. It was a terrible cocktail, superbly written up by Richard Davy in *The Times*. The British at that stage could afford to sneer: their universities were still of the older model, and selected students quite rigorously. When, at Cambridge, an attempt was made to occupy the central administrative building, the students had to be told that its functions were quite vague, that a committee met from time to time. The building was occupied, and the reactionaries at Trinity College were mobilized, some of them arriving with hunting shotguns. The occupants had to be protected by the police as they left the building.

Government financing of universities had been generous enough to start with in France, but in the later sixties there were cutbacks, and the education minister, Christian Fouchet, proposed a new system of selection, to cut numbers by one third. He also announced that 'the university' should be 'industrialized', precisely the language to annoy anyone working in one. There had been student strikes in the French system before, at Nanterre most notably in the previous November, but now the dam burst. One particular grievance was that boys could not spend the night in girls' residences: the sort of prescription which in the past would just have counted as common sense. Now, perhaps because of the Pill, there was a *climat de saturnales* in places where *l'austérité faisait prime*. It was exploited by a *vedettariat delinquant* with *l'histrionisme dont Cohn-Bendit fut un talentueux prototype*. Daniel Cohn-Bendit was a clever manager of groupuscules that would otherwise have collapsed in squabbling; and he was also well aware that, as de Gaulle challenged the supremacy of the dollar, any sign of trouble in France would be welcome in Washington. Although a fatuous American political scientist had pronounced France to be one of the two most stable countries in the world, the temper was rising outside the glossy world of the new technocracy and the film-set sparkling buildings of André Malraux's cleaned-up *beaux quartiers*. At Nanterre a minister (of 'Youth') called François Missoffe visited in January 1968, to open a swimming pool. There he encountered Cohn-Bendit, who complained that Missoffe's book on 'Youth' had nothing to say of sexual problems. Missoffe said that he was not surprised, given Cohn-Bendit's looks, that he had sexual problems and that he should dive into the swimming pool to sort them out. It was the start of troubles. The sociology building was 'occupied', the administration called in the police, and the 'Tet Offensive' in Vietnam supplied the students with an occasion for militancy, complete with denunciations of *l'école des flics et des patrons*. There were counter-attacks by extreme right-wing students (and there were thick rumours, to the effect that the CIA were behind these, because it wanted to destabilize de Gaulle). At any rate there was 'a mass of manoeuvre', its strength increased because of the half-hearted attempts at repression by the Nanterre rector. The thing spread, on 3 May, to the Sorbonne itself. There, there was an affray with the police, semi-encouraged by the rector, and eighty of them were injured by flying brickbats.

Magistrates sentenced four students to brief terms of imprisonment, and tempers rose, elsewhere, as well as in Paris. By the night of 10/11 May barricades had been put up in the Latin Quarter, the highest – three yards – rather suitably in the rue d'Ulm, where stood the poor old ENS, the teachers' training school that had produced the grave ancestors of whom these students were a weird offspring. The students attempted to produce their own left-wing ideology.

However, it was sloganeering: 'the beach lies under the street', 'bourgeois medicine does not cure, it repairs'. There was an odd cult of Maoism and the names of sages were invoked, but as Leszek Kołakowski says, 1968 yielded no political thought worth mentioning, and although François Maspéro and others produced a spate of writing, none of it lasts. The extraordinary thing was that France fell into a sort of paralysis for the month of May. This was because the Paris events gained momentum through various other elements, which had nothing to do with them. There were younger workers at the Renault automobile factory outside Paris, just waiting to escape from trade union and Communist control so as to make their own 'demands'. The order police, the creation of which dated back to the conditions of near civil war in 1947, were quite widely hated, and were made up sometimes of Corsicans who had organized *ratonnades* against Algerians back in 1958: even solid middle-class neighbours of the barricade-manning students would offer them food and drink. There was a sexual element as well – an English homosexual with a white Rolls-Royce drove along the embankment having the time of his life in the back of it and the Communist poet Louis Aragon, whose wife, Elsa Triolet, had died not long before, emerged in pink to cheer on a demonstration on that side of the fence. The television and radio journalists were vastly annoyed at efforts by the State to control their output, and when de Gaulle wanted to make a speech rallying the people, he could only do so under heavy guard, from the top of the Eiffel Tower, with technicians from outside, and – another by nature left-wing group looking for State money – the film-makers set up a 'States General of the Cinema' to try to stop the Cannes Film Festival on 18 May. By 21 May 10 million people were on strike. There were of course academics, delighted with their quarter-hour of fame, and even a cohort of high-school pupils ritually joined in. One of them, chased by police, jumped into the river and was drowned when caught in the mud of the Seine. That soul provided the martyr. May the 23rd and 24th saw a further explosion of violence, with burned cars and an attempt to set light to the stock exchange. The automobile workers at Boulogne-Billancourt even turned down a large wage increase and for a time struck revolutionary attitudes.

But this was of course just an accumulation of self-importance and holiday-wanting; Annie Kriegel in her memoirs bubbles over with contempt, and so do many others, whose writings easily outlive the contemporary celebratory literature (the historical echoes, of the 'June Days' of 1848, were obvious enough: the outstanding comments on these were made by Tocqueville in his memoirs or by Flaubert in *L'Éducation sentimentale*, mocking the Iberian accent of an international windbag; even Victor Hugo in *Les Misérables* shook his head and thought that, in the end, the rebelling workers would have to be 'shot down, but respectfully'). Of course the State deserved 1968, because it had expanded education far too fast, and its supposed 'technocratization of the university' was leading, quite predictably, to the manufacture of clones – bearded sloganeers and shrieking girls on the one side, besuited briefcase sandwich-lunch know-it-alls on the other. But 1968 was in itself a fiasco, if a sinister one; it would fizzle out unless there were a revolutionary party organized enough to take advantage. It was here that the French Communist Party might have moved. It did not. Lenin had already spoken viciously of left-wing infantilism; the trade unions did not want control to slip into anarchist hands; and in any case de Gaulle had proved very useful to the USSR. He had stood up to the Americans, especially in matters of world finance, and he had disrupted NATO; by a fitting twist, he had even departed on a state visit to Communist Romania when the May events were under way. The French Party therefore did not move. De Gaulle himself staged a theatrical coup, vanishing for three days at the end of the month (he consulted the army in Germany, and got assurances of support, in return for release, from prison, of the military dissidents of 1962). His prime minister, Pompidou, cleverly announced that there would be elections, and the various potential political successors then got busy with campaigning (Mendès France and Mitterrand were both involved, in a cautious way). Students in any case had their exams to think of, and by mid-June the last occupants were cleared from a Sorbonne area that had now become rat-infested. Come the elections, there was an enormous governmental majority – 358 seats out of 485.

France had been there before, and such majorities made for what had been called the 'unrepeatable Chamber' (*Chambre introuvable*) – a reactionary majority so large as to threaten moderate and sensible voices within the government itself. But in this case, the boys and girls of 1968 had understood how to deal with a bureaucracy: a box-ticking culture which would run scared, and politicians in any event knew perfectly well that education brought cantankerous postbags and endless self-important lecturing, for no political gain. The government resolved on compromise and consultation; in other words, ran away. The politicians had been terrified, and simply gave in to demands for 'autonomy' and the rest; from that day to this, the universities in France have had to admit anyone with the right paper qualifications, themselves a very debased currency. French higher education survived with the 'Grand Schools'; the state universities became, as Besançon said, 'third world' and vast damage was done to the cultural resonance of which French governments were enamoured. This coinage, worldwide, was now debased.

Not much noticed at the same time, there was another university crisis which portended far more than the circus of May 1968 in Paris. In all of the university disturbances, there was one that took a lead for perversity, and it was not to do with left-wing infantilism. The University of Louvain in Belgium had a very long and sometimes outstanding history. Its official history (*Katholieke Universiteit Leuven*) is a noble book, and an epitaph. Humanism and its greatest figure, Erasmus, had flourished there. In the eighteenth century it had somewhat fossilized, students having to discuss (in Latin) such questions as 'Did Adam and Eve pay each other compliments in the state of innocence?' There was an inflation, and the window-cleaners had to be paid in gold; the clerical elite flourished while the juniors were starvelings. In 1794 came one of the great scenes of university reform, when, after their victory at Fleurus, revolutionary generals in their twenties occupied the place, stabled horses in its precincts, eventually, in 1797, abolished it, and exiled the Rector to French Guyana. It was restored in the nineteenth century and became a greatly respected Catholic university. In Belgium at that time French was the language for educated people, although Louvain itself stood in a Flemish hinterland. The university was an elite place of the old-fashioned sort, with a considerable intellectual and social life, 'characters' abounding; as such it attracted envy and resentment, but its products spoke for themselves, and Louvain was a leading European university with much international resonance. Its library was famous. With the student expansion, there were by 1960 more Flemish-speaking students than French, and some of them demanded Flemishization ('Netherlandization' as it was called, though almost no one thought of joining up with the Dutch, who had no objections to the use of French, a world language). In fact the halls of residence had already been 'Netherlandized' in part in the fifties, and some classes were already 'parallel'. But nationalism of this sort was an itch only made worse by scratching. There was a further problem, that French-speaking (or French-leaning) parents at the university naturally wanted French-language schools in the town itself. There were demonstrations against these supposed 'caste schools' and it did not help that the university hospital doctors used French, sometimes unable to understand a distraught Flemish peasant mother with a sick child. In fact the doctors took a lead in what followed, and some of them made a property fortune out of the scouting of planning laws (the town acquired the usual hideous academic concrete). The real problem in Flemish eyes was that nearby Brussels, cosmopolitan and French-speaking, would spread like an oil slick (*tache d'huile*) and Frenchify a corridor to Louvain. In 1965 there were Flemish demonstrations to the effect of 'All Walloons Out' and Flemish students solemnly turned their backs on the procession of professors coming out of St Peter's Church at the start of the academic year. The most that can be said for all of this is that at least no-one was killed, though there were some bruises. The Rector, Mgr Honoré Van Waeyenbergh, lost control, and though the bishops solemnly said in 1966 that the idea of two

Catholic universities, one French and one Flemish, was absurd and expensive and impossible, they could not control the situation either. In January 1968 the French section was transferred to another concrete place at Woluwe, a suburb of Brussels, and has hardly been heard of again. Neither has the new Flemish university, which now, quite absurdly, uses English to express its international character. This time round, there would be no Fleurus, no horses stabled in ancient colleges, no deans sent to Guyana, but a great institution had died just the same.

But the fall of French at Louvain was only a small piece of a far larger picture: the wrong road taken in 1968. The European university also died, becoming, as the German equivalent of George Orwell, Hans-Magnus Enzensberger, said, a 'karst'. A brilliant French commentator, Marc Fumaroli, wrote an essay in 1992, 'The Cultural State', lamenting what had happened: France, he said, was turning into a huge version of Venice as she stood in the 1790s, before Napoleon had annexed her: wonderful architecture, many displays that impressed the tourists, but an air of deadness just the same. The State had built up an empire over Culture, studding Paris with *grands travaux* – a new opera house at the Bastille, a new and huge library, various 'culture houses', including a glass pyramid at the Louvre, the largest museum in the world, and ancient palace of the kings of France. There were enormous exhibitions and shows, and many references to 'spaces of culture' or 'places of culture'. The greatest of these was the celebration of the 200th anniversary of the French Revolution, in 1989. It was supposed to represent the Rights of Man, but the best thing that came out of it was another clever book, René Sédillot's *Le Coût de la Révolution française*. Yes, France had had a revolution in the name of equality and liberty, but she had then lost her leading position in Europe, being overtaken by England and Germany. Still, in the 1950s, French civilization had attracted vast numbers of foreigners, and in the 1960s the Fifth Republic began to support it more lavishly than ever before as a national asset. The results were supposed to impress foreigners with the grandeur of France, and the monuments of Paris were scraped clear of centuries of grime, to look like filmsets. However, the effects of state patronage bore out what Charles Fourier had said a century before: 'What the State encourages, withers; what the State protects, dies.'

A mania for public support of Culture spread over France, sometimes with preposterous results. In Provence you could read that 'the Regional Council dynamizes the plastic arts'; there was 'a micro-climate of contagious euphoria' with publicly funded art, and museums, spreading all over the place. The château de Chambord only very narrowly escaped acquiring what was described as an enormous breughelian pyramid, supposedly to celebrate the Renaissance. All of this was supposed to protect French culture, but its output compared quite badly with that of the 1950s, when, in small, private theatres, Ionesco and Beckett were performed. The new managers of French culture were very often anti-American, denouncing the establishment of McDonald's on the boulevard Saint-Michel, but they themselves were really in the grip of another dictatorship altogether, that of East Berlin and Moscow: on the tower block outskirts of Paris there were 'avenues Maurice-Thorez' or 'stades Rosa-Luxemburg' that were as grimly Communist as anything you might have met in Romania. In fact, 'State Culture divided Arts and Letters into functionaries and clients'. Typical of its output was a film, *Germinal*, which sought to revive a world of working-class passions, of the old French Left, with France's best-known actor, Gérard Depardieu, in the heroic role. The film had no effect: it was, as Tocqueville had said of an earlier French revolution, that of 1848, 'men warming their hands at the ashes of their grandfathers' passions'. A more interesting film was Andrzej Wajda's *Danton*, which showed a gloomy picture of a revolution eating its children. But Wajda, having lived through a genuine revolution, in Communist Poland, knew what he was talking about, whereas the French were only turning out wooden propaganda.

Most European countries had public support for the Arts. The Germans had inherited a tradition by which several, sometimes quite small, territories or towns had proudly maintained their local arts; the British, as ever, were better when it came to private gatherings and support – for instance, for the Hallé Orchestra – but they also had, in the BBC, a sort of Ministry of Culture, promoting music and literature through the radio. France, from the 1920s, tried to keep the language ahead, in a world role, subsidizing schools all over the globe; in the 1930s French film and theatre had been well ahead. However, much of this had to do with education, rather than public support for culture: it was simply a fact that the French were very well-educated indeed. In 1959, when the Fifth Republic was set up, Culture became a national totem; in fact, a sterile, old-Venice form of it was superimposed onto an educational system that, notoriously, declined, and a national television that was both censorious and comical. In Germany, state-led art sometimes reflected self-hatred. In France, matters were more complicated: the shapers of culture were motivated in part by the claims of national grandeur, but in large part also by contempt for what was bizarrely called the 'French desert'.

It was said that the State had neglected its artists. This was in some measure quite true: it had not given great public commissions to, say, Cézanne. It had also allowed the sale of many modern paintings to foreigners. In the Third Republic, there had been a reaction against the cultural pretensions of earlier French governments, but there is no evidence at all that the civilization as a whole suffered – quite the contrary: the world beat its way to Paris. In the sixties cultural pretensions returned; but France interested the world less and less – though, to be fair, some of this was the world's, and particularly the Anglo-Saxon world's, fault, as knowledge of foreign languages ran down. In the fifties supposed decentralization of culture had been encouraged, at least in the theatrical world. What, in practice, this meant was that small versions of the Paris model went up everywhere, to the detriment of local character. This went together with a Communist notion that literature had been corrupted ('bourgeois') since the Revolution, that it needed to purify itself: such was Sartre's attitude, in 1948, and, in 1953, Roland Barthes's (*Le Degré zéro de la littérature*). They were contemptuous of cliché, dismissing even genuine, interesting and highly successful figures such as Édith Piaf or Charles Aznavour or Maurice Chevalier or Georges Simenon. The accent was on Brechtianism – 'angry young men' – as against the boulevard theatre: it was all modernism, and the hope was that the epicurean, *avant garde* dilettantism of the *art déco* world would be generalized. As Fumaroli says, this did indeed happen: within a generation, robustly bourgeois figures were going in for their version of bohemia, and popular culture more or less collapsed into out-of-date copies of Atlantic rock music. In the Third Republic, academe, not 'culture', had reigned: as a young education minister, Jean Zay, said in his memoirs, the greatest test was not to speak in the Senate, but before the professors gathered in the higher education council. In fact he did very well – commissioning the Palais de Chaillot, and getting Robert and Sonia Delaunay to decorate the technical pavilion of the exhibition of 1937. It was simply nonsense to write off the Third Republic as a cultural desert, but such was the tone. Later, Communist influences became very powerful, but an initial impulse came from Vichy. In 1940, with the great defeat, there were calls for a cultural purification of the country, and a General Secretariat for Youth was established, in which Catholicism and the army played their part. At Uriage a new school for administrators was set up, the beginnings of 'technocracy', and a Catholic thinker, Emmanuel Mounier, 'the poor man's Heidegger', developed 'personalism'. One of Vichy's cultural ministers wrote, 'Diriger l'art, c'est lui permettre de s'accomplir.' A central part of this thesis was that the French universities had somehow let the national culture be frittered away in scholarly aridity, in egalitarianism. Mounier did have a reading list, but it was skimpy, and his accent lay elsewhere: he wanted to escape from the alleged academicism of literature and museums. These ideas were well-meant, in the sense that they were inspired by a feeling that ordinary people deserved a higher culture than, hitherto, they had had.

Such were the germs of the technocrats' attitude to Culture, and after the war they were filtered through Communism, which won an enormous influence. Vichy even launched an idea of great public fetes. In this, it could rely on Rousseau, who disliked the Italian theatre and wanted demonstrations of unity; Wagner was a similar influence, and led straight to the megalomaniac producers Max Reinhardt, Gordon Craig and Erwin Piscator manipulating the whole theatre, and using light, especially, to dominate a mass. The idea of theatre as awakening – here applied for left-wing purposes – was very old, and into the 1970s it was being used in western Europe, sometimes absurdly. Could television and film take its Brechtian place?

These notions came together, in 1959, with André Malraux – one-time hero of the Left, now de Gaulle's minister of culture. Like so many intellectuals, he was out of touch with the liberal democracy which had in effect triumphed in 1945, and, like so many, he talked of some 'Third Way' between capitalism and Communism, which was a false way of putting the whole problem. France thus became in 1959 the first democratic country to acquire a Ministry of Cultural Affairs, and it went on to spread far and wide, in the very propitious environment of the French State, larger than elsewhere. Malraux's budget had been small, and his *Maisons de la Culture* did not flourish, but, under Pompidou, elements of grandiosity took over. This especially concerned the Centre Beaubourg, but throughout the provinces and even in Paris small replicas pullulated. There was an entirely misleading idea that this was a continuation of Louis XIV's practices, but, now, there were far more bureaucrats than artists, and it all had to do with a very modern phenomenon, 'leisure'. The State's monopoly extended, notoriously, to television, with a great noise as to protectionism against supposed cultural imperialism, cheapening, etc. and in the 1980s proceeded to grandiose nonsense – 'the clangorous fiasco of the Bastille [opera], or the absurd project of creating a National Library, by its nature a private matter, in the very centre of a gigantic Leisure Complex' or even some enormous French version of the Las Vegas Strip, a 'Champs-Élysées of Culture', including Versailles.

Much of this came about with the ministry of Jack Lang, in 1981. On one level, it was popular, his team grinning away in the Kennedy–Servan-Schreiber manner. Culture, said Lang to *Playboy*, was to be fun. As the eighties drew to a close, Culture even gave the socialists a new lease of life, their original inspiration having failed: there was indeed fun, even though the other ministries – the economy, foreign affairs – became grim-faced as the problems began to accumulate. To begin with, the Malraux project had been very serious indeed, as befitted a country that had gone through so much, up to the Algerian war. Then 1968, an explosion of imbecile hedonism, had occurred. Theatre had begun this process and Lang himself had run a festival at Nancy that was supposed to be innovative, thought-provoking, etc. in the Brechtian manner. At least it had some sparkle, whereas the cultural commissars were taking over elsewhere (Louis Althusser's *Notes on a Materialist Theatre*, or Sartre's thoughts as to 'a proletarian theatre').

In 1969, the Nancy Festival started a sort of annual commemoration of 'the revolution of 1968', the general idea being a French Woodstock or Berkeley. Patrice Chéreau added the war of the sexes to the Brechtian war of the classes; or there was an American, in 1971, who staged a seven-hour dumb show, brilliantly illuminated, which Aragon said was the best thing he had ever seen. Lang was sacked from the Théâtre de Chaillot, in 1974, having destroyed the *art déco* frescos that had once seen Gérard Philipe's triumphs, but took his revenge, claiming that France was still a cultural desert. In 1981 the ministry announced there would be 'recognition of the cultural habits of the young, rock, jazz, photo, scientific and technical culture. Local radio . . . Introduction of the cultural dimension of the politics of social and professional inclusion for the young' (*sic*). Six *groupes de réflexion* were set up, and no doubt various useless institutes in the education ministry where Alain Besançon's one-time Communist friends found their places, burrowing away in the State like some sort of termite, pre-programmed and leaving nothing to record their passage but little heaps of pulverized dirt. Tocqueville had written a famous passage:

> Au dessus (de cette foule innombrable) s'élève un pouvoir immense et tutélaire, qui se charge lui seul d'assurer leur jouissance et de veiller sur leur sort. Il est absolu, détaillé, régulier, prevoyant et doux. Il ressemblerait à la puissance paternelle, si, comme elle, il avait pour objet de préparer les hommes à l'âge viril; mais il ne cherche au contraire qu'à les fixer irrévocablement dans l'enfance.

Lang in 1981 even announced that 'culture is the abolition of the death penalty! Culture is the reduction in the hours of the working week! Culture is respect for countries of the third world! Each member of the government has an obvious artistic responsibility.' Wooden language followed:

> the ministry entrusted with culture has, as its mission, to permit each and every French citizen to cultivate their capacity for invention and creation, to express their talents freely, and to obtain the artistic training of their choice . . . to contribute to the spread of French art and culture in the free dialogue between the cultures of the world.

France now adopted the stereotypes of Greenwich Village, giving up her own clothing and popular music, but a good part of the inspiration was really Soviet, in that Lenin had maintained a commissariat for culture, under Lunacharsky, together with various Bolshevik women – Krupskaya, Trotskaya, Dzierzynska, Kameneva, etc. It had Lito – Direction of the Book, which purged libraries, Muzo for music, Izo, Teo, Foto-Kino and Chelikbez, the special commission for the elimination of illiteracy. Lunacharsky had said, 'taking power would be pointless unless we could not make people happy'. Narkompros collected its avant-garde, and there remained, for Malraux's generation, an illusion – 'an ultra-modern Parnassus, working together with an ultra-modern state to ultra-modernize a people that was innocent, but stupefied by religion and the old order'. But the library purging was soon followed by poets and artists. Fascism, with *dopolavoro* and *Kraft durch Freude*, followed.

Against this European happiness-by-State came the American style, happiness by democratic entertainment, an immense force. Even by 1946 there was an initial test – one condition for an American loan was that American films should be freely distributed, as against the existing quota, by which French films had to be shown four weeks out of sixteen. American films then invaded – in 1947, 388 were shown, whereas French ones fell from 119 to 78 that year. In 1948 the US films were taxed, and the money was passed on to French film-makers. But the fact was that Holywood was very good. State protectionism in France turned the cinema over to coteries, anxious to do down the *idées reçues*; François Truffaut alone, or nearly, holding out for the older values in the national tradition. Fumaroli remarks that it has been a good thing that French wine-makers never had a state subsidy or were forced by coteries to make an avant-garde wine. But the way was now open for a Ministry of Cultural Affairs, with the inevitable coteries frightened by popular success and denouncing 'Americanism' while being dazzled by its techniques, though this ultra-modern America was in reality at variance with America's own traditions. French Communists took up the cause, and the Central Committee collected some big names – Picasso, Aragon, Léger, Irène Joliot-Curie, quite in the style of Comintern media mobilization in the thirties. Russian films, etc. were shown in fellow-travelling organizations such as *Les Maisons de la Pensée Française*, and Fumaroli wonders how far these ideas percolated, as the state 'structures' spread, and of course culture offered at least relief from the endless wooden language and the tiresome agitprop. In time, many left the Party but stayed, at state expense through *Maisons de la Culture*, etc., with 'gauchisme', and 1968 showed how Brechtism replaced Marxism of the old sort. Kremlin-Beaubourg, Kremlin-Bastille then got going. Jack Lang, for instance, said of Cuba in 1981 at a Unesco conference in Mexico that it was 'courageous', that 'culture is above all the right of each people freely to choose its political order', as against the supposed domination of culture by a multinational financial system. There was much denunciation of the American film festivals at Deauville, but the denunciation itself was really that of Greenwich Village, sexual liberation, drugs, etc. Lang subsidized French rock groups that imitated obsolete American ones and made a great fuss of rap. That ministry was even encouraging a confrontation for alleged creativity between the museums and a noise called 'tag'. The only answer would have been to defend French culture via the schools, but instead Lang tried to fight Americanization by adopting what the American liberals made of it – alternative lifestyles, marketing, social and racial problems – and bringing Disneyland to France. There were gruesome events such as a *Fête de la Musique*, endless music of all sorts launched simultaneously, everywhere, in the manner of a campaign against smoking or for seat belts. There was in June 1995 a business on the place de la Concorde for SOS Racisme, a nowadays discredited organization, with reggae and pop groups subsidized by the ministry, looked on with favour by Jacques Attali, and Jack Lang, with 300,000 people there for the weekend, including tourists, with huge screens and amplified music, the ministerial faces projected. It was supposed to be an enormous campaign against racism, complete with campaign buttons (*touche pas à mon pote*), in connection with the celebrations of 1789.

There were of course in the Ministry of Culture (as it was after 1976) the older institutions, the museums and archives, with enormous international authority, with well-chosen exhibitions, in the usual dusty and slow-moving scholarly atmosphere. Now, the ministry introduced dynamism, etc., and its exhibitions were glossy and shallow as against the older style of long-lunch apparent laziness (in the great days of the BBC Third Programme, three-gin lunches were standard). Fumaroli says 'the ready-made smiles of the modern, dynamic techno-crat disguise a mourning'. Hence the saga of the Bibliothèque Nation-ale. Even with Malraux (who instituted the *Maisons de la Culture*) there had been ideas of juxtaposing the modern and the medieval, and the idea won after 1988, as the socialists ran out of any other ideology. This led to imitation of the Grand Louvre scheme, and I. M. Pei's absurdly misplaced *Maison de la Culture. Lieux culturels* followed, with all the audiovisual paraphernalia. Strange it was that these arti-facts were not really shown on television at all, where they would indeed have had access to millions if that was the intention. The State did not let go of television, and a modest cultural channel, la 7, can only be seen very expensively, on cable, and by fewer people than watched the original Eiffel Tower transmitter in 1935. Besides the electoral considerations, the ministry's own assumption, that there is a huge public for culture, would automatically be disproved as there would indeed only be a small number of viewers for such a channel, and in any case they were quite likely just to ignore television. There is the example of the Centre Beaubourg, getting in a year as many people as watch a successful TV show in a single night. But the museum itself attracts no more people than when its pictures were tucked away in the Palais de Tokyo. Visitors spend time in the side-shows but do not pay to enter as they were supposed to do. There was conscious imitation of the Eiffel Tower (1889), renowned worldwide, and Beaubourg, the Louvre pyramid, Opéra-Bastille, the Géode de la Villette, l'Arche de la Défense, and then the tower-books of the Tolbiac library were repetitions on the theme. The crowds that visit do indeed silence criticism but the real visitors remain quite stable in number. The things have been a touristic success, and nothing else. Books got the treatment as well, and libraries acquired multimedia trappings, until the Direction du Livre had the idea of the Très Grande Bibliothèque (Paris libraries generally being understocked). The Beaubourg's own library took in as many visitors as the museum upstairs, people sitting on the floor and notices warning of pickpockets. The Très Grande

Bibliothèque was supposed to keep the old French books and as well to be an 'information library', but the two purposes (however much talk there was of the technical difficulty of keeping books in the old BN and the need to computerize the catalogue) were different. The old library was meant for an elite – or a minority, if that is the right word – and yet it was supposed to coexist with a crowd of sightseers (*badauds*). Fumaroli remarks that no-one expects non-sportsmen to come onto football pitches, or non-dancers to take the floor in discos. 'The superposition of two libraries, by nature incompatible, on the same architectural site, itself in any event conceived to attract the robot-tourist' caused a debate that had been simmering all along, since 1959. The public who had always gone to the museums and the Comédie-Française were oppressed by this supposed cultural democratization. The Lang ministry was the apogee of modish bureaucratic creationism, all geometry and Le Corbusier, with a vast budget. But what was there to show for it all? This 'Culture' was used as a grandiloquent, triumphalist alibi for the ruining of the old university and the humiliation of its scholar-teachers, as 'social sciences' take over from the old humanities, which truly had the apparatus of scholarly disciplines to offer. Television became the real queen of the battlefield, a mighty engine of egalitarianism, which simplifies and coarsens to the point of caricature the worst features of what Montesquieu called the general spirit of a people. Curiously enough, the men (much more often: it took time for the women to catch up) of 1968 frequently went on to prosper in the media, as they did in Germany as well. That year had much to answer for.

16

Atlantic Crisis 1974–1979

Of this period, the fall of Saigon and Phnom Penh in April 1975 was the great symbol – the greatest military and economic power on earth defeated by a small and very determined Communist state. It was a symbol of greater resonance than even earlier such instances, such as the evacuation of Canton in 1949, when Chiang Kai-shek had fled to Taiwan, with his broken army (and the museum treasures of ancient China). In Saigon, there was a general panic, for all the world to see on television, as the helicopters whirred off the roof of the American embassy, crowds of people clutching desperately at the struts. Of course, the supposed peace agreement of 27 January 1973 had been fraudulent, a face-saver for the Americans, and there was a considerable Northern presence in the South. Heavy weaponry was moved along the jungle roads, and 100,000 men came in from the North, with tanks and SAMs. The total force available stood at a million men, regulars and *guerrilleros*, most of whom did front-line service, whereas Thieu's American-trained 750,000 men suffered for the enormous 'tail' on which the Americans insisted: in effect six men in the rear for every one at the front. Thieu tried to extend his own control in the Mekong Delta, but that only overextended his forces – by now, at least partially, far better than before, and offering one of the might-have-beens of the affair. Then came the oil crisis, depriving the South Vietnamese air force of fuel, which the Americans would only dole out from watering cans; and inflation became much worse. By autumn 1974 the Northern leaders had decided upon a two-year 'general uprising' and early in 1975 seized territory adjoining Cambodia, capturing huge amounts of supplies, at that only eighty miles from

Saigon. Nixon had promised to 'respond with decisive military force', but he was now politically dead, and Thieu was abandoned, to the cheers of Congress.

The Ho Chi Minh Trail, no longer the romantic Guevara pathway, was now double-tracked and paved, with intersections that required traffic managers, and ended close to Saigon. In fact the South could be cut in half, and the North had another advantage, that small attacks in the centre would drive hordes of refugees in panic towards the sea and Saigon, blocking all the roads and preventing the Southern army from moving effectively. That is what happened – a chief city bombarded and isolated, with refugees crowding the roads and even the ports, paralysing the ships. South Vietnamese soldiers themselves panicked, rushing to save their families. A truly ruthless regime would just have machine-gunned the refugees and driven them in a different direction, but Thieu was not made of such stuff, and instead just ordered complete retreat out of the Central Highlands. Masses of troops picked their way through masses of refugees, moving in buses, lorries, private cars, bicycles, all overloaded with people, from babies to aged ancestors, those who fell being crushed by the vehicle behind, while the North Vietnamese threw shells into the crowds. Forty thousand people are said to have died on this exodus, and over $1bn of materiel fell into North Vietnamese hands.

Now came collapse. Thieu hoped to hold on with enclaves that would get American support – Da Nang on the coast, together with Saigon and the Mekong Delta. But, once again, the Northern commanders applied ruthless methods, using refugees to paralyse the defenders' movements, and attacked towards Hue, a city already vastly demoralized by the Buddhist troubles and swamped in refugees by the North Vietnamese attack of 1972. On 24 March the old fake-imperial city, tinkling bells and all, collapsed, and a million refugees now fled towards Da Nang, where the Americans had had their fortress-port, or tried to get away by sea, clinging to anything that might float. By 29 March Da Nang was falling as well, as official America turned a disdainful back (the ambassador even tried to prevent a decent man, Edward J. Daly, president of World Airways, from sending two Boeing 727s to the city, flying on the first one himself.

After landing, his aeroplane was mobbed by thousands of people, some 270 of whom were finally jammed in, under gunfire, and, badly damaged, the aircraft limped heroically back). Then all the other coastal towns fell, Cam Ranh Bay, the great American base, after only thirty minutes of fighting; one airport was captured with more than sixty grounded aircraft. By early April the North Vietnamese had cut off Saigon, and were able to shell Bien Hoa airfield. Cambodia was collapsing as well: on 12 April 276 Americans were evacuated from Phnom Penh, which should have been a sign to the still disbelieving Thieu. He hung on to office for another week, desperate to see the B52s return. Instead, he learned on 23 April that President Ford, speaking at a university, had announced that the war in Vietnam 'is finished as far as America is concerned'. His audience stood up and clapped.

The evacuation of Saigon had itself been held off, to forestall panic, but panic then took hold, as a formation of captured Cessna A-37s bombed the presidential palace. The famous scene came on 29 April, with the helicopter evacuation from the embassy compound itself. Up and down, on film, 6,236 people were taken off through crossfire, the large machines lifting off from the walled-in yard, the smaller ones from the roof; 662 flights were made between Saigon and ships eighty miles away, the crews managing matters with great efficiency and such decency as could be mustered; and the end came at 5 a.m. on 30 April, when the ambassador left. Now, every South Vietnamese who could get away made for the American Seventh Fleet, helicopters landing so fast that they had to be pushed overboard as soon as the occupants had been got out, to make space for the next one: 675,000 refugees were brought to the United States. On 30 April a North Vietnamese tank smashed through the gates of the presidential palace. The stand-in president, the selfsame Duong Van Minh who had once destroyed Ngo Dinh Diem at the Americans' behest, wanted formally to capitulate. He was told that he no longer had anything to give up, but was allowed, on the radio, to say a few words to the effect that that was that. In Cambodia, at the same moment, there was a similar collapse, as the Khmer Rouge moved in to a silent Phnom Penh, filled with a foreboding that was entirely justified.

To start with, the opponents of the Vietnam War were jubilant: the 'People' had triumphed, the Americans and their lackeys were scuttling ignominiously away, as 'Whites', in this scenario, were supposed to do. The Communists were even on a best behaviour that comes as a curious shock after the experiences of mismanaged American triumphs, a quarter-century later, in Kosovo or Baghdad, when army engineers were replaced by private contractors. The North Vietnamese worked to get the electricity and water in Saigon going, and for a time there was recovery. But this solicitude for the Saigon population did not last for very long. The usual tyrannical procedures were applied, with attempts at heavy industrialization, and collectivization of agriculture, in a country wrecked by a quarter-century of war. Even the Mekong Delta, from which rice had been exported, saw famine. Anyone connected to the 'old order' was 're-educated' in gruesome camps and a secret police had the usual field day. Vietnam was distinguished only by a phenomenon known as the 'boat people', as a million people (estimates differ) bribed their way onto open boats to escape, over pirate-ridden seas, to countries such as Malaysia or even Australia, where they were not greatly wanted. About 750,000 of the Chinese minority were floated off from 1978 onwards, taking years to become, eventually very successfully, integrated elsewhere. Meanwhile, Vietnam relapsed into the traditional hostility towards China, and there was even an absurd war. In Cambodia matters were even worse. A provincial peasant and largely teenage Communist Cambodian guerrilla force had started up: the Khmer Rouge. These were led by one Pol Pot, who, though not a great academic success in France, had learned the usual stew of exterminatory Communism that flourished in those parts (Enver Hodža in Albania, and for that matter Andreas Papandreou in Greece, had had the same training). Maoism had glorified the revolutionary peasant, whereas Marx had regarded peasants with contempt – 'quadrupeds' (as the French Left saw them). Mao had demonstrated that the peasants were after all revolutionary, that the evil really lay in the towns, where money was made, and foreigners flourished. A sort of mad peasant ideology resulted. On 17 April 1975 the Khmer Rouge invaded the Cambodian capital and declared that townspeople were abolished: 2.5 million people were killed, sometimes horribly, or starved, or worked to death, until the Vietnamese invaded. In later years, 'boat people' and the 'killing fields' of Cambodia (revealed by an enterprising Hungarian television journalist, Aladár Chrudinak) counted as glaring evidence that the Americans had been right in fighting the Vietnam War, and wrong only in the method with which they had fought it. This is a debate that goes on.

There was another great symbol of this period – 'Watergate', and the fall of Richard Nixon. It was as if the gods had wanted to take a revenge, in black humour, for Nixon's weasely behaviour over Vietnam, for the original offence was comic, and we might even apply Hegel's remark as to 'the terrifying infinity of the particular'. Nixon's staff were caricature business school types, sandwich lunches, workout sessions, confusing efficiency with efficacy: no imagination at all. John Ehrlichman was a Christian Scientist lawyer who objected to Nixon's drinking and refused to work with him unless it stopped. The drinking did in fact stop, more or less, and Nixon's judgement did not improve: without a drink he became charmless and gauche. The Chief of Staff, John Mitchell, exuded silent strength, misleadingly, but he had a first-class record that made Nixon feel inferior, and brought out the nasty, frustrated and unscrupulous side of the President. Junior staff, tails wagging, organized a break-in at Democrat headquarters in the Watergate office building, in the hope of finding discreditable papers. The affair was bungled, lies were told, and Nixon, his head in Chinese clouds, did not follow the trivialities. Then he lied as well. Then the lies were recorded, as well as his reactions to the revelation of this. Then the people who tried to find out about the recordings were harassed, and then more lies were told.

Lying about (and obsession with) trivialities, and subjecting opponents to this or that survivable illegality, were not new in American politics, or for that matter the politics of most other countries. Roosevelt himself had been guilty. The Watergate break-in had even occurred in a defensible context, because secret documents had been 'leaked' to *The New York Times* (about Vietnam) and national security was threatened. But Nixon depended upon a wooden, two-dimensional staff, and National Security people who might have understood something about proportion had been cold-shouldered. The Republican establishment's candidate had been Nelson Rockefeller (who lost, because he had divorced a wife of thirty years' standing, and discovered the sixties in his own sixties) and they did not like Nixon: 'such a common little man', said Theodore Roosevelt's daughter. Over Watergate, they may even have stabbed Nixon in the back. At any rate, a huge fuss in the media, preoccupying them as the internal and external affairs of the United States went from bad to worse, led to a threat to Nixon of impeachment, a formal condemnation by Congress which might have led to bankruptcy and imprisonment. On 9 August 1974 Nixon resigned. He was given a formal pardon in exchange, by his unchosen successor, Gerald Ford, who was next in line, mainly because he was not a thief, like the previous Vice-President, or an alcoholic, like the other alternative. Not America's brightest moment.

There was far, far more in the background. The October crisis of 1973 introduced a period of terrible instability, when quite sober commentators could assume that the End was Nigh. OPEC now appeared to be almost a villainous operation from James Bond, with a palace headquarters on the Vienna Ringstrasse. The earnings of oil exporters rose from $23bn in 1972 to $140bn in 1977. There was a fourfold inflation of oil prices, and then an eightfold one; stock exchanges collapsed, banks failed, and a tidal wave of petro-dollars engulfed the world, enriching by far the least worthy recipients. Golda Meir, in Israel, remarked that Moses had wandered in the desert for forty years, leading his people to the only place in the Middle East that had no oil. But it was on the whole America's own doing. The oil producers, left to themselves, would have been far too disunited for common action, and their common strategy at OPEC did not in fact last for very long. But the fall of the dollar in 1971 pushed them together: why accept valueless paper dollars? The same was true, though not to the same extent, for producers of other raw materials – coffee, tobacco, copper, rubber, iron ore, meat as well – and prices shot up, even in 1971, two years before the oil shock. The problem was symbolized by the Brazilian city of Manaos, deep in the jungle. There, once upon a time, rubber had appeared, and the place became opulent: famously Dame Adeline Patti, the great opera singer of the 1890s, appeared there. Then rubber was produced elsewhere, and Manaos relapsed back into semi-jungle. Now, the Middle East was becoming a huge Manaos.

At least in the epoch of Manaos, there was one commodity that ruled everything else, including money: gold. International prices were stable, or even inclined to go down gently, because the main trading countries' currencies were based on the Gold Standard. If more gold had been produced then no doubt prices would have risen, but there was a very limited supply of it – roughly what could have been stored in a house (silver was far more plentiful, and therefore unreliable). Up to 1914, and in most ways even 1931, most currencies could be exchanged into gold on demand. In practice it was of course inconvenient and unsafe for gold to be carried around in any quantity, but paper money based on it was trusted, and there were few openings for the manufacture of paper money on the scale that occurred in the 1960s. If you had a profit, you might keep it safely in paper – and very handsome, dignified paper at that. Now, the inflation of the paper dollar meant that, on top of low prices, the producers were getting money of questionable value, itself declining in purchasing power (and looking more and more crumpled and grubby). The only answer was for them to combine and to create scarcities, as the oil producers in 1973 elected to do.

But the volume of paper-money purchasing power in the Atlantic countries meant that an increasing amount of money chased goods, with the inflationary results that would follow. Primary produce of all sorts, including food, now rose in price: in the USA even in 1971 wheat went up by 50 per cent. As an instance of what happened, there is the index of prices paid for 'Omaha Choice Steer' of roughly one ton in weight. In 1951, at a time of rising prices in the Korean War, the price was $35. In the 1960s it varied around $25. Then in 1969, 1970 and 1971 it started to rise – $30 and above – reaching $36 in 1972 and $45 in 1973, where it stabilized until 1978, when it reached $50, and then in 1979 almost $70 (the figure then stuck for almost a quarter-century). Inflation was telling and prices since 1956 have risen ten times: a Florida bungalow in the early 1960s cost $35,000 with interest at 5 per cent, but a decade later stood at four times as much with a higher rate of interest, and there was more to come. Inflation on this scale was general, and when it affected oil prices, it threatened the existing order at its base. From August 1972 to August 1973 meat and fish rose by 40 per cent and *Business Week* feared that the USA would become another Brazil, a place with endless zeros on the torn and smudgy banknotes. An ounce of gold reached $875 in 1980 (as against $35 in 1970) and the dollar, having stood at four Marks, fell close to two, with a somewhat lesser fall against the yen. In August 1971 it had finally come off gold, and had gone down. Sharp-sighted foreigners could see the dimensions of the problem to come, though Nixon and the advisers at Camp David 'closed the gold window' apparently quite casually, the Secretary of the Treasury dismissing complaints: the dollar is our currency but it's your problem. American exports then flourished at the expense of other countries'. Weaselling protection against them then set in, and unemployment increased all round. Late in 1972, in the library of the White House, the German chancellor, Helmut Schmidt, tried to sort things out, and for a time the foreign exchange desk officer of the Federal Reserve, Paul Volcker, even flew around in a windowless aircraft from place to place, with a view to fixing things. It was no good: there was a tidal wave of money moving against the dollar, and lines in the sand were engulfed. By now there was so much money held in places quite beyond the West's control that nothing much could be done, and the speculators were just given their heads. Currencies now, in March 1973, floated against each other, the values yo-yo-ing; in June the dollar fell to 2.28 Marks from 2.83, then rose again because the Americans had oil, then fell again in 1975, and fell drastically when the Shah of Iran ran into trouble at the turn of 1978–9. With such uncertainty as regards money, trade suffered, and unemployment grew. But so did prices.

It was a strange inflation. Ordinarily, when prices started rising, there was a heightening of activity as people worked harder to make ends meet, or for that matter dealt in the black economy (as had happened in post-war France, Italy or Germany). In 1974 this did not happen. The American economy declined by 6 per cent between 1973 and 1975, and unemployment rose to 9 per cent. This was in defiance of the rules, because money had indeed been spent – and spent, and spent, and not just on Vietnam. Nixon had not reversed the sixties programme – quite the contrary. A budget of $5.5bn in 1964–5 became $144bn by 1993; welfare spending rose twenty-five times by the end of the seventies, taking half of the budget and three times the earlier share of the GNP (12 per cent). Under Johnson, permanent deficit-financing had become the rule, as distinct from conscious additions strategically thought through: $3.7bn in 1966 became $8.6bn in 1967 and $25.1bn in 1968. In March 1968 the Treasury Secretary protested that this would bring down the dollar, and so taxes were put up, such that there was even a surplus in 1969 – the last time for a generation. Thereafter control was lost, and by 1975 federal spending had reached $332bn, the deficit being over $50bn. By then government spending was taking almost 25 per cent of the entire output of the economy. All of this added to the national debt, which started to climb. It had reached $271m after the war, fell somewhat as a proportion of GNP until 1965, and then, under Johnson, grew and grew.

Nixon had to wrestle endlessly with the external problems, including of course that of the dollar's world role, and he neglected the internal problems – finding Congress difficult to deal with, and anyway lacking powers to deal with it head-on. The Constitution itself in effect left the State sometimes paralysed: it was weaker in many ways even than the Swiss central state (where on occasion the cabinet had nothing to do but play cards). By contrast, the legal machinery was much more developed: there were 312 lawyers per 100,000 people, as against 190 in Germany and 134 in England. Given that the President could be frustrated by Congress and/or the Supreme Court, if they so decided, the very system of government was not well-equipped to deal with a general crisis, and in 1973 much went wrong.

With Nixon's resignation, the United States went into a sort of tailspin. The inflation – or rather 'stagflation' – went together with a, for the USA, very strange phenomenon, that much of business now appeared to fail: some of the greatest names in American business got into trouble, symbolized by the fall of one of the largest modernizing enterprises of all, the Penn Central railway. Chrysler itself was saved by the Republicans only as a national symbol: by 1980 the collapse of public services was such that 88 per cent of Americans went to work by automobile. 'The pursuit of happiness', in the foundation charter of the United States, has always struck foreigners as funny. That is a misunderstanding of the original, which was just a polite way of saying 'money' ('commodity' is a similar euphemism, and in English 'honorarium', 'remuneration', etc. have the same function). As the seventies went on, the expression could only be used with irony. Much of the country – in its way, the real part – was still innocent and old-fashioned: churches got a billion dollars for building, twice what public hospitals got, and the modern ills of family breakdown and drug addiction passed these parts by. But overall the country was paying for the very obverse of the pursuit of happiness, and there was a sort of civil war. It was an extremely strange period. Hollywood became anti-patriotic, and embarked upon a campaign of anti-American film-making, with Robert Redford in the lead, though he had several less talented imitators. But there was hysteria at large. Senators George McGovern and Ed Muskie referred to Nixon in apocalyptic terms: 'one-man rule', 'this tyrant'. The 'Pentagon Papers' affair, in 1971, which had then led to Watergate, was a disaster for the whole concept of national security, encouraging babyish attention-seeking among journalists without the talent of the pioneers in the business; and a campaign was launched against the old CIA, its assorted enemies being cast as martyrs (e.g. Seymour Hersh's work on the Chilean coup in *The New York Times* in 1974). Various radicals were acquitted, and there were the usual conspiracy theories as to the Kennedy assassination, even a House committee accepting primitive legendry as to how the Mafia had caused it. Tom Wolfe wrote a superb little essay, 'Radical Chic', on the attitudinizing of New York money at social events staged on behalf of grotesque killers.

Politics fell into paralysis, and foreign policy for a time became mouthings. Congress was now cutting the powers of the presidency. In November 1973, even before he fell, Nixon had faced a Resolution preventing him from sending troops overseas for any length of time if Congress did not formally give support, and the Jackson–Vanik amendment of 1973–4 put an obstacle in the way of his policies towards the Soviet Union, by cancelling favourable trade arrangements if Moscow did not cease harassing Jewish would-be emigrants. In July–August 1974 Congress again paralysed US handling of another strategic headache, on Cyprus, where first Greeks and then Turks had intervened. Both were in NATO, and each had treaty rights to invoke;

Cyprus mattered because there were British bases there, and the island was on the very edge of the Middle East. One set of Greeks attacked another set of Greeks, and there was a Turkish minority with paper rights, which the Turkish army then invoked, occupying a third of the island. The enraged Greek lobby intervened, against the advice of Kissinger, who felt that it was giving up the chance of a long-term solution in order to vent short-term steam, a judgement proven correct. That autumn Congress restricted the CIA, and in 1975 frustrated any positive policy towards Angola, where a civil war killed off a fifth of the population. Endless new committees in both Houses now supervised aspects of foreign affairs, and the old congressional committees which had been notorious for insider dealings, with long-term chairmen who knew which levers to pull, were replaced by an allegedly open system in which nothing worked at all. The staff monitoring the White House rose to 3,000.

The seventies were a period when the formula of fifties America appeared to be failing, and there was a symbol of this. The very capital of capitalism was in trouble. New York was reigned over by a Mayor John Lindsay, a man in the Kennedy mould, who shrank from making enemies. The city's workers were collecting wages that, with inflation, bought less and less; in 1968 the rubbish was not collected for a week, and rats ran through the streets of Manhattan. The sewage workers then struck, and from Harlem hundreds of thousands of gallons of raw sewage floated along the river. This (1971) was the background to the famous riot, in which 'hard hats' working on building sites near Wall Street and the World Trade Center attacked anti-war protestors demonstrating there. The protestors fled, to fight (successfully) another day. Lindsay had attitudinized in their direction, decreeing that the city administration's flag should, in mourning, be put at half-mast. He was forced to restore it to celebration mode, but then found another and much more damaging way to deal with the situation. He made bargains with the unions. In the USA these often had some association with organized crime, and might turn into protection rackets. The transport workers got an 18 per cent salary increase, an extra week of vacation, and fully paid pensions; the district councils, bureaucrats, had higher wages and were allowed retirement after

1. and 2. **Old business.** The former Chief of the High Command, Wilhelm Keitel, fails to persuade the Nuremberg judges not to hang him, while a delighted former finance minister, Hjalmar Schacht, signs autographs after his acquittal, September and October 1946

3. and 4. **Germany in 1946.** Berliners collecting firewood in the Berlin Tiergarten, and a tram filling with passengers in Dresden

5. and 6. **The chilly Communist future.** The young Erich Honecker being voted first chairman of the Free German Youth; a post-Christmas meeting of the French Communist Party at the Vel d'Hiv, Paris, complete with gloomy Christmas tree, both January 1946

7. and 8. **Aftershocks.** Surviving Jewish families fleeing from Poland in the summer of 1946 following anti-Semitic violence; the origins of the American space programme: a V2 rocket being fired in New Mexico, August 1946

9. and 10. **The end of the British Empire.** British troops pulling casualties from the rubble of their headquarters at the King David Hotel, Jerusalem, July 1946, and Greek Communist prisoners in Salonica with 'The British Must Go' spelled out in French on their shirts, March 1947

11. and 12. and 13.
The Cold War coalesces.
George C. Marshall with
Vyacheslav Molotov,
March 1947; Jan Masaryk
and Edvard Beneš in
Hradčany Castle, March
1947; Mátyás Rákosi at
his desk

14. and 15. **Stalin.**
Stalin celebrates
his seventieth
birthday at the
Bolshoi Theatre,
January 1950;
from right to left:
Beria, Malenkov,
Vassily Stalin,
Molotov, Bulganin
and Kaganovich
carrying Stalin's
coffin, March 1953

16. and 17. **Communism on the March.** Chinese Red Army troops during the assault on Shanghai, May 1949; Korean refugees fleeing from Communists in the north, with frozen rice paddies in the background, January 1951

18. and 19. **Hungary 1956.** Partisans with the corpses of secret policemen, Budapest, November 1956, and a Soviet tank in Budapest later in the same month

20. and 21.
Colonial delusions. French African troops at Port Said (the shortly to be blown up statue of Ferdinand de Lesseps in the background); British troops posing for a street photographer in a different part of the same town, November 1956

22. and 23. and 24. **Leaders.** Georgy Malenkov about to watch Arsenal play Manchester United during a visit to London, March 1956; Nikita Khrushchev and Władysław Gomułka at the United Nations, September 1960; John F. Kennedy and Dwight D. Eisenhower leave the White House for the former's inauguration, January 1960

25. and 26. **The non-Atlantic in the ascendant.** Two symbols of Communist glamour: Yuri Gagarin and Fidel Castro; the Berlin Wall at Potsdamer-Platz, August 1962

27. and 28. **The Atlantic in trouble.** Some of the hundreds of thousands of white settlers fleeing Algeria, May 1962; captured American airmen being paraded through the streets of Hanoi, July 1966

29. and 30. **The new Europe.**
Ludwig Erhard and Charles de
Gaulle at a dinner hosted by
Konrad Adenauer, September
1962; Willi Stoph and Willy
Brandt, May 1970

31. and 32. **Prague 1968.** Nicolae Ceauşescu and Alexandr Dubček, Prague, August 1968; Prague later in the same month

33. and 34. **The 1970s.**
Leonid Brezhnev,
southern Russia, summer
1971; Richard Nixon and
Henry Kissinger, Paris,
December 1972

35. and 36. **Cold War spin-offs.** Salvador Allende with his new head of the Chilean armed forces, Augusto Pinochet, August 1973; Sheikh Yamani and Edward Heath in London to discuss the oil crisis, November 1973

37. and 38. **Awkward social occasions.** President Carter, King Hussein and the Shah, Teheran, January 1978; President Tito and the Prime Minister, James Callaghan, Heathrow, March 1978

39. and 40 and 41. **Good and bad populism.** Helmut Schmidt, April 1977; Jimmy Carter, September 1978; Süleyman Demirel, the great Turkish survivor, May 1977

42. and 43. **The men who made Thatcher.**
General Galtieri (*centre*) with Admiral
Lambruschini (*left*) and Brigadier General
Graffigna, Buenos Aires cathedral, May
1980; Arthur Scargill, Orgreave colliery,
May 1984

44. and 45. **Couples.** Ronald Reagan and Margaret Thatcher, June 1984; Nicolae and Elena Ceauşescu with folkloric Romanian children, *c.* 1985

46. and 47. **More couples.**
Elizabeth II and Rupert Murdoch,
Wapping, February 1985; General
Wojciech Jaruzelski and Pope
John Paul II, Warsaw, June 1987

48. and 49. **Cold War spin-offs.** President Mohammed Najibullah meeting Soviet troops, Kabul, October 1986; Prime Minister Turgut Özal meeting Ronald Reagan, April 1985

50. and 51. **The end.** The East German leader Egon Krenz about to lose his job, with Mikhail Gorbachev, Moscow, November 1989; Boris Yeltsin earlier in the same year

twenty years; the teachers received increases of 22–37 per cent. Lindsay made New York the capital of crime. In the 1960s it had 7.6 murders per 100,000 people and from 1971 to 1975 21.7.

It was of course a racial matter. Crime was associated substantially with non-whites, including the Puerto Ricans. Jonathan Reider, in his well-known study of the white backlash in Canarsie, Brooklyn, said that his interlocutors 'spoke about crime with more unanimity than they achieved on any other subject, and they spoke often and forcefully ... one police officer explained that he earned his living by getting mugged. On his roving beat he had been mugged hundreds of times in five years.' In a notorious case in 1972 the police chief ordered all white policemen away from a hospital, when he gave in to the black rabble-rousing politicians Louis Farrakhan and Charles Rangel rushing in to defend criminals who had killed a policeman.

The crisis of 1973 wrecked the city's finances, as stock exchange dealings fell, whereas welfare costs remained fixed. New York City was only narrowly saved from collapse in 1974, though Lindsay himself had by then given up, and in the later 1970s ordinary city services often came apart – snow not shifted; in 1977 a power failure that lasted for almost thirty hours, during which there was a great deal of looting. As was said, the cheerful city of *Breakfast at Tiffany's* turned into the bleak battleground of *Midnight Cowboy*. Around this time, too, came a further extraordinary flouting of ancient rules: the release of mental patients onto the streets, as asylums were closed. Progressive-minded specialists had urged this, and New York acquired a sort of black-humour chorus to its problems. And so any American big city had the horrible sight of mentally ill people roaming the streets and combing through the rubbish. Much of this went back to sixties bestsellers, whether Michel Foucault's *Madness and Civilization* (1965) or Thomas Szasz's book of 1961, *The Myth of Mental Illness*, and it was the judges who ruled that this had something to do with human rights. The overall sense of these works – Laing's the best-known – was to the effect that madness was, in this world, a sane response, and there was something to be said for this view. Much the same happened as regards crime. Progressive-minded criminologists had been arguing quite successfully for non-use of prison, but crime rates doubled in the

1960s whereas the numbers in prison actually fell, from 210,000 to 195,000 (by 1990 they had risen again, to one million), in accordance with modish behaviouralist ideas, and in the later 1970s, although there were 40 million serious crimes every year, only 142,000 criminals were imprisoned. The National Rifle Association membership grew from 600,000 in 1964 to 2 million in 1981. If the police and the courts would not defend Americans, what else were they supposed to do?

Contempt for ordinary Americans also showed in the interpretation of the desegregation laws. The worst cases happened over school segregation. Boston schools that served poor districts were dictated to by judges who unashamedly sent their own children to private schools. The Civil Rights Act of 1964 had expressly stated that there would be no enforced bussing of children from one district to another to keep racial quotas. But the Office of Education in the Department of Health, Education and Welfare issued regulations in defiance of this. The argument was that if there were not sufficient white children, then segregation must be occurring. The courts backed this in 1972. Almost no-one actually wanted the bussing, but it went ahead, with riots and mayhem, and there was a move out of town, and a rise in private-school enrolment (from one ninth to one eighth). In the north-east racial isolation became worse than before – 67 per cent of black pupils were in black-majority schools in 1968 and 80 per cent in 1980 (more than even in 1954). There were horrible stories at South Boston High, where black children were exempted from fire drills out of fear for their safety if they left the building. A journalist, J. A. Lukas, wrote the classic book on the story, all the more gruesome because the grand liberals did not have to have anything directly to do with their handiwork. Michael Dukakis lived in a decent suburb and sent his children to private school; Edward Kennedy used St Alban's School, and the liberal journalists of Ben Bradlee's *Washington Post* did likewise.

Where was American democracy? Law was passed by an apparent 'Iron Triangle' of lobbyists, bureaucrats and tiny subcommittees. The Democrats (now essentially controlled from the north-east) reformed the House in such a way as to remove the old men from committee chairmanships, as from October 1974, when one of them became involved in a sex scandal involving a whore. The old system had been able to deliver votes, for instance for the Marshall Plan, but it could also be used to stop left-Democrat aims because experienced chairmen knew how to do it. A San Francisco congressman, Phil Burton – he supported Pol Pot in Cambodia, in 1976 – was backed by labour, but the result, with many now open committees, was that lobbyists flourished, and the small print of enormous legislative documents contained provisions to satisfy them, quite often unnoticed by scrutineers. It became impossible to get the budget in on time, and there had to be endless 'Continuing Resolutions' which simply enabled the government to go on spending as before: in 1974, $30bn more; between 1974 and 1980 spending (beyond defence) rose from $174bn to $444bn.

It was not surprising that so many Americans felt hostile to the whole process, and a radical, Christopher Lasch, wrote powerfully as to how a bureaucracy-dominating elite had taken power from people to run their own lives. He particularly despised the endless fuss made about cigarette-smoking – it started with a ban in Arizona, in 1973, on smoking in public buildings – but this was a frivolous period, the landmarks down. What Leszek Kołakowski called the politics of infantilism went ahead. Alvin Toffler pronounced in 1970 that the future would amount to endless leisure. For some, it did. In 1970, 1.5 million drew a disability pension, but 3 million in 1980; one tenth of the nation's families was headed by a single woman, living on welfare. Paul Ehrlich in 1968 looked at *The Population Bomb* and asserted that there would be famine in the 1970s, and thought that pets should be killed, to save resources. One man made his name in the seventies with the claim that there would be a new Ice Age, and made his name again twenty years later with a further claim that global warming would mean apocalyptic floods. The wilder shores of the sexual revolution were explored, Niall Ferguson remarking that the only people who wanted to join the army were women, and the only people who wanted to get married were gays. Feminism, a cause that went back to hesitant beginnings under Kennedy, was vigorously promoted through the courts, and quotas for 'positive discrimination' were allowed – although Congress had never voted for this. Equality was applied, with many absurdities resulting (Edward Luttwak got himself off guest lists when he pointed out that heavy military lorries, driven by women, might crash because the driver's legs were not strong enough for the controls). In Ohio women were at last 'allowed' to lift weights heavier than 25 pounds; in February 1972 the ghastly little word 'Ms' was allowed in government documents; women were 'allowed' to enter sports teams' locker rooms; in New York women were permitted to become firemen; and in 1978 women were allowed to serve on naval vessels, ten of the first fifty-five becoming pregnant. Here was America at its witches-of-Salem weirdest.

The economy itself was losing the lead that it had had over all others, and, again, inflation had much to do with this. Unions, on the whole, could resist it, at least in the big industrial firms, where blue-collar wages kept up. Labour was all-important for the Democrats, and AFL–CIO grew, up to 1978, as 'corporatism' prevailed, but it was increasingly not so much blue-collar workers as soft-professional teachers in the lead. There were alarms as to the competitiveness of American industry. Kenneth Hopper, a Harvard Scottish warhorse, noted ('American Machinist Special Report' of July 1970) that output per hour in factories had increased by 20.1 per cent between 1961 and 1965, but by less than half of this figure in the following five years; the growth in take-home earnings fell from 23 per cent to −1.5. The point was that 'of the major nations of the world, the US reinvests the lowest proportion of its GNP' – 16.6 per cent as against 23 per cent in Germany and somewhat more in France, or 34 per cent in Japan, such investment including machinery and housing. In engineering, from the mid-fifties onwards, investment was far lower, per $1,000 deliveries, than in Europe or Japan (about $12 as against $60–80), and fixed assets were even below England's. There was some official dishonesty involved in defence of this: a strange myth was propagated by the OECD that American equipment was only four to five years old, that investment had really been quite adequate, that overinvestment needed to be taxed. The Department of Commerce knew better. America, or parts of it, had been vastly spoiled and had not had to work; even in 1968 some essential structures were over fourteen years old. Congress sometimes ascribed the inflation to business's desire for capital investment, but in fact new equipment was indeed needed, and what had confused the figures was tax. Depreciation allowances were unreal, and old equipment was recorded as relatively recent. There was also much grumbling that Americans had a low propensity to save (6.1 per cent of their income, whereas the German figure was 13 per cent and the Japanese 20 per cent). But only a fool would have saved in countries where inflation ran in double figures and interest rates in single (or, after tax, half of these).

This was an era when the vast industries and dam projects of the New Deal era lost ground. General Motors, ITT, Union Carbide, US Steel went on in the old way: Cadillacs and Chevrolets were much the same as before, representing strange and classless aspirations for boat-like motor cars; but the Japanese were more subtle. The American share of automobile sales went down from 32 to 19 per cent, of steel from 20 to 12 per cent, and in manufacturing generally from 26 to 20 per cent (1981). The standard of living fell below that of Germany or Sweden, as the GDP per head stood at $6,000 to Switzerland's $7,000. All in all, much of American industry was now 'rust belt'. The trade deficit with Japan rose ten times in a few years (to 1978) to $11bn and Japanese goods accounted for a quarter of imports. A good part of the economy appeared anyway to be unreal. In January 1968 credit card debt amounted to $1.5bn, 5 per cent of which went on car loans, and by 1982 grew to $64bn (and by 2004 $576bn). The great new fortunes were built on borrowed money, and inflation now helped to wipe out the debts. Meanwhile, governments struggled to find money for essentials, and America's infrastructure was shockingly bad. The notion of a direct rail link between Kennedy airport and Manhattan was beyond America's powers, and no new runway was added to Los Angeles airport between 1970 and 2000. Health care in the United States became yet another piece of black-humour surrealism: a great deal of money spent, but 50 million people not covered by the existing system, such that infant mortality was greater than in blockaded Cuba.

The Great Society was running into the sand, and so were the Democrats, now badly divided between Northern, liberal wing, Southern illiberal wing, and corrupted city-boss body. By this time, there was no commanding figure on the Democrat side to stand for the presidency, and 'Jimmy' Carter emerged, from a peanut farm; he had been Governor of Georgia. When his mother was told that he was standing for the presidency, she reacted: president of what? He scraped in with 40.8 million votes to Ford's 39.1 million. Carter's regime symbolized the era (1976–80). It was desperately well-meaning. It jogged; it held hands everywhere it went with its scrawny wife; it prayed, Baptist-fashion; it banned smoking where it could; it sent bossy women to preach human rights in places where bossy women were regarded as an affront to them. There was a whole lobby around these in the Carter administration, and it took over part of the State Department. Carter's initial idea was to make the presidency popular: hence jumpers and jeans, and a dispersal of the Nixon trappings (the parade ground uniforms were sold to Bolivia). The man started his day at 6 a.m. and was generally exhausted; his wife was somewhat more ordered, and sometimes attended Cabinet meetings. There was fighting between the State Secretary, Cyrus Vance, who had had direct experience of Vietnam, and Zbigniew Brzezinski, as National Security Adviser, who resented the world's not putting him on the same level as Henry Kissinger. He was one for verbiage: 'the need is not for acrobatics but for architecture' were his words of wisdom to the world. Carter was a hapless fellow, everything, sunny side up, curdling: even after his lengthy retirement, as he kept pushing himself forward as a sort of sexless Clinton, the pattern prevailed, as North Korea fired missiles over Japan about two weeks after Carter had announced that she did not have any, and as Haiti collapsed into mayhem after he had announced that the great and good had come to power there. There was a similarly naïve attitude to matters Soviet. Carter scrapped the B1 bomber unilaterally, and cancelled the neutron bomb (telling an enraged Schmidt only later). There was also an absurd neglect of the Soviet navy – the expansion of which went back to the Cuban Crisis in 1962, after which 1,323 ships of all classes were built, to the Americans' 120 major surface battleships and 188 nuclear submarines. In 1975, through Cuban proxies, the Soviets moved into Angola; and Ethiopia collapsed, on the edge of the now volcanic Middle East.

This regime will be remembered only for its failures. Of these, inflation and the mismanagement of the oil problem were the worst, and together they badly weakened the country. The only success of the time was the Egyptian–Israeli agreement (Camp David in September

1978, followed by the treaty in March 1979, but its Egyptian maker, Sadat, despised Carter so much that he did not even say in advance that he proposed to visit Israel). Carter's worst failure came over energy policy. The great problem was American. There was huge demand for the oil companies to be controlled because of what were said to be 'obscene' profits (the word probably intended was 'obese' but the mis-use has stuck). True, the profits had been enormous, rising from $7bn in 1972 to $16.5bn two years later, because oil which had been bought at the old price was sold at the new, and chemical operations had also flourished, given the weakness of the dollar, which encouraged exports. But the companies had been nationalized abroad, and their profits overall were, if anything, somewhat below the American average. Besides, oil policy had become a terrible tangle. Nixon had imposed price controls in 1971, to stop the then prevailing inflation of 5 per cent, and these had been kept, with extraordinarily complicated rules, for oil. The standard reporting requirements for the Federal Register required 200,000 respondents and five million man-hours; and 'for the oil industry [it] became more important than the geologist's report'. The direct costs ran into thousands of millions, and there were tales of extraordinary waste and maladministration. The regula-tion was meant to ensure fair shares, and to bring back refineries that had been kept out of service. It seems only to have profited lawyers. Administrations lurched, unwilling to accept that the price mecha-nism was in the end valuable. President Gerald Ford, in January 1975, talked nuclear power and coal; ecologists went to town. However, two things were at last put through. The Alaskan Pipeline, set to cost $10bn, was allowed; and in 1975 American automobiles had to have fuel efficiency standards. In 1977 Carter took over, appointing a multi-purpose warhorse, James Schlesinger, as his maker of energy policy, in effect hoping for rationing because a CIA report of 1976 had predicted another oil shortage. In his plaintive moralizing way, Carter wanted oil use to be subject to even greater regulation, and proclaimed (April 1977) 'the moral equivalent of war', subsequently dismissed as the acronym 'MEOW'. The point was that US oil prices were well below the world level, with absurd effects – the US at times even subsidized imports. A complicated effort was now made to revive coal, and to loosen the controls on natural gas: a very good time for lobbyists. Utility companies, oil producers, liberals, ecologists, coal producers all fought, and Schlesinger himself said that the decontrolling of natural gas had been 'Chinese water torture'.

It was true that America was experiencing tissue regeneration under all of this. Whereas in other countries people tended to stay close to where they were born, Americans packed their bags and moved. Modern industries could shift, given air-conditioning technology, to the old South, the south-west and California, now gaining population at the expense of the north-east, and by 1964 California, with 30 million people, had become the largest state, Texas soon following. Shoots of ultramodern industry were coming up, and much ingenuity was shown as regards substitutes for oil. But the middle and later seventies were a demoralizing period.

17

'The British Disease'

The overall Atlantic crisis was displayed at its worst in England, where the entire civilization had – with a Dutch contribution – started. The positive sides were enormous: the rule of law, the Industrial Revolution, a habit of non-violence in politics. France, rights of man and all, had not contributed anything like so much to the world and, comparing British experience with French, Edmund Burke had said, 'We go from light to light; we compromise, we reconcile, we balance.' In the nineteenth century the British had had to face the problems of the modern world, the organization of what came to be called 'mass society'. They had done so, preserving and adapting old institutions, using them for new purposes. For instance, local administration was carried out through the vestry, and the Church of England had a social role; the colleges of Oxford and Cambridge, which were originally religious places, of a sort that collapsed on the Continent, made for world-class universities. The oldest and most adaptable of these institutions was of course the monarchy itself, and in 1953, when Queen Elizabeth II was crowned, complete with archbishop, sacred oil, orbs and sceptres, it was an extraordinary spectacle, watched by tens of millions on the relatively new black-and-white television sets. A film-maker of genius, Lindsay Anderson, remarked, later on, that the monarchy was a gold filling in a mouthful of rotten teeth. That fitted the England that emerged, a generation after the coronation. However, the early fifties were a good time. Western Europe was not yet quite competitive, British exports did well, and there were good markets in the old imperial area. Decolonization during the 1950s had been, at least in comparison with French experience, a success, and the new

309

Queen became a considerable expert in it. At home, taxes on income were absurdly high, but there was no tax on fortunes made out of equities, and the banks were generous with overdrafts, charging a low rate of interest. The old England (and Scotland) had an Indian summer, and the great Victorian cities, with Glasgow in the lead, were still the great Victorian cities of industry and empire. But the later fifties showed that this could not last.

Her worldwide troubles in 1947 had led to the creation of an Atlantic system; now, her domestic ones revealed its central weaknesses. The great British economist John Maynard Keynes had somehow lent his name to the Pursuit of Happiness: he could reconcile welfare with progress. Government waved its wand, the poor had money transferred to them from the rich, spenders were encouraged rather than savers, the economy grew accordingly, and unemployment was kept low. 'Keynesianism', though no-one could quite pin down the Master, reigned, and dissident economists were unfashionable, or even slightly ridiculous. Their chief argument against Keynesianism was that it would promote inflation: if governments overtaxed then money would go abroad, and an overhang of paper money would translate into higher prices; in the end, when workers, through trade unions, wanted higher wages to defend themselves against a rising of basic prices, then they would expect inflation in the future, and want even higher wages. That would in turn add to the paper money and to the inflation. There were a few bright sparks who suggested that there was a relationship between the amount of paper money and pyramids of credit on the one side, and rising prices on the other. This was called 'monetarism'. Such bright sparks were not fashionable. In the sixties, the Keynesians made the running, had the answers, were constantly in the newspapers and on television, and then, in the seventies, ran into very choppy waters.

The oil crisis had its worst effects here, and the quadrupling of energy prices pushed England into a trouble that called in question the whole post-war order. Strikes in the seventies meant that the average worker was not working for nearly a fortnight every year ('average' is not the right word: large unions alone were involved, and not all of them) whereas in the fifties the figure had been three days.

The Prime Minister, Edward Heath, who had the face of a large and angry baby, would harangue the nation on a television that was switched off after 10 p.m. In 1974 he launched an election distinguished by the abstention of 2 million of his natural supporters, lost, and was replaced by a man who pandered to the unions. The Stock Exchange sank to a pitiful level and banks went under. The country was about one third as well-off as Germany, and in parts of the North there were areas that even resembled Communist Poland. In 1970 a rising figure in the political-media world of London, Ferdinand Mount, remembered that, from the capital, 'the main railway line to the north passed through great swathes of devastation – industrial wastelands with rows of roofless workshops – the roofs had been removed in order to avoid taxes'. Why had this decline come about, in a country which, after the war, had been still the second-greatest exporter in the world? It was partly that the pound had become a very strong currency, and latterly because there was oil in the North Sea, but the fall of exports was really to do with 'poor quality, late delivery, trade union restrictions, timid and defeatist management'. In fact Keynes himself, towards the end of the war, had bitterly hoped that the Germans would still have enough bombing power to obliterate some of the worst-managed industries. As things were, the obliteration happened painfully a generation later.

There was of course a great British problem, that the old industries had been the very first in the world, and, to a lesser extent, that their old markets were declining. In its way, the London Underground symbolized the entire national problem. It had been the first network in the world and was a triumph of engineering in the 1860s. But back then tunnels had to be extremely deep, whereas a generation later engineering had advanced and the Paris metro, say, was far shallower. London was stuck with a museum piece, and still is (the government at the time of the Millennium opting, quite characteristically for governments of the epoch, to build an entirely pointless structure, the Dome, at great expense instead of appealing to Londoners to put up with trouble for five years in order to have a state-of-the-art transport system). British industry entered upon a decline, and the means selected to stop it only made things worse. The facts were indeed as

Ferdinand Mount had said, an awful litany of uncompetitiveness, and it had happened to other country-empires in the past. An economic pundit of the sixties, Thomas Balogh, opined that England was going the way of Spain: she too had run an empire upon which the sun never set, and in the seventeenth century had declined very rapidly, as the contrast, to this day, of North and South America shows. But this was the wrong parallel. There was a much closer one, with Holland. The British Empire had not been, like Spain's, a military-religious affair, involving wide settlement and the forcible conversion or assimilation of natives: it had been, like Holland's, a commercial business, and it was abandoned when commercial logic dictated as much. Once India had gone, in 1947, there was little sense in trying to retain the rest in the face of local nationalists who, if given their way, would agree to keep the commercial ties going.

In fact the thirties had seen what amounted to a collapse of prices in the goods that made empire worth the game, and in any case the expense of running empire became prohibitive, especially after the Second World War. In the mid-fifties the imperial trade was still larger than the non-imperial, and there was a last flourishing of old exports and capital investment. But then Europe recovered spectacularly, and these markets counted for more and more, quite soon half of British trade. Governments in the later fifties therefore wanted rid of colonies; a process of decolonization got very rapidly under way. The older colonial hands (and some of the younger officers, who were hard-working and idealistic) knew that problems on the ground were not simple, that decolonization was not a matter to be rushed in case majorities coalesced around expropriation or worse of minorities. That was to be the pattern in many places, from Burma to Cyprus, but by now the British had had enough of these endless insoluble problems, and colonies were abandoned, helter-skelter. There was a formula: identification of least unpalatable power-wielder; minor member of royal family declares country open; Union Jack wobbles down masthead, cock-feathered-hatted governor at the salute; a few tears here and there; old hands stay on, to manage schools; new hands arrive, as advisers; native dances begin; new flag wobbles up; new anthem is sung; parliamentary mace is handed over; mayhem begins.

Opinions vary as to why this happened and as to whether the British could have avoided it; but at any rate they were able to walk away with very, very few casualties, and kept bases and markets.

But history was conspiring. As with Holland, the initial and enormous success of industry inspired imitation, competition and overtaking; protected markets did not help, as creativity suffered. The trade unions were in part responsible, but so also was a supine and spoiled management that allowed the unions to get away with it. Then the declining industries were taken over by the State, which turned out to be even worse at management – the story of the sixties and seventies. Economic creativity shifted into banking, to lending abroad, and the City of London on the whole attracted the bright and mobile, not British industry. The same had happened with the Dutch two centuries before: the great yards of Rotterdam, where Peter the Great had worked and learned, rotted, and so did the myriad of small and tiny enterprises in the city's hinterland, where endless wooden and iron parts had been ingeniously turned out in the past. Much the same now happened to Glasgow and its hinterland, which in 1914 had been responsible for fully one third of all ship-launchings; as Germans, Norwegians, Japanese, Koreans turned out mass-produced shipping of low cost and tolerable quality for the growing trade of the fifties and sixties, the Clyde and the Tyne were no longer able to compete, and the little Coatbridges and Bellshills to the east of Glasgow also went down. Liverpool, one of the grandest Victorian cities, was the worst affected, and its middle classes tended to move out, to Cheshire or the Wirral. These flourished. The comparison with Holland and Zeeland is an interesting one. Curiously enough, Catherine the Great started the extraordinary collection of the Hermitage, in the Winter Palace at St Petersburg, when she bought the collection of the long-term and legendary British Prime Minister Sir Robert Walpole, with Dutch money. She then failed to pay the Dutch back, and Holland went down.

The details of the British performance were overall dismal, at least if compared with Germany and France. The figures were endlessly repeated in gloomy articles in this period, as British commentators recognized what was happening (it was obvious enough just from a train window). In Germany and France, in the period 1960–73, management and workers just produced more per hour every year. Their productivity rose at 5.7 and 6.6 per cent respectively, as against a British figure of 4.1, and in the 1970s the gap grew. By then, on the official figures, Britain was even worse off than East Germany, and West Germans – especially a Hamburg Anglophile like Helmut Schmidt – shook their heads. The British share of world exports declined – one quarter in 1950, 14 per cent in 1964, under 10 in 1973. German exports rose from 7 per cent to one fifth, and then, in 1973, over 22 per cent. France stood at 10 per cent throughout. But the French direction of trade shifted away from colonies, which had accounted for nearly half of trade in 1952 but only one tenth by 1977. The Common Market accounted for the difference. The American share fell from over one quarter in 1950 to one fifth in 1964 and then one sixth in 1973, but of course the smaller share was quantitatively far larger. Japanese trade rose from almost nothing to 8.3 per cent in 1962 and 13 per cent in 1973. There was always an argument that the British decline was not really a decline at all, that the country had started from an artificially inflated position, that it was bound to lose ground as other countries learned, and therefore that there was nothing to worry about. But there was, and the collapse of British industry in the period after 1950 is a dismal story, in which areas that had been well and truly on the map of civilization shrunk into its edges. In the nineteenth century intelligent Germans asked why they were not British. A century later it would (or should: there was not much informed interest in Germany, and in 1989, when the Wall in Berlin came down, there were only eighty-nine passes in higher-level German in the entire London school area) have been the other way about.

Geoffrey Owen's account of this is the most illuminating, as it examines various industries in turn to look at the problem in detail. There are various long-term and short-term questions. The longer-term ones are of considerable historical interest, and the quality of history written in the past generation in Great Britain is head and shoulders above that found elsewhere: the National Archives are the best in the world, though reaching them on the British transport system is itself a considerable test for scholarship. England had somehow modernized without 'modernizing': the political system consisted of living fossils, and there was not even a written constitution.

In the 1960s, as the country slipped, there was much head-shaking, and a small tidal wave of ink was spilled on reform of this or that part of the historical legacy – especially the matter of class. However, there was one recent inheritance that was hardly challenged at all: that of the Labour government in 1945. It was bathed in a golden glow of togetherness. In 1965 A. J. P. Taylor published his *English History 1914–1945*, a brilliant book, and he (strongly Labour) ended it with the characteristic line, 'Men no longer sang *England, Arise!* But England had arisen, just the same.' Fifteen years later, as he looked out over rubbish-strewn streets in a not very fortunate part of London, his savings eaten by inflation, he was not so sure. Was there one single piece of legislation in that brave-dawn era which he would not have repealed? There had been widespread nationalization of industry and transport. They had a captured state market, and they provided employment – the National Health Service, providing medical attention cost-free, the largest non-military employer in Europe. But the record as the sixties and seventies went on was dismal. Nearly £100bn had been invested in the nationalized concerns and the annual return was –1 per cent. By 1982 nationalized industries had cost over £40bn in write-offs. The automobile-making British Leyland cost, in a ten-year period covering the seventies and early eighties, £3bn, and most of the once great British automobile industry became an international joke. In other countries, the failure of nationalized industry was not taken as self-evident. In England, it was a sort of non-violent protection racket, and to have a telephone installed or a piece of gas equipment repaired took the sort of little black-humour epic that Communist countries knew so well. However, the nationalized industries had not appeared for no reason: private concerns were not an advertisement for the alternative. In fact they themselves often appealed for state money, and became in effect nationalized.

The great British staples had been coal, shipping, textiles. Grand Victorian cities had been built up on that basis, Glasgow, Birmingham, Liverpool, Manchester especially, which Taylor knew so well, and in their great days they had been as much pioneer cities as had been, say, Boston. Even in the 1950s, the staples were holding up, in part because markets in the Empire had been protected. Cotton textiles still amounted to half of exports in 1950, but India and Hong Kong had been allowed to export with an agreement in 1932, and England became a net importer of cotton goods at the end of the decade, for the first time since 1750. The war had at least got shipping going again. But in the 1950s there was also an absolute decline and later in some cases even a collapse; it affected some of the very industries upon which the thirties recovery had been based.

Shipping was a British disaster area. After 1945 there had been a world boom, as trade grew, and by 1975 world shipping output had risen to 36 million tons, as against the pre-war 2 million (at worst) and 7 million (at best). For a time the British went on as before, with 1,324 launchings in 1950 (almost two fifths of the entire world figure). The chief shipping centres, especially Glasgow, flourished: those ranks and ranks of cranes, stretching all along the Clyde estuary, with an entire culture to match, and, at its educational heart, the Royal Technical College, which trained generations of engineers and maritime specialists from all over. In 1950 the British merchant fleet was a quarter of the world's. But then came decline – 172 launchings in 1985 – by which time the British fleet was only a small fraction of the world's. Some of this was 'unfair' in the sense that strong competition, and a desire to cut costs and to avoid the detailed regulation that was coming up, meant that there was an enormous growth in foreign registrations (e.g. Panama). Some of it had to do with pride in quality: those Clyde-built steamers sometimes had an extraordinary finish, no longer in demand. But a great deal had to do with new technology, at which Norway and Germany became more adept, with oil tankers and container ships: these were ugly, sometimes prefabricated and welded together. Japan, as the Korean War went ahead, boomed. By 1956 she had overtaken Britain, where yards were too small and apparently dominated by skilled men defending their position at the expense of technology that might have been used by people with lesser skills – an old, old problem.

Steel was another sad story. By 1914 the USA had become the largest producer, but two fifths of British steel was made for export, and in 1939 (despite legend) Germany was not ahead. After 1951 a large European market became the main stimulus, but England had not joined the European Coal and Steel Community and therefore missed much. German steel had not been nationalized, because the Allies had shrunk from relaunching it, and this saved Germany from the formula that did such harm to British steel (which was twice nationalized and denationalized). In the fifties there was a seller's market: even small plants made money, and when a delegation from Port Talbot in Wales went to Chicago as part of a scheme organized by the Anglo-American Council on Productivity it did not even mention trade unions as part of a problem. Governments attempted to plan, as governments tend to plan where steel is concerned, and placed plants for political reasons, at Ravenscraig and Ebbw Vale, respectively in industrial west-central Scotland and Wales. The ECSC on the Continent, by contrast, forced producers to rationalize, rather than to appease local interests, and an integrated market grew up. French strip mills supplied German car factories, and themselves used German coking coal; and there was an American system of pricing that allowed for more competition than in Britain. When Lorraine lost its advantage to Brazil and Australia, and inland steel became less competitive, plants were shifted towards the sea ports (Bremen, for instance, arose because of Dutch–German collaboration, as did, on a greater scale and for other goods, Rotterdam). The French constructed Usinor at Dunkirk. In Germany, Vestag was broken up in just the right way, with successor firms of appropriate size for specialization and competition – hence Krupp, Mannesmann, Thyssen, Hoesch. Germany had had less Marshall aid than other countries, and the financing for this came from a levy of the steel-users in 1952, with consequent closer attention to what was done with the money. Output then trebled in the early fifties. Japan managed a similar feat later on, her exports rising from 6 per cent of all in 1960 to 23 per cent in 1973, by which time British Steel had become almost comic. The labour force, of 340,000 in 1969, was at least one third too large. Nippon Steel produced 520 tons per man per year, Thyssen 370, Bethlehem Steel 180 and British Steel, in 1975, 122. By 1980 British steel cost a third more than German, and subsidies were far larger – in the latter half of the seventies, the equivalent of DM14bn, to the Belgians' DM3bn and the Germans' DM1bn.

The most obvious hammering for the country came from the motor car industry. In 1960 BMC had been comparable in size with Volkswagen; in 1975 it folded. By 1990 Rover was a subsidiary of British Aerospace, and was sold in 1994 to BMW (subsequently being resold). High-level craftsmanship had traditionally been rewarded in the British domestic market, whereas the American was able to use flow methods (as in the celebrated Taylorism) for a less variegated product. In the early 1950s the continental Europeans had not properly started again and British output was simply swallowed up in the export market; there was much flair to the MG sports car, for instance. However, after the Treaty of Rome, intra-European trade started up, and boomed: the Volkswagen became *the* symbol of the German recovery. The British, without much thought, turned it down. But local British occupation officers decided to support the Volkswagen manager's efforts to restart the factory; the French had greater foresight, and invited the maker and part of his family to Baden-Baden, in their occupation zone, to see what might be done; they then imprisoned him for alleged war crimes. But the British insight was not followed up (and in similar style the British turned down the offer of Danish Lego). Early on, British production ran at half a million cars, 400,000 of them exported (in 1950), whereas the German figures were 219,000 and 69,000. Then, in 1960, there were 1.35 million British to 1.8 million German – not far from half in both cases being exported. France had re-entered the market, with over a million cars (half exported). Part of this reflected tax levels – the Germans' tariffs being half the British level (30 per cent). The French and German markets were also simpler, such that the famous Beetle and the Renault 4CV could match it easily, whereas British cars – the Jaguar and the Rover – were more imposing (and sold well in the USA). Ford showed what could be done by proper management, and by recruiting of graduates who would learn in the practical American way. But there were still problems of fractured unionization, of small firms not co-operating in the German style, of an overvalued currency that made British products more expensive than German or French ones.

By the early sixties there was uneasiness about all of this, and it was translated into politics. Fifties England had been run, as far as finance was concerned, in budget-balancing style: the overseas position was too fragile for anything else. The rules were slightly bent in 1958, as the reigning Conservative Prime Minister, Harold Macmillan, bid for popularity in a pre-election year. His three Treasury ministers resigned, but the protest was waved aside, and an election in 1959 was triumphantly won, with the victory slogan (not quite accurately quoted) 'You've never had it so good'. This was true enough, and the wartime generation remembered the vegetable mess of 'Woolton pie' and taxation that, from quite a low level, took half of an income. Now, the working classes were earning good money, and often lived in subsidized ('council') housing; they were beginning to take holidays abroad, as the pound stood relatively high. Astute middle-class people acquired property, with generous tax relief, for small sums of money, which could be borrowed cheaply. The truly astute ones invested in equities, the rise in the values of which was again not taxed, and if a bank gave you an overdraft, you could be well-rewarded for doing nothing at all. Fifties England was the last gasp of the Victorian era, but acid was running through the system.

There followed almost two decades of self-consciously big government, in the spirit of H. G. Wells. In the Edwardian period he had been the very archangel of Progress – a career of extraordinary diligence and doggedness, triumphing over illness, divorce, lowly social origins to become a major novelist and a commentator with a deep knowledge of the natural sciences. He spoke for a world of classless technicians, by preference scientists, and condemned the older world of monarchs, horses, Latin and peasants. From 1964 to 1979 there was a dismal descant on H. G. Wells and even, in the form of C. P. (Lord) Snow, a caricature of him. This was the era of Wilson (Labour) and Heath (Conservative), which for historical purposes can be regarded as a seamless web. The initial Labour government in 1964 was led by Harold Wilson, a scholarship boy from Leeds (itself one of the grand Victorian cities, but the southernmost of them) who had taught Economics at Oxford. He recruited a team that was the brightest, in terms of education, that the country had ever produced, except perhaps for the Liberal Cabinet of 1914. One or two of their autobiographies were of very high quality, Denis Healey's especially (he was an excellent German-speaker and knew music properly). They also instinctively believed for the most part in the virtues of planning, in Snow's case making silly remarks about the Soviet Union; they greatly expanded education, putting up new universities and expanding old ones in a manner that now looks foolish.

However, they fell foul of twin problems: the balance of payments and the trade unions. In England inflation stood generally somewhat higher than elsewhere, and the trade unions were blamed for being greedy. In Germany the unions were 'responsible' and had their own stake in the system. The British ones were much less controlled and there were vastly more of them, competing with each other as much as with the alleged bosses. Wages rose, without much reference to productivity, and since the pound was overvalued, exports suffered because they were too expensive – quite apart from the problems of quality and delivery that were coming up. The French had had a great problem with large Communist-controlled unions, but they ruthlessly devalued to keep down export costs and to deter importers. But the Wilson government opposed devaluation, partly because London was reconstituting foreign investment quite cheaply, partly because they had foreign debts to pay, and partly because the overvaluing of the pound meant that running military enterprises, whether 'east of Suez' or in Germany, was cheaper; besides, a third of world trade was conducted in pounds sterling, which meant a great deal of money for the City of London. The Americans, with a very large stake in the system, would give support. However, trade was more or less free, foreign goods were cheap and of decent quality, and there were constant alarms as to the British balance of trade. Governments were reluctant to cut spending (and in any case the deficit of the balance of payments came about through military expenditure abroad). They were severely criticized for not spending more, and foreigners speculated again and again against sterling. In November 1967 it was devalued (from $2.80 to $2.40) but the pressure did not really go away, because the British problem was too great: attempts to play a world role and at the same time to spend money on various domestic temptations. An attempt in that direction even cost Labour an election. In 1971 a new Conservative government came in, under Edward Heath. He was a hapless and virginal figure, who to begin with talked the language of private business, and soon ended up adopting the same policies as Wilson: big government, the saving of industries such as shipping that were in trouble. A National Enterprise Board, an Industrial Reorganization Corporation, ruled the roost: meetings of these included civil servants and trade union officials, as well as businessmen to whom titles were awarded (the businessman's definition of a knight was 'a man who failed to say no when he should have done'). There had even been an absurd parody of a National Plan, the offices of which contained a lavatory without a lock or paper, and its head, deliberately put there by Wilson so that he would discredit himself, drank too much.

British government interventions of this sort were not successful. In the automobile world, they went almost comically wrong. In the 1960s there was the almost inevitable response to competition, the creation of a large corporation, British Leyland, itself after 1974 directed by a National Enterprise Board (under the head of Reed International) and before then vaguely responsible to the Industrial Reorganization Corporation. However, tax again distorted affairs. It became sensible for British businesses to pay their people in 'perks', such as motor cars, and a standard, not very interesting range then appeared, which did not match Mercedes or BMW in engineering. To these, the Swedish Volvo offered serious competition, and since the British had a free-trade agreement with Sweden, offsetting the Common Market, Volvos took the top of the market. By 1980 three fifths of the motor cars sold in Britain were imported. Leyland's management did not deal with the crisis as Arnold Weinstock had done with electricity, that is by cutting management costs and building reserves of cash. Instead, in 1972, they tried to negotiate with trade unions and craftsmen, and the Board refused to bring in outside advisers. The oil crisis of 1973, and then the inflation, brought a financial crisis, and the National Enterprise Board put in a large sum of money; Alan (Lord) Bullock recommended three levels of union co-responsibility ('partnership' in the German manner). But it was all pointless. Union troubles rose, to the point of ridiculousness, and by 1980 under a million British cars were produced, one third of them for export, whereas France had 3 million and Germany 3.5 million, between half and two thirds being exported (in Germany Volkswagen had faced a crisis, but Helmut Schmidt had refused to bail it out as Leyland had been bailed out). Japan had already entered the world market, taking a quarter of American sales, and even building factories in the United States.

Intelligent people did not need statistics to learn about the decline of the country; they only needed to take the boat train to France. By this time, British problems seemed to be falling into a vicious circle, of inflation, of problems with the pound, of problems with the balance of payments, of problems regarding unions and management alike. In 1971 unemployment began to rise, reaching not far from one million, while at the same time inflation stood at 9 per cent – not what was supposed to happen. Heath saw the answer in three directions. After a few weeks of pretending that he would 'free' the market, he was soon (February 1972) into the business of subsidizing collapsing indus-tries, and then imposing controls on wages and prices (November: the 'U Turn'). But he would make up for this. First of all would be govern-ment spending. Then would come attempts to deal with the union problem, whether by agreement, or by law. Finally, there was 'Europe': the magic that had worked in France and Germany would work in England as well.

The first two tacks ran into headwinds. Money was splashed around, interest rates were reduced from 7 to 5 per cent, and bank lending was less controlled; taxation was cut by £500m and post-war credits were repaid. At the same time public works were undertaken, particularly in the north – famously, an elaborate concrete bridge with hardly any traffic on it. There was an explosion of bank lending – £1.32bn in 1970, £1.8bn in 1971 and almost £7bn by 1973. Another expansionary budget followed in 1972, with tax cuts of £1.2bn. In 1972 the floating of the pound allowed inflows from abroad, and new credit-giving institutions were allowed to emerge, offering and taking loans in conditions no longer subject to the controls of the past. For a time, this seemed to work. Unemployment did indeed fall to 500,000, but this was classic fool's gold. The 'fringe banks' for a time did well out of property prices, which had a dangerously more important role in England than elsewhere, and unlovely concrete spread and spread and spread.

But then came the oil shock. Even food prices trebled by 1974 as against 1971, and the bubble burst in November 1973, when the minimum lending rate was pushed up to 13 per cent while public spending was cut back by £12bn. One of the new banks could not obtain credit, and the other banks had to set up a 'lifeboat'. It was not enough. The Bank of England itself had to move in, in the winter of 1974–5, and a well-connected bucket shop concern, Slater Walker Securities, had to be rescued in 1975. The Stock Exchange collapsed. Heath's effort to spend his way through the strange 'stagflation' had thus come to grief, and inflation by 1976 reached 25 per cent.

In this dismal tale came a damp squib: since the later 1950s the importance of the European recovery had been plain for all to see. Germany boomed and boomed, and so, despite 1968, did France. Italy was also picking herself up in a remarkable way, and by 1970 any Englishman could see for himself how far his country was lagging behind. By 1960 British governments appreciated that their might-have-been alternative, the former imperial lands and some of the smaller European countries such as Finland and Austria, did not give them quite the same weight as would membership of the European Economic Community. Besides, the Americans were very keen to have Great Britain as a member, for the obvious reason that she would act as an Atlantic bridge for them, in a hostile view, to walk upon. The British tried in 1962–3 and were told 'no' rudely and in public by de Gaulle, who wanted to build up Europe as a sort of 'third force'. He did it again in 1967. After his resignation, and after the shock of 1968, there were more realistic French governments and de Gaulle's successor, Pompidou, could see, with the shocks of the world's financial system in the early seventies, and the American disaster in Vietnam, that the Atlantic system needed buttressing. On the British side the various mishaps of that period caused a good part of opinion to wish that, like Italy, England could be governed by foreign-made rules, since the domestic ones were so demonstrably not working. Besides, on both sides of the political divide, senior politicians believed in big government, erecting concrete blocks of some hideousness in celebration of it. The Europe of

Brussels did much the same, and the tourism shops in that city even sold ballpoint pens with a paper-clip as pocket-attacher. In 1972–3 the Heath government pushed British membership, and did so in some desperation. It signed away British fishing rights, condemning pictur-esque fishing villages to decline as floating fishing factories vacuumed the fish out of the sea. It also had to accept the Common Agricultural Policy, which put up food costs for the poor by £25 per week, and deprived former colonial territories of an appropriate market, all the while getting the ordinary taxpayer to pay. Still, 'Britain in Europe' appeared to be the only way out of the troubles of the Heath–Wilson period, and in 1975 a referendum confirmed British membership. Italians had constantly voted with enthusiasm for not being governed by Italians. Now the British did the same. Heath had quite unwittingly done that service to the cause he most believed in. But Europe offered no immediate relief, quite the contrary.

The attempt to deal with the union problem was farcical. It had split the Labour government in 1969. Heath tried to deal with it by law, and made the law look an ass: jailing dockers, however repel-lent they might be, in peacetime, was a *reductio ad absurdum* of Marx's *Eighteenth Brumaire*, called for ridicule, and got it. London, at the time, was plastered with government posters explaining an incomes policy of percentages of percentages minus some figure that had been thought up for the lowest-paid, and the face of the Prime Minister on television was an invitation not to bother voting at all. Heath's incomes policy did not get off the ground; it was sabotaged by the miners in 1972 and fatally in 1973–4. A Prices and Incomes Board was established (under one Aubrey Jones, a marketer of soap powder in the 1960s). Of course, it was absurd for some central body to be controlling such details unless it had the equivalent of wartime powers. But the Atlantic world attempted such things, even under another supposed conservative, Nixon. The whole thing tended to freeze pay as it stood, 'relativities' being a minefield, i.e. who was paid more than whom for what. The Cabinet, to its bewilderment, found itself discussing what the secretaries should be paid. With the Coal Board, there were immediate problems, because miners saw them-selves as essential, could also discern that the rise in oil prices would make coal very desirable, had their wages politically determined, and did not see why their daughters should earn more as hairdressers. In 1972 they put in a claim for 27 per cent and 10,000 of them besieged the Saltley Coke Depot outside Birmingham. This was settled. Dockers then wanted their slice.

In the end it was the inflation that caused much of the trouble, but there was as ever in England an historical element. An extraordinary British anomaly, a tribute to the very high standards of the past, was that the trade unions were subject only to the criminal law: gratuitous mayhem, of a kind that no-one, in the English nineteenth century, would have expected. In 1906 a Liberal government anxious to please labour produced a trade union law that assumed common decency. The matter was not even debated, so that the then worthies could devote their oratorical talents to the Irish Question. The trade unions' power to 'picket', i.e. to deter potential customers and strike-breakers, was unchallenged. That power was not supposed to include violence, but there was nothing to prevent strike pickets from roving around to stop firms that were indirectly involved in the affairs of the struck-against one. A would-be mining revolutionary, Arthur Scargill, sent men with brickbats to raid the power stations and stop the use of coal, and the police stood by, helpless. In the docks, a similar protection-racketeering prevailed. In the event, power was switched off for much of the day, and industry itself went over to a three-day week (during which it produced more than in the previous 5½-day week). In February 1974 Heath narrowly lost an election, and Labour returned, this time producing a 'social contract' with the unions which was received with derision. The general idea was that there would be a 'fairer' society – i.e. direct taxes on the better off that would reach almost 100 per cent – if the unions restrained wage demands. They could not control their own people and the overall inflation was such that they were required to put in for higher wages in any event.

The public service unions now started. From 1961 to 1975 central government employment had risen by 27 and local government by 70 per cent. The NUPE (National Union of Public Employees) grew, from 265,000 to 712,000 between 1968 and 1978, and in 1973 came the first National Health strike, which included consultants. Jack Jones became a figure of power, as head of the TGWU, the largest of the unions, pushing for an extension of union power over Labour. It was he who produced the idea of a 'social contract', an echo of the 'social partnership' of consensus-minded Catholics. There would, he promised, be moderation in wage claims as a consequence. There followed some preposterous calculations as to permitted wage rises. As in the United States, these were soon shown to be imbecilic. Jack Jones apparently dictated academic salaries, and some deluded dons, unable to believe that an enlightened government could do this to them, demonstrated in mortarboard and gown outside Downing Street with the electric slogan, 'Rectify the Anomaly'. By June 1975 weekly wage rates had risen by up to one third, and by summer 1977 inflation stood at 13 per cent and wages rose by 14 per cent, the better-paid workers now paying marginal rates of income tax. In fact taxation was wicked, in the sense that it was destroying the good. A married man with two children had take-home pay of £70 per week in December 1973, but £63 in 1977; by 1979 the incidence of taxation was growing, such that there were 2.5 million more taxpayers than in 1974, but the government's own poverty figure was £55 per week for a married man with two children. There was every incentive, therefore, for said married man to abandon his family and sue for 'benefit'. A million people earned less than £55, the lowest 10 per cent of earners in the National Health Service earning £48, and the overall average itself was now low: £80 in industry generally or, for the 2 million local government workers, less (dustmen earned £56). Anthony Crosland, the ideologist of modernized Labour, became a near alcoholic. His final contribution to the country's future was to destroy the selective grammar schools that had been a great glory, and a means to inspire and promote bright children from poor backgrounds. This was done in the name of equality: schoolchildren were all now to be brought up in the same huge 'comprehensive' schools, and examinations were increasingly rigged to demonstrate that these unlovely places were a success. As ever, in England, when equality was in question, all that happened was the proletarianization of the lower-middle class.

England had the dearest labour and the cheapest management, and a spiralling down began. The public debt was added to, by over £10bn in 1975–6, and at the same time the GDP fell (by 1 or 2 per cent in the middle seventies). This compared badly with the German or Japanese experience, and even the American, because inflation in those countries was much less (in Germany even in 1975 6 or 7 per cent). England could only compete by selling London property to the new oil money, and was not exporting goods; the 'pump-priming' strategies of the era meant that none-too-good manufacturers were able to sell indifferent goods to the domestic market. The balance of payments deficit increased to £1.5bn in 1975 and a sterling crisis broke early in 1976. Healey himself decided boldly on a new programme of cuts in spending, and recognized that wage demands and inflation (plus an exchange rate of $2 to £1) made the country uncompetitive, and the government was divided (Wilson himself resigned in March 1976). In the latter part of 1976 the IMF was called in, to reinforce Healey's existing strategy, and the cuts went ahead – the first and in some ways the only truly serious cuts made. A humiliating 'Letter of Intent' had to be signed by the British government, one of the founders of the IMF. By the autumn, Wilson's successor, James Callaghan, was publicly warning his own supporters that they would have to give up the idea of spending their way into employment: 'Higher inflation, followed by higher unemployment. That is the history of the last twenty years.' By 1976 the Treasury itself was somewhat converted to the idea of monetarism, a limitation of the quantity of money such that inflation could be contained. But the conversion was not enthusiastic. The Bank (and the City) expressed greater enthusiasm.

It was an unhappy time, the country winding down, and a slow crisis started. In 1976–7 the world economy did pick up, as the oil-shock money was recycled back to the industrial and exporting countries (which grew overall at 5 per cent). But the British economy was by now too fragile to gain much more than a respite, and inflation still ran high – 25 per cent in 1975, 16 per cent in 1976 and in 1977 (earnings keeping apace until 1977). As the pound was now a petrol currency, it naturally rose; keeping it down meant selling it, and that made for inflationary pressures, compounded by the inrush of Arab money. Still, there was a respite, unemployment not much above a million, and inflation down below 8 per cent in 1978. The respite did not last long.

Seventies England finally fell apart over an absurd wrangle about Scotland. The vagaries of the electoral system had made the government dependent upon a few Scottish Nationalists. Theirs was a cause not worth discussion: careerist soft-profession mediocrities with no sense of their own country's considerable history. They had to be placated, and a referendum was staged as to independence. It failed, and, without the votes of the few Nationalists, the Labour government collapsed. It did so as the economic strategy also collapsed: the comic arithmetic of the pay policy anyway fell apart because in far-away Teheran the Shah lost his Peacock Throne, and in the ensuing panic oil prices doubled. Iran was the second-largest oil producer, and revolution there affected 5 million barrels per day. Production was suspended for ten weeks after 27 December 1978, and then recovered only to 2 million. By June 1979 the price of Saudi Light Crude had risen from $12.98 to $35.40, and there was a very harsh winter in the USA and Europe; the spot price affected marginal, non-contracted oil, and some crude-oil prices – Nigeria's for instance – even reached $40 per barrel. In Britain, with inflation rising, the barriers broke. The TUC wanted 22 per cent, not the 5 per cent they were supposed to accept, and various strikes began in the winter of 1978–9. Callaghan, who himself said that if he were younger he would emigrate, confessed that there was a strange new tide a-flowing, and he was right.

By this time, the government's policies were spreading havoc. The headmaster of an infants' school in a small Berkshire town wrote to parents whose children usually had school dinners that they would have to go home because of a strike. He added: 'we cannot allow you to provide packed meals instead, as this could be regarded as a form of strike breaking'. The heart of the whole wretched problem was expounded by a valiant economist of the Right, Walter Eltis, who said that if at Oxford in 1965 the question had been asked as to whether an absence of growth, inflation, unemployment and a balance of payments crisis could coexist, the answer would have been yes, but only in an underdeveloped country. The Bank of England noted in 1975–6 that the real return on investment was now zero. By then taxation of salaries had reached 83 per cent and on interest or dividends, 98 per cent. The government was in no condition to face trouble from the unions again, and there was more panic; the City refused to buy government stock, mistrusting it; interest rates rose above 10 per cent again, to 14 per cent by May 1979, when the next election happened. The annual debt – 'public sector borrowing requirement' – almost doubled, to some £10bn, but even then some effort had to be made to control public sector wages at a time when the government was taking three fifths of the entire national income for itself. In the summer of 1978 the unions rebelled against the system, the Ford workers leading the way, and by the winter there were surreal strikes, including dustmen and even body-buriers. But England, messy as she was, was not without creativity, or even tissue regeneration. There was to be a reaction against all of this. Edward Heath had been dismissed as leader of the Conservative Party, to his own and his supporters' great surprise. Margaret Thatcher replaced him, to his disbelief. She meant business, at last.

18

Europe: The Phoenix Flops

In the early 1950s Moscow had been frightened at the prospect of a Europe headed by a rearmed Germany, and in alliance with the United States. Stalin had tried to bully the Germans; in the early years of Khrushchev there had been fewer crude ploys, but then he too had become a bully, exploding huge experimental bombs and serving ultimatums over Berlin. The West only closed ranks, and NATO became quite sophisticated, with an intelligence network and, in some countries, even a shadowy, underground organization. But by the 1970s matters had changed. Nixon and Kissinger needed to stop the Vietnam War somehow, and had approached Moscow in May 1972 with proposals for détente. They were couched in terms of disarmament – SALT I, the Strategic Arms Limitation Talks – and the American bait was a credit deal over grain shipments, easings of conditions for Soviet visits to the USA, etc. The Americans' threat was of a deal with China, and the context was a division that had been emerging since Khrushchev's last years: he had withdrawn help and refused Mao the secrets of the bomb, and Mao responded with a sort of offended nationalism. In 1969–70 there were Chinese–Soviet armed clashes on the river Ussuri, a disputed border, and the Chinese responded to the American opening. But it was not just the Americans who appeared. West Germany launched her own probe, known as *Ostpolitik*, and she was offering hard-cash concessions. Was this the opening that the Kremlin had been looking for since 1952, and the 'Stalin Note' offering German unification in return for neutrality or, as it was called by now, 'Finlandization'? Germany was after all vulnerable, and official Europe had no teeth.

At the time Europe certainly seemed to the outside world to be a miracle of prosperity, without the concomitant crudities of the United States. However, she remained less than the sum of her parts. The European Community itself (to use the shorthand) was not particularly efficient: quite the contrary, it stumbled along drearily. Its institutions (and its flag) went back to the early fifties, and the Coal and Steel Community: a court, an assembly, and a High Authority to sort out the very technical technicalities of who was to produce what at which price. Jean Monnet himself had become bored with his creation, and its European outcrop was generally used as a parking place for failed politicians whose vanity needed to be salved. The first president of the Commission had been Walter Hallstein, possessed of negative charisma. Later on came heavy-lecturing worthies, the heaviest and longest-lasting a German Widmerpool, Günter Verheugen. It was all desperately uninspiring and even in some ways fraudulent. At the heart of this multinational community was Belgium, subject to the most absurdly provincial nationalisms; even Luxemburg dressed up its dialect, the Dutch equivalent of Liverpudlian, as a national language. In the 1970s, to give the Community some sort of personality and appeal, a parliament was set up, with direct elections. This was again, as with everything touched by the then French president, Valéry Giscard d'Estaing, lifeless and even ridiculous.

A British journalist of genius, Catherine Bennett, wrote an article about it in 1991. She had unearthed a British Labour member of the European Parliament, one Glyn Ford, who claimed to be so busy that he could not make appointments. 'Anyone wanting a little of Mr Ford's time must wait beside the telephones dotted around the bars and hallways, bleeping him now and again, for a gap to occur between the seven simultaneous meetings which Ford says he has "all day, every day".' He had been an MEP since 1984 and was 'Chair of the Committee of Inquiry into the Rise of Racism and Fascism in Europe', 'which', as he explained, 'was pretty high profile, *and* I was made the Parliament's spokesman on Star Wars'. By 1986 he had produced a report with fifty recommendations, and a Solemn Declaration. The grandiose 'hemicycle' had its ushers, its interpreters for (then) nine languages, its electronic voting gadgets (when they joined the EU the

Finns learned how to jam their pencils into the 'yes' button and go and have a drink), and speakers had four minutes to address a variety of topics – bananas, mud flaps, cordless telephones, gay rights, etc. Committees would meet to draw up reports that might go to the Commission, be translated, presented to the Parliament, then 'debated. Then amended. And translated. Votes are taken on amendments. Amended, finished proposals go to the Council of Ministers which meets infrequently, in secret. If they dislike the proposals, the Ministers discard them.' As Bill Newton-Dunn explained, it was 'very unsatisfactory, an enormous confidence trick'. The domestic parliaments had in effect given up power to the European Community, but had not been replaced by a democratic body with any power, either. Instead, talk. There was a Women's Committee, which felt 'that insufficient care is paid to the fact that women have to be fitted into working life differently from men'. As Miss Bennett says, 'a selection of thick documents, one running to 75 pages, all available in all nine languages, all to be thrown away, suggested that this indeed is the kind of thing members of the Women's Committee say to each other in their sessions without end'. This all went together with lavish offices, in Brussels and Strasbourg, with generous travel and daily allowances, etc. 'Tell them they're lucky and the honest ones say, yes . . . Others snap, "You should see what the chauffeurs and interpreters get paid." Or "The Italians get £70,000" . . . MEPs are freed, like the members of the Sealed Knot society, like the lions at Longleat, to act out their parts in a great, elaborate sham . . . Looking at them, listening to them, it's hard to know what is worse: their expensive, conceited charade of a Parliament, or the prospect of it ever becoming the real thing.'

This reflected one of the great developments of the seventies, the rise of the 'soft professions'. Deeper down, it also showed the increasing powerlessness of parliamentary bodies in general as bureaucracy and technology made semi-secretive committees and lobbies more powerful. The soft professionals, demanding a European policy for gays or women and the like, were expensively used to hide the shift of real power. Besides, the experience of any multilingual parliament was not encouraging, and Margaret Thatcher in a later speech made mock of such bodies as the Austrian before the First World War, where proceedings became chaotic and even budgets could be produced only by decree. The secretiveness of the Council and the Commission, the sheer loftiness of their civil servants, and the extraordinarily slipshod ways with money were notorious. In the seventies matters were made worse because the machinery worked almost ridiculously slowly. Creating a unified market was supposed to mean the ironing out of endless small differences. The bureaucracy was not in itself very considerable and did not amount to more than that of an English local government. However, it did involve far more people, in the separate countries, as they went through the European laws and had to apply them. The ways of these bureaucrats were, to outside eyes, very strange, and involved a degree of petty bullying noticed in every country. As an Italian said, it was an age of bureaucratic micro-persecution: no smacking of naughty children (a French father was imprisoned in Edinburgh) and increasingly no smoking. Europe became unpopular in England because shopkeepers could be arraigned if they went on marking goods in the old weights and measures, rather than in the metric system. There were stories as to the harmonization of condom sizes, the Italians claiming that they needed three millimetres more than the Germans, who took offence.

At a more serious level, in the 1970s various governments applied regulations on health, safety and the like in order to prevent imports: the Germans kept out foreign beers, for instance, because of their alleged impurities. The French insisted on certain classes of imports' being trundled along highways and byways for a six-month-long inspection, paid for by the importer, in Poitiers (which, on the strength of the income, wrecked its medieval centre with a corrugated-iron *Salle Omnisports* and the usual gruesome concrete). One answer to this might have been a common currency. The Europeans wondered if they could not find common ground for a dollar of their own. They were more dependent upon trade than the Americans, who could coin it in from the dollar's privileged position, and trade inevitably suffered if traders did not know what they were getting for their trade. However, from this to a European common currency was a long way, and there were detours through the Common Agricultural Policy: was the cathedral of subsidies and export-primes and import rebates and value-added tax to be translated into Marks or francs or dollars and at what rate? A Pierre Werner, of Luxemburg, commissioned in 1970 to examine these matters, came up with a central fiscal authority, though not a bank or a currency except, after a period of co-operation, in 1980. Then there was some agreement, not as it turned out lasting, that the dollar would fluctuate within agreed limits, the 'Smithsonian bands'. The pound joined this, and its behaviour – a wriggling of the graphed values in the lower percentages – gave the whole scheme its name, 'the snake'.

To keep the weaker currencies from going below the floor, there was a European Monetary Co-operation Fund, meaning that the German taxpayer would pay in order for German traders to have an artificially low currency. However, the weaker currencies were weakened by the oil shock, and the collapse in dollars meant that no-one wanted them, either. The Mark strengthened against the pound and against the franc as well, such that France dropped out of 'the snake' in 1974 and again in 1976, so that governments could go on pumping out paper money that would allegedly stop unemployment. It did, 25 per cent of the French working directly for their government, and though the French did not on paper abandon free trade, they (and the Italians) put so many informal obstacles in its way that protectionism appeared to be returning, and the effect on the arithmetic of the Common Agricultural Policy, already weird, was understood, Helmut Schmidt complained, only by one man, who could not then clearly explain it. In October 1976 there was a realignment of currencies at Frankfurt, but this suffered because the various countries had different import priorities, and there was no general agreement as to how the inflationary prob-lem was to be dealt with. At this level, Europe was part miniature protection racket, part pulpit and entirely irritating.

'Europe' had initially been an American idea, and a very good one at that. However, with the decline of American power and prestige at the time of the Vietnam War, there was also trouble with the European creation. Part of this was a straightforward outcome of geopolitics: if the USA were going to be sucked into Far Eastern adventures, Europe would have to do something for her own security vis-à-vis Russia. Part of the story was, however, financial. In the later sixties, the dollar empire was weakening; in the early seventies it fell apart. These troubles had their effects in western Europe, and the seventies were far from being the happy time that the sixties had been. France was marking time; but Italy fell into trouble. Her history had been for a very long time in counterpoint with German: Guelfs and Ghibellines, Romans and Goths: in one view, healthy barbarians coming to put life into effete southern stock, and in another, naïve buffoons coming in to be seduced and robbed, or maybe used as mercenaries (the Papal Guard to this day have uniforms of the old Swiss *Landsknechte* who fought the sixteenth-century wars). Since the war, there had been an interesting Italian descant on German history as well: a miracle, with undercurrents of gloom. Here, too, was terrorism, worse than in Germany; here, too, was head-shaking, and a failure of population growth; and for the Left – Germanic Ghibellines for the greater part – the seventies turned into 'the years of lead'. The arch-Ghibelline Paul Ginsborg litanizes: public finance fell into vast disorder, deficit growing; public industry had to be shored up; in 1971 a state institution was established to bail out even private industries, this then becoming 'an albatross'. There was welfare, but without taxes to match, and pensions represented the largest loss. Housing laws were sabotaged. The bureaucracy was a nightmare. There was another side of this, that the unofficial economy did rather well, as a new Italy, hairdressers and small artisans working away while big industry languished, was emerging, and the black economy amounted to about a quarter of the country's takings. This distorted perceptions. If governments attempted serious reform, there followed a tired choreography: capital flight, deficit, IMF, devaluation (in 1976 against the dollar, 25 per cent), deflation, factory closure and even, originally, a return to the land. In 1980 there was a disastrous earthquake around Naples. Of $40bn sent in relief, half was stolen, and $4bn went into bribes for politicians. Sicily had many roofless and unfinished buildings, put up with public subsidy and not finished by the private owner who would have had to pay tax. The context was a strange political system: the Christian Democrats were in charge all the way through, but they consisted of rival factions and their allies varied. An old political tactic had to be used. In 1975 the Communists were running out of steam, and were being taken over by other enthusiasms – feminism raised its head – and they were anyway much engaged purely in matters of administration since all of the cities except for Bari and Palermo were in the hands of left-wing coalitions. Left-wing infantilism of a sinister nature then took over. 'Red Brigades' developed, from October 1970. In May 1974 a bomb in Brescia killed eight, and another, in a Bologna train, twelve. The killing went on, amid accusations from the Left that they amounted to a provocation, and the police were slow and inept. By 1976 terrorism had started again, with an asinine hard-drugs-fuelled occupation of Rome university and battles for control of the microphones, while women slogged it out with each other, the trade union leader was shouted down, and French representatives orated in an absurd echo of the Catalan internationalist in *Éducation sentimentale*. In 1976–7 the Red Brigades killed eight and wounded Indro Montanelli, a great figure of Italian journalism, in the legs. All of this softened the Communists, who co-operated secretly with the Christian Democrats.

On 16 March 1978 came a strange episode. One of the wheezes with which the Christian Democrats kept on and on in office was to get their own dissident allies faced down by the threat of a Communist alliance – not of course a formal one, but an arrangement by which the Communists would just abstain, much as had happened with de Gaulle in 1968. One Giulio Andreotti could act as a front for these schemes. However, he was something of a puppet prime minister, and Aldo Moro, prime minister twice previously, was the long-term fixer behind the scenes. On his way to the parliament, his car was ambushed, his guards being killed, and Moro was bundled away in the middle of Rome. He was hidden for two months, issuing appeals, and the government did not give way to demands for the release of prisoners. The Communists in fact supported the government and there was even a general strike against the terrorists; but Moro's corpse was found in a car boot in the middle of the city on 9 May. Thereafter the Red Brigade killings went on – 29 in 1978, 22 in 1979, 30 in 1980. For Moscow, Italy was therefore a soft target.

But it was Germany that offered the greatest target of all. Were not the Germans, already formidably rich, now becoming a Great Power again, and, at that, in charge of Europe? However, Germany had changed.

It was common to talk of 1945 as *Stunde Null*, but the Germany that had emerged by 1960 did have long historical roots. What was now emerging, and in politics generally dull to the point of genius, was the 'third Germany', a world of petty duchies and prince-bishoprics that had been smothered in the imperial ventures of Prussia and Austria. An Englishman who knew Germany well was Geoffrey Barraclough. His *Origins of Modern Germany* (1952) was a classic: he started it with a quotation from Nicholas of Cusa, to the effect that Germany's divisions would mean domination by foreigners. The divisions went back to the Golden Bull (1356) which allowed Electoral princes, with their own capitals and coinages, to run quite free. The Church played a disintegrative role after the Investiture Contest in the late eleventh century and this also sucked Germany into Italian affairs. Later on, German history was written round the Thirty Years War, and the wreckage thereby caused; and that Catholic–Protestant war carried on in other forms far into the twentieth century. Was Germany to be united by Protestant Prussia, with her disproportionately sized army and mainly small-squireen nobility, or by Catholic Austria, with her great reach into the Balkans, her role as defender of Europe against the Turks, her fairy-tale aristocracy and her imperial rule over Slavs and Magyars? That battle had produced Bismarck, the Prussian maker of united Germany in 1871; it had also produced Hitler, who was Austrian and a believer in the unity of all Germans, regardless of religion, and therefore including Austrians. It was notoriously a formula for the end of the world: a superbly talented nation, daemonically driven. By 1943 representatives of almost every country in the world were queuing up to declare war, and in 1945, when Hitler celebrated his final birthday on 20 April, a small, bedraggled cohort of diplomats was left to totter through the rubble of central Berlin, with the wounded groaning in the lobbies of the Kaiserhof and Adlon hotels, to present their top-hatted congratulations to Adolf Hitler, raving, far below, in his bunker, as to how treachery had prevailed, that it had all been the fault of the Jews. There was a Croat; there was an Irishman; there was a Slovak; there was a Japanese. Their names were meticulously recorded in the Visitors' Book, while the Russians occupied the old Reichsbank building on the Werdersche Ufer, a hundred yards down the road. Greater Germany ended in the blackest farce of the entire history of the world, its final scene, with Hitler's fate, of all things, the only inefficient cremation in the history of the Third Reich.

Since 1947 there had been another Germany, and again it was an extraordinary success story. This time it was a Germany minus Prussia and Austria. It was a return to the old Holy Roman Empire, to a Germany where true civilization existed on a very local level, that of the prince-bishopric. And here there was another British historian, Tim Blanning, to do it justice. He was Barraclough's natural successor, again asking much the same question as to what, in Germany, had gone wrong. It was a measure of the importance for England of Germany, and Germany for England, that British historians were head and shoulders better than any other foreigners when it came to looking at what went wrong. Germany in the British mirror remains an essential question. Since 1815 Germans had been asking why they were not English. After 1950, the question should have been the other way about: why was it preferable to be German? After 1980 the question changed again, and intelligent Germans asked why they had not produced a Margaret Thatcher, just as, in 1900, they asked why they had not produced a Gladstone. But in 1960 Germany was in the ascendant. 'Neo-Nazism' would then be shouted from the world's rooftops. It was vastly overdone: there was never any danger of a Hitler rehabilitation: how could there be? In any case the constitution had sensible provisions for its own defence. It was true that the generation of 1933 preferred to pass over the recent past in silence. It had had to be prodded into recognition of the horrors of the era, and some monsters – though the case of Austria was worse – were allowed to live out prosperous lives undisturbed by justice. But the remarkable thing about the new Germany was the lack of any nationalist revanchism: Nazism slunk back to the saloon-bar-bore level at which it had started.

The German formula appeared to be succeeding along liberal-democratic lines. At Bad Godesberg in 1959 the Social Democrats had solemnly ceased to be a Marxist party, had promised to co-operate with enlightened capitalism (their chief leader, Willy Brandt, knew Scandinavia very well). In any case, this went along with the programme adopted by the trade union paymasters of the party. The institutions allowing trade unions a considerable say in large industry had also made them 'responsible' in a way that made British observers gasp with disbelief: no silly strikes, no ridiculous wage demands or inter-craft rivalries. The schools practised literacy; towns were well-organized; you could put your savings in the currency, knowing that inflation would not eat them up. And then the economy was highly successful, producing well-engineered exports that went round the world. Besides, the Germans were doing a great deal to make up for their recent past. They had done what they could to compensate the Jews, with a billion Marks paid from 1959 to 1964, and altogether DM56bn up to 1984. All of this occurred in a context that any German even of twenty knew very well: millions and millions of Germans had suffered and died in 1945–6. There were of course refugee leagues, and sometimes they made problems in political life. But it was an extraordinary comment that they did not endlessly dwell upon their grievances, got on with life, and set up museums and academic institutes where their history could be remembered. Other diasporas with grievances, especially those in the United States, never let go of them, distorted them to the point of caricature, and did damage.

The 'miracle' had meant a formula, that of the *Ordoliberalen* for whom National Socialism had indeed meant socialism. Alfred Müller-Arack had come up with the untranslatable *Sozialmarktwirtschaft*: private economic effort, legal protection against unfair competition or monopolies, protection for small business, and safety-net welfare that would look after people genuinely in need. These ideas were not entirely new; they had their rather tortured origins in the nineteenth century, when Catholics were looking for an accommodation with liberalism (itself at the time mainly Protestant and Jewish). However, the very word was ambiguous: 'need' was an elastic word. As prosperity grew, Chancellor Adenauer had read it to mean generous pensions, and these were to become a millstone round Germans' necks later on. Housing received subsidies for renting by people of low income – a sensible enough system, provided that the incomes were genuinely low, and provided again that inflation was kept under control. The 'miracle' system came under a further strain, caused by its own successful application. The Mark reflected Germany's success, and there was pressure on her government to support the weakening dollar (with a small revaluation in 1961). A country without a debt then borrowed, slightly. There were protests, but they were drowned by the noise of boom.

In the sixties everything worked well, and even superbly. The great firms – Mannesmann for instance – flourished on a worldwide scale and where the symbol of the fifties had been the Volkswagen, that of the sixties was the BMW. These firms were surrounded by a network of small and medium-sized family enterprises, which did not have counterparts elsewhere (at any rate not in England) and these specialized in a long-term relationship that included banks. These firms co-operated in the local chambers of commerce, and organized apprenticeships; the trade unions did not insist on such apprentices having much the same rate of pay as a skilled man, as happened in an England where young men increasingly did not do anything useful, and where much of big industry was soon to collapse. The chambers of commerce even made themselves useful in the foreign service, because they had their own commercial links and could promote exports with some degree of knowledge. That again was in contrast to British experience. Chambers of commerce were not well-organized, and to encourage exporting the Foreign Office assumed that it must have a role: not a wise measure, as matters turned out, because the diplomats were taken away from their proper functions and did not have their heart in the new ones. Various other factors came to Germany's aid. There was still a flight from the land, of willing and able peasants; NATO took care of defence, increasingly also of its costs; research and development money in Germany went to the civilian concerns, whereas in England much of it went into military hardware; and then again, while Bretton Woods flourished, the Mark was both strong and undervalued. Exports therefore boomed, boomed and boomed.

When Ludwig Erhard succeeded Adenauer, he showed a timeless verity, that good finance ministers make bad heads of government. He was impatient with platitudes about 'Europe', as he was a firm Atlantic free-trader; but on the other hand he mistrusted the Americans over Vietnam, and wanted some control over the nuclear trigger. In internal affairs he also lost ground, finding the powerful

Bavarian wing of the party difficult to control because, like so many skilled financiers, he could not understand social conservatism and Catholic moralizing. He was finally overthrown because of a small but significant affair. There was a somewhat larger deficit in 1965, and a mild inflation, to do no doubt with the revaluation. The Bundesbank combated this with a rise in interest rates (to 5 per cent) and opposed Erhard's plans for social spending. Erhard lost ground in an election (1965) and was then manoeuvred out in 1966.

The Christian Democratic Union had lost its overall majority, had to find a coalition ally, and hit upon the small third party, the Free Democrats. They lacked the trade union or clerical battalions, but on the other hand were formidably educated, and had regional bases here and there, especially in the Protestant parts of the south. They were themselves divided, in the manner of parties lacking a mass base, and though most of them were certainly free-marketeering, they regarded Catholics as slippery; many of them might also agree with the Social Democrats as to 'progress' in general. Germany was still an extraordinarily conservative country in matters moral. In much of the country, there was nothing between the mortuary Sunday and the Reeperbahn. Neighbours denounced each other if they did not obey ordinances about clearing the snow; landlords could be prosecuted if they allowed an unmarried couple to stay; rigid shop-hours made the towns lifeless at night, and the capital, Bonn, was a place of the skulls. The school system was built upon a supposition, enshrined in the constitution, that women would stay at home and look after the children: the school day ended at lunchtime, partly because as the children grew up they were expected to work on the farm or in the shop (compulsory education had been 'sold' with this concession a century before). Schools were also segregated between the academic and the non-academic or 'vocational' and the universities were hereditarily middle class (and themselves stuffily run). The Adenauer government even prosecuted a well-known periodical, the Hamburg *Spiegel*, for criticizing the defence ministry, thereby giving *Spiegel* a reputation for authoritative but dissident free-thinking that it has never quite lost. The most absurd of such episodes was the row made over the publication by a Hamburg historian, Fritz Fischer, of a book claiming, with vast evidence, that Germany had brought about and deliberately prolonged the First World War for imperialist purposes. There was jumping up and down, his passport was withdrawn, and Fischer was turned into a hero. Here there were grounds for complaint, even contemptuous complaint.

There was another aspect of this, quite dangerous, again for the future. The economic success had meant an influx of immigrants, 'guest workers' as they were excruciatingly known – the 'guest' was supposed to mean that they would leave once they had made their little pile. Of these, Turks stood out, and they arrived in hundreds of thousands. Generally they were from provincial Anatolia and, often enough, the Black Sea coast; in the first generation, which had grown up in a secular republic, they worked hard enough and of course tended to live together. In France, which was far freer of small-town regulation and prissiness than Germany, such immigrants duly melted, apart from a residue, in the pot. In Germany the process of integration took generations longer and, of all strange things, the third generation of 'guest workers' turned out to be quite Islamic, ferrying in its brides from Anatolian villages, such that the non-integration was perpetuated. The same had happened with the millions of Polish migrants in the later nineteenth century: they had their own churches and sports clubs, were cold-shouldered by the German trade unions, and took five generations to penetrate the Hamburg football team or the Politburo of the German Democratic Republic.

West Berlin was an island within an island, strongly affected by the presence of foreign military, and heavily subsidized. The city was led by a remarkable man, Willy Brandt, who was impatient of the small-town pieties of Bonn. He drank, chased women, and told funny stories. He had also had an exceedingly creditable career – an illegitimate working-class birth in Lübeck, a self-propelled rise through the educational system, an immediate teenage detestation of the Nazis, flight to Norway where, learning the language on the boat, he became a left-wing journalist; work for an anti-Nazi resistance network that included false passports and residence in Berlin; friends all over the place. In other countries, such men and women often turned Communist, especially when Stalin started winning, but Brandt, like other left-wing Germans (and Arthur Koestler), had seen the Communists in destructive action in the last days of the Weimar Republic, when they had co-operated with the Nazis in order to destroy the Social Democrats. Brandt (like Ernst Reuter, his predecessor as mayor of Berlin, who had spent the Nazi years in Ankara as professor of Town Planning) knew his Communists, and as mayor of Berlin he faced them down (and subsequently as chancellor also faced down the extreme Left). He understood that in a democracy the political parties should co-operate to maintain the system if the system were not to collapse. That had failed to happen in the pre-Hitler republic, where, in the restaurant of the Reichstag, the lunchtime tables would have a notice, 'Only for members of the Catholic (Centre) Party'. Rather than face cantankerous negotiations with the Free Democrats (FDP), the two main parties formed a Grand Coalition. In that way the CDU could control the conservative and Catholic Bavarians, the SPD could contain rebellious left-wing anti-capitalists, and the FDP would subdue its vanities. There was a further element. In the mid-sixties, the American involvement in Vietnam, the possibility that Germany might face a Soviet attack in isolation, brought vital matters to the fore – the future of NATO, the opportunity for a German finger on a nuclear trigger, the possibility of an Anglo-Franco-German Europe: matters that required a strong German government. The querulous Free Democrats were sidelined; so were the right of the Right and the left of the Left. The Grand Coalition emerged in 1966, with a bizarre partnership of the Nazi-resisting Brandt as foreign minister, with an oily Swabian, Kurt Georg Kiesinger (whose Nazi past was at once 'leaked' from East Berlin), as chancellor.

Even so, the Grand Coalition pulled in different ways – an element of social and school liberalization, but also a 'Stability Law' requiring savings. Whatever: the boom went on with growth again at the fabulous 7 per cent while inflation went back to a trivial level. On the whole, it was Brandt's side of the coalition that profited: if the Left were anywhere near power, and matters improved as the various elements in the old austerity proved irksome, then the CDU, representing the old virtues, would appear nagging and irrelevant. Welfare spending, 15 per cent of the GDP in 1950, edged up in the later sixties to 18.7 per cent, and did not bring about the end of the world. Brandt's standing rose. Meanwhile, the coalition came under strain. As the dollar weakened, pressure came from Washington for a serious revaluation of the Mark, and that threatened the profits of the exporters. On the Right, Franz Josef Strauss spoke for them; on the other side, Karl Schiller spoke for international finance (he won: there was a revaluation – 8.5 per cent – in 1969, two others following in 1971 and 1973). As the elections approached (1969) the small Free Democratic Party edged towards the Left, talking of educational reform, 'participation' and youth: Ralf Dahrendorf, author of a considerable analysis of Germany's problems, emerged as a radical, and beady liberal eyes were trained on the foreign ministry. In 1969 a new ('Little') coalition emerged, with Brandt as chancellor and Walter Scheel (not Dahrendorf, who was sidelined to Brussels) as foreign minister. Schiller and Helmut Schmidt, both of them remarkable and memorable figures, took over the economic ministries, with functioning corporate institutions and a provision for intelligent public spending. In time, this was to cause strain, because debts built up, but Germany, quite unlike England, had a good seventies. Even a foreign policy began to emerge.

In the sixties, bright people among the Social Democrats had argued that some opening should be made towards Moscow, towards eastern European countries especially, and that the way towards change in Berlin would be through concession, not denunciation. One reason for the Russians' behaviour over Berlin was a conviction that, isolated, it would be drained of people, and there was some truth in that: in order to keep the population up, young men who studied there were exempted from conscription, and there was much studying, accordingly, with, accordingly, a great many students, male and female, with nothing to do except make up grievances. Besides, improvements in Berlin, such as family visits, would hardly be gained through head-on collision: for that, the West was simply, locally, too weak. Even in 1963 a Social Democrat warhorse, Egon Bahr, had told a stout Protestant audience at Tutzing that there would have to be *Wandel durch Annäherung*, meaning that greater closeness would bring transformation (Brandt had been meant to make this speech, but, to his subsequent resentment, missed the cue). This line may have been encouraged by Moscow, with which another warhorse, Herbert Wehner, an old Comintern hand, still had his links; the speech occurred in the late-Khrushchev-period 'thaw', when countries bordering Germany and Austria were taking little steps of their own to make travel somewhat easier.

Then there was Soviet energy, which an expanding West Germany could do with: here, the Austrians, in 1967, were the stalking horse, offering credit terms in exchange for access to Soviet oil and natural gas. But the most important element was the change in the German atmosphere, as the post-war generation grew up and read its *Spiegel* or *Zeit*: a certain feeling of guilt spread as to what had been done in Germany's name to the countries to the east, whether Poland or Czechoslovakia. Had the time not come to revise the rigid fifties policy of recognizing neither them nor the eastern borders that had been fixed in 1945? Once Brandt had managed to dispose of his entanglements with the tiresome Kiesinger, policies of openness towards the East became a prime cause of the new SDP–FDP ('Little') Coalition. To be in favour of *Ostpolitik* was to be radical chic, as the Germans understood it: away from the smug stuffiness of the fifties. On one level, this was just common sense: it was absurd not to recognize reality on the ground, and to withhold diplomatic recognition from countries that recognized East Germany. But there was also an idea, not proven wrong in the outcome, that a soft approach would cause a fatal softening on the other side. The problem was a more general one, that so many Germans had suffered, had remade their lives, wanted unification, and detested the in any case very unlovely German Democratic Republic. The older generation, many of them born in old Prussia east of the river Elbe, had difficulty in swallowing the borders of Potsdam, in 1945, on the rivers Oder and Western Neisse.

Brandt's memoirs, fascinating up to this point, now turn into wooden language and chronology. Feelers went out to Moscow, obviously the heart of the matter, and at least by implication there was a considerable bargain: recognition of East Germany, at least *de facto*, in return for access to Soviet energy and some easing of conditions for West Berlin. The process took time, not least because the East German leadership, little Ulbricht in particular, knew their Moscow and knew that they could easily go the way of the Greek and Spanish Communists, sacrificed pawns in the greater game of Soviet foreign policy, itself now beset by fears of China. Early in 1970 Egon Bahr went to Moscow; a surreptitious link for communications was opened, with a KGB man, in a villa in Dahlem, in a prosperous part of West Berlin; a non-aggression treaty was drawn up in August. A face-saving letter, drawn up by the Christian Democrat leader, was attached, reserving Germany's right to unification; subsequently the Constitutional Court and the Christian Democrats were able to assert improvements for the ordinary existence of East Germans that Brandt and Bahr had omitted to insist upon. But the substance was recognition of East Germany, in treaties of 1971–2, preceded by a visit of one Willi Stoph, the SED chairman, to Kassel, in which he made a grotesque claim for 'reparations', and a much publicized return journey by Brandt, in March 1970, to Erfurt, by train (there were tiresome formalities against a journey by aircraft via Berlin), during which he was lionized. In December 1970 there was a treaty with Poland, and in the course of a visit to Warsaw Brandt embarrassed his hosts by kneeling at the monument to the Jewish ghetto and the uprising of 1943: by this stage the Polish Communists were making some use of anti-semitism, and Brandt's spontaneous gesture took them aback. Borders were now recognized, though the treaty with Czechoslovakia, for tiresome formal reasons, took somewhat longer. One counterpart, as with Romania around the same time, was that 'ethnic Germans' who had stayed behind in 1945 were allowed to depart: money changed hands for this.

Money also flowed eastwards for more substantial matters. The Germans soon followed the Austrian lead on Soviet energy: at Essen, the very heart of the industrial Ruhr, agreements began in February 1970. Over twenty years the USSR would supply Ruhrgas with 32 billion cubic metres of natural gas, costing (at 1970 prices) DM2.5bn and maybe, starting in 1973, for more than twice as much. The existing pipeline, which stopped in Bratislava, would go on into Bavaria. Mannesmann, the largest European maker of steel piping, was to supply the USSR with 2.4 million tons of it, and the cost would be borne by seventeen banks, headed by Deutsche Bank, repayable, through profits, over eleven years at a cost of 6.25 per cent in interest – a rate far below the inflation to come. Bonn guaranteed the deal. This was a classic method of dealing with the USSR: not genuine trade at all, but a means by which the German taxpayer subsidized his own banks and incidentally also promoted Soviet industry: a similar deal had been done even in 1931. In 1972 West–East German relations were formalized, and again there was a subsidy for the East German state; it also gained privileged access to the EEC market under West German terms, in return for making slightly less petty fuss (what the Germans called *Umstandspinsel*) over small matters in Berlin – a two-day wait for a visa at the border, East German numberplates having to be screwed on, in the freezing cold, as temporary replacement for West German ones. There was a great row over ratification of all of this, in 1972, and bribery had to be deployed, but the treaty went through. Brandt said, *now* Hitler had lost the war, and in 1971 he got a Nobel Peace Prize, from which, as happened with other men, he never quite recovered. Thereafter, vanity took hold; women and bottles succeeded each other, and his judgement went so far wrong that even he, with long and deep practice, failed to smell an obvious Communist spy in his closest entourage. The scandal eventually (in 1974) lost him office, and Helmut Schmidt took over.

There were problems below this radiant surface, and some of the Left, especially in the universities, responded hysterically: a reflection, in the first place, of the bubble status of West Berlin, and also of the expansion of student numbers. As to these, Adenauer had been quite careful, no doubt believing that the country needed only so many 'students', whereas it could not have enough apprentices, respectful of their elders and learning a practical trade. Erhard and then the Great Coalition put up the number of students, from 385,000 in 1965 to 510,000 in 1975, and though the increase passed off without incident in most places, it did cause trouble. The university system in Germany was a sort of fossilized Enlightenment, and boredom reigned. Anti-Americanism became a cause; the visit of the Shah of Iran was the occasion for a riot; the police mishandled things; a martyr appeared, one Rudi Dutschke, a student, a sort of El Pasionario, and aged forty; and there were as in the United States some sages to offer high-sounding comfort. A Norwegian 'peace researcher' named Johan Galtung referred to 'structural violence', by which he meant people getting on with their lives. The old Frankfurt School, much of which had migrated to New York (the New School) now returned, including, via East Germany, one Ernst Bloch. The Frankfurt School had been set up in the twenties, and its largely Marxist professorate had tried to update Marxism, to take account of the things that Marx had simply got wrong or over which he had perhaps been misinterpreted. Especially, this meant showing that intellectual life was not just a function of the relations of production, that culture, such as music or film, might on the contrary shape the mind of a generation and thereby alter the relations of production. The Frankfurters were then led into worlds of psychology, and from there to the study of words, the tools of philosophy. Ernst Bloch was a lion, his particular interest being in the philosophy of the preposition and the demonstrative adverb; he lectured, to awestruck audiences, on 'the not', 'the *nevertheless*', 'the *whence*' – harmless stuff, which made its impression because there was indeed an intelligentsia all dressed up with nowhere to go.

A section of that Left then took up the cause of terrorism, the 'Red Army Faction', a strangely Germanic phenomenon, the example of which spread to Italy with the Red Brigades. Dostoyevsky in *Demons* had written about such people a century before. Nechaev, spreading terror, had his ideology – essentially, 'the more, the worse'. There was a hatred of the smug world all around, a belief that random terror against it was both deserved and beneficial. Nechaev had a charisma that allowed him even to hypnotize prison guards into letting him escape, and subsequent terrorists owed similar escapes to a bourgeois tolerance in which Dostoyevsky saw the origins of the whole business. Andreas Baader looked not unlike Che Guevara, and he could ensnare young women of moralizing parental background, surprisingly often daughters of Lutheran pastors. Ulrike Meinhof and Gudrun Ensslin were the chief entrapped souls, but there was a network beyond, and it turned out to include men who subsequently rose a generation later to become even foreign (Joschka Fischer) and interior (Otto Schily) ministers. In 1967 251 people were killed in, by mistake, Brussels. In 1968 two

Frankfurt department stores went up in flames. This problem went on and on in the Brandt–Scheel period, and to begin with the German response was very weak-kneed: in part because of a fear, not unjustified, that the world would shriek 'Nazi' if it was too harsh, and in part because the federal system got in the way of interstate policing. It emerged in 1990 that the East German Stasi had been involved in training, in sending people to the Middle East. Baader himself was arrested in 1972, and there was a lull. In 1974 one of the prisoners starved himself to death; next day the president of the Berlin supreme court was killed in his home. Early in 1975 the head of the CDU in Berlin was kidnapped, and exchanged for terrorist prisoners. In April the Stockholm embassy was blown up, one person killed. The half-dozen released prisoners went to the Yemen, taking as hostage a friend of Brandt's; in December 1975 they occupied a Geneva hotel to intimidate OPEC; in June 1976 they hijacked an Air France aircraft bound for Israel, and took hostage the Jews on board. At last, in 1976, amendments were introduced into the criminal code, and judges were even allowed to exclude defence lawyers if they were thought to be obstructive; these lawyers' own communications with prisoners were subjected to controls (to prevent the smuggling of weapons). Baader and others were eventually sentenced to life, in a specially built prison near Stuttgart. Reprisals followed. The head of the Deutsche Bank was kidnapped, and in September 1976 a very prominent industrialist, Hanns-Martin Schleyer, was seized, with three of his associates. The Schleyer kidnappers demanded the release of Baader and his fellow convicts, and a Lufthansa plane was hijacked to Somalia for the same purpose. However, by now the State was responding with greater forcefulness. The plane was freed in an efficient operation, and Baader committed suicide, together with his fellow-convicts. Schleyer was then found, garrotted with piano wire. After that, matters settled down, although, here and there, the kidnaps and killings went on, right up to the time of unification and beyond.

It was a strange interlude, and there was much head-shaking in the German manner as to its significance. If ever there was a major country in Europe that had prospered, had done all of the recommended things, it was Germany. Perhaps there were indeed unhappy and resentful currents under the surface, a feeling that the country was only capable of reaching the top range of mediocrity; certainly, the cultural changes that occurred around this time implied considerable contempt for fifties smugness; there was, quite suddenly, a relentless and self-satisfied harping on the Nazi past, and Wieland Wagner, very much a product of it, to the point of running a concentration camp in Bayreuth for incarcerated rocket scientists, produced an anti-capitalist *Ring*. But there seems to have been a much more profound vote of cultural no-confidence around this time, perhaps the German women's vote of no-confidence in the Constitution: in the later 1960s the surplus of births over deaths vanished. The country was heading for a full-scale demographic crisis, and West Berlin had the lowest birth rate in the entire world, including even Communist countries such as Hungary. The problem became so serious that a French commentator, Pierre Chaunu, reckoned in 1980 that within fifty years there would be no more Germans: it was 'Mandeville's bees gone mad', individualism to the point at which there would be no individuals left.

West Germany was saved from herself by East Germany. Here was a warning as to what might happen if the Atlantic link were ever really sundered. Brezhnev might visit Bonn (1978) and talk of our 'common European home', but, as Margaret Thatcher later remarked, homes are built with walls, and the Berlin Wall was one too many. The 'German Democratic Republic' was an embarrassment. It remained a place where the inhabitants had to be contained by a wall, and a very ugly one at that, complete with minefields and yapping hounds on dog-runs, in case they all decided to move out, as they had done before 1961, when the wall was built. You just needed to travel one or two stops in the underground system, the *U-Bahn*, and you were in a different world: a brilliant and funny writer (East Germans were much funnier than West Germans), Stefan Wolle, describes 'the specific smell of the DDR, the composition of which will never properly be analysed' and 'the unmistakable harsh, lecturing tone of voice of salesgirls, waiters and People's Policemen', the grey plastic telephones, 'Sibylle' wall cupboards, the Metallkombinat Zeulenrode, flowered carpets, sagging net curtains. Berlin was dominated, through the Party, by Saxons, who counted as the fifth occupying power (historically, Saxony is an interesting case – somewhat as with Scotland, a country that never quite took off, was industrial, and supplied far more than its due share of enlightenment and civilization; had Britain ever become Communist, the Scots would also have been well to the fore). The Party leadership specialized in self-incense, with liturgical formulae, and the general aim was *Geschichte als Ereignislosigkeit*, history as the happening of nothing. Ideology became, says Wolle, the opiate of the leadership.

After the Wall went up there was an initial period of repression, with nearly 20,000 political punishments (as against 5,000 in the first half of 1961). Groups of 'Free German Youth' went round roofs, pointing aerials away from West Germany or even sawing them off, to block television (*Aktion Blitz*), but then an attempt was made at a consumer society to match that of West Berlin – little cars, washing machines, colour television and the rest. In the mid-sixties the working week was shortened (five days, nine hours) and the cult of Walter Ulbricht was reduced (Honecker taking over in May 1971 as first secretary of the central committee of the SED). The Alexander-Platz Funkturm (radio tower) started in October 1969, and in 1968 there was an educational reform supposed to bring modernity (in Leipzig the thirteenth-century Gothic university church was knocked down for the benefit of a gimcrack university building). In the mid-sixties there had even been talk of economic reform, with factory autonomy, a 'New Economic System of Planning and Management' (NÖSPL). The period was known as the *Systemzeit* on account of the supposed spread of computers and a new emphasis in education on mathematics. East Berlin became a sort of parody copy of the West, Chicago rather than Moscow being the model. But as Stefan Wolle writes, without a proper service sector the imitation could not be managed: the regime could not provide for the levels of prosperity managed in the West. It staggered into a brief consideration of reform at the time of the 'Prague Spring' but then staged an ideological witch-hunt, rewarded careerists and informers, and stopped the reforms it had briefly considered. There was even, in the hard winter of 1969–70, an economic crisis such as western Europe had not seen since 1947. A hard freeze began early in the November, there were headlines as to the 'self-sacrificial struggle of the miners in the lignite works'. Potatoes ran short, and Nasser sent some from Egypt, but in the canteens there was only macaroni to be had, and domestic fuel consisted of coal dust. The energy crisis was such that East Berlin's electricity hardly sufficed for more than the floodlights of the Wall, and trains were generally hours late in arriving.

Under Communism, you could never be entirely sure if such things were not somehow being stage-managed in order to discredit the existing leadership of the Party, and in due course there was a change. It occurred in the context of the West Germans' own *Ostpolitik*, and of course from the Soviet viewpoint it was easier to deal with some sort of flexible East German leader as distinct from Walter Ulbricht, an old Comintern man who had emerged from the Weimar Communist Party. In a meeting of the Politburo from which many members were absent 'ill' or 'on leave', and with many 'candidate' members present in a non-voting capacity, Willi Stoph presented a report highly critical of Ulbricht – badly prepared automatization of output, useless prestige buildings (hideous hotels and high-speed motorways through town centres, with no traffic). It all led to a humiliation for Ulbricht, when *Neues Deutschland* gave only a brief mention of his speech (which was not published) and some Politburo members formally wrote to Brezhnev to complain that Ulbricht was still thinking in a pan-German way, that there was a danger of upheavals in the manner of Poland in the later 1960s. In the interstices of the Soviet 24th Congress there was a decision to push Ulbricht aside (in April 1971). He died in 1973, still in theory the head of state, in a grand house in Wandlitz. His death occurred during a sporting festival, and he was made to write a letter saying that the Youth Celebrations' organizers 'should not allow their good humour to be affected by his unfortunately timed death'. His reward was that no flags were flown at half-mast. But with Ulbricht, the old DDR died as well: what remained was a hulk, disposable of by Moscow whenever circumstances suited.

19

The Kremlin Consolations

The troubles of the Atlantic West were compounded by foreign affairs. Moscow seemed to have in many ways the demand hand, with Americans and Germans coming back and forth, to offer this and that, in return for insubstantial concessions. Seen from Moscow, the later seventies were not a bad time; they ended with a classic piece of triumphalism, the Olympic Games of 1980, for which Moscow was cleaned up, acquiring some more huge buildings in the process – a hotel complex called 'International One' and 'International Two', otherwise known as the 'Hammer Horror', constructed for world trade exhibition purposes at the behest of the aged and, now, iguana-like go-between, Armand Hammer. Undesirables were cleared out of town, and the centre became a sort of Forbidden City. To the sky-scraper foreign ministry, the clients and satellites came and went; and there was a new, expanded Soviet navy going round the world, its crews coming back to port, gleefully bringing cheap jeans and ball-point pens, at home in short supply. The chief preoccupation was China, no doubt, but she was in no splendid condition; Mao died in 1976, leaving a battle for succession in a country that had experienced a grotesque version of the War Communism that had nearly destroyed Russia in 1919. True, there was a Chinese–American understanding of sorts, but America was also in no happy state. President Carter, grinning and maladroit, did not inspire respect. Europe was also not a threat – very far from it. The main NATO element, Great Britain, was in steep decline; the Germans had run to Moscow, signed away thousands of millions in return for a few old-age pensioners' trips to West Berlin, and the promise that the West Germans could pay some more millions to buy out political prisoners. Besides, matters in the West began to worsen again. The 'stagflation' period ended raggedly in 1975, and two years of relative stability followed. But then in 1978 things went sour again, with another twofold increase in oil prices, and another bout of inflation. England was in especially bad shape, and even appeared to be near collapse; another important NATO country, Turkey, was on the edge of civil war; Italy was in disrepair, her governments needing Communist support; and the Shah of Iran fled in January 1979, having been overthrown by a sort of bazaar-Islam revolution that Communists regarded with glee, not imagining that it would destroy them as well. When oil prices doubled, within a few weeks, the USSR profited.

It was true that the USSR was not itself in brilliant health, but its leaders were comparing the Moscow of 1975 with the Moscow they had known in Stalin's time, and there was no likeness. Later on, the years between Khrushchev and Brezhnev were called 'the period of stagnation', but the term is not entirely accurate: some parts of the system worked well enough, and the men who succeeded Khrushchev had had quite enough of reform schemes that went awry. His fall was arranged by men of much cautiousness who were already not young; Leonid Brezhnev had seen the Second World War, had been a minor lion in the occupation of Hungary, and was not far off sixty. The others were much the same. Khrushchev had terrified them with the Cuban gamble, and they had been much dismayed at the internal turmoil associated with his campaign against Stalinism: intellectuals such as Pasternak or Solzhenitsyn had broken free and there had even been an ugly riot-cum-strike or two in the south. Khrushchev's schemes to divide the Party between industrial and agrarian wings had been particularly convulsive, and he was overthrown in 1964, when he was seventy, for gambling. After the usual year or two of obscure manoeuvrings, Leonid Brezhnev emerged as successor, and his overall line was simple: 'Reform, reform: people ought to work better, that's the problem.' He was right; the whole system was, as an East German critic said, a permanent *Bummelstreik*, what the French called a *grève de zèle*, the only English equivalent of which is 'bloody-mindedness'. Brezhnev stopped the assaults on Stalin, and even installed a small work on the Kremlin Wall in commemoration of him. Khrushchev's reforms were reversed, and a re-reform, given the name of Brezhnev's (for a time) head of government associate, Kosygin, restored the powers of the central ministries, twenty-seven of them by 1975, with two dozen 'main administrations' covering assorted products. Khrushchev's regional economic councils were scrapped, because there was a danger that these councils would be taken over by some republican – in effect nationalist – coterie. The authority of Gosplan – the State Planning Committee – was reinforced. Of course, the centralization of things meant preposterous inefficiencies and delays. The Rosa Luxemburg knitwear factory in Kiev complained that it had to report on the fulfilment of fifteen different indicators, and authorization from above was needed even for small sums of money. An idea of the Kosygin reforms was for pretend firms to be set up, giving out a bonus to managers, as distinct from 'main administrations', but of course this led to abuse, hence demands for more central control, hence larger monopolies.

But at least corruption was under some sort of control, and there was even a hope that information technology (meaning computers) would bring dramatic improvements as regards the mountains of paperwork. Economists anxious to keep up with the West suggested computerization to deal with the tidal wave of information coming in, and Vasily Nemchinov's Central Mathematics–Economics Institute devised a new planning system called 'Optimal Functioning'. OGAS, 'a total informational processing system with an analytical function', lumbered onto the stage in 1971, but computers were distinguished only by their weight, and managers resented young computer scientists telling them what to do. Print-outs sprawled their way across dirty factory floors, and the managers just got on with managing in the old ways, but such problems were not unknown in the West. In any case, and it is one of the extraordinary features of this period, Western economists of considerable reputation took the Soviet economy very seriously. John Kenneth Galbraith, for instance, thought that the full employment that the Soviet system ensured was admirable, and whole institutes were set up in Vienna and points west to examine the workings of the Soviet economy. In England, hardly an

advertisement for capitalism, there was an institute at Birmingham
University to study the workings of the Polish economy, directed by
an Italian Keynesian, Mario Nuti; a great cemetery of information
was installed, R. W. Davies the chief undertaker. At least with economic affairs, there were some facts to deal with; libraries to build up,
and on the whole, in such institutions, the remarks of 'Solzhenitsyn
et al.' were dismissed. The grandest of these Sovietologists was
E. H. Carr, who had written a multivolume history of the Russian
Revolution and stopped it in 1929, when collectivization of agriculture happened, and the information shut down. Poor Davies, a Welsh
Communist and not a dishonest man, attached himself to the far
grander Carr, who said that murdering peasants was one of the prices
to pay for progress, to chronicle the advance of the Soviet Union
beyond 1929, and even to call his volumes on the murderous collectivization, 'The Socialist Offensive'. The next generation of students
was brought up on such tomes, and was therefore caught gawping
when the Soviet Union collapsed. (This writer will not plead innocent:
as late as 1987, he was telling students that the USSR had 'solved the
nationality problem', the worst mistake in academic life that he has
ever made, and fortunately not preserved in print. At the time, minority nationalism was causing pointless mayhem in countries that he
knew about – Ireland, Scotland, Belgium, Spain.)

People who said that nationalism in the USSR was very much alive,
and very angry, were of course right, but their evidence at the time
consisted of trivialities and impressions – a girl at a Latvian boat-race
wearing a T-shirt with a Latvian inscription; a Ukrainian Catholic
imprisoned for decades, and emerging, incoherently, with a grand
beard, to massacre English at a press conference. Vladimir Bukovsky,
a long-term victim of the system, and utterly irrepressible, could not
believe his ears and eyes when at last, in 1976, he came to the West
and was asked to lecture at the Ford Foundation and suchlike: eyes of
naïve vacancy, peering through festoons of hair, to put stupefyingly
silly questions. President Carter refused to meet him, and the Ford
Foundation missed him off the Christmas card list; in revenge, he
wrote a book, based on the Soviet archives, that demonstrated quite
how misguided they had been, in the style of the 'useful idiots' whom

Lenin had found such bores. When the founder of jogging dropped dead at the age of fifty-four, Bukovsky responded with glee.

As regards the Soviet economy of this period, Alain Besançon remarked, 'It is a strange feature of the sovietological world that a certain economic approach to Soviet reality, however knowledgeable, honest and sophisticated, meets, in people with a different approach, a disbelief so vast that they do not even bother to criticize – not knowing where to begin, let alone to inform themselves further. It is much like the attitude of the dissidents to official statistics, or the figures at which the Western economists arrive: derision and shoulder-shrugging.' These dissidents 'et al.' were of course closer to the truth than their Western critics, and their derision was even shared by the more astute elements in the KGB, such as (no doubt) Vladimir Putin. But for the moment the USSR functioned. Rockets fired off; disarmament discussions went on with Americans who could not quite reconcile the potholes in the Moscow roads with the satellites in space (New York, going bankrupt at the time?). And there was always the cultural argument. A concert by Svyatoslav Richter was unanswerable. There was something about Russia that produced musicians of a world class beyond compare. A certain conservatoire tradition, an intelligently critical public concentrating culturally because the political economy was so primitive, or just grown-up attitudes towards alcohol and cigarettes: who knows why?

In this perspective, Brezhnev becomes understandable, because the USSR worked, and the West did not. Leonid Brezhnev was now in charge of a vast system in which only the KGB really knew what was happening, through its huge network of informers, and under him that organization came to be all-important. Stalin had controlled it by the simplest of methods, a periodic cull. Now, and this was Khrushchev's contribution, such culling was not possible: to that he himself owed his life, as he said. The system worked for a time, and quite well, because of an external factor, the rise in commodity prices, and especially oil and gold. In the early 1970s Western investment also went into pipelines to carry natural gas to Germany, the lines amounting to a length four times that of the globe's circumference. By 1985 gas was almost fifteen times greater in volume than in 1965 and development might have been more had the road system been better developed (lorries, ubiquitous in the system, chugged along at less than the speed of a decent bicycle). With these sums in foreign currency, Moscow could still indulge some megalomania, and a Brezhnev could carry on in the old way: the 'A' system launched its space-shots and intervened all over the world. It even built an enormous navy, in the 1970s, and made itself felt in parts of the world that were new to it, such as the Middle East. The basis was being eaten away, but external help could be obtained, as had happened in any crisis of the system, from the Volga Famine of 1921–2 to Hitler's attack in 1941. The Western world just needed to be reminded of the importance of Russia.

It was of course true that the peoples of what the West called eastern Europe were 'captive nations'. That problem was not, in Brezhnev's eyes, enormously serious. The West had become disinterested in the subject at Teheran in 1943, when Churchill had in effect agreed to a displacement of Poland, bodily moved west into Pomerania and Silesia at the expense of Podolia and Volhynia. East Germans had rebelled in 1953, and had been widely ignored. Yugoslavia had been disaffected by Stalin, was not part of the Soviet empire, but co-operated with it, and as a Communist country worked, like the USSR, as a purported federation of nations devoted to the construction of socialism. Hungary had rebelled in 1956, and Moscow had adapted its dealings with Hungary accordingly: she had a certain room for manoeuvre, could make deals with the diaspora (like Armenia in the USSR) and even produce plans for economic reform of a sort that might at some stage have relevance for Moscow. Poland had also been allowed some headroom, and the Church was no longer persecuted. A small-farm peasantry obstinately persisted with its horses and carts, but heavy industry had been built up, and in the later seventies Western banks were anxious to invest in it, swallowing whole the propaganda that a new leader, Edward Gierek, was launching, to the effect that Poland would be the new Japan. Poles could travel to visit relatives in the West, and dissidents were picturesquely part of the scenery: the Party was a nuisance, not a tyranny. Communism, Brezhnev-vintage, was even quite a useful discipline for the Poles, whose intelligentsia, freed from romantic nationalism, became world-class.

There was a problem as regards Czechoslovakia. She was unique among the satellite states, in that her native Communists had been numerous and strong, based in a modern industry, in 1939 on much the same level as Belgium's: true at any rate of the Czech two thirds, though not for the Slovak part. Czech Communists kept much of the investment for themselves, and Slovaks groused, as they did on cultural matters, since they counted as bumpkins, not unlike the Ukrainians over the border. A constitution of 1960 was strictly centralized, i.e. making no concessions to Slovak desires for autonomy, and collective farms were stronger than in Hungary, let alone Poland. President Antonín Novotný, visiting the Slovak cultural centre, was enraged by demands that Slovak culture should be promoted by the foreign machine; like most Czechs he did not think that there was any. There were little signs that matters were not going his way; very obscurely, key figures were moved in and out (this writer, spending a few months in prison in Bratislava at the time, had his own experience: *v.* Note, pp. 371–81). In 1964 Gustáv Husák made a secret speech, in the course of criticisms by the Bratislava municipal government, which led to demands from Prague for his expulsion, and Alexandr Dubček, who had a key role in matters economic, spoke up for the intelligentsia. But it was all very small-scale.

The Stalinist Novotný went on in office; as late as 1954, several months after the USSR had started to release Stalin's victims, there was a minor purge trial, and a commission in 1957 even reaffirmed the guilt of the 1950–51 trial victims, though some were released. A huge Stalin statue even went up in 1955, demolished only when Khrushchev insisted, along with the removal of Klement Gottwald from his mausoleum. In an obscure place, much later, there was still a little 'Stalin Square'. In Czechoslovakia there was nothing like the Polish peasantry, stubbornly stuck in subsistence agriculture; nor was there anything like the Polish Church, the Czechs having inherited a powerful anti-clerical tradition. Opposition to the Communists was enfeebled from the outset because it was itself largely Communist. It talked, and then talked again.

Still, there were signs of trouble in the woodwork, and a Party congress was postponed for several months in 1962. The 1951 purge trials continued to be a cause of unease, and there was a new commission to investigate them. In 1963 it pinned the blame on Gottwald, and by implication his close colleagues, some still in high places. A Slovak journalist – Miroslav Hysko – publicly denounced them, and was not himself arrested: the old trial verdicts were, instead, cancelled. All of this was evidence of much deeper currents. Further evidence came when a report late in 1963 stated that the campaign against Slovak nationalism in 1951 had been unjustified; and from prison there emerged Dr Husák, whom the Russians subsequently chose as their man in Prague. Novotný, an elderly figure recognizably in the Stalinist mode, was careful to dissociate himself from the old guard and only four of them remained; the warhorse Slovak secretary (Karol Bacílek, a Hungarian) was displaced in 1963 by a younger man, Dubček. Slovakia, when he was a child, had been part of old Hungary, and in the capital, Bratislava, Hungarian was still the second language. Anti-Catholicism in the later nineteenth century translated there, as in Hungary, into Communism in the twentieth, and Dubček somewhat resembled Imre Nagy in that he had spent time in the USSR, his parents having gone there; from the age of four until he was seventeen (in 1938) he had lived in Russia, and he attended the Moscow Higher Political School from 1955 to 1958. However, Imre Nagy had been galvanized by Hungarian nationalism, the original sense of the word coming from Luigi Galvani of Verona, who had noticed how a scalpel that had accidentally received an electric charge made the corpse of a frog twitch. Dubček remained something of a dead frog, and even resembled one. His speeches amounted to wooden language, with at most some sense that he opposed bureaucracy. The reformers' candidate for president was also a veteran of the USSR, Ludvík Svoboda, who had had a role in the Communist takeover in 1948, as ostensibly non-Party defence minister. There was also trouble in the Czech lands. They had been highly industrialized, but were languishing: in 1961–3, economic growth had stopped, even been reversed. A Five Year Plan was abandoned, and in 1963 a team of experts under Ota Šik, who had been in the Politburo since 1958, argued for serious change, such that concerns' profits should not go to the State, and management should be properly rewarded, with prices that reflected costs. A congress in 1966 approved a new system without parallel elsewhere in that world.

The backdrop was serious movement among the writers – not of course the 630 members of their union, the usual parade of elks, but in various journals, particularly Slovak, which were uncensored. The overall appeal was to the Soviet example, with denunciations of the 'cult of personality', and even Novotný tried to come to terms, inviting the writers to the Prague castle. But by the summer of 1967 there was deadlock at a 'congress of the Czechoslovak writers', and one was even imprisoned for giving details to an exile in France. Foreign Communists – Roger Garaudy and Ernst Fischer – became involved, as campaigns went ahead against the censorship, or against Czechoslovakia's policy towards Israel. At the same time there was a burst of creativity, as Czechoslovak film made the rounds, and Milan Kundera surfaced; solemn socialism-with-a-human-face economists appeared, and Youth took a hand, protesting that repairs were not carried out in the dormitories at Strahov or that there had been a power failure. Talk went ahead, and beards nodded; the police behaved absurdly, censoring people for writing that 'science ends where its freedom ends' or, as in 1963, dismissing the entire editorship of an historical journal for publishing a review that indicated the gaps in a particular collection of orthodox texts. By the autumn of 1967 there was an atmosphere of crisis within the Party – itself greatly dominated by the proletariat – and there was a secret meeting, at which Dubček spoke, not for repression of the writers and students, but for a more suitable policy as regards Slovak industry. Novotný was pushed out, and the 'Prague Spring' burst. There was a May Day demonstration containing the banner headline 'WITH THE SOVIET UNION FOR ALL TIME AND NOT A DAY LONGER'.

Much of this was froth. The Slovak Communists wanted federalization, and had used the Prague intellectuals to force the issue, but they warned in veiled language about any repeat of Budapest in 1956, and a Soviet general appeared to say that 'international duty' would be done if need be. Courts reopened cases, and there was much foreign applause, but reality lay with Husák, not Dubček. The background was manoeuvres by the Warsaw Pact, though Brezhnev in June still had 'tears in his eyes' to the effect that he would not intervene. The fact was that the Party still functioned; though many of the central committee delegates did not appear, in mid-July Soviet language in letters was more harsh. The French Communist Waldeck Rochet appeared to suggest an answer, and on 1 August Dubček met Brezhnev at Čierna nad Tisou, in sub-Carpathian territory on the Ukrainian border (the Soviet delegation steamed back every night to Csap, to the railwaymen's club). Brezhnev simply did not want to see Czechoslovakia leave the Soviet zone, and did not trust her; the East Germans were adamant that Czechoslovakia must not become an Austria. Dubček was expected to restore the censorship, but the real problem lay with the Slovaks, who pressed for federalism, and would deal with Moscow rather than with a Prague intelligentsia full of its own words. The trick was then to find some old Czech proletarian characters who would collaborate, and that was quite easy. In mid-August the Russians started to use threatening, inquisitorial language. In the night of 20/21 August they moved in, an 'appeal' having been got together by the team that would then in effect run the country. Its furniture consisted of old trade union warhorses on the Czech side, and Slovak federalizing Communists on the other, and it was the latter who ran the regime. Gustáv Husák was installed in the presidential villa at Smichov, and Czechoslovakia then hardly disturbed the headlines for the next twenty years.

At any rate, Brezhnev in the 1970s could look on the world with a certain confidence. The West had done nothing about the Prague events, and the Germans especially were now running to Moscow, offering considerable amounts of money; they had in effect recognized East Germany and given it money, too. China was always a question mark, but Mao had left her in a very enfeebled condition, and she was even lured into a war with Vietnam. Now, events in the Middle East did call for action, and at Christmas 1979 came a clumsy lurch, one that was to prove fateful.

The Turkish generals' coup had happened at a moment of great turmoil in the Middle East. The Shah of Iran had fallen; oil prices had doubled; and the ruler of Iraq, the Stalin-worshipping Saddam Hussein, was planning to fall on Iran, to make himself master of the whole region. Meanwhile, the Americans, under the feeble Carter, seemed to be fair game, and their diplomatic staff in Teheran were taken hostage by a mob of angry students; in spring 1980 a pathetic attempt was made to rescue them by helicopter mission, which went wrong in classic Bay of Pigs style, with sand blocking the engines, and machines crashing into each other. Old men in Moscow chuckled, and moved into Afghanistan.

The last act of the USSR began very professionally, with a mixture of brute force and low cunning. On Christmas Eve, 1979, Soviet troops took over the airport at Kabul, and three days later six Soviet divisions crossed the border. The rulers of Afghanistan knew that power was precarious, and in 1979 the Tadj-Bek palace in Kabul was very well guarded – 2,500 special troops, dug-in tanks and a private guard consisting of relatives of the president. President Hafizullah Amin had himself seized power a few months before, in a coup, and had called in a special Soviet force of 500 men to complete the security system. It had been recruited among Central Asians wearing a uniform that made them resemble local, Afghan, forces. But they were in fact from the KGB and *Spetsnaz*, its 'special purpose' troops, men (Uzbeks and Tadzhiks) trained to the highest degree of physical fitness. Amin never thought that they would be a threat. He was quite wrong: there had been 343 flights into Kabul in forty-eight hours and their mission was in fact to overthrow him.

The affair was, militarily, very well prepared. The palace had been studied with a view to assault, but much care was taken to disguise the Soviet intent. The night before, the Soviet forces attended a banquet with the Afghan defenders. President Amin was extremely careful as to what he ate, but he did trust his own cooks, who were Soviet Uzbeks. On 26 December 1979, in the middle of the dinner, all who had touched the food began to roll around in extreme pain. Soviet doctors were summoned, and revived Amin with injections and a drip-feed. But they were soon followed by Soviet assault troops, who blasted their way, with foul language, through the defences, hurling grenades into the private rooms and even the lifts. Amin wrenched himself from his bed, and, in his underwear, with tubes dangling from his body, went down to the main hall to see what was happening. His five-year-old son, crying, rushed up to him, clutching his father's legs. One of the Soviet doctors said, 'I can't look at this.' Amin was killed shortly afterwards. The affair was all over by midnight, and at 12.30 a.m. on 28 December, a telephone call came through to the new Afghan leader, Babrak Karmal, from the head of the KGB, Yuri Andropov. Soviet troops were coming in to reinforce Karmal's position. They were already in control of the airports and the main roads into Kabul, the capital. All very easy: but in the next twelve years Afghanistan was wrecked as a country, and so, too, was the Soviet Union itself. Almost no-one in a senior position in Moscow seems to have recognized that this would happen. On the contrary, the decision to invade Afghanistan was taken quite casually, and was hardly even minuted. Old Brezhnev, Andropov and the senior military simply went into 'country A', as it was called. Other Politburo signatures, willing or unwilling, were collected afterwards.

They thought that they had the measure, not just of Afghanistan, but of Central Asia in general. The whole area was very backward, and when the Russian Revolution happened, the Bolsheviks found that they could rely on some elements within the Islamic world, including even the Chechens in the northern part of the Caucasus. The USSR was progress. It freed the education system from obsolete nonsense – a teacher who did not know Arabic (let alone early medieval Arabic) forcing, with terrible punishments, rote-learning of the Koran on small boys who had no notion of what they were having to memorize. Women were emancipated, and local languages were given some encouragement; customs such as month-long fasting, or circumcision, were discouraged (or worse). It was true that, as time went by, Moscow found itself relying on local power-wielders. The tribal system was tenacious, and there were also religious orders (*Sufi*) with a leader, *Sheikh*, who exercised a great deal of informal authority. When, after Khrushchev, the Russians started to deal through locals rather than Russians, these informal networks came into their own, together with a corruption that oiled the wheels. When the USSR finally collapsed, the last generation of Communist bosses quite easily took on national dress, and religion, to become presidents of the new Central Asian republics. At any rate, no-one in Moscow seems to have thought that running Afghanistan would be especially difficult. As regards her foreign affairs, the country was a sort of Asiatic Finland. Her ruler had been grateful for support against the British, and had recognized the Bolsheviks early on. He then initiated a modernization drive not unlike Atatürk's in Turkey, and since the USSR was also modernizing backward Central Asian tribal peoples, there was much over which to collaborate. In the sixties aid came from the USSR, the usual cement and chemical works, and a gas pipeline took two thirds of Afghan natural gas to the north.

Even its considerable internal problems were familiar, in the sense that, with every Islamic society, you feel you are dealing with the same pack of cards, though the distribution of suits and honour cards greatly varies. Here, in a population of 15 million, modernization brought about the usual troubles. There was a Persian-speaking upper class, which was eroded by population growth and the de-localization of politics. Women's emancipation in a Sunni Islam context of, in places, considerable conservatism was not straightforward: in Herat the men used henna as make-up (the Turkish slang for 'homosexual' is *pusht*, from 'Pushtun', the more accurate version of the English 'Pathan', the dominant group) and the women had to wear the clumsy *burka*, which hardly showed even their eyes. There were troubles between Pathans, semi-Iranian Baluchis and Turkic Uzbeks of the north, each with a different language; tribal matters counted as well, and even divided the Communists (the People's Democratic Party of Afghanistan (PDPA), set up in 1965) into two rival groups. There were also secular army officers who sympathized with Moscow, where many of them had been trained, and despised the native traditions. The party in effect depended upon university students, the intelligentsia and some administrators for its member-ship, and these, vain and isolated from society at large, split. On top of everything else, the Pathans were not confined to Afghanistan. In 1947, when Pakistan was established, 6 million of them lived there, and accounted for several Pakistani leaders; there was agitation for a 'Pushtunistan' that would have caused secession, and the Pakistanis tried to control their neighbour's affairs. Militarily speaking, Afghan-istan was so mountainous that only a genius could conquer it; the northern and southern parts were even cut off from each other until a great tunnel was driven through, at 12,000 feet, in 1964, with Soviet aid, to connect them in winter.

Once this happened, politics became less local, and factions contended for central power. A famine in 1972, and a supposedly shameful treaty with Iran, brought discontent, and while the monarch was abroad, he was overthrown, by a 'modernizer', Mohammed Dowd, with help from two factions of Communists in the wings. Dowd proceeded with modernization, on the whole leaning towards the USSR in much the same way as other 'Third World' leaders of the era. As happened in Iran, Islamists began to surface as political opposition in the 1970s, and were driven abroad. To lessen his dependence on the Communists, Dowd took a loan from Iran, and this prompted Moscow to connive in his overthrow. One of the Communist factions, led by Nur Mohammed Taraki, a writer, seized power in 1978 and launched what was described as the 'April ['Saur'] revolution'. It was strongly anti-religious, and there was cruel persecution; the prisons, hideous, were full, with 27,000 deaths, by official figures, in one of them alone (the governor said that, in order to set up socialism, he would leave, if necessary, only a million Afghanis alive, as that number would suffice for its construction). Agrarian reform was launched, and neglected the all-important matter of access to water, which was controlled by the village elders. It also took land from religious foundations (as the Shah had done) and tribal chieftains.

The party itself split, and, true to form, the rival Communist leader, Babrak Karmal, much grander in social origin, and from a different clan, was packed off to Prague as ambassador (where he was kept in waiting as Moscow's man). In the short term, a Communist regime could indeed manage to suppress Islam, because Islam lacked an international organization (such as the Vatican) and would only manage a united front of resistance if forced to. It was forced to. Herat rebelled, despite savage repression and 100,000 killings. Meanwhile, the Pakistanis were giving training in guerrilla warfare to Islamists who had taken refuge there: that way, they could control 'Pushtunistan' agitation. In other words, complications within complications, and not a place to invade.

Nevertheless, Soviet clients were in trouble, and the problem landed on Brezhnev's desk. Taraki appealed for help to Moscow. To start with, he met reluctance, and was told on the telephone that direct intervention was not possible. Kosygin showed how much the Politburo understood the situation when he said, 'Could you not recruit from among the working class?' and had the apposite answer, 'I am afraid that there is not much of a working class in Afghanistan.' Taraki was sent a hundred barrels of incendiary liquid. However, the men of experience, Andropov for the KGB and Gromyko for the foreign ministry, warned against any direct intervention. Without intervention, Taraki himself soon lost control, and was overthrown after barely a year, in September 1978, by Hafizullah Amin, a rival who had been trained in the USA, latterly at Columbia. Taraki was tied down to a bed and suffocated with a cushion; Brezhnev is said to have broken down in tears when he heard. But in any event Amin had been rebellious not just locally, but as far as the USSR was concerned: he had defied the advisers, and four of Taraki's men had even had to be smuggled out via the Soviet embassy, in nailed-down boxes. Soon, Amin was sending 'frantic' messages for Pakistan to offer some support, as he knew that the Soviets were suspicious of him. That made them more suspicious still, since Pakistan entertained good relations with China. More atrocities followed – 12,000 of the most qualified people, under Taraki and then again under Amin. Amin then tried to mend fences with Islam, which Taraki had treated with contempt.

Moscow's 'Third World' expansionism, very promising after the Americans' defeat in Vietnam, was in any case considerable. There was now Soviet emplacement in Africa, particularly in Ethiopia, on the edge of the Arabian Peninsula. The Americans' ally, the Shah, had fallen early in 1979, as had Anastasio Somoza in Nicaragua a little later; there was even a proto-Cuba forming up in tiny Grenada. Besides, the Carter administration in Washington generally invited contempt. It had lost the way over 'human rights', denouncing South Africa and Chile rather than the Soviet Union; its economic performance was woeful; the German chancellor, Helmut Schmidt, looked on Carter with derision. American Intelligence did not even notice Soviet troop concentrations a month before the invasion; nor did it understand the significance of the occupation specialist General Ivan Pavlovsky's transfer to Kabul. From Moscow's viewpoint, it was an obvious opportunity – get rid of a few obscurantist clerics, as had been done before in Communist history, and show who was boss. There was the usual puppet for such occasions – Babrak Karmal (a pseudonym, meaning 'people's flag', though he was of tribal leadership stock), who was prepared for some kind of accommodation with Islam, though himself a whisky drinker. After the Christmas slaughter in the Tadj-Bek palace, he was installed as president, with instructions to behave with moderation.

It was the start of a long nightmare, a war that, for the Soviets, turned out to be unwinnable. In the first place, the American reaction was much harsher than Moscow had supposed: not just sanctions of various sorts, including a boycott of the Moscow Olympics, which Brezhnev had planned as a showcase of Soviet professionalism, but non-ratification of SALT II, a resumption of the arms race, and the adoption of a strategic partnership with Pakistan. This was dangerous territory. Pakistan was pioneering a nuclear bomb, in pursuit of her troubles with India, Moscow's ally in the area. But there were also Islamic elements, some of which had even burned down the American embassy just before the Soviet invasion of Afghanistan. The Saudis (and various other Islamic states) condemned the USSR, and sent help to Pakistan; to its subsequent regret, the USA then gave training and help to the Islamic element. The USSR was isolated, and could not even sway the UN, which, apart from Greece and a few other countries, offered overwhelming condemnation. A few Europeans demurred, saying that militant Islam was worse than Communism, but Brezhnev's blundering meant that they had no real influence.

There was unquestionably much to be said for what the Soviets were trying to do: the dead, irrational world of small-town and tribal Islam, with its endless children, its terrible oppression of women, and its hostility to minorities, needed to be escaped from. However, the battling had already caused disruption, and in the Amin period there had been devastating disruption – 100,000 deaths and 500,000 refugees. History showed decisively that Afghans united against foreign invasion, if on nothing else. Maybe if the country had been isolated, resistance would have been destroyed, as had happened in Central

Asia. But Afghanistan bordered on Iran and Pakistan, and mountains made connections over the border impossible for the Soviets – they had 100,000 men only – to control. Seven Sunni Islam resistance groups supported from Pakistan emerged, and so did eight separate Shia Islamic ones based on Iran – forces numbering up to 200,000 men. In the old days, Islamic resistance to European empires had been hopelessly weak (except in the case of Turkey) because it had no base at all in technology. Now, technology was well within reach. Trotsky had said that Stalin had been 'Genghiz Khan with a telephone'. Communism came to an end, at least in part, because the real modern-day Genghiz Khans had an understanding of surface-to-air missiles.

The Soviets could only really control about one fifth of the country, and the Afghan army was unreliable, to the point not just of mass desertion, but of having to be deprived of weapons that might be sold to the resistance. Karmal tried through amnesties, licensing of private trade and greater tolerance for religion to make himself popular, but the regime remained as ever divided, and some of its members (including the foreign minister) were identified as Soviet agents: most things were done by the thousands of Soviet advisers attached in this or that capacity. The Soviets themselves became involved in smuggling of the Western goods that were available in Kabul, and the corruption affected the PDPA. The Soviet forces were hated, and there were atrocities (a captured prisoner might be 'under-shirted', i.e. his skin slit around the middle of his body, and then lifted off, over his head). The troops could only move about in large numbers. They responded to resistance with tremendous and unscrupulous force – a hundred peasants routinely burned in an irrigation channel where they were taking refuge, and the like; air-dropped landmines caused mayhem; 12,000 corpses were discovered in mass graves in the main prison, Pol-e-Charki. The Soviet 100,000 became 600,000, and the war caused 80 per cent of the educated Afghans to flee the country, by 1982. Kabul itself trebled in population, and by 1989 over two thirds of children admitted to hospital were suffering from malnutrition. Even in 1980 there were a million refugees, and by 1984 4 million, with perhaps another 2 million who had been uprooted in their own country, quite apart from the perhaps 2 million who were killed – out of a population of 15 million. There had been a supposed Afghan army on the Soviet side, perhaps 80,000 men, but 50,000 deserted in 1980. An atmosphere of sheer hatred developed, with the sort of self-sacrificial attitude that had animated the Vietcong, and it began to affect the Central Asians (Tadzhiks) whom the Soviets used: they were replaced by young men from the Baltic republics, whose enthusiasm for the Soviet Union was not increased thereby. In this atmosphere, the Soviets could control Kabul but hardly anywhere else, beyond highways that needed to be very intensively patrolled. They got rid of Karmal in 1986, not long after the 27th Moscow Congress, replacing him with a Mohammed Najibullah, who had been head of the Afghan equivalent of the KGB, the KHAD (his brother boasted that he had signed 90,000 death warrants), and, in a strange echo of the Greek civil war, 30,000 children aged between six and fourteen were sent to Moscow.

But the Afghan resistance did not diminish. Rather, it grew more difficult, more anarchic, more inclined, even, to fight among itself. It was based on Pakistan and Iran, the latter maintaining Shia rebels, while in Pakistan there were 380 'refugee tented villages' which maybe had the highest birth rate in the world. The seven resistance groups did not easily collaborate, and the fiercest, *Hezb* (Gulbuddin Hekmatyar), did not co-operate at all: it was, especially, at odds with the other chief resistance group, Massoud's *Jamiat* in the Panjshir valley, and religious or tribal emphases played their part, Pakistan insisting on some sort of alliance. The Shias, with Iranian support, were not involved, and themselves were divided. But money was involved: opium from Afghanistan and the frontier areas of Pakistan supplied, in 1981–2, half of the heroin reaching the West. This is a dimension yet to be explored – or, rather, there is a serious question, as to how far the Americans were encouraging both what they later called 'fundamentalist Islam' and the drug trade. The CIA had been prevented, by Congress, from getting what it thought to be proper money. Why not do drugs, through Islamists who did not mind corrupting further a Christian youth whom they already regarded with contempt? At any rate, the Afghan resistance flourished, and in 1986 the Americans were giving it Stinger missiles – missiles that enabled men on mountainsides to knock out

Soviet helicopters. They were brought in through Pakistan, and there was almost nothing that Moscow could do against this. The president of Pakistan himself was murdered, no doubt at Soviet behest, but this made no difference. The USSR had met its match. Thirty thousand Soviet soldiers were killed out of some 600,000 combatants – nothing, in comparison with what had happened on the Afghan side, but a vast amount, in terms of Soviet prestige.

Just as the Russians were moving into Afghanistan, and the Teheran students humiliated the American diplomats, there was a great change going on in the Atlantic world. Its origins went back to 1975, and can even be pinpointed to the Rambouillet meeting of November, that year. Disillusion with the post-war orthodoxies was growing; more and more people now thought that the answer must be to change them. Inflation? An unmitigatedly bad thing, rewarding vice and punishing virtue. Development aid? Theft. Détente? A lie. OPEC? Blackmailers. It was time to go back to the older scheme of things, of right and wrong, black and white. A little before the Rambouillet meeting, there had been a symbolic change in London: the Conservative Party disposed of its failed leader, Edward Heath, and replaced him with Margaret Thatcher. In America the old Goldwater Republicanism emerged in strength, with a new leader altogether, Ronald Reagan.

NOTE

I had my own spear-carrying experience of events in Czechoslovakia, spending three months in prison in circumstances that turned out to be quite revealing. I had gone to Vienna in 1963, on a scholarship from Cambridge, to study in the military archives. At the time, Hungary had begun to open up, and there was a month-long language school at Debrecen, where I took up with an East German girl. She had ideas of getting married and escaping to the West, and relations were not brilliant. Neither was Vienna: I spent my evenings more or less kicking a tin past the whores down the Kärntnerstrasse, though there was something to be had from one Christopher Lazare, onetime lover of Klaus Mann and author of one of the greatest book review opening lines ever: 'John Steinbeck is an inverted Aesop; he uses human beings to illustrate animal truths.' I had had a landlady from the Banat, who used to stir her enormous bloomers in the jam pan, and disagreed violently with me as to whether, when you cut your fingernails, the bits needed to fly off at unpredictable angles: we parted company acrimoniously, and through a Croat friend I found a splendid pair of sisters who looked after me. But it was not lively, and the next day's newspapers were sold around 6.30 p.m., when the café waiters started looking at their watches. Lazare used to eye them and ask whether, perchance, they had the newspapers of the day after tomorrow. Budapest, even then, was more fun if you knew where to go, and I had been taken round by Adam Rez, a collaborating figure like the baron in Bulgakov, who was kindly, whereas I was hopelessly naïve: *si jeunesse savait*. In February 1964 I went there by train, and there followed a set of events that would be entirely familiar to anyone knowing the history of central Europe in the twentieth century (a very good introduction is Kafka's *Amerika*, which is not about America at all: the whole book is a Vienna hotel). In the carriage was a Togolese studying agronomy in Romania. He had problems with the customs, and I endeavoured to translate ('fekete ember', etc.) as his French was all right. He had got talking to a Flemish Belgian. The Belgian opened the corridor door to a fur-coated female presence, Andrea Walder, in French. I joined the conversation, and we found things in common. She pronounced the Hungarian place names – Szekesfehérvár, etc. – correctly and I asked, sensibly, was she an academic or a journalist. She replied, 'Je suis journaliste.' 'De quel journal?' 'Vous connaissez le *Daily Express*, de Londres?' She did seven languages perfectly, and the only mistake I ever heard her make in English (she said 'insist to' with an infinitive rather than 'insist on' with a gerund: a tricky one, because all other languages do a 'for' with a subjunctive) was itself a bright one. She had the grand manner, could march up to any Ritz desk, order a suite, make a few telephone calls, and run away from the bill to another Ritz. Anyway I was quite bowled over. Arriving at the Eastern Station in Budapest, she introduced me to Tibor Karman, whom she described as her fiancé, and we had dinner somewhere grand (it was Communist Hungary, and the great boulevards of nineteenth-century Pest were very dimly lit, with no life at all except for sporadic uninviting shop windows, but there were still grand restaurants).

Tibor, as she presented the case, had had a horrible time. Karman is a name to conjure with, as I later discovered: one of them set up the *Minta* ('Model', meaning Teachers' Training) school, and his son was one of the two dozen Hungarian Nobels (it is a tribute to the relationship of Hungary and the Jews that an abnormally high percentage of Hungarian Nobels were non-Jewish, namely 17.5 per cent). As I remember it, Andrea told me that Tibor's family had had rubber plantations in Indonesia, which is quite credible. They had met, she said, during the war. Her father was a (hugely tall) Transylvanian nobleman, her mother a Viennese Jewess, and owner of a sanatorium on the Semmering, a fresh-air place for ailments, south of Vienna. The father had got the honorary consul-generalship of Monaco, and therefore flew a large neutral flag from the block on a Pest boulevard. There, when the Nazis started attacking Jews, they stuffed the house, and the Karmans must have belonged to their set. Tibor stayed there during the siege of 1945, when old Hungary collapsed. Communists took over, and were no more friends of the Rózsadomb Jews than the Nazis had been. He was then, she said, imprisoned by the Communists and tortured. There were nasty marks on his back. He had been held in Szolnok, and therefore not released in 1956, because it was under Russian control, but he had met János Kádár in prison, and played chess with him, and Kádár had let him out. Then he had been given the sort of job – hospital portering – that released prisoners got. He had, in the evenings, betaken himself to old haunts, the Grand Hotel on the Margaret Island, where the barmen and the waiters were all part of old Hungary. Foreign journalists ended up there. Andrea, escaping from writs from the Ritz, ended up there as well, reporting for RIAS in Berlin (the *Daily Express* was I suspect something of a fantasy, but she had had some sort of affair with a married English peer in London, whose photograph, of him on a horse, she kept by her bedside). She and Tibor met in that red plush and gold bar. It was Ortrud and Telramund. There was money, once the West was reached. The West Germans were offering compensation for the horrors of 1944.

More: there was a *Herr Generaldirektor* in Vienna to whom, as an SS officer, the Karmans had entrusted property, in particular some Dutch paintings, and he had deposited them for safe-keeping in the national bank of the then Independent State of Croatia, in Zagreb. That *Herr Generaldirektor* would have some explaining to do. They would get married. They went to the Hungarian government and asked for an exit visa – refused. What they needed was a useful idiot, *der Geist, der stets bejaht*. And she met me on that train.

It was not a good moment in my existence. Someone said that you can only do central Europe if you are very young or very old, and I was getting beyond my first youth. More, I had written an article in, *History Today,* and Peter Quennell had been very encouraging, though the article – it was about the Habsburg army – was probably romantic tosh (the Austrian army is a very good subject, to which, now old, I would very willingly return: anything that knocks provincial nationalism on the head is a good thing). Out of the blue in Vienna came a letter signed Michael Sissons, of the literary agency A. D. Peters, the authors of whom represented a roll-call of English literature. It said that Hodder and Stoughton wished to publish a history of the twentieth century, and would I take care of the bit up to, as I remember, 1930. Five hundred pounds on signature, $5,000 to follow – huge sums. Tail wagging, I had asked Jack Plumb, who was enormously helpful to young men, what to do, given the obvious difficulty of combining proper respect for scholarship with etc. He said take it. I did, and the signing ceremony was witnessed by the Hodder grandees – the Attenborough dynasty – with a certain amount of disbelief. They were right. Back in Vienna, I went down to the British Council library in the Harrach Palace and took out Churchill's speeches of the war, which moved me to tears. Then I took E. H. Carr's three-volume *Russian Revolution* and started to take close, handwritten notes, which took weeks (it is a very boring and even silly book). Poor old Hodder and Stoughton were not going to flourish, as I plodded through Carr's account of the problems of the Mensheviks with the trade unions, one packet of Senior Service untipped after the other, and tins kicked down the Kärtnerstrasse. I was an idiot.

But useful. Andrea and I met in Vienna, in a hotel near the Franz-Josephs Bahnhof. She did not tell me about the portable property in

Zagreb, and it was all presented on an emotional level: 'I knew the British would not refuse.' It also all seemed quite easy. There had been a well-dramatized affair in Berlin, where someone had been squeezed into the dicky-box of a low-slung Karmann (coincidental) Ghia sports car and driven below the bar at Checkpoint Charlie, on the Friedrichstrasse in Berlin. The driver had got through the first barrier in the usual way, showing his passport, and had driven in second gear through the barbed wire towards the final barrier, then revved up quite suddenly, and driven under the boom. Could I hire a Karmann Ghia, and we would squeeze Tibor into the boot? There was a twist. It would not be the Austro-Hungarian border, but the Czechoslovak. At that moment, the first drips of the thaw were coming off the ice, and there had been a deal, to earn Austrian money, on the Czechoslovak side. From Vienna, you could go for the weekend to Bratislava, the main town in Slovakia, and so close to Vienna that, in the old days, there had been a connection so easy that you could go for the night to the Vienna Opera and be back afterwards. No visa was needed, nor was one needed from Hungary, such that Austro-Hungarian encounters took place in Bratislava. All depended upon the car.

I could not drive. However, there was someone who could, called Jan Wilson. She was Australian, and had come to teach in the English school in Vienna, an outfit that had been opened up in Heiligenstadt, near the Beethoven House (there were, as it turned out, forty-seven of those, because landladies turned up screeching about dog's hair when he was in the middle of a sonata). It was run by a Lancastrian, who had been a sergeant and had married an Austrian; he spoke Lancastrian Viennese ('Righty-oh, *'nabend'*). Waifs and strays turned up, and I was teaching French to waifs and strays, some of whom – as happens, bizarrely, with these odd schools, like Russell's – went on to great things. I taught a Count Gudenus who now owns much of Guatemala, for instance, and whose ears I boxed almost mortally. Jan Wilson was, like me, hanging around, and wondering what on earth life was about. When I asked her to drive, she said yes with alacrity. I went down to a car-hire place, Liewers, on the Triester Strasse, and politely asked whether they had a Karmann Ghia. They did not, but there was a Volkswagen 1500, a car not very large – in fact, the classic symbol of the *Wirtschaftswunder*. We drove off, past these huge villas in Heiligenstadt where once Richard Cobb had wept and sung. When he was very young, in about 1934, his mother had packed him off on a Quaker network to learn German, and he had found himself in the Heiligenstadt villa of one Felix Saltén, a Budapest Jew and the creator of *Bambi*. He and his wife did not have a relationship of pure love, and she took it out on the young Richard, who spent his time in the back kitchen eating bread and dripping – the fat of fat – with the maid. His mother had given him pamphlets to distribute to the working-class quarters of Vienna, telling people where, in Czecho-slovakia, they could get help. Round Richard went, and was picked up by the police. Men in loden coats, hats with a feather in them, dragged him, kicking, the length of the Ottakringer Hauptstrasse and he said later on that what he had remembered from it all was the huge-faced women, fox-fur-eyed, holding their heads in their hands and just staring out of the double-glazed window. To accommodate the habit, there was even a little hollow built into the window sill, holding the elbows that held the head, so that it could stare. Then he was expelled, the first and not the last time in that very remarkable life. We drove past the Saltén house, and got on our way past Hain-burg, where, in 1889, the Austrian Social Democrats had launched their bid for the future, which turned out so tragically wrong. The scene was of course central Europe in *Prisoner of Zenda* mode, and we went through the Slovak border without difficulty. Hotel Devin, Tibor, dinner, what do we do next?

It was clear to one and all that this was not on. The car was absurdly small, the frontier obstacles serious. Next day, we trundled round the countryside, and it is an interesting area, as I later learned. The Csállókőz (Vel'ky Žitný ostrov in Slovak), an island in the Danube, had once had German villages, filled with harmless people (whom I later encountered, speaking a mixture of Hungarian and German, in Nassau). A scene of desolation in the snow ('Dieses Dorf hiess seiner-zeit Modern,' said Tibor). None of us had quite the courage to say that this was preposterous. Tibor lay down on the back and Andrea put a coat over him; she then sat upon him, and rehearsed a line to the effect that she was suffering from an inflamation of the ovaries –

Eierstockentzündung – which she thought would defeat the Slovak frontier guards. We then approached the frontier. It was the ides of March, 1964. So many people had that same experience – deep snow, barbed wire, guards in long coats with long rifles and red stars in uniform caps, barking Alsatians. The first barrier opened up, and we were in a column of cars going back to Vienna, which Andrea had banked on. Second barrier. Andrea had expected that there would be one guard, who would probably just have waved us through – the Slovaks' instincts are decent – but, the authorities knowing what they were doing, there were several. One looked into the back of the car, and wondered. Andrea said, 'Eierstockentzündung'. A hand went to the coat underneath, and hair was obvious. 'Sie chaben eine vierte Perzzoon in diesem Wagen.' I said to Andrea that there was no point in contesting it, and we were all led towards the customs building. Tibor stood shoeless in the snow, and bit his fingernails to the quick: he knew what would have happened otherwise, as sticks went under them. There was an interrogation that night, all of us in separate rooms. Morning came, and the customs people – decent Slovaks: I heard them say about me, 'Simpatický' – rang up the Czech Ministry of Justice people in Prague. The Czech Ministry of Justice people in Prague were pigs, insisted on rules, and so we were stuck. A police car took Jan and me to the prison, the Prokurátorská väznica v Bratislave. We stopped on the way, at a café, and they gave us an enormous *slivovica*. Then the prison gates opened, and the formalities started: belongings handed over, medical inspection, prison clothes put on – a brown number, smelling (I can recall it now) of washing, with flat shoes that you cannot run in. You go along the corridors, and if there is another prisoner coming, you are turned, face to the wall, until he has passed. Warders click keys to warn each other that they are coming. Then a cell – it was 283, and I later went back, post-Communism, Monte Cristo fashion, to see it, to wonder if the inmates needed some cigarettes. The cell then contained four young men, and I complained to the governor that the cell was too small for that number. He agreed, but said, what could he do? They were gypsies. In the old days, the gypsies used to get themselves put into prison in November, because they were fed and heated. Now there was a free market, and it was

September. There was therefore overcrowding in the Prokurátorská väznica v Bratislave. I could not criticize, and wandered down that well-known staircase reciting the *St Matthew Passion*, which, somehow, I knew by heart: *Wenn ich einmal soll scheiden, so scheid' Du nicht von mir*, in the old Klemperer version. I thought of my poor old mother, a war widow, with me as the only child – my father had been killed in the RAF in '42 – and what she must be feeling. Your first week in prison is awful, and the chap they had moved in with me was very sympathetic as I wiped away the tears that were not entirely to be stifled. He was quite an interesting lad, Kornel Karpacky by name. Our common language was Hungarian. The authorities let me have the grammar book I had arrived with, Banhidi-Jókai-Szabó, *Tanuljuk nyelveket*, and I had reached lesson ten, where they explain that the verb changes according to whether it is transitive or intransitive followed by an indirect article or a dative. The translation passages were about a Palestinian going round a textile factory. At that time, the second language in Bratislava was Hungarian. It had been the second capital, until 1918, and the Jews, a quarter of the population, had spoken Hungarian; there were also Germans who had taken to it easily enough. Kornel spoke it, with a thick Slovak accent which I myself have never, to this day, entirely lost, because his mother had come from Transylvania and his father was Slovak. He explained that life had been very difficult, that he had made three of the local girls pregnant, had had three mothers chasing after him, had made for the frontier with wire-cutters. I should not have believed this, because Kornel – who was not I think entirely balanced in mind – must have been that phenomenon of Communist prisons that everyone knows, a *Spitzel* – someone planted to find out what you are about. He did not get anything much out of me, and must have got quite sick of the *St Matthew* (I also knew the Verdi *Requiem*). At some stage, he must have been told to try a homosexual approach. The prison pants came down, and a foot-long Pan-Slav number stretched before my eyes. On it had been tattooed the badge of Fascist Slovakia, some sort of double-headed lobster. I expressed no interest, and there we were. The weeks went by. I got to know the guards. The librarian, who had good German, trundled round his books, and I said, 'Seitdem ich hier sitze, kann ich nicht umhin, *Das Kapital* zu lesen', which I then did. H. G. Wells was not really any better, though, in later life, I would gladly read both of these men, especially Wells. Forty years later, Penguin asked me to do an introduction to his *Short History of the World*, a superb perform-ance, and he is the writer whom I should want to recall from the dead. He competes with Orwell, but Orwell never dies.

The warders became friendly. 'Mész haza,' they said – you'll go home. One had served in a Slovak outfit in Italy at the end of the war, and spoke at bit of Italian, which I vaguely could manage: 'piove', in the exercise yard, where we went every day for half an hour, balancing on an isosceles triangle of half-thawed ice, and if you stood on one end, the other, thirty yards up, rose. Then it was back to the cell, warders clicking their keys, to warn each other that a prisoner was coming. The food was some sort of stew, pushed through a flap. Later on, one of the judges asked me, why did you never complain about the food, and I said, not to his enlightenment, have you ever lived in a Cambridge col-lege? I was not wasting my time, and the British went into action. The Consul-General in Prague, Ramsay Melhuish, turned up with several hundred untipped State Express, which I shared with Kornel, who, Slo-vak nationalist that he was, said that they were inferior to his own Lipa brand, the tobacco of which was so carelessly packed that the whole thing caught fire and was therefore easier to smoke. Melhuish also gave me all the works of Bertrand Russell when, in alimony mode, he wrote books called 'Power', 'Being', etc. We used to talk about the lectures of A. J. P. Taylor in the governor's office, and he was very kind to my mother, whom he put up in the Thun Palace in Prague. She was, I am afraid, dif-ficult, and he was wonderful. She came: there was nothing to be said but the prison governor took the point. At a certain point, in my cell, I heard the clumping of boots. It was the governor. He said something like:

Wir chaben einen Brief bekommen von Leuten die heissen Hodder und Stoughton und besonders von einem gewissen Herrn Sissons. Sie wollen, dass Sie einen Vertrag unterzeichnen, wonach Sie auf Ihre Rechte bezüg-lich des Buches über das zwanzigste Jahrhundert verzichten, wemgegen-über sie bereit sind, Ihnen einen nach Belieben jeglichen Buchvertrag mit demselben Entgegengesomething zu unterbreiten willig seien.

No more E. H. Carr in the Palais Harrach: instead, I said I would write a book about the eastern front in the First World War, signed the contract, and ten years later, wrote it.

It came to a trial. Neither the Czechoslovak nor the Hungarian KGB could work it out. Was I some kind of deep agent? Three months went by. I had a defence lawyer, Edgar Prisender, who turned out to be an enormously interesting man. He was the grandson of a Habsburg major-general, was, somewhere along the line, Jewish, and sprang from a family of Hungarian landowners in Slovakia. His French was near perfect (I gave him Proust, though that would not have been his cup of tea) and he had acquired decent English as well. He kept me going with vitamins – kohlrabi, a vegetable that I had not known – and came every week. I was all right, not wasting my time, but Jan Wilson had a far harder experience. She had been banged up with a gypsy prostitute, and had no language at all in common; she had stopped menstruating, and she did not have the support from family that I had. We met in Sydney much later, where she ran a market garden; never a word of reproach. I went to Australia in 1978, and would have stayed, except that it is so very far away. Jan, who was without friends and family, and did not speak the languages, behaved like a brick.

The trial was interesting. There was nothing much in the world news at the time, and they piled in. In the spectators' box were an RAF war widow, and a woman who had lost her family in Auschwitz, Andrea's mother. The interpreter – it all had to go through English, Slovak and Hungarian – was also from Auschwitz: he told me he had come out weighing 60 pounds. The judges had been fixed in advance by Edgar Prisender. They would trap the old Stalinist public prosecutor into making a fool of himself. They did. He was stupid enough to demand the maximum sentence against me and Jan, who were obvious innocents, and the minimum against the principals, Andrea and Tibor. Even then, they got six months – nothing, in terms of that system (an old Austrian woman had got nine years in Pardubice a few weeks before). Jan and I got a month, and were expelled from the country on 8 June. The Czechs – not the Slovaks – were absurdly bureaucratic, and when I wanted to take my baby son, in 1983, to see his godmother were vindictive. It needed an intervention by the Foreign Office for me to be put into a Helsinki basket.

The upshot, and the meaning, of that trial was that the public prosecutor was made to look foolish, and was got rid of. The Slovak judges rose in the land. So did Edgar Prisender. We had got on very well indeed, and I went to see a wonderful Hungarian cousin of his in Vienna afterwards, who told me, come 1968, that Edgar had been named Czechoslovak ambassador to the USA in August 1968, just before the Soviet invasion. Edgar denies this. But he escaped in 1968 and became an international patent lawyer for Ciba-Geigy in Basle. They should have made him president of Slovakia, as a prelude to the country's rejoining Hungary in a confederation. Andrea and Tibor had a different fate. The affair had obviously been embarrassing and ridiculous. The Czechs meanly made both of them serve the other few weeks of their sentences in Pakrac prison in Prague. Then they were expelled, and I met Andrea as she came over. Tibor was received with flowers and apologies by the Hungarian secret police at Komárom. Then the Austrian government went into action, and Tibor was shoved over the border at Hegyeshalom without a passport. They got married. Then they approached the SS *Herr Generaldirektor* and got nowhere. However, there were the Karman paintings, deposited in the Fascist Bank of Croatia, and a deal was done: a villa on the Dalmatian coast, in return for the de Hoochs (were they even genuine?). What happened? I have taught a prime minister of Hungary, and the brother of one of his cabinet ministers took me into Transylvania when Romania collapsed. The Slovak interior minister arranged for me to visit my old cell, number 283, in 1992, and I marched up the prison steps remembering those lines, *Wenn ich einmal soll scheiden, so scheid' Du nicht von mir.* I was very near tears. I still do not know what it was about: central Europe. But I did my stuff for the growth of Slovakia, and that has turned out quite well.

20

Reaction

Afghanistan was another gigantic dwarf, like Greece: a place, not very significant in itself, where geography and the local complications combined to make it important on a world scale. The Soviet invasion prompted a Western, particularly British and American, reaction, but that had in any case been building up, for quite different reasons, for some time. A wise observer had said, at the time of the Hungarian uprising in 1956, that the system was going to go on and on until an explosion happened in Moscow itself, which duly happened. But the origins of this went back to a change that had come about with Henry Kissinger, in the middle of the seventies.

In November 1975 the 'capitalists', leaders of the half-dozen advanced industrial countries, had met at Rambouillet, outside Paris, at the behest of the French president, Giscard d'Estaing. They stared gloomily into the fireside as they, as expected, chatted. Helmut Schmidt wondered if democracy would survive: in this period, Portugal had almost passed under Communism, and Italy was very unstable. New York was going bankrupt, and Saigon had fallen not long before. Henry Kissinger vowed that his purpose on earth was to break the OPEC cartel that was making so much of the trouble, but the inflation associated with OPEC went on. It was worst in England, at 24 per cent in 1975 (and altogether not far from 100 per cent between 1971 and 1975) and in 1976, of all extraordinary signs of failure, the IMF was called in, extracting a Letter of Intent in return for the organizing of support for the pound. Every country had some degree of inflation at this time, but the Germans and the French kept it well below British figures. How? Was it greater discipline as regards petrol use? Or moderate, responsible behaviour on the part of the trade unions? Or better management of the credit and money supply by the Bundesbank, using interest rates and bond prices to stop too much spending with borrowed money? Or European financial collaboration, which, certainly, Schmidt and Giscard greatly wanted?

These subjects came up on the Rambouillet agenda of the 'G7', as they were to be called. By now, ideas of radical change were in the air: otherwise, the Western world would be in thrall to the Arabs, and the Soviet Union, with its vast oil revenues, would predominate. A declaration promising exchange rate stability and restored trade was made; beyond that – a sign of what was to come – the International Monetary Fund was invoked, and at last given a true world role. This was the start of the celebrated formula, the 'Washington Consensus', in effect shaped by the USA. It amounted to a recognition that the post-war order, with reference in effect to John Maynard Keynes and Bretton Woods in 1944, had failed. There must be liberalization.

The problem of inflation was worldwide, but it was worst in the Atlantic countries. The USA, after the Nixon crash, was in poor shape and needed the formula itself, as the dollar went down. Newly emerging Far Eastern countries, especially Japan, were making American exports uncompetitive; great heavy industrial regions turned into 'rust belt' country, historic places such as Baltimore or Philadelphia becoming wastelands. In the USA and in England, blundering efforts were made even by supposedly right-wing regimes to control wages, but to make this acceptable to trade unions, prices were also controlled, and, with reference to the unions' supposed interest in equality, 'the rich' were to be taxed heavily. In practice, this meant tax rates of 80 per cent at a none-too-high level, and on 'unearned income', i.e. people's savings, 98 per cent. The argument behind this was that inflation was caused by excessive wage demands from trade union leaders who had become spoiled and greedy; they might give up their bad habits provided that the middle classes were taxed so hard that equality would prevail. However, the trade unionists themselves then found that they were being taxed at higher levels: there was even a danger that people who were receiving welfare payments would pay tax at 40 per cent. Improvement did not follow, and in any case the unions could always say, and this was the right thing to say, that their problem was not greed, that prices were rising, that their wage demands were defensive. 'Corporatism', English-style, was no more successful than the preposterous 'Planning' had been before it. Alternative thoughts were then thought.

There was another argument altogether as to why inflation rose, and it was advanced under the name 'monetarism'. In 1970 Milton Friedman, an American economist (who had had experience of Cambridge but not in the charmed circle of King's College: he had stayed at Gonville and Caius, where the leading light was the Budapest-Jewish Peter Bauer), gave a lecture in London to the effect that the British economists were 'naïve, unsophisticated' – more so even than the Americans of the 1930s. He noticed later on that 'the present situation cannot last. It will either degenerate into hyper-inflation and radical change, or institutions will adjust to a situation of chronic inflation; or governments will adopt policies that will produce a low rate of inflation and less government intervention into the fixing of prices.' There was, said Friedman, an alternative course: to control the supply of money. Inflation was at the source of the whole problem, and that could be stopped if governments stopped producing the paper money (most of that consisting of figures printed in bank accounts) that caused it.

The argument was not really new. Economists had argued as to the role of money for a long time, and in the nineteenth century there had been differences as to whether the supply of money and credit just reflected the demand for it, or whether it shaped that demand. The brightest brains of Europe, the British in the lead, had addressed such questions, and they could only be answered with a good grasp of mathematics, logic and history. In late-nineteenth-century Cambridge, Economics had even arisen out of Moral Sciences, the working name for Philosophy. However, along with moral questions, there were technical ones. What was money? In the nineteenth century the question almost answered itself because money was based on gold, which of course had a value. True, there was not very much gold, but a piece of nobly printed paper could be taken to the bank and changed back, if need be, into so many ounces of gold. Of course that did not happen, because gold was heavy and could be stolen, and if governments were trusted, then their paper was as good as metal – especially in England, where the gold reserve was actually quite small, less than Russia's. However, there were limits to the amount of paper that could be printed in these circumstances, and that limited bank credits. People who needed them sometimes wanted to have a wider basis for money (in the USA there were demands from farmers for silver to be used as well as gold). Keynes in the 1920s and still more in the 1930s had wanted governments to abandon these standards, on the grounds that gold was 'a barbarous relic', that a properly managed paper money would expand credit, stimulate the economy and cause employment to happen. His critics said that a paper money of this sort would mean a rise in prices, the inflation that did indeed occur in the seventies. Friedman was returning to the older ideas of monetary stability: the seventies were to bear out such wisdoms.

At the time these ideas were not at all fashionable. As David Smith says, to be a monetarist in the 1960s was 'like having an unfortunate but embarrassing affliction which people were too polite to mention'. The grand establishment at King's, Cambridge, basked in the sunlight of Keynes, and disdained monetarists, who were on the whole of a lower order. They seemed to be backwoodsmen, offering the grim formulae that had made the thirties such a black decade in the minds of the Keynesians, who sneered. As Keynes's biographer, Robert Skidelsky, has demonstrated, there was even a sexual aspect to this. Keynes broke the rules, did so in a very sophisticated way, and was never held to account for it, even though other homosexuals, including the inventor of the computer and cracker of the German codes in the war, Alan Turing (also of King's, but not as grand as Keynes), were harried to death because of it. Old E. M. Forster and George 'Dadie' Rylands, characteristic of the twenties, lived on and on, into a world where *Death in Venice* became museum piece Edwardian, and witnessed a radical change: Antonio Gramsci came to King's, which adopted the causes of 1968, discovered women, and went in for positive discrimination of various sorts. It did not flourish, eventually going bankrupt, bringing down Cambridge Economics with it: within a generation, no foreigner bothered with it, and even very few English graduate students took its doctorates. The then Provost, Noel Annan, wrote memoirs, *Our Age* (1990), explaining why this course had been adopted, and of course not just at radical King's alone, but widely across the old institutions, such as the BBC. He recognized the mistake, but the Cambridge economists of that era were part of 'our age', and they high-hatted little Friedman, happily married, quite Jewish, and very American. One of the best monetarists, Alan Walters, not of grand social origins, and initially interested in the economics of another British disaster area, transport, was turned down when he wanted support for research in a monetarist direction in the 1960s: the money supply was dismissed as unimportant.

True, there were outposts. The University of Chicago – Friedman's – was one such, and not just in economics. The USA was still in some ways an old-fashioned country, and Chicago, a place dominated by an Irish-Italian-Polish Catholic mafia much as other religion-mixed cities had been in 1900, was a place where political arithmetic made more sense than the moral algebra of Keynes. Catholic priests were everywhere far more adept than Protestant pastors at mobilizing votes, making non-Catholics pay for municipal jobs and contracts awarded to their followers. 'Who, whom?', i.e. who paid for whom, was the great question, and a simple answer to mafias was for money not to be created for them to steal. In 1956 Friedman wrote his article on 'The Quantity Theory of Money': it restated the old idea that money did indeed have an independently very powerful role in shaping the economy, and did not just reflect the shape of it. As matters worsened in London, these ideas began to surface. One of Chicago's professors, Harry Johnson, a heavy-drinking Canadian with verve, also held an appointment at the LSE, and by 1969 influential commentators in London had become interested, particularly Peter Jay at *The Times* and Samuel Brittan at the *Financial Times*. All along, there had been people – in the main, disciples of Keynes's great critic, Friedrich von Hayek – who had not liked the orthodoxies of the Welfare State. They had been derided, but, with support from enlightened businessmen, a successsful poultry farmer set up the Institute of Economic Affairs (IEA), where, in the high noon of Keynesian England, the old ideas were kept alive. The IEA published interestingly, staged provocative lunchtime meetings, and often proved to be right. Now, in the mid-seventies, it began to move centre-stage.

Its people began to take some tricks at last, as the grandees' schemes went awry. Even in 1969 there had been some official talk of limiting the money supply, and to hold the Bretton Woods line a budget surplus was prepared, in London as in Washington (the cuts in spending probably cost Labour the election of 1970: the then Chancellor, Roy Jenkins, a masterpiece of reproduction furniture who was eventually to split the party, probably wanted this, because it might bring sense to the trade unions). At the London Business School shoestring research turned out to be effective. David Laidler at Manchester predicted, for instance, that unemployment would get worse despite the spending spree of 1972, and he was right: it reached two million in 1980, even more than he had expected, while in that year the inflation rate, at 18 per cent, ought to have precluded this. But the monetarists were also accurate in predicting inflation rates of 15 per cent and 25 per cent in 1975 and 1976. Laidler reckoned that the problem with inflation was that it became self-propelling: people assumed that it would happen and behaved accordingly. He recommended keeping the money supply under control, and announcing 'targets' for it in advance. This was all very well, but there was a difficulty to be overcome, and it never quite was. How were you to define 'money'? Notes and coins were a tiny fraction of what people could spend, given chequebooks, bank loans, credit cards, and stocks and shares that rose or fell. Then again there were great complications concerning abroad: money might flow into England, according to oil discoveries or to alterations in the exchange rate. These things were very difficult indeed – and, some said, impossible – to measure, even assuming that they were worth measuring at all.

There were various measures, well-stated by a wise political commentator, Alan Watkins: 'narrow money' was that held in the Bank of England, plus deposits made by the commercial banks; 'wide', that circulating in pockets – together, these were Mo. Then there was M1, which to Mo added bank deposits that could be withdrawn on demand. There was an M2 which went out of fashion quickly enough; M3 consisted of M1, with the addition of deposits that could be withdrawn after an interval of time; M4 was this, plus deposits in building societies, where savings for house purchases and mortgages were placed. One leading theorist, Tim Congdon, regarded M4 as the best measure. However, whatever their disagreements, the monetarists could at least chalk up more successful predictions than their opponents. They also had history, on the whole, on their side, since great inflations had accompanied the French and Russian Revolutions, themselves preceded and accompanied by issues of paper money that, in the Russian case, went so fast that there was no time even to print numbers on the notes, such that people who accepted them had to ink in the numbers themselves. In the great German inflation of 1922–3, ending with 11 million million Marks to the pound, the Reichsbank solemnly denied that its money-printing had anything to do with the inflation, and when the inflation was indeed stopped almost in its tracks by the introduction of a new currency altogether, its president, Rudolf E. A. Havenstein, dropped dead.

The British monetarists had strong Atlantic connections and some found the American atmosphere more rewarding in every way. A measure of British disillusionment was a book by Robert Bacon and Walter Eltis, *Britain's Economic Problem*, which showed that the government took 60 per cent of the gross domestic product, that the public services, being 'non-marketed', crowded out private investment. There was much truth in this, demonstrated when, in the 1980s and especially in the 'long decade' that followed 1991 and the end of the USSR, different ways were tried. Then, electronics vastly lowered the costs of publishing, retailing, even transport; potential producers, and especially China, were liberated, to produce on a vast scale, and some prices fell and fell. But in the seventies, the great advances in technology were not applied in such matters as telecommunications or printing (let alone the heavy industries and mining) because of union obstruction and of course lack of investment. Everything contributed to a downwards spiral, and the critics were right to say that inflation was the chief problem. They were resisted, partly because they seemed to be offering a return to the dismal verities of the Gold Standard age. In the USA economics was much less dominated by the Keynesian orthodoxies. There the unions were markedly less strong, and there was not quite such a concentration on the virtues of full employment. The most basic assumption in England had to do with the thirties, when so many young and educated people had looked guiltily at the mass unemployment of the traditional industries, mainly in the north, and had compared it with the prosperity of the south (and maybe also thought, inevitably, that their own job prospects should have been grander than the schoolteaching or other such low-paid work that many of them found themselves doing). Keynes had said that government spending would cause employment to increase, which would then create more 'demand' and cause greater production. This had been formalized in the Phillips Curve.

Friedman challenged this. He claimed that there was only a 'trade-off between unemployment and unanticipated inflation', meaning that if people saw that inflation was coming, they would take it into account in wage demands, and unemployment would be back to the starting point. In Keynes's own time people had not expected inflation and did not know how to deal with it. The Friedman school reckoned that 'economic agents would quickly develop efficient methods of seeing through the short-term real effects of expansionary fiscal policies'. There were rejoinders: there were still economists (James Tobin the best-known) who argued as before that mild inflation was a good thing. The grand establishment – Wynne Godley and Nicholas Kaldor – even toyed with reflation behind a wall of import controls, which would imply planning of this and that, and of course a paper money subject to joyous arithmetic. On the whole, the challengers were more interesting, and serious innovation came from institutions that allowed them to flourish, such as the London Business School. They did not worry so much about the balance of payments, and appreciated that there was an international aspect to the problem of inflation: since 1971, and the end of Bretton Woods, exchange rates had widely fluctuated, the dollar being worth half of a pound and then, a year or two later, being nearly equal to it. In the circumstances, inflation. By 1976, and the arrival of the IMF inspectors, Denis Healey, who, if British Labour had been as enlightened as the SPD, would have been a Helmut Schmidt, was listening to the monetarists, and by March 1980 they were predominant. However, the often bitter, self-righteous and contemptuous arguments about monetarism were really about matters that went deeper.

Monetarism was a useful fiction. It was not a miracle cure, though it could certainly deal with symptoms, and this was noted by political commentators who had made their training in Marxism. One such, Alfred Sherman, dismissed economics as jumped-up accountancy: paper-money inflation just reflected the power of labour and the trade unions to impose transfer payments; he also saw the interest of the Keynesians themselves in the power of the State in organizing the transfers, the productive parts of the economy having to pay for it all. It was described in the United States as 'rent-seeking', as political economists tried to find a theory to fit what had been happening. A bureaucracy, complete with its own wooden language, was established to effect the transfers, and it taxed the middle: as Sherman said, the State turns everybody into a proletarian or a functionary. This was again a very old argument. It was levelled at the Counter-Reformation Catholic Church. In the later nineteenth century, Protestant countries were overwhelmingly richer and better organized than Catholic ones. Why? You cannot really point to significant doctrinal differences; nor can you say that the rich and the organizers were especially Protestant. The obvious answer, expounded in Hugh Trevor-Roper's essay on this subject, was that the Counter-Reformation Church drove the businessmen out through taxation and religious harassment. They moved from Antwerp to Amsterdam, from France to Prussia, from Italy to England. Meanwhile, the papacy built extraordinary baroque buildings, and developed an equally baroque bureaucracy of much splendour, which made generous charitable arrangements for the poor (in Latin languages, 'pawn shop' is 'mount of piety'), whereas in Protestant countries such as the Netherlands or Scotland 'sturdy' beggars were whipped out of town and churches were bald boxes, with a smaller bald box next door marked 'school'. The paradoxical outcome, in the later twentieth century, was that Catholic countries were becoming richer and better organized than Protestant ones: Bavaria and Baden, for instance, easily overtook much of northern Germany, let alone the German Democratic Republic, which was, in origin, overwhelmingly Protestant.

There was, here, one obvious line of enquiry, that in the Catholic countries conservatism reigned as regards the family and education, whereas elsewhere (including northern Germany) the changes of the sixties did great damage to both. Welfare was a case in point. Originally, welfare in the Atlantic countries had been set up on an insurance principle: you paid for 'stamps', and this guaranteed you against bad times. There were also, in the USA, many charity hospitals for the poor who did not have the wherewithal to deal with emergencies. But inflation killed such things, as it made scholarship funds for education meaningless small change; the insurance funds suffered from inflation, and the State anyway needed the money to pay for the widening gap between 'entitlement' and reality. The State won, and, increasingly in the Atlantic world, including Canada, the State took over what should have been a matter of semi-private insurance, and 'social security' just became another tax. In Sherman's view, State spending then brought about inflation.

But there was more. It also brought about unemployment. As to this, there was much worry, because especially in England unemployment had gone up and up, despite repeated applications of the Keynesian formula against it – even and perhaps especially under ostensibly right-wing regimes such as Heath's. Why? One of the leading monetarists, Patrick Minford, studied the question and did so from the viewpoint of Liverpool University. Liverpool, by 1980, was a stricken city. It had been one of Britain's grandest, with superb Victorian architecture and an art gallery, set up by the Walker shipping family, that contained the best Pre-Raphaelites. The shipping, as with Glasgow, had collapsed, but Liverpool, unlike Glasgow, did not have alternatives, and anyway had to compete with Manchester, which did. The professional classes moved out, the Victorian city declined. But Liverpool had also developed hideous housing estates, themselves a prescription for demoralization, and a spiralling down began. Any sensible observer of the scene immediately wondered: why, with so much unemployment, can you not get a taxi? The university itself had had its great Victorian days; Patrick Abercrombie, the originator of town planning in Great Britain (and of much else), had taught there, and Gladstone even talked with a Liverpool accent. In modern times, it had produced the Beatles, who, despite nonsense in the opposite sense, were quite well-educated middle-class boys. Patrick Minford (like Sherman, a one-time Communist) might well feel resentful, as a professor paid far below the inflation rate (some trade union boss having declared that academics did not rate much love and care), and he examined the paradoxes of a Liverpool that he could see crumbling before his eyes. Minford had adopted monetarism, as a surrogate Gold Standard, and now wrote on unemployment. Why was it at such a level? His answer was one that had already been offered in the great Slump. Even then, money had been spent on Liverpool, and it had not responded very well. There was a particular problem, in that Irish immigration had created what in the USA became known as an 'underclass', so bad that, even in the truant schools that were set up to punish boys who absented themselves from school, the Catholics and the Protestants had to be kept rigidly separate: there was a common bathhouse, for instance, and it was kept locked on one or other of the religious sides, in the yard, on alternate days. The same problem existed in Glasgow but there – the State in Scotland being more forthright – it was somehow kept under control. Not so in Liverpool: four decades later, money was spent, and even more; the result, said Correlli Barnett cruelly, was 'urban primitives'. Minford was less outspoken, but said much the same: if you pay people to be unemployed, they will be. More: they will abuse the system. This again had origins in Ireland, where the alienation of the Catholic Church by the Anglo-Scots in the nineteenth century had meant that it would not co-operate over birth certificates. No-one knew who was born, when. Old-age pensions were introduced in England before the First World War but Ireland was not included, because no-one knew when the claimants reached the claiming age. Now, much of Liverpool existed on the black economy: the city that had pioneered the slave trade then turned, by fearful symmetry, into Ireland's revenge on England. Men and women would want to get married as a matter of course, especially if there were children. One problem in measuring unemployment was that people lived in couples, and the wife might try for employment. She was then taxed. 'The marginal tax rates on wives of unemployed men are high and increase with his unemployment duration ... her

income risks loss of benefit.' Wives – one third worked – even lost
15 per cent of their income in tax, while the husband got something
back in 'benefit'. You did not need to be a mathematician to work out
that men and women would not marry, if they were paid not to. He
might have added that the housing policies pursued since the war had
had the same perverse effect. The couple paid a low rent, sometimes
ridiculously low, and, if they left the dwelling to take employment
elsewhere, would find a new dwelling so expensive that no money
was made. They were therefore imprisoned in unemployment, in a collapsing city, with effects upon the children that would prolong the
problem and create what was coming to be known as the British underclass. If you were in a union, you had a job, and real wages rose. But
the unions also kept people out, and the result was division: some people
working in padded employment, others not. This went together with a
proliferation of public bodies offering employment of a sort – for
instance, the 'Perambulator and Invalid Carriages Wages Council' and
the 'Ostrich and Fancy Feather and Artificial Flower Wages Council',
which covered 400,000 people. These things simply priced people out
of real work and minimum-wage laws reinforced this. Late-seventies
England was not a happy place, or, rather, what was happy was not
real, and what was real was not happy.

There were other ideas around at this time, often of great interest,
and reflecting the disillusion of men and women who had regarded
the sixties as a time of hope. Much of the inspiration, and even some
of the money, came from North America. There, the disillusion had
also run deep, and Johnson's idea of a 'Great Society' had disintegrated: as Ronald Reagan put it, 'We declared war on poverty, and we
lost.' Daniel Moynihan, originally a New Dealer and a Democrat,
made himself very unpopular at Harvard (they threatened to burn
down his house) because he said that welfare was causing black girls
just to do without husbands, and bringing about the disintegration of
the black family; that was producing an 'underclass' of hopeless
misfits who, again through welfare, were paid to reproduce themselves. Education also produced its counter-revolutionaries, who had
even, at the very end of his life, included John Dewey himself, the
architect of progressive education. The United States was big enough,

and decentralized enough, for new ideas to be tried out here and there. But was this possible in an England that was centrally run?

Disillusion with the sixties was now quite widespread. The educational reforms of that decade – comprehensive schools – had demonstrably done nothing either for better education or for social mobility. The concrete architecture that had replaced old and solid Victorian buildings was widely hated, outside architectural bodies, and go-ahead local authorities in the USA even began blowing up the more offensive of the 'projects'. However, whereas with monetarism there was at least a chance of changed financial ways, the bureaucracies and interest groups involved in these things were not easily changed: short of some coup, they were even irremovable. A very disillusioned figure of the era was John Vaizey. Here was one of the bright young men of the fifties, a clever man, married to a clever art historian (whose brother had written about Orwell), with a background in poverty and for that matter crippling illness: during the war, he had contracted polio, and had been cured by the then methods, which were torture chamber stuff, as he was clamped into a plaster straitjacket for a year, to be fed, immovably on his back, wartime rations. He studied a very difficult subject, the economic effects of education, and wrote well; Labour put him into the House of Lords. But trade-union-dominated England was not for him, and he recognized his mistake. In the seventies, he described it: the more criminology, the more crime; the more sociology, the less community; he could have added, the more economics, the less money. There were many such cases. Noel Annan was also extremely clever, a man for any committee needed to pronounce on the Arts, the BBC, the Royal Opera; but his *Our Age* is a rueful piece of work, trying to explain quite why his generation had deliberately subverted the wisdoms of the ages; again, it was domination by trade unions that he most resented. In the later 1970s the best British literary editor since Cyril Connolly, John Gross of *The Times Literary Supplement*, though again sympathetic to Labour, was being driven to distraction because he had to deal with obdurate print unions for days on end every month; in the end they closed him down for a year. There were in all areas ideas of much radicalism on both sides of the Atlantic. In hardly more than twenty years, England changed extraordinarily. Orwell had noted that football crowds behaved as if they were on church parade, and there was remarkably little crime. By the 1970s football hooliganism had become such that, in West Germany, the owners of small hotels in the vicinity of an international game put up notices to the effect that the English were not wanted. In the later 1970s there were warnings, and in the new 'think-tanks' set up on an American model, and following the success of the IEA, hard-hitting pamphlets were produced. The mood was set for reaction, but its cause was, as yet, far from won. The various social reforms, and the change in institutions such as the universities or the BBC, were very difficult to combat, and in any case there was no agreement – far from it – that there were problems other than lack of money. There might be a specific British problem to do with uncontrollable trade unions, and perhaps even over the management of the money supply, but that did not automatically discredit the whole structure. Besides, there was always the hope that membership of the European Economic Community would bring an improvement.

Here was another illusion, though a forgivable one, shared by almost anyone in the educated classes. If in 1973 you moved to Europe, you could see that things worked. France had picked herself up, had world-class concerns, and was almost twice as well-off as Britain. Northern Italy was heading in that direction. Especially, the legend of miracle-Germany lived on. The pound sank and sank against the Mark – it had started at twelve, and was coming down to two – and if you came back to Heathrow airport from Cologne or Munich, you either sat in a traffic jam for two hours, getting into London, or you took the underground railway for an hour or so, trundling through endless Actons, whereas in Munich you reached the centre of town from the airport in a quarter of an hour, because someone had taken the point that traffic from airports was not the same as traffic from suburbia. The Americans had never really understood why Great Britain had kept herself apart from Europe, and pressed strongly for her joining it: Henry Kissinger characteristically remarking that it was tiresome to have to make six telephone calls instead of just one, to a counterpart in Brussels. With a cross-party arrangement, British governments duly joined, and, with some media management and some mendacious language, their decision was confirmed by referendum in 1975. Their negotiating position was weak, they were in a hurry, and they were easily outmanoeuvred by the French. Concessions, later regarded as absurd, were made. The country paid more than its fair share of the European budget, and accepted provisions as regards agriculture that proved expensive and corrupt. One positive thing did emerge: the European Court, to which British law was now subject, decreed that trade unions did not have the right to enforce membership ('the closed shop'), and that, in time, was to counter the protection racket ways that had been developing. But, in the short term, 'Europe' did not turn out to be the answer, because Europe herself was losing steam.

Germany looked, in informed British eyes, miraculous. In November 1972 the SPD–FDP coalition won handsomely, and although the Left did make a spirited effort to take over important places, it was always defeated by factors without a British counterpart: the liberals of the FDP controlled essential ministries, with foreign affairs and finance, while the trade unions, quite happily part of 'the system', did not get in the way of sensible management of the oil crisis. The Bundesbank defied governments' attempts to spend money that they did not have, whereas the Bank of England blew hard into asset-bubbles. The Left might make a great deal of noise; Brandt, increasingly and rather sentimentally tolerant of these things, isolated himself, and somehow grew down. Bismarck used to say, *On revient toujours à son premier amour*, and Brandt's own weakness, as he grew older, drank more, and showed off to the women, was for the Left of his youth, a split-off from the Communist Party which was quite close, during the Spanish Civil War (in which Brandt had been present), to the POUM, the anarchist element in Barcelona that Stalin had had put down. He became, in a word, vain and silly. His memoirs are very revealing, and they almost typify Graham Greene's comment, that you live until you are thirty and then remember. In Brandt's case the memoirs are full of life until about 1955 and then the machine takes over the ghost: his version of *Ostpolitik* is hardly more than toponymy. His judgement clearly went, and in his closest entourage he was tolerating a clammy East German spy, Günter Guillaume, who, eventually found out, caused Brandt to resign when the FDP foreign minister, the machine-man Hans-Dietrich Genscher, revealed this. Helmut

Schmidt, the power in the party, dismissed the Left as 'half-baked students' who confused the crisis in their own brains with a general crisis; and he went ahead with an interesting strategy. There would be *Ostpolitik*. Germany would recognize the post-war borders, and maintain proper relations with Poland especially. Given that, in the previous generation, millions of Germans had been driven out, a great many of them dying on the way, this required much dignity and sense, whereas in comparable situations elsewhere – the Armenians, the Greek Cypriots, or for that matter the Palestinians – self-pity, distorted history and cries for vengeance went on and on (and on). But there would be no sentimental nonsense as to how Left would understand Left; Germany remained firmly in and with NATO, and, when he had to explain why Marks were spent in defence of the staggering dollar, Schmidt was forthright: they defend us, therefore we support their currency. More generally, Schmidt had a strategic sense that good relations with Moscow would in the end mean that a deal could be done there, wiping out East Germany. So it proved. Helmut Schmidt, who smoked heroically on television, aged ninety, and said of Herbert von Karajan that his life had been all discipline ('loathsome'), was one of the later twentieth century's none-too-many interesting political figures.

Schmidt took over in 1974, and Germany managed the oil shock quite successfully. Motoring on Sundays was banned; traffic in cities was subjected to controls. To this day, the traffic mess of a British town would be unthinkable in a Germany where elementary enlightenment in such matters – a limit to the number of buses, and a prohibition of deliveries by vans and lorries after 8 a.m. is normal – comes as a matter of course; it is also true that, in spending public money to offset the effects of industrial crisis on old industrial cities, the West Germans were again very successful. Essen, heartland of the old Ruhr, suffered from the competition in iron and steel from up-and-coming countries such as Korea. So did Sheffield. Sheffield, like other northern English cities, was then swamped in ugly, badly planned concrete, with hardly any effect upon employment, and none at all upon prosperity. Essen was simply more intelligently managed, because local government, trade unions and employers knew something and could co-operate for the greater good. Perhaps the essential element was the federal system: if one of the big states embarked on a mistaken strategy, it would have to compete with alternatives practised elsewhere. This happened over education. Left-wing local governments offered an equivalent of the comprehensive schools that were pushed through uniformly in Great Britain, and, at that, schools which kept open all day, in such a way that housewives could work. These *Gesamtschulen* were, as in England, not only, on the whole, unsuccessful, but in some cases scandalously so. Parents then migrated to another state that had managed these affairs differently. One result was that the balance of prosperity shifted south, into Bavaria and Baden. Another result, some years later, was that the *Gesamtschulen* improved their ways. Again the question came up, why was England not Germany, rather than the other way about?

However, Europe was not going to be the answer to England's problems. Whatever its prosperity, there was a sense that, somehow, its creativity was going. It could repeat past glories, and the Bayreuth of Wieland Wagner splendidly did so. But where were the great films of yesteryear, where the interesting architecture, and where, increasingly, the young generation? Overlaying it all, there was a cultural malaise, as the Germany of the 'miracle' generation bored its children, and still more its grandchildren; the universities were to suffer over this. Hans-Magnus Enzensberger, the German Orwell, moved over the border to Denmark, and just despised his native land: he notes, for instance, that at some time in the later eighties Chancellor Helmut Kohl's New Year Address, on television, was got wrong: they played the previous year's address, and no-one noticed. Enzensberger was bored, but was bored by the wrong things. He noted, quite rightly, that television was the opiate of the masses, that people would just look at a row of dots on the screen as if it mattered, that there were seventy people writing doctoral theses on one poet. But he was the product of a world that hated its grandparents, and shook its head at its parents. Of course, it was true that families mattered, but did there have to be a law by which a wife could not take a job until she had performed her housewifely duties? That made sense, but only if the tax system supported fathers, and the sheer costs meant that the State taxed, and did so in defiance of its own rules. Problems were coming up in this, and though the coalition government did try to modernize, it did so superficially. The intelligentsia were bored. Bayreuth put on strange interpretations of Wagner, and Horst-Eberhard Richter produced a 'Physicians for Peace' movement, recording that 'we men must learn to overcome the militant image of masculinity'. Heavy, charmless, sentimental German Protestants hawked their consciences round the world, and chicken-muscled women in shorts were to be seen in the vicinity of the old *Teutonia-Haus* in the old Istanbul street of steps, looking patronizing right and left, and regarded with wonder by the locals: why *were* north European women so unappetizing? And yet Germany was *the* admirable European country, if you judged these things from the viewpoint of an England in which nothing worked. In the early 1980s England was going to produce an extraordinary counter-attack.

There was more. Helmut Schmidt had a sense of strategy, that Germany could be a model for East and West alike, and the country could take a lead in Europe. Here, he encountered France. The decline of the dollar maybe made some opening for an alternative world currency, the euro. However, there were severe difficulties. True, there was a successful economic community, but the economies were quite different, and England especially, where property had a preponderant part, and there were worldwide interests, did not fit.

French and German budgets were very different: in France deficits were second nature, whereas in Germany the Bundesbank had its rules and could operate independently, to encourage saving. The Common Agricultural Policy took up almost all of the European budget (a uniform fraction of the value added tax, itself varying from place to place) and if the franc went down against the Mark then there were problems as regards adjustment of the sums to be paid to farmers in the way of subsidies. In the end, a European common currency could just mean Germans paying Frenchmen to do nothing, and the British were as usual in the middle as regards the dollar. Even Helmut Schmidt shook his head at the complications.

The Germans went doggedly on, trying to find some formula for sensible foreign exchange. This really boiled down to some scheme by which the German taxpayer would pay for it, and in 1979 the French graciously agreed: a European Monetary System was founded, authorizing governments to draw unlimited credit to defend their currencies. Schmidt called this 'part of a broader strategy for political self-determination in Europe', and then had a battle with the Bundesbank, which would have in effect to create inflation in Germany in order to pay for irresponsible finance in France and Italy. The decreed rates, originally variable only by small percentages, had in the event to be widened, and there were also controls on capital movements – all of this a breach of the free-trade rules. In the early 1980s France even had a preposterous rerun of the Popular Front, and controls on 'capital' meant, for a time, that travellers could not take cash abroad. The bourgeoisie then re-enacted the suitcase-to-Switzerland part of the French historical scenario. Early in 1983 this farce was stopped, and two Frenchmen of guile, Jacques Delors, and his Treasury secretary, Michel Camdessus, were able to point to the high unemployment, the high inflation and the general bankruptcy of state concerns as evidence that 'Europe', rather than the go-it-alone Popular Front line, was the answer.

By the turn of 1978–9 the conviction grew that international co-ordination was not possible, given the weakness of the dollar. Trade would suffer, and inflation would rise. That summer, 1978, the dollar fell, interest rates rose, and Carter imposed wage–price stops. He organized swaps of credit, and issued US bonds denominated in yen and DM. This was designed to help the 'real' economy – thought to be in good condition – to ignore the financial fluctuations, held to be 'unreal'. Poor Carter was unlucky. The world was about to be hit by a second oil shock. Late in 1978 Iran boiled over. Here had been a sort of showcase of modernization. The rulers of Iran had looked to the example of Atatürk's Turkey in the past, a country where the alleged or real backwardness of Islam had been overcome. Rulers of Iran had a history of misunderstanding Turkey. Atatürk had not really persecuted Islam at all; he had tried to limit the excesses of religion where its ambitions to control the State, and education, were concerned. The Turkish state had also been honest, whatever its mistakes. The Shah of Persia broke both of these rules. Besides, Turkey had no raw materials to speak of, and money was scarce: austerity reigned. In Iran money in enormous quantities poured out of the ground, in the form of oil, and the Shah became for a decade or so the figure of which his title, 'King of Kings', spoke. The great of this world paid him court. His self-understanding caused him to look down on assorted Arabs as wild tribesmen; and Persians by tradition also regarded Turks with much resentment, because (as to a degree with the Hindu nationalists on the subject of the also Turkic Moguls) they were alleged to have thwarted the otherwise obvious course of the great and Aryan Persian civilization towards the patterns of the West. In fact (a fact very frequently denied) a good third of his subjects were Azeri Turks. The Shah did not regard them with much favour. He had launched a gaudy programme of modernization, expecting (a mistake much made elsewhere) that Islam would vanish once Moslems understood that the world offered rewards for those who abandoned the rules of a very strict religion. Why bother with chastity and virginity tests in an age of contraception? Money was spent – most grotesquely, on a ceremony at the ancient city of Persepolis, where the King of Kings sat on a golden throne and dispensed patronage to an assortment of academic specialists and emissaries of the world. Money was also stolen. Teheran acquired huge traffic jams and vast concrete buildings. Western parasites arrived, middlemen of middlemen. An inflation got under way, which left the bazaar people, with their habits of thrift, of saving even empty jars and used boxes, impoverished, while the speculators were enriched. Part of the educated middle-class youth turned Communist, and the Savak, the secret police, did not treat them gently. They took up an alliance with the Islamic opposition, and they, too, suffered from a patronizing arrogance, leading them to see these people as just infantry fodder for a revolution that would soon turn Communist – an illusion that the then Soviet advisers also shared and promoted. Strikes and demonstrations began. The final push came from Carter. Persuaded that the Shah's regime was too oppressive, that America's mistake in the past had been to alienate the Castros and Allendes through CIA action, he encouraged the Shah to hold back. In the same way, his official representative at a human rights gathering had solemnly stood up and apologized for his country's handling of Allende and Chile. And so the Shah was overthrown. But his successors were not Communist at all. Over the turn of 1978–9, after various governments had passed in and out, the Ayatollah Khomeini took over, a grim, elderly figure whose prescription was theocracy, the Rule of Saints. The Saints manifested themselves in mobs of students, in gruesome executions, in parades of black-garbed women vociferously demanding that Westernization, in particular the ways of 'satanic' America, should be put down. This left the Communists nowhere: they – who after all did represent women's rights and much else that Islam did not wish to see – received as much persecution as the rest, if not more. The Western oil companies, where they did not at once leave, were expelled, subject to persecution or worse. Accordingly, oil prices went up all of a sudden: they doubled. Another version of the troubles of 1973?

To start with, paradoxically, the dollar rose in value because in times of trouble the world, including Iranian Islamists, used it as money of last resort. Dollars also flowed back to the USA, again for reasons of safety. Gold rose from $200 per ounce to $875 in 1979 as the Middle East produced crises – the Iran hostages affair, and then the Soviet invasion of Afghanistan. Carter himself had somewhat turned, appointing William Miller of the Fed to the Treasury and Paul Volcker of the New York Fed to run the American equivalent of a central bank. There was to be a meeting of the IMF at Belgrade late that summer. Volcker received lectures from Helmut Schmidt and once returned to the USA that October he announced that the defeat of inflation would be the Fed's main target. Interest rates would rise as much as necessary, and there would be direct control of bank reserves. American opinion had been the most important factor, but it also mattered that the Germans were rebelling. After all, at the Bonn summit in 1978 there had been a great deal of resentment of the Americans' ways, and even threats as regards trade; there were large imbalances as states reacted differently to the second oil shock, and the Europeans' Exchange Rate Mechanism had been called into existence to provide for some stability in a world dominated by the fecklessly managed dollar.

This was an absurd way to manage world trade and international money. It also encouraged mathematical-minded parasitism on an enormous scale. At a scrape with a felt-tip pen in Japan, or by a fax, or the touch of a computer button, elsewhere, huge sums of money could move from one currency to another, in search of a profit based on some even tiny movement of interest rates or bond yields. By 1992, $880bn went through the machines every day – one third of the value of the whole of the world's annual trade. In 1987 that process was already well under way, when it amounted to a tenth of world trade. This was in effect a huge and grotesque comment on the 'Triffin Dilemma', and that man had identified the central problem of Bretton Woods almost before the ink was dry on it. The Americans themselves suffered 30 per cent inflation in the 1960s, and yet unemployment reached 6 per cent in 1971 and New York City went bankrupt in 1974. Latin American countries borrowed joyously in paper, built upon paper, and ran into great trouble, as their rich just moved the money out, into property in Miami, where a crime wave emerged. Here were contradictions of capitalism in neon lighting, and most media commentators on the Continent scoffed. Could not Europe produce a currency that meant something? The Mark (the Swiss franc played a similar role) might then represent real, sensibly managed money. One way was the setting-up of a European currency, a standard in a fluctuating world. They tried. It was not easy, because Carter was rather stupid. Schmidt had to repeat things to him, more than once, for him to understand, and the two men ended up regarding each other with wonder, the one in a cloud of cigarette smoke, and an experience of the Eastern Front of the Second World War, the other with very little experience of anything at all except his mother.

Meanwhile, the oil money was floating around, waiting to land wherever it could find even a tiny percentage of profit, and it moved into Latin America and central Europe, especially Poland, the rulers of which were projecting themselves as a new Japan. When Citibank left Okęcie airport at Warsaw, after signing the deal, the plane was delayed on departure because a drunken baggage-handler crashed his vehicle into it. That debt built up, and up, and even Professor Congdon worried enough about it, in 1986, to write an alarmist book. It was not necessary: the debt was simply not paid, or, rather, the American taxpayer paid it. The West, in the summer of 1979, was in poor condition, and Europe was not producing the answers. Creativity would have to come from the Atlantic again, and it did. Margaret Thatcher emerged in May, and Ronald Reagan was elected President in 1980.

21

Atlantic Recovery: 'Reagan and Thatcher'

Ronald Reagan and Margaret Thatcher each brought to bear some of the core beliefs of their civilization, which included (among others) Hollywood and a belief in facts. Ronald Reagan had been an actor, a Rooseveltian Democrat, and he had escaped from a past in a way that commanded respect – his father a drunken failure, his mother a shrew. He had pushed his way forward, via a degree in simple-minded verities at an obscure college, through sports-commentating, to Hollywood. There, he had been repelled at the tactics of the Left, in the actors' milieu. Actors' politics are generally repellent: in the Middle Ages they were refused a proper burial, and in the French Revolution they had been well to the fore in revolutionary activities. The Revolution did not have a sense of humour, but they had been given the job of enforcing the price-maximum in grain. Peasants, to avoid selling the grain, had fed it to their animals, which at least they could consume, and a trick was to detect the grain husks in the animals' excrement, a task for which actors were especially selected by the reigning revolutionaries.

In the later forties in Hollywood, the McCarthy scare fell darkly upon the land, and there were victims, none of whom lost his life, though some, in employment, were for a time under an eclipse. It was certainly true that, as Vladimir Bukovsky says, if you looked at the twentieth century through Hollywood, you would have no idea what it was about. Its wallet, as was said about the Third Republic, was on the Right, but its heart was on the Left, and it felt guilty if in, say, *The Killing Fields* or *Dr Zhivago* Communists were mentioned in a bad light, or even at all. In that period Reagan seems to have guessed that these actors were being manipulated, and he became spokesman for the Republican cause: he was even divorced for 'extreme mental cruelty', his then wife tending to go along with the martyr-histrions. He had many gifts, especially as a talker. Provincial American politicians tended to be lecturing and charmless. Jeane Kirkpatrick, for instance, talked as if she had a carriage-shift bell in her larynx and qualified for the French phrase, 'She listens to herself talking.' Reagan was not like that: he told funny stories, and even, against his opponents, acted them out. There was a revealing scene when Berkeley students protested against his proposals to make them pay money for their education: past screeching demonstrators, Reagan adopted a creeping pose, and said, 'Shsh,' That disarmed even the screeching protestors, and worked very well on television, which, of course, Reagan had had in mind. As Governor of California, he had known how to goad his enemies into making allies for him. When the time came, in the crisis-ridden atmosphere of Carter's America, he quite easily defeated any north-eastern and moderate Republican candidate, and was adopted. In his way, Reagan was a Nixon with charm, for he did not lock himself away, like Nixon, and there was an element of steel as well, in the sense that he knew that the United States represented something. He had charisma, such that people around him delivered, without quite knowing why. He was also quite indolent, and would semi-doze through Cabinet meetings, eating endless jujubes, a habit he had taken up in order to stop the cigarettes that everyone had smoked in earlier decades. Not for him the Carter regimen of rising at six and ploughing through endless paper, before jogging scrawnily in shorts, holding his wife's claw-like hand, around the grounds. Nancy Reagan was no doubt a facelift too far, but she had seen him through crises, and knew how to deal with the Californian tuxedos whose activities had not made good publicity for Nixon. The White House machine, by now very large, worked messily, and there was a constant changeover. There were complaints. Apparently more efficient machines, both his predecessor's and his successor's, consisted of clockwork but worked to little effect. Ronald Reagan managed to get the big things right, sometimes despite crushing bombardments from people who ostensibly knew them much better than he did. In 1987, for instance, the most respected financial expert on Wall Street, Felix Rohatyn, wrote a vast article in the *New York Review of Books* to explain that the debt and the deficit would wreck the country. Reagan sailed on regardless, and was proved to be quite right. East-coast America was nonplussed, and was vengeful enough to have Reagan missed off the guest list for the Harvard Tercentennial celebration in 1993, whereas a parade of mediocrities such as Ford and Carter was welcomed. In fact, Carter was so full of sour grapes that he did not even give Reagan more than an hour or so of pre-paratory talk when the changeover occurred, and was appalled that Reagan did not take notes. Reagan had his revenge. Carter had asked him to send a telegram to the South Korean president, asking for an opposition leader's life to be spared. Reagan sent it, but added that he so wished that he, too, could deal with university mayhem by con-scripting students. Americans were good at everything, except losing. They were about to win an enormous victory, and the most interest-ing question about 1981 is why it did not foresee 1989.

The same question occurs about Great Britain. Margaret Thatcher in 1979 had a very difficult hand to play, and though she was a very different figure from Reagan, she ran into similar opposition: famously, almost all of the grand names in British economics denounced her to *The Times* in 1981, just as England was becoming, once again, an interesting country. But it was not just the economists. No Prime Minister can have met such sheer hatred since David Lloyd George, whom the Right had loathed because he had fought, in his way, for the class-eroding England that had ended up under trade union rule in the 1970s. Writers, actors, philosophers: off they rode, and a meet-ing of the PEN club in Lisbon, where various well-known writers of the world were expecting to protest about the fate, generally under Communism, of their peers, had to listen, in utter bewilderment, as the English contingent went on, and on, and on about Margaret Thatcher, whom most continental Europeans vaguely respected, as a woman fighting her corner in a man's world. A high point of such criticism occurred when Dame Mary Warnock, a *porphyrogenita* of the long-bottomed-knicker progressive Edwardian world, mother of five, philosopher called to any committee requiring pronouncements as to public morality, headmistress of a famous school but also wife of the Oxford Vice-Chancellor, was interviewed about Mrs Thatcher. She did not have much to contribute as to privatization or the money supply, and the high point came with a strangled 'that *voice* . . . those *hats*.' In such circles Mrs Thatcher was regarded as utterly without culture, but there again was a mistake. She had grown up in a provincial world where application to schoolwork was very important, where you read the national classics. There was a revealing occasion in 1989 when François Mitterrand staged the Bicentenary of the French Revolution. He had made quite an effort, and had a shiny Paris on show. Mrs Thatcher arrived by the new Channel Tunnel and gave an interview to *Le Monde* as to what she thought of 1789; and her remarks were in favour of the English way of doing things, what with individual rights rather than Rights of Man. Her reward was to be placed in an obscure place in the official photographs. She had her revenge. The official party was taken to a performance of a revolution opera, *André Chenier*. It was a hot night, and the opera lasted for four hours. The party was then taken to the new Impressionist museum, a brilliantly converted railway station at the Quai d'Orsay. Protocol had forgotten an essential: that after four hours' exposure to second-rate opera, the guests might need to visit the lavatory. Upon arrival at the museum, they found only one, down a flight of steps, which Margaret Thatcher naturally had the right to use first. She took her time, emerging from the steps to find a small platoon of African heads of state, in their tribal finery, squirming. She was then taken, alone, round the museum by its director, Françoise Cachin (granddaughter, as it happens, of a Comintern stalwart), who later said that, of all the politicians she had taken round, Margaret Thatcher was the one who showed the greatest interest and asked the best questions.

Oxford, also famously, rejected her candidacy for an honorary degree in 1985. That was unworthy behaviour because she was, after all, an Oxford graduate, and had become the first woman Prime Minister, a considerable achievement in itself (and when she finally fell, in 1991, she was given an extraordinarily respectful and indeed moving send-off by the high druidess of feminism, Germaine Greer, at a time when her friends were all shouting for glee). Once upon a time, these honorary degrees had meant something: in giving them to Tchaikovsky and Verlaine in the days when Oscar Wilde had been given two years' hard labour for homosexuality (Verlaine had served two years in Mons, in Belgium, but for shooting Rimbaud in the thumb, having missed) Oxford had shown decency. Then the things became an excuse for a party, as humble academics could for a moment shine in the spotlight turned on someone else, and picturesquely garbed worthies, having been told in a solemn address that the truth was in the middle, could process through the Cornmarket, past Burger King, W. H. Smith's, three clothing chain-stores proclaiming sales and the overweight Liverpudlian seller of the *Big Issue*.

Besides, she was engaged upon a course of action for universities which, however misguided in tactics, was sensible enough in strategy. Inflation was the worst enemy of educational institutions, wrecking scholarship funds, libraries, laboratories. It meant leaking roofs, moonlighting academics and generally the end of serious universities. If Oxford existed at all, it was to give out scholarships to young men and women who could not otherwise have been there – Margaret Thatcher's case. These scholarships had become small change, the university sent round its ablative absolutes in used envelopes, and then launched an appeal for funds that put the needs of the Bodleian Library – the only major university library in the world where you could not go round the stacks – sixteenth equal with crèches for laboratory assistants. Mrs Thatcher did at least have a programme to deal with this. Both she and Ronald Reagan had in the first instance to deal with this financial operation which, underneath, was a political contest. It amounted to a June Days, of a sort, and England – though not America – did produce, in one Arthur Scargill, a barricade artist whom a great many people would have liked to shoot down, *Misérables*-fashion, with respect. The crucial date was 6 October 1979, when an American measure was decisive in much the same way as 15 August 1971 had been. The Federal Reserve put up interest rates to almost 20 per cent, at which level credit would become very expensive, and businesses would crash. At the same time, exchange control was abolished in London. Pounds went abroad, especially to the United States, and business also crashed in Great Britain. This, after a very difficult period, worked. No two decades could have been more different. England came back onto the world stage, and Margaret Thatcher became a figure of worldwide significance. But she had a very hard fight in the first two years, much harder than did Ronald Reagan.

Margaret Thatcher came in on 3 May with a larger swing than any other politician since Clement Attlee, and the right size of majority – forty-three, enough to survive, not enough to encourage greedy zealots. There was one gambit that was essential for her. The Anglo-American crisis brought wise heads together. In Heath's time, the American connection had been weakened, Heath showing his usual ineptness when it came to intuition of reality. But there was an Atlantic strand in the Tory party, and it had powerful consequences, especially through NATO and the international financial institutions. As soon as Margaret Thatcher was elected, she made it her business to travel to the USA. There, she established herself rapidly. She also guessed at the importance of Ronald Reagan – at the time, thought to be of such little account that, except for Margaret Thatcher, even as late as 1977 he was given only polite, cursory treatment when he came to London. But there was a very bright and energetic group of younger people in Republican circles who were thinking hard about what had gone wrong, and what had to be done. Margaret Thatcher became quite widely known in the USA, and in 1979 Carter gave her forty-five minutes in the White House, more than he had given Mitterrand. He complained that she had done all the talking; but she had something to say, and England, not in good condition, provided the perfect rather crumbling sounding-board. What had been commonsense saloon bar grumbling was well-orchestrated and now became a swelling chorus, with some challenging thinking behind it.

There was also quite a good team, professionally managed. A sensible strategy for the trade union problem was worked out by an astute and affable businessman with a military background, John Hoskyns. The press spokesman was Bernard Ingham: a Yorkshireman, at times a stage Yorkshireman, and a one-time left-wing journalist (on the *Guardian*), he managed public relations very well. An astute television producer, Gordon Reece, knew about modulated voices and suitable hairstyles. Ronald Millar, a playwright who could manage one-liners, and John O'Sullivan, a *Telegraph* journalist who could structure a speech, made a Thatcher public performance memorable. She herself knew about oratory, and she got better and better on television, as she knew how to answer back (a warhorse of the BBC, Robin Day, helped). When asked how it felt to be the first woman Prime Minister she said, 'I don't know, I've never experienced the alternative.' In fact, she probably did not give the matter much thought, though she was very good indeed at the feminine-as-leader, since she knew when to be Circe and when to be the nanny from hell. In the end these were reasons for her downfall. She was notably bored by the company of women not on her own rare level, and they, at night, resentfully chewed husbands' ears; on the other hand, men such as old William Whitelaw, loyal, a believer in the party, old-fashioned and bluff, did not much like it when she caused them to burst into tears about being late, or told the Foreign Secretary, also a loyalist, that he was being so boring that someone needed to open the window and let in some cold air so that the Cabinet could wake up. Resentments were stoked up. However, so also were loyalty and affection: there were no stab-in-the-back memoirs. Number 10, Downing Street, was well-managed, and when she left office, the staff were in tears, because, whatever the pressures upon her, she had always been personally very kind to them, remembering to give words of comfort if any had had troubles. At any rate, as her political secretary, Ferdinand Mount, said, 'Far outweighing minor weaknesses, she radiated a sense of possibility.' It made a change. There had not been a Prime Minister of this ability since David Lloyd George. She was to sink in the end into the subconscious of the world, in that taxi-drivers from Valparaíso to Vladivostok or Istanbul would have favourable things to say, perhaps the last British figure ever to have this effect (Princess Diana being the shadow). What she had to do took a very great deal of courage.

Inflation had two sides, an internal one to do with government behaviour, and an external one, to do with the amount of money going from one country to another. The first involved endless argument about 'cuts' – governments just spending less, or not providing credit, or preventing banks from providing credit: there were variations on that theme, familiar in the old days as 'open-market operations'. That was one aspect of monetarism, and in the early eighties the internal manufacturing of inflation did matter a very great deal in an England that had simply been irresponsibly governed: the government deficit of 1970, nil, had reached £10bn in 1975, and it was probably no great wonder that, as questionable banks and property speculators and toilers in the local government bran-tubs flourished, the trade unions also could see no reason why their members should be excluded. There had been much talk of the 'Swedish model', in which the trade unions co-operated in wage policies that suited national needs, and the temptation to follow that model was considerable. The French Left, taking over under the Communist-supported Mitterrand, tried yet another of its 'singing tomorrows', and found that the original Swedish example was crashing. Here, with a small population in a vast country containing raw materials – especially newspaper- and even medicine-making timber – that the world prized, was a chance for socialism in one country if ever there was one. This was all the more so as the country had avoided wars; there is even an argument that had Sweden not traded with Germany, the world wars would have ended two years before they did.

However, the 'Swedish model' had observers gasping: rich, well-organized, some world-class products and also a very elaborate welfare system. There was very high taxation – even, in one notorious case of a writer who was hit for capital gains and income tax on a bestseller, 108 per cent (one of the system's architects, Pierre Vinde, later deputy secretary-general of the OECD, operated it with humour: this writer asked him on a plane journey to Colombia, did he not appreciate the damage that such tax rates did. He said, yes, of course, but he enjoyed the screams of pain from the smug bourgeoisie). There was no poverty, on the other hand, and egalitarianism had gone so far that use of the polite, unfamiliar form of the word 'you', a feature of all continental languages, was abolished. There was an underside: 70,000 Lapps were sterilized, on the grounds that they were not worthy of reproduction, a practice continued into the 1970s. But the 'Swedish model' was not what the outside world thought it to be. The Lutheran Church (which organized the first strikes) had pushed for a corporate solution to labour problems: employers, State, unions. This had been very successful in the 1930s. But it then encountered problems: women entered the labour market, got divorced, and argued for an elaborate system of social welfare, which indeed developed, with very high taxes to match. The system coasted on for a while, and the great Swedish concerns exported as before, but it was on notice. The currency ran down, inflation mounted, and the country, most prosperous of places in the sixties, drifted down to seventeenth on the list by 1980; some trade unions deserted the system. The great architect of Swedish social democracy, Olof Palme, lost an election, and his party lost another one, more convincingly, a decade later. Palme himself was murdered, probably by a Kurd. As Andrew Brown writes, 'You might say that he devoted his career ... to ensuring that no Swede would ever need to experience the American combination of material poverty and boundless optimism, and that he succeeded so completely that ... he left a country where no-one was poor and no-one had room for optimism.' Finland was a more interesting place, her leaders considerably less keen on preaching morality to the rest of the world, as Swedes tended to do. At any rate, the 'Swedish model' was no longer of interest.

Versions of the internal inflationary problem had happened before, and there was even a sort of *Ur*-version of a cure. France had attempted this, with 'austerity' programmes that did not quite succeed until de Gaulle came in. Italy had carried it out in the later 1940s, in the teeth of a Communist Party. But the origin in modern times went back to Germany, after the First World War, when, at the end of 1923, a cross-party government just set up a new currency altogether, wiping out the national debt, rewarding people who had property, and expropriating the savings or earnings of people still dealing in the old currency. The programme meant a year or two of extreme discomfort, as the government cut back its spending, and although the established trade unions accepted it, it also meant unemployment for the hundreds of thousands, and latterly millions, who not only were not protected by them, but were actively excluded, because they offered cheap competition. In 1948 the Germans had pushed through a similar reform, but had had to do so under Allied occupation, and at a time when trade union power was greatly weakened by the millions of refugees willing to work for very low wages. Such reforms indeed amounted to a brutal business, but the rewards for the pain were clear enough, a year or so down the line. At bottom, that was what the monetarists in London and Washington were doing, and in 1981 there were indeed fears that civil peace might break down altogether.

Where the monetarists faced difficulties, which were never really resolved, was in the external aspect of inflation. In conditions of free trade and money movement, inflation could be imported. The German Bundesbank, with the lessons of 1923 and 1948 well within living memory, was naturally concerned to keep inflation down, and was independent, in so far as any central bank can be independent. On occasion it had arguments with governments, and on the whole it won them. However, whatever the Bundesbank did, it could not stop foreigners buying Marks, and increasing the domestic money supply; Germany, too, suffered inflation in the 1970s, though at a considerably lower rate than did England. Now, the British had acquired, of all oddities, a petro-currency. Oil had been found in the North Sea, and the rise in oil prices meant that it was worth exploiting, expensive and difficult as this clearly was. Foreign money therefore poured into the pound, and to London came Arabs, acquiring property. How did all of this affect the British money supply, and what should be done about it? The answer had to be in international co-operation among the first-rank countries, the G6 or, with Canada, G7. And since that in turn depended on monetary policy in each of these, they had to march in step. In the end, the contest of internal and external monetarism was won by the external side's managers, when the price of the dollar was brought down very hard at the Plaza Agreement of 1985. There is a case to be made that that was the end of the Reagan–Thatcher experiment: thereafter it was back to business as usual. But in 1979 a determined effort was indeed made.

International co-operation was essential. The reform would have to come from Washington, and from Washington it duly came, though with some prodding from the German central banker Otmar Emminger. Paul Volcker, an austere and in private life heroic figure, was now presiding over the management of American public finance, and he was converted to monetarism, in effect by Emminger. On 6 October Volcker woke him up, at a meeting of the IMF in Belgrade, to say that American interest rates would be put up as far as necessary to stop the dollar slide. Carter, by now, was simply furniture, and the unheard of dollar interest rate, of almost 20 per cent, was introduced. That pushed the dollar up to over 3.3 Marks in the years 1980–85. This had very great international complications, some of them near disastrous: Latin America, debt-ridden, with interest to be paid out of native paper but in dollar terms, was in tremendous difficulty. The world's exports even fell by 11.2 per cent in the years 1980–83, and overall there was no growth at all in the world economy. Such was the dark international context for Margaret Thatcher's accession in May 1979. Reagan's United States could somehow absorb interest rates at this level, because of a unique feature of the civilization: Americans moved, and expected to, from parts of the country that did not work to parts of the country that did. Besides, the bankruptcy laws were far easier than in England, and bankruptcy was almost par for the course. Foreign money moved to the USA in any case.

The British also got foreign investment, given North Sea oil, and of course the income from it helped as regards budgets. But the problems were more difficult to solve: the pound was absurdly overvalued, at $2 in 1979 and $2.50 in 1980, very helpful for buying American assets, very bad for exports. This was a very unfortunate context in which to proceed, and it took Margaret Thatcher time to find her way. She had had to keep men from the Heathite past, very ill at ease when it came to forceful confrontation. Alfred Sherman remarked of one of them, John Gummer, that in an age of plastic kidneys and iron lungs someone might have thought up an artificial backbone. Peter (Lord) Carrington was the very archetype of dogmatic appeaser, a dangerous man, very astute, his wife an excellent listener, likely to bring out the best in any interlocutor. He was made Foreign Secretary, and was from all points of view a good choice, in that his short-term talents were extremely effective, and he did not much care about the medium term in any event. He had been party chairman, a job he detested, as he did not much care for the Tory grass roots. His own career had been about appeasement, at the highest level. In 1945 he had been on the sidelines when the anti-Communist Yugoslav and Soviet troops had been tricked into death or the camps at the hands of Tito or Stalin: why bother with niceties when geopolitics were at stake? There had been similar espousal of bureaucratic roughshod-riding when he was Minister of Agriculture in the fifties, having to defend an indefensible takeover of private land (the Crichel Down scandal) by a public body for wartime purposes that had long lost validity. Similar realism applied when it came to trade union protection rackets at home. With decolonization, the British had had quite enough, and a certain pattern set in – identify the least unappetizing would-be successor, arrange some commercial deals, ignore the subsequent massacres. Carrington, who was a land-owner, had interests in Africa (as director of Rio Tinto-Zinc). Quite early on, he turned his talents on Rhodesia, where the least unappetiz-ing man of power was thought to be the Marxist Robert Mugabe. In 1980 'Zimbabwe' became independent, the USSR was held off, and the settler would-be independent aristocracy had a guarantee of exist-ence for a longer time than was usual.

There were problems, too, with the civil service. John Hoskyns was unimpressed by the government machine: here were men with substantial pensions, inflation-proofed, who had no particular brief against public spending, and whose ways meant committees and paper. Mrs Thatcher was no respecter of them and interfered sometimes in detail with the budgets, much to the civil servants' resentment. She did not like the ridiculous figure (83 per cent at a none-too-exalted level) of direct taxation: 'no group is more important' (than the pro-fessional middle class) 'and yet none has been more put through the mangle ... between the rollers of progressively penal taxation and discriminatory incomes policy.' She saw the very existence of these civil servants, and the width of their powers, as the problem, or part of it. So she was rude to them. She even visited them in their offices to find out who was who: she remarked, 'I make up my mind about people in the first ten seconds, and I very rarely change it.' There was a welcoming dinner at No. 10, Downing Street for the Permanent Secretaries: 'one of the most dismal occasions of my entire time in government,' said Mrs Thatcher. Later, it was a different story: the civil servants defeated the outsiders such as Hoskyns, who, by 1982, walked away. She complained that there were just too many state servants – 24 per cent of the workforce in 1961 and 30 per cent in

1979 – which was no doubt true, but despite the hysteria of her opponents, she had not come to power with a military coup, could not exile the bureaucracy, and in any case soon found that getting rid of one part of government meant installing another part. In the end this was to be a fatal problem. 'Cutting back the State' was very difficult, at any level from local administration to 'Europe', which bored and bewildered her, and with which her relations were difficult. Her relations with Chancellor Kohl never recovered from a first meeting, at which she and the interpreter, Alexander Lieven, a Russian émigré prince who had run part of the BBC World Service, told each other funny stories until Kohl, not pleased, finally understood that his wisdoms were not being interpreted.

Margaret Thatcher also had a ball and chain: she had to honour promises made by the outgoing government, including a 25 per cent wage increase for public employees, arranged by some commission that had tried to work out how many secretaries a deputy manager was worth, and the like ('relativities'), etc. Edward Heath glowered from the back benches, and there was much snobbish sneering. Problems mounted. There were terrible monsters of Heath–Wilson industrial gigantism: British Leyland and British Steel together pushed the budget up by £3.3bn. Average earnings rose by 20 per cent in 1980, but there was a slump in industrial output (of 12.8 per cent in 1979–81) and by the winter of 1980–81 unemployment (including school leavers) reached 2 million. By the early 1980s the West Midlands, industrially and not so long ago not much behind the southeast, was stricken – those square miles of devastation that Ferdinand Mount travelled through; and yet in May 1980 inflation stood at 22 per cent. There were some immediate reforms – for instance, an end to the absurd arrangements by which workers on strike could claim 'benefit' rather than take strike pay from their union. The abolition of exchange control on 23 October 1979 was of great importance for the future, because British investment abroad made the City of London again a financial centre of the first importance. However, the monetarists were finding their way, and the initial budget of 1980 was a mixture – Alan Walters said, as it turned out rightly, that the money supply had been too tightly held. There was too hard a squeeze

417

on credit. The new Chancellor could not fail to borrow, to pay for welfare costs, which shot up, but at the same time, with support from his junior ministers (John Biffen and Nigel Lawson), he could see that real austerity would be needed as regards the money supply. It was in the name of 'monetarism' that the programme went ahead: a step-by-step policy was announced, to bring down M3. A very confusing pattern followed, with expenditure cuts being announced, but in the first three years the monetary targets were not met; it was only in 1983–4 that monetary growth at last came closer to the aims of 1980.

At first, cunning and caution were on display when it came to the problems that had destroyed the Heath government and then Labour. John Hoskyns, in 1980, said that Mrs Thatcher had been 'too gentle' over public service pay and the trade unions. But there was a legitimate enough fear of a battle, especially with the miners. Their leader was a case of life imitating art. A famous British film, *I'm All Right, Jack*, with a star of genius, Peter Sellers, had made mock of British industrial relations – smooth crooks in charge of industry, vainglorious would-be Stalins in charge of the trade unions. Arthur Scargill was Peter Sellers, down to the body language: strutting walk, bald-patch-covering hair arrangement, humourlessness. But he was single-minded, and from an early age had absorbed a sort of Red epic, as a small boy no doubt striking in the mirror attitudes drawn from one of those lifeless Soviet paintings of the October Revolution: single-handedly he would bring down capitalism. The question on his side was how to keep his troops together. The miners were not unpatriotic, and had no interest in killing capitalism. They were also divided, in that some (a few) coal mines were quite profitable, while others, in a sane world, would have been closed down long before. The whole business was complicated because there were better, cleaner and cheaper sources of energy – not least, oil and gas, coming on stream from the USSR or for that matter the North Sea. In 1980, with the 'second oil shock', petrol was still expensive, having doubled in price, but how long would that last? A mixture of sophisticated energy policy and obsolete Marxism-Leninism was involved, and Scargill was determined to make life difficult for Margaret Thatcher and the 'capitalists'. He had already helped destroy the Heath government. Marauding bands of striking miners had attacked the power stations, so as to keep them from getting coal. The lights had gone out, as the power stations failed, and Heath had been left blustering angrily into the nation's television sets. The unions had then been invited to take responsibility for running affairs, after Heath had been overthrown. They had not proved to be any good there, either: running the country was not their job. But the lesson learned by Margaret Thatcher and her allies was a valuable one: do not act precipitately. In her first year she used ministers who talked, with every evidence of conviction, of finding common ground with the unions, and her keener supporters were disappointed. Civil servants made trouble in March 1981, refusing to pay pensions. The miners threatened to strike, in response to a plan to close twenty-three obsolete pits, with 13,000 jobs. Here, the Prime Minister gave way: it was not the moment to fight. An initial round with the miners was conceded, with a flexibility that surprised. But inflation, itself driving the miners and other unions, had to stop. She was dismissive as to three-cornered German solutions – suitable for regimented Germans, no doubt, but unworkable anywhere else. As with other matters German, she was right but for the wrong reasons: the institutions of the (untranslatable) *Sozialmarktwirtschaft* really worked because there was reasonably sound money.

British institutions were dealing with a rubber currency, and proper planning was not possible. Besides, as costs rose, employers looked to machinery, new technology, to reduce them. There was such new machinery in printing. Newspapers could just take news from an agency, and dispense with many journalists; the money would come from advertising. Accordingly, the National Union of Journalists, then led by Denis MacShane, took a lead in stopping provincial newspapers; not just stopping, through strike pickets, their delivery, but also trying to stop, through 'secondary picketing', the functioning of the agencies. MacShane even won a court case, and the *Times* itself was closed down for a year. In the same style, private steel companies lost £10,000,000 per week in a fight that had nothing to do with them. Here again was a characteristic affair. Heath had overinvested in steel before the 1973 oil price rise. The Clyde had been given the deepest deep-water jetty in Europe, but Rotterdam obviously had a vastly more important role, and a far better infrastructure because Dutch and German unions had not had to be placated as British ones had had to be. In 1979 the transport and steel unions had fought for six months over access to the Hunterstone Ore Terminal, as it was called, and cargoes were actually diverted to Rotterdam, there to be transferred to smaller cargoes for despatch to the deep-water jetty – a symbol, among many, of what was going wrong. British Steel took £3bn in public money and made a loss in 1979–80 just the same. Alone of the national corporations, British Steel was trying hard to modernize, to shed labour and expenses. Businesslike, it could not offer the 20 per cent the miners were given. The workers struck and 'blacked' private steel producers. In time, European law could be invoked against such practices, and a small start was made in an important process: that unions could be made liable for damages. As things turned out, sense, after three months, prevailed. The steel union leaders were not stupid; they realized that they had an industry which, if successfully modernized, could compete, with high wages. British Steel did continue to modernize its labour practices quite effectively, preparing the way for a privatization that was very successful: a sign that, pre-privatization, there were essential changes to be made.

Whatever the troubles of the first year, there was no doubt as to Margaret Thatcher's determination to avoid 'decline on the instalment plan'. It was true that target plans for the money supply (a 10 per cent increase, at most) were overshot. Unemployment had gone up by almost one million, and manufacturing output was in decline, as exports became dearer through the strong pound. It was an immensely difficult time. She was under attack, open and surreptitious, from men such as Chris Patten and other Heathites, and knew that she herself was irreplaceable: 'If I give up, we will lose. If I give that up, I just think we will lose all that faith in the future ... I hope that doesn't sound too arrogant.' Earlier, there had been breaches in her line – the inflation-upgrading of 'benefits' (£1bn) and an increase in defence estimates even though everyone knew, at the time, that defence could have been more prudently and more productively handled. Even John Hoskyns said that, if a U-turn were intended, it should be done quickly. In the winter, unemployment touched 3 million, and output fell by 6 per cent. But in January 1981, just as Alfred Sherman was losing influence (his own fault: he lectured at length on the private telephone line as to his own merits and deserts), Alan Walters joined the financial team (in 1975, like several others, he had gone to the USA, out of contempt for what was happening in England, where he had a post at the LSE). He and the Chancellor, Geoffrey Howe, had agreed on a measure of the money supply (Mo, crude but reasonably accurate given the inflow of foreign money) and said the deficit must come down, from its £11bn. This meant higher taxes, and of course at least a stop on further spending. Walters called this 'the biggest fiscal squeeze of peacetime' as 'benefits' were not index-linked whereas inflation stood at 21.9 per cent.

That was an outright challenge. At the time, there were 3 million unemployed, three times as many as in 1979, and the real figure, given some manipulation of the figures, was probably considerably higher. Up to 1982, manufacturing output had fallen by 15 per cent, the GDP by 5 per cent. Mrs Thatcher's anchor figure, Whitelaw, did not think there would be an election victory: probably a 'hung' parliament, without any natural majority. Besides, as Hugo Young says of this period, 'another count on which ministers were vulnerable was their detailed failure to achieve what they said they would achieve by the methods they said they would use'. Taxes had not been reduced, except for people earning more than twice the average, and the doubling of VAT had affected the poorest hardest. No-one really knew how to measure money: M3 had grown by 65 per cent from 1980 to 1984, as against the 24–44 per cent expected. No-one, as yet, had noticed that privatization would be this government's real innovation. The only bright spot was the fall in inflation (from 21.9 per cent in May 1980 to 3.7 per cent by May 1983). At the turn of 1980–81 there were ugly scenes, and what even appeared to be race riots. Interest rates, because of the dollar's movements, went up to 16 per cent. The economists were almost all in favour of spending. A new political party, set up by Labour grandees who had also been distressed at the turn of events, was winning in the polls, and at her own later party conference the level of grumbling was such that she had to acknowledge it in her speech, saying, 'the lady is not for turning'. Some of the more obvious critics left the Cabinet (including Sir Christopher Soames, responsible for the civil service, who berated her for twenty minutes: 'he was, in effect, being dismissed by his housemaid'). It was Margaret Thatcher herself who stiffened Howe's faltering resolve: and when she saw Walters before the budget, as she was packing hats in the private flat at 10 Downing Street, she said, 'You know, Alan, they may get rid of me for this. At least I shall have gone, knowing I did the right thing.' In any case, she was sceptical, or even contemptuous, of the welfare system: 'I asked myself how people could live in such circumstances without trying to clear up the mess and improve their surroundings. What was clearly lacking was a sense of pride and personal responsibility – something which the state can easily remove but almost never give back ... television undermined common moral values ... The results were a rise in crime (among young men) and illegitimacy (among young women).' She simply thought, 'Oh, these poor shop-keepers' as she saw the mayhem on television. In her memoirs she rightly says of the 1981 budget, 'I doubt that there has ever been a clearer test of two fundamentally different approaches to economic management.' There was much anger when the budget appeared (Tory enemies heard of it only a few hours before). It was famously denounced by 364 academic economists, including the best-known names, in a letter to *The Times*. It was their profession's suicide note, and economics as a subject moved substantially to the United States, where the 'orthodoxy', as these Keynesian views had now ossified, was seriously under challenge. In England, apart from pockets here and there in academe, interesting economics came from financial journalists, a few of whom taught at business schools (this writer will again not plead innocence: he submitted an article to *The Times*, suggesting that the overall atmosphere was similar to that of the last years of the Weimar Republic, and that deflationary budgets might be fatal. The editor, the brave Charles Douglas-Home, spiked it).

Far from collapsing, as these academic economists warned, the economy began to move up, headed by the Stock Exchange, in spring 1981. As 1982 began, exports recovered, and retail sales rose. Investment returned, and property prices moved up again. At least the government's determination to deal with inflation was not, now, doubted, and that had its own effect, for confidence returned. The very clever Nigel Lawson was now at Energy, with a brief to prepare for trouble with the miners. He had devised the Medium-Term Financial Strategy, which laid out plans for budgets and monetary growth in a credible way, a more sophisticated method of presenting monetarism. It was the start of the 'Golden Eighties', and any economist with a sense of history ought to have known that its verities were being reasserted. There were blocks – 'rigidities', they had once been called – to the proper exploitation of this in an England so strongly marked by the recent past. In America, Donald Regan was saying in public that Margaret Thatcher had failed for not being radical enough, but, as she replied, in England 'socialism' had just made more inroads than in the USA. She had indeed had a very difficult time, but her success made the enemies more devious, and there were even modest gifts in the following budget, as the Medium-Term Financial Strategy – the money supply – was revised, to make life easier. The criticism of this was that the lady was reverting to old practices – not carrying out the serious cuts, the change in the way of life that the original Thatcherites had wanted. They began to drop away, or to lose their sense of fight. But they had had a good moment.

22

Reagan

As happened with Margaret Thatcher, one immediately interesting thing about Ronald Reagan was his enemies. They wrote him off as a lightweight, a product of the Californian television world. The intelligentsia had of course been very strongly on the side of Roosevelt, and had again been very strongly – gushingly so – on the side of Kennedy. Reagan could hardly have been more different. He was sixty-nine when he took the presidential election in 1980, and showed not much evidence of serious education – nothing remotely comparable with Kennedy's grooming at Harvard and the London embassy. He also offered simplistic answers that the professionals regarded with derision and disbelief. 'Virtually brain-dead', said the *New Republic*; 'a seven-minute attention span', said the *New York Times*; 'amiable dunce', said Clark Clifford, grand old man of Cold War affairs. Word went round that he had more horses than books. He also went in for presidential fol-de-rols that struck the great and good as kitsch. His predecessor, the worthy Carter, had sold off Richard Nixon's operetta guard uniforms, but Reagan had near replicas made for his own, and pranced happily around as the band played 'Hail to the Chief'. Besides, Reagan's answers to economic or national problems struck most professional commentators as absurdly simpleminded. His relations with academe went from bad to worse, and Harvard shuffled rather clumsily out of giving him an honorary degree, which was awarded instead, for some reason, to Lord Carrington. But Reagan was much loved outside such circles. The apparent nonentity won by a landslide because he could talk to voters worried about taxes and government inefficiency, and he could do so with humour and style – not for him the upraised-finger repetitive moralizing that came naturally to so many of his allies. Of the federal government, he remarked, 'If it moves, tax it. If it keeps moving, regulate it. And if it stops moving, subsidize it': a neat enough way of expressing the irritation felt by so many businessmen and property owners at government doings in the age of Johnson's Great Society. On the whole, businessmen do not make good politicians, and Ronald Reagan was useful to them.

His period as Governor had not been particularly successful. He had a Democrat legislature, and although relations with it were surprisingly good, he was in no position to put through what would soon be called a 'conservative' programme. Taxes did not go down, and government spending went up; however, Reagan did gain an important bridgehead in what would soon be called the culture wars. In the later sixties, there were endless problems with academe, particularly Berkeley. Not long before, it had stood out as a successful state – as distinct from private – university, and the central European émigrés to California had clustered there. Franz Werfel had made a great deal of money out of a book, turned into a film, about Lourdes (the nuns of which had saved his Mahler manuscripts from the Nazis) and he was very generous in supporting other exiles, such as Schoenberg, who lived in straitened circumstances. Thomas Mann was less generous. A curious link between Reagan's Hollywood period and his time in office occurred with the Communist element. At Hollywood, film music had been composed by central Europeans, such as Erich Korngold or Max Steiner (who composed the music for *Gone With the Wind* – as it turned out, Hitler's favourite film). There was Hanns Eisler, whose brother Gerhart was not just Communist, but chief link with the Chinese Party (and who broke with his sister, Ruth Fischer, when her Communism turned dissident) – the very type of astute Communist who knew how to stage-manage front organizations. At Berkeley, philosophers came, of whom the last, Herbert Marcuse, taught heady stuff as to liberation. Berkeley set itself up as a rival to nearby Stanford, which was privately funded and dominated by a business school. Here, two Americas confronted each other: the one anarchic and on-the-road, the other briefcase-wielding and be-suited before its time. The Berkeley anarchists of course behaved absurdly, and Ronald Reagan could make some political capital out of them ('a haircut like Tarzan, walked like Jane and smelled like Cheetah'). The president of the University of California system, Clark Kerr, refused to discipline students who were wrecking classes and taking over buildings; like many, many others, he shrank from appearing oppressive. On the whole, the natural scientists also wanted to get on with their hard work, and frequently regarded their colleagues in the Humanities as offering only 'recreational subjects' which did not matter very much. They therefore tended to vote 'soft'. Universities everywhere in the USA were set on a path leading towards 'Black Studies' and the rest, and the great outside public shook its head. Reagan helped the regents to get rid of Clark Kerr, and there were confrontations with students, where, again, Reagan's allies were generally helpless – either blundering or expostulating. Reagan found ways of disarming the demonstrators. They were generally fairly shallow and they handed tricks to the quick-witted Reagan: when they said they were the new generation, that in his youth he knew nothing of aircraft, television, etc., he had the good answer that this was true but that his generation had invented them all. Besides, he knew perfectly well that, on television, the rebarbative, shouting demonstrators would only make for sympathetic viewers and votes. He had a presence of mind and a light touch that set him quite apart from the preachy, humourless figures mostly to be found in his own political camp, the money-mad doctors with rimless spectacles from Pasadena, the evangelical versions of Dickens's Reverend Melchidesech Howler of the Ranting Persuasion, and the rest. Whatever his shortcomings as Governor, he had one sure way of uniting his camp: he became somehow the chief figure of a general movement against the sixties. As such, he entered a sort of political subconscious, symbolizing something greater than himself.

After 1974, when he had to retire as Governor, Reagan faced some wilderness years. But events in the later 1970s went his way, as they did Margaret Thatcher's. The *National Review* had been set up by William Buckley in 1955 as a sort of *épater les bourgeois* venture, to spit in the progressive winds of the age. In 1964 Barry Goldwater had forlornly stood as Republican candidate against these winds, and had got nowhere – he had even made the cause ridiculous, as it seemed to be associated with grasping and very provincial people from Arizona, a state quite fraudulently claiming to be rugged and individualistic, which would hardly have existed at all had it not been for the enormous amounts of money poured by the government into making the desert green. Goldwater had taken the Republican nomination by surprise, for it would normally have gone to an East Coast figure, in this case Nelson Rockefeller: but his divorce alienated proper-minded supporters. There was of course more to it. The Republicans were beginning, even then, to establish themselves in the South, because the Democrats had started advancing the cause of black rights, at the expense of state rights, and a great shift of the parties was under way. The Democrats under Johnson became *the* sixties party, and collected votes from, for instance, great numbers of women who now, for the first time, were in employment and, at that, often public employment, of course dependent upon taxes. The Republican vote – or at any rate support, since Democrats in the South did not always change party allegiance – grew in Democrat areas, such as Texas or California. In California, in 1978, there was a remarkable straw in the wind, Proposition 13. There was a property tax, which was sometimes cruelly high – for instance, affecting elderly homeowners who did not have much income. With inflation, as house prices rose, so did the tax assessments, and the money was not even spent locally: it was redistributed, following Federal prescriptions for the equalization of school funds and the like. The state constitution allowed referenda, and there was a great taxpayers' revolt, despite an alignment of almost the entire Californian establishment against the Proposition, which passed by a large majority. It was a sign of things to come. With the inflation of the 1970s, many none-too-well-off people were paying more tax than before, simply because the levels at which higher tax was paid were not shifted upwards to take account of the lower value of money ('bracket creep'). A programme of tax reduction therefore made sense, though of course it was also a direct attack on government employment.

'Conservatives' in the American case needs inverted commas. In England, to which the word properly belonged, the Conservative Party

was indissolubly associated with Church and State; its leaders spoke
with a different accent, ate at different times, and had institutions to
defend that had no equivalent in the United States. If anything, the
Conservative Party was by far the earliest and most successful version
of continental-European Christian Democracy, but since this closely
involved the Catholic Church, there was a huge difference. In economic
matters, the Christian Democrats were not necessarily free-marketeering
at all, and the British Conservatives had operated a Welfare State, with
a great deal of nationalization, without demur until Margaret Thatcher's
ascent in 1975. The American 'conservatives' were unavoidably different: far more inclined towards the free market, hostile to big government, generally keen on decentralization to the level of the American
states, and radically opposed to the welfare system that had developed
since Johnson's 'Great Society'. In the 1980s, they had their hour: they
had the presidency, controlled the Supreme Court and the Senate, and
were close to control of Congress generally. But as events were to show,
the American Right was very divided. Tax-cutting and limited government were one cause; so was monetarism, the campaign to stop inflation; but so too was moral resentment, a feeling that the country was
disintegrating; and there was also an element that disliked the moral-
izers, whereas, on the question of free-marketing or abandonment of
regulation, it agreed with them. Keeping this coalition together was
very difficult and in the 1990s it fell apart.

Reagan somehow kept it together. He had simple answers, in what
was known as 'The Speech'. It was easy enough to show example after
example of government wastefulness and inefficiency, or Communist
wickedness, and in 1980 'the little man' generally felt that he was being
penalized whereas he was working normally to bring up his family
decently. This was also a moment when the Right recovered its intellectual energy: no longer was it the apologizing me-too Republicanism
of the Eisenhower era. In the sixties, there had been powerful books of
the J. K. Galbraith type, on the evils of unregulated capitalism and the
virtues of Keynesianism. Now, there were powerful books on the other
side. Richard Perle and Jeane Kirkpatrick had been firm Democrats,
consulted by Carter. After seeing how he ran his administration, they
went over to Reagan's side, and so did a further cohort of New York

Jews, originally of the Left. In 1980 that side was winning the arguments. Keynesianism as understood in the sixties had produced 'stagflation', and an alarming fall in American productivity (as Joseph
Stiglitz concedes in the preface to his *Roaring Nineties* of 2003). There
was more than room for a return to older economics, for which Milton
Friedman was the chief spokesman. The *Wall Street Journal* under
Robert Bartley displayed panache in this cause. Later on, in 1996, he
produced *The Seven Fat Years*, a sparklingly written account of this
time. In the later seventies, he commissioned economists – and considerable ones – to write in derision of the Carter era. The school became
known as 'supply-side', useful shorthand but no more than that: the
'supply-siders' were arguing perfectly seriously that taxes were too
high, and were having perverse effects; that if they were lowered, the
government would in fact get more money, because taxpayers would
not refuse work or avoid tax in complicated, expensive accounting
devices. They might even use the money for productive investment.
Stiglitz and many others now dismiss these ideas, but in the short term
they proved, as Bartley shows, quite right. Then there was the extraordinary deterioration of the conditions in which big-city Americans
lived: squalid housing, grotesque crime rates. Myron Magnet, a scholar
of English literature who knew his nineteenth century, wrote (in 1993)
The Dream and the Nightmare and it was easy for him to catalogue
the failures of the 'Great Society': as Reagan said, 'We declared war on
poverty, and we lost.' There was also a failure, though a more complicated one, as regards America's racial problem. 'School bussing, more
public housing projects, affirmative action, job-training programs,
drug treatment projects ... multi-cultural curricula, new textbooks,
all-black college dorms, sensitivity courses, minority set-asides, Martin
Luther King Day, and the political correctness movement at colleges'
had only led, all in all, to rather greater apartheid than before. Magnet
went too far in ascribing all of this to the culture of the sixties: it all
followed in a pattern of social engineering that had longer origins.
However, his facts were incontrovertible: something had gone very
badly wrong, and the bleakness could easily be extended as far as
education was concerned. Here again, progressive ideas obviously
failed. Charles Murray (*Losing Ground*) spelled it all out, tellingly and

uncomfortably. In 1965 Daniel Patrick Moynihan had foreseen the problem; and twenty years later, three of five babies born in central Harlem were illegitimate. Welfare payments made this possible, and girls became pregnant while men refused to marry. The wisdom of the ages knew perfectly well what the family was for; there was a more complicated wisdom, developed in medieval Christianity, that considered the harm that charity might do. 'Blessed are the poor' was one line; but clergymen who considered the matter knew how charity could be abused and become counter-productive. At any rate, by 1980 it was clear enough that the 'Great Society' had gone badly off the rails. The same considerations were of course well-known in Britain, but not to nearly the same extent, and, there, the immediate problems confronting Margaret Thatcher were to do with the trade unions. At any rate, by 1979 the pendulum had swung firmly towards the Right, and the interesting books reflected this.

Reagan was of course helped, as ever, because his opponents underrated him. Carter was even quite pleased at the nomination of a washed-up actor with eccentric political views. But it was Reagan who won the exchanges. Carter mocked him, saying the economy was in depression; what he meant was 'recession' but did not know the difference. Reagan was quick off the mark: 'A recession is when your neighbour loses his job. A depression is when you lose yours. And recovery is when Jimmy Carter loses his.' Of course the establishment – what Vladimir Bukovsky calls the new American elite – did not like this but, in the event, the election gave Reagan a comfortable victory. Carter then went off to obscurity, subsequently returning in the 1990s to inform the world that North Korea would agree not to develop nuclear weapons or that Haiti would turn into a proper democracy, announcements very rapidly falsified by events. With this hapless figure, the sixties came to an end.

In January 1981, as he took over, Reagan announced that there should be tax cuts and a reduction in domestic spending; he promised prosperity. However, as with Margaret Thatcher though for different reasons, he ran into problems. There were severe enough limitations on his power but in any case the 'conservatives' were implicitly divided and this showed, after initial reverses. Reagan had pledged to cut public spending, and blamed it for many ills, including inflation; at the same time he had promised to cut taxes. There was a difficult context, because interest rates (at almost 20 per cent) were so high. Private enterprise could no doubt take up slack that came from a reduction of public spending, but not if credit were so expensive: any small business would need it to keep going. Besides, Reagan was not the only wielder of power: there was a Democrat-majority Congress, there were separate states with spending rights, and there was a legal system of fabulous interferingness. Public opinion was a constant concern, and the media thereby seemed to have enormous importance – the maker and breaker of presidencies. Besides, any President would inevitably find himself dealing with foreign affairs – one complication after another, with vociferous lobbies attached. Not an easy set of cards to play.

Divisions emerged rapidly enough. Jack Kemp especially had been arguing that tax cuts would more than pay for themselves. This was a popular enough cause. The average family income in 1970 was under $10,000, and as that figure, on paper, rose, the tax rate went up by 20 per cent, though the average income in 1980 was buying about 20 per cent less than in 1970. In, say, Germany, the high taxes at least bought decent public services. Not, for the most part, in the USA. However, there was a vast constituency for social security, especially Medicare and Medicaid, the costs of which went up and up (while also leaving millions of people without health insurance). There were also endless lobbies for this or that subsidy, especially the farmers: a cow cost $2 per day, before it had even started to chew the cud or be milked. A very tortuous campaign went ahead, through a Democrat-dominated Congress (with a slight and unreliable Republican majority in the Senate). Reagan turned out to be a very astute manager. His style was less than hectic: he refused to do early-morning meetings. The team that he had chosen spoke with different voices: a James Baker, more or less in conventional mould, could, as Chief of Staff, talk lobbyists' language, whereas a David Stockman, managing the budget, addressed fears as to deficits. Reagan could also use television as a professional, and outflank Congress in that way, with an appeal to public opinion. Above all, he did not preach or offend, and his relations with the Democrat Speaker, Thomas 'Tip' O'Neill, were friendly.

In 1981 legislation brought a tax cut of 25 per cent, in slices – 5 per cent at once and 10 per cent for the next two years. The top rate of tax fell from 70 to 50 per cent and by 1985 tax was supposed to be indexed against inflation. By 1988 the top rate had fallen to 28.5 per cent. There were concessions elsewhere, for retirement savings and the like. So far, so good. Reagan was also shown to be right as to the effects: the better-off did not avoid tax, and income from them went up, not down. In 1986 a new tax law brought the marginal rate down from 50 to 28 per cent but cut out some loopholes, and there were only three tax brackets. However, business and other taxes did in effect rise.

David Stockman, at the Office of Management and Budget, was a man of fiscal rectitude, and he could see an immediate problem: a deficit. It stood at $50bn in 1980, and under Reagan, by 1986, reached $200bn. When he left office, the overall debt had increased by $1,500,000,000,000 (1.5 'trillion', though the word is not correct). Stockman was a free-market convert (originally from the radical Left) and set himself to attack 'forty years . . . of promises, entitlements and safety nets', i.e. the welfare state as it had grown up since Roosevelt's time. The problem here was not just the poor, for whom the welfare state had been designed. There were many middle-class 'entitlements' as well, and the health schemes were notoriously prodigal. There were also arrangements to subsidize the buying of houses on mortgage – great federal institutions, quite strictly regulated. Meanwhile, Reagan himself had encouraged the Defense Department to put up its budget, and according to Stockman, its Secretary, Caspar Weinberger (one of Reagan's Californians) in effect dictated government finances. Stockman talked to congressmen with a view to having taxes put up, not down, because of the deficit and 'leaked' news that he had sabotaged the tax cuts, but Reagan did not dismiss him until 1986, when Stockman went on to Wall Street. His memoirs are a long statement of contempt: both for the endless political subsidization ('pork barrel') that went on, sometimes by small-print subterfuge, and for Reagan's own management, which he thought very weak and even reckless. Military spending took priority, and from 1981 to 1987 went up from under $200bn to nearly $300bn. But it was not just defence: Stockman catalogues case after case of special pleading, as each congressman expected a favour or two in return for his vote. His was a curiously unstable career – Harvard theology, the anti-Vietnam Left, free-marketeering, money on Wall Street and, in 2007, an indictment for fraud.

At any rate, he could not convince the powers that be, and became a fifth wheel. The Reagan administration went along with social spending. There were 'cuts' – in 1981 $35bn, as food stamps and student loans were cut back. A redundant employment agency was closed down and fuel prices were freed. These 'cuts' were overall rather trivial, but, as ever in this period, there were dramatic howls. Even Daniel Moynihan talked of 'devastating cuts' and a well-known liberal economist, Robert Reich, said that it was 'the return of Social Darwinism' – the same hysteria as appeared in Britain. But Reagan could not cut back significantly: he went on spending, and could afford to do so because the GNP rose by a third – equivalent to the entire German economy. David Frum (*Dead Right*) is scathing. He notes that Reagan's old Californian associate Edwin Meese, though supposedly overseeing the entire administration from the 'conservative' angle, and subsequently Attorney-General, wasted time, ran an office of legendary confusion, and protected spending programmes from Stockman's axe – orange-growers, for instance, who were very firmly regulated as to how much each could produce. In February 1981 he trumped Stockman by announcing that all the chief programmes (Medicare, etc.) would be safe. In the same way, the despised Department of Education was not closed down, as had been, to wide enthusiasm, promised. Carter had rewarded his teacher allies with it, and the Reagan allies regarded it as pernicious. But on it went, to a budget of over $20bn in 1989: it was a useful field for patronage, particularly its Civil Rights side. William Bennett, an interesting thinker, was put in charge, and went around making speeches that electrified audiences, but his department blithely went on as before, with bussing schemes and federal instructions as to how schools should teach. The budget went up from 1981 to 1989 and the rise accounted for three quarters of the 50 per cent increase in federal education spending. Yet America's educational performance went down, at any rate as far as schools were concerned. Literacy was barely above the level of poor countries, although spending was considerable. Perhaps the worst case occurred with farmers.

They had borrowed to buy land in the 1970s and then faced high interest rates, with declining prices for land and crops. The government offered credit to a maximum of $2.5m per farm, and even forgiveness, and the extra $20bn farmers received in 1986 was three times the federal contribution to families with dependent children. Overall, spending rose from $808bn to $1,114bn. Reagan's own record looked somewhat better, in terms of government share in GDP, only because some big bills – the savings and loan debacle – came in after he had gone. He had said that he would try to undo, not the New Deal, but the Johnson Great Society. However, an essential part of that had been Medicare, which paid most of the health costs of the elderly, over sixty-five, even when they were not at all poor. This had cost $64m when it began in 1966, and reached $32bn in 1980 and over $200bn by 1997. The usual explanation for this was that medical technology and drugs had a higher inflation rate than anything else, although quite why was not easy to see: usually, technology depressed costs. Reagan had begun by denouncing socialized medicine as likely to end up with problems of this sort, but, once in office, he of course could not attack such a large and powerful constituency, and, as happened with variations anywhere else, was reduced to tinkering with cost caps. By 1993 Medicare alone took 11 per cent of all federal revenue, having grown at 12 per cent per annum. Besides, the huge inflow of Medicare money made every other form of health care more expensive, and employers were paying more into the system instead of raising wages and giving people money to spend directly, which might have caused them to question costs. Here was a monster out of control.

The Left captured culture (broadly defined) and education, much as happened in England. Its denunciations of Reagan-and-Thatcher were loud, frequent and generally absurd. 'The eighties' passed into history as a decade of 'greed'. There was an element of truth in this. The outstanding feature was that the better-off got better off, and the *Economist* was able to speculate, plausibly, that there was a return to the hereditary bourgeoisie, of substantial upper-middle-class families keeping their fortunes intact and passing them on to children and grandchildren, which had been a considerable feature of the English past. One aspect of this was certainly the reduction of top tax rates in the USA.

For whatever reason, it did indeed have the effect of increasing government income from the top taxpayers, as the 'supply-siders' had claimed (to ridicule) would happen: 50 per cent. The top 1 per cent had paid 18 per cent of all revenues in 1981 and 28 per cent in 1988.

Still, there were 'Seven Fat Years', and this needs explanation. Median family income rose in 1990 dollars from $33,500 to $38,500. Five million new businesses emerged, and 18 million jobs were created. The stock market doubled in value, and inflation fell to a negligible figure: especially, oil prices declined, such that America returned to a cheap-energy world. It seems fair to say that the critics of the 'supply-siders' simply failed to foresee this, and, when they could not deny it, reckoned that it confirmed their own orthodoxies. Reagan characteristically remarked that a sure sign that it had worked was that it was no longer called 'Reaganomics'. There was extraordinary criticism, still, and particularly of 'the deficit', which critics in other circumstances would have shrugged off. It was substantial, at 6.3 per cent of GDP in 1983, but with economic growth fell to 3 per cent in 1987, where it had been in 1981. Other countries had larger deficits; the American one mattered, because it brought in imports and thus carried other countries out of depression. It was also very easily covered by capital imports, since the world invested in America. The real objections to Reagan were of a different order altogether: they had to do with the displacement of 'hegemony'. The Californian business cronies with whom Reagan filled his Cabinet could not have cared less for the opinions of J. K. Galbraith, despised the seventies, regarded universities as pollution. Reagan himself, criticized for not having economists around, remarked, why should he: his Cabinet consisted of millionaires.

Was it true that 'the middle' was stagnant and 'the poor' were poorer, while there was 'obscene' wealth? Such was a theme of critics in all areas. There was no doubt as to the money made out of money: Wall Street entered legend, as did the London City. In 1980 there were almost no billionaires, and in 1989 there were over fifty. There had been under 5,000 millionaires; then there were 35,000. There had been 500,000 people with assets worth one million; then there were 1.5 million. In England there was a joke that a millionaire was just someone without a second mortgage in Fulham, so far had house prices risen. Then again, the 'middle' was not 'stagnant' at all, given that the percentage of families earning $50,000 (1989) rose from 31 to 36 per cent, thus rated (no doubt misleadingly, but the losing 1984 Democratic presidential candidate, Walter 'Fritz' Mondale, regarded an income of $60,000 as defining 'rich') as 'affluent'. There was also a huge increase in charitable giving – more than $100bn in 1990, an increase of over half in the decade.

Besides, poverty, as ever, defied generalizations. A student was poor, and so was a pensioner, even if living in a large house. People moved jobs, and got divorced, before rebounding. Then again, there was the 'underclass' – a problem that hardly existed in countries such as Sweden, where people who refused to work faced severe punishment, unthinkable in the USA. It was of course true that economic change greatly affected whole classes of people such as blue-collar workers and (some) farmers, but that was not a problem peculiar to the eighties: it had been a strong feature of the seventies, when the expression 'rust belt' came to describe Sheffields or Baltimores or Pittsburghs that had previously been steel towns, now facing competition from much cheaper producers abroad. In the 1980s, on the wreckage of these older industries, new ones shot up, generally referred to as 'service', but in themselves requiring sophisticated machinery. The computer was sometimes held to be as revolutionary as the railway had been for the nineteenth century. But the proper comparison is with the automobile, which had brought about the 1930s recovery in the industrial West. The recession released capital and labour in a great wave, and after the initial troubles the country boomed. But so did important places beyond the USA.

23

Brumaire: Two Coups

But it was not just the internal blockage that gave Reagan his financial troubles. He had also decided on a course of rearmament, known as the 'Second Cold War', and it proved expensive, only really justified by a belief that matters could not be left to drift. The background, as in most matters, lay in Carter's failures. The experience of détente had not been positive, and part of the Reaganites' strategy was a challenge to the USSR. This included defiance over weaponry. It also meant a new spirit in the CIA, rather cowed since Vietnam days: why not challenge the Soviet Union directly? Its civilian economy worked, everyone knew, badly. Why was it now building a very large navy, exploiting any advantage on the edges of the Middle East – Ethiopia, then Afghanistan – and probing mineral-rich southern Africa? The spirit in the United States became antagonistic. European misgivings were swept aside; a 'working breakfast' between Alexander Haig, the Secretary of State, and Helmut Schmidt, early in 1982, was marked by enraged shouting, over Poland. At the time Caspar Weinberger was preparing a document as to how the offensive should be undertaken. The general idea was to identify which technologies really mattered to the USSR, and to invest 'in weapon systems that render the accumulative Soviet equipment obsolescent'. William Clark for the National Security Council said that 'trade and finance should emerge as new priorities in our broader effort to contain and roll back Soviet operations worldwide'. But it was not just trade and finance or even brilliant new weaponry, such as 'smart bombs' and laser-beam anti-missile technology. The Americans had looked hard, since the Vietnam disaster, and considered what had gone wrong; and they now had two concrete cases from which to build up arguments.

The twentieth century was to end with a grotesque joker from the seventies crisis pack. In 1999 a very frail 84-year-old Chilean general, long in retirement, was arrested in London, in the watches of the night, in his hospital bed. The general, Augusto Pinochet, had his drip-feed detached, and he was taken off to prison, there to face charges that related to events that had occurred a quarter-century before, half a world away from London. The legal details were also bizarre. A Spanish judge, who had himself served a dictatorship quite faithfully as chief prosecutor, had issued a warrant for the general's arrest, on human rights charges; it was to Spain, not Chile, that the old man was supposed to be extradited. But, in Spain, even had he been convicted, he could not have been imprisoned: people over seventy-five were let off. The Pinochet case was, in other words, absurd.

But it was very deeply felt, by the general's enemies. The 'Pinochet coup' on 11 September 1973 had acquired worldwide significance, and was viciously remembered by the generation of 1968. The Chilean armed forces had struck, and deposed one of its heroes, Salvador Allende, the Marxist president of Chile. He died when his presidential palace was stormed, and became a martyr. Pinochet was said to have overthrown Chilean democracy and, with sinister American advisers, to have initiated a reign of terror: there were voluble exiles, with tales of 'disappearances', of mass executions in football stadiums, of torture in dank basements or freezing, sub-Antarctic camps. When the people of 1968 came to office in Washington, with President Carter in the later 1970s, they wanted to distance themselves from Pinochet. The Americans had been involved in the coup, which was even said to have originated with the CIA, and Carter accused Nixon of destroying 'elected governments, like in Chile'. In 1977 the US representative at the United Nations Human Rights Commission in Geneva stated his 'profoundest regrets' for the 'despicable ... acts of subversion of the democratic institutions of Chile, taken by certain US officials, agencies and private groups'. It was characteristic of the hatred displayed that the *New York Times* ran sixty-six articles on the Chilean affair and the opposition to it, but only three on Cuba and four on Cambodia.

Allende had died as his presidential palace was stormed in the 1973 military coup – suicide, in all likelihood, though even in 1990 his wife was claiming murder. It was the end of a three-year attempt to turn Chile into a popular, socialist democracy, and much romanticism was attached to Allende by a cohort of foreigners, such as the British Communist Brian Pollitt (who also had experience in Cuba, and whose books, along with the multivolume E. H. Carr history of Soviet Russia, were burned when the military took over) and the Frenchman Régis Debray, one-time supporter of Che Guevara in Bolivia. At this time, in the outcome of 1968, of the Vietnam wars of the intelligentsia, there were romantic films. There was, for instance, Z, in which the veteran Yves Montand played a left-wing Greek politician, done to death by the Colonels who had staged a military coup in Athens in 1967, allegedly with help from the CIA. It was (like the later *Midnight Express*) a very well-made film which, like so many such, distorted reality.

Allende became the absent hero of a film, *Missing*, by the maker of Z, Costa Gavras, and he stood, in a vague way, for 'liberation'. There was a revealing little scene when he was overthrown. A left-wing young girl, in jeans, was told by a policeman that, once order had been restored, she would be wearing a less provocative set of clothes. In the Latin, Catholic world at the time, modesty was still required, clothing was political, and divorce was forbidden. Women had had the vote in chile since 1949, but there were separate polling booths for men and women, even in 1973, and although the country's problems were obviously owed in large measure to demographic pressure, clinics for contraception were not opened. There was an element of cultural war in the Chilean affair, and Allende was recognizably a liberation figure, promising equality, liberty and fraternity, or at any rate socialism. In reality, Chile would be remembered, not for the Allende experiment, but for the 'Pinochet solution' – a period of authoritarian rule, during which economic reforms could be carried out, without political disruption. This happened, and Chile, on the whole, prospered. Democratic ways were restored; Pinochet did indeed organize a free election, and when it went against him, he retired without fuss, only with a proviso that he and others should be given immunity from prosecution. In 1975, after General Franco died in Spain, forty years after launching

a brutal civil war and then a full-scale Fascist dictatorship, his successors agreed that the slate would be wiped clean: no prosecutions, of
either side. But Pinochet's enemies were in no mood to wipe slates.

There was another military coup, seven years almost to the day
after Pinochet's, on 12 September 1980, in Turkey. Military coups do
not generally turn out at all well, and in Latin America they had been
both frequent and ridiculous – men in preposterous uniforms, with
epaulettes like fruit tarts, seizing power and then appointing their cronies and relatives to state posts, as in Peru. Argentina, once a very
prosperous and advanced country, had been wrecked in a pattern of
demagogues and attitudinizing generals (in 1980 a 'junta' of senior
armed forces commanders). In the case of both Chilean and Turkish
coups, the matter was far from simple, and the similarities are striking. If there is such a thing as a good coup, both succeeded in their
aims: order was indeed restored; new economic rules – monetarism,
of a sort, and worked out under IMF supervision – were brought in;
after a bad patch, prosperity grew; democratic elections then happened. The costs in terms of bloodshed were also limited – in Chile,
far less than with similar coups in Brazil or Argentina, which had not
received attention from film-makers or *The New York Times*. The
Left in both countries was, however, comprehensively defeated, and
remained very bitter for decades afterwards.

Since universities had been at the centre of the trouble in both countries – in Turkey there had even been policemen standing in the corner
of lecture rooms – there was much voluble complaint. A work that was
very frequently read at this time was Karl Marx's *The Eighteenth Brumaire of Louis Napoleon*. It is the great-great-grandfather of *Z*. There
had been revolutions all over Europe in the spring of, 1848, but the
one that got the greatest attention of the world was French: would it
repeat the experiences of 1789, Rights of Man, abolition of kings, aristocrats and, this time round, bankers? There was a Republic; in the
June Days of 1848 part of the city was taken over by enraged, unemployed building workers (the first political photograph taken was of
a barricade, from a rooftop). The middle-class National Guard, with
troops and an assortment of rowdies from what Marx called the
Lumpenproletariat, meaning in effect 'underclass', dealt bloodily with

this, and 15,000 men and women were summarily executed or exiled. To Marx, this was the class war, and so it was for any observer of it; there were some very clever ones, not least Alexis de Tocqueville, who had written about democracy in the United States. He called the June Days a 'servile war', comparing them with the slave rebellion, under Spartacus, that had rocked ancient Rome. The liberals who were really behind the revolution of 1848 were nonplussed. Finally, there was the army: 'the uniform was the peasant's national costume' and the army 'the dregs of the peasant *Lumpenproletariat*'. So: bankers, seedy journalists, a huge bureaucracy, isomorphous magnitudes of peasants, an army of bravos led by opera-mustachioed generals in corsets, and the clergy, but all of it likely in the end to fail. All of this, read in a university in Santiago in 1973 or in Istanbul in 1980, meant a great deal more than the long-ago historical events that were involved. The opposition to these military coups felt strongly that it had had history on its side, that it had been cheated. To this day it is vindictive.

Allende had been a veteran figure of Chilean politics – a Marxist, claiming that he wanted 'a Chilean road to socialism', i.e. without the assorted bloodbaths. He was a Valparaíso doctor and a cultivated man, reading widely, playing the guitar, able to discuss paintings. In Catholic countries, the anti-clerical tradition often did push doctors and engineers to the Left, and Allende therefore had a considerable number of intellectual cousins in Latin Europe: they agreed with his diagnosis of Chile's condition, and a prominent member of the French Left, Régis Debray, who appeared in Chile, might easily point to the comparisons of Allende and Mitterrand, later the French president. In some ways it was a *Kulturkampf* as tended to happen in Catholic countries. They had a view of the world that went quite logically from macro-America via capital and 'comprador class' – minority or foreign middlemen – to micro-paterfamilias and the foreman cracking his whip at downtrodden peasants.

Such people applauded when Allende stated his creed at the United Nations late in 1972, in a speech that the American ambassador called 'one of the most memorable speeches ever heard in the great hall'. It was a classic statement of a view, then widely held, that countries such as Chile were held back by 'international capitalism'. Multinational firms extracted raw materials such as copper, paying low wages, and the copper would soon run out. If there were protests, these firms would bribe local politicians; 'the power of corporations is so great that it transcends all borders'; 'we are victims of a new form of imperialism, one that is more subtle, more cunning, and for that reason more terrifyingly effective'; 'the financial-economic blockade against us . . . is oblique, subterranean, and indirect . . . We are the victims of almost imperceptible actions, generally disguised in phrases and declarations that extol respect for the sovereignty and dignity of our country.' One problem was that the great corporations repatriated the profits from their investments, many times over, such that Chile, and Latin America generally, had contributed $9bn to the rich countries over the preceding decade. Chile, potentially a rich country, therefore lived in poverty, apart from the hangers-on of the multinationals; 'We go from place to place seeking credits and aid, and yet – a true paradox of the capitalist economic system – we are major exporters of capital.' The Chilean answer must therefore be – nationalization of the country's resources: as Lenin had put it, the expropriation of the expropriators, though Allende did not quote him. There was this to be said for him, that copper had declined in price, unlike other raw materials, from £620 per ton in 1969 to £412 in 1972: the vagaries of international capitalism. At the time, many people would have agreed with Allende as to this *dictionnaire des idées reçues* on the reasons for the troubles of the 'Third World'. In fact, the Americans accepted the diagnosis often enough and in an effort to improve their popularity had produced a sort of Marshall Plan for Latin America, called 'Alliance for Progress', in 1961. They spent $20bn but, not being in occupation, found that much of the money went to thieving oligarchies.

But was Chile 'Third World' at all? She was very varied in character, with 9 million people over 3,000 miles of coastline, stretching from the sub-tropical copper-producing north to the near Antarctic south: great estates here, small peasant plots there, with modern cities and Indian tribes, a considerable problem of population growth, and, on the outskirts of the towns, *callampos*, shanty towns (literally, 'mushrooms'). Half of the population lived in the central valley, and large estates accounted for 80 per cent of all land, up to the 1960s; there was a native Araucanian Indian population, though in scale it did not compare with those elsewhere in Latin America (the Chileans having exterminated many). Chile had in some degree faced the same demographic problem as Latin America as a whole, where the population went up from 211 million to 261 million between 1961 and 1968, and by 1984 had reached 408 million. In Chile it grew at almost 2.5 per cent every year, a figure matched today by Uganda, which has the fastest-growing population in the world, and the cities began in places to be choked. The same was true of Turkey in the same period, adding the population of Denmark (4 million) every year to herself. As with Marx's Paris, shanty towns, 'dangerous classes', woeful sewage, epidemics were a constant reminder that revolution was at the gates.

Chile, with her weird geography and often unpleasant climate, had remained much poorer than Argentina: her people migrated there, and it was usual for them to be in such jobs as house-portering. But with a population derived from the Basque country and Galicia, she also had reasonably civilized politics. There was a moment of military takeover at a particularly bad time in the thirties, but even then it was much less nasty than elsewhere, and the military regime did not last long. There was a strong enough parliamentary tradition, but the divisions of the country were reflected in a multiplicity of parties, proportional representation doing nothing to correct this. As in so many other countries, there were unstable coalitions; the centre usually dominated affairs, and was Catholic or Christian Democrat. Marx simply did not understand religion, thought it absurd, and dismissed 'Christian Socialism' as 'the holy water with which the priest assuages the heart-burnings of the aristocracy'. But there was more to it. Many Christian Democrats had no objection whatsoever to land reform, for the benefit of Catholic peasants; they did not like banks. Their spending on welfare was considerable, and associated with an inflation that already reached 30 per cent in the later 1960s. Dating back to the worldwide slump of the early 1930s, the State was widely involved in the economy – half of industry was controlled by it, through an agency called CORFO – and although the right-wing coalition ('National Party') might have tried to dismantle the institutions concerned, and to co-operate with the Americans in the liberalization of trade and investment, the Catholics and of course the Left had different notions. There were elections in 1970, and the left-wing coalition won more votes than either of the others, though not much more than one third. Salvador Allende, its leader, was duly and constitutionally elected president, with the votes of the centre. The essential point about Catholic democracy was made in an Italian context by Indro Montanelli, veteran journalist: Liberals and Catholics said different things in the same language, Marxists and Catholics the same thing in a different language.

Allende then set about reforms and was given further support when he took office. In the first place, the Americans behaved unintelligently. Washington took alarm: another Cuba? Kissinger said at a briefing, 'I have yet to meet somebody who firmly believes that if Allende wins, there is likely to be another free election in Chile ... massive problems for us, and for the democratic forces and pro-US forces in ... the whole Western Hemisphere.' Richard Helms of the CIA wanted to stop Allende, using the small armed Right, and there was an alarmist lunch with the head of Pepsi-Cola and the editor of a right-wing newspaper. Two excitable Chilean generals were roped in, and a constitutional-minded commander was murdered. This, naturally, backfired, creating a great anti-American constituency, and thereafter the Americans behaved more circumspectly. It was then Allende's turn to make mistake after mistake, and his position was not very strong. He had almost no parliamentary majority, three of the parties in his 'Popular Union' coalition were small and likely to defect, and there was also a Constitutional Court able to block legislation where necessary. Then there was the army.

For a Marxist, here was an interesting challenge, both Czechoslovakia and Italy offering obvious points of similarity: a large Communist element (though Allende did not call himself 'Communist') in a position of some dominance. Why did Czechoslovakia get 1948, and Chile 1973? There was also Cuba, standing up to the USA and promising revolution throughout Latin America. As things turned out, Allende was a weak man, leaning this way and that way, but he started off quite well. In the first instance, Allende could advance a programme that would bring in allies from the Catholic centre, especially land reform and anti-Americanism. His coalition had two fifths of the parliamentary votes, and he took over 1.5 million hectares while nationalizing the copper industry, which accounted for four fifths of exports. He offered in the first instance money for various worthy causes – free housing, health, etc. – such that in municipal elections, in April 1971, he took nearly half of the vote. It also mattered that even then there was 25 per cent abstention – and apathy was in its way a revolutionary characteristic. His minister of the economy, Pedro Vuskovic, announced that 'state control is designed to destroy the economic base of imperialism and the ruling class by putting an end to the private ownership of the means of production', and three of the largest copper mines, American-owned, were taken over, without indemnification. Allende's first year went well, buoyed by spending of reserves and by high copper prices. He himself later on said that his greatest mistake had been not to hold a referendum on constitutional reform at that time. He was soon to run into trouble.

His Communist supporters were, at the time, quite moderate: for Moscow, relations with the USA were very important, and that might easily mean just abandoning Allende; in any case, Lenin himself had had sharp words to say about left-wing 'infantilism'. The Communists had some 15 per cent of the vote but they also controlled the trade unions, and they appealed to Radomiro Tomić's Christian Democratic Left for a common reformist platform. But there was also a romantic Left in Latin America, the MIR, or Movement for the Revolutionary Left, and it was not very interested in such reformism. Quite the contrary, it provoked. It set up the *Che Guevara Población* around 'bourgeois' Santiago, and installed 1,200 families in occupation. The great symbolic figure, Castro, came for a three-week visit at the end of 1971, during which he made inflammatory speeches: 'we have already learned more than enough about . . . bourgeois, capitalist liberties', etc. Allende himself shook his head with disapproval at the antics of the MIR, which denounced his 'reformism' as an 'illusion', and wished to take power at once, by arming the inhabitants of the shanty towns. Land expropriation took, in all, 9 million hectares of land, and in some cases the land had already been occupied by peasants; and this even affected farms with no more than eighty hectares. In 1972 the university boiled over, as thousands of students went off to the countryside for 'consciousness-raising' exercises; by now, thousands of foreigners were flocking in to participate in a socialist revolution, and the secretary-general of Allende's own socialist party, the upper-class Carlos Altamira, announced that the battle with 'the bourgeoisie and imperialism' though postponed was on the cards. Nationalizations went ahead, and the United Nations Economic Council for Latin America contained Marxist economists who gave Allende their sanction. The parliament gybed at this, and some of the nationalization was pushed through by a device close to fraud. A law already in existence allowed firms to be sequestrated if they were badly managed, and it was easy enough for Allende to push up wages, drive a firm into bankruptcy, and then sequestrate it; strikes might have the same effect. The State had run forty-three enterprises in 1970 but, by 1973, had 370 on its books, as administrative chicanery was used to demonstrate that they had been incompetently run in private hands. At any rate, Allende was bypassing Congress, by executive action, and this naturally threatened American investments, which, in copper and with the multinational ITT, were considerable. Nixon, late in 1970, had resolved to give no credit to Chile, while also using the US influence to prevent others from giving it.

If Chile had been Cuba, no doubt matters would then have come to a breach. But Castro had come to power in the outcome of a revolution that had destroyed the old army; there was no parliament or constitution of any significance. Allende did not have Castro's tools. Without dollar support, by September 1971 inflation was going up. It always was a problem in the state-dominated Chilean economy, with a balance of payments deficit, and with swollen employment rolls and pay-packets; Allende imposed price controls. These had the usual effect, of driving down supply, and, besides, the consequence of the land seizures was also to cause shortages, which in turn could be made up only through imports, of $280m (including French chickens). These led to the creation shortages and queues, and there was a sign of things to come when 5,000 middle-class housewives, banging saucepans, were met by teargas.

Matters worsened up to the summer of 1972, as, even on official figures, the cost of living rose 163 per cent. The government tried to control prices (through a Cuban in the Directorate of Industry) but hardly knew what it was doing: the lorry drivers, on whom Chile, a very 'long' country, depended, went on strike, and the queues lengthened. 'Planning' had been reinforced, and what it entailed was the taking on of more and more labour for concerns that were unsuccessful: 'floods of red ink on the books of nationalized firms,' said the American ambassador (himself not at all anxious for any kind of American intervention: he did not do his career any good). Investment fell off, as people bought black-market dollars or went abroad. One outcome of the land reform was predictable: harvests dropped by one quarter in 1973. Trade union elections were 'rigged', so that ordinary workers' behaviour could be dictated, despite their own wishes, from the radical Left, and such 'rigging' became easy enough because so many workers were standing in queues or otherwise making ends meet: apathy, the abstention of the voters, generally does occur on a great scale in the course of a 'revolutionary situation'. Even in the great October of 1917, in elections for the trade unions, most people did not bother to vote, because they were tired, bored and bewildered. The Bolsheviks got their majority at last.

At the turn of 1972–3 there was a long-standing row over the free press, much of which was of course bitterly critical. A great newspaper concern was squeezed by the government, with taxes and extra rules, and it was threatened with bankruptcy and expropriation – an obvious way of preventing opposition media from operating at all. In the University of Chile there was a long battle between the Christian Democrat Rector and a Marxist governing board. The Left seized the television station for eight months, and was able to defy court orders; there was a clique of journalists at the government's bidding, and the print or delivery unions were used to muzzle the right-wing *Mercurio*. There were restrictions on travel, though many of the better-off and mobile had already left, foreseeing the worst. In the summer of 1972 Allende was making no effort to control the MIR in the universities, perhaps hoping to provoke the Right into a premature uprising. On top of everything else, and despite promises made to the Christian Democrats, a law for 'Unified National Education', which would affect the private schools, was to be pushed through at the turn of 1972–3. But Allende had gone too far.

He now faced challenges. His actions were undertaken by executive authority, and he was regularly condemned in the parliament; the majority against him was just short of the two thirds needed to overturn his presidential veto, and the constitutional court became involved (though it shrank, as yet, from conflict). The Christian Democrats joined up with the Right, to face elections in March 1973, and, with claims of electoral corruption and fraud, took over half of the vote. As small shopkeepers went on strike, the government attempted to take over the also striking lorry drivers, and met its match: nails welded together as tyre-bursting devices, lorries hidden in forests, or banded together in such great numbers as to require regular siege. Perhaps, if the Chilean Left had been adequately led, it would have staged its revolution: after all, no Communist worth his salt would have bothered about hostile parliamentary majorities. Armed peasant squatters and shanty towns would have been 'Red Guards', there would have been a terroristic secret police, Communists would have penetrated the army and elections would have been 'rigged' with ballot boxes 'stuffed' with fake votes – the story of any Communist takeover in peacetime. These things did indeed happen, but on a small scale, and the Left seems to have succumbed to infantilism – supposing that it was destroying the economic base of imperialism, whereas the reality was just play-acting. True, Jacques Chonchol, the agriculture minister, romantically pursued his land reforms, and a Communist ideologue, Volodia Teitelboim, stirred up the shanty towns; the interior minister, Carlos Prats, went with Allende to Moscow in November 1972, and workers themselves struck against the lorry drivers' strikes, but none of this amounted to a serious attempt to take power in the Communist manner: indeed, when a mass demonstration was staged against 'Fascism', Prats shrieked from his podium, 'If you are against Fascism, jump!' A hundred thousand people then jumped. The Soviet ambassador, standing next to his American colleague, remarked that there were more effective ways of fighting Fascism. But if Allende could not seize power, he could at least create chaos, and that was Chile's condition. He had printed money – more than a 100 per cent increase in 1970, 171 per cent in 1971, with a deficit of 40 per cent in 1972 and a 163 per cent increase in the cost of living. There was a small sign that the armed forces would intervene when a brief mutiny occurred, squashed by other elements in the military. Allende then mobilized some Red Guards, and alienated the military in general.

But he was now being widely condemned. The government itself was beyond the law; the coup, though long drawn-out and ineffectual, was Allende's, not the army's. General Pinochet was acting quite constitutionally. In June 1973 an all-services committee of fifteen drew up contingency plans for a takeover, although they were not put into effect until 9 September. Some study was made of the little Soviets that the Left had established in the shanty towns; there were photographs of people to be arrested, and since the army could search for weapons, the soldiers had an opportunity for arrests. Allende himself would not opt for a revolutionary way forward – he did not 'arm the workers' – but he would also not act against the extreme Left, although even the Communists were uncomfortable with it. In the summer of 1973 matters went downhill – a 40 per cent devaluation, an attack by the government on Catholic schools, a collapse of export earnings, strikes by buses and even by doctors, and another strike by truck drivers, threatened by nationalization; there was a constant parliamentary crisis. Congress, the constitutional court and the controller-general (who oversaw the legality of administration) all condemned the government, which argued that, if all cabinet members signed a document opposing a decision of the court, then that must stand; whereupon the opposition introduced proceedings to impeach ministers, whose signatures would then not be valid. In the end, there were rumours of a mutiny in the navy at Valparaíso, instigated by the revolutionary-minded Altamira. In another attempt to placate the military, Allende agreed to the removal of his own general, Prats, and his place was taken by Augusto Pinochet. That day – 22 August – the Chamber of Deputies passed a resolution declaring that Allende was outside the law and the constitution.

This had happened before in Chile, when a president, disavowed in 1891, had killed himself. Allende contributed a note of black farce, arguing that in the cold and rainy winter, there would be flour only for three days, and by the end of August the generals were in more or less constant session, confronting a situation of anarchy. The lorry drivers' strike was into its second month. On 2 September airline pilots, dentists, chemists and the merchant marine struck. Women demonstrated again, banging saucepans, and were met by counter-demonstrating women and young men hurling rocks; on 6 September Allende made an extraordinary speech, indicating penury to come. By 9 September all of the senior figures in the armed forces had agreed on the plans for a takeover. The American ambassador was given an indication, and it is probable that the CIA were involved, though the Americans were in general quite prudent, having been caught out in the hopeless effort, three years earlier, to stop Allende.

The coup itself came in the early hours of 11 September. It was easy enough: troops took over television, blocked the roads, imposed a curfew. Allende, in the presidential palace, had his guards, but there was not much that they could do against aircraft firing rockets into the building. In the event, the building on fire, he seems to have shot himself with a rifle that had been an elaborate present (his remains were examined in 1990 and suicide was confirmed). In all, perhaps 5,000 people were killed, and thousands went into exile. They were generally articulate, and mobile – Chonchol, who had been the supposed mastermind of agricultural reform, taught in a French university. The conscience of post-Vietnam America was touched, and even in the twenty-first century, the name 'Pinochet' resounds; his family is harassed by courts. But the Chile which he took over was in a condition of collapse, and Allende had been condemned by any and every constitutional institution. Pinochet's real crime was to show that the Left had had its day: the Moneda in Santiago was the Winter Palace of the Left.

The 'Pinochet solution' – its example was to grow and grow – became a spectre, haunting the Communist world. This turned out to be in the sense of a ghost-face literally true. The Communist leader Luis Corvalán was exchanged for a Soviet dissident, Vladimir Bukovsky, at an airport in Switzerland (oddly enough the American ambassador there, demoted for behaving correctly, had been ambassador in Chile at the time of the coup). Corvalán proposed to fight underground, and, to do so, had plastic surgery in Moscow, after which, with a false passport, he went back. His underground activities were unfruitful; in 1987 Pinochet, by then leader of a tolerably prosperous and ordered country, agreed to hold proper elections, which Corvalán wanted to contest. He had to be smuggled back out to Moscow for a reverse face change, to qualify for his old passport. The Eighteenth Brumaire did indeed repeat itself as farce, though black.

It had an equivalent in Turkey, also in the context of a near civil war and of inflation, though in this case that of the second, doubling, oil price shock rather than the first, quadrupling, one. On 24 January 1980 the *Guardian*'s Turkish correspondent, David Barchard, arrived at the railway station in Ankara, from Istanbul. It was on that very day that the prime minister announced economic reforms along Pinochet-solution lines, courtesy of the International Monetary Fund. Ankara was an inviting theatre for these. His taxi could not go far up the hill to Çankaya, the modern part of town, where the diplomats and professional classes lived. The street lights had gone out, and he had to struggle with his luggage through the snow, all the way to the hotel. On most such nights, at the time, it was usual to hear gunfire. Turkey was experiencing an acute version of the general crisis of the later 1970s, and there was a grim surrealism to it all. This or that part of town was controlled by one or other of the warring political groupings, and in the preceding year roughly twenty people were being killed every day in the country at large. The Middle East Technical University had been set up, with American money, as a tribute to Turkey's loyal membership of NATO, in the 1950s. It had excellent facilities, and a setting quite rare in the centre of the Anatolian plateau, because it was well-watered and wooded. The battling inside it was such that the American ambassador's car was set on fire (curiously enough, he – Robert Komer – had been in charge of the 'Phoenix' programme in Vietnam) and policemen controlled the lecture halls, taking names. University authorities, brought up in the liberal tradition, wrung their hands in helpless lamentation; one, in Istanbul, was assassinated, with his daughter, in his car. In the capital, electricity stopped functioning except for six hours every day, and the town was dominated by a foul-smelling smog – product, mainly, of the cheap and low-quality coal, from mines on the Black Sea, which was all the fuel most people could afford. Little girls walked to ballet school with face masks. There were queues for elementary items – lavatory paper, olive oil and the like; you could be arrested for having a packet of foreign cigarettes, an offence against the tobacco monopoly. One scene in particular symbolized what had happened. Well-trained economists, statisticians, met in the ministry building to devise the next five-year plan, complete with complicated calculations about foreign trade, much of it bartering. The entire session proceeded by candlelight, and the bureaucrats wore their overcoats. Inflation, represented by grubby and crumpled notes that had passed fast through market hands, was at Chilean proportions, and the situation was comparable: another Brumaire. The generals took power on 12 September, seven years almost to the day after Pinochet. Here, too, something of an economic miracle followed; here, too, free elections were soon allowed; here, too, a good part of the educated population never forgave.

There were of course obvious differences between Chile and Turkey: the one colonized, the other a colonizer, with a fivefold difference in population (though there are interesting points in common between Turkey and Spain). But the chief matter in common was America, and if Washington wanted to simplify things, then there were many points for comparison. Chile, until Allende, had been part of an American system. So was Turkey, and September 1980 shows remarkable similarities with the September 1973 that brought Pinochet to power. We can assume that the Turkish generals had examined the story of Pinochet. The choreography was similar. They are not likely to have read *Eighteenth Brumaire*; one of their complaints at the National Security Council was that Marx was given an import licence, at the expense of other, more pressing uses for paper.

It was the end of a dream. For two generations, Turkey had counted as a model of successful Westernization, and crowning acts in that had been democracy, participation in the Korean War and membership of NATO – much of it a straightforward outcome of Stalin's bullying. The country had emerged from the wreckage of the Ottoman Empire at the end of the First World War, and a leader of genius, Kemal Atatürk, had established her independence. He went on with Westernization.

In 1923, when Turkey was at last independent, she had a very poor infrastructure (railways, at that time, for Anatolia, the equivalent of a Moon landing) and under Atatürk there was an extension of elementary hygiene, given that the very capital, Ankara, was subject to malaria and the French embassy was the station buffet. Progress happened; 700 German professors, headed by Einstein (he did not stay for long, because he was expected to teach and did not want to), arrived when Hitler came to power; Istanbul saw for a time the best German university in the world; Turkish opera singers such as Leyla Gencer had their place in the repertoire; the 'Fisherman of Halicarnassus' became a vastly translated author; Galatasaray Lycée or Robert College in Istanbul, Ankara College in the capital – where Denis Hills taught, as a refugee from post-war England – produced graduates who could teach Western civilization to the multitudes. Ankara University, where Ernst Reuter, later the mayor of Berlin, taught Town Planning, had a School of Political Science (Mülkiye) that had its *esprit de corps* and laid down Westernizing models. It produced a good part of the foreign ministry, and the foreign ministry, after 1950, was anxious to co-operate with the Americans. They, for their part, recognized an ally, and encouraged it towards democracy and elections.

These did not prove to be a simple matter. Turkey had been built on waves of refugees, from the Caucasus, the Balkans and the Crimea, and they had brought with them the 'nation-building' techniques that they had had to learn in a very cruel way from the 'Christian' states that had taken over. You got rid of minorities; 7 million people had had to flee to Anatolia, and they made up half of the urban population of republican Turkey, with villages of their own dotted up and down the land. There was hardly a family that did not remember tales of disaster, and even the government quarter of old Istanbul had been swamped by these refugees in 1912. From the Balkans, the Turks had learned how a new nation was to be established. This was a business involving considerable artificiality – for Romania, even the name of the state was false, since the original 'Romania' had been the Latin kingdom of the Crusaders in Thrace; Bulgaria was cobbled together by American missionaries; in Greece the need to classicize run-of-the-mill but, for the peasants, unknown concepts was sometimes funny. In

Turkey there was also a new national language, because the peasants needed to be made literate, and could not manage that under the existing Arabic script; words had to be invented (Ernst Reuter, who had been a prisoner of war in Kazakhstan, knew something about Turkic languages; he was put on the language reform commission within months of his arrival from Buchenwald concentration camp, and advised learnedly on the Uzbek word for this and that, designed to displace the Ottoman original). In economic matters, state boards were established to run this or that industry; people were arrested for selling the national currency without authorization; police and army were powerful; in Turkey the capital had even been moved away from sophisticated, historic and cosmopolitan Istanbul, to Ankara, in the bleak centre of the Anatolian plateau. There, you did not hear a mosque, and people of country dress were turned away if they appeared. The Western admirers of Atatürk did not really see this side of things, and he himself had a considerable sense of moderation, knowing when to stop. In his day, the Christian minorities were recognized as necessary, or even vital: they were Turkey's passport to the West. When Hitler started his campaign against the Jews, Turkey's doors were opened to (some of) them. Four and a half centuries before, the Jews of Iberia had been expelled by the crusading king. The Sultan had let them into his empire, and their descendants, many of them converts to Islam, contributed much to thirties Turkey, which was run with a sense of mission. Atatürk, who had saved his people from conquest and massacre, had enormous charisma, and now stands as a symbol of an old-fashioned Progress, of which Turkey's neighbours are not exemplars. He died in 1938, and his successors suffered from excessive caution.

Enlightenments eat their parents. The medical improvements, considerable in their own way – in Ankara, malaria had been a mass killer until the Republic, with its Çubuk reservoir and its devoted doctors – also resulted in a demographic explosion. This was worst in the partly Kurdish east, where polygamy, starting for a boy in his midteens, with a girl even younger who was soon ditched, was standard, though not legal. Then again, as France had discovered post-Napoleon, education creates an unappeasable intelligentsia; a Russian reactionary,

Konstantin Leontiev, sagely said that, in Russia, 'the tavern does less damage than the school'. The best products of the educational system, as with developing countries from the Third Republic or united Italy onwards, went into technical services and were very good indeed, but there were others, hanging discontentedly around the media or the educational institutions, and thinking that they knew it all. This was to be an enormous problem in the Turkish seventies, more or less as happened in Chile; and such men and women tended to look on the peasantry, trooping into the towns, as isomorphic magnitudes like a sack of potatoes. Migrant peasants occupied huge areas on the out-skirts of the main cities, especially Istanbul. By law, they could not be evicted if they managed to put up a house during one night's work. These 'night constructions' (*gecekondu*) formed rings round historic Istanbul and Ankara, a terrible affront to modernizing Turkey. Ankara had been planned by central European architects and their Turkish associates in the 1930s, and they had aimed higher than this.

Migrant rurals even besieged the old part of Ankara, where Atatürk had established the modernizing State. You could leave the official entertainment palace of the foreign ministry, where, once, Atatürk had danced the waltz with Western ambassadresses, and perhaps dis-cussed the principles of Bauhaus architecture with Bruno Taut, lumi-nary of Weimar, Moscow and Tokyo. (Taut, out of gratitude, said that he would design Atatürk's catafalque gratis. He then designed some-thing resembling a huge gilded eggbox. The Turks did not know how to respond. Taut let them off the hook by himself dying, and being buried in it, at Edirne.) Then you would smell kebabs, and have to avoid large, religious-clad women driving their brood along the pave-ment towards a multifarious bazaar. Istanbul's population grew from 2 million to 10 million (and by some accounts, even 15 million). There had been 12 million Turks in 1922. By 1950 there were 20 million, by 1975 35 million and by 1980 45 million. The infrastructure could hardly respond to this. Schools were too few, the electricity network was overburdened, and even the sewage system suffered. It was a var-iant of what western Europe had undergone in the later nineteenth century, but on a much greater scale, and in a much shorter time. In the 1970s order was breaking down.

All enlightened, reforming states encountered a political problem: how far could liberty be sacrificed for the sake of progress? This problem was well-known in Russia or Spain, two countries with which Turkey had a great deal in common. Pushkin had said that 'the State is the only European in Russia', and in such countries the army had a role in public affairs that it did not have in more advanced places. It took in ambitious boys from the provinces, sometimes even the peasantry, gave them discipline and education, and so caused them to rise in society (e.g. the chief of staff in 1960 came from a tobacco-farming family, and a later military saviour, Kenan Evren, was the son of a bank clerk in the Balkans). Military schools taught medicine and engineering, and the Turkish officer corps had had a role in the modernization of the country ever since the early nineteenth century. Under Atatürk – himself, in Salonica, a one-time cadet, refugee from a religious school – this went on: the army was at the centre of the State. On the other hand, there was much pressure for political change, in the direction of greater freedom. In the later 1940s there was a split in the ruling single party, the Republicans, partly because of foreign pressure, and partly because the two wings grew further apart. The Republicans, under İsmet İnönü, represented bullying Westernizing virtue, and İnönü had a statue of himself, bigger than the National Monument itself, designed for Taksim Square, where once had been an Ottoman barracks. But there were rivals, interested in prising open the State and, in some grubby cases, using primitive nationalism to expropriate the property of the minorities, especially the quarter-million Greeks in Istanbul. They were also prepared to open up to the peasantry, especially as regards the legalization of religious practices that the Republicans had regarded as ridiculous. The Republicans were by this stage unpopular, as they were associated with a police state.

In 1950, under American pressure, İnönü allowed free elections, and the free-market, liberalizing element, established as the Democratic Party, won an enormous victory. The old Republicans survived in any number only because local prefects had done deals with Kurdish chieftains in the east, whose tribes voted *en bloc* as instructed. The Democrats were in power for ten years, and started well: American aid flowed in, some of the state restrictions were lifted, a large concrete mosque was put up in the middle of Ankara (with a supermarket underneath) and the Democrats' leader, Adnan Menderes, won respect abroad because of his NATO connections (he said, 'Whatever America does is right by us'). Then came the worst mistake of modern Turkish history. The Greeks of Istanbul occupied much of the best real estate and ran the best shops; they were half of the stock exchange. Some were even deputies of the Democratic Party. On 5–6 September 1955 there was a riot in the European part of Istanbul, and the great avenue running through it, once called Grand' rue de Péra, was filled with broken glass and goods flung out of shop windows, while the police stood by. This was ostensibly done because the Greeks on Cyprus were behaving intolerably against the Turkish minority, but the main factor was simply greed, and stupid greed at that, on the part of Democrat associates. The Greeks (and many Armenians) left Istanbul, except for a tiny remnant, even then – in the Fener district – overshadowed by true-believing Moslems at their truest-believing noisiest, and having to be protected by the army and the police. The Greek district was then taken over by rural migrants, and took two generations to recover. So did the country. Menderes was later executed because of this, though, oddly enough, the Greek Patriarch appeared as a witness on his behalf. The Democrats made whoopee with the budget, lost control of finance, split, had to attempt a fiddling of elections, then tried to govern in authoritarian style. They encouraged religion, whereas Atatürk had determinedly kept it out of public life. Secular Turkey hated all of this, and there was a military coup, on 27 May 1960. A general, Cemal Gürsel, now became head of state, and tried, in close co-operation with Inönü, to produce an updated version of Atatürkism. Professors of law produced a revised constitution, in the extraordinary belief that the decreeing of things on paper would mean their realization in practice. The Americans offered almost immediate recognition and $400m credit; more professors – Dutch – arrived with a Plan.

But the outcome was Menderes's revenge. In the first place, the demographic boom went ahead – by 1980 two thirds of the urban population was under thirty-five, and the villages moved to the towns (and also moved to German towns, in hundreds of thousands). The

Democratic Party had been banned, but it carried on in another form, as the Justice Party (Turkish parties sometimes have names with an almost untranslatable religious reference, to the seven deadly virtues – chastity, sobriety, thrift, etc.). The Americans had a soft spot for it, and its leader, the wily Süleyman Demirel, had worked with them, in a company that built the Bosphorus Bridge and the Middle Eastern Technical University. The Republicans, by contrast, were turning increasingly towards the Left, and old Inönü was eventually forced out by a man who had the makings of a Turkish Allende, Bülent Ecevit: very cultivated, a Sanskrit scholar, a considerable poet and quite hopeless in politics. He had to deal with a very divided party. Part of it was rigidly secularist, regarding Islam as a disease. Another part came from a very heretical element of Islam, the Alevis, who treated women as equals, drank wine in the Christian manner, and regarded the holy month of Ramazan, when nothing was supposed to pass the mouth during daylight hours, as ridiculous. Then there were Kurds, also a rough fifth of the population, whose chiefs tended towards deadly rivalry, and were generally willing to change party allegiance according to favours. Already in the early 1960s an uncomfortable pattern was setting in. Roughly 40 per cent of the vote would go to parties with some form of religious programme; another 40 per cent would go to their opposites, some of them veering towards the Left. Then there would be small parties, set up to champion a leader's ambition. But the large parties themselves only held together if there was a leader with all of the strings in his hands, prepared to behave dictatorially and even corruptly. Coalitions succeeded each other, and the army waited in the wings. A counterpoint of bullying and irresponsibility then went ahead. The trick in politics was to establish personal influence, whether to do favours for your electors at home or for your friends in the capital. There was an element among the educated youth that wandered off into terrorism – much as had happened with 'Land and Liberty' in Tsarist Russia, where students had imagined that the masses could only become seriously revolutionary if the police made their lives hellish, by mistake. They provoked trouble, and brought another military coup in 1971, a pointless one. As happened in Chile, the Turkish Left had a great deal more responsibility for its fate than it ever, generally speaking, admitted to.

In the seventies, Ecevit with his rough 40 per cent matched Demirel, with his rough 40. In the hothouse atmosphere of the other 20 per cent, there were strange growths. Certain parts of Turkey had a strongly Islamic tradition, especially Konya, south-east of Ankara, and the Erzurum region, far to the east. Here, in secular eyes, were brainwashed peasants with a vengeance, but the real point was hatred of the corruption that came from Istanbul and Ankara. The leader was a professor of water engineering, Necmettin Erbakan, who had taught in Germany and had been a colleague of Demirel's; if he got anywhere, it was because his hands were clean. Ecevit took up an alliance with him, both sides anxious to repel the military, in 1973. Demirel could to some extent rely on another small party, the Nationalists, whose real power came partly from inflation. In an inflationary period, small suppliers, not paid on time by large receivers, suffered. A visit from Nationalist bully-boys would cause debts to be repaid faster than if the business had gone through the courts, and in populous, unsavoury areas the Nationalists did tolerably well. The Nationalists also tended to do well in districts close to areas of Kurdish or Alevi migration, such as Gaziosmanpaşa or Sütlüce in Istanbul. It was a dismal period, each party throwing money at voters (Ecevit even paid twelve of Demirel's men cash, to desert their party and join his, as ministers for this or that: one suggestion was 'weather-reporting'), and inflation got under way. The oil shock meant that the economy, almost entirely dependent upon imported energy, ran down; it survived only by contracting debts, which went up from $2bn in 1970 to $20bn in 1980. Between 1975 and 1980 there was also an eightfold rise in prices, as the government's deficits became uncontrollable, covered only by paper.

Matters were made worse because relations with the United States turned sour. This had to do with Greece and Cyprus. That island had become independent in 1960, and the position of the Turkish minority – one fifth of the population – was supposedly guaranteed under the constitution, which reserved certain rights. Great Britain, Turkey and Greece were supposed to guarantee the constitution, with a right to military intervention where required. Quite soon after independence, Greek Cypriot nationalists started to persecute the Turks. This was not wise. Left alone, a third of them would have become Greeks, a third would have emigrated, and a third would have remained as picturesque folklore, cooking kebabs and dancing in a masculine line as evidence of the great tolerance towards minorities displayed by Greek civilization. Instead, there was stupid and nasty persecution, beginning at Christmas 1963 with the killing of a wedding party. A United Nations force arrived to hold a 'Green Line' supposedly separating the two sides. This meant, as such 'peacekeeping' ventures generally did, that excuses were found for the stronger side, which then pushed the Turks into small enclaves, mostly dependent for survival on foreign charity, itself sometimes diverted by Greek Cypriot officials. Potatoes rolled around the floor of the customs shed at Famagusta, because the sacks were slit open. Matters then became pointlessly complicated, in the manner of the Levant. There was a military coup in Greece in 1967, and in 1974 there was a coup within the coup, which led to crypto-Fascists taking power. They tried to overthrow the government of Greek Cyprus, assuming that its leader, Archbishop Makarios, was playing up to the Soviet Union, given that Cyprus stood on the edge of a Middle East which was, just then, boiling. A civil war on Cyprus resulted, a number of Greeks disappearing. The local Turks, held together by a remarkable figure, Rauf Denktaş, could justly fear a return of persecution, expulsion, but Ecevit and Erbakan, with their unlikely coalition, were presented with an opportunity. The Turkish army went in, and, given the paralysis of America, through Watergate, and England, through money, was not resisted. In the outcome, the Turks occupied nearly one third of the island, and resisted international condemnation. The Turks of Cyprus remained poor and isolated, but they survived. Denktaş said, quite rightly, that they had avoided the fate of the Gaza Strip Palestinians. Nevertheless, the simple solution – recognition of Turkish Cyprus's independence – evaded international bureaucrats, and a good part of the Turkish Cypriot population simply ended up in London.

In Turkey, Ecevit became hugely popular. He decided to exploit this, with an immediate election, which would let him dispense with his odd-bedfellow Islamic ally. But parliament would not allow early elections, and fell into paralysis; when they were held, six months

later, Ecevit narrowly lost. Demirel and the smaller parties put forward a 'National Front' government, with a majority of four seats,
early in 1975. In the provinces, and some of the ministries, the smaller
parties, Nationalists and Islamists, used their power disproportionately for changes of personnel; and besides, their strength was such
that an institution designed to train clergymen (*Imam-hatıp*) was
opened for ordinary schoolchildren, segregated between boys and
girls, and subjected to solid religious education, including koranic
Arabic, which Turks simply repeated syllabically, without understanding; prizes went to the *hafiz*, who knew the lot off by heart. They had
been started (in effect) in 1951, and grew from seven to over one hundred in 1975, and 383 by 1988; in 1971 they were functioning at
middle-school level as well, and were teaching 300,000 pupils. Half
of the curriculum was religious, and the secularists grumbled. Under
Demirel's National Front governments (1975–7 and after the June
election, 1977–8) the desecularization of modern Turkey, in a sense,
got under way. In some universities, during Ramazan, the canteens
closed; there was tension between observers and non-observers since
the observers got up early to have something to eat before sun-up, and
woke up the non-observers by their talk about football and so forth,
while non-observers' smoking after lunch similarly irritated observers; there were fights and, on occasion, ambulances. The call to prayer
was now heard, loudly amplified, in the very centre of great cities, and
in Ankara there was a big row when the mayor put up a statue of one
of the secularists' symbols, the stag of the Hittites (Indo-Europeans,
not Arabs), and the religious-minded interior minister stopped construction again and again until the courts ruled otherwise. On one
level, no doubt desperately childish, but on another deeply serious,
and to do with the nature of the country and the upbringing of children, especially daughters. At any rate it divided the country very
deeply. Perhaps Demirel and Ecevit themselves would have preferred
to co-operate, as the great industrialists (Vehbi Koç and Nejat F.
Eczacıbaşı) wanted them to do. But each was prisoner of his supporters, in no mood to compromise. When Ecevit visited an Alevi centre in
Cappadocia (Hacı Bektaş) his cortège was fired on by the orthodox
Sunni in Nevşehir; in the mixed town of Maraş a regular battle

developed between Alevis and Sunnis, and a hundred people were killed. The police lacked training and equipment, as only seventeen of sixty-seven provincial sections even had a camera; and the prisons were in chaos, some of them unable to pay their telephone bills because prisoners abused their rights to long-distance telephone calls (in a country where in any event talking on the telephone is a national curse). In 1979 a Fascist murderer, Mehmet Alı Ağca, was able to slip out from Ankara prison, where he had been tried for the murder of a famous newspaper editor, Abdı İpekçi (from an old *dönme* family, a stout secularist, and descendant of Jews who had converted). Ecevit sought a way through the mess with a combination of nationalism and restated left-wing orthodoxies. He approached the Soviet Union (in vain) for oil; he toured Yugoslavia and irritated the army chiefs by praising its supposedly non-professional and voluntary territorial defence system. In 1978 he made a considerable blunder, of refusing to apply for membership of the European Economic Community at precisely the same moment as Greece did apply. His government fell apart, and Demirel returned, with a minority government.

Demirel could at least bring back the Americans. There had been a revolution in Iran, hitherto America's ally. Turkey was needed again, even more so when the Soviet invasion of Afghanistan happened, and support was offered. However, this would mean new men. Demirel therefore had, as under-secretary for planning, a very clever one, Turgut Özal, who had worked in the World Bank and knew America very well indeed. His title was lowly; in that way, he would not appear to be a political threat to better-known people. However, the under-secretary for planning had the right to countersign anything; Özal became the centre of the regime. On 24 January 1980, as the *Guardian* correspondent struggled up through the snows towards Çankaya, Turgut Özal produced his set of economic measures. But to put them through was very difficult: Demirel's was a minority government, and parliament was by now so paralysed that in 1980 the deputies would not agree on a new president: in farcical repeats, they voted more than one hundred times without result.

The financial position was terrible – a debt of $20bn, with low exports and high inflation. And by now the 'Friedmanite' medicine was proposed, the businessmen's association, TÜSİAD, being in sympathy. Ecevit in effect lost the Americans' confidence that summer (oddly enough he never gained the Russians' – they preferred to deal with Demirel, as they did not want a 'Finlandized' Turkey, which would be too unstable). American backing meant an end to giveaway finances, strict austerity over credit, a wage freeze. Erik Zürcher, a considerable commentator on Turkey, who wishes it were Holland, mutters about the 'Pinochet solution', and that is right. The army was preparing to restore order. In fact its chiefs conducted meetings, in theory to head off civil war, in reality to take power. In December there was a formal meeting at the old Selimiye Barracks in Istanbul, where Florence Nightingale had once nursed. Then, it was decided simply to let the politicians make such a mess that no-one could conceivably object to a coup, which is more or less what then happened. Demirel and Ecevit would not agree on a coalition of 'repair', Ecevit denouncing the Özal proposals of 24 January. He remained incorrigible – even secretly approaching Erbakan for informal alliance, and refusing a deal with Demirel.

The army could obviously have moved in at this moment, and already had the martial-law powers to do so. However, it had blundered over earlier coups that had proved to be pointless: you took power, your general opined on television at 3 a.m. to the national anthem, professors of political science wrote you a constitution and then, after a short while, you got Demirel back again: *burasi Türkiye*, i.e. that was Turkey for you. The army therefore bided its time, heeding the Leninist lesson of 'the worse, the better'. In 1977 already, 230 people had been killed, one fifth of them in Mayday events in Taksim, in Istanbul, when the Left had been shot at. After that, the figures were between 1,200 and 1,500 every year. In Trabzon, on the Black Sea coast, guns were routinely carried, and were frequently used: there was almost a war between town and gown, in the latter case, the Black Sea Technical University. But there were endless cases reported casually every day in the newspapers. A good review of this aspect of things was produced in Ankara (1992) by the National Security Council – *12 September in Turkey and After*. It is the country as the generals then saw it – everything divided, with unions of Left and Right for police and teachers, but the Left itself also dividing, and sometimes murderously. The book takes day-by-day excerpts from newspapers. On 5 January 1978 there were fist-fights in parliament, an Ankara café was machine-gunned, a bomb exploded at Istanbul High School, with fifty-one people killed and 444 wounded that month; a car manufacturer was asking for a price rise of 400,000 Turkish lire (over $8,000 at the rate of late 1979, while on 24 January devaluation brought the dollar to 80 lire, from 47). In September 1979 the Islamic party's leader was ranting against 'the tyranny applied by Zionism ... all Westerners will be eliminated'; a headline runs, 'Gazi Teachers' Training School in Ankara was occupied by 800 right-wing students' – the deputy dean of Political Science at Istanbul university was strafed in his car by four terrorists, including a woman, and there was further shooting even at his funeral. On 2 September 1980 twenty people were killed; on the 3rd twenty-nine, including the three-year-old son of a police sergeant in Bingöl, a largely Kurdish town; on the 4th eighteen; on the 5th a nightwatchman, a village head and his son in Adana, and two more people in cafés in Istanbul and Eskişehir; the Konya prison was raided, and seven people freed; there was a murder in Fatsa on the Black Sea, and, next day, five more in Ordu, along the coast; a raid at Diyarbakır, the chief Kurdish town, got away with 2 billion lire. On 6 September it was the Islamists' turn, when beards, green flags, Arabic, and Islamic dress appeared, with slogans to the effect that 'Iran is the only way', and demands for the introduction of the shariah law. When on 12 September General Kenan Evren took over, face on television to national anthem, tanks in streets, he rightly made the point that two years' terrorism had cost the country almost as many casualties as had the three-week battle of the Sakarya, in 1921, which had saved Turkey from the Greeks.

The terrorism went on almost to the last moment – a cinema queue machine-gunned in Mersin, a bag-bomb killing six in Kurdish Siirt, and after a great demonstration against NATO it was discovered that the slogans on the posters had been booby-trapped: fifty of them had to be cleared. On the last day, the army leaders were careful. General Evren saw the acting president for tea and gave nothing away (for which he later apologized, as he did to the defence minister Ihsan

Sabri Çağlayangil, who had not been told, although that, given his political instincts, may have been by choice). Lights went out gradually in the military buildings. Abroad, people did guess, and Nuri Çolakoğlu, for the BBC in London, certainly knew. However, the senior American general was only told five minutes beforehand, even if the chief American expert, Paul Hentze, seems to have been in the know (he was able to tell Carter, at *Fiddler on the Roof*). Then, in the evening, the directors of television and the post office were invited to headquarters and politely detained. Under escort, they went off to block the telephone connections of the deputies and links with the outside world (incidentally, somewhat more professionally than happened in Poland, where soldiers, in December 1981, smashed the telephone wires with heavy axes). The politicians lived in their own compound, and it was easy enough to proceed there. The general behaved humanely. He knew that Turkish politicians, some of them given to heavy overeating, might have heart attacks if faced by soldiers at 3 a.m. He therefore arranged for their best friends to accompany the arresting parties, and to be first visible when the door opened. The arrests went ahead smoothly enough, and the various men met in the VIP lounge at Esenboğa airport, on their way to internment at Gallipoli. One thing the military *had* learned: not to make martyrs. There was to be no hanging. The politicians were personally banned from entering politics again, and the parties themselves were also banned. But the imprisonment was in easy circumstances, and did not last for more than a few months in most cases. The military had also learned from previous coups, and, perhaps at American behest, from the experience of Chile, although this cannot be demonstrated one way or the other. The deputy chief of staff, Haydar Saltık, planned the operation ('Flag') and in a fifteen-page typescript outlined certain essentials: for instance, the need to suppress the small parties. There was a certain fear that in the *gecekondu* districts the army would not be able to appear, but things went quite smoothly – the army had timed the coup very well, and it was greeted with great relief in nearly all quarters, from Joseph Luns at NATO headquarters (who embraced the Turkish ambassador, Osman Olçay) to ordinary Turks in Anatolian small towns. The only hitch was that the central television aerial could not, for some time, be made to work – the signal to the units to move. The general made his broadcast, on lines by now somewhat traditional, but this time the generals had learned: they did indeed promise a return of democracy, but not at once. Parties were banned. But Turgut Özal went ahead with the IMF programme of 24 January. As was already happening with Pinochet, this was 'the Washington consensus' in action, and it was to work remarkably well.

24

The Eighties

The 1980s have entered history, in much the same way as the twenties or the sixties or for that matter, before them, the *fin-de-siècle* nineties have done. Pinning down such things is not possible: pedantic historians can even claim that such decade moments do not exist. They do. Perhaps this is just a matter of technology: bikes, typewriters, telephones; the motor car; the Pill. The eighties were marked by the computer, or perhaps just money. However it is to be explained, there was a *Wirtschaftswunder* in the Atlantic world; though there was no tangible symbol, as had happened for the German original with the Volkswagen, because much of what happened, happened in cyberspace. The money translated into conspicuous consumption, often of a repulsive sort, at all levels, but all in all the 1980s deserve the name *The Seven Fat Years*, title of a famous book on the subject by Robert Bartley of the *Wall Street Journal*.

The decade began with lamentation, talk of a crisis in capitalism and of a Second (or Third) Cold War, but quite quickly, by 1982–3, things improved. The 'Anglo-Saxons', including Australia, were to see money in a way not experienced except maybe in the USA of the 1920s. In 1990, even taking inflation into account, the American GNP was nearly a third larger than in 1982 – equivalent to the entire German economy. Overall, the standard of living rose by close to a fifth and 18 million new jobs were filled. The output per hour of American labour – productivity – grew by 10 per cent, manufacturing grew by nearly half, and exports almost doubled. So did tax revenues. There was a British counterpart, although the 'mix' was very different, as manufacturing fell by roughly one quarter, and 'services' took its place: southern England boomed. In 1984 Ronald Reagan was re-elected, the first President since Eisenhower to have two full terms, on the basis of a 'morning again' campaign that took advantage of the boom, and the extraordinary confidence that came with it. He had more electoral votes than Roosevelt, and his opponent, Fritz Mondale, who stood on an old-fashioned platform of tax increases for 'the rich', was sunk without trace. Margaret Thatcher was similarly triumphant – three electoral victories in a row, and even, though *in absentia*, four. The performance was extraordinary, comparable to de Gaulle's. It showed the British capacity for tissue regeneration, in defiance of all the self-imposed odds, and, though this may turn out to be the country's last moment as world leader, the Thatcher government produced prototypes that were widely followed. But it was uphill work, to start with, the stage being cluttered with toxic historical furniture, with the last gunboat, and the last gasp of the industrial 'triple alliance' that had produced the strange death of liberal England seventy years before.

In 1982 Margaret Thatcher was under heavy attack from all sides: one of her best allies, Norman Tebbit, had it right when he said that he bore the scars of many wounds, mainly in his back. Then came an extraordinary episode, bringing modern themes together, including that of military dictatorship in Latin America. There was one such, a junta, in Argentina, the modern history of which had been one of squandered opportunities. Far from copying Pinochet, the military in Buenos Aires regarded him as a poor cousin, and cast about for ways to gain cheap popularity. A national cause of sorts existed, in a remaining British colony, the Falkland Islands, a few hundred miles from their coast. Take it over by force; the British would simply be grateful that some forlorn colonial outpost, which cost the taxpayer money, would be taken off the expense list. Relations between Argentinians and British were good; casual conversations showed that no-one in London cared about the Falklands one way or the other. Besides, British defence policy was a mess. In the later 1970s naval pay was so low that sailors had to moonlight. In 1980 there was a moratorium on defence contracts; there was absolute resistance to aircraft carriers and no-one would pay for the Falklands. On the other hand,

Argentinian regimes were generally so awful that the Falklands lob-byists did not have any trouble in convincing the Left of their cause. However, the Argentinians misunderstood. They assumed that they would have American support or at least understanding. After all, the USA had become heavily involved in Central America, where Argentina's support was needed: there was semi-clandestine military co-operation, the Americans supplying training and weaponry. In this atmosphere, taking the Falklands seemed to make sense. The American ambassadress at the United Nations, Jeane Kirkpatrick, was assumed to be influential, and she had written what was thought to be an important article – saying that the USA should tolerate lesser, banana republic authoritarian regimes.

In December 1981 a General Leopoldo Galtieri seized the dominant role in the Buenos Aires military junta, and he appeared as the ultimate in comic, circus-uniformed rulers, an 'El Supremo' out of *Hornblower*. In March 1982 he tested the waters: his troops landed on South Georgia, a remote, frozen place from which the British had conducted surveys of the Antarctic. Then, on 2 April, he invaded the Falklands. In London there was disbelief: a senior Foreign Office man caught the mood when he gasped, they cannot treat a major power in this way. Parliament was specially recalled, and was in boiling mood, a mood that even affected the left-wing Labour leader, Michael Foot. The navy was full of fight, and of course anxious to show that surface ships were still needed. Sir Henry Leach, First Sea Lord, had the qualities to per-suade Margaret Thatcher that a naval force could and should be sent; he called the reductions in naval spending 'the greatest con-trick of the century'. He also much admired Margaret Thatcher's decisiveness and remarked, accurately, that if nothing had been done 'we would have woken up in a different country'. She herself liked military men, whereas she tended to dismiss diplomats; she now took a great gam-ble. She would fight, guessing that she would have American support where needed. This was correct, and state-of-the-art Sidewinder mis-siles forced the Argentinian aircraft to fly low, such that many of their bombs did not explode, because the fuses had been mistimed. A British expeditionary force was put together with speed and efficiency, and embarked for a campaign, 8,000 miles away.

The fact was that British opinion had now divided, with, on the whole, educated people questioning the whole venture and, on the whole, uneducated people cheering on what the popular press called 'our boys'. On the face of things, this was, as a German book's title ran, 'the absurd war' – the last of the Royal Navy, embarking on a voyage of 8,000 miles for a nearly valueless set of islands, the inhabitants of which could, with a fraction of the cost, and greatly to their advantage, be resettled on one of the not dissimilar Scottish Hebrides. However, the Argentinian junta behaved with grotesque obstinacy, refusing American mediation, and waving aside even Latin American efforts. A proposal was made for the British ships to stop a thousand miles from the Falklands, and that was ignored (it was, in any event, unreal). An elderly battleship, the *Belgrano*, was first directed towards the islands, and then away from them; it was sunk on 2 May; 368 sailors drowned. Later, a great fuss was made, to the effect that it had been sunk so that Margaret Thatcher could simply ignore further attempts at mediation. Not many people believed these assertions at the time, and no-one does now. It is clear that the junta were in no mood to offer any concessions, even to common sense. War was war, and developed its own momentum, beyond the helicopter accidents hitherto seen. Two days later *Sheffield* was struck by an Exocet, twenty-one lives being lost. It was an old ship, with too much aluminium, and chaff, to distract the missile, was not used because the ship was broadcasting, and there were other near disasters, but, with both patience and determination, the Prime Minister was showing the generals and admirals, says Hugo Young, 'every quality they least expected in a politician'. She also needed luck: there were large and vulnerable ships at stake, including, with some symbolism, the *Queen Elizabeth II*, which had been constructed in a conscious recall of the great days of Atlantic shipping. But morale was high, and the operation was professionally conducted.

On 25 April the British retook South Georgia, along with a particularly vicious Argentinian officer. The Chileans gave considerable help as well, in radar intelligence and efforts to divert Argentinian strength. The Argentinians' chief weapon, the French-made Exocets, proved to be less deadly and accurate than expected – on three occasions they did not explode, and the Argentinian pilots were operating at the extreme end of their fuel range, so that they could not manoeuvre easily. In any case the French gave covert help to the British. On 21 May came the landings, and the shivering Argentinian conscripts were no match for professional soldiers; after three weeks, on 14 June, they surrendered, as a celebrated British journalist, Max Hastings, spearheaded the advance into Port Stanley by marching into the local pub and ordering a beer. Margaret Thatcher's gamble had succeeded, and as her biographer writes, 'it was an event of stunning political impact all over the world'. Quite accurately, she said, 'we have ceased to be a nation in retreat'. The junta in Buenos Aires fell, its victims liberated in great numbers. After Margaret Thatcher's loss of office, there was a gathering of representatives of peoples in whose liberation she had had a hand – central Europeans, Slavs, for the greater part, who each sang a national song. She was very touched and grateful when a representative also came from Argentina. She herself of course shot up in popularity at all measure: why was 'that woman' getting away with successes that had escaped her supposed betters? In Scotland the Secretary of State thought that it was all like a 'Nuremberg rally' of vulgar triumphant nationalism, and a particularly lugubrious Foreign Secretary remarked that instead of having a cavalry officer, they had 'a corporal'. Visits by Pope John Paul II and Reagan, within weeks, became part of the picture. As she told an interviewer, rightly, 'there was a feeling of colossal pride, of relief that we could still do the things for which we were renowned'. But in some ways it marked the high point of the Thatcher period: a courageous budget was associated with economic recovery, and the Falklands campaign with a great sea-change in international affairs.

The 'high eighties' were under way. At the time, only a few people sensed the breakthrough to come. Arthur Seldon of the IEA did, but academe was almost solidly refractory, and the dead hand of Edward Heath still lay upon much of the Conservative Party itself – so much so that the creative thinkers of the first Thatcherite hour tended to despair, as, returning to Downing Street from a good lunch on strategy, they were confronted by committees and devil-in-detail agendas. The election of 1983 was an easy win: as with the Democrats in the

United States, the main opposition party had talked itself into a corner, had split, and anyway offered nothing more than a rerun of the later 1970s. Considerably less than half of the working classes voted Labour, which became almost a regional party, as a north–south gap opened up. There was only one Conservative seat left in Scotland – aptly, at Bearsden outside Glasgow, the northernmost outpost, once upon a time, of the Roman Empire, which was commemorated by a piece of wall and the first recorded Scottish utterance, to the effect that Rome created devastation and called it peace. That sentiment was expressed, less pithily, by its author's descendants, as the impetus came from southern England, in the accents of which the Prime Minister spoke. And southern England boomed. This should have given prosperity to the north as well, but there were formidable difficulties, especially to do with a system of 'social' housing that stopped labour mobility.

Later on, Mrs Thatcher did admit that she wished she had handled some of the real, longer-term problems earlier. This was right: Britain became a country where local government, education, health and transport were sometimes lamentably behind those of other European countries. However, there was always the excuse, a perfectly fair one, that major enemies had to be disposed of first. 'The conflict between good and evil' was what Mrs Thatcher saw at work in British politics. Nationalized industries, an absence of competition, parasitical trade unions, inflationary finance and taxation which destroyed the most valuable habits and institutions: these had to be defeated. She had already chipped at the unions' privileges – the right to picket had been limited, and in 1982 individuals' rights as against their unions were greatly increased (union funds became liable for damages in the event of unlawful action). Public service strikes had occurred, and perhaps, through calculation, had been allowed to last longer than they needed to do before being settled: inconvenience or worse to the public from transport or civil service unions was a great help to the government. But early in 1984 the challenge came from what had been the most troublesome element of all, the National Union of Miners. There was some play-acting involved in this: attitudes being struck. Arthur Scargill was an extraordinary fellow, who thought that he could overthrow the Thatcher government as other miners' leaders had defeated Heath's. This was to mistake the enemy. The Thatcher government (in this case, Nicholas Ridley and Nigel Lawson) had made sure that there were reserve stocks of coal, for energy and heating. The police were better paid so that their loyalty could be rewarded. A sustained effort was also made to persuade the trade unions of 'a new realism' (the phrase used by their general secretary, Lionel Murray – characteristically in the new England, 'Sir Len'). Some – the electricians, who understood what could be done with computers – were to be easily persuaded. Scargill, and some old-fashioned unions, had to be defeated. At the time, this appeared to be an all-important cause if England were not to sink into the 'Third World' status that so many people predicted for her.

Meanwhile, Scargill had said that opposition of an extra-parliamentary order was legitimate, the government not having had a majority of the vote. In characteristic apocalyptic style, he announced that 'extra-parliamentary action will be the only course open to the working class'. What he meant was action contrary to his own union's rule book. He could on his own authority organize a banning of overtime. He could only organize a strike by flouting rules to gain a majority, which he did, in a tradition that went back to Lenin's own management of the Russian socialists in 1903: 'Bolshevik' means 'majority', the first, in this case, of many lies. But the government's intelligence connections were sufficient for a rival union, based on profitable pits with the chance of substantial wages, to challenge Scargill. The Coal Board was now managed, not by comfortable upper-class appeasers of the Carrington class, but by an elderly Scotsman, Ian MacGregor, who had been brought back from America and who knew a great deal about managing such matters: he had already proved his worth at British Steel, though, there, he had had intelligent union leaders to deal with. He announced that loss-making pits would have to be closed, that a third of the miners (70,000) would have to be given compensation, and Scargill responded absurdly, as if he wanted all of his men to continue with their obsolete, filthy and dangerous jobs. He banned overtime in October 1983, and then, with ridiculously inappropriate timing, started a strike on 6 March 1984, at the end of winter. Most productive pits did not follow; attempts to picket and stop the (Nottingham) miners failed, despite a murder, because the police were firm. Scargill, with a baseball cap that went badly with this image of the last Leninist insurrection, failed to break through a police line. Then again, the power stations functioned, because stocks of coal were high, and imports, even from Poland, a supposedly Communist country, went ahead. This time round, government legal action was successful, as it had not been in 1972. In August, for instance, some of the miners took their own union to court over its failure to stage a proper strike ballot. A writ was even delivered at the Labour Party conference. Scargill tried to involve other heavy-industrial unions, the famous 'triple alliance' of coal, docks and railways which had been very effective with strikes in the past, back to before the First World War. The government had already managed to privatize some of the docks, and the pockets of dockers who still maintained a local monopoly were isolated and relatively powerless – as well as, in Liverpool, bereft of sense. The railwaymen were simply bought off. This time round, new technology – always an enemy of these old unions, at least if they had an unregenerate leadership – had weakened the old guard. British Steel, for instance, managed with Ro-Ro and free ports; it would no longer be held up by absurd dockland practices, which in the Heath era had involved gangs simply standing, watching other gangs do the work. There was much sentimentality as to the 'communities' of the miners, and efforts were made to enlist middle-class sympathies, which had mattered so much in the seventies. But in the end Scargill had a self-destructive urge, and, early in 1985, the strike crumbled. Yes, it had cost a great deal – the Coal Board had losses of over £2bn. MacGregor himself, who had been less forthright, in private, than Margaret Thatcher would have wished, was dissociated within weeks. Curiously enough (and an echo of earlier patterns) the loyalist miners and civil servants were not rewarded, getting only small pensions. It would have been fitting had they been given decorations, but the honours system in England was for appeasing enemies rather than rewarding friends. Still, the old industrial unions, which had made so much trouble for earlier governments, Labour and Conservative, had in effect been defeated.

Coal and railways were of course the old world. One of these union troubles concerned the new – at that, an immensely important part of the new: the media. The British press had been greatly respected, especially The *Times*, and it generally managed its affairs with genial informality that somehow, mysteriously, produced results (there was a practice of shutting the leader-writer in a room with a typewriter and two bottles of wine, which went on until one such writer was found slumped over his machine, having typed the word 'notwithstanding'). Under William Rees-Mogg, in the later seventies, economic journalists such as Peter Jay or Tim Congdon had hard-hitting things to say. However, the paper made severe losses, and there were great economies to be made if new machinery were to be used in printing. The printers' unions – there were three – resisted and fought each other. After vicissitudes, the newspaper was acquired by a very hard-headed Australian, Rupert Murdoch, who already owned tabloid newspapers that caused some head-shaking as to crudeness, intrusion into private lives and what was soon to be called, in America, 'dumbing down'. When the *Belgrano* was sunk in the Falklands War, one headline, 'GOTCHA', became famous. However, Murdoch knew how to deal with people, quietly dealt with a rival union altogether, set up a building in the dock areas, which had become derelict because of the dockers' unions' ways, and abandoned the original building in central London overnight. The newspapers were instantly produced, by the new methods, without interruption. Early in 1986 there were battles between enraged printers and the electricians or distributors, with police support: not a day's production was lost, and the printers' unions came to terms (on television, Murdoch was asked what he would recommend a striking printer now to do, and said, laconically, 'Find another job'). Some of the journalists took the printers' part and refused to co-operate, suggesting that a Murdoch *Times* would betray the newspaper's status. Others took a different view, and the editor of the *Sunday Times*, Andrew Neil (like MacGregor a Glaswegian), spoke for many when he took the radical Thatcherite line and advocated an Americanization of the country. Rupert Murdoch astutely used the profits from London to establish an empire all over the globe. He was much hated, but in the end was following an old media pattern: the *Manchester Guardian* itself had only got away with its moralizing because of the profits made by its sister newspaper, which reported the horseraces. However, here was now an empire based on mountains of debt, with mountains of profit, from media of all sorts which could make or break governments. At around the same time, in London and New York, banks moved into the same world; vast fortunes began to appear from thin air. The Reagan–Thatcher era was associated with a new economy, in which industry of the classic sort meant a degree of backwardness, much as had happened with peasant agriculture in the later nineteenth century. Brazils and Koreas metal-bashed; Turkey produced 90 per cent of the televisions sold in England, and the main road from Istanbul to Kayseri and Antep was choked with container lorries bearing goods to central Europe. London and New York plucked money out of the air.

The tidal change had much to do with technology. Its history proceeds in great leaps. In the middle of the nineteenth century, one of these had involved the railway; electricity had marked another, essentially in the early twentieth century, when it had enabled coal-poor countries such as France and Italy to acquire modern industry (aircraft and motor cars being an obvious instance in both cases). Now came another huge leap, in one view the greatest ever made – electronics, 'information technology'. In 1980 there was a video cassette recorder in only 1 per cent of American households; by the end of the decade, in three fifths. Cable television, by then, reached half of households – earlier, 15 per cent. Turner Broadcasting survived near collapse and then, by the time of the Gulf War, had become the worldwide network, flattening the old network news programmes. Telephones in 1980 had been very basic, not much beyond the models of fifty years before. Ten years later, there was almost no limit to what they could do, including photography. The old Bell system had encountered some animosity, and in England the national telephone company, like the utilities, was widely regarded as a producer's conspiracy against the public. Cheap long-distance transmission made for a vast change in this, and the old land-line monopolies were broken (although in some cases they managed to retain a great deal of their power). Cellular phones, fibreoptic cable, flourished, as did the fax machine, which was displacing the, also often despised, earlier methods of post offices. The biggest single item in this technological revolution was the personal computer.

In 1981 there were about 2 million such: seven years later, nearly 50 million – IBM the initial leader, followed by Apple Macintosh in 1984. By 1989 'a visiting Russian scientist would be impressed by the computer equipment of his American counterpart, but moved almost to tears by the computer equipment of his counterpart's secretary', says Robert Bartley, the *Wall Street Journal*'s poet in residence, and eighties consumption boomed, to the point at which American clothing or even food styles ran round the entire globe, even, at least for men, in Iran, where there was a forthrightly anti-American regime. The illustrations are endless. The basis was demand from people in new types of jobs – in the USA the participation of women went up from 51 to 57 per cent: almost 60 per cent of families had two earnings (the average family size declining somewhat, to 2.63 members) and the traditional single-earning family now accounted for one quarter of all households (as against nearly one third in 1980). One quarter of the new jobs came from business services and health care; computer and data-processing services led. Some of this followed economic first principles, as they had been established in the nineteenth century. Depression released energy from labour and capital – perhaps women belong in both categories – that had been poorly used. Interest rates, falling, enabled sharp-sighted businessmen to pay for new technology. This process, in the Atlantic world, had been delayed in the 1970s as governments tried to keep the old going – the old now including their own selves – although their unproductiveness was notorious, whether it was bureaucracy or nationalized public utilities. In the USA that process was not as strongly resisted as in western Europe, and there was a whole new breed of entrepreneur – odd, somehow ungrown-up, unappetizingly dressed and outstandingly successful when it came to the understanding of the strange new technology. Steve Jobs and Stephen Wozniak invented the first personal computer in Jobs's garage in 1976, and their Apple I and Apple II machines beat IBM itself to market. In 1980 they issued their first public stock, brought the Macintosh onto the market in 1984, and by the end of the decade Apple was ninety-fifth in the *Fortune* list of 500 companies. Another genius who failed to complete his university course (Harvard) was William Gates, who started a small company in 1975 and bought a computer operating system for $50,000; it became Microsoft Disk Operating System, MS-DOS. In 1986 Microsoft raised over $60m by going public, and by 1990 it had thrown Apple and IBM into a defensive alliance: but Windows software had become so popular that a new version, DOS 5.0, sold a million copies in a month. There were other examples – Mitch Kapor, a former disk jockey and instructor in transcendental meditation (Lotus 1-2-3 in 1983, sales of nearly $700 million in 1990); Philippe Kahn, who came to Silicon Valley in 1983, used a clever ruse to persuade a trade magazine to accept an advertisement on credit, raised $150,000 of sales thereby, and set up Borland International, which, in 1991, was the third-largest supplier of personal computer software. There were many similar examples in other industries. For instance, the possibilities for genetic engineering were already clear, in 1980, when Genentech was the pioneer, raising $300m in the capital markets and, by 1984, putting its synthetic insulin in circulation, with sales of almost $500m by 1990. Frederick Smith had suggested a national overnight delivery service – Federal Express, which struggled for a decade until 1980 and then took off as an American institution, with, ten years later, sales of $7bn. There was also Tele-Communications Inc. for cable TV, with sales of $124m in 1980, $3.6bn in 1990; Turner Broadcasting had sales worth $50m in 1980, but $1.4bn – as CNN – ten years later.

There was a considerable revolution, in other words, though it also had its victims. The once great firms came under competitive pressure, and they had to cut costs – 'downsizing', as it was unlovably called. The largest 500 companies lost 3.5 million jobs in the eighties, General Electric, for instance, falling from 400,000 to 280,000 employees. The huge conglomerates of the 1960s started to dispose of branches that were not central; and there was a tendency towards small holding companies that simply managed the incentives for almost autonomous operating companies (of these, Kohlberg Kravis Roberts – Wall Street – was a prototype). Gone – or almost – were the days when businesses were comfortable, showing off with huge buildings and endless trotting secretaries. Many companies fell sharply – nearly half of the *Fortune* list of 1980 was not there by 1990. The losers quite often had merged, and there was much anger against investment bankers' willingness to finance hostile takeover bids: the short-term results, to impress shareholders, that made their offers attractive, ran the complaint, might mean immediate asset sales that would run counter to long-term investment. But manufacturing itself did not decline, and employment in it did not decline as fast as in the *Fortune* list. Manufacturing still accounted for almost one quarter of the GNP. What did happen was that productivity, output per man, rose, and did so substantially. It rose at 3.6 per cent per annum and the answer was that management 'fat' had been cut, while there was elsewhere a burst of creative energy from the Wozniaks and Gateses (plus illegal immigrants). There was, at work here, a characteristic American quality – it had been shown during the Second World War – of rationalization and risk-taking in pursuit of profit. There was a new financial idea, venture capital. Someone had to raise the initial money for patents, lawyers, etc. for a start-up company; it was a matter of guessing which one. Governments had shown that they were not good at such things, and British mistakes in this respect had been splendidly comic – a prize, stiffly contested, going to the supersonic Concorde.

A molecular biologist, Herbert Boyer, held the patent on techniques for gene splicing. Genentech was founded by two venture capitalists, Thomas Perkins and Robert A. Swanson. By 1980 the market value of the company was $300m. In 1991 Genentech sold part to Roche Holdings for $2.1bn, and an option on the remainder at a price that would have been one hundred times Genentech's earnings of 1989. Genetic technology is exactly the industry that central planners would love to have developed, but the bureaucracy's record was very poor, and in the USA congressional lobbying might also have affected the result. As things were, the eighties were a demonstration that venture capital could produce much better results than 'industrial policy' ever did.

What caused all of this? Robert Bartley reckons that it was a direct consequence of the tax cuts, both in Great Britain and in the United States, and he cites Thomas Perkins, who was chairman not only of

Genentech but also of six other, smaller concerns, and who had been at the start of Compaq and Sun Microsystems, as asserting that a tax cut 'should make it far easier to raise funds, and it will bring the entrepreneurs forward'. In 1975 there had been only $10m of new net capital, and in 1977 $39m. In 1978, following the first tax cut, the figure was $600m, and with the Reagan tax bill of 1981 over twice this. When the tax cuts appeared in reality, in 1983, the figure quadrupled. Then, in 1986 and later, as increases in the capital gains tax came (from 20 to 33 per cent), the figures fell again, to around $2bn in 1988 and 1989. Initial public offerings, where firms first went public, showed a similar pattern – under thirty per annum from 1974 to 1978, then 103 in 1979 and 953 in 1986 (falling thereafter to 186 in 1990). The public offerings amounted to $9bn in 1972 (constant dollars) but only $142m in 1974, rising to $2bn in 1980 and $24bn in 1986. By 1988 they were back to $6bn. As for England, as John Hoskyns said, a man would have had to be mad to attempt to be any sort of entrepreneur in the 1970s, and the Thatcher governments' tax cuts did indeed bring in much greater revenue because people worked harder and more inventively. However, there is devil in the detail, not least because some of the new ventures depended in the end on government money – in California, especially, from the largesse of the Pentagon. The other large source for venture capital was foreign, of course, especially where high technology was involved, and that also was brought about by government action, because of the way in which the dollar was managed. The world could not do without it, as the universal currency, and the Americans took what in the foreign-exchange world was known as an 'arbitrage profit' – the old word was 'coinage-clipping' – on an enormous scale. Japanese and British money flowed into the United States. 'Deregulation' broke down some of the internal dams.

Since the great Slump of the 1930s, government regulation in the US had followed government regulation. Banks had got themselves a bad name, and thousands collapsed, the managers running away with people's savings, in some form or another. There always had been a dislike of money-out-of-money people in the United States: Jefferson thought, for instance, that Hamilton's proposal for a Bank of the United States was intended to restore the monarchy; Andrew Jackson was similarly ill-disposed; William Jennings Bryan famously denounced the 'Cross of Gold' upon which honest farmers were said to be crucified. It was easy enough in these circumstances to make a great fuss about crooked finance, and it was no doubt true that behind every fortune lies, if not a great crime, as Balzac claimed, at least a few corner-cuttings. When things went well, these passed unnoticed. When things went badly, various highly placed money-men were found out. Regulations of a fairly stringent sort were then imposed by the Roosevelt administration to make sure that banks did not do it again: 'the money-changers have fled from their high seats in the temple of our civilization. We may now restore that temple to the ancient truth,' said Roosevelt. This was not really fair. The causes of the great Slump of the 1930s went far beyond the crimes or corner-cuttings of some money-men. It was the high priests themselves who had done for the alleged ancient truths – an absurd tax increase in 1932, in mid-Slump; an absurd tariff, Smoot-Hawley, which had destroyed foreign trade in 1930; a grotesque mismanagement of the money supply and the arbitrary shutting down of 6,000 banks; a pig-headed unwillingness to value gold properly and thus provide internationally valid credit; an equally pig-headed obstinacy as regards Europeans' paying their war debts promptly and in full, while at the same time discrimination went ahead against their exports. In such a context – it destroyed parliamentary democracy almost everywhere – the crimes of some money-men amounted to small beer. However, they caused an irresistible demand for regulation. The same happened over housing. The 'thrifts' took money from savers and lent it to mortgagers, i.e. borrowing short and lending long, with an easy profit margin and a foreseeable income, but through a 'Reg Q' which limited the interest that they could charge for mortgages. The inflation of the seventies knocked the props from the system: the existing interest rate on mortgages could not be pushed upwards to match the fall in the value of the dollar, and savers clearly would not keep money in any bank if they wanted to preserve its value – they would look for higher interest elsewhere (the bonds sold by private companies or even the government), or they would switch into gold, or something that would not go away. By 1978 the amount of money in funds tripled, to almost $10bn, and reached over $40bn the following year (and in 1982 over $235bn). In 1980 the thrifts asked for help, as they lost funds, and 'Reg Q' was abolished. The 'thrifts' were allowed to invest beyond home mortgages, even offering credit cards, and there was, later, a similar relaxation in Great Britain for the equivalent, the building societies. Bricks and mortar, greatly rising in value, offered apparently solid collateral, and pyramids of credit then built up on that basis. But such deregulation happened elsewhere, and banks became free in ways that they had not been since 1932. By 1985 there was lamentation in advanced educational institutions to the effect that economics, business schools and banks were attracting far more students than ever before. A classic of this period, Michael Lewis's *Liar's Poker* (1989), reveals the world of Salomon Brothers. He had been a graduate student at the London School of Economics, despised the concentration at his native Princeton on two-dimensional economics, but, almost by chance, was wafted into a world in which his starting salary was twice that of his professor, and then made cruel mock of the whole greedy and stupid business of the bond market. Tom Wolfe's *Bonfire of the Vanities* remains the outstanding novel of the decade and perhaps even the half-century. He too had made his observations on the trading floor of Salomon Brothers, once a rather staid and safe Wall Street house, turned into a sort of perambulatory worldwide casino.

The money thereby let loose might well be directed towards assets held by the State – in most countries, many. Here, again, was one feature that made the Thatcher government stand out, abroad as well as at home – privatization. In the later nineteenth century, most enlightened people had wanted the essential pieces of the economy – water, railways, etc. – to be run by the State, especially if the companies running them were foreign, as was the case in, say, Russia. In old Austria, trains were stopped at the border because the company had not paid some debt or other. In England such private companies went on for longer than elsewhere, especially France, but in the course of the world wars the State moved in, and by 1979 the 'commanding heights' – ports, steel, aircraft, railways, etc. – had been taken over. It was now the State's turn to experience criticism, and there were even attempts to explain theoretically ('public choice') why there was such truth in

Nietzsche's great line, 'What the State has is theft; what the State says is lies.' Why theorize? Anecdote existed, in mountains, to bear him out. Even the recipients of 'benefit' in Oxford went on a sort of reverse strike at the slipshod and inhuman ways in which they were paid their cash (1984). However, as any government had discovered when it came to privatization (Konrad Adenauer had tried it to a very limited extent), there were very severe difficulties. The arguments against privatization (it should really be called 're-privatization') were considerable, and who would want to take over these tremendous loss-makers, with their in-built over-employment, incompetent or demoralized managers, huge debts and gigantic pensions commitments? As regards education or public health, there was also a very great political problem: the National Health Service in Great Britain, giving medical care at any level for nothing (at any rate in appearance), could hardly be reformed without patients' having to pay something directly, as happened in, say, Spain or Sweden, but any government suggesting this would have lost the next election, or three. There was a possible halfway house, of introducing what was supposed to be 'internal competition', but Nigel Lawson, a chief privatizer, aptly quoted the saying that applying private sector discipline to the state sector was equivalent to painting stripes on a donkey and calling it a zebra. In time there was to be a cavalry charge of such donkeys in British higher education and the health service, but privatization, otherwise, went ahead in areas that greatly deserved it.

An element of luck supervened. The nationalized industries had no admirers, and the only arguments of substance concerned what had gone wrong: the nature of the beast? Unions? Management? Inflation? At any rate, privatization, to begin with, was just a way of raising money. Steel, coal and Leyland dominated the early agenda, as these cost taxpayers £300 each (in 1995 money). In 1982 a few small things were sold off, such as government shares in British Petroleum and the National Freight (lorry) company. Then, with Lawson as Chancellor in 1983, half of British Telecom was sold off: an enormous success, amounting to the largest equity offering in history. The shares were undervalued, and buyers had to be rationed, but they made windfall profits at the same time. One of the early charging donkeys was also a low-level loan scheme for students who would then pay low-level fees to their universities (less than their parents would have paid for a few weeks in a crèche). Bright undergraduates took the loan, bought the shares, sold them and paid off the loan at a profit. In 1984–5 assets such as railway hotels were sold off, with beneficial results, and the nationalized industries were told they might raise prices (and they even made a profit in 1989). By 1989 half of them had gone to shareholders, and 650,000 workers left state employment, nearly all with shares. As the journalist Simon Jenkins says, 'the biggest transfer of assets out of state hands in the history of democracy' was the sale of council housing – 1.25 million people were able to buy their dwellings from the local council, instead of paying 'social' rents which, though in themselves sometimes ridiculously low, represented a trap: immobility, no capital. In the 'projects' (the American equivalent) of a Liverpool or a Manchester, single mothers lived without cost, but also without hope. Selling off such housing was a creative step. Great Britain again became a pioneer, but again suffered for it, in that mistakes were inevitably made, which other countries, following, would know to avoid. Water, gas, Telecom, though prepared for privatization, were not groomed to expect competition – they would in effect be monopolies, and BT soon showed that it could fall behind others. Regulation was heavy-handed, and Ferdinand Mount correctly noted that the degree of regulation and public subsidy was such that what in Britain was called 'private' would probably have counted as 'public' on the Continent. The later privatization of the railways was near farcical (and Mrs Thatcher herself had always opposed the scheme, as too complicated): it would have made more sense just to concrete over the railways and substitute buses on the roads thereby acquired to a central terminal. Mobile telephones worked less well and more expensively in England than they were to do in Azerbaidjan. However, no-one really knew how privatizations should be executed; the Treasury was only interested in taking the money, and reducing the annual borrowing figure; the privatizations were rushed and the shares were undervalued. Rolls-Royce shares were nine times oversubscribed, ports thirty-four times, British Airways twenty-three times, at a cost of £25m to the taxpayer. However, this was uncharted territory, so mistakes would be made. At the least, regulation did become more open and there was an obvious gain in efficiency as against the old, dreadful, days. That managers' salaries now reflected private sector ones of course created some adverse comment, but the overall degree of efficiency was noted later on. In the old days, nothing had worked and no-one had earned anything.

As the 'high eighties' went ahead, a great wave of money swept over the Atlantic world, and the outcome was a long boom – ninety-two months of growth, compared to fifty-eight in any earlier period (outside wartime, as with the Vietnam era). No recessions got in the way of the compounding of growth: 1984 was spectacular enough – almost 7 per cent growth – but the other years are remembered for the extraordinary prosperity of the Atlantic world. Geoffrey Owen, an expert on this dismal subject, shows how even the motor car industry was recovering. In 1984 Toyota and Nissan were adopted and invited, and Michael Edwardes could simply close the hopeless Merseyside plant. Jaguar was privatized, and some of the excessive manpower was at last shed, but the new models were still not much of a success (even in 1986 there were of course industrial-policy Conservatives arguing for continued support) and in the end the Japanese were brought into north-eastern England to show the way forward. Honda–Nissan insisted upon a single-union agreement, as did Toyota–Honda at Swindon. By 1997 output was 1.7 million cars and exports accounted for a million of them. The world of the sixties albatross had at last been overcome, but essentially through foreign management. By 1988 100,000 new firms were registered. As Bernard Connolly remarks, 'the bullishness of the country' became visible. Business investment rose by 20 per cent. The adaptation of advanced computers to financial transactions somehow catapulted London back to the centre of the world's money, and as the bond market got under way, older divisions between deposit banks, operating on classic old-fashioned lines, and investment ones, involved in speculation, were elided. In October 1986 came an important moment, deregulation of the City, otherwise known as 'Big Bang', such that old-fashioned banks and stockbroking firms gave up their staid ways. Venerable (and well-run) establishments such as Lawrence, Prust were bought up by a Deutsche Bank anxious to escape from the stuffy confines of Frankfurt, where, it was said, there *was* a night-life, but she went to see her aunt on Tuesdays. In New York and London the money poured in, and in the British case Alan Walters himself called it a 'miracle', comparable with the earlier German one, for there had been steady growth since 1981, weekly earnings had risen by 14 per cent in real money between 1983 and 1987, and inflation had been held below 5 per cent.

However, as the money poured into government coffers, what next? It mattered that Margaret Thatcher was now a world figure. As with an American presidency, the possibility always existed that a British Prime Minister would escape into foreign affairs. To begin with, she had been rather contemptuous of these international gatherings – what had begun as a decent enough idea for small, informal gatherings soon degenerated into a media circus, and at meetings of the G7 the final communiqués would be drafted before the people had even met. Photographs and television images with foreign leaders were thought (mysteriously) to win votes. Besides, abroad there was sometimes adulation – none of the abuse shouted back home. Patriotism could be on display, without any sniggering. It also mattered that NATO had come under considerable pressure. In 1982 there was a great fight over the placing of intermediate-range ultra-modern missiles on European soil, and vital countries, Germany, especially, saw enormous demonstrations against this, a matter in part of KGB manipulation which Bukovsky, from Politburo documents, was able to demonstrate. In this atmosphere of the 'Second Cold War', as commentators called it, the transatlantic link became all-important. Margaret Thatcher took her eye off the domestic ball, and moved on to what appeared to be a much larger one, foreign affairs. Instinctively, she did not like the Foreign Office: it was too 'European', talking platitudes, and inclined not to be as fervently Atlantic as she was. If the Americans took a hand in anti-terrorist action, as they did in the spring of 1986 against Gaddafi in Libya, then Mrs Thatcher could follow her instincts and offer support. There had been an outburst of terrorist killings, organized from Iran or Libya or elsewhere, and at Christmas 1985 nineteen people had been killed at Vienna and Rome airports. Three British hostages were taken in the Lebanon and killed, and her view of such things was that proper retaliation should be made. It duly was, and the problem greatly lessened, though she was regarded as reckless in the usual quarters. In general, she remained forthright in her opposition to the humbug of Third World goody-goodies, Scandinavian ladies, lecturing and the like, and at the waste-of-time 'summits' which now proliferated she was at 'new levels of manifest arrogance'.

Such bluntness went down well, domestically, and it was no doubt utterly deserved: the British had given away too much for membership of the Common Market and the cant of 'North' and 'South' needed to be dismissed. But there was similar and greater cant at home, and here the lady was being sidetracked. More and more, foreign affairs took over: the endless grind of domestic reform was too exhausting, and the divisions on the Right too difficult to bridge. Increasingly, too, matters European came centre-stage, generally in a cantankerous way. For a good generation the Common Market had been bumbling along, but in 1985 Margaret Thatcher herself had promoted the 'Single European Act', which was supposed to simplify things. It would end the hidden protection devices and stop the endless haggling over uniform standards that got in the way of trade. But, unnoticed at the time, that same Act allowed the larger countries, and of course Germany especially, to override opposition provided they could take on a lesser ally or two. This meant that in matters of some importance the British might be outvoted and yet compelled by the Europeans to go ahead. 'Europe' took attention that diverted and exhausted; it was also in the end destructive of constitutional ways. The British Parliament soon found itself nodding through great heaps of small-print legislation in obedience to European directives, and since Parliament had absolute power, the police were soon prosecuting people who illegally killed bats in their attics, and the absurd persecution of smokers got under way.

Deregulation, privatization, the existence of powerful computers that could be programmed to buy and sell at an advanced level, with endless manipulations of complicated IOUs ('swaps', 'options', 'warranties'): much of it came down to mortgages on bricks and mortar, whether the Colombian embassy in Tokyo being sold to pay off the national debt, or a broom cupboard near Harrods in London being sold for £35,000. As ever in such a world (after Louis Napoleon's Eighteenth Brumaire there was a similar bonanza with property in Paris, and even a form of unit trust) there were figures, part child, part ogre, who understood the system, made vast sums of money mainly by borrowing from people who did not, and discredited the system as a whole. There had been Armand Hammer, who had managed to make money in Stalin's Russia, with a monopoly for the sale of pencils made on a German model, just as every child in the USSR needed a pencil for the expansion of schooling – Stalin ended this in 1929, but Hammer was allowed, in compensation, to take two waggonloads of icons and art, confiscated from the original owners, out of the country; he set up shop in Park Avenue, used the profits to buy oil in the early 1930s, when its price was very low, and then boomed: at the end of his life, while watching cricket at Lord's with the Prince of Wales, he was harassing his sister-in-law for the $15,000 that he had lent to his much less successful brother for a life-saving operation which had failed. There was Robert Maxwell, fraud to the core, claiming to be a Czech, but in effect Hungarian (he had been born in what had been north-eastern Hungary, and cut his teeth, financially, on cross-border smuggling). He survived by doing his own people out of their retirement fund, and died by drowning, probably suicide, in circumstances that were never cleared up. In the USA 'junk bonds' created fortunes and led to discredit of the whole system. These involved a real risk, being bonds raised against the possibility of taking over, via the stock exchange, some firm or other, allegedly badly managed and overextended. In 1980 such bonds raised $5bn, but by 1986 almost $50bn, falling back to around $35bn thereafter. Their chief architect, Michael Milken, made himself vastly unpopular and eventually was imprisoned (though on a lesser offence). He financed Turner Broadcasting and many other well-known, now well-established, concerns, and two thirds of the 'junk bond' money went quite productively into such corporate growth, not into the spectacular takeovers. It was all, in the end, brought about as a consequence of the seventies inflation, and the distortion that that had produced, but there was a great deal of head-shaking. Economists stuck in the Left could be waved aside. Those on the Right, with views as to probity, not so, and the best were worried. In the mid-1980s Tim Congdon wrote in warning against what was happening, and was followed a decade later by Peter Warburton. They were proven right, but only a decade later, in 2008, when the bubble appeared to collapse, and trillions disappeared, the exports of Japan (at this moment of writing) dropping a quarter in a month (January 2009). But such works appeared in the 1980s to be wolf-crying. Michael Milken might be led off, to boos, in handcuffs. But a far greater drama was going ahead elsewhere: Moscow and Peking had noticed what was happening.

25

Floréal

Moscow and Peking had supposed that the Third World would rescue them. In the Russian Revolution, the Bolsheviks had really won because they had recruited the earliest version of it: you could tell assorted downtrodden Eastern peoples that colonialism was the enemy, that Marxism was the friend. After they had won the civil war, in September 1920, the Bolsheviks had staged a congress of 'the toiling peoples of the East' at Baku on the Caspian; 2,000 attended, some taking time off for their prayers, others trading, and had been addressed first of all by Grigory Zinoviev, the head of the Comintern, screeching his Moscow-Jewish German, and then by the Turkish Enver Pasha, nephew-in-law of the Sultan, former commander of the Turkish army, who addressed them as 'comrades', and flounced out when he was told he could only have five minutes (he responded by circulating his vast address). The enemy was imperialism. There was obvious sense in this strategy, as was later displayed in China in 1949, and Vietnam in 1975. The Russians had accordingly gone into the Middle East and Africa, a process culminating in the invasion of Afghanistan. On America's doorstep, they had taken up alliance with the revolutionaries of Nicaragua, who agreed – as had happened with Republican Spain in the civil war – to pretend to establish a popular front rather than a people's democracy, so as to rope in Western allies who would not have liked an outright Communist takeover. But in 1983 the Third World was not working out as intended. Iran had gone very badly wrong. So had the invasion of Afghanistan. And two very vulnerable places, Chile and Turkey, had shown that the Soviet formula was quite misplaced. The eighties economy was defeating not just Marx, but Lenin and Mao Tse-tung as well.

The most characteristic book of the eighties was written not long after the decade ended, Francis Fukuyama's *End of History* (1992). The title seemed funny when the book appeared, and seemed even funnier afterwards, but it was not senseless. The claim (a quote from Hegel) was that democracy and capitalism ('free markets') had spread from period to period after the Second World War, that dictatorships, Communism, wars, etc. would be things of the past, and that the world would move more and more in the direction of, say, Denmark. The essential was a decent level of prosperity, after which politics could move from Third to First World. Walt Rostow, back in the 1960s, had said much the same about industrialization. A point came when a country could 'take off' into self-sustaining growth: England at the time of the Industrial Revolution, Germany somewhat later. 'Big picture' books of this sort were easy enough to pick apart, but they did connect with a substantial literature of Europe around 1900, when it was perfectly obvious that Western civilization had produced something unique, which needed explanation, and which countries such as Japan or Turkey might copy. Fukuyama's contribution was only hesitantly stated. Its centre was that a modernizing dictatorship, or at any rate a period of rule without real elections, might be necessary for the 'take-off', whether political or economic, to be arrived at. The question would have been accepted by any Communist in the 1930s: the peasants, Marx's quadrupeds, would only accept progessive change if they were forced to. Modernization from the Left was a standard line, and was accepted very widely indeed. Since the Second World War a school of development economics had emerged, with the Swede Gunnar Myrdal in the lead, and its adepts were all around, whether in Africa or Latin America, arguing in effect that the peasantry and the small bourgeoisie should pay for heavy industrialization, courtesy of the State.

But in 1976, by the time Mao Tse-tung had died, that scheme of things looked much less promising. China, after all, had gone through convulsions, disasters, tens of millions of people dead of starvation, and the USSR was also hardly an advertisement. Development economics had grown out of the Marshall Plan, and something had gone badly wrong: the more aid, the more backwardness, however you were to explain this. In remote relationship, much the same happened with the Keynesian assumptions as regards public spending and unemployment: much of England was Third World, in German eyes, though there were only low-level civil wars. And now there was a Pinochet, creating considerably more prosperity than anything Communist; quite soon thereafter, 2 million Soviet citizens were taking refuge in, of all places, Turkey. What was going right, and what, wrong?

In Chile, in the first four years, to 1977, the aim was consolidation of the regime, a depoliticization of life, and a suppression of political parties and labour unions: farmers to farm, workers to work, students to study. There would have to be a currency reform, to put an end to the inflation: the State, printing its own money, was paying for its hangers-on at the expense, in taxes and rising prices, of people just trying to do a useful job outside the system. These matters had been analysed by political economists since the time of Adam Smith, two centuries beforehand, and economists in that tradition had swept the board in the nineteenth century. The State should be confined to its proper functions, in the way of defence, the rule of law and a money the value of which could be trusted. This brought about extraordinary progress in the later nineteenth century. But then had come 1914 and the big State had seemed to be the answer: world wars and the great crash of 1929, when finance and trade had collapsed, had seen to that. But this generated problems of its own, and these had been obvious enough to a particular school of political economists in central Europe even before 1914. The Austrian empire had been a very peculiar place, never really captured by western European liberal economics. Even in 1914 it employed a quarter of the population, and there was a legendary tragi-comic bureaucracy, the tax laws taking up three huge volumes, printed in two columns in small print on thin paper. Lawyers swarmed, and the general atmosphere was summed up by the great journalist of the era, Karl Kraus, when he said that Vienna was an asylum where you were allowed to scream. By 1934 there was a semi-dictatorship, trying to assert financial (and other:

divorce was banned) orthodoxies. Its leader, Engelbert Dollfuss, faced a revolt from the Left. The army brought up artillery against a huge fortress-like public housing development called Karl-Marx Hof in Heiligenstadt, otherwise an upper-middle-class district; shells flew. The photographs of that, in the snows of February 1934, became one of the great Comintern tableaux, and two very prominent British Communists, one of them a major spy, became involved with left-wing Austrian women of that vintage. But that atmosphere also produced a school of political economists who looked upon the whole business and wondered what had gone wrong with the comfortable certainties of 1914. Like Keynes, they had a weakness for answering the problem in terms of mathematics. Hayek and Schumpeter had got out, via London, to Chicago and Harvard. Ludwig von Mises got out to Switzerland, and the oddest remark made, upon the outbreak of the Second World War, was made by him at Bern station to Wilhelm Röpke, later the architect of the West German economic miracle, whom he encountered by chance, as he transferred from Istanbul to Switzerland: if the Anglo-French free-trade treaty had been ratified by Louis Napoleon, this war would not have happened. In its surreal central European way, this stated a truth: countries that ignored the economic rules would distort everything and end up with a disaster. This ended up with the bombardment of the Karl-Marx Hof by the artillery of Prince Schönburg-Hartenstein. It also ended up with the Pinochet coup. The University of Chicago took in the Austrian school, Hayek in particular. In the USA universities competed with each other, and there was freedom in ideas. Chicago had always striven to acquire a character different from the Ivy League places, which listened to grand siren voices from England. Milton Friedman and others of his tendency worked there. In Chicago, at any rate, there were young men and women who had listened to what Hayek and his disciples had to say, and there were young Chileans who had attended the same classes. There had, since 1956, been a formal link between Chicago and the Catholic University in Santiago. In Allende's Chile, Friedman had much to chew upon, and Pinochet's Chile became the test case for an experiment that was to prove to be of worldwide importance.

Allende himself had stood on what appeared to be a formidable rock of thinking. Why was Chile poor, much poorer than Argentina? The Argentinian Raúl Prebisch argued powerfully that in Latin America big estates counted as a bottleneck, and in Chile they predominated – 80 per cent of the land held by 7 per cent of the farms, each with a thousand hectares on average, whereas 37 per cent of the farms held 0.2 per cent of the land. These figures seemed to reflect 'social injustice', and development economists argued that, because there were so many very poor peasants, there was not proper demand for industrial goods. The rich just imported them, and otherwise did nothing for economic growth except employ servants who, in the poorest countries such as Haiti, themselves employed servants. In the USA, there was a great deal of head-shaking as to what had gone wrong, the role of the USA included. Kennedy, as part of a campaign to limit the appeal of Castro, promoted an 'Alliance for Progress', with grants of money for 'structural reforms' in Latin America, and the Chilean Christian Democrats promoted land reform, though they did so prudently: carried out too quickly it could damage production. There was a problem for Chile, in that half of the population lived in the central valleys, not in the immense areas to north and south: vast estates on endless tracts of valueless land hardly made any difference, one way or the other, and some of them worked efficiently enough. They would have worked more efficiently, as experience was to show, had Chilean produce been freely bought and sold in the richer markets. But these protected their own agriculture: no-one knew Chilean wines until much later. Over the pace of land reform, the Christian Democrats split three ways, and their alliance with the Right disintegrated, which was the background to the election of Allende. That had ended in tears.

The concomitant of the big state was printed money, which produced inflation, and inflation distorted everything. Augusto Pinochet led the field in what was to become a powerful counter-attack. His first move was to cancel the 300 per cent wage increases sanctioned by Allende, and some of the controlled basic prices were hugely increased. The great mass of the population had had its energy sapped, and accepted the immediate troubles easily enough, though no doubt the presence of the military helped. The essential move was to restrict the output of paper, which in turn meant a drastic curtailment of the State's spending. There was no great secret in this: you needed some foreign support, high interest rates to prevent an expansion of borrowing, devaluation, and maybe bond sales at a well-judged rate, to attract some of the excess paper. These things had been done in 1923 in Germany, and a great inflation, which had brought the Mark to 11 billion against the dollar, stopped more or less overnight, in the context of a Communist takeover in Saxony (suppressed by the army, in what was known as a *Reichsexekution*) and then Hitler's first attempt to seize power, with the *Putsch* in Munich. There, the change had come about because, at last, a government stretching from some way into the Left to some way into the Right had been strong enough to maintain control. There were problems in the short run, with bankruptcies and unemployment, but there followed an economic recovery. Now, the first step in Chile was to carry through the money reform. Reducing inflation is a slow business, and in 1974 it still stood at over 500 per cent. Milton Friedman came on a visit in March 1975, and an economic recovery programme was announced. There were three phases of liberalization – the first to 1977, then a council of state in 1981 and a constituent assembly in 1985 with direct election every eight years provided for. A constitutional article forbade attacks on the family. Control of inflation meant, not just management of a paper currency, but attacking the causes of the inflation – what a prominent English politician, Sir Keith Joseph, with excellent American contacts, famously addressed at this time.

There would have to be a dismantling of the State. It meant privatization, to encourage efficiency through competition. The State, with ignorant investment of other people's money, with over-employment, with automatic further credit from some puppet bank and with inappropriate political appointments, could in effect ruin concerns to the point at which no-one would buy them. No-one would make a profit out of them. In Chile some of the firms taken over by Allende had not been so ruined, and by 1978 all of the 259 sequestered firms had been returned to the stockholders, and ninety-nine others were sold off cheaply, mainly to conglomerates. There were two concomitants. The peso, though stable enough, was devalued, to the point at which imports from Chile became very cheap, and a further concomitant concerned the outside world: trade was widely liberalized, with foreign competition allowed. Tariffs sank to 10 per cent by 1978. There was a recovery, led by exports, and not just by the copper and other raw materials that Chile produced. There was now a property boom in Santiago, and there was a rehousing of the poor, away from the shanty towns into tower blocks well-segregated from middle-class areas, which experienced a property boom, because the tax on capital gains in property was abolished, and conglomerates (*piranhas*) made great gains out of the proceeds. Prices, generally, were removed from controls. On the sixth anniversary of the coup, Pinochet made a speech referring to the 'seven modernizations', which included a new labour code, and a new principle, of privatization, to be followed. This latter included social security: there would now be competition among private firms to provide insurance, rather than blanket coverage by the State. The new principle meant that education was also devolved – first onto the municipalities – while private schools were encouraged. The University of Chile and the Catholic University had been placed under the military, and were now expected to be self-financing. Privatized universities now became part of the intellectual agenda: this reflected the success of the American model, as against the decline of state universities in every other country.

Sergio de Castro became finance minister in December 1976 and surrounded himself with Chicago Ph.D.s who proposed textbook answers to the various problems. These became, quite soon, the stock-in-trade of the Western world, from the Atlantic to Turkey. There would be liberalization of foreign trade, and an end put to the practice of import substitution; the peso would be devalued as far as might be necessary to promote exports. On the other hand, credit would be restricted and interest rates put up in order for inflation to be stopped. These two aims were not always easy to combine, because high interest rates could push up the value of the peso, which might damage exporting. There was a further problem, that the course of privatization brought, at least in the short term, unemployment, although to some extent public works were used to counteract this. Given the overwhelming strength of the army, there was of course nothing that the trade unions could do while the reforms went ahead. Wages fell in purchasing power by half. Then matters began to improve, as the end of inflation meant that people started to save again.

The regime then had to contend with the 'second oil shock', when, in 1979, petrol prices doubled, and the country suffered from further difficulties when, in 1979, the British and Americans launched their own inflation cures, with a great fall in demand in 1980 and 1981. The rise of the dollar disrupted the exchanges, and in Chile, in 1982, there were many bankruptcies – 824, as against twenty-four in normal times, and unemployment reached beyond 20 per cent, while output fell by over 14 per cent. In 1983 the unemployment figure rose to 28.5 per cent and inflation also went up, from 9.9 per cent to 27 per cent. One problem was that the peso had been overvalued, and there had not been proper supervision of banks, which took dollar loans and lost the money in speculation. The de Castro team imagined that there would be some automatic adjustment, but by 1983 Pinochet himself realized that he must contain the crisis by state action. The claim was that the rich grew richer and that the gap between them and the poor widened – a not improbable claim. By 1978 conglomerates had emerged in force – Vial controlling twenty-five companies, Cruzat-Lorrain thirty-seven of the 250 largest ones, and six conglomerates held over half of their assets; there were press empires, and two of them took over 75 per cent of social security arrangements. Banks borrowed heavily from foreign fringe banks and then somewhat later ran into difficulties. In the later seventies interest rates were low and there was much borrowing once inflation had been halted: imports, debts and interest costs grew in 1980–81 as the dollar rose, and by 1982 a debt problem had emerged (in 1973 it had stood at $3.67bn but by 1982 it was over $17bn). The *gremios* – new private companies – suffered from foreign competition and in the last years of the seventies there were 1,338 bankruptcies. Even Vial and Cruzat-Lorrain went bankrupt and some bankers were prosecuted.

De Castro left office, succeeded by a more flexible man, José Piñera, who reorganized the entire world of pensions and welfare, devalued by 35 per cent and imposed tariffs again – not part of the original programme at all. Some of the banks were taken over, and their debts were underwritten by the State. Real wages were held down; they had fallen by one third between 1973 and 1975, and even in 1989 were still 90 per cent of the 1970 level. There was some labour unrest in 1983 and the copper workers staged a day of protest against the police, but wages were generally held down, and growth, at over 7 per cent, returned. Now, trade opened up: for instance, Chilean wine could be exported, and enterprising farmers worked out how they might grow new fruit – kiwi for instance. Once recovery was in place, by 1986, there was more privatization – utilities, mining and some services, and the banks that had been taken over were also sold off, as going concerns, this time with military money involved as 'people's capitalism'.

After that, recovery happened, as it did, famously, throughout the Atlantic world, and by 1986 Pinochet was confident enough to introduce the transition back to democratic practices. Pinochet had appointed the mayors and had organized local government to favour his rule – thus municipal change meant that in Santiago there were very rich boroughs and also very poor ones that could not pay their way. The number of boroughs went up from sixteen to thirty-two and the Santiago area was enlarged for development, out of which of course money was made; and the poorer elements were shifted in much the same way as was done with Glasgow, as the boundaries stretched to the Andes and farmland was cleared. The *pobladores* were moved out of middle-class areas, and their old areas gentrified: 150,000 people were moved out of shanty towns, where they had sometimes been squatters. The *población* of La Hermida was shifted away from middle-class Ñuñoa to a new area called Peñalolén with a per capita income under 1 per cent of Ñuñoa's. A prosperous area such as Providencia with a population of 116,000 did well from the decentralization money and in the five years after 1982 built health clinics and night schools, whereas La Florida, with nearly 200,000 people, could hardly have a wooden day-centre for children. Self-help groups started. The rich, in the eighties, had the life of their equivalents in every other country, mobile telephones, jeans and business schools well to the fore.

With education there came a certain militarization, with soldier-rectors in the Catholic University and the University of Chile; patriotism was to be stressed, and there were purges. As an American writes, ineffably, the generals 'disagreed with the vision of a university as a place for the free exchange of ideas'. Beyond twelve specialist areas the universities lost their monopoly in the sense that any private entrepreneur could offer any subject. Business schools proliferated (some sixty). Readers of *Eighteenth Brumaire* complained into their beards; tuition fees were introduced and the state support for universities fell from two thirds to half. The exiles went to town: they now understood how dangerous for their cause was the growing prosperity of the country. Perhaps this accounted for the stupid chasing of the prominent exiles by DINA, the Chilean secret police.

Early in 1988 a 'No' (to Pinochet) campaign started (with American help for the opposition, at least with computers). In October 1988 the 'No' campaign succeeded; the architect of the recovery in 1983–6 joined the 'No' campaign, and in the election Pinochet lost. A middle-road Catholic, Patricio Aylwin, at the head of a sixteen-party coalition, formed the government in March 1990, having become president elect in December 1989. Soon, there was a woman president, and, a few years down the road, the ancient, wheezing Pinochet was arrested in a small-hours raid on his hospital bed in London. Margaret Thatcher went into battle on his behalf, and he was released after a few very embarrassing months. As he left England she gave him a silver Armada Plate, originally designed in celebration of the defeat of the Spanish Armada by Sir Francis Drake in 1588. The Spanish were very angry indeed. But, in the end, the arrest of Pinochet was the best comment on his reign. He was not a man of much interest in himself, but he deserved well of his country, and pursuing him in old age to London was childish vindictiveness.

Turgut Özal in Turkey was in some ways a comparable figure. He was the product (indirectly, and not the cause) of a military coup, and his problems and solutions were Pinochet's, although the Turkish army conceded free elections quite quickly, such that octroyed solutions, as in Chile, were not, in anything other than the short term, possible. As with Pinochet, the intelligentsia were very hostile, and with the two films *Midnight Express* and *Yol* they produced damning, superbly made and, as with most political films, mendacious evidence. But as the outcome of the Turkish coup of 1980 the country was on the map again, and a figure or two spells it out. Turkey, in 2000, counted as twentieth economic power in the world. F16s made in Kirikkale, in the middle of Anatolia, won prizes. Istanbul had become an important financial centre, and the standard of living, overall, was such that Russians migrated to Turkey. At home, they died at sixty; Turks died at seventy. Back in 1923, when Turkey started off, she had been very backward. In the 1970s, the country was still in large part backward, and almost torn by civil war. By 1990 there had been a transformation, and Turkey was the only country between Athens and Singapore that attracted refugees – 2 million of them.

The repression after the Turkish coup followed Pinochet lines. The army had bided its time, and then moved massively. From 1980 to 1984 there were 180,000 arrests; 65,000 people were imprisoned, 40,000 were sentenced, and there were 326 death sentences (though in the end only twenty-seven executions). On the other hand, twenty-six rocket-launchers and 750,000 handguns were seized, and the casual killings stopped overnight. Meanwhile the politicians were kept aside – the nationalist Alparslan Türkeş with the Islamist Necmettin Erbakan on Uzunada near İzmir, the others at a village near Gallipoli. Hundreds of the politicians were banned. A new constitution was adopted, by referendum, in November 1982, and an election was held a year later; but this time the politicians were supposed to act under severe restriction. The system of proportional representation was abolished, because it had allowed small parties to make the running, and a vote of 10 per cent was needed for any representation at all in parliament. There would be State Security Courts with great powers, and order was at last restored. On previous occasions the generals, taking power, had tended to scratch their heads and drift, but now, in 1980, they had a strategy in mind: the political confusions must be stopped, and that meant coherent behaviour. There was one very significant difference with Chile: it was not a general who took power, the senior one, Kenan Evren, contenting himself with the mainly ceremonial presidency, and spending his time painting (at which he was good).

The overall idea seems to have been to collect moderates of the Demirel and Republican sides perhaps under the leadership of one of the generals' trusted Republicans, such as the veteran Turhan Feyzioğlu. Oddly enough, the old politicians, even in internment, held to illusions, perhaps precisely because their internment was so mild; they never imagined that the National Security Council could do without them, and Demirel, especially, was constantly being telephoned by senior civil servants and politicians whom the generals consulted. One man was essential – Turgut Özal, the international money-man. He was not particularly keen to have any sort of state-oriented political team in charge. The generals, for their part, despised the politicians, and when they found they could not easily re-form a civilian government, on 18 September they simply handed full powers to the commanders of the martial law districts and nominated an admiral as prime minister. Özal was happy enough with this solution, for he could push through the economic reforms that he and his business friends wanted to see. Authority tended therefore to settle lower down in the pyramid, and Özal found it coming his way, as under-secretary of the plan.

Özal did not believe in plans – he used to laugh, as to how, coming back through the customs at Istanbul airport, he waddled, because he had worn layers of smuggled tights for his wife in thick layers, to avoid paying duty. He had worked at the World Bank and been an irrigation engineer. Turks older than him would also have been engineers or economists, but they would have been from the urban middle (or higher) classes, and secular. Özal was the product of the Turkey that they had created, in so far as education and mobility had reached far into the depths of Anatolia, and had affected places such as Malatya, where he came from. He was part Kurdish, and in religion belonged to one of the stricter orders (*tarikat*: the often-used 'sect' is a mistranslation, because the differences are in practice, not theology). An engineering training, at the Istanbul Technical University, had not dented the piety, and when he was at the World Bank he had his prayer mat at the ready. No drink, of course, but far too much to eat, and far too many cigarettes (the combination killed him almost absurdly early, in 1993: as with Atatürk, who had also died far too early, this time from cigarettes and *rakı*, you wonder what would have happened if he had gone on longer, for he was a great creative force). Özal was obviously the Americans' man, and he could deliver the IMF. He might just have remained as the vital cog in the generals' machine, but events pushed him into prominence. The generals did not, on the whole, like him: they were very firm secularists, were generally from Western-leaning Thrace or the Aegean, and were even sometimes of Alevi origin, regarding ultra-pious Islam as so much ju-jitsu. Besides, they, without complaint, worked within the State and did not in their heart of hearts see why the economy could not be run like the army, orders issued and obeyed. They even tried to run politics through a dummy party, with two others to represent a sort of *emredersin* ('yessir') opposition.

The reforms announced on 24 January 1980 had followed lines that the IMF and Washington had been recommending with increasing insistence since they had proved to be successful in Pinochet's Chile. Price controls were at least relaxed, and the state enterprises lost less – \$62m as against \$290m earlier. Quota lists for imports were cut to six months, as against the earlier twelve, and the trade deficit continued, but the IMF gave a standby credit of \$1.25bn – the greatest ever given to date. An essential was to stop the inflation, which meant initial pain, as it did in Chile or for that matter England. There would be serious devaluation – in effect, almost by half – and there would be reliance on an export-led recovery. This would mean freeing foreign exchange from controls – and in Turkey these had been very onerous indeed. You even paid a tax if you left the country. Taxes in general were heavy, and if you bought anything at all, you were required by law to keep the sales record. There was very widespread evasion, the black economy accounting for a good half of sales, and at some stage the system would have to be overhauled, but the budget must first of all be brought nearer to balance. Of course these things were difficult to achieve, and the civil service was deeply unsympathetic; the generals were very irritable, and the large private concerns would much have preferred to co-operate with Demirel, whom they knew (not least as a Mason) from old. Özal, in the eyes of the establishment a rough peasant, though nominated deputy prime minister, was quite isolated, and when the generals sensed his ambition, they drove him out. But he came back, for an odd reason.

The January measures of 1980 could only really be pushed through if, initially, wage levels were held back. This was difficult. Half of the economy was controlled by the State, with monopolies of this and that, and the trade unions were powerful. There were subsidies for (some) agriculture, and there was elaborate protection for the Koç industrial dynasty, the head of which, old Vehbi, was very astute indeed. (He owed his origins to Ankara. As a small boy he had seen Armenians and Greeks going around on horses, whereas he had his donkey; he wondered how you got a horse. As he grew up, he got the franchise to sell refrigerators in the main square of the town, which had meanwhile become the capital. An oak forest was to grow from this acorn.) The Karabük works on the Black Sea, started with Soviet help and finished with British, produced indifferent steel with coal, from nearby Zonguldak, of atrocious quality, but everything was interlocking, and the system resisted liberalization on 24 January lines. Telling the workers not to have index-linked wages at a time of high inflation was very difficult indeed. Stopping strikes for a time was easy enough, as in Chile, but for how long? Initially all that happened was that the banks were freed from the restrictions hitherto prevailing. Gold was freed altogether; banks now kept four fifths of their hard-currency earnings instead of handing them to the State. It became legal to hold dollars (or Marks), and the Turkish currency was devalued, from 47 to 80 lire against the dollar; there were fourteen further devaluations up to May 1981, as the government did not bother with the exchange rate. This meant, for the banks, very easy money indeed, as you just shifted in and out of Turkish money as and when, making a huge profit if you happened to have warning that a devaluation was forthcoming. Interest rates were unnaturally high, in Turkish money, and inflation or Turkish paper-money creation tended to rise faster than the dollar. Given the world recession that continued until the turn of 1982–3, the liberalization in Turkey was not an easy matter, and the money that it generated, given the odd combination of liberalization and restriction, produced profiteers and Ponzi (pyramid) schemes. There was, in Turgut Özal, too much of the grasping provincial, and his (second) wife loved flashy jewellery; her sons were very badly spoilt. This was a Turkish (and Russian) peculiarity. In western Europe, money took four generations to move *Buddenbrooks*-fashion from four-square local dealer via business corner-cuttings and divorces to neurasthenic aesthete. In Turkey, the dynasties mostly did it in two generations.

Özal's own fingers were burnt, and he dropped out of politics for a while. Then, in time for the election of 1983, he returned (from a weight cure in the USA, where he fell to 13 stone, but no doubt also took time off to talk in Washington). Of all oddities he, standing with a permitted opposition party, ANAP or 'Motherland', now gained in popularity precisely because the generals, with their dummy parties, had had to bear the brunt of the blame for the liberalizing policies that Özal himself had introduced. Besides, the Americans regarded him as extremely useful. Their own interest was straightforward, the big base at İncirlik, on the edges of Iran, Iraq and Syria, with a network of listening posts and small garrisons stretching from Sinop on the Black Sea through Diyarbakır on the Tigris. When the Russians went into Afghanistan, the Americans found themselves in alliance with Islam, and, in Turkey, Özal had his links in that quarter (as indeed had Menderes before him, also, for much of the time, the Americans' man). In 1983 there was an election, and ANAP swept in. Boom ensued. The gamble on exports was a success, as they doubled (to $6bn) between 1980 and 1986; for the first time, Turkey became a part of the world economy, selling manufactures rather than just raw materials. Money poured into Istanbul, especially, and the growth rate also doubled (to 7 per cent in industry).

But there was at the heart of it all a great problem. Özal's regime was based mainly on relatively upstart Istanbul (or İzmir) money, and provincial Anatolia was also coming into the picture (places such as his own Malatya, and more especially Antep). The men who emerged in such places were generally pious, though in a rather lazy and not consistent way, and under the generals of 1980 Islam made much progress. It was helpful against Marxism, or at any rate might counter the role of so many Alevis, heretical and easily secularized, on the Left. In the seventies, the observation of Ramazan, the fasting month, when nothing – not a cigarette, not a drop even of water – had been supposed to pass the lips, sunrise to sunset, had not been much observed: how, in a hot month, in a proper job in a city, could that fail to turn people into murderous vegetables? Now, its observance grew. In the two decades after the 1980 coup Turkey became in some degree desecularized, and even in the very centre of Istanbul, the *ezan*, the five-times-a-day call to prayer, resounded, microphones turned up. In Galata the techno-music stopped somewhere around 3 a.m. and then, with dawn coming up over the Bosphorus, the first (from his accent, Kurdish) *muezzin* cleared his throat very audibly in the Ağa Cami near the Galata Tower, and charged full-tilt, followed by ten others, for a good hour. Of course, these things were not as intended by the military in 1980, and one of them, driven to distraction by the waking of his small child, finally shot a megaphone, but they had opened the door, to their subsequent regret.

One particular set of measures did considerable damage to the country's public image. The generals had become enraged with the leadership of the universities. Decree 1402 after the coup allowed dismissals and there were some forty, who made a noise; beyond that, some 15,000 fled abroad, there to spread news of the Pinochets' taking over of the country (ten or more years later, they were looking foolish, and many returned). The fact was that the universities had often become ungovernable, or at any rate were not controlled. Now, a Higher Education Council was set up, with strict control of appointments, and İhsan Doğramacı ran it. He set up the first of the private universities in what might be called the European space, Bilkent (it means 'science park'). Doğramacı was an organizer of genius. He had studied the American system, because the old European (and Turkish) system had been failing. That failure was obvious, everywhere. The State took on too much, expanded the number of students, jerry-built horrible buildings; educational reforms meant that the students were less and less well-prepared (in England, spelling became a problem) and inflation then impoverished everyone and everything. The American system was better prepared to resist these developments, and Bilkent was stamped out of the ground as a private university. Doğramacı (originally a paediatrician, from a grand Ottoman-Iraqi family) took a long view. A university enriched its surroundings, such that people would want to live within the area, driving up property prices. He therefore took over some barren land south-west of Ankara (there were still wolves on the campus, ten years on), and developed a partnership with two banks and a construction company, Tepe Holding. The State gave the water and electricity (and grants for research, mainly scientific), and the companies' profits went into the endowment. The other third of the income came from fees. As Istanbul and İzmir flourished in the middle and later eighties, parents were prepared to pay $10,000 in tuition fees provided their children got a decent education. That meant good English, and there was already a critical mass of Turks to adapt to that. The weight was on the natural sciences, and good connections opened up with the United States, but there were also schools for business and tourism, for which, again, parents were prepared to pay. As income was generated, the university could expand: the academics had very decent accommodation, and the professional classes of Ankara started moving to the housing that went up around Bilkent, complete with the services that their American equivalents would expect – a shopping mall (Real, complete with its Praktiker, a German do-it-yourself shop, and the British Marks and Spencer). Profits from it all went back into the university, which spiralled upwards. It spent more on its library than did ten British universities put together, and the internet connections were of international class. Since Bilkent was not bound by state regulations as regards salaries, it could afford to pay the academics decently, and a good half of the staff consisted either of Turks returning from the USA or of foreigners. Here was another upwards twist in the spiral: they needed a good English-language school, and the Bilkent School, again, became *the* prestige school in Ankara, taking over from the old Ankara College, where Denis Hills (and many other legendary men and women) had taught. Keeping all of this together involved a feat of organization and leadership, and İhsan Doğramacı's son, Ali, who had taught engineering at first-class places in the USA for twenty years, could keep all the balls in the air. He took over the rectorship, had charisma and intuitional judgement, and, within twenty years, put Bilkent on the world's map. It was an extraordinary performance.

İhsan Doğramacı, who had been offered senior political roles and turned them down, instead worked at the very infrastructure of the country, a sort of counter-Gramsci. He braved extreme unpopularity, deserved well of the Republic, and received the best sort of flattery, in that there are now two dozen imitations of Bilkent in Turkey, and private universities all over the European area.

America in a Turkish mirror made for a contrast with Chile. In Chile there was a general in charge, and there were no elections for ten years while Chicago economists sorted things out. Then she experienced the end of history. Turkey did not, although there was a brave try. There, the army did not want formal power: no Pinochet. It was happier with professors of Political Science, and wanted figureheads. Turhan Feyzioğlu had thought that he would be indispensable to the generals, as an old, reliable republican alternative to the wayward Ecevit. There, he was wrong: this was a military coup with a big difference. This time round, the generals had thought things through; Turkey was the front line of front-line countries; it would not do for it to be run on non-democratic lines; there would have to be a democracy, the only one for a considerable number of miles to the east, north and south. Democracy generally meant Demirel, whom the military did not want at any price. They got Özal instead. In his way, he was a sort of South Korean politician, and this was an era when South Koreas shot into worldwide prominence, more interesting and productive than assorted European Legolands where a large part of the gross domestic product consisted of divorced men's taxes, paying for other men's divorced wives to have jobs as divorce counsellors, all paying VAT. He did not believe in the State, or at any rate not the Republican, Atatürk state. Özal was the IMF's trusted man: he had served at the World Bank for two years, and worked closely with the Sabanci dynasty, where he understood directly the virtues of private enterprise (as distinct from state-dependent enterprise, the Sabancis being, on the whole, less dependent than other great enterprises) and the German government helped. As director of the employers' union, he had been quite tough. Demirel had been his original patron, though as Özal rose the relationship became tense (in 1990 Özal put up a memorial to Menderes, and Demirel, who regarded himself as rather more successful, was put out; he brought back the bones of Enver Pasha from Kirghizia as a come-back, the Democrats being children of the Young Turks).

Özal won in 1983 because he had outmanoeuvred the generals. They took the blame for the 24 January measures, and the Özal party, ANAP, counted as opposition. His reign was very Second Empire, even to the point where, at its end, *horizontales* arrived from the Soviet Union in battalions (and caused such havoc among traditional religious marriages on the Black Sea coast that a law was passed against adultery: like the Atatürk hat law, it was a declaration of intent, much criticized by humourless people). Money showered, old quarters of Istanbul were bulldozed for motorways to take fancy motor cars, and there were always the *tarikat* connections to make hand wash hand in Anatolia (in Özal's case, the Nakshibendi, who were quite open: his main Kurdish ally, Kâmran İnan, was one of their leaders, a Sheikh, with a Lausanne degree in law and a Swiss wife). Islam in Turkey was not at all dissimilar from Catholicism in Italy, and this had long, long origins. Even in mid-Byzantine times, Anna Comnena had divided the Anatolians into Greeks, barbarians and semi-barbarians, meaning the Turks. Özal was a very clever man, sitting on his exercise bike (it failed: he was huge) and zapping CNN, driving a BMW at absurd speeds, taking parades in a baseball cap and telling the generals to turn up to lunch. He was a far more interesting man than the wooden Pinochet, and moved his country forward in an extremely interesting direction. But he failed. The problem goes back to 1986, the return of inflation. Özal gave up, and was diverted, like Margaret Thatcher, into foreign policy, an entertainment not vouchsafed to Pinochet, who could get on with the job.

Özal's government did remarkably well in the first period, with a cabinet largely made up of American doctorates and engineers (the chief Treasury minister, Kaya Erdem, clearly knew his business). Currency liberalization had to be pushed through the hostile bureaucracy; its style had been to present 13,000 pages, now reduced to fifteen; it retained valuable property – large offices, summer houses, shares, gold, etc. Inflation fell back – roughly to 30 per cent – as protection came down (only 200 items being banned for import; by 1988 thirty-three needed approval, and after 1984 only three were entirely prohibited). Tariffs, wharf charges, VAT had meant that the real rate of protection stood at around 60 per cent (c.i.f.) and it had often changed. Motor cars had incurred duty of 112 per cent in 1980, 145 per cent in 1986, 74 per cent 1989. Exporters' tax rebates were accelerated, and after 1980 they were allowed to retain $40,000 and then more (earlier there had been compulsory clearing at the central bank, to pay for imports). The exchange rate itself was unified, as against the variable earlier rates, and income tax, hitherto the largest item on the revenue side, was cut from 40 to 25 per cent, and on companies to under 50 per cent, while VAT was raised at 10 per cent. Up to $3,000 could be bought per person, without restriction. Later, this was altogether freed. By 1987 income tax contributed only a quarter of income, indirect taxes one third. Parts of the country began to flourish, particularly the ultra-Western areas – Istanbul and the north-west, İzmir, some places on the south coast; there was a shift in trade towards Europe, and a growth of part-manufacture, particularly for Germany. By any index, Turkish prosperity was growing. One sign was the freedom to travel – people could now move more than once every three years, though a hundred-dollar tax remained until 1996.

However, there was much difficulty as regards the disciplines of monetarism: how could government expenditure be reduced? It was all very well to liberalize foreign trade and currency exchange: these things were vital. But what Pinochet had done in domestic matters was a different matter altogether, and here Özal was stuck; perhaps he even wanted to be stuck, because he had an excuse to channel state funds in the direction of his friends. Privatization might have been an answer, but in practice there were great problems – not least because the constitutional court kept striking down the proposals on the grounds that they were against the national interest. Public spending took a quarter of the GNP in 1980, a fifth in 1984, slightly more than that in 1987, and there was a constant deficit, 3–5 per cent of GNP, to which the State boards' deficits might be added (6 per cent). The outcome was chronic inflation. Up to 1985 the lira had fallen steadily, in fact faster in dollar terms than in domestic prices. This was, overall, healthier than the alternative which set in after 1985, when Turkey joined efforts at managed exchange rates. After 1985 domestic prices rose faster than the dollar. More paper emerged from the Turkish printing press, and it could be freely exchanged for dollars, as insurance, at a crawling-peg rate. Time deposits could be held at will and switched, after very large interest rate gains, into dollars, and the upshot for anyone with savings was a 25 per cent tax-free annual dollar profit.

The technicality was that the dollar rose from 14 lire in 1975 to 47 in 1979, 76 in 1980, 163 in 1982, 225 in 1983, 522 in 1985, 1,422 in 1988 and 2,609 in 1990 (by March 2000 it had reached 600,000, and in 2003 1.6 million). The US price index rose from 56.6 per cent of the figure for 1985, reaching 95 per cent in 1981, after which there was stabilization (by 1990, 113). From 1985 to 1990 the Turkish price index rose from 100 to 769. In other words, the Turkish currency was appreciating by roughly 25 per cent every year against the dollar. By then, about half of the Turkish money supply was in dollars (or Marks). If you had access to foreign currency you could, with sufficient agility, make substantial (and tax-free) interest. In this way the banks became lazy. There has never been an inflation quite like the Turkish one. With that level, either the currency takes off into hyperinflation, as in Latin America, or there has to be some stabilization, usually exceedingly painful and sometimes with blood on the streets. This did not happen. The technicians at the central bank were very competent, knowing how to judge interest rates and bond yields. But beyond that was always the notion that Turkey was too important to be allowed to go: the IMF would always step in (as indeed it did). But this was hardly a healthy business: inflation was a sort of hidden taxation, hitting especially the poor, and it rewarded parasitism or even straightforward criminality. The Left of Bülent Ecevit had failed in dealing with this, and so, in the event, did Özal, though his failure was much more interesting: eventually, his legacy was to be taken over by an astute Islamic party endorsed by the Americans. House prices in Istanbul at the highest level showed what vast sums of money were available, in a country whose nominal GDP per head was at least in theory of Third World type.

In effect there were two or perhaps even four economies at work in the Özal era, apart from the criminal (drugs-related) one. Exports did very well indeed with the reduction of corporation tax and tariffs. They accounted for one fifth of GNP in 1989, more than double what they had been ten years before, and considerably more suitable for a country without oil. Export earnings grew at almost 20 per cent annually, from 1980 to 1988, which was all the more remarkable as world trade slowed in the early part of that period. Their character also changed. In 1976, agriculture had accounted for two thirds (just over a billion dollars) but by 1989 18 per cent ($2.1bn). Industrial exports rose from one third ($600 million) to four fifths ($9bn) and manufactures accounted for nearly all of this, as distinct from half-finished items. Textiles accounted for half, followed by chemicals and then steel, of which Turkey had hardly supported any in the 1970s, despite the enormous Karabük plant. Now, Turkey's exports were worth $1.5bn, an astonishing feat, given where she had started from. There was also a change of direction. The Middle East took more, in volume, but much less, in proportion; OECD countries, and especially Germany, now took two thirds of the exports. It became quite common for representatives of Turkish businesses to travel the world, probing markets – not a feature seen by the world since the later sixteenth century. Turkey could now, at least on economic grounds, advance her candidacy of the European Common Market which had been tabled as early as 1963; Europe in 1981 had accounted for about a quarter of trade, but by 1995 well over half ($28bn). In fact she weighed more than all other candidate countries put together, and then some. The same had of course occurred elsewhere, especially with Japan, in the fifties, and South Korea and Taiwan in the sixties. Was Turkey now catching up, and why had it taken her so long? The short answer was: other 'miracles' had had an American occupation. Turkey had a semi-demi American occupation, and Özal was its symbol. Overall it had been a great success, but the price was debt – the international one rising from $13.5bn to $40bn, interest on which took 70 per cent of export earnings. By 1997 the World Trade Organization was optimistic about Turkey – noting that exports had grown by 11 per cent per annum as against a general 7 per cent. The Istanbul stock exchange, trading $300m every day, was among the top four of the 'emerging' ones; imports at $67bn, and exports at $57bn (including the estimated $10bn–15bn to Russia) were creditable, especially in the light of Turkey's past. The Bosphorus was three times busier than the Suez Canal.

Americanization was the watchword, and not one greatly liked by the old republican establishment. It stood for a sort of Turkish sixties, and in not dissimilar circumstances – in 1980, 60 per cent of Turks had lived on the land, and there was then a great flight, as happened a generation before in Italy or Spain – and it happened at every level. There was insider dealing in politics, and Özal's own family was involved. The Emlak Bank would make loans, its manager taking part of the proceeds, where no other bank would have lent; eleven state banks gave out loans that no private bank could have contemplated. In the cities there was illegal building, some of it of such poor quality that it collapsed in earthquakes that left stoutly built housing blocks unimpaired. Özal just waved such corruption aside: to him, as to others of his way of thinking, it was less expensive than honest but idiotic state wastage. But the Westernization of Turkey went ahead in other ways. Students went to the West in great numbers – 25,000 to the USA. On the military and scientific level, the co-operation was intense: in Britain and the USA there was a substantial Turkish professional emigration, whereas in continental Europe 'the Turks' were, on the whole, of rural origin.

Private business might flourish, but much of the economy was still in the hands of the State. This was the same unhappy business as elsewhere – 2 million workers retiring early and underproducing, in factories varying in output from steel to pickles. Public enterprises undertook about a third of manufacturing. The State owned over half of the usable land, i.e. excluding mountain and forest, and there were a million farms and small plots, many simply squatted. The army owned almost one fifth of Ankara (often distinguished by tree-planting, sign of a military presence), and there was famous clientelism at work, with soft loans. Özal himself believed in privatization but this was difficult – it even constituted a vicious circle. There was not enough capital in Turkey; it could only come from abroad; but because of inflation, and perhaps also opaque business practices, this would not happen until finances had been stabilized, which could only happen through privatization. Otherwise the budget deficit just went on and on, worsening in 1986 when ANAP spent money for the election (in which its vote fell to one third, although this meant two thirds of the seats). Privatization did not happen – or at any rate only on a small scale (under $3 bn in eleven years). Meanwhile, state managers became demoralized; there was not much investment (and the railways especially suffered, though the resulting lengthy journeys could be romantically old-fashioned). The Zonguldak mines (employing 30,000 people) would have cost less had they simply been closed down; meanwhile, foreign investment banks for some time made fortunes out of advice to then naïve Turks, and nothing much followed. Özal's one real contribution was a build-operate-transfer system for capital projects, by which foreigners could make their profit for some years before transferring the project to the State (as happened with the Bosphorus Bridge).

The Özal years split the country. The foreign trade element had done enormously well, and continued to do so; and this was far from being just a matter for Istanbul and İzmir, as there were places far to the east, such as Antep, that were lifted off, and the new motorways through Kayseri, the chief town of Cappadocia, to the east and south became arteries of European trade. The perennial question, as to whether Turkey could become a member of the European Union, was debated endlessly at ministry level, but it was in effect being settled by voting with feet, or at any rate wheels. Maslak, where once, during the Crimean War, the French army had trained on the European shore of the Bosphorus, saw one Manhattan-ish skyscraper rise after another, and the multinational hotels also built. It meant the ruin of parts of the city, an especially scandalous instance being the destruction of the old Park Hotel, next to the former German embassy in Gümüşsuyu. It had been a Pasha's house, had been turned into a grand hotel, and in its place half of a gruesome car park went up until it was stopped. The counterpart was that, as the money poured in, so did migrants. The city became, like Mexico City, a megalopolis, and although old Stambul survived, it was squashed in with concrete or clapboard suburbs, each taken over by a region in the east. It was a demonstration of the trickle-down effect, in that the crumbs from the tables of Maslak rolled down into Sütlüce, and the parking arrangements of Galata were taken over by a Kurdish mob from Bitlis, near Lake Van.

The later years of Özal have a shadowy resemblance to the later years of Margaret Thatcher, when the machine ran beyond the monetarist desert and entered upon richer and much more intractable soil. The real parallel for this is Italy, in the Christian Democrats' blue period: a veneer of piety, and the sound of the till. 'Social control' was maintained by Islam, but the ANAP itself split, on religious matters: at a conference, the culture minister even fought a very large minister of state as to whether the Aya Sofya should become a mosque again. Özal, putting in his wife as chairman of the Istanbul branch, distanced himself from the *kutsal ittifak* element, the 'holy alliance'. There had always been an element of Islam to the Özal mixture, and it some-times seemed to be taking over – for instance, in 1988–9 the old ques-tion, whether women should be allowed to wear head-coverings in universities, came up, a matter of vast symbolic importance that Özal himself preferred not to take up: he said, just leave the question alone, dealing with it is for later. His supporters wanted their girls to be virgins when married, and (in theory) thought drink the mother of all evils. There was another side to this, perhaps Iranian in origin: secu-larists were assassinated, and even Moslem modernizers. By 1989 the ANAP was down to one fifth of the vote in local elections, Inönü's (renamed) SPP taking nearly one third; the ANAP majority was now artificial. By 1991 new elections put Demirel ahead of ANAP by under a quarter, and bizarrely he struck up an alliance with another old dispossessed party, the SPP ('Socialist' etc.), now renamed Repub-lican (CHP), and this introduced a period of political kaleidoscopes, governments of various coalitions succeeding each other until 2002, when a sort of Islamicized (and American-leaning) version of ANAP appeared, as the Justice and Development Party. Özal had really failed with the resumption of inflation in 1986, and the clash of the external and internal economies. The same had happened with Margaret Thatcher, and, like her, he now made his reputation in foreign affairs. However, Turkey had some real weight, not least as the only Moslem country in the world, apart from Jordan, with serious credentials (as a wise historian, Hasan Ali Karasar, remarked, 'Islam, politics, economics – choose two'). How would she use it? The most imaginative answer would have been the annexation of northern Iraq, on the lines of the National Pact that had been pushed by Mustafa Kemal sixty years earlier.

Iraq came up. Saddam Hussein was possessed of megalomania, and the country that he ran, an artificial creation from the First World War, contained dissident elements, held together by oil money. He stood between Turkey and Iran, which, run by megalomaniacs, was Shia, from a branch of Islam so different as almost to constitute a different religion. The key factor was that, in northern Iraq, there were Kurds. That opened up, for Turkey, an enormous problem, the greatest that she had had to deal with. The Kurds are a people who never took off as a nation. There are perhaps 25 million of them, spread over Iran, Iraq, Syria and Turkey, where they formed the bulk of the population of the south-east, bordering Iraq. Kurdish, like Iranian or Hindi, is an Indo-European language, and some of the words are recognizable to a western European ('new' is *nu*; 'me' is *min*; 'two' is *du*; 'four' is *char*, cf. French *quatre*; 'valley' is *dal*, cf. German *Tal*; and the grammar is fairly familiar). In Xenophon's *Anabasis* people called *Curtaroi* are mentioned. His 10,000 Greek mercenaries, unpaid, unwept and unsung, were finding their way back home from fifth-century BC Persia, came to a river in some mountains, and found *Curtaroi* offering attitude on the opposite bank. They wondered what to do, encamped. Next morning, they found the *Curtaroi* engaged in fisticuffs, and crept past towards the sea. Nearly two millennia later, at the time of the Crusades, the Arabic *Ekrad* (plural for 'Kurd') were well-documented as mountain warriors, of whom the great Saladin was one ('Selahattin' in Turkey is generally a Kurdish name). But they were split up over various states, and the language was never standardized. It has divided into several variants, and though a specialist can recognize what is being said, people on the ground have to communicate in Turkish or Arabic once they leave their home area. There were historical differences noticeable even in the sixteenth century, as Kurdish emirates fought; and there was even rivalry between the two chief Moslem brotherhoods of the area, the Kadiri and Nakshibendi.

One of the chief Kurdish elements in Iraq, the Behdinandi, simply refused, under the British Mandate, to use the Sorani Kurdish that was expected, and preferred Arabic. The outstanding pioneers of these matters were Russian and British, in this case D. N. McKenzie. In Turkey the chief Kurdish language is called Kırmanç, but it is split into dialects (Dimili) and there is another version, possibly a different language altogether, called Zaza. There are theories to the effect that the Zaza-speaking Kurds are not even of Kurdish origin. Some may even have been Armenian, and when the Turkish army found PKK – Kurdistan Workers' Party – corpses, these were sometimes not circumcised. At any rate, regardless of the linguistic divisions, many Kurdish parents did not want their children educated in anything other than Turkish, so that they would get on in life. In Van, in the 1960s, there was the moving sight of young men studying in the street lights, with a view to just getting on. Most did: there was intermarriage, and, whatever was said about the Kurdish question later on, most Kurds voted for ordinary Turkish parties and, if they went into politics, shot up that tree. Turkey was simply so far above Iraq or Iran in terms of interest and development that no Kurd in his senses would have wanted to live anywhere else. However, something went badly wrong. A terrorist movement, the PKK, developed, and made the running for the latter part of Özal's reign.

The Turkish government and army were blamed for this, but it was simply not an easy question, and the Kurds themselves did not know what the answer was. In the end, this had to do with a more general failure, that of the Turkish Left. It had had its chance in the 1960s, and it was even not far from power in the 1970s, when Ecevit ran things. However, it did not know what to do with the Kurds, regarding them as a weird amalgam of Armenians and gypsies. It did not help that Kurdish society (many parts were much less than that whole) was significantly different, in that Şafi Islam reigned, harsher than the Turks' Sunni version. Ordinary Kurds (there were many extraordinary Kurds) behaved differently towards women, especially, who did not rate very highly: polygamy went on, though given religious rather than legal sanction, and there was a great demographic problem. This imposed a terrible strain on every sort of infrastructure, and matters were again complicated because the south-east of Turkey worked by dry agriculture. The State had responded with a scheme for great dams to divert the water of the two biblical rivers, the Euphrates and the Tigris, towards irrigation and hydro-electricity, but this would take time, and in any case the profits went towards the tribal chiefs, the *Agas*, who mainly ran affairs in these parts, clan-fashion. The Turkish Left were no good at these matters, and bear some responsibility for the troubles that followed. Sprigs of Istanbul grandee families, Henri Barkey or Çağlar Keyder, thinking beardedly about their own local version of *Eighteenth Brumaire* and looking to jobs in America, could hardly be bothered, at the Ankara School of Political Science, with some hairy peasant from Siverek called Abdullah Öcalan.

Öcalan was a megalomaniac, given to comparing himself with Mao and Lenin. His family background was not entirely unlike Stalin's, in that he had a weak, henpecked (*sılık*) father and a bossy (Turkish) mother. His first enthusiasms (like Stalin's) were religious. His first intention was to work in the State, but as a student he encountered Kurdish nationalism. This had complicated origins. There had always been uprisings by Kurds against the State but they did not have a nationalist side until late in the day. There was no doubt a vague idea of Kurdishness, but the realities were religious and tribal. The Republic, declared in 1923, was secular, and the last Caliph was dismissed in 1924. In 1925, and again in the 1930s, there were Kurdish uprisings, the last one (in Dersim, from 1936 to 1938) put down with much harshness. On all occasions, the State used tribes against each other – they had fought all along, whether over access to water, or over some hereditary grievance such as sheep-stealing, and in any case some were strictly Moslem, adhering to the *Şafi* version of Islamic law, which required its adepts to perform ritual ablutions if they had been in the same room as a foreigner or a woman, while others were Alevi. By the later sixties, Kurdish banners figured in student demonstrations. In 1969 'eastern revolutionary cultural hearths' were set up in Kurdish towns, but after the coup of 12 March 1971 the organizers fled to Europe.

Öcalan went on to a surveyors' school and then the department of Political Science at Ankara University, which had been a training ground for the bureaucratic elite of republican Turkey (it was called Mülkiye, after an Ottoman equivalent, but the original inspiration had been the modernizing École des Sciences Politiques in Third Republican France, also a country that took a very robust view of peasant dialects). As the university civil war of that period got under way, he was associated with the Left (and spent seven months in prison after the coup of 1971) and took up with his Krupskaya, Kesire Yıldırım; but no-one remembered anything much about him. The university Left, usually products of the professional class and as likely as not to regard themselves as way above village Kurds with a background in surveying, probably played its part in driving him towards Kurdish nationalism. They seem to have regarded him as a possible police agent as he talked 'in a very gauche [*toy*] way' about a Kurdish state, and the Turkish Left hardly bothered to include Kurdish banderoles.

The custom, at that time, was for small student groups to gather at the Çubuk reservoir park outside Ankara, where families might go for excursions at weekends – reservoir parks, as with Rooken Glen outside Glasgow, being a hallmark of progressive towns, but in this case out of sight of the police. There, on 21 March 1973, the PKK appears to have been founded, although its formal establishment came a few years later, in a village of Lice district, in the south-east, in Diyarbakır province, on 27 November 1978. Before this, Öcalan sent off representatives to the Kurdish east, there to spread the word, and setting up assorted protection rackets. For this, they used the grievances of one tribe against another, such as, for instance, the government's grants of agricultural machinery to one rather than another – in this case, on the Syrian border, the Süleyman and Paydaş clans, respectively for and against the government.

PKK propaganda is entirely predictable, written in wooden language, and based on the analysis of almost any Third World Communist movement of the era. There is 'imperialism'. It has local supporters, the 'comprador class', among the bourgeoisie of the State; in the particular locality there is 'feudalism', in this case the Kurdish tribal leaders and their hangers-on. Women are oppressed. Religion is regarded as part of the oppression. There are rivals on the Left, but they are potentially treacherous – they might just come to terms with 'imperialism' or at any rate show no sympathy for the cause of national liberation. The Turkish Left, in this case, was dismissed as 'social chauvinism', another well-worn phrase (it went back to the 1920s) – 'feudal petty bourgeois and children of family', meaning Henri Barkey and Çağlar Keyder. And now, in 1978, came the 'First Congress' of what is almost the last National Liberation Front of the old school and this time round there were Palestinian (and Bulgarian) connections. Öcalan's outfit elected its central committee, its organizational and political bureaux, and had its officials for media affairs, military affairs, etc. The name was now changed to 'PKK' and its manifesto was issued. It invoked a version of Kurdish history, going back to the Medes, and emphasized the Indo-European as against Turkic origins of the people; it talked of 'Turkish capitalism' in the 1960s, referring to *toprak ağaları* ('landowners') *ve kompradorları*, and developed a version of the Vietcong programme, for a 'national democratic revolution' in which the 'working classes' would take the lead; these, it was claimed, were emerging from the peasantry; the enemies were 'feudal, comprador exploitation, tribalism, religiosity [*mezhepalık*] and the slave-like dependence of women'.

Here are Dostoyevsky's *Demons*: a gathering of perhaps two dozen people, most of them vaguely educated (Selim Çürükkaya, an interesting defector, says he was very impressed by Öcalan's reading: he himself had struggled up from a village, and Alevi-Kurdish, Zaza-speaking, background, and had managed to graduate from sheep-watching to a high school at Mersin on the south coast; another was a schoolteacher of Laz background, i.e. Moslem Georgian, from the Black Sea coast). Of the original members, seven were killed on Öcalan's orders as 'agents', five fled, and were denounced as traitors, and another five, though not classed as traitors, were downgraded. Two committed suicide, and another was murdered by a rival group in northern Iraq. Öcalan's own wife fled, with another of the originals, and set up a rival PKK ('Vejin', though, here, for translation, the Indo-European is not helpful) in Paris. The first action occurred in July 1979, at Kırbaşı, a village in Hilvan. The area was run by a tribal chief, Mehmet Celal Bucak, who was also deputy, for the Justice Party, of Siverek. The PKK's strategy – following the Maoist one – was to ally with one tribe against another; the Bucaks, strong in the Urfa region, were at odds with the Türks. The PKK blamed 'feudalism' for the plight of the Kurds, and decided to make an example. In the event, they attacked a Bucak during an *iftar*, the fast-breaking dinner celebrated in Ramazan, and wounded the chief, though they also killed a maid and a small boy. The main activity thereafter was partly to fight the Turkish Left, but also to levy a tribute on the timber trade of a government minister. At the turn of 1979–80, as the military stepped up arrests, Öcalan became alarmed, and before the coup of 12 September 1980 he moved to Syria. At this point the PKK became heavily involved in the politics of the Middle East.

In fact his style became very much that of a Middle East dictator. The truth was that Öcalan himself despised the Kurds as *zavallı*, 'poor mutts', who could only be kept in place by Stalinist methods. In 1980, established in Syria, he took up links with one of the two large Kurdish factions in Iraq, Celal Talebani's PUK, based on the Iranian side (and using its own language), and he opened up a training camp in the Bekaa valley in Lebanon, copying his ways from the PLO. Its attitudinizing leader, Yasser Arafat, had been allowed to address even the United Nations, generously conceding that he would deposit his revolver on the lectern as distinct from leaving it in its holster. Kurds: Palestinians? For Turks and most Kurds, unimaginable, but how should the problem be dealt with? Games were then played, the basic reality being that the Kurds moved in hundreds of thousands to western and central Turkey, and became assimilated. But the south-east remained a problem.

The Turkish state operated an alliance, never entirely reliable, with the other Iraqi Kurdish group, Mustafa Barzani's PDK – Kurdistan Democratic Party – and four-cornered fighting might then develop; there were also problems, from time to time, with the Syrians, who sometimes opposed Saddam Hussein, with whom the PKK had, on the whole, good relations. In this atmosphere, Öcalan built up his own cult of personality, and ran affairs very strictly. One former close associate, Selim Çürükkaya, defected in the end, and wrote memoirs. He had come from a village, struggled up to the teachers' training school at Tunceli, and spent eleven years in prison, there organizing hunger strikes. Then he was smuggled out, via Greece and Serbia, to Öcalan's camp – the 'Mahsun Korkmaz Military Academy', where there was much marching about by young women in camouflage suits and boots. His estranged wife was there, and she had turned into a Rosa Klebb: she ticked him off for smoking, saying that no-one smoked when the Leader was present; she even ticked him off for crossing his legs, such informality being an offence against discipline. The camp was full of informers, and it had its own prison. The place was, generally, run by men who, in Turkish prisons, had not 'resisted', as Selim Çürükkaya claimed he had done, but had obeyed orders (a small version of the problems that arose in the satellite European countries after 1945, between Communists who had spent their time in Moscow and Communists who had been part of the anti-Nazi resistance movements). Öcalan himself was puritanical in sexual matters, though he did surround himself with a little group of fanaticized young women; the camp even had its own Orwellian language, imprisonment being called *uygulama* or 'treatment', and there were provisions for self-criticism sessions, with detailed questionnaires being served on people who had emerged from prison, as to their conduct before and during the imprisonment. There was even a version of the witch-hunt against Trotskyists in the Stalin era – one Mahmut Şener, then exiled in Germany. There was a grotesque leadership cult, Öcalan issuing a sort of catechism, comparing himself with the Mahdi, with evocations, in the Party Central School, of 'The way of life of *Apo*, the way of work of *Apo*, the way of striking [enemies] of *Apo*'; after grandly named congresses ('Congress of Victory') there would be purges and liquidations. *Apo* was supposed, in Turkish, to mean 'Daddy', but it was also the name for the German terrorists of the seventies, *Ausserparlamentarische Opposition* ('non-parliamentary opposition'), and the PKK's prose was very Germanic.

The PKK learned its tactics from a school that, by 1984, was already quite venerable. It had a political wing, ERNK, which took twelve of the sixty-five seats in the exile parliament, a dummy body which reflected the Greek Communists' ways in the Second World War, of ELAS/ETAM. But there were other instances. Mao Tse-tung had matched his Communist guerrillas with village politics, and

General Vo Nguyen Giap in Vietnam had famously succeeded by similar methods. In the case of the PKK, tribal politics had a similar part, but this time there was a different element, in that small-town intelligentsia were recruited. Schoolteachers, emerging from the peasantry, had had a role in terrorism as far back as the Russian anarchists and the Armenians who had learned from them. The argument was that atrocity would cause counter-atrocity. The Turkish authorities would overreact against simple villagers, whose sympathies would then be with the rebels. Later, in the 1990s, there was also forced recruitment of boys and young men, just as had happened in the Greek civil war, who could be made to take the blame for an atrocity. It often happened that, upon capture by the army, they would spend time in Diyarbakır prison or elsewhere. There, they would receive lessons in Marxism. This had been a device of Balkan Communists between the wars, and, both in Greece and in Yugoslavia in the early thirties, the Communists took a fifth and more of the vote. In Greece, for instance, they took votes from the Macedonian minority, from the dock workers of Salonica, from the tobacco-growers of Thrace and from children of the refugees who had arrived from Anatolia. Add the sons of some rich and educated families, and you have a model for the Communism of the whole area. A great book, *Eleni*, describing how, in a village in north-western Greece, the locals could be made far more radical than they might otherwise have been, is the prototype and, curiously enough, after Orthodox services in Greece collections would solemnly be taken to buy rockets for the PKK. Its managers had learned from earlier practices, and they behaved atrociously. In 1985, in a village of Çatak district in Van, they killed a man and his two baby daughters, and then poured paraffin on the house to burn it down, with the wife and two children, of eight and ten. In February 1987, using Turkish uniforms as camouflage, they shot up four houses, in Şırnak, when the villagers guessed who they were, the women and children fleeing. Road ambushes, even stopping local trains, were frequent enough in Bingöl and Bitlis, the travellers being killed with Kalashnikovs. Another speciality became economic targets – the ferro-chrome works and their clerks. Obviously, from the PKK point of view, the more

economic distress, the better. Another method was to prevent education by the simple enough device of shooting schoolteachers – over
one hundred. In April 1990, in a village near Elazığ, they attacked a
primary school, roped in the teachers' wives and children, and shut
them up in the headmaster's room. Then they killed a teacher. His
wife, pregnant, was spared, but when she said that she did not want
to survive, they obliged. There was another element. In accordance
with Kurdish ways, young men were married off very early, produced
two or three children, did their military service, took a second wife,
and then a third one. The boys of the first marriage found their mother
last in the queue, old before her time; children of the more prosperous
years were favoured. According to Turkish military intelligence, the
PKK recruited such boys. Of these, there were many. Naturally, local
poverty helped the PKK, which then perpetuated it – shooting up
chicken farms, for instance.

The State responded as it had done since the first Kurdish rebellion
in 1925, nominating 'village guards', who were given weaponry. These
tactics were dangerous, in that the guards themselves might hand over
the weaponry, and the PKK specifically attacked them – sometimes
wiping out entire families or even villages. The army could hardly
defend each and every mountain hamlet, and in the later 1980s it was
outmanoeuvred: in much of the south-east, the PKK controlled roads
as soon as night fell, and it took the military some time to work out
proper tactics. These were harsh – the forced evacuation of hamlets,
the population being despatched to towns, especially Diyarbakır,
which doubled and trebled in size, with hastily erected tower blocks
and tent cities. Foreign journalists, seeing the resultant overcrowding
and misery, blamed the Turkish state, and its officials, in turn, were
sometimes clumsy in handling this – expelling critics or even putting
them on trial. Martyrs were created. The wife of the mayor of
Diyarbakır, Leyla Zana, demonstrated upon taking the oath in parliament: she used Kurdish and created an uproar (though she went on
to take the oath formally in Turkish). She received an eleven-year
sentence, and the European parliament took up her cause. All of this
allowed the PKK to make the running when it came to propaganda

in foreign countries, particularly in Germany (which tolerated the PKK networks), France (where an Institut kurde was set up) and Belgium, which stood host to a Kurdish parliament in exile that was in effect controlled by Apo (though in the end he worked against it). In Sweden there was an ostensibly enlightened policy, of allowing immigrant children education in their own languages. Absurd preaching teams from Sweden then arrived in south-eastern Turkey, with a view to standardizing Kurdish, in a country where basic textbooks were lacking.

But there was also an ostensibly non-terrorist Kurdish political element, which gained parliamentary representation in the early 1990s when it struck an electoral pact with a left-wing party. It itself was promoted by the leader of the Türk tribe, Ahmet, using the tribal patronage machine as his brothers had earlier (1967) been involved with the Republican or Justice Party, depending upon the swings of local patronage. Twenty-four members of the ruling family had been killed in vendettas, and Ahmet Türk was himself imprisoned on suspicion of concealing a member of the PKK. However, he resurfaced as a purportedly moderate, culturally oriented, would-be politician. Through a political group that called itself variously 'People's Democratic Party' or 'Democratic People's Party', demands ostensibly of a purely cultural nature could be advanced – arguments for education in Kurdish, for instance, which appeared to be entirely reasonable but in practice would have required the creation of a standardized Kurdish with a far bigger vocabulary, i.e. almost the same creative effort for a Kurdish State that had gone into the making of the Turkish Republic itself. Why, thought most Turks and Kurds, bother? The party operated summer schools in Romania. There was a further problem, in that a good part of the Kurdish population of the southeast was strongly religious, and there was fighting between militant Islamic groups and the PKK, which was, at least in the first decade, very strongly secular, and dedicated to the emancipation of women. One prominent Kurd, Abdülmelik Fırat, grandson of Sheikh Said, might have served as overall spokesman for the cause, but the secularism of the PKK put him off. In the later 1990s the Turkish Kurds in the south-east divided between nationalists, with PKK connections of this or that depth, and Islamists; elsewhere in Turkey their votes simply went to the existing Turkish parties. In all of this, Greece was well to the fore. There were training camps on Greek soil, and Greece was the favoured place for PKK people to be smuggled through, via Belgrade, to Syria. Rich businessmen, army officers and politicians all took a hand and in the end Öcalan was kidnapped by Turkish military intelligence from the Greek embassy in Kenya. Western Europe played its part. The Kurdish cause was taken up by some French people, including Danielle Mitterrand, in 1989, in connection with the revolutionary bicentennial. In Italy the Communist network could be used, as was shown when Öcalan in 1998 was forced out of Syria and tried to find refuge among allies in Italy, the government of which, for a time, was craven and would not expel him, despite Interpol most-urgent arrest warrants. There was an element of smuggling of people and of drugs into western Europe which made the PKK merge with existing criminal networks, and a constant barrage of propaganda put the Turks on the defensive. They themselves did try manfully to respond to such Western criticism. For instance, one result of the film *Midnight Express* was for Turkish prisons to be run on liberal, reformist lines, the prisoners assembling, running much of their own life, and equipped ultimately with e-mails or cellular telephones. In the outcome, they became little Marxist universities. Eventually, the authorities felt strong enough to decree a change of regime, with single cells, where prisoners could not be intimidated. There followed hunger strikes by people whom the terrorists simply nominated. Later, as the cause became more desperate, there was a similar attempt at suicide-bombings, and various girls would again be nominated to pretend to be pregnant, and then blow themselves up against a state target. These were not in fact successful – the girls lost their nerve, blew themselves up in the wrong place, or simply could not go along with it. Of a dozen suicide bombings, only two succeeded. There had been a moment, in the early 1990s, when Turgut Özal appeared to be suggesting some sort of Turkish–Kurdish confederal arrangement and there was even a long wrangle in the cabinet, when the *éminence grise* of Turkish politics, Kamran İnan, himself of prominent Kurdish origin (he was related to the Bucaks), argued the cause. Özal's suggestion, if in fact it was seriously advanced, was very unpopular. But it would have been a good thing.

For Turks, and great numbers of Kurds, the answer was assimilation in Turkey. This was very far from senseless, but the bad feeling that had developed since the 1960s was difficult to overcome. For Turkey there appeared to be two solutions – one, the assimilation of millions of Kurds in the more prosperous west and south; two, the advance of the GAP project, the bringing of water and hydro-electricity, on an enormous scale, to south-eastern Turkey, through a project of endless dams and hydro-electrical works, to bring prosperity and hope to an area beset by dry agriculture, a demographic nightmare, and endless throwing away of rubbish. A whole team of social engineers was attached to this project, to bring education to the children and enlightenment to the women, to remind them that polygamy and chadors (the word means 'tent') did not have to be their lot in life. Which would win: Kurdish nationalism, or a modern Turkey, following the European patterns? Özal's success was to make Turkey prosperous enough for this problem to have a worldwide dimension. His failure was not to see it through, with a strategy. And that was the verdict on the eighties as a whole.

26

Chichikov

What *was* Moscow to make of 1983? Three things were clear enough. The economic crisis in the West had not proved deadly, for a start: quite to the contrary, the eighties boom was under way, and the most interesting Russian comment was a question, why, with an education system five times better, do we have an economy five times worse (a question still not answered: perhaps the answer is that real mathematicians are not interested in arithmetic). Then again, there was China, which, having made an enormous and murderous mess of her version of War Communism, was now flourishing mightily with her version of the New Economic Policy. Finally there was the Middle East and its oil. Blundering into a quagmire in Afghanistan, the USSR had lost all around, and her out-stations in the Third World were liabilities.

But so too were the satellites in eastern Europe. None of these countries was an asset, and the exports of Comecon, put together, amounted to about two thirds of Mexico's. They took Soviet oil on cheap terms, and in public relations terms were headaches. The worst case was Poland's. Historically, the relationship had been a poisonous one, of bullying and self-pity, a sort of permanent *vierge folle* and *époux infernal*. Rousseau had told the Poles: you cannot stop them from swallowing you; make sure they cannot digest you. Balzac had offered different advice: get on with practical life and make yourselves indispensable to the Russians. The Poles in a sense did both, because they did develop a first-rate intelligentsia, but instead of being loyal Communists, or even, like Czechs or Slovenes, just progressives of the sort that Communists could use, they marched off in a different direction altogether and produced the most vibrant political Catholicism in the world. Frenchmen, trained from earliest infancy in anti-clericalism, could not believe the crowds they saw in Poland welcoming the Pope. 'Like the Ayatollah,' sniffed one of those Frenchmen.

There were great differences between Poland and the other 'bloc' countries. In the first place she had a 'mass of manoeuvre', a population coming on for 40 million, and still, in the 1960s, expanding, and that because of a second considerable difference: a large peasant population, still set in the old days, with hay-carts trundling along on the roads. That in turn reflected another great difference, that the Western Allies had had some sort of formal rights as regards Poland, and even Stalin shrank from applying the full-scale Soviet formula there. Some version of due process had to be gone through, and collectivization of agriculture, the expropriation of private peasant plots, would have excited resistance. A consequence of all this was that the Catholic Church remained powerful – much more so than in Hungary, where there was a strong Protestant tradition, or Czechoslovakia, where anti-clericalism was also strong. Poland was different.

The Communists after the war had attempted 'modernization', the development of big industry, and, in the areas taken from Germany, that was not unpromising. There already was substantial enough mining, and a steel industry was built up. The old Kattowitz – Katowice – was a grim nineteenth-century barracks of a town, and it now acquired a Communist overlay. An enormous stadium was put up in the centre, as an open challenge to the Church that would otherwise have dominated the area. In Cracow, which was very Catholic and proper, a gigantic steelworks, Nowa Huta, went up, and the general idea was that with sport, women's emancipation and a healthy proletarian work-day rather than mindless peasant agriculture, a new Polish version of 'Soviet man' would emerge. But the early, Stalinist, programme was carried through by a small group of mainly Jewish Communists, and they were broken when Khrushchev denounced Stalin in 1956.

A 'native Communism' took their place, under Władysław Gomułka, himself to a limited extent their victim, and he was prepared to co-operate with the Church and the peasants, and the intelligentsia as well, on the understanding that, with 'modernization', matters would go his way. This did not happen: on the contrary, the intelligentsia resented the censorship, and encouraged student revolts. The regime fought back, identifying the Jewish origins of many of the people involved, and drove some of them out. A characteristic victim of that moment (1968) was Leszek Kołakowski. Interwar Poland had crashed, especially with the failure of the Warsaw Uprising against the Nazis in 1944, and a good part of the intelligentsia, seeing the Red Army coming in, became, if not Communist, then at least sympathizers. It was a version of a fairly old Warsaw problem: Russia, whatever her appalling features, worked, and Poland, whatever her admirable ones, did not. Kołakowski, philosopher and historian of ideas, went along, and even helped falsify electoral returns in 1946: why bother accurately recording the votes of the Polish peasantry, obstinate clowns (the original of 'clown' is a Dutch word meaning 'peasant') and boors (ditto). A sojourn in Moscow caused some shock; but he was an enthusiastic supporter of Gomułka and the promise of a new Poland. Then the 1960s brought disillusion. He wanted to answer the central question of why reform Communism was not working. This was not a subject that he could openly address. He therefore addressed it in ingenious disguise: in *Religious Inspiration and Church Link* he wrote what purported to be a work of history, about the Dutch Calvinist Church of the early seventeenth century, when the (Arminian) effort to humanize it had failed, against the Counter-Remonstrants, who were enthusiastic about damning people. He had learned Dutch more or less on the train in order to write this book, a long one, hardly penetrable by the censors or for that matter anyone else. But it was enough to predestine him to exile, the more so as his wife was Jewish, and there followed the sort of distinguished career that put Poland back on the world's intellectual map for the first time, in effect, since Copernicus in the sixteenth century. The three-volume *Main Currents in Marxism* is a classic. But in his disillusionment Kołakowski was in good company. Student revolts saw Gomułka off.

In the seventies the opposition gradually built up. As elsewhere in the 'bloc', intellectuals were a main element, and in ordinary circumstances this could be a ticket to nowhere: 'daring arguments, tame conclusions', as A. J. P. Taylor had said of Vienna in 1900. Beards talked 'civil society', and Thomas Aquinas was much brandished in the wind. Among the intelligentsia of western Europe, and especially in Italy, there was a desperate desire for some connection with the real proletariat. This was generally a hopeless cause, and so it also proved in Hungary and Czechoslovakia. Marx had said that 'the conjunction of the proletariat and the intelligentsia' would bring Communism; he had gone on, to the effect that 'philosophy cannot become reality without the abolition of the proletariat and the proletariat cannot abolish itself unless philosophy becomes reality'. In Poland these words came to mean something; and of all revenges on Marx, through the medium of the Catholic Church. The French observer who dismissed the masses' religious enthusiasms as Ayatollah-like had it entirely wrong: the Church, historically, had been adept at raising the cause of the poor, and besides, in Poland, it was *the* national institution. Workers could be mobilized by priests, and this was to happen again and again as the seventies went ahead. The intellectuals went along, and found themselves having to talk common language with priests in a way that had no counterpart elsewhere. But it mattered also that the workers were galvanized by other factors: an industrialization that worked out very badly. In that decade the Communist Party (it had a different name in Poland) had also embarked on a supposedly unifying and national strategy, economic growth.

Gomułka's successor, Edward Gierek, was a miner (he had quite good French, having worked in Belgium) and he wanted to profit from German *Ostpolitik*. He would make Poland 'a new Japan'. His relations with Valéry Giscard d'Estaing and Helmut Schmidt were good; there was money to be had from the banks, stuffed with Arab dollars; Poland could export, as did the Far Eastern miracle-countries. Investment came in, and the skies above Upper Silesia – the Katowice region – turned a vague green, as factories pumped out their chemical smoke. For a time, this succeeded. Output rose by 11 per cent per annum and real wages by 7 per cent (1971–5). But consumption also shot up, as food to the value of $3bn was imported every year (in a country that, before the war, had exported it). However, Polish goods suffered for lack of quality, and when the second oil shock occurred, in 1978–9, the market for them went down. The external debt, at

$20bn, could not be easily serviced, and investments, often pointless, were already taking 40 per cent of the national income. The 'new Japan' was looking instead at North Korea. Prices, preached the regime's own economists (there had been quite a vogue for the sending of bright and orthodox Poles to business schools such as INSEAD), would have to go up, to take account of production costs. However, most workers could only see in that the privileges of the Party, and strikes began. The private butchers were permitted to sell the best cuts of meat, and could charge almost twice for them. Now they were permitted to sell cheap cuts as well, which affected ordinary consumers. The Lublin railwaymen got it into their heads that the lack of meat was caused by exports to the USSR, and they welded a train to the railway line heading east. At that, Gierek was summoned to explain himself to the General Secretary, Brezhnev, and a frigid communiqué resulted (in July 1980): 'an exchange of information as to the situation in their respective countries'. In the docks of Gdańsk there was a stubborn woman, one Anna Walentynowicz, who worked a crane. There is always something of an imponderable about these working-class troubles in northern Poland: in that region, a great number of the people forcibly moved from the Ukraine had settled, including Polish Ukrainians ('Ruthenes') from the mountains of the south. Their children had inherited resentments to work out; and Anna Walentynowicz was herself from Rovno, in what had been a mainly Ukrainian area of old Poland. At any rate, she was refractory. She had been a good Communist and worker to start with – had even been decorated – but now she protested, and was dismissed, even though she only had a month or two before she would have reached the age of retirement. The workforce took up her cause, and there emerged another remarkable figure, Lech Wałęsa. Here was a good Catholic – eight children by the same wife – with a career as a fitter. He was also an organizer, and 13,000 people struck on 14 August 1980, in protest at the dismissal of Anna Walentynowicz. They occupied the workplace, the Lenin Shipyard. Priests were well to the fore. A trade union, Solidarność ('Solidarity'), emerged from this, and the very name had Catholic overtones, *solidarietà* in Italian, involving charity and co-operative movements, under clerical patronage.

A central matter, here, was that the Pope was a Pole. Karol Wojtyła was elected on 16 October 1978, having been Archbishop of Cracow, the most religious city in Poland. He had risen from the pious lower-middle class, and brought enthusiasm to everything (he was even in his youth a good amateur actor). He knew his Communists, and told people, even in 1946 when he was just a parish priest, 'Don't worry, they'll finish themselves off.' But he was also a good tactician: the formidable Cardinal Prince Sapieha promoted him, and when he went to Rome, though he did not like the changes in the Church that came with Vatican II, he was careful not to make a personal issue of things. He was also a considerable intellectual, very well-read in Catholic philosophy and able, when he invited the world's philosophers to the Vatican, to hold his own. Other Popes before him had either been deeply troubled about the modern world, not really knowing what to do, or perhaps too keen to go along with it. John Paul II – the name he took – had no doubts. He really came from the triumphalist world of the later nineteenth century, when Leo XIII, with *Rerum Novarum* in 1891, had made an effort to reconcile Catholicism with socialism. Here, Leo had quoted Aquinas from the thirteenth century – when 'capitalism' had started – and tried to identify a Christian answer. The Conservative Party in England belonged in this context, and the Christian Democrats in Italy and Germany were exemplars; perhaps, even, the most interesting question in France is why there never was an equivalent. Pope John Paul certainly had the measure of the modern world, and had a good idea as to how it might be managed. For instance, he did not bother very much with the media, and had his chauffeur read out a fortnightly summary of the press in the back of the car. He did not bother very much about the secular pieties, such as democracy, which he probably associated with ugly women and uneatable food. However, he had a wonderful sense of timing, of stage presence (much admired by Sir John Gielgud), and a papal appearance was a memorable occasion. In Poland the audiences were in hundreds of thousands. It was the man and the hour. On 13 May 1981 Mehmet Ali Ağca tried to kill the Pope. There was a Bulgarian connection; Ağca himself was a Turkish Fascist who had already murdered the editor of a Turkish left-wing newspaper and had mysteriously escaped from his prison. The circumstances have never been explained, even by Ağca himself after long years of incarceration: he seems to have lost his mind. But it would not have been stupid on the KGB's part to want rid of this Pope: for he did destroy them.

Communist Poland now disintegrated, at any rate down to its most basic parts. Gierek had a heart attack, was even imprisoned for a year and in the event he died in 2001 aged not far off a hundred. He was succeeded by a nonentity, Stanisław Kania. Communist Poland was now down to its essence, the army, in the shape of General Wojciech Jaruzelski. On 9 December 1981 Marshal Viktor Kulikov, as head of the Warsaw Pact forces, moved on Warsaw. On the 12th, at night, roadblocks were set up, borders were sealed, and special troops moved on the telephone exchanges with long axes to cut the wires abroad. At 6 a.m. on came the general, national anthem to the fore, sternness of gaze, while tanks patrolled the streets outside. It was a military coup. In military form, Jaruzelski was almost a fossil of the Kołakowski generation. It was not that he believed in Communism, but he did believe that the Poles must find a method of living with Russia, that the great mistake of the country's history was to fail to do so. A good part of the aristocracy had thought the same, sometimes with a corrupt side, in the Convention of Targowice in the age of Catherine the Great (1792). Some priests at that time had behaved in a suicidally nationalist manner. Pope John Paul was determined not to let this happen again: the Church would this time have a strategic sense. He managed matters in Poland. He had gone there in May 1979, to an audience of 400,000 in Plac Zwyciestwa, and through Cardinal John Krol in the USA he had a good contact with Reagan. This Pope was not at all popular with the media, but the morning Mass in the Vatican was crowded as never before. In June 1983 he returned to Poland. This time round, a million people turned up for the Black Virgin at Częstochowa, and some pilgrims betook themselves there from Warsaw on their knees. The Politburo in Moscow were apoplectic. They had Afghanistan on their hands, and no-one wanted to repeat the experience of Prague in 1968 let alone Budapest in 1956. The only hope was that the Poles would themselves do something.

In September–October 1980 there were agreements of the government with Solidarność, in the context of a strike threat, and coal output going down by 90,000 tons and inflation at 12 per cent. In mid-January 1981 Jaruzelski took over the government – a weird figure, be-corseted because of lumbago, and wearing dark spectacles because of eye problems that went back to the privations of resettlement in 1940. He did ask Brezhnev for troops but the entire Politburo voted against this: he would have to do it on his own. Nine million Poles were now in Solidarność. On 3 April 1981 he and Kania, the Party chief, by now, as was solemnly recorded in Politburo minutes, a very serious drunk, went to Brest-Litovsk. Solidarność held a conference in the autumn and there were Soviet descents on Warsaw – the head of ideology, Mikhail Suslov, and even the minister of foreign affairs, Andrey Gromyko. The Communist Party sacked all but eighteen of the Central Committee and Gierek was the scapegoat as the economy now crashed: there was not even tea to be had at hotel bars in Lublin. By November 1981 matters were in place for a declaration of martial law. A colonel, Ryszard Kuklinski, told the Americans. Jaruzelski took over the Party and tried to have Solidarność in a subordinate role, which Wałęsa refused; on 13 December 1981 WRON, the national security council, of fifteen generals and a cosmonaut took over. Wałęsa was put in a comfortable villa with his wife (seventh time pregnant) and apologetic generals. It had been Gomułka's and he was there for seven months. There was no European reaction – quite the contrary, as Claude Cheysson even said, 'socialist renewal' was at stake. There were problems as soldiers took over the mines and the Seym produced a huge reform package that meant decentralization, etc., but it led nowhere. There were over 10,000 internments, and over 150,000 'prophylactic discussions' but the overtones were farcical. If you lifted the hotel telephone you were told 'Rozmowa kontrolowana', meaning that someone was listening. That the tape was old and wheezing did not inspire fear, and conversations with the Polish intelligentsia anyway consisted of funny stories.

At any rate, Moscow was having considerable difficulty in digesting Poland, but there was worse. Could Poland digest the Soviet Union? There was an imponderable, television. Telecommunications were now such that in the furthest reaches of the Soviet Union truth could be told: people would know that they lived 'like dogs', as Richard Pipes's fellow traveller had known in fifties Leningrad. Maybe in Brezhnev's time the blockage of information meant that most Soviet citizens imagined that the West still lived in the world of Dickens's novels, that the imperialized Third World was only waiting for shining tomorrows courtesy of Moscow. But cameras could now be dropped in the remotest places, from there to beam instant images to a waiting world (Robert Harris's *Archangel* has a good description of the process). In East Germany Western television had generally been available, such that the inhabitants were under no illusions as to the relative poverty of their living conditions – as Enzensberger said, Communism was the highest stage of underdevelopment, and East Germany was a state that *sich selber mitmacht*, an imitation of itself, as Musil had called Austria-Hungary. This line was now true of the Union of Soviet Socialist Republics. What was to be done? A sign that matters were going out of control was that the secret police took charge.

This situation was not at all new for the bosses in the Kremlin. In 1921 the West had not followed the Bolsheviks' pattern. There had been no revolution, or at any rate not a 1917, in Germany. By rights, the Germans should have produced one, and for a few weeks there had been workers' and soldiers' councils on the Soviet model. But then there had been deals – the Social Democrats with the generals, the trade unions with the bosses – and the final revolution was not Lenin's but Hitler's. Moscow had responded by finding common ground with Berlin. Now there was a wooden replay of this, an effort to separate the Europeans from the USA. 'Our common European home', an old tune of Molotov's in 1954, came up again under Brezhnev.

In 1921 Lenin had responded quite creatively. In the short term the Revolution had failed. There was famine, and there were revolts. In 1920 the peasants were given a New Economic Policy, by which private buying and selling had again been allowed. Then there had been an approach to the Germans, and German industrialists and even military officers had co-operated with the new Soviet Union. Bolshevik diplomats put on white ties, appeared in the West, talking good French, and money came their way. On the whole, the West did not really understand 1917. Why could the Bolsheviks not be bought, like everybody else? Now in the 1980s, as Moscow saw the failure of everything, everywhere, that calculation came back in great force. Lenin is said to have said, around 1921, that there were Western 'useful idiots' who would talk about feminism or ecology or town planning or humanism and who could be put on the same platform as Bolsheviks whose intentions were to take over the planet. Now Moscow came up with the last useful idiot, Mikhail Sergeyevitch Gorbachev, in himself an obviously decent man, whose task was to soft-soap the West. Seeing him in action, Yuri Lyubimov, a theatrical producer of genius, scratched his head and wondered as to whom Gorbachev reminded him of. He said, at last, 'Chichikov', the anti-hero of Gogol's *Dead Souls*, who worked out a scheme for buying serfs whose deaths had not been recorded – a scheme which in the short term makes Chichikov appear to be a great landowner, but which ends in farcial collapse. In the Soviet Union, there were many equivalents.

The statistics of the seventies could not conceal a slowing down and even a reversal of the economy. Labour was no longer migrant, and construction – its forte – slowed down. In the sixties labour began to run short, then in the seventies arable land, then in the eighties fuel, energy, petrol, and, as Vladimir Bukovsky puts it, 'the system turned out not even able to pillage itself efficiently'. More and more of the GNP – one third in 1980 – went on investment, and a rough fifth went on defence, but the investment led nowhere. The statistics were in any case fictional, and in 1987 the economists Vasily Selyunin and G. I. Khanin challenged the whole set, claiming that the national income had grown far less since 1928 than had been suggested; growth rates had declined from the 4 per cent of the later sixties to 1 per cent; any growth was a statistical illusion, ascribable to inflation. It is an extraordinary fact that the most vociferous anti-Communists, starting with *Reader's Digest*, understood such things much better than all the institutes set up for sympathetic study of the Soviet economy (for which 'production' would be an apter description). Time was to come when, at St Antony's, Oxford, a Polish or Hungarian professor, didactically bearded, in a shiny brown suit, would lecture on such subjects as the possibility of market reforms under Socialism, and be discovered, a little later, buying Marks and Spencer female underwear from his expenses. Outdated technology and the exhaustion of plant caused shortfalls, and the quality of consumer goods was dismal; and, besides, the printing of money was causing a great overhang of deposits in savings banks, of 20 billion roubles in 1965 and 91 billion in 1975 (in 1985 more than twice that).

Technology, here, was the prompter. Already in 1975 Yuri Andropov, head of the KGB, had noted with alarm the rise of new 'smart' American weaponry. The 'smart' bombs were one aspect, but there was much more. A French historian of philosophy, himself a one-time Communist, Alain Besançon, wrote the best analysis of Soviet Communism (called 'Anatomy of a Spectre'). It had an 'A' system, which was very 'A', an illustration that the Revolution was better at the best than the West. That was the Bolshoy, the satellites, the foreign ministry, sophisticated people speaking languages. There was a 'B' system, very 'B', which produced the consumer goods. There was a surreptitious 'C', which was the reality, and in which everyone lied and stole. When Communism collapsed, it was the 'C' system which came to the top. Now, in 1980, the 'A' system was under challenge. Its missiles were being frustrated in space. But the 'B' system was challenged as well, since ordinary people could understand how dismally 'real existing socialism' looked after them, in comparison with what happened in the West. Men and (they tended to be more acute in Russia) women in the intelligentsia worried, and wrote memoranda. Other citizens responded differently, and stole or lied with greater sophistication. In modern society revolution is not possible. The alternative is sabotage, and that was what was happening: a permanent *Bummelstreik*, as Stefan Wolle said of East Germany.

Alain Besançon has a passage to illustrate the problem:

Take a statement such as 'The USSR with an annual output of 145,000,000 tons of steel is the first metallurgical power in the world'. Everyone knows that the USSR produces fewer cars than Spain, that its domestic appliances are not comparable with ours, that the railway network is hardly longer than India's, that the motorways are far inferior to France's, and that production of tanks, however ultra-lavish, cannot account for more than one or two million tons of steel. What, therefore, can this figure of 145,000,000 tons mean, given that it is higher than that of Germany's and Japan's put together, while they produce about twelve million cars and much else? The conclusion has to be drawn that these 145,000,000 tons include

(1) Production of real steel
(2) Production of low-grade steel
(3) Production of useless steel
(4) Production of steel for rust
(5) Production of pseudo-steel and
(6) Pseudo-production of steel

There were other comparisons, for instance with Spain, and on the official figures these meant something. However, again reality – a mere glance at a Moscow market selling shrivelled potatoes or dubious meat – told a quite different story. The USSR might be compared with, say, India, but even then there were problems. If you saw Soviet advisers returning from such places, their suitcases would be full of tomatoes, bunches of ballpoint pens, hams, jeans. The USSR had in fact less foreign trade than Belgium, fewer cars than Brazil, fewer telephones than Spain. The writer Boris Souvarine had said in 1938 that the very name 'USSR' contained four lies. He had gone on:

> rights of man, democracy, freedom – all lies. Five Year Plans, statistics, achievements, results: all lies. Assemblies, congresses: pure theatre, staged. The Dictatorship of the Proletariat: a huge imposture. Spontaneity of the masses: meticulous organization. Right, Left: lie upon lie. Stakhanov: liar. Stakhanovism: a lie. Radiant life: lugubrious farce. The New Man: an old ape. Culture: barbarism. The Genius Leader: an obtuse tyrant.

Resistance took various forms. One was a strike by women. They no longer made children, and (as the writer Sonja Margolina said) complained that the system had turned the men into babies, with no pride or responsibility. From 1965 to 1985 the population had risen from 230 million to 275 million, but the average growth rate fell from 1.8 to 0.8 per cent, and there were large regional disparities. The

Russian rate fell from 13.1 per cent around 1960 to 5.7 per cent in 1985, the Ukrainian from 9.4 to 4.3 per cent. Estonia and Latvia had the lowest birth rates in the world. However, the Tadzhik rate was much higher – a 50 per cent increase in a decade. Besides, the death rate rose, uniquely among advanced countries. A man died at seventy in 1969, at sixty-two in 1979, and infant deaths were not even recorded if they occurred in the first year. In 1986 a quarter of the district hospitals had septic tanks for sewage disposal, and a fifth had no running water. Yet abortions, given the absence of proper contraception, ran at 7 million cases per annum as against 4.9 million live births. Family size dropped to 3.5 persons in Russia and even less in the Baltic, though it still stood at around 5 in central Asia. Meanwhile, a woman's lot was not a happy one: three quarters of women were involved in manual labour, including construction, and certain professions, notably schoolteaching, were feminized (75 per cent). It was they, too, who queued, losing twenty-one days per annum even in 1970.

Meanwhile there was another classic sabotage-cum-escape, alcohol, and under Brezhnev alcoholism turned into an epidemic. In 1979, perhaps 18 million people passed through the sobering-up stations (*vytrezviteli*) run by the militia, and a tenth of the population of Leningrad was arrested for drunkenness. In 1980 50,000 people died of it, and if murders are included, 200,000. It accounted for half of the divorces – in the towns of European Russia, half of the marriages – and divorce (at 250 roubles) was quite expensive. All in all, alcohol was said to take 10 per cent of the national income. In the factories business could not really be done after midday, often enough, and the Poles reckoned that there was a 'morphology of Communism' in that piggy-eyed, fat and flushed faces showed the results of complicated negotiations between power-wielders, left by their assistants to sort out common problems in false alcoholic concord.

One challenge to this might occur: criticism by educated people behind the scenes. It was here that the kitchen table played its part, and of course the KGB knew very well what was happening, whether because of bugged conversations or because their own families joined in. Andropov was well aware, for instance, that young people were performing the theatre of the absurd – Beckett, Ionesco or Pinter, for instance – at home, and reported as much to (of all things) the Politburo. The immediate answer was to attempt diversions, bogus controversies in journals and the like. There was also a 'Talmud' of 400 forbidden subjects such as the statistics of infant mortality (the census was stopped) or grain output. The relative freedom of Khrushchev's time went. A challenging historian, Alexandr Nekrich, was exiled for telling the truth about the terrible disasters of 1941. P. N. Volobuyev, head of the Academy's Institute of History, had impressed his Western hosts in the sixties, and was dismissed. There had been a clever historian of the central question of Tsarist Russia, the agrarian one – A. A. Tarnovsky. He had contributed to a multivolume series on Russia's history that was not bad at all. He was packed off to Siberia as a schoolteacher, and the orthodoxy was maintained by one S. P. Trapeznikov, who recycled Lenin on radiant-tomorrow lines. Tarnovsky is said to have died of drink. Curiously enough the Central Asian historians suffered less, and rehabilitated their nations.

In 1980 Mikhail Gorbachev was elected to the Politburo, by twenty years its youngest member. There had been signs of a rethink in the system, but at the top level it carried on much as before. The Olympic Games were the last old-fashioned piece of triumphalism and by now Brezhnev was only just capable of doing his job. He died in November 1982 and was succeeded by another piece of old furniture, in this case the KGB's Andropov, who had once crushed Budapest and in the seventies had had charge of persecuting the dissidents, especially Aleksandr Solzhenitsyn. He was sixty-eight, and soon fell badly ill, dying in February 1984. In turn he was succeeded by old Konstantin Chernenko, the protégé of Brezhnev, himself elderly and suffering from emphysema. He died in March 1985, and Gorbachev at last emerged. His supporters were the *institutchiki*, men who made a proper study of 'capitalism' in the USA or western Europe, were fluent in the languages and knew the factual background. In the seventies, as part of the détente strategy, new institutes had been set up, for the study of the world economy or international relations in general, and they did not have illusions. Viktor Dakhichev became quite outspoken, as had Khrushchev's son-in-law, Alexey Adzhubey before him, to the effect that West Germany could be cultivated: why wreck relations with that economic giant for the sake of useless lumber in Brandenburg and Saxony? Or Yevgeney Primakov, in the Institute of Social Sciences that trained people from the Third World, himself a fluent speaker of Arabic and Persian, who could easily see that the USSR was getting nowhere in a Middle East that found it repulsive and backward. In the Central Committee machine, the International Department, successor of the Comintern, men argued for a new course in foreign affairs. Relations with the European Left had led nowhere: NATO had survived the lengthy campaign against the placing of missiles in Germany. That department had been run for a generation by Boris Ponomarev, and no doubt its support for Gorbachev was part of a campaign to unseat that old man, which in 1985 duly happened. After that, there were new faces: Georgy Arbatov for the USA, or Aleksandr Yakovlev, sidelined in the foreign ministry, both of them fluent in English and flexible in manner; Gennady Gerasimov, Georgy Shakhnazarov and Fyodor Burlatsky had all been modernizers associated with Andropov. It was in its way 'police liberalism', which went back to Beria. The KGB knew how far things had gone wrong, and, with a view to shaking up the old men, saw that a degree of public criticism and respect for law would be helpful, quite apart from the good impression to be made abroad. The Party and the KGB had had a host–parasite relationship, even (terms changed) before 1914. Now, the parasite was given responsibility.

Gorbachev himself was not really as revolutionary a figure as these men sometimes claimed. He had climbed the Party ladder from the provinces – Stavropol in the south – as head of personnel in 1963, then, in 1966, as deputy secretary. He did not have foreign languages, but he did have a wife who, as the crack ran, weighed less than himself, and she was educated. His protector, Fyodor Kulakov, regularly met Soviet leaders, such as Suslov and Kosygin, as they came to the Black Sea or the Caucasus on holiday, and that put Gorbachev on their map. In 1978 he went to Moscow as a secretary of department in the Central Committee, with responsibilities of an agricultural nature, but was still quite lucky, in that Kulakov had to take the main responsibility for what went wrong in that domain, and lost his place in 1980 to Gorbachev, who became a full member of the Politburo. It was a meteoric rise. Suslov and later Andropov, for the KGB, bestowed their blessing, and Chernenko even let Gorbachev chair the Politburo in his wheezing absences. Other old men died off – Dmitry Ustinov late in 1984, having run defence for years – or finally just retired, as with the long-term prime minister Nikolay Tikhonov. At any rate, Andropov's men did emerge in the Politburo by rapid advance, but they, or perhaps their wives, could not compete with Gorbachev. He was sent on a dramatic mission in 1984 to see Margaret Thatcher. The Western Right had recovered, and was prospering; if there was a symbol, it was the re-emergence of England in the first few years of the Thatcher period. She was back on the map again, and was the most obvious place to start if there were a new strategy, of appealing to Washington. That visit was a success. As Margaret Thatcher said, it was not what Gorbachev said: that was wooden language of the old style. It was his eyes. Upon the death of Chernenko, Gorbachev was put forward as general secretary by Gromyko, by now himself aged, who made a remark about his 'iron teeth'. There was nothing startling about his early pronouncements: 'we have no need to change our policy. It is correct and truly Leninist. We have to pick up speed and move forward to . . . our radiant future.' In his first year he applied himself in the usual way to installing his own men, and in March 1986, when the 27th Party Congress elected the secretariat and the Politburo, half of the members were Gorbachev appointments. Other purgings caused the change of fifty-seven senior functionaries and 40 per cent of the Central Committee members – the second-highest turnover since the death of Stalin. The average age fell to sixty, and by June 1987 two thirds of the government had been replaced. By 1988 25,000 militiamen had been sacked, 1,500 with a conviction, and in Uzbekistan there was an almost complete turnover of the Central Committee.

Someone had said in 1956 that Communism would go on until there was an explosion at the head, in Moscow. By 1980 the empire indeed had its problems, and this time round the United States would not co-operate in keeping it going. The curious thing about this period is Reagan's perception in 1981 that as regards the USSR the 'last pages are even now being written'. People ostensibly far better educated took a quite different view – for instance, James Schlesinger

and Paul Samuelson, quite apart from the vast majority of sovietologists, who still viewed things through the Vietnam prism. NSD(ecision)
D(irective) of March 1982 (repeated in 1983) meant to 'neutralize'
Soviet control of eastern Europe and there was a deliberate attack on
the Soviet economy; in January 1983 the ambition was even to change
the USSR fundamentally. This was also a return of the CIA, which
had become demoralized in the Carter years, its budget and staff
(14,000) run down. Now, with William Casey (who had greatly helped
Reagan when, in 1980, the money was running short) and Caspar
Weinberger (an old friend of Reagan's who understood technical
advances), there was a change: the cautious East Coast men were sidelined; proper studies of Soviet hard-currency flows and the like were
made; and the National Security Council contained allies such as William Clark and Richard Pipes and Admiral John Poindexter (who
continued until driven out in 1987 by the Iran–Contra affair). This
new team was secretive – Casey flew around in a black plane with
living quarters – and only two or three people around Reagan were in
the picture: even George Shultz, the Secretary of State, learned of the
Strategic Defense Initiative only a few hours before its announcement.
Reagan himself hardly bothered with the arms-limitation business
that takes such a large place in the works of Don Oberdorfer or Strobe
Talbott, and dealt directly with Casey, an old hand from 1941–5, his
memories going back to Allen Dulles's time. Reagan was by now
somewhat deaf, and complained that Casey's voice sounded like a
scrambler telephone.

Weinberger's intention had been to find ways to render Soviet technologies obsolete. There was an especially vulnerable point, the Siberian pipeline. Here was the great legacy of *Ostpolitik* and détente, a
huge project, financed by a foreign and mainly German consortium,
that guaranteed the energy supply of central and western Europe; it
would give Moscow a vast income and of course leverage in West
German affairs. Moscow naturally knew that work on the pipeline
could be interrupted through technical or legal obstruction. The
Soviets had tried to offset the foreseeable pressure by pinning down
work on the Siberian gas pipeline by contract, even to intermediate
levels, but had neglected one aspect – the rotor shafts and blades

driving the gas turbines for the forty-one compressor stations along the 3,600-mile Urengoy pipeline. General Electric made these, and was now prohibited from providing them. A Soviet team based in Cologne found that a French machinery maker, Alsthom-Atlantique, could make them, even then under a General Electric licence. The government allowed it to act in Moscow.

Meanwhile evidence built up that the Soviets were indeed in economic trouble – the trade surplus of $200m in 1980 had turned into a deficit of $3bn in 1981, and the USSR was having to pick up Polish bills, which weakened its capacity for credits in the West. Gold sales rose from 90 tonnes in 1980 to 240 in 1981, at that with falling prices: a clear sign of trouble. Early in 1982 American agents were sent to Poland through the Israelis, with the Church turning a blind eye: the idea was to co-operate with Solidarność people in hiding. An Israeli contact, manager of a shipyard in Gdańsk, took delivery of equipment for Solidarność, to maintain the pressure from underground, which was smuggled in from Sweden, apparently as tractor parts. Jacek Kuroń sent Reagan a letter from prison to the effect that a mass insurrection could come about: a letter that Reagan kept in his desk. The Warsaw embassy now had a four-man electronics team that could pick up most Polish traffic, and there was, by April, an underground co-ordinating committee which could communicate; there were flurries of activity. There were forays with American diplomats, but it was not the embassy that really mattered: the decoy work was useful.

A continuing point was with the Saudis. Weinberger had Arab friends, particularly Prince Fahd, the apparent heir, whose sons had been educated in England and the USA – a flamboyant spender and gambler, who had apparently opposed the oil price increase in 1973. He saw Saddam Hussein as a help against Iran, the more so as an underground Shiite organization was now active in Bahrain and Saudi Arabia. Weinberger went to Saudi Arabia to work out details, especially for a rapid deployment force that Carter himself had started – with provision for 300,000 US troops. In May 1982 Casey was in Saudi Arabia. The administration had done its best to prevent Congress from revealing the extent of Saudi investment in the USA, at the expense of some bullying by the CIA in Congress. Now, the point was to co-operate against the USSR in oil production – delaying the gas pipeline would contribute – the more so as Soviet oil would displace Saudi in such markets as Belgium. In 1982 Soviet sales to western Europe did increase by about a third and Saudi markets were pressed. Casey and the Saudis did a deal – the US would make things difficult for the USSR (and of course Iran) and the Saudis would do their best to push down prices (in itself this naturally helped the then depressed American economy). Casey also encouraged the Saudis not to use Palestinians, judged unreliable and possibly pro-Soviet; and Fahd wanted to support Islamic movements in Central Asia. Something was done in that direction.

Meanwhile vulnerability assessments of the Soviet economy were prophetic, convincing Casey (and Reagan) that the economy, dependent on the West for machinery to exploit the raw materials, was indeed about to implode and besides, as the terms of trade worsened, the OPEC countries would have less money with which to buy Soviet weaponry. In the 1970s Soviet earnings had risen 272 per cent, whereas oil exports had risen only by a fifth. Herbert E. Meyer, Casey's chief banking and energy adviser, reckoned that each dollar in the price of oil meant a thousand million for Moscow. It was clear that both a British company, John Brown Engineering, and the French firm wanted to take over the supply of turbines for the Siberian gas pipeline project, and Casey could point to the $15–20bn per annum that would accrue. There was an important Chinese dimension to all of this. The Chinese took over from the Iranians as watchers of Soviet missiles; they supplied Soviet equipment to the resistance in Afghanistan; they maintained a Radio Urumchi for Central Asia. The Americans relaxed CoCom for them, the multilateral agreement to limit the export of the most advanced technology. On 23 March 1983 Reagan made his Star Wars speech – he would exploit Soviet weakness in the new generation of electronics. CoCom was tightened up, and 1,400 illegal shipments of high-tech equipment were seized (to 1987). Another wheeze was for dummy companies to sell fake technology such as flawed blueprints for gas turbines. Meanwhile the US was doing twice as much defence procurement as in the 1970s – 10,000 tanks and 3,700 strategic missiles. In 1984 Weinberger was aggressive at NATO in Brussels, as there always was a US component in the advanced technological items: that was one basis of the American recovery. The Pentagon budget for research and development had doubled and the Soviet defence budget was supposed to have risen by 45 per cent as well, to take account of proton beams. Gromyko accused Reagan to his face of using Poland as a lever and of trying to 'exhaust' the USSR into 'surrender'.

Meanwhile oil prices went down. Twenty dollars per barrel was regarded as the right price for the USA, whereas in 1983 $34 prevailed. US energy imports would drop from $183bn to $70bn, or 1 per cent of GNP, as these imports (5.5 million barrels) accounted for a quarter of all. The Saudis took only $1.50 to produce a barrel, and Fahd visited Reagan early in 1985. The basic calculation was that a drop in the price of $5 would raise the American GNP by 1.4 per cent, bring down the deficit and reduce inflation. In effect the Saudis financed the Contras in Nicaragua. They then had to double output and agreed to do so; Nigel Lawson also wanted this, and the USA, by running down her own stock (held in salt caves in Texas), could drastically cut prices at will. The British did cut prices to $30, and OPEC went below that in 1983. The Soviets responded by sending Haydar Aliev in his English suits and Italian shoes to see Hafiz Assad, who had cut the Iraq–Syria pipeline in order to help Iran; the Saudis feared Iran and wanted Stingers and AWACS. The Saudis also worried that natural gas was replacing oil (1984). There were by now 1,700 US troops in Saudi Arabia, and the AWACS arrived; it was the same deal as with the Germans in the 1970s – support for the dollar in return for defence. Casey told the Saudis in advance that there would be a 25 per cent devaluation of the dollar in 1985 (the Plaza Agreement) and they acquired non-dollar assets to offset the fall in the oil price. Through Edgar Bronfman of Seagram (cover for the CIA) Casey had another channel towards Israel, which required reassurance as to the help for the Saudis. In August 1985 the Saudis started raising their output from 2 million to 6 million barrels and then 9 million such that prices fell to $12 by June 1986, a loss to Moscow of $1.4bn. Bush – a Texas oilman – did not like all of this and there were rows with Reagan. But by 1986 it took five times as much Soviet oil for a given piece of German machinery.

Meanwhile the Afghan crisis mounted. The CIA shipped its weapons and tried to keep President Muhammad Zia-ul-Haq clean, but the Soviets responded with bazaar bombs and drove refugees into Pakistan with a view to destabilization. William Casey expressly said that this was America's revenge for Vietnam. Bagram airbase was attacked by the mujaheddin, and twenty aircraft were destroyed by Chinese-supplied rocket-launchers; several senior Soviet officials and military were killed in Kabul. In January 1985 Soviet plans were known in advance (use of *Spetsnaz* night attacks with a van to interrupt mujaheddin communications). NSDD-166 of March 1985 was intended to end the stalemate and was to allow serious weaponry and not just the Carter harassment idea. There were 120,000 Soviet troops in Afghanistan in 1985 but the mujaheddin had night-vision and precision-guided weapons as well as satellite intelligence, and even a device to identify a pilot's voice as belonging to a particular unit. The oil pipelines were sabotaged; Kandahar airport attacked; Najibullah nearly murdered; 450 prisoners taken by Ahmad Shah Massoud ('Lion of the Panshir'). By 1985, from Oleg Gordievsky (who defected in 1986) and other sources the encouraging news came back that the Siberian pipeline had been cut in half and was two years behind schedule in construction; the turbines were inadequate. Then the Stingers arrived, in July 1986: a 'fire and forget' weapon, meaning that the aimer could fire and then not remain exposed to counterfire. The missile could go up to 15,000 feet at 1,200 miles per hour. The mujaheddin first used it on 25 September 1986 and there were two strikes near Jalalabad airfield, and further ones over Tadzhikistan. In December 1986 Gorbachev told Najibullah in Moscow that there would have to be a withdrawal. His own Central Asian territories began to rumble, as in Alma Ata a rampage followed the fall of Dinmukhamed Kunayev and his replacement as boss of the Party by a Russian.

Gorbachev, in the first two years, talked. He talked and talked. Generally, what he said was long-winded and even impossible to unravel; the book that he subsequently produced launched a word, *perestroyka* or 'reconstruction', which entered the world's vocabulary along with *Sputnik* and *gulag* as the Soviet contribution. So did another, *glasnost*, meaning 'openness to criticism'. This was supposed to be revolutionary but in practice it was quite old. Ever since the early days, under Lenin, Bolsheviks had been well and truly aware that all was not well, that bureaucracy was somehow getting in the way of the original spirit, and calls for *perestroyka* had been made in the 1920s, sometimes by someone ambitious for the leadership. That criticism was suppressed – the intelligentsia muzzled, imprisoned or worse – made the problem worse, and *glasnost* was again quite an old cry. In effect all that was being done, in the first two years, was consolidation of Gorbachev's position and the establishment of his coterie of ambitious advisers. The principal change was in foreign affairs, where a new approach was made to the Western Right, with a view to some dramatic arrangement as to arms control and a diminution of Western support for the Afghan rebels. There were other obstacles, such as CoCom, which did not stop the export, but made it expensive. And in any case the Western Left, especially the German, had proved to be of very limited utility; it was even being dropped by Moscow before Gorbachev himself emerged. At any rate there was a new era in relations, because, quite suddenly, Soviet representatives turned out to be agreeable drinking companions, quite willing to talk freely. This made, already, a huge change with the past and a great number of journalists, used to the restrictions of earlier years, allowed a natural Russophilia to emerge. It was a tribute at least to the public relations machinery in Moscow, which had been very wooden for a generation and was now learning fast. But in the first two years, and for that matter throughout Gorbachev's six years in office, *perestroyka* remained a matter of words. The powers that be ranted on about the virtues of central planning, and amalgamated five huge ministries dealing with agriculture into one very huge ministry, which spewed out regulations to the collective farms even more frenetically than in Khrushchev's time, and was not heard of within a year or so. Investment in heavy industries went up, the economist arguing for this, one Abel Aganbegyan, himself rollingly mountainous, being sent abroad to explain that there was new thinking in matters economic. Though gushed over by naïve Russian-speaking females at Oxford, he did not take in Margaret Thatcher, who knew her economics.

There was a strange moment in the summer of 1985 which was characteristic of underlying realities. Since 1918 Moscow had refused to pay a very large sum owed to the British, partly because of war debts and partly because oil companies had been expropriated without compensation. At each Anglo-Soviet meeting, the British side would propose a discussion of this, and the Soviet would refuse. But in that summer the new foreign minister, Eduard Shevardnadze, greatly astonished his interlocutors by saying that the matter might indeed be discussed. There was some Tsarist Russian money still held in London, at Barings Bank, and that sum – a fraction, but £40m – was now handed over, in final settlement. It all had to do with the son of Duncan Sandys and grandson of Churchill; he had connections with oil, and when the deal was done, it turned out that everybody had been cheating everybody; they all sued. But the Moscow PR machine was in action. It had always been easy for Moscow to rope together writers and actors, traditionally the most absurd commentators on public matters, no doubt because subject in a higher degree than other professionals to a combination of vanity, boredom and resentment of the capricious free market. Now a clever attempt was made at the television audiences, by people who had watched American television and the mass media. They had appreciated the importance of the visual, now that devices could convey images almost 'live', to masses of people who would take in a very simple message. 'Gorby' became a star, especially in Germany, where his book was on the bestseller list for mysterious months and months.

Back home was another matter, and there Gorbachev was far more of an Andropov than his admirers in the West thought. One thing the regime did do, and it greatly damaged its own finances. Russians drank, and governments, proclaiming a monopoly of drink production, made money out of it. This weird episode was studied by Stephen White (*Russia Goes Dry*). Russians famously had a weakness for drink, and there was public understanding for drunkenness. A good part of the State's income, in Soviet as in Tsarist times, came from the spirits monopoly. There was a puritanical side to the early Communists, who staged 'battles on the alcohol front', but drink was quite an easy way of keeping the people quiescent, and the battles became bottles. By the seventies there was an evident problem, and the census revealed less and less of life in the USSR – sixteen volumes for 1959, seven for 1970, but only one, summary, for 1979. Figures for life expectancy were suppressed, and after 1963 the figures for alcohol consumption were 'managed', almost ignoring moonshine, which represented nearly half of the consumption. The ten litres per head of 1965 turned into fifteen in 1979, but from the railways alone 7 million litres were stolen, and nearly a tenth of families spent 40 per cent of their income on spirits (which were relatively expensive). Under Gorbachev the statistics re-emerged, revealing that life expectancy had fallen to sixty-two for a man and that pure alcohol consumption per capita had risen four times since 1940, and consumption of all drink as much as eight times. The KGB stated that university students drank all day; 15 per cent of the population was alcoholic; and *Pravda* was complaining that building workers started only on Tuesdays or that collective farmers were useless after midday. The police under Andropov even went round the bathhouses arresting absentees, but they could hardly interfere with the third of the workforce that was absent in order to consult a doctor.

Not long after Gorbachev acceded, in May 1985, a campaign against drink began. He himself did not touch it, and had inveighed against it long before. He had allies as well – a reformed alcoholic named Mikhail Solomentsev in the Central Committee, and Yegor Ligachev, chief secretary in Tomsk, which he made 'dry'. Others protested, even Aliev in Baku, and Nikolay Ryzhkov, the later prime minister, who simply said that Prohibition had never worked. Boris Yeltsin in Moscow protested, but did none the less close nine tenths of the wine shops. State output went down; vines were uprooted in the Crimea, in Georgia and – most disastrously – in Nagorny Karabakh. That area, formally part of Azerbaidjan, was largely Armenian in population, but had been handed to Azerbaidjan early on, as a way of softening the blow of Soviet conquest. Wine was a principal product, and its suppression (and a subsequent calamitous earthquake) meant general impoverishment, and a considerable worsening of relations between the two peoples. But the campaign against alcohol was, generally, farcical. In Moscow there were only seventy-nine places to drink, and hotels would not serve alcohol until 2 p.m. Some towns declared themselves 'dry', and drunks were sacked or fined. Diplomatic gatherings were widely deserted, but of course the counterpart was a rise in the output of moonshine, as had happened in twenties America. A Temperance Society by 1988 had 428,000 branches and over 14 million members, three quarters of them over thirty. Fifty films were suppressed because they showed drunken scenes; on the radio *La Traviata* was shortened to cut out the drinking; an 'agitational steamer' went down the Volga, and medical research teams jumped onto the bandwagon, working from the Serbsky Institute of Criminal Psychiatry, with an enormous research centre for the causes and consequences of drink (one head of department was sacked for suggesting moderation). In 1986 there were victories – output of vodka down by a third. Men were denounced by their mothers-in-law and packed off to 'cure-labour prophylactorias' without any judicial process. However, it was all more than somewhat ridiculous. Very little could be done to stop people making *samogon*, and of course they did this with ingenuity. The rural background of so many told them how. There was even a computer-programmed process, and it was often superior to the state product (and sold for more). Sugar sales from 1985 to 1987 reflected this, increasing more than they had done between 1970 and 1980, and yeast also boomed, for instance in Kamchatka. Fruit was stolen in large quantities, and criminal gangs went around with tankers full of neat spirits. In Tatarstan there was an underground distillery in the very Party headquarters; a fishing trawler was found to contain 576 bottles of vodka to celebrate the navigator's wedding; soldiers used to shave the top of their heads and then place upon them a piece of bread, soaked in boot polish that had been left to melt into it under the sun for a day or two. One workman in Vladikavkaz complained on behalf of his hundred-odd fellows that 'ordinary people have no holidays and everyone walks around in a foul mood, like jackals'. In 1988 the whole campaign was relaxed, and soon collapsed. By 1993 Russians were ahead of Frenchmen as drinkers, but over sixty drink factories had been destroyed and there were thousands of hectares of uprooted vineyards, whether in Yalta or in the Caucasus; Georgian wines had been famous. Now, even Armenia suffered, because she had produced the corks. It all added to the great tension and the disruption of supplies in general that went ahead in 1987–8.

27

Restoration

As Goebbels, bombs raining down on his ministry, and the Russians liberating Auschwitz, had noted in his diaries, when he heard about the Yalta conference, the real battle between the Allies had not been about Poland; it had been about Germany. So it was, and forty years later the Yalta settlement was starting to unravel, beginning, for that matter, with Poland. However, the crucial decisions were taken in Moscow, as a clever Hungarian had predicted, back in 1956. The 27th Congress of the Party, held at the turn of February/March 1986, was the stage. At the time, no-one really noticed what was happening: the proceedings of the Congress amounted to the usual tidal wave of liquid concrete. The Party rewrote its statutes, modifying earlier remarks as to class war and imperialism. Even Xan Smiley, astutest of the foreign correspondents, and the *Economist* did not notice that something decisive had happened – a forgivable mistake (this writer has reason to hope), given the needle-in-haystack nature of truth in that system. But what was really meant was that Moscow was giving up the Berlin Wall. Within months, Solidarność was discussing a new Poland, and within a few more months the Berlin Wall had indeed gone, and so, thereafter, did everything else go, including, by 1991, the Union of Soviet Socialist Republics itself. There was a romantic theory that this had been achieved by 'We, the People', a theory that could only elicit a chuckle from the grave of Andropov. The people were Mussorgsky extras, in an operetta where Polish pretenders made trouble for Old Believers. The Politburo were stupefied by Poland: they would not send in troops, and knew that their Polish puppets were lost: what *were* you to do with hundreds of thousands of pilgrims, marching on their knees, to a religious symbol? If the proletariat went on strike against the Communists, how were you to deal with it?

Martial law had been declared at the end of 1981, and had solved nothing: Poland still had the debts, and after a week or two the black market ran things as before. In effect it was the Pope (with the American embassy) that now ran affairs. In June 1983 he returned to Poland. If he had called for a revolution, it would have happened. He did not. The virtues of capitalism and democracy did not much interest him and in 1984 Jaruzelski himself said that the Church was an ally. There was a curious aspect, that many of the people in the Reagan administration were Catholic: Haig's brother was a priest, and there was William Casey at the CIA. Oleg Bogomolov, for the Institute of Socialist Relations, had written a report in 1978 about what the Pope would do. It is worth noting that both Khrushchev and Brezhnev, with Ukrainian involvement, disliked the Uniates as fake. John Paul went again in 1987 and three quarters of a million people attended the Mass at Gdańsk. There had been a referendum on economic reform, boycotted at the behest of Solidarność, and strikes had followed in the spring (1988). Lech Wałęsa was needed, and in January 1989 he appeared on television again. Mieczysław Rakowski took over as prime minister, and in February 1989 there was a round table over the price increases. The elections then occurred in June, and by now Gorbachev and the Pope were co-operating. Gorbachev informed Cardinal Agostino Casaroli in Moscow in the ineffable words: 'The most important thing is the human being. The human being must be at the centre of international relations. That is the point of departure for our New Thinking.' And he did release the Lithuanian Cardinal Vincentas Sladkevičius, after twenty-five years in prison. In return he had a present: the Virgin of Fatima had promised that Russia would be freed. In the summer of 1989 Poland acquired a non-Communist government, the members of which undertook to leave the Communists alone. Opinions greatly varied as to the wisdom of this, and Alain Besançon made himself unpopular, as he talked of another Convention of Targowice, or sell-out. But was there a serious alternative? Gorbachev, by now doing the rounds of 'our common European home', had to act over Poland, and if the

Church and the Americans pushed the Poles towards a compromise element, so be it. But he would also have to get rid of ugly, tiresome little Honecker as well.

Poland was really about Germany, and another important People's Democracy also supervened. Act two was set in Hungary. János Kádár, the general secretary, had promised some economic liberalization and had impressed Mitterrand. Hungary had always had a strange relationship with Austria, and Austria was now, in her way, a considerable success story. Why was Budapest, capital of what was in the end a rather more interesting civilization, such a lifeless ruin? Something of an effort was made to do something with Budapest, and at least the Váci utca and the old Gerbeaud café were very smudgy copies of the Herrengasse and the Sacher in Vienna, though if you went two or three tram stops down the Rákóczy út you were well and truly in the Communist bloc. Kádár was a prime opportunist, and the Russians needed him: he was very adept at making sure that he had no obvious successor. Besides, there was an enormous and very influential Hungarian diaspora, and after *Ostpolitik* its members came back and forth – latterly in the shape of George Soros. Hungary built up the largest per capita dollar debt in the world, $2bn, but the industrial showcases were not a success. In the recession of the early 1980s exports to the West ran down, and half of the earnings were needed just to pay the debt interest. Wages were blocked, there was notable inflation, and purchasing power fell by 15 per cent. Hungary had a degree of liberalization, Kádár announcing that who was not against was for, and there were opposition movements, with openings in the press. By 1985 there were public meetings, and in 1987 when Kádár was already 75 there was something of a turning point: the state enterprises were allowed to charge their own prices, but on the other side personal taxes were introduced. Imre Pozsgay circulated a document by the main economists, saying that the regime had led the country to near disaster, and in March 1988 – the anniversary of the revolution in 1848 – thousands of demonstrators gathered in Budapest. Viktor Orbán started to make his reputation as orator (and eventual prime minister). At the next Party conference, Kádár himself was voted out, and at another anniversary, the execution of Imre Nagy in 1958, the end of the Party itself was spelled out. Nagy had said that he feared being rehabilitated by his own executioners and that is what happened: the Communists shed their name and carried on as social democrats, or even as liberals.

Soviet leaders all along had tried to split Germany from the Atlantic alliance. In the later 1970s Brezhnev visited Bonn. There were German neutralists, and it even became chic in West Germany to talk as if all differences with the USSR could somehow be smoothed over. But the central problem remained, that the State which called itself the 'German Democratic Republic' was an embarrassment. It remained a place where the inhabitants had to be contained by a wall, and a very ugly one at that, complete with minefields and yapping hounds on dog-runs, in case they all decided to move out, as they had done before 1961, when the Wall was built. Erich Honecker was saying that the Wall would last for fifty years, and there was another very odd aspect to it, that many Germans agreed. Hans-Magnus Enzensberger wrote an essay saying the Wall would be an historical curiosity, and there were many West Germans with egg on their faces when it came down.

The East German state had already been reduced to a formality, kept going by the West. The Lutheran Church managed the sale of prisoners – 2,300 in 1983 and 1984, and emigration was anyway going ahead: a worker cost DM 50,000 and a graduate DM 200,000. From 1965 to 1988 30,000 were thus bought out, for DM 2bn. Thirty thousand left legally every year while about 40,000 managed to escape (1961–88) and ten-day family visits went west (1.3 million in 1987). In 1981 East Germany owed $13bn and that took 43 per cent of export earnings; the Soviets did give loans but also cut back on cheap oil (hence the stink of lignite in Erfurt). In July 1983 it was Franz Josef Strauss (ambitious to be foreign minister) who negotiated with East Berlin – West German banks lending an interest-free billion Marks and another billion in 1984. The East Germans had reduced their trade with the West generally but it rose with West Germany. There were no customs barriers, and Strauss extracted two secret notes from Honecker as to the relaxation of border controls so as to prevent the strip-searching of children. Richard von Weizsäcker, as mayor of West

Berlin, used to cross the border to discuss the *S-Bahn* and matters of pollution as no predecessor had done. Schmidt visited Honecker in 1981 and Honecker wanted to return but there were problems with Moscow and the Czechs and Poles, and besides Moscow had said that there would be no more such rapprochement if the Euro-missiles went ahead. Honecker therefore had to say in 1984 that he would not go, although in 1987 he indeed did. There he found a West Germany that gave him a welcome.

The SPD to Schmidt's great disapproval now flirted with him, and in 1985 Oskar Lafontaine, minister-president of the Saarland, talked of accepting a separate nationality; in 1986 he even proposed a nuclear-free zone, though there had been the absurd ceremony for twenty-five years of the Wall, including a preposterous DDR stamp of a young girl giving flowers to soldiers shooting refugees. There was even a ridiculous 'Values Commission' of the SPD and the Academy of Sciences in East Berlin, and when the end came the Lutheran Churches were forbidden to ring their bells. It remains extraordinary that Bonn did not see the end coming: it was only in the spring of 1989 that Chancellor Kohl told the French he could see great problems coming for the East German state. In 1988 9,000 East Germans had got out through a country of the bloc where holidays were allowed – mainly Poland. In 1989, in the summer, tens of thousands moved out via Hungary and Austria. This was voting with feet, and Moscow did nothing to prevent it. The heart of the whole business was Germany. Russia and Germany had had the key relationship, and by 1988 the Gorbachev team were in creative mode. How could they get rid of Honecker and his colleagues? The answer lay in Hungary. The prime minister, Miklós Németh, had been promised DM500m if the border were opened (April, in Bonn). In June 1989 Gorbachev came to Bonn on an official visit. He told Kohl that whole areas of the USSR might need immediate help. Kohl consulted no-one and said the first despatches would happen at once. The East German parliament had approved of Tiananmen Square and on 13 June Gorbachev said that it would not happen in Red Square, and the communiqué of 13 June in Bonn spoke of 'self-determination'. Much was made of an East German resistance that was now mostly stage-managed. The

Protestants were restive and 120 young protestants who sat in before a church, protesting against local elections with their 98.5 per cent yes vote, were arrested, but then the church went to court over the electoral fraud and the prisoners were released (May). Even the SPD 'Values Commission' protested in March against long prison sentences for the Justice and Peace Work Circle. In July at the *Kirchentag*, or Church congress, there were clashes and from then on at the Nikolai-Kirche growing numbers appeared every Monday protesting at not being allowed to go west: curious that Saxony, the heart of the wretched state, was also its end. Honecker was quite remote and cushioned by Stasi reports, but on 10 September the Hungarians opened the border with Austria.

Hungary's foreign minister, Gyula Horn, himself a 1956 represser, opened the border for the thousands milling around Sopron and had sent his deputy, László Kovács, to ask the Russians, who made no objection; anyway the wire and mines had gone. Twelve thousand transports of East Germans went off in three days and some with little Trabants, while 7,000 in the Warsaw and Prague embassies left by trains through East Germany; another 10,000 invaded the Lobkowitz gardens in Prague. Three months of high drama followed. Communists dropped out of the Polish government and Wałęsa took over. On 7 October the Hungarian Party changed its name to 'socialist' and on 23 October, the anniversary of the Revolution, the Communists' own parliament proclaimed the restoration of the republic plus old flags. There was an equivalent in Berlin, as various efforts were made to vary the SED formula; there was even a last appearance of the Menshevik USPD (Independent Social Democratic Party of Germany) element, as *Neues Forum* was allowed at last in October, with a well-meaning earnest painter, Bärbel Bohley, to make critical comments about consumer goods and the refugees. The Leipzig church became too small, as the 5,000 marchers of 25 September became 10,000 a week later: even the factory militia started to be used with the police. Honecker did not mention it at all, but on 6–7 October Gorbachev visited for the fortieth anniversary – ritual kissing at the airport, Politburo servility and a soggy little joke from Honecker. The Russians were openly in ridicule mode, and Gerasimov remarked, 'If you are late it's a life sentence.' Next day at a Politburo meeting Honecker went on about the success of the East German microchip and later denounced the 'large-scale manoeuvre' against him; indeed, Valentin Falin, the reigning German expert, seems to have encouraged Hans Modrow, the Dresden secretary, and Markus Wolf, the espionage chief, to get rid of this tiresome little know-all. They no doubt encouraged the demonstrators for Gorbachev on 9 October in Leipzig, 120,000 of them on the 16th. Apparently ammunition was distributed, but half a dozen people supervened, including Kurt Masur of the Gewandhaus. On the 18th Honecker resigned, with others, for 'health reasons': Soviet generals were privately saying that if the Wall went they would not intervene, and Shevardnadze had said as much to James Baker on 25 September. The extraordinary aspect of it all was the slowness among West Germans, and some of them were downright silly, right up to the last moment. The Left had been trapped: even Bahr in November 1988 was saying that talk of unification was 'environmental pollution', though he later tried to take credit for it. Some of the CDU put 'Europe' before unification and Strauss himself was making money out of the Moscow trade. Peter Glotz, an otherwise intelligent man who saw through the Yugoslav problem, rejected use of the word 'unification' as late as 21 October 1989. Norbert Gansel saved the Party's honour when he recommended the expression *Wandel durch Abstand* as the hundreds of thousands of East Germans fled. Joschka Fischer for the Greens said, 'We should strike the reunification commandment from the constitution', in 1989 of all years, and Otto Schily had said the same in 1984. Both men went on to high government posts. Certainly no-one seems to have given any thought to how West and East Germany could be properly unified, and the subsequent story was unhappy: very high unemployment and empty cities.

Egon Krenz at fifty-two, representing 'Youth', took over. He had noisily approved of Tiananmen Square and had been head of Internal Security. The satirist Wolf Biermann called him a 'standing invitation to flee the republic'. This figure now talked democracy on television, there was an amnesty for Republic-flight on 27 October and the clergymen managed the demonstrations that went on with 250,000 shouting, 'Wir wollen raus.' Krenz went to see Gorbachev and sacked five of the Politburo members. The Czechs then released their own East Germans (10,000) and now even in the Alexander-Platz on 4 November hundreds of thousands took to the streets shouting, 'Wir sind das Volk.' One and a half million had applied to leave permanently and 120,000 had already left, only a quarter legally. On 6 November the government said anyone might go for a month, and then resigned. Television now broadcast everything and Modrow was invited to take over. Cars from the West were no longer searched. There was a fear that the Brandenburg Gate would be stormed, and on 9 November Günter Schabowski, an East Berlin politician and member of the SED Politburo, made a muddled utterance as to exit visas, while a rumour went round that the Bornholmerstrasse crossing would be opened. The streets filled up and Vopo – Volkspolizei, or People's Police – water cannon were used against people climbing the Brandenburger Tor, but other people attacked the Wall with picks, and on 10 November the Gedächtniskirche bells rang out as crowds mingled in the Kurfürstendamm; a Rostropovitch concert was held for the Stalin victims at the Gate itself. The East Germans gave out 7 million exit visas, and almost half of the population left. The absurd French Communist Georges Marchais sent congratulations to Krenz, although he was not to last too long.

On 11 November Kohl telephoned Gorbachev to reassure him and there was a to-do about unification – Mitterrand visited Bonn and promised support and then did what he could to delay it, attempting to use Margaret Thatcher, who was somewhat wrong-footed. There were maybe illusions as to the survival of East Germany as a sort of Austria, and for two weeks after 9 November Moscow seems to have supposed that East Germany would keep going under the reform Communists. This was quite wrong, and the German events inspired imitation. In astutely managed parties there was anticipation. Czechoslovakia was slow off the mark, but demonstrations started on 17 November and on 24 November Miloš Jakeš, the General Secretary, resigned; a new Party hierarchy came in: the demonstrations carried on, and on 10 December old Gustáv Husák went, to be replaced by museum pieces of 1968.

George Bush and Gorbachev were to talk. This was a secret affair at the outset, apparently suggested by General Jaruzelski, the previous July. Shevardnadze and Baker had talked in Paris about Cambodia and much else and Aleksandr Bessmertnykh with his outstanding English managed things: Bush and Gorbachev met on 2–3 December on tossing seas off Malta, an odd echo of the original Yalta. It was the seventeenth 'summit' and a list was ticked without teams of experts: there was understanding about German unification and by this stage the Soviet economy had been unravelling so far that Gorbachev was somewhat desperate for German credits and membership of the international economic institutions. By June 1990 he even told Congress as much, unaware that he was being recorded. In July Kohl came to Stavropol to discuss Soviet army withdrawal and Gorbachev agreed that East Germany could be in NATO: the German payment in the end amounted to DM60bn. However, it seems all to have gone back west, to Swiss accounts held by people who understood what was happening. The crisis now affected the Soviet Union itself. Just as the 28th Congress got going Ryzhkov ineptly announced price rises and in summer 1990 its component peoples (or their local bosses) began to break away.

There was a strong element of *mise-en-scène* in what had happened: the revolutions, though presented as such, were staged by the KGB. The general idea was to replace the old guard with 'reform Communists' such as Krenz who would be acceptable in the West. On 17 November a provocation was staged by the Czechoslovak secret police, at the order of a KGB general, Viktor Gruchko: a student demonstration was set up in Prague, and was fired on, complete with a student victim (who was filmed, walking away, once his 'death' had been recorded), and, this time round, back came Alexandr Dubček, flanked by Václav Havel, quite willing to co-operate with Gorbachev over German unification. Romania's was the classic case. Ceauşescu was a true grotesque, and besides had on occasion challenged Moscow. He had held all possible jobs, and moved in relatives as he vacated them. A press law of 1974 laid down prison sentences for the diffusion of unauthorized information, and illegal crossing of the border attracted a sentence of three years; even the typeface of typewriters had to be registered with the Security Police, and informers were every-where. The absurdities of the regime hardly had bounds: for instance, in 1967 contraception was made a crime and since abortions then grew to outnumber live births, that too became a crime, punishable with ten years' imprisonment (1984). Ceauşescu had been very anxious to outdo Tito, and indeed he flourished because the West cultivated him. He was three times in Washington, and was so impressed by the fireside chats in the Oval Office that he had his own fireplace installed and kept lit even at the height of summer. His wife had aspirations as a natural scientist, and was awarded an honorary doctorate by London University. As she was being led out to execu-tion, her last words were, 'How can you do this to an honorary doc-tor?' Ceauşescu described himself as the 'Danube of Thought', and his stock-in-trade was a stupid nationalism, making much of the Latin connection (because of which the country's name was changed from the Greek 'Rumania' into a 'Romania' which had been used to describe the Crusader and Latin state in Constantinople). But the 1980s went badly. Reagan did not have Nixon's tenderness for Ceauşescu: the minute a reformist regime appeared in Moscow, he had lost his utility. The IMF did not renew its loans, but he went ahead with manic projects – tearing down old Bucharest, putting up a vast palace, and agro-villages which were meant to deprive peasants of any individual-ity. There was a Hungarian minority in Transylvania, and culturally it had a bad time, though the Hungarian towns were generally better-off and cleaner. In much of the country the people lived at a very low level, with revolting food and energy shortages.

A stage revolution was organized. Ion Iliescu was Moscow's man and Ceauşescu had offended the Russians with his demands for abro-gation of the treaty of 1940, which had allowed Stalin to annex the largely Romanian Bessarabia. Another stalwart was Silviu Brucan, a former ambassador in Washington; on occasion he wrote anony-mously in the Western press; he was also visited every week by the correspondent of *Pravda*. In February 1989 Brucan, with five other senior figures, wrote an open letter to Ceauşescu, accusing him of 'discrediting socialism, isolating Romania and failing to respect the Helsinki agreements'; when at the United Nations Romania was attacked by the French prime minister Michel Rocard, and the Human Rights Commission proposed an official visitation, the Soviet Union did not use its veto. Meanwhile there had been another piece of decisive action in Budapest. The chief foreign correspondent of Hungarian television, Aladár Chrudinák, was a brave and resourceful man who had managed to film the Cambodian horrors and reveal these in the West. Now he went to Transylvania, interviewed a young clergyman, László Tőkés, and extracted from him a line to the effect that the wall of silence and lies had to be broken. Ceauşescu's machine then went into action. He used Tőkés's superior, the Bishop of Nagyvárad (it was a peculiarity of Hungarian Calvinism that it had bishops), to have him transferred from Timişoara in the Banat to a remote village in the mountainous north. Tőkés and his pregnant wife were then defended by parishioners, and the local Romanian population joined in (16 December). On the 17th the police used truncheons, even against the women and children who had been put at the head of the protesting demonstration, and Ceauşescu, on the verge of leaving for Teheran, complained at the 'softness' of the police. Troops opened fire, or so it was claimed, and rumours spread, partly through Budapest television, that thousands had been killed (Yugoslav television claimed 12,000). Ceauşescu broke off his visit to Iran, and decided to stage a mass meeting in his own support: thousands of people were brought in to demonstrate outside the Central Committee building, with orders to condemn the supposed Hungarian separatists – a device that in the past would have worked. However, this time round, it did not. A group of young people started shouting, 'We are the people', and there were catcalls. Bafflement spread over Ceauşescu's face and his wife – the microphones had not been switched off – said, 'Promise them something.' He then promised a wage rise, but the offer was swamped, and, hurriedly, he made off, in a helicopter from the roof. On 22 December hundreds of thousands of people collected, and there was a general strike in Timişoara. Elsewhere, there were isolated outbreaks as crowds attacked Security Police buildings in Sibiu and Braşov, both in Transylvania, but the damage was very limited: much of the alleged fighting was staged, bullets deliberately fired in the air. This looked like revolution, but it was carefully managed, and Iliescu, wrapping himself in religion and nationalism, took over. Ceauşescu was subsequently tracked down, but of course he knew what had happened: 'my fate was decided at Malta', when Bush and Gorbachev had met; 'everything that has happened in Germany, Czechoslovakia and Bulgaria has been organized by the Soviet Union with the help of the Americans.' He was shot, after a masquerade of a trial, in which the chief judge himself committed suicide. Iliescu, who had managed very cleverly to avoid contamination, took over, with a government of former Communists; soon he too was using 'the organized discontent of the masses' to put down the dissidents. This 'revolution' had been a *montage* if ever there was one, down to faked massacres: but it was soon followed by the greatest *montage* of them all, the coup of August 1991 in Moscow.

The 'dissent' that had the greatest explosive potential was indeed national. It was one and perhaps even the main factor in the very creation of the USSR that Russia consisted of several nations, some tiny, some large, some Slav, some Turkic. If you included the Ukraine among them, then half the population was non-Russian. The early Communists had found allies among these peoples, one remark being to the effect that the Revolution had been made by 'Latvian rifles, Jewish brains and Russian fools'. Moslems in the Caucasus and Central Asia, like the Tatars in Russia proper, had made common cause with Lenin and at one level were rewarded, in that early schooling and basic newspapers were made available in native languages. However, in Stalin's time Russification became the rule, and with let-ups from time to time so it remained. Because the regime operated strict censorship, the nationalist discontent hardly showed; when it did, there were vast camp-sentences for the people involved. In the 1950s semi-thaw, here and there, discontent emerged. Stalin had deported whole peoples, of whom a third would die during or just after the transport to some Central Asian waste, and the regime could also divide and rule, setting peoples against each other by the award of some territory to a different republic. This was done when the Crimea was handed to the Ukraine by Khrushchev, or, earlier, when Nagorny Karabakh, widely Armenian, was assigned to Azerbaidjan, in the capital of which, Baku, there was also a substantial Armenian population. Russians flooded into the Baltic states, though less so to Lithuania, for whatever reason. What was so very strange was that the Russians themselves were poorer than most of the others, imperial people though they might be, and the contrast with the satellites (except for Romania) was even more striking. Estonians ate 87 kilos of meat per head per annum and Russians 66 kilos; Estonians had three times as many motor cars; Baltic consumer goods were of higher quality as well; Azerbaidjan ate better because private plots were larger and less threatened. Russians muttered that they were parting with cheap energy to make these things possible, and also grumbled at the low levels of culture in Central Asia, which swallowed investment and made babies. However, as regards nationalities, tectonic plates were shifting.

Something of a Russian cultural revival got under way, with, in 1965, a society for the preservation of old buildings (something vastly needed) with 15 million members. A cult of Andrey Rublev developed; Suzdal was restored as a 'museum city' and the Golden Ring towns, little Moscows, complete with jewel-like Kremlins of their own, such as Uglich or Rostov, followed. Historians who wished to avoid overt politics could work on medieval themes, and there were writers who lamented what was happening to the language and to nature itself (particularly Valentin Rasputin, but also a Kirghiz, Cingiz Aitmatov, who, later on, was promoted as an instance of multi-nationalism). There was always at least potentially an anti-semitic element in this, given that Jews were crudely accused of hating old Russia. Religion was, again, potentially involved in this, and the regime kept a close eye upon it, not a single bishop being appointed without Central Committee say-so. Orthodox clergymen sent to the West, for the World Council of Churches, were straightforwardly agents, spouting Moscow's lines on peace. A council of religious affairs and KGB oversight meant infiltration and control, though in Central Asia (and especially in Chechnya) resistance was stoutly managed, the more so as Islam was a way of life and not just a cult. Khrushchev, in pursuit of modernization and the creation of 'new Soviet man', persecuted religion, and since it could buttress nationalism closed churches. In 1981 another atheist campaign brought about the demolition of 300 of them, mostly in the Ukraine, while the devout might also lose their jobs, and monks were sometimes sadistically persecuted. Khrushchev had also been quite harsh as regards lesser nationalities, and little Siberian peoples could almost be wiped out with drink. Under Brezhnev, there was some lightening, and ethnographic institutes studied the lesser nationalities quite thoroughly. Brezhnev himself spoke, at the 23rd Congress in 1966, of the need for 'solicitude' as regards 'peculiarities'; he also claimed that 'the national question is now resolved completely and irrevocably'; Andropov remarked that Russian 'has entered quite naturally into the lives of millions of people of all nationalities'. Brezhnev's policy had been to appoint loyal 'natives', which led to some odd outcomes.

There was even a weird descant on the old French line, applicable in a surprisingly large number of countries, that 'the south governs and the north works': Ukrainians made up over 80 per cent of the Politburo in 1979. Under Petro Shelest and then Vladimir Shcherbitsky, a Ukrainian but also a Russifier, Kiev went its peculiar way as the Moscow centre came to rely on local 'barons' who could promote their own nationality, though in the form almost of a freemasonry. In this way, Haydar Aliev in Azerbaidjan or Leonid Kravchuk in the Ukraine were able to emerge as national leaders when the USSR itself disintegrated; in Central Asia the transition was even smoother. There, a system not far from apartheid developed, as Islam was a way of life almost independent of institutions, and there was almost no way of controlling, say, circumcision (although a fatwa pronounced it unhealthy in 1962). The four Sufi *tarikat* flourished surreptitiously, and Murids avoided contact with non-Moslems; after 1970 the proportion of the European population declined, and Moslems rose from one eighth to one fifth of the whole. Only in Kazakhstan did the Russian element rise, in proportion. To placate the locals, the great Uzbek monuments at Tashkent and Samarkand were restored, partly as a gambit in foreign policy, given Moscow's closeness to the Arabs. But mosques were also closed down, and only twenty men were allowed to go on the Mecca pilgrimage every year. This was not reflected in Moscow, where there were few non-Slavs, but, short of Stalinist methods, there was no way to run the localities except through these locals, even if Andropov tried to break the system in the Caucasus by having 'workers' representatives' somehow pushed in.

In the early 1970s, while accepting the Germans' *Ostpolitik*, Andropov had told the Politburo what, in effect, the strategy was. The Soviet Union was falling behind the United States, and in areas that mattered, as distinct from kitchen equipment. He even hinted that, one day, the Soviet Union might just abandon central and eastern Europe, as a liability. Get rid of the Berlin Wall, cultivate good and profitable relations with Germany, fall back within the Soviet borders, and use the respite to recoup: it was not bad, as Leninist strategy, and in effect the various coups of 1989 were in some degree provoked or stage-managed, though none quite as obviously so as that in Romania. So far so good: Gorbachev was hero of the hour in the West, which, Germans in the lead, did indeed offer a great deal of money. However, Andropov's strategy went wrong: he had clearly utterly underestimated the threat that would come, within those borders, from separatist nationalism, and officials had always claimed that Communism had solved the problem. But in 1990 this began to spread – in the event, overnight destroying the entire Soviet Union.

The process was devious, but the main lines were clear enough. Already in the later 1970s there had been a great many detailed studies as to how reform should be conducted, and at the 27th Congress, early in 1986, these had been implemented. After 'acceleration' there was to be 'reconstruction', the famous *perestroyka*. Great slabs of prose were then written about this, but the Party shrank back from any sort of private property, and the most that emerged was permission for a few small co-operatives. Later on, there was talk of 'joint ventures' with the West, a scheme by which the West supplied capital and knowledge, and the Soviet side the land. For the moment very few of these emerged, and they did not last for long, as the Western investors soon found themselves losing money through this or that administrative trick, what the French call *chicane*. Then there was the even more famous *glasnost*, 'openness' or perhaps just 'criticism': the intellectuals, the periodicals, the press were now free to discuss earlier taboo subjects. Ridiculous pieces of censorship were set aside, as for instance with the great writer Mikhail Bulgakov, and the historians were supposed to become less dishonest. This, welcomed universally, was not quite what it seemed: Bulgakov had been quite widely read in pirated editions, and no-one really needed to be told about the crimes of Stalin all over again. It can even be said that when, later on, some archives were opened, there were remarkably few 'revelations', or at any rate there was very little that came as a surprise. Still, what there was, in a Soviet context, was remarkable enough, and in Germany there was 'Gorbymania'. By 1989, under pressure to show democratic credentials, Gorbachev did allow a Congress of People's Deputies, in which roughly a fifth of the members had been freely elected. In that context, Russian nationalism now emerged in great strength, as the figure of Boris Yeltsin took the lead.

Yeltsin was an odd hero, yet another of those sinister clowns whom Russian history throws up. His background was pure Party, and he was mayor of Moscow from 1985 to 1987; there he criticized Party privileges, and attacked Gorbachev himself. He was then humiliated and sacked. However, he had his friends, and they were now advancing the cause of Russian nationalism: Russians were poor, and blamed the ungrateful empire for this; get rid of it, and keep the fabulous material resources of Siberia. Yeltsin was elected to Gorbachev's Congress in 1989, and now set about conquering the power structures of Russia, as distinct from the Soviet Union: he became in effect president of a 'sovereign' Russia in 1990 (though formally only in 1991). Russians were supposed to obey him, and not Gorbachev; there were clashes. However, quite obviously, he knew how to manage powerful Russians, such as Anatoly Sobchak, the mayor of Leningrad, and these powerful Russians were responding to the evidence of collapse. By 1990 the economy was running down, as there was an explosive increase in paper money, translated into a black market that occupied more and more of output. Worse, the various regions had developed their own networks, independently of Moscow, and these were now pushing 'sovereignty' – the first, Estonia in September 1988, the pebble announcing the avalanche. Panic-buying emptied the shops; by spring 1991 there were demonstrations of 150,000 people in Moscow, and Yeltsin took the lead. By this time the Party's sharper men (there were not many women) were preoccupied with their own survival, and took up shadowy contacts with Western banks: thousands of millions went abroad, and the gold reserve disappeared (when the whole system fell apart in August 1991, the two men most obviously in the know as to this, Nikolay Kruchina (the treasurer) and Georgy Pavlov (the finance minister), committed suicide in circumstances that, for Kruchina, might suggest murder).

As nations declared 'sovereigny' – i.e. would not obey Soviet laws – and as mass demonstrations caught the attention of the Western media, Gorbachev responded initially by repression. Of course, once nationalism was released in this system, it expressed the frustration and rage that Communism produced; it was doing precisely the same in Yugoslavia, itself a little version of the USSR, complete with its Western subsidies. Troops were used in Lithuania, in January 1991, as had happened in Baku, in the Caucasus; but this time round, they were answered by mass demonstrations in Moscow itself, let alone in Baku. It was Yeltsin who now held the cards, and Gorbachev attempted to sort out a new constitution for the various peoples of the USSR; but this did not solve anything, the more so as there were now quite serious strikes, even in Byelorussia. In August came a mysterious affair: the putsch. Men whom Gorbachev had recently appointed, including the head of the KGB, appeared on 18 August, with tanks, on the streets, while Gorbachev was ostensibly on holiday on the Black Sea. They would take power, and to begin with the world took them seriously. However, this was almost a farce. One of the plotters, at a press conference, had obviously been calming his nerves with drink; fingers rapped nervously on the table. The tanks, on their way to Yeltsin's headquarters in the Russian parliament, stopped at traffic lights, where old women with shopping bags banged on their sides, shouting at the drivers. Yeltsin was not even tracked to his country house; Sobchak in Leningrad was not touched, and rallied that city at once; the Yekaterinburg KGB came out for Yeltsin. In the event, the putsch disintegrated within three days, and the plotters flew to see Gorbachev, asking what to do. It had all been a clumsy manoeuvre, to make out that Gorbachev must be supported against 'dark forces'. The whole affair ended within a week, allowing Yeltsin to appear as saviour of his country, as he stood on a tank and denounced the plotters; but the probability is that he had tricked them into thinking he would support them. At the end, Russia became independent, and the Communist Party was banned. But it left a country in many ways ruined, and bright men and women all over now wondered how they could turn it into a normal European country. Quite naïvely, to begin with, they looked at the Western model.

28

'Ending History'

As the Iron Curtain collapsed, there was much interest in the causes and consequences. The Left was mainly taken by surprise, and was (and, again mainly, is) quite unable to account for what had happened: Susan Sontag remarked honestly and pertinently that *Reader's Digest* had been closer to the truth all along. But the academic observers of the bloc scene were also caught napping. A British expert on international relations, Philip Windsor, remarked, seeing the fall of the Wall on television, that it was the end of an empire; when his companion asked whether he meant the Soviet one, he said, no, political science. Very, very few people in the West had foreseen the end – the first was a 25-year-old Frenchman, Emmanuel Todd, whose *The Final Fall* (1976) seems to have been inspired by rock music, listened to in a shabby student flat in Budapest. Earlier, in 1970, a very brave Russian, Andrey Amalrik, had guessed, on the basis of day-to-day impressions, that the end was coming, though he got the date wrong. Grave seniors, the world over, shook their heads at such perversity, and when Gorbachev appeared, there was a sort of parade of guards of 'useful idiots', including J. K. Galbraith, who thought that the achievement of full employment was the great strength of the USSR. This writer will not plead innocence, having informed students until 1986, though not in print, that the Soviet Union had 'solved the nationality problem'. But it is clear now that the most reliable guides all along had been the shunned 'Cold Warriors', men such as Alain Besançon, Robert Conquest or Vladimir Bukovsky, whose accounts (in *Jugement à Moscou*) of his dealings with American foundations read tellingly: when he explained to them, back in the 1970s, what was really going on in the

Soviet Union, he was no longer welcome, and was even missed off the Christmas card list. In the same way, most of West German academe and much of the media was entirely taken aback when East Germany imploded. There is a counterpart in economics, where the 'supply-siders' of the early eighties had been widely dismissed, with derision, and had then turned out to be right, in so far as economics is about prosperity.

In 1991 there was much triumphalism on the Right, the more so as, by a quirk of history, the fall of the Berlin Wall more or less coincided with the fiftieth anniversaries of the Marshall Plan and NATO or, for that matter, of the German Federal Republic itself (celebrants of which could often only mumble a half-remembered and rather soppy version of the old national anthem). It was an Atlantic hour, a triumph of American power, soft, as exemplified by CNN, and hard, as exemplified by the IMF. The Fukuyama thesis, that the West, catchily described as free market and democracy, had won, had captured Japan and South Korea, and would go on turning all countries of the world into versions of Denmark, sounded quite convincing. But which 'West'? For most of the world, it was Reagan's United States – and not the European countries that practised the minor virtues, such as thrift, failing to make babies and padding their pensioners.

Efforts were made to parade the European Union (as it was soon to be called) as an alternative model, of 'Rhenish' as distinct from 'Atlantic' capitalism. On one level, Europe, or at any rate the Europe of the Single European Act, unquestionably did good, in that it could break into stagnant pools of local protectionism, and for a Spain or a Greece, emerging from stupid military dictatorships, joining Europe was important for morale and in a limited degree finance. The same was, on the whole, true for former Iron Curtain countries, which got German investment and remittances from migrants to the West. But, as generally happens with multinational organizations, Europe was good only at dealing with limited and well-defined problems. Her efforts on the world stage were laughable – never more so than when the then presiding officer, a Luxemburger named Jacques Poos, turned up with two other worthies at the start of the Yugoslav civil wars in 1991 to warn against nationalism – in this case, that of the Slovenes, who were ticked off for thinking that their country (an elephant beside his own) was large enough to indulge in independence. At bottom, Europe was itself in any case an Atlantic creation, and French aspirations to make it independent of the United States very speedily broke down. Lacking armed forces, it had only two lines in foreign affairs: 'Me, too' to the Americans, and then 'Oh, dear' to the Americans.

Even the 'Swedish model', long and finger-waggingly upheld as a sort of 'third way', broke down. It had thrived, with a small population sitting on raw materials, had thrived further because it had stayed out of both world wars, had done well out of the export of arms, while its political establishment moralized at the rest of the world. Up until the 1970s, Swedish Lapps had been sterilized in tens of thousands on the grounds that they, stunted in growth and drunken in habits, were not worthy to reproduce themselves. In the 1990s, Swedish delegations were appearing in Turkey to reproach Turkey for her handling of the Kurds, a handling that most certainly did not include sterilization. By 1990 Sweden herself had slipped from being second most prosperous country in the world to being seventeenth, and was overtaken by Finland, a former colony, where affairs were less pretentiously managed. In 1990 the only European of any serious interest in the former Communist bloc was Margaret Thatcher, herself, of course, no great respecter of the European Union.

Great numbers of hungry, intelligent Russians (and others from the old bloc) came west, with a view, often dewy-eyed, to learning what the secret had been. Others did not need any such training. Communism had had, in the form of Alain Besançon's 'C' system, its own hidden, brutal and corrupt form of a market, and vicious figures made enormous fortunes out of the Soviet rubble. Russia then went through a very difficult decade, most Russians becoming disillusioned. The end of the Soviet empire was of course the culminating moment of the eighties, but there was an air of anti-climax to it all, as with most such moments, including Victory Day in 1945. Besides, this particular victory would clearly bring great problems, the worse for having been so widely unforeseen by the bureaucracies that had come into existence in the era of détente in the 1970s. Yugoslavia, the very model of Communism-with-a-human-face brotherhood-of-peoples, exploded, and the unification of Germany brought headaches of unemployment and mass migration to the prosperous places of the West. After a year or two of patriotic euphoria, the European countries of the former bloc were mainly taken over by variants of reformed Communists, now generally learning to talk another wooden language, that of 'Europe'; their young migrated, their agriculture generally languished, particularly when European regulations were used to suppress the old-fashioned ways with, say, ham or smoked fish or wine that might have let them be competitive. Much effort went into making out that this was all a great success for Europe, and for a brief period there was even a parody of the old Sovietology, in which 'transition' from Fascism or Communism was solemnly studied, as if there could be any conceivable comparison between Spain and Russia except at the most superficial level. But the reality after 1990 was, mainly, depressive, and the collapse of population growth almost everywhere demonstrated as much.

However, even the extraordinary showcase boom of the eighties came to an abrupt end, as American and German financial problems introduced a recessionary period. Japan herself, where an asset bubble had enabled the Colombians to sell their Tokyo embassy and pay off the national debt, now stuck and shrank. Ronald Reagan had retired in 1988, succeeded by the much more conventional George Bush I; Margaret Thatcher herself lost office in November 1990, manoeuvred out by her own party and especially by the Europe-minded element. The pound had, despite her misgivings, been put into the emerging European single-currency arrangements. Quite soon, her misgivings were shown to be right, as the strains proved too much: interest rates, set by mainly German needs, rose to such a degree that credit was choked off, recession followed, and the pound was pushed out again, much to the benefit of astute speculators. Reagan was lucky to the end, in that he managed to retire before the bill had to be paid for a piece of extraordinary maladministration.

For well-intended reasons, Americans had been encouraged to buy houses on mortgage in the 1930s through federal-regulated institutions, Savings and Loans (as happened with the building societies in England). The interest paid by buyers was fixed, which made sense when there was not much inflation, as, until the 1960s, was mainly the case. However, these institutions, borrowing money, had to pay the going interest rate, which in the 1970s became double that of the interest rate that could be charged from their own borrowers. Money went elsewhere. In 1980, with Paul Volcker's 20 per cent rate, the Savings and Loans were in trouble, and bankruptcy threatened. If Reagan had adhered to his own announced principles, the hundreds of insolvent institutions would have been allowed to collapse, but in the depression of the early 1980s he shrank from this, and in any case the troubles in the end were not of his making. The government insured deposits up to a value of $100,000. With this collateral, the institutions could borrow a great deal more. In 1985 they could have been shut down for a comparatively modest sum, but the Reagan administration itself encouraged easy credit – deregulation and an Act of 1982 allowed the Savings and Loans to move, beyond simple mortgages, into the world of speculation, and a further move abolished the rule that there had to be at least 400 shareholders: from then on, they could be owned by a single man, thereby empowered to borrow huge amounts of money on the basis of deposits guaranteed by the US government. On top of this, the amount of his own capital that he had to put in was decreased to 3 per cent of the money out on loan. The problem was further put off by accounting rules that allowed losses to be unreported for ten years, during which the institution might go on as before. So the more buccaneering of these institutions went on, especially in Texas, vastly over-building office blocks and the like; by 1990, of the 2,500 that survived, only half could be considered healthy. Some 750 Savings and Loans then went bankrupt, costing $160bn dollars and causing damage to house-building: depression then followed, in 1990, as the bill came in, and it wrecked the presidential career of Reagan's successor.

The heart of the problem was Reagan's unwillingness to apply free-market principles to residential housing: nearly 40 per cent of mortgages were guaranteed, whereas in 1970 almost none had been. In 1988 the failure was evident, and, with the deficits, even the tax cuts were reversed, partly formally, but mainly by stealth, as social security contributions went up and up. Federal spending rose by nearly 3 per cent per annum and income by 2.5 per cent: this made for a large deficit, overall of nearly $1.5tn. Defence spending had been part of the story, but only part, and in any case as the arms competition with the USSR ended, it in effect paid for itself in the end. In fact by 1986, to offset the deficit, taxes were raised, and endlessly rising social security taxes nullified the Kemp–Roth tax cut of 1981 for most people. In other words, the Reagan Revolution was something of an illusion, and the same might be said of the Thatcher Revolution. In England, too, taxes were if anything higher and the size of the State had hardly been diminished at all.

Besides, as the economic tide went out, various grasping monsters were beached, as indeed had happened in 1930, and that again gave 'the eighties' a bad name. In 1934 the Stavisky scandal had almost destroyed republican, democratic France, since government ministers and parliamentary deputies had been found to be involved in an upended credit pyramid, the apex of which stood in the municipal pawn-shop of Bayonne; the Madoff running it was found dead in mysterious circumstances. Now, in New York, life imitated art, in this case Tom Wolfe's *Bonfire of the Vanities* and Oliver Stone's *Wall Street*: the makers of 'junk bonds' vanished into prison as recession pricked their bubbles. In London the empire of Robert Maxwell collapsed. He (repulsively: the baseball cap making it worse), larger than life, was a lie from the start. He was not, as he claimed, a Czech and therefore a gallant ally. He was born in an eastern part of Czechoslovakia which had been part of Hungary, and where the local (Hassidic) Jews all spoke Hungarian. His name was the Germanic 'Hoch', the Hungarian for which is 'Magas', no doubt the inspiration for his Anglicized or Scotticized 'Maxwell', to which was attached the army rank of 'Captain', when he became a Labour MP. His money came from Soviet connections: he had bought up the patents of German scientific magazines for a song in Soviet Berlin, and he performed useful services for the Soviet Communist Party, which probably paid him by letting him know in advance when they would be selling gold or timber, so that he could one-way-bet-ly speculate accordingly. When the Soviet Union collapsed, Maxwell stole his pensioners' money and then fell overboard from his yacht, in mysterious circumstances. His US equivalent, Armand Hammer, was not caught, though upon his death he was found to have left, net, very little money. Both Hammer and Maxwell used a small orchestra of lawyers to silence enquirers.

By 1991, therefore, the critics of the eighties appeared to be justified. The notable books on the subsequent period – for instance, Joseph Stiglitz's *Roaring Nineties* or even Edward Luttwak's *Turbo-Capitalism* – rather shook their heads. Later booms and busts (most recently the crash of 2008) caused a veritable vibration of heads, and the 'decade of greed', as the eighties had been called, once more came in for condemnation. It is of course legitimate to ask what went wrong, and when. However, in this, the critics of the eighties were misleading. The great weakness in books of the Stiglitz type, knowledgeable and well-intended as they unquestionably were and are, was to suffer a strange nostalgia for the seventies; in fact one very good reason for the triumphs of 'Reagan-and-Thatcher' was that their critics were not only very wide of the mark, but disagreed badly among themselves, and were themselves products of the seventies, when their orthodoxies had indeed proven calamitously wrong. The record of development economics, for instance, is unimpressive; countries such as Tanzania, spoiled with World Bank largesse, spiralled down in planning, whereas South Koreas and Taiwans, with hardly any help at all, shot up. This phenomenon made the reputation of the economist Peter (Lord) Bauer, also of Hungarian origin (and also Jewish, but he was educated in Budapest at the grand and otherwise anti-semitic Piarist School, since his father, a bookmaker, had agreed to put a red line through the debts of the chairman of governors, a Count Sigray). His observations did not earn him a Nobel Prize, but, nowadays, the critical literature of the 1980s can mainly only be read as a sort of archaeology, turning up the urn burial practices of some once great tribe, the terror of its neighbours. This irrelevance applied still more when it came to the artistic artefacts of the anti-eighties. British film had a wonderful tradition to it, classics such as *The Third Man* still watched. In the 1960s, the film schools had been sixtified, in the sense that their students were supposed to develop an updated version of 1930s social realism, allied with hyper-active (or hyper-passive, in the

German case) camerawork. Public subsidy was then showered upon films that would otherwise have been utter financial flops, the beneficiaries afterwards rounding upon the subsidy-givers to complain at their parsimony. In the opera, one *Fidelio* after another evoked Pinochet and the SS; you would hardly have been surprised to find the Dove in *Parsifal* represented by a B-52 bomber over Vietnam. There was a characteristic episode, in the context of President Mitterrand's celebrations of the bicentenary of the French Revolution. The Bastille: ideal place for a popular opera, ran the thinking. The episode was chronicled by Maryvonne de Saint-Pulgent in her *Syndrome of the Opera* (1991) – vastly over-budget, vastly late, strikes at the opening, peacock-screeching between major participants, flouncings-out. Opponents of the eighties very frequently missed the entire point, and only really showed how accurate had been their own critics of the later seventies. However, it was true that the decade had not ended as these self-same critics had wanted. What had gone wrong, and where?

It is curious to see that, in 1986, there was some crisis, in itself insignificant but generating headlines, that seems to have marked a caesura on the Right. Ronald Reagan's administration was lamed by 'Irangate'. After Vietnam, Congress had found ways to stop intervention abroad by the CIA, regardless of any national interests that might be involved. Nicaragua had undergone a revolution in 1979, and the 'Sandinistas' who took charge talked Cuban language; Central America was full of combustible material, and American interests were at stake. The CIA wanted to keep a counter-revolutionary movement (the 'Contras') going and found a complicated way round the congressional prohibition: through Israeli mediation, a deal was done with Iran for the release of hostages, some of the proceeds going under the cover to the Contras. Nothing much about the affair was quite what it purported to be but the Washington media were only too happy to have another Watergate, and though Reagan always protested innocence, some of his senior staff suffered. This coincided with the much larger failure, in 1986, to clean up the overall mess that had become of the budget – an objective that had been stated in the first Inaugural. 'Irangate' was a symbol that the Reagan Revolution had failed, at least in its own terms. By 1993 the tax take was almost where it had stood in 1980.

There was an odd parallel in Britain around the same time, an affair known as 'Westgate'. A small helicopter company called Westland was in trouble, and wished for government help because of defence exigencies; but the American company Sikorsky proposed to buy it. The defence minister, Michael Heseltine, was a vain man, able none the less to arouse enthusiasm at Conservative Party gatherings. He strongly believed that there should have been a government strategy for industrial regeneration, and had tried, in stricken Liverpool, to do his best on a local scale. He had spoken up for local government, even when the Prime Minister (in 1983) wished to close down the rather attitudinizing left-wing apparatus that in theory ran London. He also believed in a European zone. Now he argued that a European consortium should save Westland. More generally this reflected a belief in 'regional policy', German examples of which he had no doubt heard of. It was true that in the once industrial powerhouse of Germany, Nordrhein-Westfalen, regional policy had been practised such that towns like Essen, which, had they been in England (or France), would have been stricken in the manner of Liverpool, had recovered. But in Germany, which had nothing like the British problem with inflation, planning could proceed on a relatively confident assumption that costs would not go beyond bearing (and there were also solid critics in Germany of regional policy: it seemed to hold the richer parts back while doing little to improve the poorer parts). Besides, local government there was simply more competent. Now it appeared that Heseltine, whose talents had not, he thought, been adequately rewarded, was using the Westland case to push his way into the Department of Trade and Industry, a monster that reflected sixties gigantomania in a hideous concrete building. He stirred up the more corporatist-minded of his business friends, and was indiscreet in his pursuit of his aims. There were leaks to the press about a warning to him, and it came to a Cabinet meeting early in 1986 at which Heseltine lost his temper, resigned there and then, and stormed out. There were even pompous complaints to the effect that constitutional government had 'broken down'. It was no doubt true that, by now, the Prime Minister was bypassing some of the Heathite arrangements, and Heseltine's coup failed. However, sufficient mud stuck to the government and there was more muttering complaint. One minister on the way down was permitted to take such blame as there was, and another, on the way up, delicately indicated that there might be a leadership crisis. 'Westgate' was of no interest to even a narrow public, because the country had much else to ponder.

If we look for the moment at which the impetus of the early eighties gave out, it would be 1986, the year of these insignificant symbolical twists. In that year, the seventies came back again, with attempts to rig currencies along lines satisfactory to the powers that be; Europe adopted the Single Market, promptly misused in an anti-market sense; and it became plain that the Thatcher government had lost its overall sense of direction, becoming, as the great historian of government S. E. Finer noted, 'an unimpressive and unhappy government'. This coincided with a further great problem, that inflation, which had brought this government to power, now returned. Nigel Lawson had been an imposing Chancellor, commanding confidence, and in his own view he was irreplaceable. In March 1988 he brought down the top rate of income tax from 60 to 40 per cent, and the standard rate to 25 (from 27). Labour politicians howled, with the usual shouts that the rich were being given privileges, while the poor suffered. The tax reduction made sense, of course, as it had been shown the advanced world over that if taxes were put at a sensible level, people would not strive very energetically to avoid paying them if they knew that they were getting something in return. The tax reductions cost £6bn, not, by 1988, a large sum, and if they contributed to rich taxpayers returning to the country, there would be no loss at all. In any case, the government's accounts were in surplus, the first time since 1969.

A far more insidious problem lay in the world of international finance. In 1985 Lawson had in effect abandoned the original monetarist strategy. Instead, he wished to control inflation, as part of a worldwide effort, through the rate of exchange. In 1985 there had been a parallel movement in the United States, and the finance ministers of the main countries met, in an agreement – the Plaza – to bring down the overvalued dollar. These attempts to control the world's money were not usually successful over the medium term, nor were they now. In February 1987 there was another agreement – the Louvre – to bring the dollar up again. There was then a disagreement between the Germans and the Americans, provoked by some unguarded vinegary statements by James Baker, now a dominant figure in the Reagan administration, and, on the whole, a force for uncreativity. The new trouble was a fear that the dollar would have to be protected by high interest rates, and in October 1987, the midst of the great eighties boom, the stock markets crashed. Understandably, the finance ministers then agreed to cut interest rates, pumping credit into the world, and generally fearing that there might be a repetition of the Slump of the 1930s. In reality these fears were entirely overdone. The stock markets quite soon recovered, and much of the problem had had to do with ultra-new technology, which put the market's usual herd instincts into fractions-of-a-second velocity. A credit boom was already under way; it went ahead, and inflation went up. But in England there was more to it. Lawson had decided that his best method of controlling inflation was to link the pound with the most stable currency on the Continent, the *Deutsche Mark*. In a way, this was inconsistent with his earlier stance. He had been an efficient manager of the sound-money Medium Term Financial Strategy, an attempt, not senseless, at domestic financial management. However, the Single European Act was emerging, and the Americans were trying to recover control of the dollar; and there was in truth almost no way in which domestic money could now be measured, because Britain had recovered as a trading and foreign-currency-dealing nation. Inflows of foreign money were vast, much of it connected with Japanese investment. The British balance of payments had been suffering, because oil prices declined, and Lawson took the circumstances of 1985 as guide: the pound had indeed declined by 16 per cent against the Mark, which would of course add to inflation.

In 1986 these circumstances were to change, as the boom went ahead. 'Big Bang' meant that the City could bid for world financial supremacy, and 'popular capitalism' was an enormous success, with a great part of the population now owning assets in property or even shares. The City firms turned into 'security houses' as in New York, and the wonder occurred that the British sold automobiles again, even if they were from foreign-managed factories. The British addiction to buying property meant that credit based upon property assets was in heavy demand. In natural circumstances, this would have meant a rise in the pound, just as in the Reagan boom the dollar had risen. Any deficit on trade would be met, as in the USA, by foreign investment. However, that was not Lawson's idea, and he preferred to control the pound otherwise. Lawson agreed with the Bundesbank that the pound would be kept at just under DM3, i.e. if it threatened to go higher or lower, he would change interest rates and sell foreign exchange or bonds accordingly. This allowed him, of all things, to cut interest rates in October 1987, and again in the March, to 7.5 per cent.

But, as things turned out, DM3 was too low: with foreign investment pouring into 'booming Britain', the pound was undervalued, and inflation was a consequence. This link to the *Deutsche Mark* was intended to attach Britain to the Exchange Rate Mechanism (ERM), which was the Europeans' contribution to world financial stability. Lawson had argued for this in 1985, when the monetarist recipes turned out to be inadequate. Back then, Margaret Thatcher had resisted – she preferred the markets to set exchange rates, and anyway disliked handing sovereignty to the Europeans. It was a sign of her loss of power that Nigel Lawson started to devise his own exchange rate policy, 'for which there are few precedents in modern economic policy-making'. The chief civil servant was not told until after several months had gone by, and the Bank of England just did what it was told, without asking why. Margaret Thatcher found out from an interview in the *Financial Times*, and on 7 March 1988 heard from her own people that their opposite numbers at the Treasury themselves disagreed with the policy. She at once told Lawson that the pound must rise, which it did, to DM3.10. Lawson, though humiliated, survived because of his triumphant budget. But the economic climate began to worsen, in the sense that inflation was returning, and now the demand for a link with the ERM, to prevent the inflation (as the French *franc fort* was alleged to be doing), became very very strong.

The French had high unemployment, because credit rates and the franc were kept high. But this was 'Europe', an apparently sacred cause. An excellent account of the problem appears in Bernard Connolly's book, *The Rotten Heart of Europe* (1995). Writing as a European civil servant, he exposed the rough dealings of Brussels, and the machinations to which Lawson exposed himself.

In the inflationary boom of the later eighties, as stocks and house prices doubled and trebled, the popularity of the Reagan and Thatcher governments was unassailably strong; and, besides, especially in Margaret Thatcher's case, they had demonstrably dealt with at least the short-term problems confronting them in 1979. It would not be wrong to say that she had turned round the temper of the country. The same was also obviously true of Ronald Reagan, as witness his triumphant re-election in 1984. However, both had been sucked more and more into foreign affairs. The ending of the Cold War was quite well managed, and was maybe the last moment at which a British Prime Minister could claim a true world role (although she had an unnecessarily carping tone when Germany was reunited). But both in London and in Washington, when it came to matters of the longer term, the Right fell apart. Here again, those critics with their hearts in the seventies can be dismissed out of hand as irrelevant. It was certainly correct to observe, as did the reactionary critic Anthony Daniels (a prison psychiatrist with considerable qualifications), that the British had achieved the feat of becoming much richer while also having a more uncomfortable life. But the seventies-minded commentators were quite mistaken in blaming the rising crime and growing coarseness on 'the Thatcher cuts' or an alleged ethos of 'greed'. The problems had been well in evidence before, and had even caused the rise of Margaret Thatcher in the first place. If she can be faulted, it would have to be in failing to take up a strategy to deal with such problems. The Atlantic, or 'the Anglo-Saxons' if we are to include Australia, struck French observers as undergoing a sort of social crisis, for all the money, or perhaps because of all the money, that was pouring out. Plantu, the cartoonist of *Le Monde*, wrote the line, 'socialism is the hope of Europe', and then drew three representative British figures

– the Prime Minister saying, 'What's Europe?', the banker saying, 'What's socialism?', and the young street hooligan saying, 'What's hope?'. 'Yob' was the reinvigorated word used for this last figure, while 'yuppie' entered the language to describe the noisy young products of the financial revolution.

England was visibly changing in very unpleasant ways. In 1944 Orwell had called attention to British orderliness: football matches resembling church parades; Richard Hoggart in a famous book thought that the working classes' future would be a sort of 'virtuous materialism'. By 1990, in a neat little Westphalian town, before some football match, there was a notice, 'English people not served'. Richard Tawney had done much to develop the Welfare State. When he died in 1962, he can have had no idea of what, very shortly, was to come about. For him the best things in England were stable families and internal peace. No policeman even needed a Perspex shield until 1977, let alone a gun. In 1955 there were fewer than 1,000 crimes per 100,000 people, a figure steady since the middle of the nineteenth century. It crept up to 1,700 in 1960, 2,600 in 1965, 3,200 by 1970, over 5,000 by 1980 and 10,000 by 1990. In Sunderland there were 480 armed robberies in 1980 and 5,300 in 1991. Again, the facts of family breakdown were incontrovertible. In 1942 10,000 divorces occurred. There was a Divorce Reform in 1969 and in 1971 there were 100,000 divorces. This was expected to be the last of it – unhappy marriages at last over. But there have been at least 100,000 divorces per annum ever since, even where children are involved. In 1990 there were nearly 200,000 divorces, but the figure then levelled out because people did not marry. In 1971 under one in ten births was illegitimate; in 1981, the figure was 13 per cent and in 1990 nearly one third, 50,000 of them to teenage mothers.

That children born in such circumstances would probably go wrong was simply a commonplace of the wisdom of the ages. From the sixties, an often asserted line was that, where there were problems, these had to do with money. It was of course true that single-parent families had less money, and three quarters of unmarried single mothers were indeed on 'income support'. For many years, the evidence was fought over, but in the United States, where the whole problem had come up earlier, a long-term study had been made, and by 1993 the evidence was published. It showed that 'the dissolution of intact two-parent families is harmful to large numbers of children ... [It] dramatically weakens and undermines society.' It was not difficult to make a list of the stupidity, cowardice and lying that had been involved in denying this common-sense generalization. Even the educational pundit A. H. Halsey, who came very close to apologizing for his own part in the creation of the world of the 1990s, could not help blaming 'Mrs Thatcher' because the housing estates where the mayhem occurred were broken down and poor, although he admitted that family breakdown had caused his own educational reforms to fail. But for governments to deal with these things is obviously difficult; the best writing on this subject is by Margaret Thatcher's own one-time political secretary Ferdinand Mount, whose *Mind the Gap* (2004) argues for a restoration of civil institutions, even the Church. In the United States, so much larger and with a far higher degree of decentralization, various answers could be variously tested, and it was there, rather than in England, that some progress was made as regards such problems, vigorously identified by Charles Murray or Myron Magnet (*The Dream and the Nightmare*, 1993).

In matters to do with society, the Welfare State, the National Health Service and education, uncreativity was on display. Perhaps this reflected an obsession with 'information technology'. Computers, programmed for this or that, were supposed to replace manned offices, and there were fantasies as to how 'paper' would just disappear. Boxes would be ticked, managers would know how, automatically, to respond, and if need be management consultants could be brought on to advise. This was to confuse efficiency with efficacy, and it was extraordinary that the Thatcher governments went in for a degree of centralization that enfeebled 'the little platoons' which had so distinguished British history. Ferdinand Mount noted in effect how the growing central state had turned everyone into a functionary or a prole: exactly what had been said in the later 1970s. Government was not cut back at all. True 600,000 workers – a seventh – had been moved from public to private sectors, but the effort meant that more, not fewer, public servants were required, and Mrs Thatcher even appointed a minister to the National Health management board – precisely what was not supposed to happen. The government did indeed try to manage the civil service better but the Welfare State had become a great monster, the DHSS having fifty volumes of rules created since 1980. Samuel Finer said that Margaret Thatcher was 'historic rather than historical': greater for what she represented than for what she did. Businessmen were asked to look at the whole problem. In 1984 there had been some improvements, some money saved by elimination of the more extravagant absurdities, such as the experiment-rats that cost £30 each. But most of this was tinkering.

English education had suffered from the abolition of the grammar schools in the later 1960s. The head of Margaret Thatcher's political centre, a Welsh non-conformist, had 'an almost fanatical horror of the way education was now done in schools' but where could he restart? Reform meant a parade of acronyms which, not long before the 1987 election, *Die Zeit* could mock unmercifully (a German correspondent in London, with an English wife and modish Hamburg views, lamented that his fourteen-year-old son, taken from his German school, was being diseducated). A National Curriculum was hammered out and hijacked by the educationalist bureaucracy; a universal examination called GCSE was installed, absurdly easy for some, impossibly difficult for others. Melanie Phillips listed the resulting woes, in a book, *All Must Have Prizes* (1996), which took all the tricks and had no effect. George Walden, who could handle the international comparisons, also wrote in the same sense, also to no effect. The minister in charge, Kenneth Baker, was himself a businessman, a believer in head office intervention, who did not see that without the threat of dismissal for the delinquent branch officials and of bankruptcy for the main firm itself such ways of doing things did not work. As Walden sadly pointed out, the fact was that the politicians (and many of the bureaucrats) could side-step the entire mess because they, like a rough tenth of British parents, used private ('public') schools which were often world-beaters. Margaret Thatcher herself had briefly been Minister of Education when the calamitous comprehensive reform had been going ahead, and had herself abolished many of the grammar schools. She later regretted this. But it was strange that the government waved aside its own supporters. There were similar problems in the USA, but there (as, to some degree, in Germany) there was such decentralization that good ideas could be tried out locally, in defiance of an educational establishment that a forthright Reaganite, William Bennett, dismissed as 'the Blob', with its weasellings and jargon (though even he proved ineffective at controlling it).

The preposterous over-centralization was on display over universities. A sage at the London School of Economics was Elie Kedourie. He wrote a pamphlet called *Diamonds into Glass* which summed up the problem: that the spending of money on the second rate would destroy the first rate. At least the American system was mixed, public and private of various sorts, the tax system encouraging towards the private side. If a Cornell collapsed in chest-beating self-righteousness, a San Diego would manage its affairs differently. The world's young wanted to go to American universities, and European ones, easily within living memory a target for bright Americans, no longer attracted them. As Kedourie showed, in the thirties and forties British universities had been very good; the 'boffins' of the Second World War had worked wonders, with radar, jet engines, penicillin, nuclear physics and much else to their credit. Such facts were then misinterpreted, and the problem, as ever, went back to the later 1950s. Back then, national decline had had to be addressed. The spending of money on universities looked like an obvious start, the more so as universities always complained about money. A great man, Lionel Robbins, was commissioned to write a report, which doubled universities, created thirty-two polytechnics, and asserted that there must be 'parity of esteem'. Architects made (ugly) whoopee, concrete went up and, as Noel Annan said, 'all students could be given a Rolls-Royce higher education', modelled on Oxford. In fact British education was set to be the beggar's Oxford. It was a variant – on a small and therefore potentially rescuable – scale of the Continent's experience, which had led to 1968. The fact was that Robbins's report had set up 'financially unviable arrangements' after 1958 that 'no country could afford'. The

Thatcher government continued this, without embracing an alternative and creative course. In due course it made the problem even worse, by upgrading polytechnics, and thus doubling the number of universities.

Here again at work was the vociferous irrelevance – or downright humbug – of the critics. They went on as if the universities were wonderful, and as if there were a straight line between higher education and national prosperity, an argument easily defeated by the instance of Romania, which produced more graduates in the natural sciences than anywhere else, and where the lights frequently went out. Such thinking, in England, had caused provision for women students to take places in the natural sciences which, at considerable cost, they then failed to take up. Oxford 'dons' were especially pleased with themselves, whereas the conversation at their high tables would generally have made the exchanges in the bus stop in the rain outside seem exhilarating.

In the early 1980s there was a cut in public grants, of 5–8 per cent, and teacher–student ratios did rise, because of the overall attempt to control government spending and inflation. This had started under Labour, and, with Mrs Thatcher, it did not last for very long. Private money easily made up the gap, and the number of dons did not decline: it rose, from 43,000 in 1981 to 47,000 in 1987. Even by the somewhat questionable measure of published papers, the British were producing a third more of them per capita than the French and Germans, and twice as many as the Japanese (even then the index of such papers did not include periodicals started after 1973). This did not stop a wave of hysteria: Sir Denis Noble at Oxford started a campaign, 'Save British Science'. *Nature* and *New Scientist* produced endless doom and gloom. A Sussex 'unit' referred solemnly to the 'catastrophe that we face as a scientific and educational nation', and there were loud references to a 'brain drain'. A *Times* letter signed by over a thousand people in 1993 claimed that civilian research and development had declined as a proportion of the GDP, but that ignored the fact that the GDP had gone up considerably in the meantime: one thing that was very obvious all around in the 1980s. These claims simply did not square with obvious evidence. The Royal Society itself showed that, apart from some very high-profile moves to the USA, there was not even much movement abroad among the 300,000 people whom it surveyed: only about twenty-four per annum, easily made up for by immigration. 'Save British Science' was just the usual euphemism, verging on hypocrisy, of an older complaint. Academic salaries were going down relative to others, and especially in terms of housing costs. Junior pay was less than in the police or even the National Health Service. A professor earned three quarters of a medium-grade civil servant's pay in 1979, and half in 1996, but the problem predated the Thatcher government, academics' pay having been arbitrarily held back in the early and middle seventies. A distinguished American applied for the Drummond Chair in Economics at Oxford, and was accepted. He received his first month's salary and enquired whether it was intended to cover removal costs. When informed that it was the salary, he realized he had made a mistake, having assumed that the figure quoted in the job advertisement had been a monthly rather than an annual salary. Such nonsense had to do with inflation and, more broadly, the attempt to fund too many universities on a sort of watering-can principle, Oxford professors having the same salary as sages of the sticks; and British students, like Continental ones, were hardly expected to pay anything at all for their higher education. As Kedourie said, it would have made sense to give each university an endowment of £50m and then let them sink or swim. Instead, by the end of the decade, 'managerialism' was being applied to the universities, and the principle was introduced of student loans. For students able to do summer jobs these were pocket money, for others, not enough to live on. The Treasury put on a ceiling of £420m, and the banks refused to operate the scheme as collecting the debts might alienate customers. Eventually a loan company was established (in Glasgow) but in 1995 the Brezhnevite results were plain to all – an eighth of the loans irrecoverable, a backlog of 17,000 unanswered applications, only one in twenty-seven telephone calls answered, and an assessor appointed who managed to adjust all of seven cases in five years. Meanwhile, in pursuit of student numbers, the universities abandoned entrance qualifications and adulterated their courses, with 'modules' to be picked and chosen. Did this contribute towards graduate employment? No. Only two thirds of graduates got a job or professional training within months and at Sussex one quarter of the graduates seem simply to have chosen unemployment in preference to some job as a receptionist or stacking shelves.

Meanwhile, the Thatcher governments responded with greater doses of managerialism, as with the schools; costs were held down arbitrarily: small, possibly creative, departments were closed down, for minuscule savings that turned out to be costly, such that Middle Eastern or Balkan studies imploded, much to the country's loss when both areas turned out to make for great international crises later on. A White Paper even asserted that 'If evidence of student or employer demand suggests subsequently that graduate output will not be in line with the economy's needs government will consider whether the planning framework should be adjusted' – meaning, no money. In 1987 one Lord Croham reported in business-schoolese, and a fake 'market' was set up, in which the universities were to 'compete' for funds. This meant encouraging them to produce publications, which could be totted up. The overwhelming majority went unread. The 'bidding' system was of course dominated by a single 'buyer', the government, which held down fees. Even clinical medicine was paid for at just over £5,000, and politics rated £2,200 per student, roughly what might be demanded by a decent infants' school for a term. Even then, the fees were supposed to include 'research'. As Simon Jenkins remarked, 'What is so strange about [these] higher education reforms is how little headway was made by the Right.' Government cack-handedness was such that it mismanaged a scheme for early retirement. In principle there was something to be said for clearing dead wood and promoting the young. However, academic salaries were already so low that even a three-quarter pension was not to be lived on. What happened was that the dead wood stayed, whereas men who could find another job took the pension and then moved on – 4,500 of them in 1985, generally from departments that were specially favoured, such that 800 new posts had to be set up. There was a puzzle at the heart of it all. British universities had produced brilliant results at a time when nuclear physicists had to go through a committee to get higher-quality box-wood for an experiment, and had to break in to the

Cavendish Laboratory after 6 p.m. to see how their experiments were going. By the 1980s they had a level of money that could be described in the words of the Habsburg prime minister a hundred years before as 'supportably unsatisfactory'. Where were their split atoms and radar and penicillin? There are imponderables in the world of academe, and quantification – box-ticking – could drive them out. The world, at any rate, voted with its feet and preferred America, warts and all.

The disintegration of the Thatcher government can be dated from the early months of 1986. Triumphalism reigned, and for the most part deservedly so. However, there was no strategy to deal with longer-term problems, and, almost casually, an expedient was found for a shorter-term one: the Poll Tax, which, by 1989, was causing great numbers of the MPs to think that they would be vastly defeated at the next election. Local government in Great Britain had once worked remarkably well, in an apparently messy way: the great Victorian cities had led the world in prevention of epidemics, in provision of transport and even as regards schools, where the half-dozen semi-public institutions of each, such as Glasgow High School or Manchester Grammar, were of legendary quality. The local owners of property paid the bills, and controlled the results. Then came votes for all, industrial decline, inflation and sixties grandiosity. Great cities put up concrete housing estates – soon hideous and crime-ridden – and local government descended often enough into corrupt stagnation, most voters not bothering, and the rest supporting a system by which absurdly cheap rents made it unprofitable to look elsewhere for employment. Meanwhile, property-owners paid. In London, 75 per cent of the income came from voteless businesses. Of 35 million local voters, only half paid rates. As a matter of principle, the rates were both inadequate and provocative of much anger, because they could be unjust: an elderly widow paying the same as a working family next door, on the one side, more than a better-off family in a public-rented house on the other, and more than a widow in some better-run place across the street. London was absurdly run, more or less by Whitehall but with fifty non-elected bodies and a general misunderstanding as to what made Paris work. Only a fifth of people on the various boards were elected, and there was the usual modern English problem that acronyms mean mess.

Was there not some way of sorting out the mess? There were wrangles between government and local government, especially London and Liverpool, where high spenders proposed to ignore government guidelines for the control of inflation. The only way to deal with this was to set a rates 'cap' and here there were battles, one problem being that if the government 'capped' rates, it would necessarily be responsible for the 'cuts' that followed – old folks' homes closed, etc. How could this problem be solved? There had been inquiries, six since the war, but there seemed to be no alternative to rates, from property. In the USA there was a local sales tax, and the country was easily large enough to have endless variety. Neither there nor in Germany did central government take detailed control of local finance, and in both cases there were large units, 'states', which produced somewhat different and healthily competing ways of doing things. The Heath government had attempted a reform along these lines, ending up with things that were too large to be changed or too small to be effective. Local government was an unrewarding karst of a subject, and the matter was now dealt with in an almost casual way. Had local government's powers been confined, what followed might have made sense. As matters came to a head, there emerged the most absurd piece of reactionary triumphalism since Charles X of France, in 1830, had appointed as prime minister a man who had visions of the Virgin and decreed a closure of the press. The revolution of 1830 quickly ensued.

It was called a service charge. In theory, high-spending and inefficient councils would be penalized by their own voters, because the service charge would be so high, higher than in comparable areas. Nigel Lawson and one or two others demurred, but in January 1986 the plan was introduced, with preparation time of ten years. Parliament's system of select committees strangely allowed it through, and a one-time Heathite, scorned by Sherman, and greatly promoted thereafter, introduced the Bill more or less without criticism, so long as he was given money (over £5bn) to smooth its passage. There were to be safety nets and rebates, complications that made the Bill very difficult to understand. Nigel Lawson argued that the best thing would be to remove education from local government responsibility, as it accounted for half of its spending. At any rate, serving bills for several thousand pounds on a family not used to paying anything at all was not a sensible method of gaining popularity, especially as so much of local government was inefficient and pointless (Oxford had forty times as many AIDS 'counsellors' as there were AIDS victims). By 1989 a large number of Conservative MPs were feeling their heads. The details, as monks, the disabled, etc. had to be exempted, were surreal.

All of this amounted to a *piano* and chromatic version of a funeral march, but there was another version in the major going on very loudly at the same time. The government had failed in its aims, a failure concealed by some magnificent victories, and above all by the legendary status of its leader. Neither in England nor in the USA had 'the State' really been cut back. The concomitant, inflation, now returned. By the end of 1988 house prices were rising by almost one third per annum. In 1987 the consumer price index rose by only 2.7 per cent, but in 1988 it was rising and in 1989 was at 15 per cent – more or less the figure with which this administration had started. The pound slid, and the balance of payments registered alarm. To all of this, the European lobby in London responded with cries for closer co-operation with the Europeans. The Confederation of British Industry was important in this respect. It consisted mainly of well-established businessmen of the older type, not expert in finance, and brought up in the corporatist world of the seventies, when businesses really flourished only through their links with a then all-governing government. The *Economist*, the *Financial Times* and a small host of respected commentators all blamed the troubles upon failure to join the ERM, the early stage on the way towards a European currency, in the context of the Single European Act. The monetarists had been waved aside, and the one-time Chancellor, Geoffrey Howe, was now in favour of some British co-operation with the would-be European currency (he had recently and very uncomfortably given up smoking). So was his successor, Nigel Lawson (soon to give up eating). Charles X had been overthrown by his cousin Louis-Philippe, a man for the wallet, and the Orleanists now gathered, to conspire in London.

The point as to the ERM was that it was the product of a world of two decades before, the failure of the Bretton Woods system. It could only really be made to work if there were real partnership, i.e. if the German Bundesbank agreed to support currencies such as the pound that were based on very different economies from the high-saving German one. Any restriction of credit, in pursuit of exchange rate stability through higher interest rates, would mean unemployment, but the ERM had become a sort of totem, and the Americans, who had invented its original version, were in support. 'Europe' was a sort of *deus ex machina* for dealing with intractable internal problems, as the Italians, welcomingly, had found, and as Mitterrand in France, needing a bomb to blow up his allies on the Left, astutely discovered when his wooden Brave New World collapsed in 1982–3. It became, as a nineteenth-century English radical had observed of foreign affairs, a sort of outdoor relief for a sort of aristocracy, and for that matter the Foreign Office, not, generally, having much of a role, and having weakened its *esprit de corps* with half-baked positive discrimination, now found a role: it could interpret the awful complexities of Europe for politicians who had many other things on their minds.

A Sir David Hannay was apparently deputed to 'Europeanize' Margaret Thatcher, to inform her of the advantages of the institutions of what was supposed to be a united Europe. She took up the invitation to address the training school for European bureaucrats, the Collège d'Europe, at Bruges, in Belgium. Even then, she went not out of enthusiasm but because she had to be in Luxemburg anyway. Just then, the 'president' of the European Commission, Jacques Delors, was promoting his own candidacy for renewal quite vehemently: Germans, latterly, had been collecting such functions (as Manfred Wörner had done with NATO) and Delors wished to keep his. He went the rounds, making European speeches, announcing that within six years there would be a real government and a real parliament, responsible for '80 per cent' of all laws passed in Europe. A few weeks later, the British Trades Union Congress gave him a standing ovation, as he sketched a picture of a left-wing Europe, with social benefits and low unemployment. In September 1988 Margaret Thatcher made her Bruges Speech, having lost from the draft a good part of the Foreign Office emollients, and made a characteristic assessment of Europe as she saw it – she played up the British contribution, but then told truths, to the effect that Brussels had been painfully slow and reluctant as regards the freeing of markets and capital movements, and that 'we have not successfully rolled back the frontiers of the state in Britain only to see them reimposed at a European level, with a European super-state exercising a new dominance from Brussels'. It was a good swan-song; but the fact was that she had already lost the campaign. 'Europe' was marching on regardless, and even Geoffrey Howe, the Foreign Secretary, regarded the speech with 'a weary horror'.

There were Europeans of some enthusiasm in influential positions all around; they, too, were somewhat shocked. It was put about that there was no such ambition for a European federal state, that 'federal' meant something different to the Germans in particular, that it was all xenophobic fantasy. In 1988-9, interest rates were rising, with inflation, and the ERM appeared to be the solution. It was quite widely advocated by very influential people, and the Americans, by now, were in favour of it, because it would support their own efforts to control the dollar's value abroad. In the spring of 1989 a report, given the name the 'Delors Report', outlined what should be done to unify the Continent and its various currencies. Robin Leigh-Pemberton, Governor of the Bank of England, had signed it. It outlined 'stages' towards unity, in a manner supposed to be non-committal but in practice very influential. The fact was that a very powerful establishment wanted the Europeans' 'stages', and certainly the ERM. Margaret Thatcher had, as ever, a large voting army. But many of her senior officers were near mutiny. The Delors Plan was supposed to be discussed by European heads of government in Madrid, in June 1989. The Spanish expected to make their first important mark at this, their first presidential European 'summit'. The Prime Minister rejected this, but then found that even in private the people to whom she listened disagreed. Both Howe and Lawson asked for a joint interview on 25 June 1989 and threatened to resign. She gave way. At Madrid, she did agree to 'Stage One', though privately adding to Charles Powell, 'We can't stay in this bloody common market any longer.' The full-scale European Monetary Union had been postponed, but ERM, as a stage towards it, had been in effect endorsed.

That summer, the post-war Conservative Party started to disintegrate. The Poll Tax was supposed to take effect in the spring (1990) and the party stood low in the opinion-soundings. At that point, one of her few remaining allies, Nicholas Ridley, spoke indiscreetly, as he was wont to do, and denounced the ERM as 'a German racket designed to take over the whole of Europe'. The sentiment was wildly expressed, and it was an exaggeration: but, as with much that Ridley said, there was truth in it, in so far as German credit conditions would have to be valid for all of Europe, and that, in Britain, would mean high unemployment. Misfortune again came when some Irish terrorists assassinated Ian Gow, a wise adviser, and his successor as Parliamentary Private Secretary was not, by far, of the same class (he even wanted to extract a public oath of loyalty from the MPs). The middle party took Gow's seat at a by-election, with a very large majority. There was of course the perennial stalking of the foreign stage, but Margaret Thatcher's great moment had passed, with the waning of the Soviet Union. Her last act was to stiffen the resolve of the American President, George Bush, when Saddam Hussein invaded Kuwait in August 1990.

The next round of exhausting European wrangling was set for Rome, with the Italians chairing proceedings. Early in October, the concession, to join the ERM, was at last made. But the Europeans wanted more, an advance towards the Delors stages for proper unification. In their view it mattered much more, now, because, without formal unity, an enlarged Germany might be a great and malevolent force once more. One of the 'stages' involved an irrevocable commitment to monetary union (as it happens, with fixed exchange rates planned for 1994). Mrs Thatcher hated the 'grand and vague words' of these European occasions, and disliked what they portended. She said, about the tired metaphor of not taking the European train as it was leaving the station, that 'people who get on a train like that deserve to be taken for a ride'. She denounced the Italians' 'mess' of a presidency, and said, in Parliament, in grand-actress style, 'No, no and no' to all three Delors proposals. Howe resigned, and wrote a powerful letter; when the party chairman attempted to explain this away, he spoke on 13 November very powerfully indeed in the House of

Commons, apparently much of the statement at the dictation of his wife. And then Margaret Thatcher had to face re-election as leader of the party. She won, but by a very narrow margin and under a strange rule that required a second-round election. It was of course an extraordinary humiliation for an outstanding figure, though in British affairs it had happened before, not least to Churchill. Her ministers, on the whole, told her that they would not support her, and in the end Denis Thatcher told her that that was that. The next day, 22 November, there was a brief, tearful Cabinet. She broke down, and had to start the business again. Then she had to appear for a final Commons debate, on a motion of no confidence. She spoke with a command performance, perhaps her greatest speech ever; one of the greatest occasions in the history of the House of Commons. The eighties had been a magnificent counter-attack: just when the enemy thought it had won, its ammunition dump had exploded. The look on the faces of the seventies was a poem. But what did the eighties do, in England and America, with the victory of the 'Seven Fat Years'? It had been in so many ways the best of times: Russia back in the Concert of Europe, China returning as a great world civilization, a recovered Germany with an entirely healthy relationship with her neighbours, an Atlantic that had recovered its vitality. There had been downsides to the eighties, perhaps those associated with democracy by the classical writers. But it had been the most interesting, by far, of the post-war decades.

Further Reading

Richard Pipes, in his two-volume *Russian Revolution*, had the good idea of naming the hundred essential books. My own list, with inevitable injustice, is even more of a thimble in an ocean. For general accounts, there are Eric Hobsbawm, *The Age of Extremes* (1994), which is excellent on the troubles of capitalism, and Paul Johnson, *Modern Times* (1983), excellent on the troubles of Communism. In both books there is much with which creative disagreement happens. Obviously the uses of technology are enormously important in the making of this period, and it would be easy to list two-dimensional works of praise. They should be put in the context of David Edgerton, *The Shock of the Old* (2006), which shows that 'modernism' is not what it purports to be.

As a general account of the Cold War, I have mainly used a splendid French account, Georges-Henri Soutou's *La Guerre de Cinquante Ans* (2001), but another French book, André Fontaine's *Après eux le Déluge, de Kaboul à Sarajevo* (1995), covers the last decade or so of Communism, very readably. John Lewis Gaddis, *The Cold War* (2005), is a very efficient survey, and his *The Long Peace* (1987) bears re-reading, but see also David Reynolds, *One World Divisible* (2000). The world of arms negotiations was covered in admirable and dogged fashion by Don Oberdorfer, *From the Cold War to a New Era* (1998).

For the world of 1945, Tony Judt, *Postwar* (2005), and William I. Hitchcock, *The Struggle for Europe* (2003), complement each other. I wonder if the Communist takeovers can ever be satisfactorily covered. Vojtech Mastny, in *The Cold War and Soviet Insecurity* (1996), is too much of a Menshevik Internationalist, but he intuits a great deal. Hugh Seton Watson wrote a book sixty years ago, when he was very young, *The East European Revolution* (1950), that has never been replaced. The Czechoslovak coup was covered by Karel Kaplan in a very dense book, *The Short March* (1986). Memoirs of the era, and of course the literature, are probably the best introduction, given that the story line, set in trade union minutes and the like, is not gripping. Nicholas Gage, *Eleni* (1983), is a superb story, but cf. David Close, *The Origins of the Greek Civil War* (1995), C. M. Woodhouse, *Modern Greece* (1991), and Czesław Miłosz, *The Captive Mind* (1958). David L. Bark and David Gress, in *A History of West Germany* (2 vols., 1993), cover everything thoroughly, but there are entertaining memoirs, e.g. Noel Annan, *Changing Enemies* (1995); see also Wolfgang Benz, *Die Bundesrepublik Deutschland* (3 vols., 1983). Paul Ginsborg, *A History of Contemporary Italy* (1990), and Jean-Pierre Rioux, *La France de la Quatrième République* (1980), are very well crafted. I have a considerable weakness for Correlli Barnett, *The Lost Victory* (1995), as an examination of the sometimes absurd illusions of the British.

The background to the Marshall Plan has been well examined from Western sources. Michael Hogan, *The Marshall Plan* (1989), and from a German perspective Gerd Hardach, *Der Marshall Plan* (1994), are important. They need to be complemented by Alan S. Milward, *The Reconstruction of Western Europe, 1945–51* (1984), and *The European Rescue of the Nation-State* (2000). W. Roger Louis, *Imperialism at Bay* (1978), covers the end of European empire, and cf. Christopher Bayly and Tim Harper, *Forgotten Wars* (2007). John Gillingham, *European Integration 1950–2003* (2003), builds on the author's examination of Jean Monnet and his works. Daniel Yergin, *Shattered Peace* (1978), is still useful on American reactions.

On the history of the Soviet Union generally, John Keep, *A History of the Soviet Union 1945–1991* (2002), is useful, but see also Amy Knight, *Beria* (1993). William Taubman, *Khrushchev* (2003), David Holloway, *Stalin and the Bomb* (1994), Jasper Becker, *Hungry Ghosts* (1996), Stéphane Courtois, *Le Livre noir du communisme* (1997), Jonathan Spence, *The Search for Modern China* (1991), Jung Chang and Jon Halliday, *Mao* (2006), and Jonathan Fenby, *The Penguin*

History of Modern China (2009), have been my most important sources for the Communist world in the post-war period. Simon Leys, *The Chairman's New Clothes* (1971, trans. 1977), is another wonderful book; also, when it appeared, unpopular.

On the end of European empire, see Keith Kyle, *Suez* (1991), Scott Lucas, *Britain and Suez* (1996), Alistair Horne, *A Savage War of Peace* (1973), Georges Fleury, *La Guerre en Algérie* (1993), Avi Shlaim, *The Iron Wall* (2000), Chaim Herzog, *The Arab–Israeli Wars* (1984), and Jean Lacouture, *De Gaulle* (2 vols., 1993). René Rémond, *Le Retour de De Gaulle* (1983), is a good summary of the problems of the late Fourth Republic.

'The Sixties' is an enormous subject. I have a weakness for Arthur Marwick, *The Sixties* (1998), but it was devastatingly reviewed by Roger Kimball, whose own contemptuous remarks as to universities were recorded in *Tenured Radicals* (1990). The same theme, with a very brave attempt to associate it with longer-term factors, comes up in Allan Bloom, *The Closing of the American Mind* (1987). Lara V. Marks, *Sexual Chemistry* (2001), records the emergence of the Pill.

On the political side, see Robert Dallek, *An Unfinished Life* (2003), on JFK, and his *Flawed Giant* (1999) on Johnson, and Robert E. Quirk, *Fidel Castro* (1996). Of books on Vietnam, I single out despite very strong competition Michael Lind, *Vietnam* (2002), Frances Fitzgerald, *Fire in the Lake* (2002), Mark W. Woodruff, *Unheralded Victory* (1999), and Gabriel Kolko, *Vietnam* (1986). See also Margaret Macmillan, *Nixon and Mao* (2007). Jonathan Aitken, *Nixon* (1993), is sympathetic.

The worldwide inflationary consequences of this era are documented by Harold James, *International Financial History in the Twentieth Century* (2003), and Barry Eichengreen, *The European Economy since 1945* (2007). Niall Ferguson, *The Ascent of Money* (2008), is a superb exercise in perspective, with sharp comments as to particular instances of greed and stupidity. Daniel Yergin, *The Prize* (1992), examines the most important element in the inflationary crisis of the 1970s and has also become a classic.

The counter-attack of the later 1970s and the following capitalist boom of the 1980s are recorded in Arthur Seldon, *Capitalism* (1990), Edward Luttwak, *Turbo-Capitalism* (1998), Paul Craig Roberts,

The Supply Side Revolution (1984). Andrew Brown, *Fishing in Utopia* (2008), is a sympathetic account of the failure of the Swedish model. Graham Hancock, *Lords of Poverty* (1989), attacks the business, or racket, of international aid. It owes much to Peter Bauer, *Reality and Rhetoric* (1985).

American demonstrations that the welfare system had failed are legion, but see especially Charles Murray, *Losing Ground* (1984), and Myron Magnet, *The Dream and the Nightmare* (2000). Daniel Yergin and Joseph Stanislaw, *The Commanding Heights* (1998), are triumphalist.

Chile emerges with Nathaniel Davis, *The Last Two Years of Salvador Allende* (1985), and Mary Helen Spooner, *Soldiers in a Narrow Land: The Pinochet Regime in Chile* (1994); and Turkey in Andrew Mango, *The Turks To-day* (2004), Nicole Pope and Hugh Pope, *Turkey Unveiled* (2004), Hamit Bozarslan, *La Question kurde* (1997), Anne Krueger and Okan Aktan, *Swimming against the Tide* (1992), and William Hale, *Turkish Politics and the Military* (1993). A good account is Mehmet Ali Birand, *Thirty Hot Days* (1985), but we are not spoiled for Turks' own accounts of their recent history.

For British affairs, we are indeed spoiled. Hugo Young, *One of Us* (1989), is understanding of Margaret Thatcher's approach, though at the time he was a considerable critic. Richard Cockett's *Thinking the Unthinkable* (1994) is a classic about the IEA. The memoirs of Denis Healey (1989), Nigel Lawson (1992) and of course Margaret Thatcher herself (1993 and 1995) record the era. John Hoskyns's *Just in Time* (2000) is a little gem as to what went wrong, right and wrong again. Ferdinand Mount, *Mind the Gap* (2004), is an immensely thoughtful exercise. Melanie Phillips, *All Must Have Prizes* (1996), is another on education. In general, Alan Sked, *An Intelligent Person's Guide to Post-War Britain* (1997), and Richard Vinen, *Thatcher's Britain* (2009), can be strongly recommended.

The fate of the eighties 'revolution' in the Atlantic world causes headshaking. The poet of the era is Tom Wolfe, *The Bonfire of the Vanities* (1987), but there are precursors of great power, *Radical Chic* (1970), *The Painted Word* (1975), and *From Bauhaus to Our House* (1981), making mock. For England, Simon Jenkins, *Accountable to None* (1995), is a brilliant book. David Frum, *Dead Right* (1995), shows how developments in finance derailed affairs in the USA. By contrast, Lou Cannon, *President Reagan* (1991), accepts he was wrong about the deficits. Niall Ferguson, *Colossus* (2005), shakes his head. A very thoughtful account of the USA is John Micklethwaite and Adrian Wooldridge, *The Right Nation* (2004). The grubby underside of the 1980s appears in Michael Lewis, *Liar's Poker* (1989), and Tom Bower, *Maxwell* (1988), while the strange cultural impoverishment is well displayed by Eric Schlosser, *Fast Food Nation* (2002), and *Reefer Madness* (2004). The thoughtful will find much thought in Seymour Martin Lipset, *American Exceptionalism* (1996), Michael Medved, *Hollywood vs America* (1993), and Robert Hewison, *Culture and Consensus* (1995). Since the financial upheavals that came with the end of the Reagan era, there have been a great many alarmist and even contemptuous accounts, notably from Paul Krugman, e.g. *Peddling Prosperity* (1994). Joseph Stiglitz, *The Roaring Nineties* (2004), has less than the usual problem, of failing to explain why the seventies did not roar. Robert L. Bartley, *The Seven Fat Years* (1995), is another classic on the Reagan years and what went wrong. Kenneth Hopper and William Hopper, *The Puritan Gift* (2007), is a splendid demonstration of the fantasy world of the business school. Finally, a work of futurology which, unlike so many, survives: Hamish McRae, *The World in 2020* (1994).

On the end of the Cold War, aside from Soutou and Fontaine, cited above, there are good essays on separate subjects. John O'Sullivan, *The President, the Pope and the Prime Minister* (2006), and Peter Schweizer, *Victory* (1996), set out the Reagan–Thatcher strategy. On separate theatres there are good books, e.g. Walter Lafeber, *Inevitable Revolutions*, on US involvement in Central America (1984) and an excellent English account, Simon Strong, *Shining Path* (1992). It notes the Kurdish connection of the Peruvian *Sendero Luminoso*. Christopher Kremmer, *The Carpet Wars* (2003), and Henry S. Bradsher, *Afghan Communism and Soviet Intervention* (1999), cover the Afghan tragedy. As an Islamic dimension developed, self-pity and resentment emerged with Edward Said's *Orientalism* (1978), of which there is a stupendous destruction job done by Robert Irwin, *For Lust of Knowing* (2006).

For the end of the Soviet bloc, the once sniffed-at Right clearly had the best of things. Vladimir Boukovsky, *Jugement à Moscou* (1995), is a wonderful book, for some odd reason only partially translated into English. It was based on Politburo documents and much else; see also Evgeny Novikov, *Gorbachev and the Collapse of the Soviet Communist Party* (1994). There are two further French accounts: Françoise Thom, *The Gorbachev Phenomenon* (1989), and Alain Besançon, *Présent soviétique et passé russe* (1980). More conventional accounts are John B. Dunlop, *The Rise of Russia and the Fall of the Soviet Empire* (1995), and, by a veteran of sovietology, Archie Brown, *The Gorbachev Factor* (1996). Another view is Ben Fowkes, *The Dissolution of the Soviet Union* (1997). Ronald G. Suny, *The Soviet Experiment* (1998), is important for the nationality dimension. Charles Maier, *Dissolution* (1998), shows how the end of East Germany was planned from Moscow. Jens Hacker, *Deutsche Irrtümer, Schönfärber und Helfershelfer der SED-Diktatur im Westen* (1992), and Stefan Wolle, *Die heile Welt der Diktatur* (1998), show how it had to be done in the teeth of considerable unenthusiasm from West Germany.

Finally, Europe. Its ever-closer union does not make for an interesting story line, and that side of things is best confined to efficient short accounts, such as Michael Maclay, *The European Union* (1998). European success stories are of course there: Charles Powell, *España en democracia 1975–2000* (2001), and John Hooper, *The New Spaniards* (2006), splendidly discuss the case of Spain. However, other than in the British case, the 'European' story is on the whole one of head-shaking and pessimism. Marc Fumaroli, *L'Etat culturel* (1992), is a brilliant book on the displacement of the old university by an ever-grinning ministry of culture. H.-P. Schwarz, *Die gezähmten Deutschen* (1985), wonders why German policy is either 'me, too' or 'oh, dear'. Bernard Connolly, *The Rotten Heart of Europe* (1995), is dismissive of Brussels manoeuvring, and David Marsh, *Germany and Europe* (1994), shows how very keen the Germans were to have, in the flat turn of speech, a European Germany rather than a German Europe. David Smith, *Will Europe Work?* (1999), is a good piece of Atlantic scepticism. As to where we all go from here, the latter chapters of Niall Ferguson's *Ascent of Money*, not greatly interested by Europe, not vastly admiring of the bankers' role, but very taken up with the relationship of the United States and China, are a very good pointer.

Index

Montesquieu, Charles de Secondat,
baron de 289
Montgomery, Bernard, 1st Viscount
Montgomery of Alamein 63
Moon landings 122
Moore, Barrington 217
Morgan, Kenneth, Baron 10
Moro, Aldo 336
Morocco 143
Moscow:
alcohol prohibition 551
Hotel Lux 27, 33
Khrushchev as Party head
112, 117
Olympic Games (1980) 353,
368, 540
Oriental Workers University
213–14
post-war rebuilding 100
see also Kremlin
Moscow conference (1947)
2, 3–4, 39
Moslems:
Greece 16
India 11, 13
Pakistan 11
Palestine 15
Vietnam 213
see also Islam
Mossadegh, Mohammad 136–7
overthrown 137, 256, 263
motor cars see automobile industry
Mounier, Emmanuel 283
Mount, Ferdinand 311, 312, 411,
417, 484, 585
Mountbatten, Louis, 1st Earl
Mountbatten of Burma
14, 141
Moynihan, Daniel Patrick 393,
430, 433
Mozart, Wolfgang Amadeus 196
Muggeridge, Malcolm 54, 85,
139, 208
mujaheddin 547

Müller-Armack, Alfred 339
multinational corporations 167,
248–9, 441–2
Munich 163, 395
Münzenberg, Willi 23
Murdoch, Rupert 475–6
Murray, Charles 429–30, 585
Murray, Lionel 'Len', Baron Murray
of Epping Forest 473
Musil, Robert 535
Muskie, Edmund 299
Mussolini, Benito 139, 195, 196, 198
Mussorgsky, Modest 553
My Lai massacre (1968) 224
Myrdal, Gunnar 86, 177, 491

Nagasaki 5, 20
Nagorny Karabakh 550, 564
Nagy, Imre 130, 133–4, 360, 555–6
Najibullah, Mohammed 370, 547
Namur 61
Nancy Festival (France) 284–5
Nanking 89, 90, 91
massacre (1937) 85, 91
Nanterre, University of 274, 275
Naples:
earthquake (1980) 335
student population 272
Napoleon I 155
Code Napoléon 151
Napoleon III see Louis Napoleon
Nasser, Gamel Abdal:
and Algerian independence 137,
140, 142, 144, 265
and Aswan Dam 137, 138, 139
coup of 1952 136
death 263
disasters of regime 263, 265
Egyptian–Syrian union 188, 257
pan-Arab nationalist ambitions
136, 137–8, 142, 144, 264–5
Six Day War (1967) 265
and Suez crisis 138–9, 264–5
National Archives (British) 314–15

Saladin 515
Salisbury, Harrison 84
Salomon Brothers (bank) 482
Salonica 16, 76, 456, 522
SALT (Strategic Arms Limitation
    Talks) 237–9, 240, 330, 368
Saltén, Felix 376
Saltley Coke Depot 325
Salzburg Festival 247
Samara (Kuybyshev) 33–4
Samarkand 566
Samuelson, Paul 543
San Francisco 177
San Francisco Treaty (1951) 96
Sandys, Julian 549
Santiago, Chile 445, 450, 496, 498
    Catholic University 493, 496, 499
    University of Chile 447, 496, 499
Santiago de Cuba 199
Sapieha, Cardinal Prince 29, 532
Sartre, Jean-Paul 282, 284
Saudi Arabia:
    and Afghan war 368
    and Iran 544–5, 546
    oil production 38, 256, 257, 264,
        269, 544–5, 546
    and Yom Kippur War (1973)
        264, 266, 267
Savak (Iranian secret police) 401
Savings and Loans crisis (USA)
    434, 574–5
Saxony 350–51, 495
Scargill, Arthur 325, 409, 418–19,
    472–4
Schacht, Hjalmar 19, 154
Scheel, Walter 344, 349
Schenectady, New York 169
Schiller, Karl 344
Schily, Otto 348, 559
Schlesinger, James 307, 308, 542–3
Schleyer, Hanns-Martin 349
Schmidt, Helmut:
    background and character 314,
        344, 397

and Britain 314
and Carter 306, 367, 402, 403
economic policy 297, 322, 397,
    399–400, 402, 403
and European Community
    334, 383
and Gierek 530
and Honecker 557
on the Left 397
Minister of Finances 344
Ostpolitik 397
Rambouillet summit (1975) 382
and Reagan administration 437
succeeds Brandt as Chancellor
    347, 397
Schoenberg, Arnold 425
Schreiberhau 50
Schuman, Robert 59–60, 108
Schumpeter, Joseph 161, 493
Scotland:
    comparisons with Saxony 351
    Conservative Party in 472
    first recorded Scottish utterance
        472
    nationalism 328, 356
    Protestantism 390
    referendum on independence
        (1979) 328
SDP (British Social Democratic
    Party) 421–2
'Second Cold War' 437, 467, 486
Second World War:
    bombing of Germany 9, 18
    British victories 6, 9
    German capitulation 18–20
    Japanese surrender 5, 87
    Soviet victories 5, 18, 100,
        105, 106
    Victory Day (1945) 573
SED (East German Party of Social-
    ist Unity) 108, 346, 350–51,
    558, 560
Sédillot, René, Le Coût de la
    Révolution française 280